Spreadsheet Modeling for Business Decisions

The Mcgraw-Hill/Irwin Series   Operations and Decision Sciences

*Available only through McGraw-Hill's PRIMIS Online Assets Library.

Spreadsheet Modeling for Business Decisions

First Edition

John F. Kros
East Carolina University

Boston   Burr Ridge, IL   Dubuque, IA   Madison, WI   New York
San Francisco   St. Louis   Bangkok   Bogotá   Caracas   Kuala Lumpur
Lisbon   London   Madrid   Mexico City   Milan   Montreal   New Delhi
Santiago   Seoul   Singapore   Sydney   Taipei   Toronto

McGraw-Hill
Irwin

SPREADSHEET MODELING FOR BUSINESS DECISIONS

Published by McGraw-Hill/Irwin, a business unit of The McGraw-Hill Companies, Inc., 1221

Avenue of the Americas, New York, NY, 10020. Copyright © 2008 by The McGraw-Hill Companies, Inc. All rights reserved. No part of this publication may be reproduced or distributed in any form or by any means, or stored in a database or retrieval system, without the prior written consent of The McGraw-Hill Companies, Inc., including, but not limited to, in any network or other electronic storage or transmission, or broadcast for distance learning.

Some ancillaries, including electronic and print components, may not be available to customers outside the United States.

This book is printed on acid-free paper.

1 2 3 4 5 6 7 8 9 0 QPD/QPD 0 9 8 7 6

ISBN   978-0-07-352513-6
MHID   0-07-352513-8

Editorial director: *Stewart Mattson*
Executive editor: *Scott Isenberg*
Developmental editor II: *Christina A. Sanders*
Marketing manager: *Sankha Basu*
Project manager: *Gina F. DiMartino*
Production supervisor: *Debra R. Sylvester*
Coordinator freelance design: *Artemio Ortiz Jr.*
Associate media project manager: *Xin Zhu*
Cover design: *Studio Montage*
Typeface: *10/12 Times New Roman*
Compositor: *Laserwords Private Limited, Chennai, India*
Printer: *Quebecor World Dubuque Inc.*

Library of Congress Cataloging-in-Publication Data

Kros, John F.
    Spreadsheet modeling for business decisions / John F. Kros.
       p. cm.—(McGraw-Hill/Irwin series : operations and decision sciences)
    Includes index.
    ISBN-13: 978-0-07-352513-6 (alk. paper)
    ISBN-10: 0-07-352513-8 (alk. paper)
    1. Decision making. 2. Problem solving. 3. Management—Mathematical models. I. Title.
HD30.23.K77 2008
658.4'030285554—dc22
                                    2006033971

www.mhhe.com

Brief Contents

Table of Contents

Chapter 7
Introduction to Forecasting   259

Chapter 8
Introduction to Optimization Models   281

Preface

OVERVIEW AND PURPOSE

This text focuses on five fundamental topics of business decision modeling; in addition, the text emphasizes the effective communication of results to the appropriate business decision maker. Overall, the text strives to educate managers in the process of becoming more effective and efficient problem solvers. Ten chapters capture the topics. Although traditional texts include many other topics, I have attempted to identify the core methods used by managers in their everyday problem-solving situations and offer students a process to improve their own critical thinking, management judgment, and communication with their end-user clients.

CHAPTERS AS BUILDING BLOCKS

Each chapter is a building block for the next topic and contains numerous links to previous material so students can integrate the information into their own decision-making and analysis process. Examples as well as exercises are presented that guide students in forming their own decision-making process, understanding the output from their analysis, and communicating that analysis in written and verbal form.

COMMUNICATION OF BUSINESS DECISION MODELING— REPORT WRITING

A special section in each chapter is devoted to the communication of decision-making and business decision modeling results in written and verbal form. In addition, an appendix is provided that details the communication of specific techniques discussed in the text and illustrates proper presentation of results.

These special communication sections and the appendix are developed to link the burgeoning management scientist's internal understanding of the material with a practical framework for proper language, format, and presentation skills to successfully deliver results to a real-world audience.

THE INTENDED AUDIENCE AND MARKET

The text is intended for introductory management science, quantitative methods/business analysis, and business decision-making courses. The text could be used in a sophomore/junior-level undergraduate curriculum and/or a graduate-level MBA curriculum in a domestic or international setting. Examples and case studies include regional, national, and international situations, scenarios, and solutions. The text is flexible, with special features for a graduate curriculum that undergraduate courses could make optional.

SOFTWARE PACKAGES AND SUPPLEMENTAL MATERIAL

The trend of increased use of software packages, spreadsheets, and integrated case studies is taken into consideration in the text through numerous examples and the early incorporation of spreadsheets and software. Supplementary software programs, such as TreePlan, @Risk, and other add-ins for spreadsheets, are also integrated in the textbook. The text details the use of the simulation software and decision tree add-in programs in Chapters 4 and 5.

INTENDED LEVEL OF THE COURSE

The author believes that the text is broad enough to satisfy the needs of a "survey course" in management science, but specific enough to satisfy upper division "elective" courses or graduate-level MBA courses in quantitative methods or business decision making. In addition, the author believes the text is highly adaptable, especially in the case of MBA programs and the tendency of late to offer shorter 1.5 credit hour classes. The proposed text should be positioned as:

1. An alternative to lengthy technique specific texts.
2. A multiuse text for undergraduate and/or graduate courses.
3. An interactive text filled with up-to-date examples, case studies, and software.
4. A text that develops a link between internal understanding of the material and practical frameworks (verbal and visual) for presentation of results to a real-world audience.
5. A text that can be used in a regular 15-week semester course or in a shortened 10-week quarter-based course or in a 1.5 credit hour graduate-level course.
6. A text that provides detailed instructions including "rule-of-thumb" sections, which explain items such as software use, writing and presentation guides, real-world applications, and expert opinions.

CONTENT OF THE TEXT

The text provides the most important and useful topics within business decision models while at the same time preparing students to apply those topics to real-world problems, to integrate the use of common software packages into their analysis and solutions, and to prepare written and verbal conclusions from that analysis.

Instructors and students who view business decision modeling as an integrated, continuous course and not as a series of techniques somehow loosely connected will especially be interested in this text. This text is highly suited to those instructors who teach in an alternative scheduling atmosphere, most notably the standard 15-week semester. In addition, instructors seeking comprehensive guides on the use of available software, real-world applications and case studies, and written and verbal communication skills are a target.

The inclusion and integration of communication skills relating to the written and verbal dissemination of analysis and results is a distinctive approach in this text. In addition, the use of comprehensive help/study/example guides within the text is unique.

THE STORY—THE ROAD LESS TRAVELED

So you may ask, "Why write a textbook?" Well, after attempting in vain for numerous years to find a text that included the topics I wanted to cover, but was not a 25-chapter behemoth, and also challenged students to become better problem solvers instead of formula-memorizing robots, the logical and final conclusion was …

… if you want it done right, do it yourself.

Therefore, I set off on the book writing road. And after many emails and meetings with publishers, colleagues, friends, and family, this text actually was finished. But like any academic writing, it is truly a work in progress, continually being made better. I hope all who read this work and those who attend a course wherein the material is taught enjoy it and take away something. I encourage any suggestions for improving the text and/or the material contained within.

Acknowledgments

As always this effort would not have been possible without the support and guidance of numerous colleagues, friends, family, and all those poor souls who had to listen to me bounce ideas off them, or for that matter anyone who just had to listen to me!

I want to thank my wife Novine and my daughters Samantha and Sabrina for always being by my side and encouraging me in their special way when the light at the end of the tunnel starts to dim. Samantha is 4 years old and always reminds me that she loves me and so do Barney and Dora. Sabrina is 2 years old and expects much from the National Champion Texas Longhorn football squad this year as well as a completely successful year from the Nebraska Cornhuskers football team. Thank you Novine, Samantha, and Sabrina and I love you very much.

To three extremely dedicated and bright graduate students, Alan Fang, Catherine Linnes, and Stephanie Leung, for their countless hours of work, revisions, and late-night e-mails, I extend my heartfelt thanks and look forward to working with you more in the future.

I thank Christina Sanders and Scott Isenberg of McGraw-Hill for their guidance, patience, and assistance in the publishing process.

To my colleagues who took time out to read the rough drafts, thanks and I told you I would mention ya'll somewhere in the book:

Alan Abrahams
University of Pennsylvania

Eric Abrams
McKendree College

Kenneth Ahdoot
Alexandria MD, VA

Marvin Brown
Grambling State University

Michael Brusco
Florida State University

Mark Clements
Northwest Missouri State University

Jerrell Cogburn
University of Texas San Antonio

Pierre David
Baldwin-Wallace College

Scott Dellana
East Carolina University

Robert J. Divis, EMC²
Phoenix, Arizona

Eric Drabkin
Hawaii Pacific University

David B. Gathman
iNet Solutions, Conshohocken, Pennsylvania

Kingsley Gnanendran
University of Scranton

Ray Henry
Clemson University

Nathan Hunt
Ronald A. Chisholm Limited Moscow, Russia

Christopher Keller
Indiana University

Ronald R. Klimberg
St. Joseph's University

James B. Kros
Dell Financial Services, Austin, Texas

Jennifer M. Kros
Citicorp, San Antonio, Texas

Kathy A. Kros
Computer Tots, Wixom, Michigan

Herbert Lewis
Stony Brook University

Ajay K. Mishra
State University of New York at Binghamton

Marco T. Morazan
Seton Hall University

Jeanette Mori
Hawaii Community Foundation, Honolulu, Hawaii

Nick Popoff
Blue Circle Cement, Detroit, Michigan

Steve Puryear
IBM Inc., Atlanta, Georgia

H. Neal Sievers MD
Chicago, Illinois

Jim Sapp
*eSapp Consulting LLC,
Indianapolis, Indiana*

Ronald D. Schwartz
Florida Atlantic University

David Schilling
Ohio State University

Minghe Sun
*University of Texas at San
Antonio*

William J. Swank
George Mason University

Thomas F. Wood
James Madison University

Mahmoud M. Yasin
East Tennessee State University

Zack Wassmuth MD
Austin, TX.

Chris Zak
*Charter Net Health Care, Fort
Worth, Texas*

Chris Zobel
*Virginia Polytechnic Institute
and State University*

To my parents, Bernie and Kaye, who have always supported me, even when they don't exactly know what I am writing.

Thank you to the University of Virginia, Systems Engineering Department, for graciously allowing me to use the lab in the revision process along the way.

To all of those who received email attachments, Dr Pepper–stained hard copies, or random sheets of paper scribbled with half-blown ideas, I appreciate all your input or for that matter the simple fact you took time to look at my work and listen to my ramblings. And to anyone whom I have forgotten to mention, thank you very much.

John F. Kros, Ph.D.

About the Author

John F. Kros has a bachelor of business administration from The University of Texas, a master of business administration from Santa Clara University, and a Ph.D. in systems engineering from The University of Virginia.

During his graduate work, he took time out and was employed for several years by Hughes Network Systems (HNS), in Germantown, Maryland. At HNS his responsibilities included: master scheduling, capacity planning, inventory control, and quality assurance/ISO 9000 auditing and training. HNS is a major manufacturer of electronic circuit boards, DSS satellite dishes, cellular phone and switching equipment, high-speed cable modems, and network computer satellite systems.

John currently is an Assistant Professor in the Marketing and Supply Chain Management Department in the College of Business at East Carolina University, in Greenville, North Carolina. He teaches the Business Decision Modeling and Business Operations Management courses and every once in a while is allowed to teach an undergraduate mathematics or decision-making course.

His research interests include: design of experiments, multiobjective decision making, Taguchi methods, and applied decision analysis. He is a member of the Institute for Operations Research and Management Science (INFORMS), Production Operations Management Society (POMS), and the Decision Sciences Institute (DSI). John has published in *Quality Engineering*, *Quality Reliability Engineering International*, *Industrial Management and Data Systems*, the *Journal of Business Forecasting Methods and Systems*, *Computers and Operations Research*, and the *Journal of the Operational Research Society* and in numerous INFORMS and DSI conference proceedings.

He enjoys spending his free time with his beautiful red-headed wife, Novine, and their two beautiful daughters, traveling, snow skiing, vegetable gardening, spending time with his family and old fraternity brothers, watching college football, and attempting to locate establishments that provide inexpensive food and liquid refreshment. Suggestions are always welcome!

Chapter **One**

The Art and Science of Becoming a More Effective and Efficient Problem Solver

Learning Objectives

After completing this chapter, students will be able to:

1. Describe the process of quantitative problem solving
2. Describe the use of business decision modeling in quantitative problem solving
3. Understand the application of business decision modeling in a real situation
4. Discuss problems using quantitative problem solving techniques
5. Be cognizant of computer and spreadsheet use in business decision modeling

Chapter Outline

Business Decision Modeling in Action—Algorithm? What the Heck is an Algorithm?

Introduction

Algorithms, algorithms, algorithms everywhere! What is an algorithm? Where does this stuff come from? This question probably takes you back to those nasty word problems in math class, remember, "If a train leaves Chicago at 6 A.M. traveling at 60 mph and a train leaves Omaha at 7 A.M. traveling at 80 mph …."

Algorithms = step-by-step solution process

Even though some of us may not have very fond memories of these sorts of problems, we use algorithms on a daily basis. Algorithms are really step-by-step methods for solving a problem. Algorithms are set in motion when you order a hamburger at a fast food restaurant or when you book your airline reservation.

Algorithms, Computers, and Problem Solutions

How does this apply to us today as future managers, supervisors, and entrepreneurs? Well, with the advent of the computer in the 1940s and the further proliferation of that concept on to our desktops, the way we use mathematics to solve problems is getting a huge boost. The power of today's computers has added a new dimension to using algorithms to solve problems and to solve problems more effectively and efficiently.

Faster, Cheaper, and Better

Algorithms have allowed businesses to solve problems faster and to provide goods and services cheaper and better.* The study of these algorithms for problem solving is called quantitative methods (business decision modeling), management science (MS), or operations research (OR). This text will provide a solid foundation in what business decision modeling is and give numerous examples on how it is used to solve problems. This text will give you the ability to solve complex problems effectively and efficiently out in the real world.

THE ART AND SCIENCE OF USING BUSINESS DECISION MODELING TO BECOME A MORE EFFECTIVE AND EFFICIENT PROBLEM SOLVER

The art and science of becoming a more effective and efficient problem solver is what this book is all about. Readers are invited to develop skills and judgment in becoming more effective and efficient problem solvers. Sections on the communication of results are introduced to aid in the decision and writing process. Real-life problems are addressed throughout the text to integrate the theory with practical applications.

Techniques as well as mathematical models are presented for seeking solutions to these problems. The ability to produce professional-quality reports is a major goal of the text. The text

* Kevin Maney, "Higher Math Delivers Formula for Success," *USA Today*, December 31, 1997.

strives to educate managers in the science of problem solving using critical thought and judgment. This process will aid in the management of real life, unstructured, messy situations.

Definition of Quantitative Business Decision Making

What is business decision modeling? There are actually a number of different words used to describe the business decision modeling discipline and a number of different definitions used to characterize it. A few are listed below:

> "[Business decision modeling] **is** the application of a scientific approach to solving management problems in order to help managers make better decisions."

> "… is the application of quantitative analysis to managerial decision making."

> "… may be described as a scientific approach to decision making."

> "… is the study of decision making in the operations function."

So which do we follow? Which is correct? Before we try to decide this, let's take a quick look back at those definitions and scan them for any similarities. There are many similarities that exist.

- All definitions mention the idea of decision making.
- Those in charge of the decision making are managers.
- The managers are making decisions on the basis of a scientific approach or set of rules.

These definitions are not the only definitions. When looked at as a whole, however, the different definitions do have a common theme. What about the different names being used? In actuality, business decision modeling tends to be referred to by numerous monikers. In fact we see the following names used in just the four definitions used above:

- Management science
- Quantitative analysis
- Operations research
- Operations management

At times, business decision modeling and the aforementioned names are used interchangeably. Just take a look at the name of the course, what department and what school the course is taught in and the terminal degree of the professor teaching the course. You can start to get a feel for how closely all these names are interchangeable. It should be noted that even though each of these monikers has similar elements, there are subtle differences between the definitions and names.

Overall, as we travel through the text, challenge yourself to begin to make your own definition of what business decision modeling is with respect to your own background, field of study, industry, etc.

Areas of Business Decision Modeling Application

Armed with these definitions, a student of business decision modeling needs to next think about areas where business decision modeling concepts and techniques are used.

Table 1.1 provides a description of the types of industries that use business decision modeling and its uses. The areas listed below are just a sampling of the places business decision modeling concepts are employed. In the process of studying business decision modeling, one should begin to see the numerous applications that affect our everyday lives. Each day as you drive to school, go shopping, access the Internet, or go on vacation, stop and take a look around and ask yourself is business decision modeling at work here?

Companies Using Business Decision Modeling Concepts

As we look around to recognize areas where business decision modeling concepts are applied, we also need to be aware of companies involved in these applications. Many companies directly associated with the areas listed in Table 1.1 use business decision modeling.

Margin notes:

Business decision modeling is the application of a scientific approach to solving management problems.

The terms management science, quantitative analysis, operations research, and operations management are at times used interchangeably to describe the discipline.

Business decision modeling techniques and models are used in many areas that affect our everyday lives.

TABLE 1.1
Areas of Business Decision Modeling Application

Industry	Industry
Banking - Banking and credit card management - Loan portfolio management	Airline and travel - Reservation ticketing - Flight and crew scheduling
Manufacturing - Inventory and capacity planning - Quality control	Marketing - Consumer preferences - Market research
Entertainment - Queuing/crowd control - Demand forecasting	Information technology - Computer programming - Networking efficiency

TABLE 1.2
Companies Using Business Decision Modeling

Company Name	Operational Activity
SABRE Decision Technologies	Airline reservation systems
Capital One, GE Capital, Providian	Banking and credit card management
CSX and Union Pacific Railroads	Rail shipping
Matson Ocean Liners	Over-the-water freight shipping
McKinsey, Accenture, Ernst & Young, AMS, Boston Consulting Group	Management consulting

Table 1.2 contains a brief list of companies using business decision modeling in their daily operations.

This list is by no means exhaustive. There are many more companies that use business decision modeling concepts in their everyday operations and that effect us in our everyday lives. The challenge for the student of business decision modeling is to keep your eyes open and continually observe if the companies that provide you with goods and services use business decision modeling.

The Business Decision Modeling Process

Business decision modeling is actually a process for solving problems.

The previous sections included a definition of management science as a rational systematic approach to problem solving. In addition, areas of business decision modeling use were detailed and companies that use business decision modeling in their operational activities were listed. Overall, as students begin to become acquainted with the discipline, it should become clear that business decision modeling is actually a process for solving problems. This process resembles what is called the *scientific method* for solving problems.

The business decision modeling process, depicted in Figure 1.1, follows these general steps (1) identification of the problem, (2) definition of the problem, (3) modeling of the problem, (4) initial model solutions and feedback, (5) review and iteration, and (6) implementation. Each of the six steps will be analyzed individually after a brief history of business decision modeling.

Figure 1.1 **Business Decision Modeling Process**

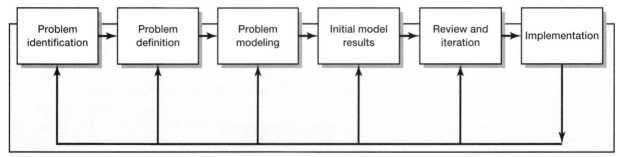

Feedback/review/evaluation

Business Decision Modeling Throughout the Ages

A Brief History

HISTORICAL OBJECTIVE

Until the middle of the last century, most industrial enterprises employed only a few workers. As companies expanded, however, it became less feasible for one person to manage all of the new managerial functions of the business effectively. New scientific methodologies were developed to provide assistance to each new type of managerial function as it appeared.

As more specialized forms of management emerged, so did more specialized subfunctions, such as statistical quality control, equipment maintenance, marketing research, and inventory control. Whenever a managerial function is broken down into a set of different subfunctions, a new task—the executive function of management—is created to integrate the diverse sub-functions so that they serve efficiently the interests of the business as the whole. The executive function evolved gradually, as did organizations themselves. However, increasing demands were made on the manager who in turn sought aid from outside the organization that gave rise to management consultants.

ORIGINS OF BUSINESS DECISION MODELING

Business decision modeling can be partially attributed to World War II, since many operations sought to bring mathematical or quantitative approaches to bear on military operations. Business decision modeling has characteristics that include economics (known as econometrics), psychology (psychometrics), sociology (sociometrics), marketing (marketing research), and corporate planning problems. The growing complexity of management has necessitated the development of sophisticated mathematical techniques for planning and decision-making.

Some areas of business decision modeling, such as inventory and production control, and scheduling theory, have grown into subdisciplines in their own right and have become largely indispensable in the modern world. The potential of computers and information systems as new tools for management forced the non–technically trained executives to look for help in the utilization of the computer.

OPTIMAL INFORMATION AREA

Operational Research Society Web site at http://www.orsoc.org.uk/home.html

OpsResearch.com Web site at URL http://www.opsresearch.com/OR-Links/index.html

Professor Hossein Arsham's Applied Management Science Web site at http://ubmail.ubalt.edu/~harsham/opre640/opre640.htm#rintsites

THE BUSINESS DECISION MODELING PROCESS

Quantitative Methods/ Management Science Time Line	Time	Major Milestones or Accomplishments
	1890s	Frederick Taylor develops the field of "scientific management."
	1900s	Henry Gantt develops a charting process widely used today. The Gantt charting process is the precursor to packages such as MS project.
	1910s	A. K. Erlang investigates waiting time for telephone callers and formulates the first measure of average waiting time in queuing theory.
	1920s	Walter Stewart introduces the concept of quality control charts, the precursor to employee empowerment through total quality management.
	1930s	John von Neumann and Oskar Morgenstern develop the fundamental concepts for decision theory and analysis.
	1940s	The field of operations research comes to the forefront with the advent of World War II. The first electronic computer is developed.
	1950s	The Operations Research Society of America (ORSA) and The Institute of the Management Sciences (TIMS) were founded to foster further study of operations research and management science. Scheduling and project management techniques, PERT and CPM, are developed by DuPont, Sperry-Rand, U.S. Navy, and Lockheed.
	1960s	Large corporations begin to use operations research techniques to solve problems more efficiently and effectively as computers become common tools in industry. The Decision Sciences Institute is formed to further the study of teaching and research in the field of decision science.
	1970s	The Apple microcomputer and VisiCalc, the precursor to the common spreadsheet, are developed.

**Quantitative Methods/
Management Science
Time Line**
continued

Time	Major Milestones or Accomplishments
1980s	The personal desktop computer is widely marketed and specialized business decision modeling software packages begin to proliferate (e.g., Lotus123, Quattro Pro, and Excel).
1990s	TIMS and ORSA merge to form the Institute for Operations Research and Management Science. Laptop computers now run complex software and tackle problems larger than the best computers from the past.
2000s	Students of business decision modeling can gather data, perform complex analysis using their home computers, and communicate the results via the World Wide Web at speeds unseen in the past.

Step 1: Problem Identification

Identifying the problem that exists is the first step in the business decision modeling process. Many experts believe this is the most critical step. If we do not identify the problem correctly all of the subsequent steps are worthless. A statement of purpose, thesis, or set of goals is generated here.

Step 2: Problem Definition

Once we have identified the problem we must clearly define the pertinent variables, those variables' parameters or limits, and any assumptions regarding the real world that apply to the situation at hand. If we do a poor job of defining the problem, our model may be inappropriate. Definitions regarding the problem must be linked to the problem identification and set of goals established therein.

Step 3: Problem Modeling

Models can be of a high-level/abstract nature or a more numeric/concrete nature.

Problem modeling can take on two common forms: the abstract, or high-level, model and the numeric, or concrete, model.

Individuals or gr oups attacking a problem many times begin with the abstract model and work towards a more specific model.

Abstract, or High–Level, Models

Examples of abstract models are flow diagrams and charts or graphs that physically describe a system or set of components or put structure to the definitions created in the problem definition section. Figure 1.2 is an example of a high level flow diagram used to model the transfer and shipping of goods in a particular region.

**FIGURE 1.2
High-level Flow of
Goods Model.**

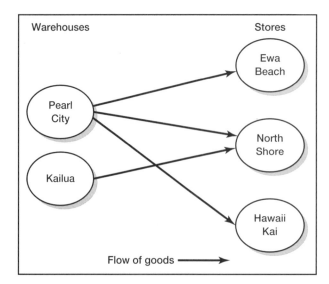

Numeric, or Concrete, Models

High-level models are used primarily in the early stages of the business decision modeling process but many times are carried forward, added to, or modified and also used in the specific modeling stage. Most often the specific models used in business decision modeling are mathematical in nature. These models consist of mathematical relationships that integrate the variables, parameters, and assumptions from the problem definition step into a set of mathematical numbers and symbols. A simple example of a specific model is the relationship of revenues and costs to profit. The numeric model that computes the profit the firm generates is in general,

$$\text{Profit} = \text{revenue} - \text{costs}$$

In fact, businesses use the equation for profit all the time.

Financial profit is defined as revenues less costs and is considered a basic financial model.

Overall, models can become very complex and can include numerous mathematical equations and relationships. The individual topics covered in this textbook will present numerous models for solving many different types of problems. Some of the models we will study tend to be very specific with strict assumptions and definitions, while others are general and can be applied across many situations, scenarios, and disciplines.

Step 4: Initial Model Results

After the problem has been identified, defined, and modeled, business decision modeling techniques are used to generate an initial solution. The word *initial* is used here because the next step in the business decision modeling process is the review and iteration step. Any business decision modeling professional would agree that rarely do we get everything perfect and generate the exact answer the first time around. Moreover, in real-life problems are messy and unstructured, and it may take a number of attempts to generate a model that is adequate and/or produces a satisfactory solution. In sum, as students of business decision modeling, we must develop the critical process and not a set of individual stand-alone techniques.

Step 5: Review and Iteration

Managers must review model solutions, or "do a reality check," on the output.

The review and iteration step is a time for what some call a *reality check*. Why should we as managers take a step back?

As you probably noticed in the earlier examples, mathematical formulas and simple algebra were used to create solutions or recommendations. The term reality check is used here because of the underlying theoretical nature of mathematics, the mathematical relationships developed in the modeling step, and the earlier definitions and assumptions made in the problem definition step. The review and iteration step encompasses the concept of critical thinking. To be an efficient and effective problem solver, we must develop critical thinking and judgment with regard to the solutions and recommendations that result from the models used.

This critical thinking or judgment is manifested in this step by literally stopping, reviewing the last four steps, and asking yourself a series of questions like the following:

- Does everything look okay? That is, does it all check with reality?
- Did we get an answer that pertains to the problem/goals we identified in step 1?
- Have any of the assumptions or definitions from step 2 changed, or should new assumptions be introduced?
- Is the model we developed functioning properly; i.e., are the answers we obtain feasible and applicable to the real world?

Overall, one of the most compelling reasons for the review and iteration step is to avoid making recommendations or presenting solutions that have no basis in the real world. We must also note that no model is ever perfect, so it is advisable to conduct sensitivity analysis. Good business decision modelers always do a best-, most likely-, and worst-case analysis. There will be numerous discussions of sensitivity analysis throughout the upcoming chapters.

Business Decision Modeling Behind the Scenes

The RAND Corporation

The RAND Corporation was established during World War II to further and promote scientific, educational, and charitable activities for the public welfare and security of the United States. In the early years, RAND's efforts were focused on national security issues, but as time passed, RAND aimed to tackle society's most pressing problems. The unique assembly of researchers, scientists, engineers, humanists, mathematicians, aerodynamicists, physicists, chemists, economists, psychologists, and members of other professions collaborated routinely and effectively to address problems and concerns of people around the world and at home.

The key players in the formation of RAND included General H. H. Arnold; Edward Bowles of MIT, a consultant to the Secretary of War; General Lauris Norstad, then Assistant Chief of Air Staff; Major General Curtis LeMay; Donald Douglas, President of Douglas Aircraft Company; Arthur Raymond, Chief Engineer at Douglas; and Franklin Collbohm, Raymond's assistant. RAND became a nonprofit private organization on May 14, 1948, and was able to obtain loans from Wells Fargo Bank and Union Trust Co. Later, in July 1948, it received further funding on an interest-free loan basis from the Ford Foundation for an amount of $1 million. Four years later, the loan from the Ford Foundation enabled the establishment of the RAND-Sponsored Research Program, which furnished staff with the means to conduct small nonmilitary research projects. This marked the beginning of the diversification of RAND's agenda and was the first of many grants to RAND by the Ford Foundation to support important new initiatives.

Some of RAND's early contributions include providing the foundation for the U.S. space program, digital computing, artificial intelligence, and even laying the building blocks for today's internet technology. Theories and tools for decision making under uncertainty were created, and basic contributions were made to game theory, linear and dynamic programming, mathematical modeling and simulation, network theory, and cost analysis.

RAND Corporation's website is at http://www.rand.org/

Step 6: Implementation

Implementation of the model, solutions, and recommendations is the last step in the business decision modeling process described in Figure 1.1. As future managers, we will be using the models developed and/or the results and recommendations from those models. In the business world, managers must make decisions in order to keep their businesses running, sell products, and service customers. This is in stark contrast to what many academians or theorists consider the last step of the process.

The implementation step, although the final and possibly the most critical step in the process, is often ignored. At times, necessary changes to a so-called normal way of doing business are revealed and in turn certain individuals may choose not to adopt the results or recommendations of the process due to reluctance for change. This way of thinking needs to be avoided. If the process solution is not implemented; the entire process was a waste of time and money.

BASIC FINANCIAL MODELS

Basic financial models such as profit = revenue – cost are used in many places in the real world.

Most of the basic business decision modeling models arising in business and economics applications involve the use of the profit equation. The next sections will detail the general profit equation and discuss cost and volume models, revenue and volume models, profit and volume models, and break-even analysis.

Three Parts of the General Profit Equation

The general equation contains three parts: profit, revenues, and costs. The general equation looks like this:

$$\text{Profit} = \text{revenues} - \text{costs}$$

Financial cost is generally made up of fixed and variable components.

Profit, revenues, and costs are related to the volume of items produced and sold. Algebraically all three parts are functions of the volume of items produced, volume of items sold, and the prices of those items. Each part of the general equation can be broken down into a mathematical equation detailing the specific relationships that profit, revenue, and costs have to volume.

Cost and Volume Models

Total costs tend to rise as volume of production increases.

The cost of producing a product comprises two major cost components, fixed and variable. Fixed costs are the portions of the total cost that do not depend on the level of production volume. Fixed costs do not change, hence the name fixed costs. Variable costs are the portions of total cost that are dependent on the level of production volume. Total cost is the sum of fixed cost and variable cost.

Let's take a surfboard manufacturing firm as an example. The firm, Surfboard Inc., knows it takes $100,000 to set up the shop for the production of the surfboards. This cost doesn't change as the number of surfboards goes up or down. It is considered fixed and is incurred even if no surfboards are made. The firm also knows that it takes $100 in labor and materials to produce a surfboard. Therefore, $100 is the variable cost associated with how many surfboards are produced. The resulting cost volume model for producing x surfboards is written as

$$\text{Total cost} = \$100,000 + \$100x$$

where

$$x = \text{number of surfboards to be produced}$$

$$\text{Total cost} = \text{fixed} + \text{variable costs of producing } x \text{ surfboards}$$

The total cost for the firm can now be calculated by using the equation presented above. For example, if the firm decides to produce at a volume of 100 surfboards, or $x = 100$, the total cost is calculated as

$$\text{Total cost} = \$100,000 + \$100(100) = \$110,000$$

Business analysts and economists use this model to describe how the total costs of a firm change as the volume produced changes. This is called *marginal analysis*. In the case of costs, the marginal cost is defined as the rate of change of the total cost with respect to the volume produced or x in our equation. From the total cost equation above, we can see that for each extra surfboard produced, the total cost would rise by $100. The marginal cost is equal to the variable cost in this case.

Revenue and Volume Models

Managers are also concerned with the revenue stream associated with producing products. A model relating revenue and volume produced can be created. Let's use Surfboard Inc. again as an example. The firm realizes $300 for each surfboard it sells. Therefore, the total revenue for the firm can be written as

$$\text{Total Revenue} = \$300x$$

where x = number of surfboards to be produced.

As in the case of costs, business analysts and economists use this model to describe how the total revenues of a firm change as the volume produced changes. Once again, this is called *marginal analysis*. In the case of revenues, the marginal revenue is defined as the rate of change of the total revenue with respect to the volume produced, or x in our equation. From the total revenue equation above, we can see that for each extra surfboard produced, the total revenue would rise by $300. Obviously, if the firm sells one more surfboard it would receive another $300 in revenue.

In general, revenue is the price of a unit multiplied by the quantity of units sold.

Profit and Volume Models—Putting It All Together

As we have discussed already, profit is made up of revenue minus cost. The last two sections detailed the relationship between revenue, cost, and volume. Since profit is made up of revenues and costs, then profit must also be related to volume. On the assumption that the firm can sell all the surfboards it produces, we can develop an equation for profit based on volume.

As was stated earlier, profit equals revenue minus cost, and if we combine the revenue and cost volume equations, the total profit equation can be written as

$$\text{Total profit} = \text{revenue} - \text{costs}$$
$$= \$300x - (\$100,000 + \$100x)$$
$$= \$200x - \$100,000$$

Therefore, we can see that total profit is related to the volume of surfboards, x, that the firm produces.

Break-Even Analysis

The managers of Surfboard Inc. have been asked to figure out how many surfboards the firm must produce and sell to break even. The term *breakeven* refers to the relationship between revenues and costs. Specifically, breakeven is the level of production and sales at which revenue and cost equal each other. After developing the relationship between profit and volume of surfboards produced, the managers can answer this question, using the profit equation and some simple algebra.

Breakeven refers to the point at which total costs equal total revenues.

At the break-even point, the firm sells enough product to cover total costs, but neither garners a profit nor incurs a loss.

Using the profit equation derived above, let's attempt to find, by trial and error, the break-even point. First let's allow volume of surfboards to be produced and sold to equal 400, i.e., $x = 400$, and calculate profits as follows:

$$\text{Total profit} = \$200(400) - \$100,000$$
$$= -\$20,000$$

The manager would conclude that at a volume or level of production and sales of 400 surfboards, the firm would incur a loss of $20,000. However, if the volume of surfboards to be produced and sold is equal to 600, i.e., $x = 600$, profit is calculated as follows:

Break-even analysis can be modeled graphically or numerically.

$$\text{Total profit} = \$200(600) - \$100,000$$
$$= \$20,000$$

One can see that at a level of production and sales of 600 surfboards, the firm would realize a profit of $20,000. Using simple logic, the manager can conclude that the break-even point must lie somewhere between a production and sales level of 400 to 600 surfboards. We can develop a simple equation to help us find the break-even point of any profit equation. The first step is to set revenue equal to cost. This is done by using the profit equation and setting it equal to 0. The resulting equation is

$$\text{Total profit} = \$200x - \$100,000 = 0$$
$$\$200x = \$100,000$$
$$x = 500$$

The manager can conclude that the firm must produce and sell at least 500 surfboards to cover all costs and break even.

Graphical Break-Even Solution

This relationship between revenue, cost, and profit can be graphed to show all possible combinations of volume and resulting profits. Figure 1.3 displays this graph along with the firm's break-even point, fixed cost, total cost, total revenue, profits, and losses.

In addition, a general relationship for computing the break-even point can be established. If we allow x to equal the number of units produced and sold (i.e., the volume) and we allow P to equal the selling price per unit, then total revenue can be written as

$$\text{Total revenue} = Px$$

Cost can also be represented in the same manner, where fixed cost is represented by FC and variable cost is represented by two symbols, Vx. The x is the same x as stated above and represents the number of units produced and sold. The V is equal to the variable cost associated

FIGURE 1.3
Graphical Break-even Analysis

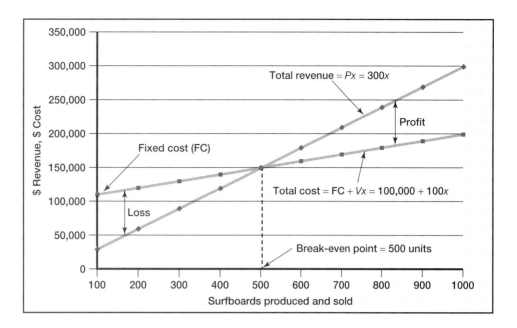

with producing an extra unit. Total cost is written as

$$\text{Total cost} = \text{FC} + Vx$$

Combining these relationships, we can write total profit as

$$\text{Total profit} = Px - (\text{FC} + Vx)$$

The break-even point is calculated by setting total profit equal to zero and solving the resulting equation for, as follows:

$$\text{Total profit} = 0 = Px - (\text{FC} + Vx)$$

$$\text{FC} = Px - Vx$$

$$\text{FC} = x(P - V)$$

$$x = \frac{\text{FC}}{(P - V)}$$

The general equation for numerical break-even analysis is

$$x = \frac{\text{FC}}{(P - V)}$$

Given this relationship, a manager who knows the firm's fixed cost, sales price, and variable cost per unit can easily obtain the firm's break-even point.

COMPUTER-GENERATED SOLUTIONS USING SPREADSHEETS

Computer spreadsheets have made solving problems such as break-even analysis much easier for managers

Throughout the text business decision modeling problems will be modeled and solutions proposed by using computer software packages. In some cases, all the student must do is follow the instructions, input a set of data or parameters into a model template, click a solve button, and then interpret the resulting solution output.

In other cases, students will be asked to model problems by using whatever method they believe is adequate. This type of activity develops the critical reasoning and judgment skills needed to effectively and efficiently solve more complex problems.

Solving Complex Problems Using Spreadsheets

With the advent of the personal computer and the basic spreadsheet program, managers now have at their fingertips the tools to analyze a vast range of real-life problems. As we progress through the text, it will become apparent that spreadsheets are a powerful means of formulating, modeling, and solving complex problems. We wish to promote the use of spreadsheets as a logically self-contained and simple method to model problems. By no means, however, are we advocating that spreadsheets are the be-all, end-all solution to business decision modeling and/or real-world problem solving.

Students will find that the text starts out with simple model-building concepts and spreadsheet solutions and builds toward higher-order models with more complex formulations. Some models will be built from the ground up and others will be generated by using spreadsheet add-ins or specialized software. This progression is meant to help the student develop modeling, critical thinking, and judgment skills as well as to introduce them to numerous business decision modeling techniques.

The author firmly believes that students must understand the underlying business decision modeling process and not just "point and click" their way to computer-generated solutions. At times the business decision modeling discipline has been accused of supplying students with software or spreadsheet models that spit out problem solutions, while students understand neither how they were generated nor how they should be interpreted. This text provides a foundation in the construction of models, including those developed in conjunction with spreadsheets, the use of specialized software, and the ability to interpret the results that these software packages generate.

Spreadsheet Solution for Break-Even Analysis Problem

The break-even analysis problem given above can also be solved by using a spreadsheet program such as Excel. The following steps illustrate how the surfboard break-even problem can be modeled and solved in an Excel spreadsheet.

1. Open Excel and a new Excel worksheet.
2. In cell A1, type **Break-Even Analysis for Surfboard Inc**.
3. In cell A3, type **FixedCosts =**. Proceed to cell B3 and type in the value associated with the fixed costs of manufacturing surfboards. For our example, type in **$100,000**.
4. In cell A5, type **VariableCosts =**. Proceed to cell B5 and type in the value associated with the variable costs of manufacturing surfboards. For our example, type in **$100**.
5. In cell A7, type **Price =**. Proceed to cell B7 and type in the value associated with the selling price of a surfboard. For our example, type in **$300**.
6. In cell A9, type **Break-EvenPoint =**.
7. In cell B9, type in the following formula for the break-even point: $= B3/(B7-B5)$

Cell B9 will then contain the break-even point for our surfboard example. Figure 1.4 displays how this will appear on an Excel spreadsheet.

FIGURE 1.4
Excel Spreadsheet for
Break-even Analysis

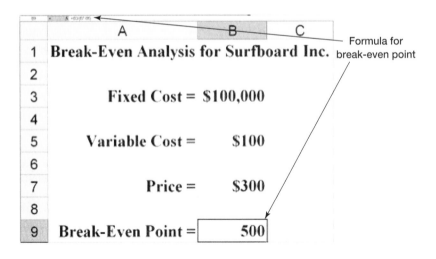

WRITING BUSINESS DECISION MODELING REPORTS FOR BUSINESS

Reports comprise analysis, conclusions, and recommendations. The quality of the final report is a function of the quality of the content and the quality of the packaging. A beautifully packaged report that has meaningless analysis is as worthless as a powerful analysis that is packaged so poorly that it never gets read. You must have both quality content and packaging to present an effective report.

General Rules of Thumb

It has been said that people tend to be persuaded more easily if a story or anecdote is used to prove a point. In many cases, managers must provide statistics or numbers to convince a client. However, most conclude it is more effective to give a short anecdote before providing the statistics.

There has been much written about business report presentation. There are a few areas that definitely apply to business decision modeling reports. These areas are crucial to helping your client understand your analysis. Areas of utmost importance when writing business decision modeling reports are:

1. **Use common, everyday language.** The terminology and symbols used in business decision modeling at times are very complex. Your client may not be familiar with this terminology or the symbols used. If possible, avoid the use of technical jargon but use your knowledge of business decision modeling to translate the technical terminology into phrases that your client can understand.

2. **Be concise; tighten up your writing.** Get to the point. Managers do not have the time to read lengthy, ill-written reports. In fact, many managers will not continue to read proposals that do not quickly reveal the purpose and recommendations of the author. The writing and revising process aids dramatically in reducing the superfluous material in a report or executive summary. The process of writing and revising your work is difficult but a very rewarding task.

3. **Use graphics to aid in the explanation.** There are many opinions on whether to include graphics, tables, and visuals in a report and/or executive summary. Overall, professionals in the business decision modeling and technical writing disciplines would agree that the proper use of graphics, tables, and visuals is a must in effective report writing. A few general guidelines do apply:

   - **Labeling**. All charts, graphs, and tables must be labeled.
   - **Size**. All charts, graphs, and tables should be large and easy to read.
   - **Position**. All charts, graphs, and tables should be contiguous. If possible, do not split visuals over two pages.

In summary, visuals should aid the client in understanding your material. They should not cloud or distort the information.

Creating a Structure

One of the most important issues in creating effective business decision modeling reports is to know the goal of the report and to create a structure that guides you through the analysis and writing. A common report structure is as follows.

Executive Summary

Introduction—Background

Problem Statement—Purpose

Analysis

Conclusions and Recommendations

Executive Summary

The executive summary is the **most critical piece** of the final report. In reality, most busy executives never read beyond this section. Think to yourself how many times you have actually read a report cover to cover; most of us skim the introduction, read the executive summary, and then skip to the conclusions/recommendations.

How much detail should be included in an executive summary? The rule of thumb is the shorter the better. An executive summary is the report in miniature that covers key findings, conclusions, and recommendations. A number of good reference documents on writing executive summaries are listed at the end of this section.

Introduction—Background

The length and the style of the introduction and background section may differ depending on the audience and the problem at hand. This section should be kept to a minimum and should outline the problem and its background as decided on by the client and the report analysts.

Problem Statement—Purpose

The statement of purpose, or problem statement, can be included in the introduction but many times is set apart for effect. In addition, this section can provide details and information about definitions and assumptions made in the analysis.

Analysis

This is the heart of the report. The model of how the problem is solved must be presented here along with the "what if," or sensitivity, analysis. Sensitivity analysis will be defined and detailed in Chapter 4. Anyone who is still interested after reading the executive summary will peruse this section, looking for verification and validation of the outcomes seen earlier.

This section must be written very clearly and completely and should include charts, tables, and other graphics. On the other hand, do not overdo it. Excessive use of tables, computer printouts, or mathematical formulas in the body of the report is highly discouraged. Use appendices to house this material and provide proper reference in the body of the report.

Conclusions and Recommendations

The recommendation section should sum up what the analysis section and the sensitivity analysis concluded. At a minimum, a restatement of the choice or decision to be made accompanied by the implications of that choice or decision must appear. In other words, explain to your client what the best alternatives are, the process to begin exploring those options, and the associated costs, profits, etc. After the conclusions and recommendations section, an appendix can be used to house technical information, computer output, calculations, and/or complete mathematical models.

Executive Summary Example for Surfboard Inc.

The sample document below is an executive summary for the Surfboard Inc. model developed earlier in this chapter. The executive summary should be used by students of business decision modeling as a guide for future writing. It must be noted that it is only one example and executive summary style may change, depending on audience and content.

Since the executive summary is the only document presented it must both explain the problem facing Surfboard Inc. and provide recommendations in a limited amount of space.

Executive Summary for Surfboard Inc. Break-Even Analysis

TO: Eddie

FROM: Business Decision Modeling Consulting Group

Introduction:

Surfboard Inc. is seeking a break-even analysis for its North Shore operations. The objective is to find Surfboard Inc.'s break-even point given its cost and pricing structure. We are assuming the firm can sell all surfboards produced.

Current Cost and Pricing Structure:

The current cost and pricing structure is summarized in Table 1:

TABLE 1

Surfboard Inc, Manufacturing Firm Cost and Pricing Information

Cost Category	$ Costs	$ Price per Surfboard
Fixed cost	$100,000	$300
Variable cost per surfboard or average variable cost	$ 100	

Profit Equation

On the basis of the above information, costs and pricing, a general profit equation can be established. This equation is listed below.

$$\text{Profit} = \$200 \times (\text{number of surfboards}) - \$100,000$$

The breakeven point quantity is equal to 500 surfboards. Hence, Surfboard Inc., at the current cost and pricing levels, must produce at least 500 surfboards to break even.

Break-Even Graph

To illustrate this point in relation to other production levels, a break-even graph has been constructed. The graph relates various levels of surfboard sales/production to the resultant levels of profit, revenue, and costs. Figure 1 displays the break-even graph.

Conclusions:

Figure 1 illustrates that the break-even point in number of surfboards is equal to 500 surfboards. Surfboard Inc. will incur a loss at sales/production levels of less than 500 surfboards and garner a profit at sales/production levels of greater than 500 surfboards. Total Revenue is defined on the graph as Px (price multiplied by quantity) and Total Cost is defined as $FC + Vx$ (fixed cost + variable cost multiplied by units sold).

FIGURE 1.5

Surfboard Inc. Break-even Graph

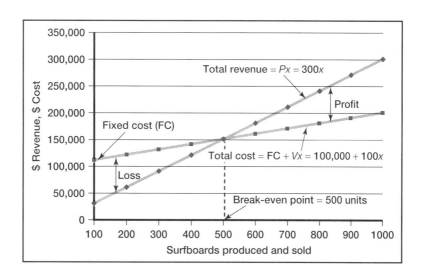

Optimal Information Area

Bricklin, Dan. "Dan Bricklin's Web Site," at **http://bricklin.com/history/sai.htm**

Decision Sciences Institute, at **http://dsi.gsu.edu**

Institute for Operations Research and Management Science, at **http://www.informs.org**

Mattessich, Richard. "Early History of the Spreadsheet," at **http://www.j-walk.com/history/spreadsh.htm**

Power, Daniel. "A Brief History of Spreadsheets," at **http://dssresources.com/**

Trick, Michael. "Michael Trick's Operations Research Web Site," at **http//mat.gsia.cmu.edu**

"VisiCalc '79," Dan Bricklin and Bob Frankston, *Creative Computing,* November 1984, vol. 10, pp. 122, 124.

"VisiCalc Production Ends," *PC Magazine,* August 6, 1985. vol. 4, p. 33.

References

Ackoff, Russell L., and Maurice W. Sasieni. *Fundamentals of Operations Research*. New York: John Wiley & Sons, 1968.

Beer, Stafford. *Management Sciences*: *The Business Use of Operations Research*. New York: Doubleday, 1967.

Hillier, F. S., and G. J. Lieberman. *Operations Research*, 4th ed. San Francisco: Holden-Day, 1987.

Holtz, Herman. *The Consultant's Guide to Proposal Writing: How to Satisfy Your Clients and Double Your Income*. New York: John Wiley and Sons, 1998.

Locker, Kitty. *Business and Administrative Communication*, 4th ed. New York: Irwin/McGraw-Hill, 1997.

Ragsdale, Cliff. *Spreadsheet Modeling and Decision Analysis*, 2nd ed. Cincinnati: South-Western, 1998.

Sant, Tom. *Persuasive Business Proposals: Writing to Win Customers, Clients, and Contracts*. New York: American Management Association, 1992.

Silk, David. *How to Communicate in Business: A Handbook for Engineers*. IEE Management of Technology Series 17, 1995.

Smith, Charles B. *A Guide to Business Research: Developing, Conducting, and Writing Research Projects*. Chicago: Nelson-Hall Publishers, 1991.

Taylor, Bernard. *Introduction to Management Science*, 6th ed. Engelwood Cliffs, NJ: Prentice-Hall, 1999.

Problems

1. Rick Miles runs a CD-making business. He forecasts demand for his CDs at 5000 for the next year. He charges $20 per CD sold. It costs him $2000 in fixed costs a year to run his business and $2 per CD in variable costs.

   a. What are Rick's revenues?
   b. What are Rick's costs?
   c. Does Rick make a profit?

2. The Scheinbach computer company manufactures computers wholesale. The company's fixed monthly cost is $45,000, and its variable per computer cost is $525. The company sells the computers for $925. Determine the monthly break-even volume for the company.

3. Kathy runs her own computer education business. She needs $4000 a year to pay the leases on the computers she uses. She estimates she will have 400 pupils for the next year. Each pupil pays $200 for the education. However, it costs Kathy $20 to $30 per pupil in supplies and overhead.

   a. What are Kathy's yearly revenues?
   b. What are Kathy's average total costs? What is the range of Kathy's costs?
   c. Does Kathy make a profit? What is the range of Kathy's profit?

4. Wayne owns a shaved ice stand. He sells 700 shaved ice cups per month at $1.50 each, making the total revenue $1050. Each shaved ice costs Wayne $0.50 and he has fixed costs of $750, making his total costs $1100. Therefore, he realizes a loss of $50 a month. Help him determine what his break-even point is.

5. HPU Graduates is a start-up microbrewery in Pahoa, Hawaii. Its fixed costs to produce beer total $8000 per month. The variable cost to produce their beer is $3.00 per case of beer. It sells its beer to one hotel only, and that hotel has said it wants 550 cases this month. What price does HPU need to charge to break even?

6. The VA-TX Company is going to present a new product in Santa Clara, California. In this event, VA-TX will present a seminar with a coffee break. The auditorium's capacity is 500 people. The cost of renting the place is $4000/day, utilities included. Moreover, the cost of the food and drinks is $5 per person. After some other experiences, the company knows that 50 percent of the audience buys its product, which is priced at $75. Is Santa Clara a profitable place to do this kind of campaign?

7. Eric runs a chiropractic center in Mililani. The annual fixed costs for operating Chiro-Care clinic is $222,000. The variable cost per patient treated is $55. The price billed for each visit is $136. Currently, he has around 2500 visits a year.

    a. Is he making a profit?

    b. He doesn't think he can increase demand, so he is thinking about a cost-cutting measure for his variable costs. What would his variable costs need to be in order for him to break even at 2500 visits a year?

8. John is thinking about getting into the tourism business in Oahu. He will take visitors on a whole-day trip to the main tourist spots on the island in a new van he is planning to buy. He would like to know how many tourists he has to move daily to have a before-taxes profit of $1000 per month so he can save that money. He will work 25 days per month.

    His costs for the new business would be as follows:

    Variable costs per day trip per person

    >   Gasoline: $ 30

    >   Maintenance: $ 5 (oil, tune-ups, wheels, repairs, etc.)

    Fixed costs

    >   Leasing and insurance: $ 1000 per month

    >   Personal expenses: $1000 (the minimum amount he needs for living expenses) per month

    He is planning to charge $ 45 per visitor for a day trip.

    Using the break-even formula, John will need how many daily travelers in order to achieve a profit of $1000 per month?

9. The Thai Corporation has sales subsidiaries around the world. As a rule of thumb, each new established subsidiary should be able to reach its break-even point during year 2. After 18 months of business activity in Thailand, The Thai Corporation's Thai sales subsidiary generated a sales volume of 200,000 units. Its variable costs are $5 per unit and fixed costs at this level equal $750,000.

    a. In year 2, at a sales price of $17 per unit, how many units does the subsidiary need to sell in order to break even?

    b. Do you think the company will make a profit if last year's sales are a good indicator of future sales?

10. The VA-TX Company has noticed when it advertises, it dramatically increases the amount of customers who buy its product at seminars. With advertising, VA-TX expects the audience to buy the product at a price of $75. The cost of renting a place is $4000/day, utilities included. Moreover, the cost of food and drinks is $5/person. If VA-TX assumes at a minimum it will sell 124 units, what would be the upper bound on advertising dollars (i.e., where would the the company break even?).

11. Bradley is a sales associate for VA-TX. He has suggested that if the company would provide an open bar at the end of the seminar, sales would rise. The open bar would increase the variable cost per customer from $5 to $7.50.

    a. With the same fixed cost structure, how many sales would VA-TX have to make to break even?

    b. How does this compare with the break-even point(s) in Problem 10?

12. Bernie Hsiao runs a lamp-making business. He has two lines of lamps: antler lamps and fishing rod lamps. It costs him $10,000 a year to run his business (labor, materials, and overhead). The estimated

demand for antler lamps is anywhere from 100 to 200 units. The estimated demand for fishing rod lamps is 300 to 400 units. He charges $2000 for antler lamps and $200 for fishing rod lamps. However, he incurs $750 in variable costs per antler lamp sold and $30 for each fishing rod lamp sold.

a. What are Bernie's expected/average revenues from antler lamps? What are Bernie's expected/average revenues from fishing rod lamps? What is the total expected/average revenue Bernie's lamp business could generate? What is the range of total expected/average profit?

b. What are the expected/average costs associated with the lamp business? Identify the costs associated with antler lamps, fishing rod lamps, and costs associated with both.

c. Does Bernie make a profit in the case of low estimated demand for each lamp?

d. Does Bernie make a profit in the case of high estimated demand for each lamp?

e. If half of the fixed costs are attributable to antler lamps, how much do the antler lamps contribute to this profit? If half the fixed costs are attributable to fishing rod lamps, how much do the fishing rod lamps contribute to this profit?

Chapter Two

Introduction to Spreadsheet Modeling

Learning Objectives

After completing this chapter, students will be able to:

1. Understand the process of spreadsheet modeling
2. Understand simple spreadsheet concepts (layout, formula bar, active cell, etc.) terminology (cells, text, calculations, etc.), formatting of cells (borders, shading, naming, etc.), and referencing (relative, absolute, etc.)
3. Develop skills in creating simple formulas and formatting spreadsheets
4. Create a spreadsheet to store and process numerical information
5. Learn the basics of the following spreadsheet functions: Goal Seek, Solver, and Curve Fitting

Chapter Outline

Business Decision Modeling in Action: Using Spreadsheet Models

Introduction
Background
Categories of Models
Models versus Modeling

Process for Modeling
Why a Process for Modeling?
The Problem-Solving Process
Goals in Spreadsheet Design

Basic Spreadsheet Concepts
Layout of a Spreadsheet
Reference Cells and Ranges
Relative References
Copying Formulas
Absolute References
Mixed References

Business Decision Modeling Throughout the Ages: A Brief History of Spreadsheet Modeling

Applied Spreadsheet Modeling—Goal Seek
Example 1
Applying Number Format to Cell
Naming Cells
Creating Data Tables
Creating Charts Using Chart Wizard
Sensitivity Analysis

Using Goal Seek

Basic Excel Functions
Mathematical Operators
Built-in Functions
Basic Functions
Statistical Functions
Logical Functions
Using Lookup Functions

Applied Spreadsheet Modeling—Using Basic Functions
Example 2
Using MIN Function
Using IF Function
Using VLOOKUP Function
Expected Profit from Demand Probabilities
Sensitivity Analysis

Applied Spreadsheet Modeling—Using Solver
Building the Spreadsheet Model
Using Excel's Solver
Analysis of Results
Modification of Constraints and Rerun of Solver

Business Decision Modeling in Action: Using Spreadsheet Models

Client Problem

The staff of Schlumberger was confronted with a resource-intensive ordeal during each reporting period. Budget planning posed a resource drain on the accounting staff because time-intensive manual editing of spreadsheets into various required company formats.

Solution

Beyond Technology (www.beyondtechnology.com) is a widely recognized Microsoft Excel VBA development firm. Beyond Technology develops financial and engineering applications, with special expertise in budget planning, forecasting, investment portfolio analysis, decision support systems, and data modeling. Beyond Technology worked with Schlumberger on a strategy integrating various components of its financial reporting. The first step in the model was developing a planning/project costing model for worldwide budget administration, consolidation, reporting, and analysis. Beyond Technology included a multicurrency break-even model—a vision of the organization's chief controller—to perform "what if" analyses across the company's manufacturing and engineering enterprise. Microsoft VBA functions were used to automate hundreds of time-consuming manual tasks, freeing professional staff to concentrate on the business.

Financial Tools for Negotiation: Examples from PricewaterhouseCoopers

PricewaterhouseCoopers (PWC), at www.pwcglobal.com, is one of the world's largest professional services organization. The group helps clients to clarify their thinking and strategies through the application of analytical and quantitative techniques. Transaction analytics achieves this by using a variety of techniques, including uncertainty and risk analysis, financial modeling, and systems thinking—a means of mapping the causes and effects of business drivers.

Business Question: How Can We Target Our Customers Individually?

A PWC client wanted to target its existing customers more accurately, building stronger relationships and encouraging brand loyalty, maximizing value from its data. PWC initially developed a spreadsheet-based campaign-planning tool for the client to use and identified a number of new opportunities for the client to build customer profiles. This tool enabled the client to select individual customers for a marketing campaign, drilling down to price sensitivity for individuals, and provided an accurate measure of the financial return for the client.

Business Question: How Can We Evaluate Our Product Options?

PWC built a product strategy decision matrix for the client, which needed to evaluate the different product options available before committing to further development trials. PWC built a decision tree and evaluation matrix to structure the product options, develop criteria to evaluate each option and develop metrics by which to judge the evaluations (including total attractiveness, overall probability of achievement, overall confidence rating and product utility).

INTRODUCTION

Life itself requires one to make countless decisions. What field am I going to concentrate in? Which job offer should I take? Whom am I going to marry? How much should I invest? Making good decisions is a very difficult task. One has to evaluate the numerous courses of action available and choose the best alternative.

In the business world, managers are faced with the same need to make endless qualified decisions. Often managers use spreadsheets as a convenient and useful tool in their analytical toolkit besides experienced guesses to help them make better decisions.

Most spreadsheet models are mathematical formulations.

Spreadsheets accept inputs based on a mathematical relationship with logical assumptions and provide outputs that are insightful to an analytical manager. The power of spreadsheets comes from their flexibility, i.e., the ability to instantly provide the results (output) when one varies its inputs.

By itself, a spreadsheet does not make decisions; it only serves as a tool for managers. Managers have to analyze the decision alternatives before choosing a specific plan for implementation. Models, when properly formulated, can greatly enhance decision making. They also provide structure and quantifiable results, and thus credibility, to the decision-making process.

This is the very essence of using quantitative methods for business decisions.

Background

Most spreadsheet models tend to begin as a mathematical model. Do not be afraid of these terms in the mistaken view that only experts in spreadsheet modeling or higher mathematics can harness the power of spreadsheets for analytical decision making. A simple mathematical model tends to be a quantitative representation or approximation of a real situation. Let's begin with a very well known and well used mathematical model for business modeling—the profit equation:

$$\text{Profit} = \text{revenue} - \text{expenses}$$

The profit equation represents a well-defined functional relationship between revenue and expenses. In simple mathematical terms, profit is a function of revenue and expenses.

$$Y = f(X_1, X_2)$$

where Y represents profit and X_1 and X_2 represent revenue and expenses, respectively.

We could also say that profit depends on revenue and expenses. Therefore profit represents a dependent variable Y, whereas revenue and expenses are independent variables X_1 and X_2, respectively.

When modeled properly into a spreadsheet, the revenue and expenses will be the *inputs* to produce the corresponding profit result, which is the *output*.

Functions can be quite complex, involving multiple independent variables as well as intermediate levels of independent variables. The level of expenses could be further dependent on level of activity, as represented, for example, by sales commission for each product sold. Such expenses are known as *variable costs*, in economic terms. Revenue may also depend on unknown variables such as demand.

Not all business problems have a clearly defined functional relationship between the dependent and the independent variables like the profit equation. We will discuss in the next section the different categories of models that can be classified on the basis of the characteristics of the relationship between the variables and characteristics of the values of independent variables.

Categories of Models
Descriptive Models

The first category of models you are likely to encounter in the business world are called *descriptive models*. Descriptive models simply describe the current situation or system facing the manager. These models tend to have a well-defined relationship between the independent variables (inputs) and the dependent variable (output). Often this translates to a well-defined mathematical formula such as that of a profit equation, where profit is the output. However, the values of the independent variables such as demand are not within the decision maker's control and thus are uncertain. With this type of decision problems, we may use management science techniques such as simulation, as well as queuing, PERT and inventory models.

For example, you currently manage the Waikiki branch of XYZ convenience stores and you believe long lines at the cash register are deterring potential customers from entering the store and making purchases. The manager wants to build a model that reflects the current situation at the store but that will also be able to improve the current situation if possible. The number of customers entering and making purchases varies and has to be estimated or simulated in order to determine the profit.

Prescriptive Models

Prescriptive models on the other hand prescribe solutions for a manager based on the problem defined. Here the relationship between the independent variables and the dependent variable is well defined and the values of the independent variables are known or within the decision maker's control. All we need in order to solve the problem is to determine the values of the independent variables (inputs) that will produce the best possible value for the dependent variable (output).

For example, as an operations manager of a bakery, you may know your inventory of flour, butter, and eggs as well as the labor hours available and the rate of production, but you need to find out how many sweet buns you can produce in a day on the basis of this set of known variables. You may wish to find the optimal number of buns to produce in order to maximize profits while having a limited number of resources available. Another example is a typical investor's problem. How should your limited funds be allocated between different investments in order to maximize returns without exceeding a certain level of risk? Overall, a goal of descriptive models is to generate a solution concept early in the process, whereas a goal of prescriptive models is to better understand the requirements before generating a solution.

Deterministic Models

Deterministic models assume all relevant inputs are known with certainty. Perhaps the most common and popular deterministic modeling technique is mathematical programming.

Stochastic/Probabilistic Models

Stochastic or *Probabilistic models*, on the other hand, assume that some inputs are not known with certainty. This text will present probabilistic modeling techniques such as decision analysis, simulation, and forecasting.

Predictive Models

The final category of decision problems are known as *predictive models*, where the objective is to identify the form of the functional relationship between the dependent variables and the independent variables, as it is unknown. In order to do this, we need to predict how these variables relate to each other, given that the values of the independent variables are known. Several management science techniques such as regression analysis, time series analysis, and discriminant analysis can be used for this purpose.

For example, a marketer believes that the demand for its rejuvenating cream is dependent on price and buyer's age as well as advertising. Here demand is the dependent variable and price, age, and advertising are independent variables. However, the relationship that relates

Descriptive models describe situations.

Prescriptive models vary inputs to reach a desired output.

Deterministic means with certainty.

Stochastic means involving chance or probability.

Predictive models aim to set up functional relationships between dependent and independent variables.

these variables to one another may be unknown. Thus the marketer will have to analyze the relationship, using techniques such as regression analysis of past buying behavior in order to identify the function that relates these variables in a reasonably accurate fashion. Another example is to use historical stock prices to predict the relationship of the current stock price and the underlying index it is traded in.

Models versus Modeling

Good managers learn modeling and not specific models.

It is important to stress that it is not necessary to memorize a particular model to solve real-world problems, but rather to understand the importance of modeling. Modeling is more of a process, where we abstract the essence of a real problem into a model, spreadsheet, or other medium.

PROCESS FOR MODELING

Why a Process for Modeling?

In general, the problem-solving process is made up of a number of steps including a feedback loop.

The intent in this chapter is to demonstrate a general approach to the model-building process in a spreadsheet environment versus covering specific models. The advantage is for the student to complete this course with the ability to apply the knowledge and practicum of spreadsheet modeling to a wide array of business fields, whether it is in information sciences, marketing, finance or human resources.

A few general points before delving into the salient points of the problem solving process.

Initially, a process-driven modeling approach forces one to think logically about the problem at hand. In other words, one must consider in a given situation what elements can be controlled and how they are logically related. In a waiting line situation, the number of customers in line is related to the rate at which the cashier serves each customer. Also the probability that potential customers walk away from a purchase is related to the length of waiting time (also quantified as the number of customers waiting in line multiplied by the average service time taken by the cashier).

In addition, you may be unfamiliar and probably intimidated by the need to conduct spreadsheet modeling for your analysis. This course is taught with the intention of guiding the uninitiated through the basic uses of Excel by way of practical application of the various case studies you and your colleagues will be put through. This chapter will also run through a number of Excel functions that will be useful for a variety of problem-solving applications.

Finally, the problem-solving process that is described in this chapter represents good practice for modelers who are faced with a wide variety of problems rather than a particular problem. The steps we describe here will aid you in how you may logically think through the problem at hand and the steps you may need to take to solve and implement it with greater success in the real world. This may seem redundant to a few of you, as you may possess a natural analytical mind-set; however, it is still important to understand how modeling fits into the entire problem-solving process to be an effective modeler.

The Problem-Solving Process

Step 1: Problem Definition

Normally, those people closest to the business would identify the problem when there exists a disparity between a desired scenario and the actual situation, such as when profits are not as high as anticipated, and the manager wants to understand the underlying cause. Often the manager may have a general idea of the problem but is not be able to clearly define it. The analyst or the manager required to model the problem and conduct an analysis has to sort through the information provided and determine the root problem. Identifying the real problem requires insight, investigation and a certain amount of skepticism.

The result of deriving a proper understanding of the situation at hand would include a clearly defined statement of the problem, the manager's objectives (the dependent variable) and various related parameters (or independent variables). The manager may want to identify what is causing profits to fall, where the objective is to maximize profit. The related parameters could be price, demand, productivity of the sales force, and related expenses.

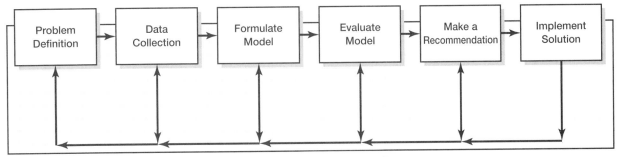

Feedback Loop - Review and Revise

A major mistake in trying to define a problem is to have a solution in mind based on gut feel or even business instinct. Although it is quite common for managers close to the business to believe their view is quite accurate in this respect, an effective modeler who remains objective on the outset may discover insights overlooked by the manager.

Remaining objective is very important in modeling.

Step 2: Data Collection

This stage is not extensively covered, although it is implied, in the rest of the text. Market researchers spend hours collecting data through observation, interviews, surveys, sorting through the organization's historical data, or surfing the Internet. In the chapter on probability, Chapter 3, we show an example of how one may derive a usable function of demand by determining whether demand is normally distributed from a statement given by the manager. Note that very often the data we collect are at best approximations of actual behavior. For example, it is impossible to accurately predict demand on a daily basis for 365 days of the year. The important thing is to understand what is relevant (i.e., critical factors) and how it affects your problem.

Step 3: Formulate Model

After defining the problem and gathering the necessary data, the manager must formulate a model of the problem. Depending on the objective, the model may be descriptive, prescriptive, or predictive. If a manager is faced with various alternatives, such as to increase the sales force or lower the price, to improve profitability, the model has to be descriptive to compare the results of conducting what-if scenarios on a given situation. On the other hand, if a manager who wants to maximize profit while varying the parameters with certain constraints may use a prescriptive model to determine the optimal price or the optimal number of sales people. The model may be a defined mathematical formula, such as the profit equation. The model may be predictive to help define the formula with known variables, such as determining the beta of a stock through a regression analysis of historical stock prices.

Models can be descriptive, prescriptive, deterministic, stochastic, or predictive.

After choosing the appropriate modeling technique for the problem, we can use Excel to apply the relevant model. This is when the inputs (or variables) and formulas are entered into the spreadsheet to achieve outputs for the model.

Step 4: Evaluate the Model

After model formulation, the model has to be evaluated to determine if the model formulated in step 3 is in fact an accurate representation of the problem. There are two ways to do this. You can enter various known inputs to see if the model accurately depicts the current situation. Alternatively, you can vary the inputs to see if the model generates reasonable results.

Evaluation is completed to ensure the model is accurate.

If the model produces awkward results, the modeler will have to evaluate whether the formula and inputs entered are accurate. If they are, the modeler may have to relook at the model, as a crucial constraint (e.g., labor hours must be less that 50 hours per week) or even a crucial variable (e.g., state law requires any nurse seeing critical care patients to be a registered nurse) may have been overlooked.

Testing the results of the model against known results helps ensure the structural integrity and validity of the model. This step is vital as it provides feedback to the modeler to modify the model before it is presented to the manager or client.

Step 5: Make a Recommendation

What-if questions and sensitivity analysis must be part of the recommendations of the model.

Given the spreadsheet model is formulated correctly, the next step is to use the model to analyze the problem it represents and evaluate the alternatives. This may require you to ask several what if questions and conduct sensitivity analysis. In other cases, if the model is prescriptive, it may provide an optimal solution. Often we make estimations for numerical inputs into a problem, besides providing an optimal solution; sensitivity analysis also provides insightsabout how the model works.

Either way, the modeler has to make a recommendation that best meets the organization's objectives. In real-life situations, the modeling team would also have to present and explain their recommendation as well as the workings of the model to the organization.

Step 6: Implementation and Feedback

Implementation may be the most difficult step of the problem solving process.

Even if the model is robust and provides an optimal solution, the hardest part is the implementation step. This is because people in general are naturally resistant to change. One way to ensure buy-in and receptivity is for the modeling team to involve the end users from the onset and preferably have them involved in the entire problem-solving process. Besides improving adoptability, this practice would also give modelers a better understanding of the problem and identify bugs in the model early on, reducing the time required to modify the model. To further ensure that the solution will be accepted, the solution/model should be flexible, with user-friendly interfaces.

This leads us to discuss some basic goals in spreadsheet modeling design in the next section.

Goals in Spreadsheet Design

The primary purpose of spreadsheets is to communicate information to managers.

The primary purpose of spreadsheets is to communicate information to managers. Therefore, the primary design objective in most spreadsheet models is to present the relevant parts of the problem clearly, logically, and in a manner that is simple to comprehend. The output of the spreadsheet model should be correct and consistent.

The model should be constructed such that a manager should be able to retrace the steps followed to generate the different outputs from the model in order to understand the model and verify results. Models therefore should be auditable by a third party and not simply perceived as a black box that receives inputs and spits out results. Often the data and assumptions used are dynamic or are best estimates of a situation. Thus, a well-designed spreadsheet should allow easy modification or enhancement in order to meet dynamic user requirements.

BASIC SPREADSHEET MODELING CONCEPTS

We will describe some basic spreadsheet modeling concepts so that a beginner may be able to follow the topics and applied examples in the rest of the chapter.

Layout of a Spreadsheet

When you open the Excel program you will see from the top, the menu that begins with File, Edit, View, etc., followed by the row of shortcut keys in the toolbar, followed by a Formula bar.

An open spreadsheet is displayed with cells labeled as rows in numbers and columns in alphabets. The rows run downward vertically from 1 to 65536 and columns are viewed from left to right from A to IV. The active cell highlighted on the left hand corner, as shown in Figure 2.1, is referenced as A1. When you enter data in the active cell, it will appear simultaneously in the Formula bar and vice versa.

A standard spreadsheet layout is rows by columns.

A new workbook comes with three sheets indicated by the tabs (labeled Sheet 1, Sheet 2, and Sheet 3) at the bottom of an open workbook. We may use these tabs to toggle between worksheets. We tend not to use all the cells in a single sheet;., a complicated model may instead use several worksheets and new sheets may be inserted at the appropriate time. A useful feature of the Excel spreadsheet is the ability to link cells in the same worksheet and across different worksheets. Therefore, when we choose to vary inputs, we will see the effect of these changes within the model, which may span several worksheets (see Figure 2.1 for details).

FIGURE 2.1
Basic Spreadsheet Layout

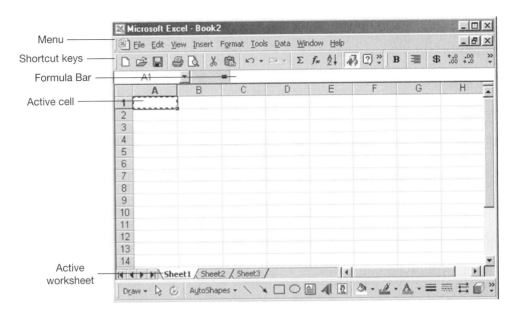

Reference Cells and Ranges

A reference identifies a cell or a range of cells on a worksheet and tells Microsoft Excel where to look for the values or data you want to use in a formula. With references, you can use data contained in different parts of a worksheet in one formula or use the value from one cell in several formulas. A cell reference A2 refers to the cell at the intersection of column A and row 2.

> In a spreadsheet, a reference identifies a cell or range of cells.

To refer to a range of cells, enter the reference for the cell in the upper-left corner of the range, a colon (:), and then the reference to the cell in the lower-right corner of the range. For example, B2:B10 refers to the range of cells in column B row 2 through to row 10. You can also refer to an entire range of cells across columns and rows. For example, B2:D10 refers to the range of cells in column B and row 2 across column D and through to row 10. D:D notation refers to the whole of column D and 2:2 notation refers to the whole of row 2.

> To refer to a range of cells, use a colon between the beginning cell and ending cell.

Relative References

When you create a formula, references to cells or ranges are usually based on their position relative to the cell that contains the formula. In the preceding range reference example, cell B2 contains the formula =A2; Microsoft Excel finds the value in A2 and enters it in B2. This is known as a *relative reference*.

> A relative cell reference in a formula is based on the relative position of the cell that contains the formula and the cell the reference refers to.

Copying Formulas

To move or copy a formula, select the cell that contains it and point your cursor to the fill handle at the bottom right corner of the selection. When you point at the fill handle, the pointer changes into a black cross. Left-click and drag the fill handle (see Figure 2.2) to copy the formula into adjacent cells.

> To copy a formula, select the fill handle and the bottom right hand corner of the cell.

When you copy a formula that uses relative references, Excel automatically adjusts the references in the pasted formula to refer to different cells relative to the position of the formula. In the following example, the formula in cell B2, =A2, which is *one cell to the left of B2*, has been copied to cell B3. Excel has adjusted the formula in cell B3 to =A3, which refers to the cell that is *one cell to the left of cell B3*.

On the other hand, when you copy a formula that uses absolute references, the cell references will not be adjusted, but remain the same.

Absolute References

Absolute references are actually cell references that always refer to cells in a specific location. If a dollar sign precedes the letter and/or number, such as $A$1, the column and/or

Business Decision Modeling Throughout the Ages

A Brief History of Spreadsheet Modeling

WHAT IS MODELING?

Modeling is the process of building a model to replicate a given situation with the ability to preview, test, analyze, or resolve potential obstacles before the actual is implemented or built. Until a few years ago, analytical modeling was rarely used in business and was viewed as arcane, and perhaps with suspicion, by most managers. Its use and application was limited to an elite few. The advent of cheap, fast computing, however, meant that computational efficiency was no longer a concern for many practical business problems. This created new exciting opportunities for end-user application.

HISTORY OF SPREADSHEETS—VISICALC

Computerized or electronic spreadsheets are more recent, and credit for this invention goes to Dan Bricklin and Bob Frankston, who created the software program VisiCalc for Apple II in 1978. Prior to Visicalc, spreadsheet computerization was possible on mainframe computers; however, this was cumbersome and clumsy. VisiCalc was created with the intention of "visualizing the spreadsheet as it was created."

LOTUS 1-2-3

By 1982 there were 18 such spreadsheet programs available in the market. A new product, Lotus 1-2-3, was introduced in 1983. Mitch Kapor, an ex-employee of VisiCorp (the company Bricklin and Frankston founded), developed Lotus 1-2-3, and his spreadsheet program quickly became the new industry spreadsheet standard. By 1985, VisiCalc was removed from the market after being purchased by Lotus. Lotus offered VisiCalc users upgrades to 1-2-3, thereby ensuring Lotus' ability to maintain a dominant market share for almost a decade.

MICROSOFT'S EXCEL

But in today's business world, the most widely acceptable spreadsheet program is Microsoft's Excel. Excel was originally written for the 512K Apple Macintoshes in 1985. By 1988, a PC version of Excel was introduced to run under the Windows operating system and was highly successful. Excel is no longer a simple electronic financial spreadsheet; it serves as a data analysis program, a database and presentation program.

OPTIMAL INFORMATION AREA

D. J. Power's "History of Spreadsheets" Web site at http://www.dssresources.com/history/sshistory.html

Thomas Grossman's "Spreadsheet Analytics" site (an excellent resource) at http://www.ucalgary.ca/~grossman/resources.htm

---

Absolute references always refer to a specific cell location.

row reference is absolute. You can either type in the $ sign to the cell reference or formula, or use the F4 key on your keyboard to toggle between the absolute, mixed, and relative cell references.

Use absolute references if you don't want Excel to adjust references when you copy a formula to a different cell. Thus, if the formula used in cell B2 was absolute, i.e. =$A$2, the formula copied to cell B3 would remain =$A$2 instead of changing to =A3.

Mixed References

Excel allows you to not only fix a specific location but also to fix a column or a row. For example, typing $A2 fixes the column A, but the row reference will be adjusted correspondingly.

FIGURE 2.2
Fill Handle Example in Excel

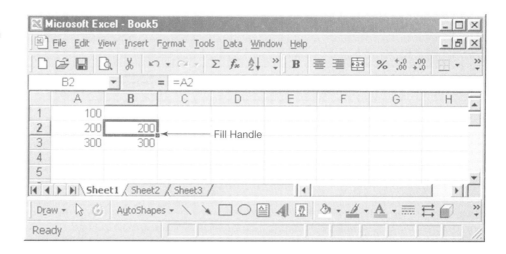

Mixed references can be used to fix a specific column or row.

In turn, typing A$2 fixes the row 2 but allows the column A to vary accordingly. An example: if a formula =$A2+B2 were copied to the cell one cell to the right and one cell down, the formula would be =$A3+C3.

APPLIED SPREADSHEET MODELING—GOAL SEEK

Excel's Goal Seek add-in can be used to solve simple models.

In order to understand the use of spreadsheet modeling, we will run through, step by step, how a spreadsheet model is constructed for a simple profit model and conduct a sensitivity analysis with a data table and chart. We will complete this example by using Goal Seek to identify the break-even level. We will also show the basics of naming cells and using number formats.

Example 1

Teez Incorporated sells printed T-shirts of various designs directly to customers at the local market for $20 per bundle of five T-shirts. The cost of renting the stand for 8 hours is $100 and Teez pays $7 an hour to Sam who sets up and runs the stand every weekend. The cost of producing a T-shirt is $1.50 per T-shirt. Mr. T, the owner of Teez, believes that, on average, he manages to sell 15 bundles a day. Furthermore, he believes that during the rainy season, the average number of bundles sold is dramatically lowered (sometimes to only five bundles), and during those days his profit is greatly reduced. Mr. T wants to know what quantity he needs to sell to break even and whether he should remain open during the rainy season.

Step 1: Problem Definition

Teez wants to know the following:

1. How will a change in the quantity sold affect his profit?
2. At what level of sales does he break even?
3. If he estimates sales of five bundles during the rainy season, should he rent the stand?

Mr. T's revenue is determined by the price and quantity of T-shirts sold. His costs include the fixed cost of renting the stand, the hourly cost of hiring Sam. and the number of hours he works, as well as the cost of producing a T-shirt. His profit is determined by deducting total costs from his revenue.

The input variables are:

Price of a bundle of 5 T-shirts = $20
Quantity sold = 15
Stand rental per day = $100
Hourly labor rate = $7; hours worked = 8
Cost per T-shirt bundle = $1.50

The formulas used are:

$$\text{Revenue} = \text{price} \times \text{quantity of T-shirts sold}$$

$$\text{Total cost} = \text{rental} + (\text{hourly labor rate} \times \text{hours worked}) + \text{cost per shirt} \times \text{number of T-shirt bundles}$$

$$\text{Profit} = \text{revenue} - \text{total cost}$$

Step 2: Formulate the Model

Enter the various variables identified earlier. For a more logical presentation of your model, inputs may be grouped and individual cells are named. We first begin with revenue inputs, which consist of the price and the quantity sold (see Figure 2.3).

Applying Number Format to Cell

The $ shortcut button formats cells into dollars and cents.

Note that after entering 20 in the cell, you may format the input into a dollar format by clicking on the $ shortcut button (indicated by the arrow) in Figure 2.3.

FIGURE 2.3
Spreadsheet Example for Revenue Calculation

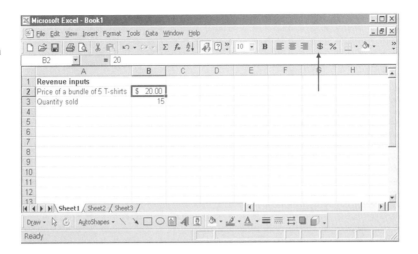

FIGURE 2.4
Example of Number Formatting in Excel

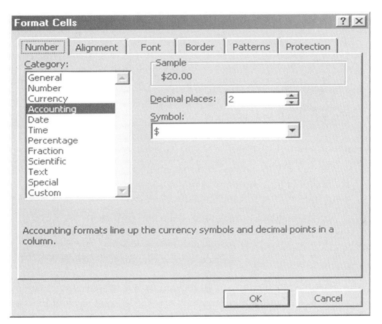

Alternatively you may use the drop-down menu of Format (found on the Menu bar) and point at Cells, after which you will be shown the dialog box in Figure 2.4. You may choose the appropriate format from the left column.

Naming Cells

To name a cell, click on the cell to be named, and then click in the Name box and type in the name of the cell.

Notice that a cell is defined by its location within the columns and rows, In the case of the $20.00 entry, the cell is defined in the spreadsheet as B2, i.e., column B and row 2. Generally it is good practice to name cells that contain formulas or global variables (price, hourly costs, etc.), as it allows the user to more easily identify the concept being modeled within the cells.

To name a cell you have to first click on the cell you wish to name. For the T-shirt example, we wish to name the T-shirt bundle price, cell B2. Therefore, click on cell B2 and then click on the Name box. Type a name for the cell and press Enter. Spaces are unacceptable in a named cell; instead you should use an underscore to indicate a space. For example, the name of B2 should be entered as "Price_of_bundle" instead of "Price of bundle" (see Figure 2.5).

Alternatively, to name a cell, first click on the cell you wish to name. From the Menu bar click on Insert, select Name by pointing at it, then click on Define. You will see the dialog box in Figure 2.6. You may choose the name suggested or you may choose to rename the cell in a simpler form. The cell refers to =Sheet1!$B$2; this should correspond to the cell you initially clicked on and wished to name.

FIGURE 2.5
Example of Naming a
Cell in Excel.

FIGURE 2.6
Defining a Name in
Excel.

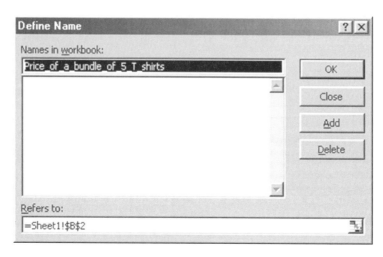

Continue with naming and formatting the rest of the revenue and cost inputs. The spreadsheet should look similar to Figure 2.7. Again, it is good practice to group inputs and outputs separately.

Next we model the revenue, costs and profits. In the Revenue cell, enter the formula (see Figure 2.8):

$$= Price\_of\_bundle\_of\_5\_T\_shirts * Quantity\_sold$$

You may manually type in the cell names or first type =, followed by clicking on the cells you need in the formula. Remember to press Enter to complete the formula. If you do type the formula, you have to type the exact names you used for the relevant cells.

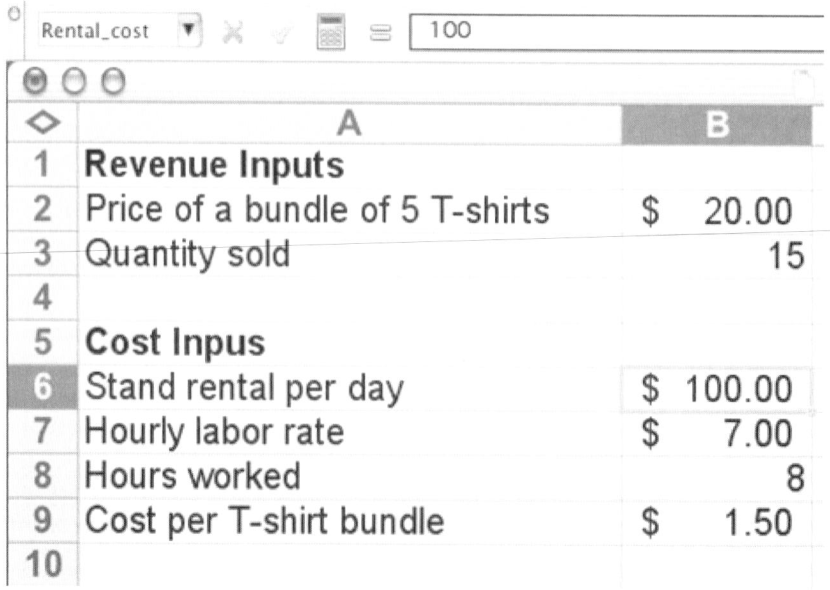

FIGURE 2.7
Example of a Formatted
Excel Spreadsheet

FIGURE 2.8   **Example of a Spreadsheet Displaying Revenue Formula**

Revenue		f_x =Price_of_a_bundle_of_5_T_shirts*Quantity_sold				
	A		B	C	D	E
1	**Revenue Inputs**				**Revenue Outputs**	
2	Price of a bundle of 5 T-shirts		$ 20.00		Revenue	$ 300.00
3	Quantity sold		15			
4						
5	**Cost Inputs**				**Cost Output**	
6	Stand rental per day		$ 100.00		Total cost	$ 178.50
7	Hourly labor rate		$ 7.00			
8	Hours worked		8		**Profit Output**	
9	Cost per T-shirt bundle		$ 1.50		Profit	$ 121.50

FIGURE 2.9   **Example of a Spreadsheet for Profit Calculation**

SUM	X ✓	f_x =Rental_cost+Hourly_labor_rate*Hours_worked+Cost_per_Tshirt_bundle*Quantity_sold				
	A		B	C	D	E
1	**Revenue Inputs**				**Revenue Outputs**	
2	Price of a bundle of 5 T-shirts		$ 20.00		Revenue	$ 300.00
3	Quantity sold		15			
4						
5	**Cost Inputs**				**Cost Output**	
6	Stand rental per day		$ 100.00		Total cost	=Rental_cost
7	Hourly labor rate		$ 7.00			
8	Hours worked		8		**Profit Output**	
9	Cost per T-shirt bundle		$ 1.50		Profit	$ 121.50

In the Total Cost cell, enter the formula:

$$= Rental\_cost + (Hourly\_labor\_cost*Hours\_worked) + (Cost\_per\_Tshirt\_bundle*Quantity\_sold)$$

and in the Profit cell, enter the formula:

$$= Revenue - Total\_cost$$

Take note that it is much more efficient to click on the relevant cells to complete the formulas. You will see from our model that for 15 bundles of T-shirts sold, Teez makes a profit of $121.50 (see Figure 2.10).

Creating Data Tables

To conduct a sensitivity analysis, use Excel's Data Table function.

To conduct a sensitivity analysis to see how profits vary with the values of quantity sold, we use the Data Table function of Excel (see Figure 2.11).

To start the process, type in cell A12 "Sensitivity analysis of Teez profits", in cell A13 type "Quantity sold", and in cell B13 type "Profit". Then in cell B14, we enter a link to the profit model by clicking on cell E9 or entering =Profit. Next, enter the trial values of the quantity sold that you wish to vary in column A. In this example, we chose values from 5 to 20 bundles. This can be as much or as little as you wish; however, the quantity chosen should be sufficient to reflect the changes in profit in order to conduct a reasonable sensitivity analysis.

The trial values of quantity sold in are entered in cells B15 to B30—values 5 to 20 (see Figure 2.12). Finally, we highlight the entire table range, A14:B30, and click on Data from

FIGURE 2.10 **Example of a Spreadsheet for Profit Calculation.**

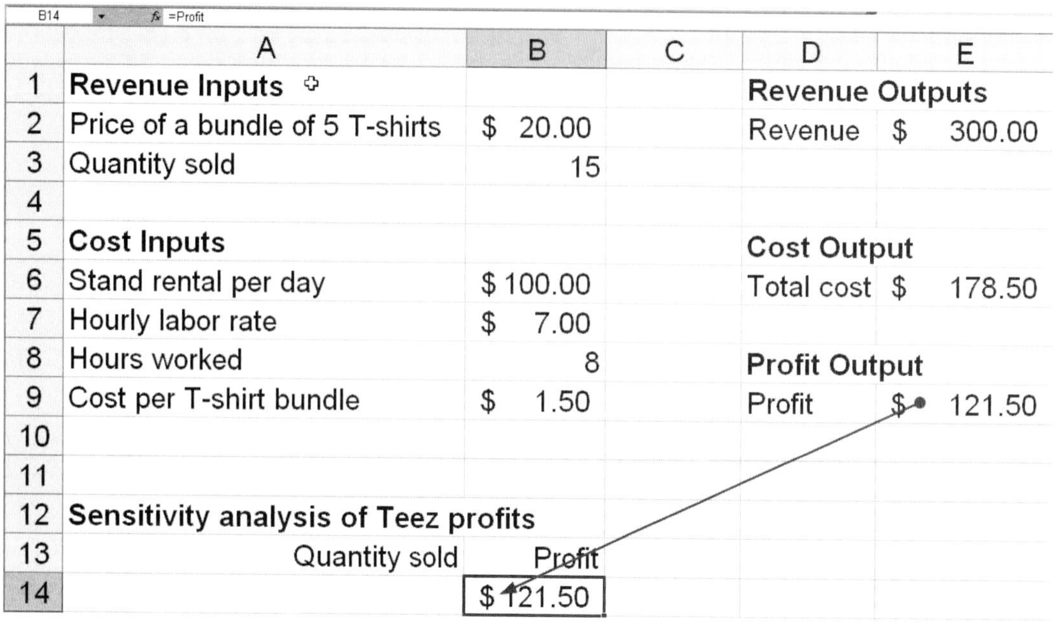

	A	B	C	D	E
B14	▾	f_x =Profit			
1	Revenue Inputs ⟳			Revenue Outputs	
2	Price of a bundle of 5 T-shirts	$ 20.00		Revenue $	300.00
3	Quantity sold	15			
4					
5	Cost Inputs			Cost Output	
6	Stand rental per day	$ 100.00		Total cost $	178.50
7	Hourly labor rate	$ 7.00			
8	Hours worked	8		Profit Output	
9	Cost per T-shirt bundle	$ 1.50		Profit $•	121.50
10					
11					
12	Sensitivity analysis of Teez profits				
13	Quantity sold	Profit			
14		$ 121.50			

the Menu bar and select Table to bring up the Table dialog box (see Figure 2.11). Here we fill in Quantity_sold in the column input cell to indicate that only the input quantity sold is listed along a column.

When you click on OK, Excel substitutes each value of quantity sold to provide the corresponding profit values and reports it in the table (see Figure 2.12).

FIGURE 2.11
Data Table Input Menu

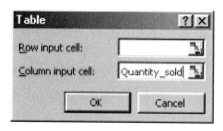

FIGURE 2.12
Data Table Outputs for Profit Sensitivity Analysis

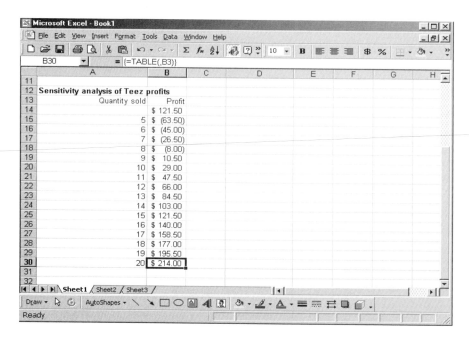

The table results show that Teez would suffer a loss if it sold eight bundles or less and make a profit otherwise. This can be represented graphically by using Excels Chart function.

Creating Charts Using Chart Wizard

To create a chart, click on Insert on the Menu bar and select Chart; the Chart Wizard dialog box will appear (see Figure 2.13). In the left column select the Chart type. Here we choose XY (Scatter); this will graph your table in a scatter plot format. Then click on Next > to go to step 2 of 4 to define your Chart Source Data (see Figure 2.14).

If you began the process immediately after creating the data table, Excel will automatically assume the data table is the Chart's source data for the *x* and *y* axes. If not, you will have to define the Data Range by either typing the location or clicking on the button on the right (indicated by the arrow), which brings you back to your spreadsheet. After that, you highlight the table data you wish to chart. In this example, it is easier to begin first by highlighting the data table before initiating the Chart Wizard.

To create a chart, click on Insert on the Menu bar and select Chart.

FIGURE 2.13
Chart Wizard Step 1 Menu in Excel

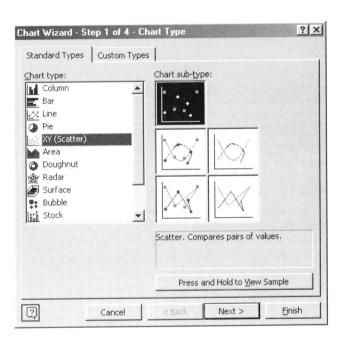

FIGURE 2.14
Chart Wizard Step 2 Menu in Excel

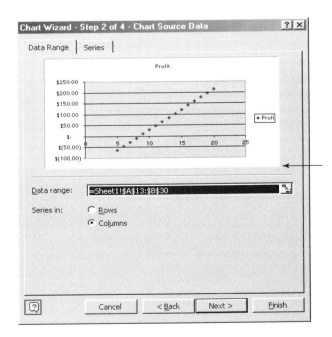

After clicking on Next >, you come to Step 3 of 4, where you customize the layout of your chart (see Figure 2.15). Here, we labeled the chart title and the *x* and *y* axes. We also clicked on the Legend tab and unticked Show Legend. And on the Axes tab, we unticked the major gridlines.

In the final step, the Chart Wizard prompts you to indicate the location of your chart (see Figure 2.16). We left the chart object in the same sheet as the model calculations for easier reference.

The final data table and the chart, side by side, make it easier for the manager to analyze the results of the data and intuitively understand that profit has a linear relationship with quantity sold. That is, profit increases linearly as more T-shirts are sold. The output is shown in Figure 2.17.

Sensitivity Analysis

As mentioned, we see from the scatter plot that profit has a linear relationship with the quantity sold. More specifically, we see that with each additional bundle sold, Teez makes $18.50.

From the chart, we see that Mr. T will not make a profit when he sells eight bundles of T-shirts or less. When Mr. T sells 8 bundles he loses $8, but if he sold 9 bundles he would make $10.50. This answers the question as to whether Mr. T should rent a stand if he expects to only

FIGURE 2.15
Chart Wizard Step 3 Menu in Excel

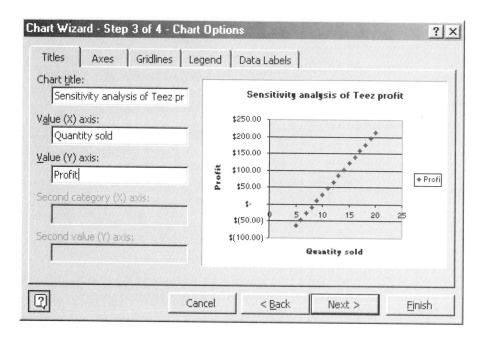

FIGURE 2.16
Chart Wizard Step 4 Menu in Excel

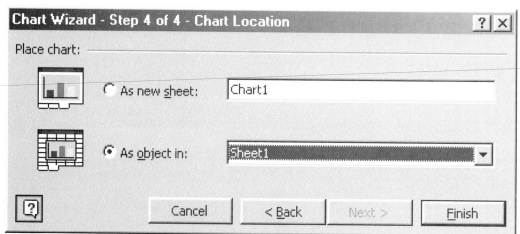

FIGURE 2.17
Final Output from Excel Chart Wizard Example

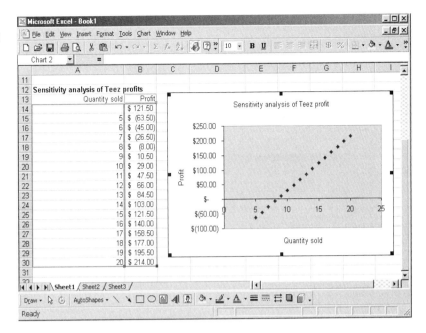

FIGURE 2.18
Goal Seek Menu in Excel

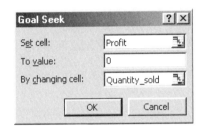

Spreadsheet models allow for easy sensitivity analysis.

sell 5 bundles of T-shirts—obviously not, as he would be losing $63.50. Although it shows the minimum number of T-shirt bundles Teez should sell, it does not quite show the exact break-even level, i.e., when profit is equal to zero.

Once again, this may be possible with a manual entry of values; nonetheless, Excel has a function called Goal Seek that will automatically compute the exact value for us.

Using Goal Seek

When you know the desired result of a single formula but not the input value the formula needs to obtain that result, you can use the Goal Seek feature. When goal seeking, Microsoft Excel varies the value in one specific cell until a formula that's dependent on that cell returns the result you want.

Here we wish to find the result where profit = 0. The single dependent input value to produce this result would be the quantity sold; this is known as the decision variable, as the profit value of 0 is achieved by changing cell quantity sold.

To implement Goal Seek, click on the Tools menu then click on the Goal Seek menu.

To implement Goal Seek, click on the Tools menu and point on Goal Seek. The dialog box in Figure 2.18) will appear. Fill in the boxes as follows and click on OK when finished.

1. Move your curser to the Set cell dialog box and click on the named cell, Profit, in your spreadsheet.
2. Move your curser to the To value dialog box and enter 0.
3. Move your curser to the By changing cell dialog box and click on the named cell, Quantity_sold, in your spreadsheet.

Excel will iterate through the possible values in the quantity sold cell to achieve profit = 0. When Excel finds a solution, the Goal Seek Status box will appear (see Figure 2.19).

FIGURE 2.19
Goal Seek Status Menu in Excel

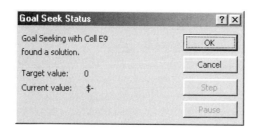

FIGURE 2.20
Final Example Spreadsheet for Teez

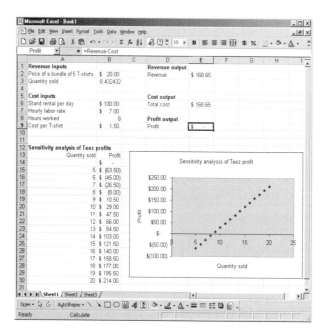

You will find that on your spreadsheet, the profit value has been changed to 0 and the quantity sold is 8.432432 bundles. Obviously it is currently not possible to sell a fraction of a T-shirt bundle. However, it at does show that in order to break even, Teez must sell at least nine bundles, since eight bundles would not cover costs. The final spreadsheet is shown in Figure 2.20.

BASIC EXCEL FUNCTIONS

Formulas enable a user to quickly perform numeric calculations in a spreadsheet.

A key advantage of using Excel is the ability to create and use formulas in its spreadsheets. Formulas enable you to quickly perform numeric calculations as we have seen in Example 1. As we mentioned earlier, you may enter a formula in the active cell by first typing the equal sign, = to indicate the beginning of a formula in the cell.

MATHEMATICAL OPERATORS

Mathematical operators commonly used in Excel are:

+ for addition

− for subtraction

* for multiplication

/ for division

^ for "the power of," e.g., 2^3 in Excel is typed as 2^3

EXP( ) for exponential, e.g., e^2 in Excel is typed as EXP(2)

Commonly used mathematical operators in Excel are +, −, *, etc.

As with basic mathematics, formulas entered in Excel are calculated in order of precedence and not just left to right. Operations inside parentheses are calculated first, followed by exponential, multiplication or division, and addition or subtraction. So the formula $= 2+3*(2\hat{\ }3)$ would first calculate $2\hat{\ }3=8$ within the parenthesis, followed by multiplying with 3, $3*8=24$. The final function is to add 2 to 24, $2+24=26$.

Built-in Functions

Excel has many built-in functions that can be accessed via the function key, f_x.

Besides entering formulas, you may use Excel's built-in functions. All functions require an equal sign ($=$), a function name, and at least one value in the subsequent parentheses. Multiple values for calculation may be separated with commas within the parentheses. We can invoke the Paste Function dialog box by clicking on shortcut key f_x to see all the functions available in Excel (see Figure 2.21). On the left column are the Function categories, and the highlighted category will reveal all the relevant Function names in the right column.

SUM(number1,number2,...)

The SUM function adds individual cells.

Under the Function category we selected Math & Trig and highlighted SUM. The function SUM adds individual cells that are separated by commas within the parentheses. Click OK and the Formula Palette opens (see Figure 2.22). The Formula Palette displays the "arguments" that the chosen function needs (the items that go between the parentheses). Required arguments are in bold; nonbolded arguments are optional.

FIGURE 2.21
Paste Function Menu in Excel

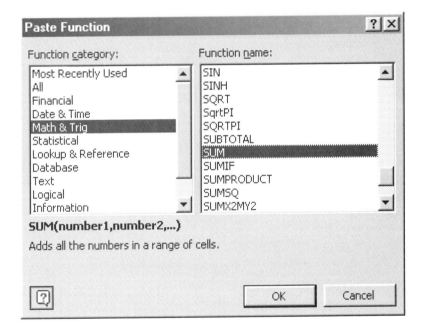

FIGURE 2.22
Formula Palette for SUM Function in Excel

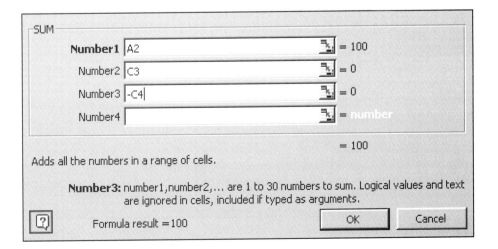

For example, you want to add A2 to C3 and to subtract C4. You may enter the following formula =A2+C3−C4 or you may type directly in the cell =SUM(A2, C3, −C4). With the Formula Palette, you may enter A2 in Number 1 tab to enter the subsequent cells or cell names.

Alternatively, you may wish to add an entire column from A2 through to A10; instead of typing each cell individually, you may use the SUM function with a range reference like = SUM(A2:A10) (see Figure 2.23).

AutoSum

The AutoSum function in Excel allows easy summations of designated cells.

There is another shortcut key that comes in handy, *AutoSum*, denoted by the shortcut key Σ. You have entered values in A2:A10. Click on blank cell A11 to indicate the location of your formula, then click on the AutoSum symbol. Depending on how your variables were entered in the spreadsheet, Excel might suggest a range of numbers to sum by displaying a blinking dotted line around it. Once you hit Enter, you will confirm the formula = SUM(A2:A10) in cell location A11 (see Figure 2.24).

FIGURE 2.23 **Formula Palette for SUM Function in Excel**

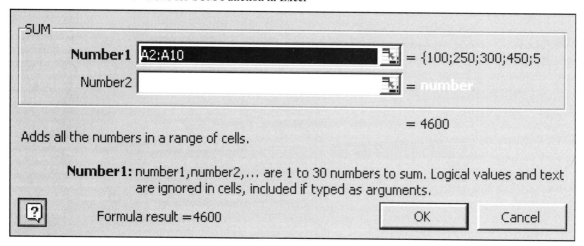

FIGURE 2.24

Example of AutoSum Function in Excel

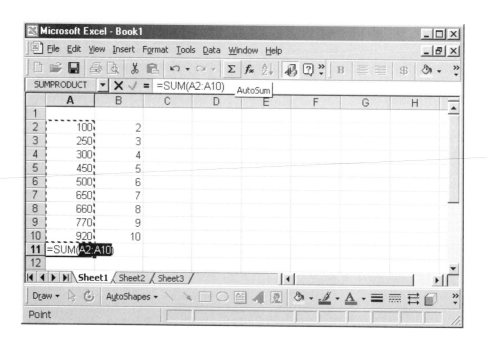

SUMPRODUCT(array1,array2,...)

The SUMPRODUCT function multiplies corresponding values of arrays of the same dimension.

Another variation of the Sum function is *SUMPRODUCT*; this function multiplies corresponding values of arrays of the same dimension and returns the sum of these products. For example, you wish to multiply the values in column A with values in column B and wish to add all of the results together. You may enter =A2*B2+A3*B3+...+A10*B10 or you can use a much simpler formula with Excel's function = SUMPRODUCT(A2:A10, B2:B10) (see Figure 2.25).

Statistical Functions

Average

Excel contains a number of common statistical functions.

From the Statistical category, the most commonly used statistical function is *AVERAGE*, also known as the mean. Average totals all the items in a list and divides by the number of items in the list.

If a cell is blank or contains text, it is ignored and not included in the total or the number of items. The Formula Palette for the AVERAGE function is displayed in Figure 2.26. The formula bar will reflect the formula =Average(B2:B10).

Median

The MEDIAN function in Excel finds the middle number of a group of numbers; that is, half the numbers have values greater than the median and half the numbers have values less than the median.

In statistics the median gives the number in the middle of a set of given numbers. The cell location will indicate the formula =Median(B2:B10). Figure 2.27 displays the formula palette for the MEDIAN function in Excel.

FIGURE 2.25
Formula Palette for SUMPRODUCT Function in Excel

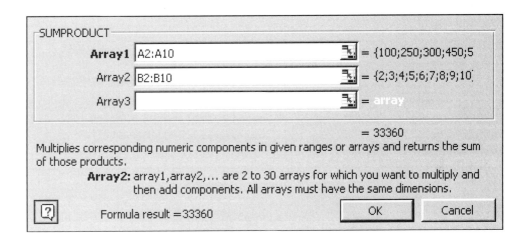

FIGURE 2.26 Formula Palette for AVERAGE Function in Excel

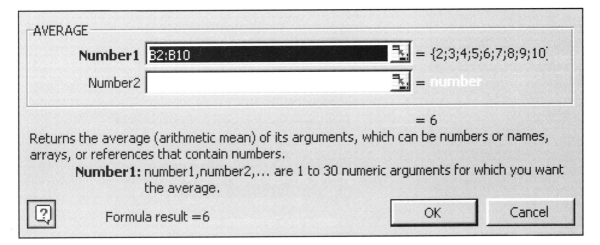

FIGURE 2.27 **Formula Palette for MEDIAN Function in Excel**

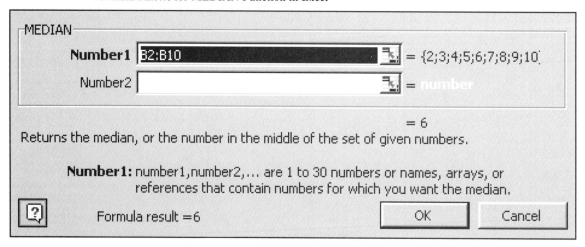

FIGURE 2.28 **Formula Palette for MAX Function in Excel**

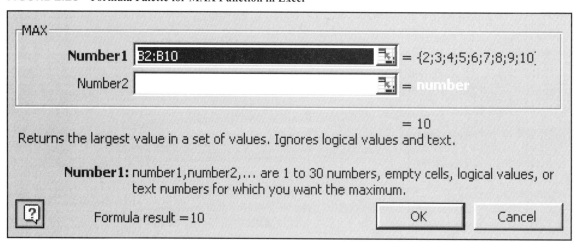

MIN/MAX Function

The MIN and MAX functions return the minimum and maximum of a data set.

With function Max(number1, number2, . . .), Excel will return the largest value among the given set of values in a list (see Figure 2.28 for the MAX function and Figure 2.29 for the MIN function). From a list (2, 3, 4, 5, 6, 7, 8, 9, 10), the maximum value is 10 and the minimum value is 2.

The formula shown would be =MAX(B2:B10) to find the largest value and =MIN(B2:B10) to return the smallest value.

Logical Functions

Logical functions in Excel return one of two possible results: TRUE or FALSE.

A logical function can return only one of two possible results: TRUE or FALSE. The IF function is frequently used because it can test for a particular condition in the worksheet and use one value if the condition is true and another value if the condition is false.

If

The IF function in Excel enables a user to create conditional tests.

Excel has a built-in IF function that enables you to create conditional tests on values and formulas. If a condition is true, you may display one value or perform a calculation. If the condition is false, you may display another value or perform another calculation. Thus the syntax of an IF function is different from that of the functions described earlier. Basically, it should follow =IF(logical_test, value_if_true, value_if_false)

FIGURE 2.29   **Formula Palette for MIN Function in Excel**

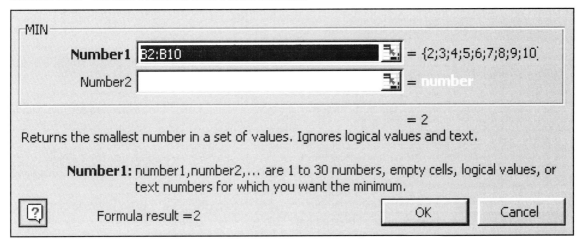

TABLE 2.1
IF Statement Example
Data

If AverageScore is	Then return
Greater than 89	A
From 80 to 89	B
From 70 to 79	C
From 60 to 69	D
Less than 60	F

The logical test is a condition that has to be met. An example is A2>200 or B2<=150. Note that >= is "equal to or greater than," <= is "equal to or less than," and <> is "not equal to." If the test proves true, if A2 is actually 300, Excel will look at the "value if true" and follow the stated action or return a value (which could also be text). Just include the function to be tested in quotes.

For example, the formula =IF(A2>200,"A","B") would return A in the cell. The next spreadsheet example will show how this can be applied to a problem. Consider, Table 2.1 as an example. You can use the following nested IF function:

$$=IF(AverageScore>89, \text{"A"}, IF(AverageScore>79, \text{"B"}, IF(AverageScore>69, \text{"C"},$$
$$IF(AverageScore>59, \text{"D"}, \text{"F"}))))$$

In this function, the second IF statement is also the value_if_false argument to the first IF statement. Similarly, the third IF statement is the value_if_false argument to the second IF statement. For example, if the first logical_test (Average>89) is TRUE, A is returned. If the first logical_test is FALSE, the second IF statement is evaluated, and so on.

Using Lookup Functions

Because Excel allows a maximum of only seven nested IF loops and too many nested IF functions become confusing to the reader, the Lookup function can be used instead to look up values in a table similar to Table 2.1. Usually this is necessary to look up a value from a list of items in order to use the right value in a formula for future calculations.

Excel allows you to look up a table either horizontally of vertically by using the HLOOKUP and VLOOKUP functions, respectively. Use HLOOKUP when your comparison values are located in a row across the top of a table of data, and you want to look down a specified number of rows. Use VLOOKUP when your comparison values are located in a column to the left of the data you want to find. From the Formula Paste function, we can select the Lookup and Reference category to find the HLOOKUP and VLOOKUP functions. It must be noted that, for the HLOOKUP and VLOOKUP functions to perform correctly, the data must be sorted in ascending order.

HLOOKUP (Horizontal Lookup) Function

To use the HLOOKUP function across an array, we need to first sort through the data in ascending order. Consider Table 2.2 entered in the spreadsheet in this form. A grade with 90 and above will be assigned the letter grade A, a grade between 80 and 89 will be assigned the letter grade B and so on.

Sorting Data

In this table, the data in the first row are in descending order, and we need to sort the data in ascending order. To sort this table of data, highlight the items you wish to sort. From the menu select Data and select Sort. The Sort dialog box will appear (see Figure 2.30).

Click on Options and select "Sort left to right" (see Figure 2.31). Then click on OK.

The table will be sorted in ascending order from left to right. The sorted table is displayed in Table 2.3.

We use cell B4 to enter the number grade we refer to as the lookup value. In cell B5, we enter the following formula (see Figure 2.32):

=HLOOKUP(B4,$A$1:$D$2,2)The result returned is the letter grade of C.

The syntax of HLOOKUP is as follows:

HLOOKUP(lookup_value,table,row_index_num,range_lookup)

The formula we used is

=HLOOKUP(B4,$A$1:$D$2,2)

TABLE 2.2
HLOOKUP Statement
Example Data

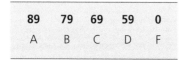

89	79	69	59	0
A	B	C	D	F

FIGURE 2.30
Sort Menu in Excel

FIGURE 2.31
Sort Options Menu in Excel

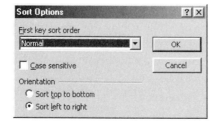

TABLE 2.3
Sorted Data for
HLOOKUP Example in
Excel

0	59	69	79	89
F	D	C	B	A

TABLE 2.4
Example Data for
VLOOKUP Function

89	A
79	B
69	C
59	D
0	F

FIGURE 2.32
HLOOKUP Function
Example in Excel

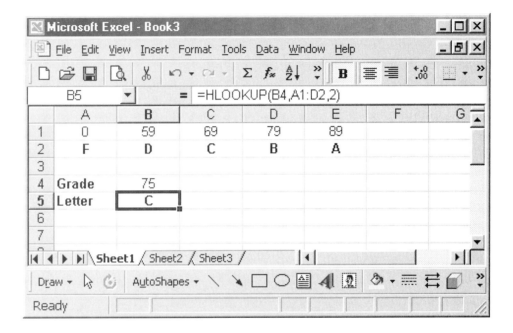

Thus B4 held our lookup value, while A1:D2 is the table reference where Excel will look up the closest corresponding value and 2 indicates that the value we want returned is found in the second row of the table A1:D2.

The argument range_lookup can take the value True or False. When we type True, Excel will find the closest corresponding to the lookup value. In other words, if an exact match is not found, the next largest value that is less than the lookup value is returned. In this case 75 had no exact match, and the next largest value that is less than 75 was 69, thus Excel returned the value C. When we type False, Excel will find an exact match. Since we did not enter a range lookup value, Excel assumed the value as True.

VLOOKUP (Vertical Lookup) Function

VLOOKUP searches for a value in the leftmost column of a table, and then returns a value in the same row from a column you specify in the table. Use VLOOKUP instead of HLOOKUP when your comparison values are located in a column to the left of the data you want to find.

Consider the table of grades in Table 2.4, where the number grade comparison values are on the first column to the left of the letter grade value you wish to find.

However, the values are in descending order, and we should sort the table in ascending order. This time in the Options select "Sort data from top to bottom" to return the format in Table 2.5.

The syntax of VLOOKUP is as follows:

VLOOKUP(lookup_value,table,col_index_num,range_lookup)

TABLE 2.5
Sorted Data for VLOOKUP Example in Excel

0	F
59	D
69	C
79	B
89	A

FIGURE 2.33
VLOOKUP Function Example in Excel

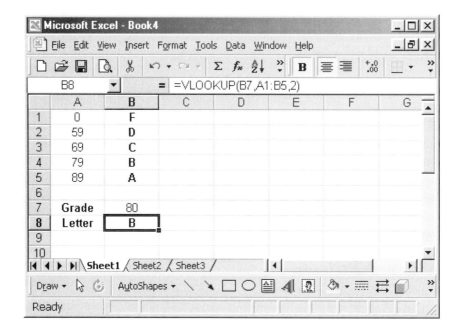

The formula we used is

$$\text{VLOOKUP(B7,\$A\$1:\$B\$5,2)}$$

The only difference is the third argument, column index number. In our formula we used 2, as the second column is where the closest or matching value to the lookup value can be found. Figure 2.33 shows the relevant Excel screen.

APPLIED SPREADSHEET MODELING—USING BASIC FUNCTIONS

A further use of functions in Excel is demonstrated here in an extension of the earlier Teez example. The model developed here is considered a descriptive model, where Mr. T wants to use the model to estimate his order quantity from the manufacturer. In the previous example, the price of the T-shirt was fixed. The expected profit is estimated with a set of probabilities of demand.

Example 2

Mr. T of Teez has expanded his operations and now sells his T-shirts in various locations. He intends to maintain the same T-shirt selling price as before; however, as we mentioned, he has to purchase more than 1000 T-shirts to attain the low price of $1.50 from the manufacturer. There are different levels of prices, and the discount table that the manufacturer uses is shown in Table 2.6. With his expanded operation, Mr. T is very uncertain about the demand for his T-shirts; the demand ranges from 20 bundles (100 T-shirts) to 400 bundles (2000 T-shirts) a week. If Mr. T has any left over, he may sell all excess inventory to a discount store for $1 per T-shirt. How many T-shirts should Mr. T order from the manufacturer?

TABLE 2.6
Quantity and Price Discount Data for Teez

Quantity	Price discount
Less than 100	$3.75
Between 100 and 199	$3.50
Between 200 and 499	$3.25
Between 500 and 799	$3.00
Between 800 and 999	$2.50
1000 and above	$1.50

FIGURE 2.34
Teez Spreadsheet Profit Model.

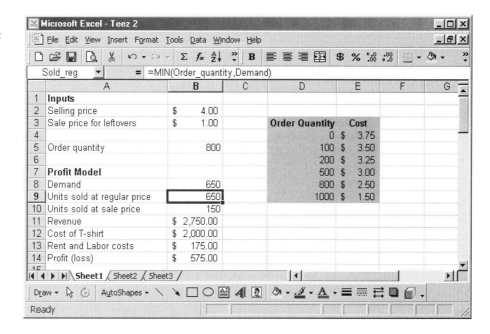

Step 1: Problem definition

Mr. T wants to know the following: How many T-shirts should he order to maximize profit on the basis of an uncertain demand and the ability to sell his excess inventory for $1?

Step 2: Formulate Model

Revenue comes from selling T-shirts at the regular price to the customers as well as from the sale of leftovers. The regular selling price is $4, while the sale price is $1. If the demand for that week is less than the quantity ordered, the number of units sold at regular price is determined by demand and excess units (quantity ordered − demand) are sold at sale price. If demand exceeds the quantity ordered, revenue would be regular selling price × demand.

To begin, first enter the data inputs we know, the selling price, the sale price, and the arbitrary order quantity and demand.

Using MIN Function

Next we use the MIN function (see Figure 2.34) in a formula to return the number of units sold at regular price in cell B9 (named Sold_reg).

$$=\text{MIN(Order\_quantity,Demand)}$$

This formula returns the lesser of the two arguments. If demand exceeds the quantity ordered, the formula would return the quantity ordered. This follows the logic that the units sold at regular price are limited by the stock on hand.

On the other hand, if demand were less than the quantity ordered, the formula would return demand. Correspondingly, the excess inventory would then be sold at the sale price.

Using IF Function

The formula used to return the number of units sold at sale price in cell B10, which we named Sold_sale, is

$$=IF(Order\_quantity>Demand,Order\_quantity-Demand,0)$$

This formula uses the IF function with the condition that, should the quantity ordered be greater than demand, the formula calculates the excess inventory (value if true). This excess inventory is the number of units sold at sale price. When the condition is violated, such as when demand exceeds the quantity ordered, the formula would return 0 (value if false). This corresponds to the assumption that, with no excess inventory, all T-shirts will be sold at the regular price, thus no leftover T-shirts will be available to be sold at the sale price to the discount store.

With the units of T-shirts sold at regular price and sale price calculated, we can enter the following formula in cell B11 to calculate Teez's revenue.

$$=Sold\_reg*Selling\_price+Sold\_sale*Sale\_price$$

There is also the issue of quantity discounts. If Mr. T orders only 800 T-shirts, his cost is \$2.50 per T-shirt. We need to use a lookup function to return the corresponding cost per T-shirt based on the quantity ordered by Teez. Other costs are fixed, such as rental and labor costs of \$175.

Using VLOOKUP Function

The formula used to calculate the cost of T-shirts in cell B11 is

$$=VLOOKUP(Order\_quantity,\$D\$4:\$E\$9,2)*Order\_quantity$$

We use the order quantity as the lookup value, where the reference table is defined by D4:E9 (color formatted in purple for clarity). The value returned is the corresponding cost per T-shirt according to the order quantity seen in the second column of the table. The resulting cost per T-shirt is multiplied by the order quantity to calculate Teez's total cost of ordering T-shirts.

Profit is simply revenue − cost of T-shirts − other costs. The formula entered in the Profit cell is

$$=B11-B12-B13$$

Sensitivity Analysis Using Data Table

Using the same method as in Figure 2.11, create a data table of Teez's profit as Demand (column input) and Quantity ordered (row input) varies. The values from 100 to 1100 is used for both demand and order quantity.

From the data table (see Figure 2.35), we can see that Teez enjoys a healthy profit for higher values of demand and order quantity. In fact, it makes sense to assume that if Mr. T ordered more than 1000 T-shirts, he would make a profit as long as demand remained above 200. But as demand is uncertain, this may not yield the highest expected profit for Teez. This also leads to the next question, "How much more than 1000 T-shirts should Mr. T order?"

Expected Profit with Demand Probabilities

In this example, the quantity ordered is decided by Mr. T and is within his control (the decision variable), while demand is not within his control. On further investigation of his sales data, he produced a probability table of demand (see Table 2.7). With these probabilities, we may calculate the order quantity with the highest expected profit and based on the probability of demand.

TABLE 2.7
Demand Probability for Teez Company

Demand	100	200	300	400	500	600	700	800	900	1000	1100
Probability	1%	2%	3%	8%	12%	16%	20%	15%	13%	7%	3%

FIGURE 2.35   **Data Table Outputs for Teez Sensitivity Analysis**

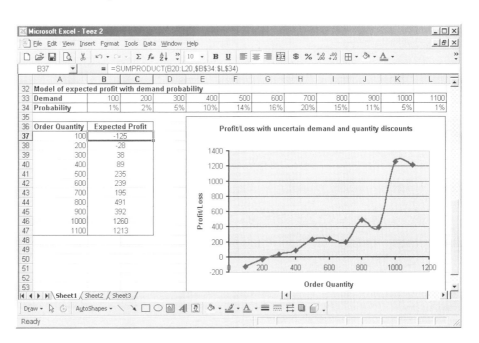

Order Quantity	Demand										
$ 575.00	100	200	300	400	500	600	700	800	900	1000	1100
100	$ (125)	$ (125)	$ (125)	$ (125)	$ (125)	$ (125)	$ (125)	$ (125)	$ (125)	$ (125)	$ (125)
200	$ (325)	$ (25)	$ (25)	$ (25)	$ (25)	$ (25)	$ (25)	$ (25)	$ (25)	$ (25)	$ (25)
300	$ (550)	$ (250)	$ 50	$ 50	$ 50	$ 50	$ 50	$ 50	$ 50	$ 50	$ 50
400	$ (775)	$ (475)	$ (175)	$ 125	$ 125	$ 125	$ 125	$ 125	$ 125	$ 125	$ 125
500	$ (875)	$ (575)	$ (275)	$ 25	$ 325	$ 325	$ 325	$ 325	$ 325	$ 325	$ 325
600	$ (1,075)	$ (775)	$ (475)	$ (175)	$ 125	$ 425	$ 425	$ 425	$ 425	$ 425	$ 425
700	$ (1,275)	$ (975)	$ (675)	$ (375)	$ (75)	$ 225	$ 525	$ 525	$ 525	$ 525	$ 525
800	$ (1,075)	$ (775)	$ (475)	$ (175)	$ 125	$ 425	$ 725	$ 1,025	$ 1,025	$ 1,025	$ 1,025
900	$ (1,225)	$ (925)	$ (625)	$ (325)	$ (25)	$ 275	$ 575	$ 875	$ 1,175	$ 1,175	$ 1,175
1000	$ (375)	$ (75)	$ 225	$ 525	$ 825	$ 1,125	$ 1,425	$ 1,725	$ 2,025	$ 2,325	$ 2,325
1100	$ (425)	$ (125)	$ 175	$ 475	$ 775	$ 1,075	$ 1,375	$ 1,675	$ 1,975	$ 2,275	$ 2,575

(Row 14: Profit (loss) $575.00; Row 17: Data Table of profit as function of order quantity and demand; Cell B37 formula: =SUMPRODUCT(B20:L20,$B$34:$L$34))

Using SUMPRODUCT

To calculate the expected profit on the basis of the probabilities in Table 2.7, we enter in cell B37 the formula

$$=\text{SUMPRODUCT(B20:L20,\$B\$34:\$L\$34)}.$$

We calculate the expected profit for each order quantity by multiplying the probability of demand with the profit for each row of order quantity that we calculated in the data table earlier. Note how absolute references are used for the probabilities before copying the formula down to cell B47 (see Figure 2.36).

Using the X-Y scatter plot, we achieve the graph that clearly shows that expected profit is highest at $1260 when the order quantity is 1000. This does not mean that Mr.T will be guaranteed to make a profit of $1260; the actual profit will depend on eventual demand. This model is a reasonable way for Mr. T to estimate how much he should order.

FIGURE 2.36

Expected Profit Calculation for Teez Company

Model of expected profit with demand probability											
Demand	100	200	300	400	500	600	700	800	900	1000	1100
Probability	1%	2%	5%	10%	14%	16%	20%	15%	11%	5%	1%

Order Quantity	Expected Profit
100	-125
200	-28
300	38
400	89
500	235
600	239
700	195
800	491
900	392
1000	1260
1100	1213

Profit/Loss with uncertain demand and quantity discounts

APPLIED SPREADSHEET MODELING—USING SOLVER

The model developed for a production planning/product mix problem is a prescriptive one. The relationship between variables is well defined and the variables are within the control of the manager. We use Excel's Solver to find the optimal production plan to maximize profits, thus prescribing a solution to the problem.

Example 3

Sweets Bakery is known for its specialty cake and custard pie, and every day there are least 15 customers willing to buy the cakes and 20 willing to buy the pies. The cake is sold for $20 and the custard pie for $18. However, the owner currently has three full-time bakers that she can trust with the recipe, each working 8-hour days. To bake each cake requires a block of butter, 4 eggs and 2 packets of flour as well as an hour of the baker's time. Each pie requires a block of butter, 12 eggs and 1 packet of flour and 45 minutes to bake (0.75 hours). This is shown alongside the cost of each ingredient/input in Table 2.8.

The owner gets a delivery of ingredients fresh daily from the supplier. Her current daily order is shown in Table 2.9.

Step 1: Problem Definition

The first thing the owner wants to have is a solution that would allow her to adjust her production plan and purchasing decisions based on these parameters. There are several questions she needs to have answered

1. How many cakes and pies should be produced to maximize profits, based on current inputs.

2. Is production capacity constrained by labor or ingredients?

3. How will production capacity change if input resources are changed?

Step 2: Model Formulation

The decision to be made in this problem is the number of cakes and pies to produce in order to maximize profit. In turn, the actual numbers of cakes and pies to produce are referred to as the decision variables of the problem. Then again, the profitability of Sweets is limited by its production capacity and demand.

To determine the production capacity of Sweets, we have to understand how production is limited by the amount of ingredients and labor used for each cake and pie. The input mix of each product can be described in the form of a closed equation.

One cake = 1 block of butter + 4 eggs + 2 packets of flour + 1 hour of labor

One pie = 1 block of butter + 12 eggs + 1 packet of flour + 0.75 hour of labor

Obviously the multiple of the number of units produced would imply the same multiple of inputs to be used for production. For example, two cakes would use 2×1 block of butter + 2×4 eggs + 2×2 packets of flour + 2×1 hour of labor.

However, we are told there is a daily delivery of supplies and three bakers who work 8-hour days. Thus, the supplies and labor available limit production of cakes and pies. This constitutes

TABLE 2.8
Ingredient and Cost Data for Sweets Bakery

	Cake	Custard Pie	Cost
Butter per block	1	1	$1.00
Egg	4	12	$0.20
Flour per packet	2	1	$3.00
Per hour of labor	1	0.75	$7.00

TABLE 2.9
Ingredient Delivery Data for Sweets Bakery

Butter per block	24
Egg	240
Flour per packet	30

the input constraints. In the spreadsheet model we have to ensure that inputs used are less than or equal to the inputs available.

Calculation of the profit is fairly straightforward. Because the model limits production capacity to less than or equal to daily demand, we are assuming that all units produced will be sold. Hence, revenue of cakes and pies is determined by the selling price and the number produced. Likewise, cost per item is determined by multiplying the input mix by the number produced of each item and the cost of each input.

Consequently, we may use Excel's Solver to solve for maximum profit, taking into consideration the production capacity and demand constraints.

Building the Spreadsheet Model

Cost inputs and price inputs should be entered first. as these are static and values that are given. Enter the matrix of values of the production input mix for both cake and pies (see Figure 2.37).

Subsequently, we formulate the spreadsheet model with the input and the demand constraints (see Figure 2.38). In the section Production Plan we put in arbitrary values of 10 cakes and 10 pies. In cell B23:C23, we enter <= to show the demand constraint in the following line (maximum sales of cake and pie). This symbol does not calculate, but serves to clarify the logic of the model.

We highlighted the cells to show these are the decision variables. Later, we will describe how Solver will vary the values in these cells to determine the maximum profit given demand and capacity constraints.

The next section shows the input constraints, defined by columns labeled Used, Available, and Excess. In the Used column, under the row of Butter at cell B28, we enter the formula

$$=SUMPRODUCT(\$B\$22:\$C\$22,B15:C15)$$

Notice the use of absolute reference for the units produced, as we then drag to copy this formula to the rest of the input constraints. This formula uses the multiple of each item produced and multiplies it with the butter input (B15:C15) and sums it up to return the total amount of butter used to produce 10 cakes and 10 pies. The other inputs used are calculated the same way.

In the range C28:C31, we enter <= again for clarity purposes to show the input constraints. Under the column Available, we enter the supplies available for daily production. Under the Excess column, we use the IF function to calculate excess supplies at the end of the day after producing 10 cakes and 10 pies. In cell E28, the formula entered is

$$=IF(D28>B28,D28-B28,0)$$

FIGURE 2.37
Sweets Bakery Initial
Spreadsheet Model

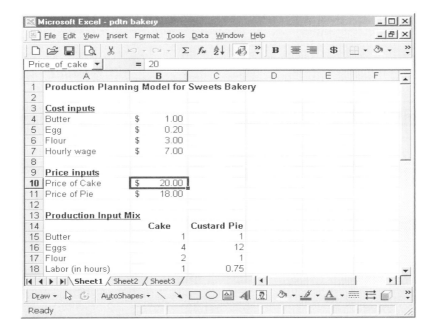

FIGURE 2.38
Sweets Bakery
Spreadsheet Including
Input and Demand
Constraints

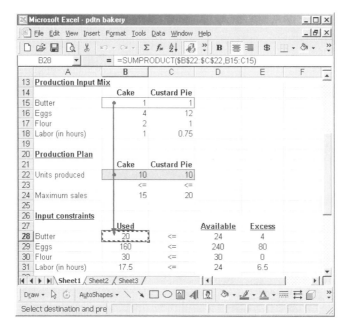

FIGURE 2.39
Sweets Bakery Final
Spreadsheet Model

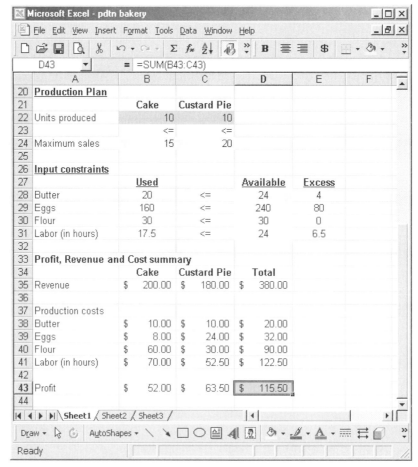

Notice the use of relative reference for the units produced, as we then drag to copy this formula to the rest of the input constraints.

Finally, revenue, costs, and profit are formulated for the spreadsheet model (see Figure 2.39). We chose to separate the calculation of revenue, costs, and profits for both the cake and the pie, so that the manager of Sweets can clearly see how each item contributes to the profit calculation.

The formulas are fairly straightforward but we will show one example for the revenue, cost, and profit cells. In the Cake Revenue cell, B35, the formula entered is

$$=Price\_of\_cake*Cakes\_produced$$

In the input cell B38, the cost cell, the formula entered is

$$=B4*B15*Cakes\_produced$$

where B4 is the cost of butter, and B15 from the Production Input Mix section is the amount of butter used per cake. In the Cake Profit cell, B43, the formula entered is

$$=B35-SUM(B38:B41)$$

The highlighted cell of Total Profit is the target cell representing the cell that Solver will solve for. In this instance, we wish to maximize profit.

Using Excel's Solver

Solver is similar to Goal Seek, where Excel will vary input cells to come up with a desired solution. However, with Goal Seek you may change only one input cell, whereas Solver changes multiple input cells. In this chapter, we will not go too much in detail about the various uses of Solver, but will demonstrate how simple it is to use to solve a profit maximization problem.

To invoke Solver, go to Tools menu and select Solver. This will open the Solver Parameters dialog box (see Figure 2.40). If Solver is not on your menu, go to the Tools menu and Add-Ins submenu, then check the Solver checkbox, and press OK. Solver should now be listed in the Tools menu. Refer to Chapter 8, on optimization, for further details on Solver and how to install it and for guidance if you have any other difficulty.

As mentioned, we set cell D43 (named Total_profit) as the target cell and select Max to indicate we wish to maximize Total Profit. In the text box of By Changing Cells, we enter the cells we wish Excel to modify in order to maximize profit. These are the decision variables B22:C22, named Units_produced.

Next, we enter the constraints in the text box of Subject to the Constraints. We do this by clicking on Add to get the following Add Constraint dialog box (see Figure 2.41).

Our first constraint is the input constraint. We know that Production Mix Inputs Used column has to be less than or equal to the values of Production Mix Inputs Available column,

FIGURE 2.40
Solver Menu

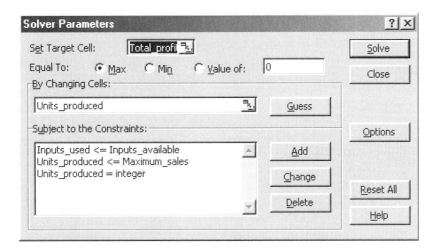

FIGURE 2.41
Solver's Add Constraint Menu

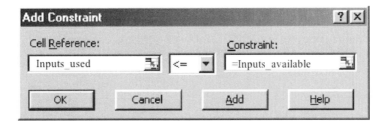

and we named the ranges as Inputs_used and Inputs_available previously. So we input the constraint as follows:

1. In the box directly under the Cell Reference label, either type Inputs_used or click on the cells B28:B31.
2. In the box directly under the Constraint label, either type Inputs_available or click on the cells D28:D31.
3. In the middle drop-down list choose the <= (less than or equal to) operator.
4. Click on the OK button and a figure resembling Figure 2.40 will reappear on the screen.

To add the next constraint, the demand constraint, we follow the same steps except that we use the name or cell references for units produced and maximum sales. Remember Units_produced, cell reference B22:C22, has to be less than or equal to Maximum_sales, cell reference B24:C24. Finally, we add the last constraint, units produced. To ensure that Solver returns integer (nondecimal) values, we follow the same steps described earlier but we enter Units_produced in the Cell Reference text box and select "int" from the middle drop-down list. Click OK to return to the Solver Parameters dialog box and click on Solve.

Shortly, the following Solver Results dialog box in Figure 2.42 will appear. Click on OK to view the solution that Excel found (see Figure 2.43).

FIGURE 2.42
Solver Results Menu

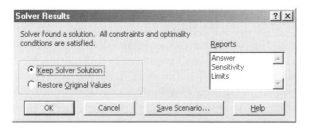

FIGURE 2.43
Sweets Bakery Final Spreadsheet Output

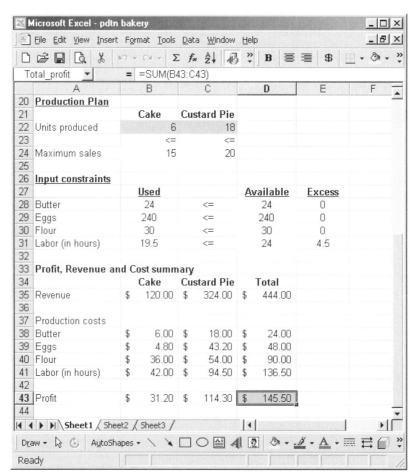

Analysis of Results

On the basis of the objective and the constraints, Sweets should produce 6 cakes and 18 pies to achieve a profit of $145.50. Looking at the spreadsheet (Figure 2.43), we see that Solver did indeed follow the constraint conditions. Six cakes are less than 15 cakes demanded, and 18 pies are less than 20 pies demanded. The input constraints are also not violated. Thus, Solver answered the first question as to how much Sweets may produce to maximize profit based on its limited resources. Specifically, $145.50 profit with 6 cakes and 18 pies.

Since demand exceeds Sweet's production capacity, we need to analyze how or why Sweets is unable to produce more. We refer to the Input Constraints section and the answer is clear in the Excess column. Observe in Figure 2.43 the Excess column indicates that all ingredients have been used in the production process, but bakers are left idle for 4.5 hours. This implies the bakers could have baked at least 4 more cakes if they had sufficient ingredients! In other words, the production capacity of Sweets is constrained by its supply of ingredients and not labor.

Modification of Constraints and Rerun of Solver

Sweets could then modify (increase or decrease) the inputs for available ingredients and/or labor and rerun Solver. The second time Solver is run, you do not need to reset the target, changing cells or constraints. Excel remembers all of these settings and saves them when you save the file.

To demonstrate how changing input resources will affect the solution, we add to our available resources 4 blocks of butter, 24 eggs, and 8 packets of flour. Total ingredient resources now include 28 blocks of butter, 264 eggs, and 38 packets of flour. The results are in Figure 2.44. Profit is now $167.45, units produced have increased to 9 cakes and 19 pies, with 1 excess packet of flour and 0.75 hours of excess labor.

FIGURE 2.44
Sweets Bakery Modified Spreadsheet Output

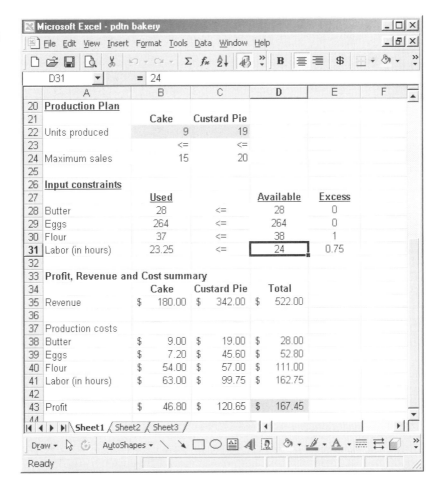

FIGURE 2.45
Sweets Bakery Modified
Spreadsheet Output

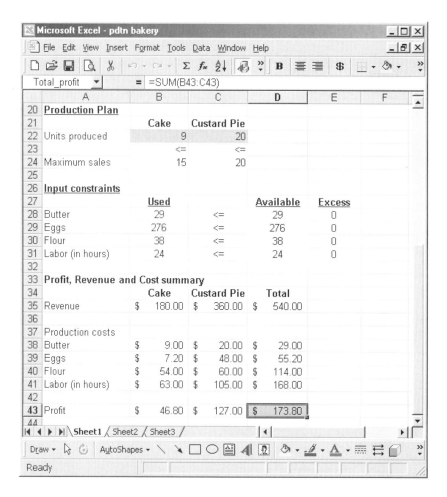

We know that a pie could be made by using the leftover 1 packet of flour and 0.75 hours of labor if we could obtain a block of butter and a dozen eggs. The problem can be modified again by simply adding one more block of butter and 12 eggs. The results of the Solver rerun are displayed in Figure 2.45.

As seen in Figure 2.45, Sweets should produce 9 cakes and 20 pies to maximize profit. In order to do so, Sweets has to increase its daily order of supplies to 29 blocks of butter, 276 eggs, and 38 packets of flour.

APPLIED SPREADSHEET MODELING—CURVE FITTING

This example shows how we may estimate the relationship between advertising and sales by using curve functions, given historical sales data. In other words, the model developed is a predictive one. We briefly explain the properties of three trend lines that can be used to fit into a scatter plot.

Example 3

Teez Company began a radio advertising campaign to promote its T-shirts. As expected, Mr. T noticed sales figures had improved since the radio ads began airing. But Mr. T wanted to know how effective this campaign has been, so he wrote down his weekly sales as well as the number of ads run during that week. The data are shown in Table 2.10.

Step 1: Problem definition

Mr. T wants to know how sensitive his sales are to the radio ads; that is, he wants to know how much his advertising campaign has been helping sales. In this case we are assuming that other factors such as price or weather are not significant factors.

Business Decision Modeling Behind the Scenes
Spreadsheets in Real Business Situations

INTRODUCTION

Decision Models (www.decisionmodels.com) provides comprehensive consultancy and modeling services based on Microsoft Excel. Decision Models has worked with Federal Express in Europe. Two major FedEx projects are the Price Rate Development Tool and a series of European route planning models.

PRICE RATE DEVELOPMENT TOOL

The Price Rate Development Tool is an Excel VBA add-in that links to a number of server databases and templates (Excel, Access, and Informix). The tool has an additional Excel menu that provides an easy-to-use set of commands and forms to allow the user to perform a wide range of pricing tasks. The tool can generate an Excel workbook on the user's PC with the following functions:

- Rate upload/download and comparison
- New rate development
- Discount matrix and rates development
- Impact analysis pivot table
- Multicurrency rate comparison and conversion

All the standard, familiar Excel functions can be used on the generated workbook. The tool has been designed to increase the user's productivity and reduce errors by automating routine calculations and administrative tasks, so that the user can concentrate on developing the optimum pricing strategies.

DESIGN AND DEVELOPMENT OF OPPORTUNITY SIZING AND SERVICE TAKE-UP FORECASTING MODEL

Another example is a model developed for Inmarsat's planned fourth-generation broadband satellite network. The model integrates research by RS Consulting, providing telephone and face-to-face interview results, demographic data, and Delphi Forecasting results. The Excel model develops worldwide 10-year volume forecasts of mobile data communication traffic and satellite service take-up, segmented by international and geographic region, economic development level, industry and product. The model factors in cellular rollout and development, price sensitivity, and channel, technology and regulatory rollout.

To maximize flexibility and future proofing, the model is dynamically generated from sets of relational tables. In addition to the standard Excel facilities, the model generator provides alternate and delta case handling, what-if audit trail maintenance, and pivot table generation.

Step 2: Build the model

The independent variable *x* in this problem is the number of advertisements that Mr. T places on the radio each week. The dependent variable *y* is the T-shirts sold during the corresponding week. In this situation we can use the help of Excel's Charting and Trendline functions to identify the relationship (function) between the variables. In other words, this is a predictive model, as the final relationship would allow us to predict how the number of ads we place affects sales.

Using the chart function, we create an *x-y* scatterplot of a chart with sales on the *y* axis and number of ads on the *x* axis. Figure 2.46 shows clearly that sales increase as the number of ads increases.

TABLE 2.10
Teez Ad and T-Shirt Sales Data

Week	Number of ads	T-shirts sold
1	10	610
2	9	520
3	6	280
4	5	260
5	11	750
6	12	880
7	7	300
8	14	1300
9	12	920
10	8	440
11	13	1000
12	7	360

FIGURE 2.46
Graph of Teez Ads and T-shirt Sales

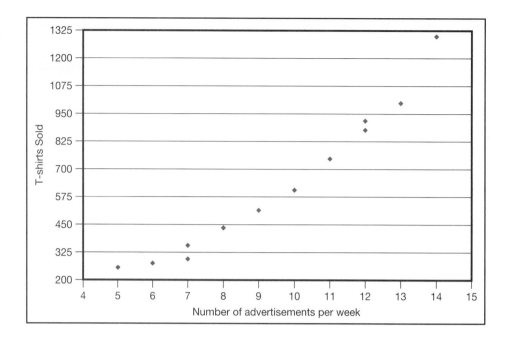

After creating the chart, select from the menu Chart and then Add Trendline. The following Add Trendline dialog box, as shown in Figure 2.47, will appear. You can choose any of the six types of trend lines, but we will focus on three: Linear, Power, and Exponential. These lines have basic equations linking the dependent variable *y* to the independent *x* with *a* and *b* as constants.

Linear Function $y = a + bx$

The linear function, used as a predictor, is defined by the general equation

$$\hat{y} = a + bx$$

Standard nomenclature is to refer to the left side of the equation as "y-hat" or the predicted value. A "hat," or caret (^), over the *y* is used to distinguish it from the original data values (the *y*) values. On a graph, this is a straight line, where *a* is the intercept and *b* is the slope. When

FIGURE 2.47
Add Trendline Dialog Box

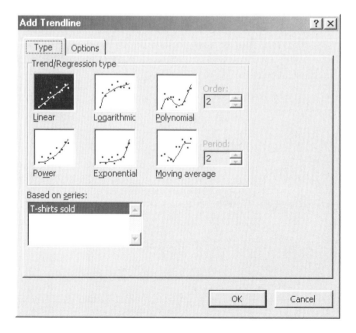

$a = 0$ and $b = 1$, then $y = x$. This means that when x changes by 1, y will also change by 1. Thus, b is also the multiple of x.

From Add Trendline, we select Linear. Then in the same dialog box, we select the Options tab and tick Display equation on the chart. The linear trend line will appear on the chart with the best-fitting linear line and the corresponding equation. Teez's best-fitting line to estimate the function is

$$\hat{y} = -421 + 111.16x$$

If we accept this function, this model is predicting that Teez will sell 111.16 T-shirts with each additional ad. As we can see from Figure 2.48, using a straight line does not appear to fit the data very well. Let us consider the other functions.

Power Function $y = ax^b$

The Power function, used as a predictor, is defined by the general equation

$$\hat{y} = ax^b$$

The power curve is determined by exponent b. In a special case when $b = 1$, the function becomes a straight line. If $b > 1$, y increases at an increasing rate as x increases. The important property of power curves is that when x changes by 1 percent, y changes by approximately b percent. In this case, $b = 1.6331$. This means when x changes by 1 percent, y will increase by 1.6331 percent.

Note also that if $0 < b < 1$, y increases at a decreasing rate as x increases; And if $b < 0$, y decreases as x increases.

This time, select Power from the Add Trendline dialog box. The trendline shown in Figure 2.49 is the best-fitting power curve with the equation

$$\hat{y} = 15.199x^{1.6331}$$

Exponential Function $y = ae^{bx}$

The exponential function also represents a curve whose shape is determined by exponent b. The general equation for the exponential function, when used as a predictor, is $\hat{y} = ae^{bx}$, where e is exponential (numerical value 2.7182 …).

If $b > 0$, y increases as x increases. The important property of exponential curves is that when x changes by 1 unit, y changes by approximately $100 \times b$ percent. In this case, $b = 0.1854$.

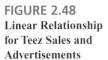

FIGURE 2.48
Linear Relationship for Teez Sales and Advertisements

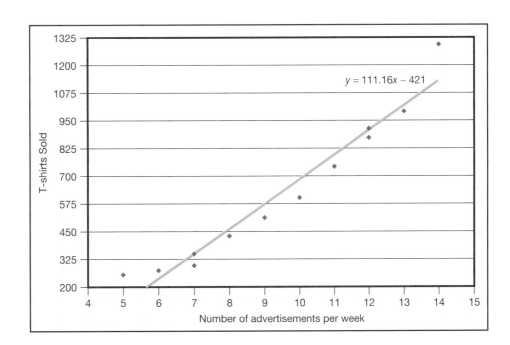

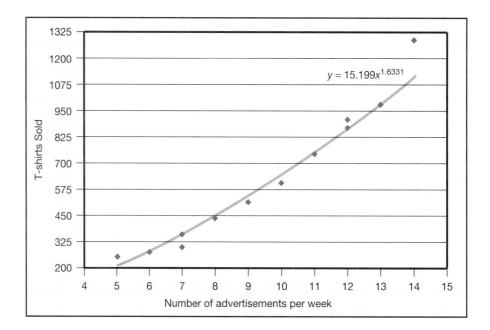

FIGURE 2.49
Power Relationship for Teez Sales and Advertisements

$y = 15.199x^{1.6331}$

This means when x changes by 1 unit, y will increase by 18.54 percent. Note that if $b < 0$, y decreases as x increases. Selecting the Exponential function, we get the best-fitting curve, see Figure 2.50, and the following equation:

$$\hat{y} = 95.466e^{0.1854x}$$

Mean Absolute Percentage Error (MAPE)

But which one of these functions best reflects the relationship between the number of ads to sales? We have to determine the curve function that will predict, with the least average error (with most accuracy), the actual data set. So we calculate the average percentage error between the observed sales and the predicted sales figure (as predicted by the respective curve function) for each row of data. This is known as the mean absolute percentage error (MAPE).

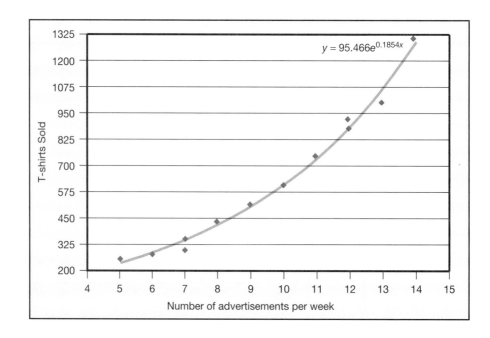

FIGURE 2.50
Natural Logarithmic Relationship for Teez Sales and Advertisements

$y = 95.466e^{0.1854x}$

The curve function with the lowest MAPE predicts the actual sales figures with the least amount of error.

$$APE = \frac{|\text{actual sales} - \text{predicted sales}|}{\text{observed sales}}$$

$$MAPE = \frac{\sum_{i=1}^{n}\left(\dfrac{|\text{actual Sales} - \text{predicted sales}|}{\text{observed sales}}\right)_i}{n}$$

We have to use each function's equation indicated on the charts to calculate the predicted sales figures for each of the last 12 weeks' data based on the given number of ads aired. Therefore, for each function we have the inputs of a and b.

Name the following inputs for each function: Linear will have linear_a and linear_b. Power will have power_a and power_b. Exponential will have exp_a and exp_b. Recall each function will predict the sales figure y, where variable x is the number of ads.

Next build a table of predicted results for each best-fitting function. Following the equation of the linear function, we enter in cell E5 the formula =intercept_a + slope_b*B5. For subsequent results the formula advances the x value from B5 through to B16. Figure 2.51 displays the spreadsheet model for Teez curve fitting model.

To calculate the predicted sales results from the best-fitting power function in cell F5, we enter the power equation according to the formula

$$=power\_a * B5 \wedge power\_b$$

FIGURE 2.51
Spreadsheet Curve-fitting Model for Teez

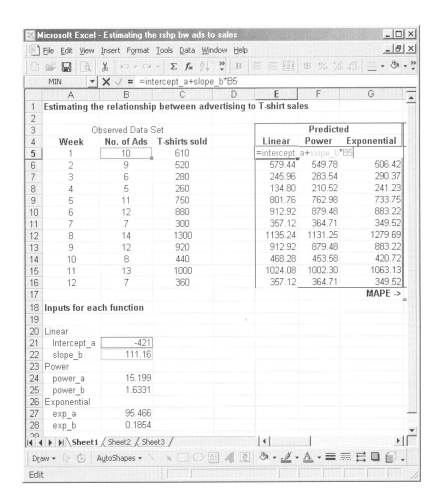

FIGURE 2.52
Spreadsheet Curve
Fitting Model for Teez

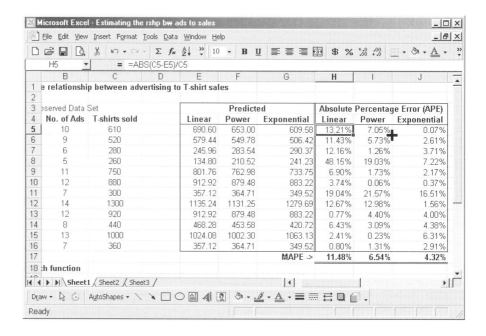

Recall the power function equation is $y = ax^b$.

To calculate the predicted sales results from the best-fitting exponential function in cell G5, we enter the exponential equation according to the formula $=exp\_a*EXP(exp\_b*B5)$. Here $EXP(\ )$, returns the exponential of the values within the parentheses.

Next, the table is extended to calculate the average percentage error (APE) for each function, using the appropriate equation given earlier. The formula you should enter for the linear function is

$$=ABS(C5-E5)/C5$$

Move your cursor close to the bottom right corner of the active cell H5 until it changes from a white cross to a black cross. Click and drag to highlight the cells you wish to copy the formula to. Excel will automatically copy the formula into the blank cells with the corresponding predicted and observed data of each row of weeks. You will see in H6 that the formula will be copied as $= ABS(C6-E6)/C6$.

You may also use absolute referencing, since column C remains unchanged. The formula may be edited to $= ABS(\$C5-E5)/\$C5$ (see Figure 2.52).

Once the weekly APE's are calculated, you can average the results to find the mean average percentage error (MAPE) of each function. In cell H17:J17, the formula is $= AVERAGE(H5:H16)$.

Since the exponential function yields the lowest MAPE, 4.32 percent, it is obvious that the exponential function would predict the most accurate sales results given the number of ads. In comparison with the earlier charts, it also appears as if more of the data set lies near or on the trend line than the other function lines.

Summary

We covered a lot of ground in this chapter. Hopefully, there was enough here for everyone to learn something new about how to apply business decision modeling methods into spreadsheet modeling. To some, the examples shown here may seem complicated at first glance, but take yourself through each of the examples and at the end you should be quite adept at building spreadsheet models. As with anything in life, all you need is a little patience and practice.

Executive Summary Example for Teez's Profit Problem

The following section presents an example executive summary for Example 2, where we discuss Teez's profit problem with quantity discounts and uncertain demand.

Executive Summary for Teez Profit Problem with Quantity Discounts and Uncertain Demand

TO: Stephanie Leung
FROM: Cua Consulting

Problem Identification

Teez Corporation has to make a purchasing decision in order to maximize its profit. The purchase price is dependent on the quantity ordered and the quantity to order is dependent on the expected demand. Given the discount schedule and demand probability, Teez has to decide the quantity of T-shirts to order.

Modeling the Problem

A spreadsheet model was developed to clearly demonstrate the relationships between discount price, order quantity and expected demand to profitability.

First, revenue is obtained from selling T-shirts at the regular price as well as from selling the leftover T-shirts at the sale price. The cost of a T-shirt depends on the quantity ordered and follows a discount schedule.

$$\text{Revenue} = (\text{demand} \times \text{regular price}) + (\text{leftover} \times \text{sale price})$$

$$\text{Total cost} = \text{other costs} + (\text{price of quantity } j \times \text{quantity } j)$$

Cua Consulting constructed a profit/loss graph based on historical sales records to ascertain the demand pattern and the likelihood of demand for T-shirts. The profit or loss is first tabulated with varying order quantities. The results are shown in graphical form in Figure 1.

FIGURE 1
Profit/loss Graph for Teez Company.

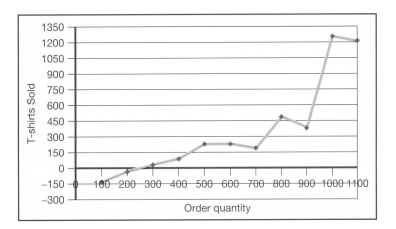

It must be noted that the profit/loss scenarios presented in Figure 1 are based on historical sales demand records. If drastic changes occur in the marketplace for Teez's shirts, then this information must be incorporated into the model and the graph redrawn.

Conclusions

On the basis of historical demand patterns, Teez Corporation should order 1000 T-shirts every month in order to maximize profit. If Teez wishes to order less than 1000, the next best order quantities are 800 and 500. Teez should not order less than 270 T-shirts, as this would result in a loss for the company. If demand patterns (as well as price or discounts) should change, Teez Company may modify the data in the model developed by Cua Consulting to review the best order quantity.

Discussion

The graph shows that Teez will not expect to make a profit if he orders less than approximately 270 T-shirts. Teez would maximize its profit at 1000 T-shirts. Although an order quantity of 1100 also returns promising profits, historical demand has never quite reached that amount. So Teez should be cautious about this prediction and embark on additional market demand study before accepting this information.

Case Study
John Woo's Cellular Connections

BACKGROUND

John Woo runs a small advertising firm. He employs 10 sales agents who need individual cellular phone service at all times. He is trying to make a decision on which cell phone package to purchase.

JOHN'S CONCERNS

John has noticed that some plans tend to "low-ball" on the monthly fee but then stick the customer with big per minute charges when the free minutes are used up. John was wary of plans like this because if his employees used a lot of minutes the per minute fees swamped any saving obtained in the low monthly fees.

On the other hand, some plans "low-balled" the "per minute" charges but stuck users with a high monthly fee. These plans appealed to customers that knew they would use large amounts of minutes, but for John he felt uncertain about if the higher monthly fees were worth the lower "per minute" charges.

PLAN OPTIONS

He has narrowed his options down to two plans; however, he is uncertain about which plan to select. Each employee uses about the same amount of airtime a month. John wants a plan that meets his current needs but will also be advantageous as his needs grow.

The "regular" plan charges a fixed fee of $55 per month for 2000 minutes of airtime plus $0.15 per minute for any time over 2000 minutes. The "executive" plan charges a fixed fee of $75 per month for 1000 minutes of airtime plus $0.09 per minute over 1000 minutes.

SPREADSHEET MODELING AND DISCUSSION QUESTIONS

Construct an Excel spreadsheet model with graphs to assist John with the following questions:

1. If John expects his sales agents to use the phone for 50 hours per month, which plan should he select?

2. Perform an analysis based on the idea that John believes his agent's average use will be 50 hours per month but knows that they will never use less than 40 hours or more than 60 hours per month.

3. How does the decision change if the agents' usage habits change and they now use the phone on average 65 hours a month, but will never use more than 85 hours or less than 50 hours a month?

Interactive Case www.mhhe.com/kros1e
Break-Even Analysis at SportsExchange

FACILITY COMPARISON AT SPORTSEXCHANGE

SportsExchange is a regional refurbisher of sporting goods equipment. It specializes in upgrading football equipment that it receives from high schools and colleges. Processes used by SportsExchange include sewing pants and jerseys, replacing pads, repairing and painting helmets, and replacing laces, snaps and elastic in pants.

The most expensive process for SportsExchange is painting helmets. Regulations that control worker safety and environmental emissions mandate a paint room that manages fumes effectively. In order to continue in its lucrative business, SportsExchange is required to invest in a new state-of-the-art painting facility. SportsExchange has identified three manufacturers of turnkey spray booths. The fixed and variable costs associated with each of the three alternatives are presented in Table 1 below:

TABLE 1
Costs Associated with SportsExchange's Three Painting Alternatives

Alternative	Fixed cost	Variable cost
A: Enviro-Spray	$500,000	$0.148
B: Spray Center	$207,500	$1.321
C: Crystal Coat	$265,000	$0.910

MODEL SETUP

Using the interactive model at www.mhhe.com/krosle, move the red (Enviro-Spray), green (Spray Center), and blue (Crystal Coat) lines to match the fixed and variable costs listed in Table 1. To change the fixed and variable costs of each alternative's cost curve, drag the colored dots on the left and right of the line to align them with the values given in Table 1.

ALTERNATIVE ANALYSIS

With the fixed and variable costs set to the values in Table 1, drag the "n" line to the volume of production desired. SportsExchange believes it will need to refinish 200,000 helmets. What is the total cost for each of the alternatives for refinishing that quantity of helmets? Which alternative appears to be the best choice (i.e.,

lowest total cost)? What alternative appears to the best choice if quantity to refinish increases to 320,000 helmets?

The cost accountants at SportsExchange may have made an error in calculating the fixed costs associated with the Spray Center alternative. They now believe that the fixed costs for the Spray Center alternative should be $150,000. If SportsExchange expects to refinish 200,000 helmets, which alternative looks the best now? What happens to the relative attractiveness of the Crystal Coat alternative as Spray Center's fixed costs decrease to $150,000?

In addition, the cost accountants have revealed that their estimate for Crystal Coat's variable cost may be too low. However, they don't know how by much they are off and would like to know how sensitive Crystal Coat is to changes in variable costs, specifically increases in variable costs. Give the cost accountants some assistance here by increasing Crystal Coat's variable costs and describe the changes that occur relative to the other alternatives.

Summary of Key Excel Terms

Terms	Explanation	Excel
Auditing toolbar	Useful for checking which cells are related to other cells through formulas	Use Tools/Customize menu item, select Formula Auditing from Toolbars tab
Cell comments	Useful for documenting contents of the cell	Right-click on cell, select Insert Comment menu item
Efficient copying	Shortcut for copying a formula to a range	Select range, enter formula, and press Ctrl-Enter
Efficient selection	Useful for selecting a large rectangular range	Pressing Shift key, click on upper left and bottom right cells of range
fx button	Useful for getting help on Excel functions	On Standard toolbar (by default)
Goal Seek	Solves one equation in one unknown	Use Tools/Goal Seek menu item
HLOOKUP function	Useful for finding a particular value on the basis of a comparison	=HLOOKUP(*valueToCompare, lookup Table, columnToRetum*)
IF function	Useful for implementing logic	= IF(*condition, resultIfFrue, resultIfFalse*)
NPV function	Calculates NPV of a stream of cash flows starting in year 1	= NPV(*discount Rate, cashFlow*)
One-way data table	Shows how one or more outputs vary as a single input varies	Use Data/Table menu item
Pasting range names	Provides a list of all range names in the current workbook	Use Insert/Name/Paste menu item
Range names	Useful for making formulas more meaningful	Type name in Name box, or use Insert/Name/Define menu item
Relative, absolute cell addresses	Useful for copying formulas; absolute row or column stays fixed, relative row or column "moves"	Al (relative), $Al or A$l ,(mixed), Al (absolute); . press F4 to cycle through possibilities
Splitting screen	Useful for separating the screen horizontally and/or vertically	Use screen splitters at top and right. of scrollbars
SUMPRODUCT Function	Calculates the sum of products of values in two (or more) similar-sized ranges	= SUMPRODUCT(*rangel, range2*)
Two-way data table	Shows how a single output varies as two inputs vary	Use Data/Table menu item
VLOOKUP function	Useful for finding a particular value based on a comparison	=VLOOKUP(*valueToCompare, lookup Table, columnToRetum*)

Optimal Information Area

Models in Business Decision Making at **http://personal.bellsouth.net/lig/b/u/burrus01/ ModelsinBusDecision.htm**

Decision Support Models at **http://www.intelligententerprise.com/010216/decision1_1. shtml?bi%7Cbusintel**

PWC Global Business Dynamics Division website at **http://www.pwcglobal.com/uk/eng/ about/svcs/bd/index.html**

Decision Support Resources, a repository of resources relating to Decision Support website at **http://www.dssresources.com**

OR/MS Today home page website at **http://www.lionhrtpub.com/ORMS.shtml**

Frontline Systems sample solutions using Solver at **http://www.solver.com/solutions.htm**

Excel Spreadsheets for Financial Modeling, including derivatives, at **http://members.attcanada. ca/-johnjaz/spreadsheets.htm**

References

Camm, J. D., and J. R. Evans. *Management Science: Modeling, Analysis, and Interpretation*. Cincinnati: South-Western, 1996.

Leon, L., Z. Przasnyski, and K. C. Seal. "Spreadsheets and OR/MS models: An End-User Perspective." *Interfaces*, vol. 26, no. 2, 1996, pp. 92–104.

Ragsdale, Cliff, *Spreadsheet Modeling and Decision Analysis W/Excel*. Thomson Learning, 2000.

Winston, W., and C. Albright. *Practical Management Science: Spreadsheet Modeling and Applications*. Duxbury Press.

Problems

1. Create a simple spreadsheet to balance your checkbook. Include rows for money in and money out, columns for each month, and sums at the bottom of each column and row.

2. Jennifer can earn 4 percent on any money she saves in her credit union account. She wants to know how much she will accumulate over 5 years if she starts with $100. Build a spreadsheet that displays this information. Use the simple equation principle*(1+interest rate) to calculate the yearly totals in Excel or another spreadsheet application. Does Excel or another spreadsheet application have a function that does this calculation automatically? If so, use the function and compare your answers.

3. Schalpfer Inc. is trying to determine whether to give a $15 rebate, to cut the price to $8, or to have no price change on a software networking product. Currently, 40,000 units of the product are sold each week for $45. The variable cost of the product is $6. The most likely case appears to be that a $15 rebate will increase sales 35 percent and about two-thirds of all people will claim the rebate. For the price cut, the most likely case is that sales will increase 25 percent.

   a. Given all other assumptions, use Excel to create a model that describes all the scenarios given.

   b. Holding all assumptions constant except the rebate claim rate, at what rebate claim rate would the rebate and price cut be equally desirable?

   c. Is the no price change scenario a good choice? When?

4. Samantha and Sabrina are opening a soda stand. They believe the fixed cost per week of running the stand is $50.00. Their best guess is that they can sell 300 sodas per week at $0.75 per soda. The variable cost of obtainng a can of soda is $0.20.

   a. Given her other assumptions, and using Excel, find the level of sales volume that will enable Julie to break even.

   b. Given her other assumptions, draw a break-even graph and discuss how a change in sales volume affects profit.

   c. From the graph in (b) discuss how changes in sales volume and variable cost jointly affect profit.

5. Ralph knows the information in the following table about processing times of claim forms at the clearinghouse he works at. He notices that as more claim forms are processed the processing time per form decreases.

   a. Fit a linear curve to the data using Excel or another spreadsheet application.

   b. Fit a power curve to the data using Excel or another spreadsheet application.

   c. Fit an exponential curve to the data.

   d. Which curve fits best?

e. Use your answer from (d) to predict the 40th unit's processing time.

Unit	Processing time hours
1	18
5	10.72
9	8.87
18	7.10
27	6.23
36	5.68

6. Copy the information from the following table into a spreadsheet. Multiply the two columns together by using a spreadsheet function such as * or the product command in Excel.

Column A	Column B
11	11
22	22
33	33
44	44
55	55
66	66

7. Graph the numbers presented in the table in Problem 6 and your answer to Problem 4. Compare the graphs. Are the graphs similar or different? Why would they be similar or different?

8. You are thinking of opening a copy shop. It costs $8000 to rent a copier for a year. It costs $0.023 per copy to operate the copier. Other fixed costs of running the store amount to $600 per month. You charge an average of $0.12 per copy. You are open 365 days per year. Each copier can make up to 150,000 copies per year.

   a. Using Excel, construct a two-way profit table (number of copiers on the left running top to bottom and daily demand on the top running from left to right) for 1 to 5 copiers rented and daily demands of 1000, 1500, 2000, and 2500 copies per day. That is, compute annual profit for *each* of these combinations of copiers rented and daily demand.

   b. Given that you rent three copiers, what daily demand for copies will allow you to break even? Draw a break-even graph to show this break-even relationship.

9. Eve Brown is trying to save for her retirement. She believes she can earn 12 percent on average each year on her retirement fund. Assume that at the beginning of each of the next 40 years, Eve will allocate x dollars to her retirement fund. If at the beginning of a year Eve has y dollars in her fund, by the end of the year, it will grow to $1.12y$ dollars.

   a. Using Excel, develop a spreadsheet model to find out how much Eve should allocate to her retirement fund each year to ensure that she will have $1 million at the end of 40 years.

   b. Are there any key factors that are being ignored in our analysis of the amount saved for retirement?

10. Chipper Payroll Services knows the demand for its services during the current year is around 50,000 worker hours and with current operations covers all customer demand (i.e., Chipper's capacity currently is 50,000 worker-hours). Chipper is planning on a 5 percent growth rate each year. Chipper's current office space and staff will eventually outgrow demand. Expanding the office space and staff depends mostly on the hours that will be worked total in the facility. If we let x = total worker-hours expanded, Chipper will incur a one-time cost of $15x$ to expand [i.e., if Chipper goes from 50,000 worker-hour capacity to 70,000 worker-hour capacity, it will incur a cost of $15 \times (70,000 - 50,000) = $300,000]. Chipper needs to expand its current space and staff, since any new business will be lost to its competitors if it cannot accommodate the new customers. Each customer serviced incurs a variable cost of $3.00 per worker-hour. It also costs Chipper $6.00 per worker-hour of capacity per year (i.e., if Chipper has 70,000 worker hours total then Chipper incurs $6 \times 70,0000 = $420,000 per year in costs). Chipper garners $25 per worker hour from its customers. Construct an Excel spreadsheet model to determine what the projected revenue, costs, and potential profits would be over the next 10 years based on the current capacity, 50,000 worker-hours, an expansion to 70,000 worker-hours, and an expansion to 90,000 worker-hours.

Chapter **Three**

Probability and Statistics—A Foundation for Becoming a More Effective and Efficient Problem Solver

Learning Objectives

After completing this chapter, students will be able to:

1. Understand graphical methods of data description—specifically histograms.
2. Understand and calculate measures of central tendency and dispersion.
3. Use Excel to construct histograms and calculate measures of central tendency and dispersion.
4. Understand the basic foundations of probability.
5. Describe mutual exclusivity, statistically independent, and dependent events.
6. Understand and use Bayes' theorem to establish posterior probabilities.
7. Explain and understand what continuous and discrete probabilities are.
8. Calculate and interpret expected values.

Chapter Outline

Business Decision Modeling in Action—A Probabilistic Medical Testing Problem*

Medical Decision Making

In recent years, there has been an increasing problem of antibiotic-resistant organisms. One of the main reasons for this is the treatment of nonbacterial illnesses with antibiotics. An example of such an organism is Group-A streptococcus, the common cause of strep throat.

Today the medical community has two methods of detecting this bacterium. One is a rapid strep antigen test, which takes around 5 minutes to test and receive results. This is easily done in a physician's office. The second is the "gold standard" and consists of a throat culture, which must be sent to the lab and can take 1 to 2 days for the results to be obtained.

Testing and Overtreatment of Nonbacterial Infections

One goal of many physicians is to not overtreat nonbacterial infections with antibiotics. The doctors also do not want to miss a true streptococcal infection. Most people would agree a quick test is better than a test that may take up to 2 days to get back from the lab. However, that quick test must also be accurate.

*This example was provided with assistance from Kenneth M. Ahdoot, M.D., H. Neal Sievers, M.D., and Zack Wassmuth, M.D.

Comparing the Two Tests

The rapid strep antigen test is much quicker and more cost-effective, but it carries a chance of indicating both false positives and false negatives. In other words, the test may not detect the antigen even when it is present, and it may detect the antigen even when the antigen is not present. To avoid this situation the physician usually takes a throat culture and sends it to the lab for testing. This test is more time-consuming (days instead of hours) and costly (around 10 times more costly).

Deciding How Reliable the Rapid Antigen Test Is

According to statistics from the medical field, the rapid antigen test produces false negatives around 90 percent of the time and false positives around 50 percent of the time. In other words, the probability that a patient was actually positive, given that the test was negative (false negative) equals 90 percent and the probability that a patient was actually negative given the test was positive (false positive) equals 50 percent. If 50 percent of the tests come back positive and 50 percent come back negative, is it possible for a physician to determine how often the test will be in error? In addition, if a person is actually positive how often will the test give the proper result?

Using Probability to Calculate the Answers

Both of the questions asked above can be answered by using simple probability. The material in this chapter will give the reader the skills to answer such questions. To answer the first question, it can be shown, using a joint probability table and the total law of probability, that the probability of obtaining an error (i.e., the total of false positive and false negative results) is 70 percent. That number is striking because it means that before the test is even given, the patient has only a 30 percent chance of being diagnosed properly.

Probability Tree Diagram for Rapid Antigen Testing

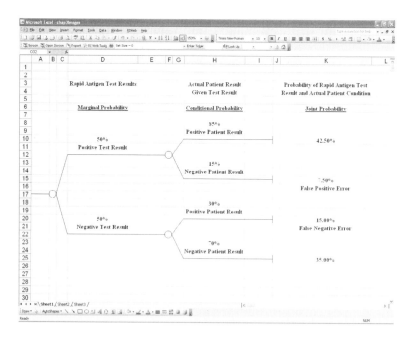

Summary

The answer to the second question is as dramatic. The probability that is sought is the probability that a patient who is positive (i.e., has the strep bacterium) tests positive. In statistical terminology this is stated: Given the patient is positive, what is the probability that they will test positive?

Statistically defined as a posterior probability, the actual probability is calculated by using Bayes' theorem. The posterior probability result for the strep bacterium example comes out to around 36 percent. With these results it then becomes obvious that doctors usually end up performing both tests and at times overprescribing antibiotics.

Optimal Information Area

Grateful Med Web site at http://igm.nlm.nih.gov.
Medical Matrix Web site at http://www.medmatrix.org/info/medlinetable.asp.

References

Corvalan, Enrique. "Evidence Based Health Care: Strategies for a New Century." presentation at the University of Arizona College of Medicine 25th Annual Primary Care Update, March 29–April 1, 2000.

Hunt, Dereck, et al. "User's Guides to the Medical Literature." *JAMA*, vol. 283, no. 14, April 12, 2000.

Peitetti, R. D., et al. "Evaluation of a New Rapid Antigen Detection Kit for Group A Beta-Hemolytic Streptococci." *Pediatric Emergency Care*, vol. 14, no. 6, December 1998, 396–98.

DESCRIPTIVE STATISTICS: GRAPHICAL AND NUMERICAL METHODS FOR DESCRIBING DATA SETS

Descriptive and numeric methods of data analysis help managers organize and interpret data sets.

The acquisition, analysis, and description of data are fundamental tasks managers are challenged with everyday. Many managers find themselves inundated with data—at times, overwhelmed and unable to glean even the most basic information from important data sets. This chapter provides some simple methods for data organization and description.

The author wishes to stress that, by learning a few basic descriptive and numeric methods of data analysis and presentation, students of business decision modeling can become more efficient and effective problem solvers. Students must begin to train themselves in the art and science of data description. This chapter will present graphical and numerical description methods and link the methods together to paint a full picture of the problem at hand.

GRAPHICAL METHODS OF DATA DESCRIPTION

Two graphical methods of data are presented: histograms and relative frequency diagrams. These methods are most commonly used to visually describe real-world data sets. It is vitally important that the student begin to look for links between the two methods and to use both methods to fully paint a picture of the data.

Histograms

Histograms relate the total number of occurrences in an event space to each other.

Histograms relate the total number of occurrences for each event in an event space to each other. Each event is represented on the x axis of the histogram while the total times each event occurs is represented on the y axis. Histograms are very common in everyday life. Many people don't use the term histogram and instead refer to diagrams depicting the occurrence of events as graphs.

As a student of business decision modeling, you have more than likely seen many histograms throughout your studies. An example could be the grade distribution on the last business decision modeling exam. If the professor gave out letter grades such as A, B, C, D, and F and then graphed them in histogram form, the histogram might look something like Figure 3.1.

FIGURE 3.1
Business Decision Modeling Grade Histogram

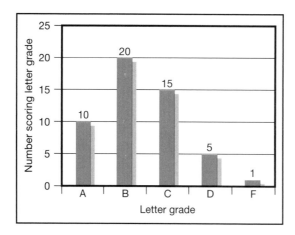

Histograms can easily be created in a spreadsheet.

Histograms are a straightforward, easy-to-construct method of graphical data description that almost everyone understands. All commercial spreadsheet packages have the capability to construct histograms. The next section will demonstrate how to create a histogram in Excel.

Relative Frequency Diagrams

Relative frequency diagrams resemble histograms but relate occurrences in an event space to each other, using probability.

Relative frequency diagrams resemble histograms but relate the occurrence of events in terms of probability. Instead of displaying the number of times an event has occurred, a relative frequency diagram displays the percentage of time each event occurred with regard to the number of total events.

Even though histograms and relative frequency diagrams resemble each other, they each give a manager unique information.

Relative frequency diagrams are used when two groups of similar data need to be compared but may differ in size. For example, students may want to know the percentage of A, B, C, D, and F grades that the whole university gives compared to the percentage of those same letter grades given by their business decision modeling professor. It would be confusing to compare the two histograms because of the difference in magnitude of the sample sets. The university may have thousands of students while the business decision modeling class may have 40 to 50 students.

Therefore, a relative frequency diagram is created. This allows the two sets of data to be compared on the basis of a common denominator, percentage histograms, throughout your studies. Let's go back to the example of the grade distribution on the previous business decision modeling exam. Table 3.1 contains the data on the business decision modeling exam grades.

Relative frequency is calculated by dividing the number of occurrences of a specific event in the event space by the total number of occurrences in the entire event space.

To create a relative frequency chart, the relative frequency of each event in the event space must be calculated. Column 3 in Table 3.1 performs this operation. In turn, column 4 contains the relative frequency in terms of percentage. Figure 3.2 displays the relative frequency diagram for the business decision modeling exam 1 grade data.

It should be noted that the histogram and the relative frequency diagram look very much alike. This is only true because of the magnitude of the numbers being in the same ratio. Each graphs gives a manager unique information about the data set being investigated. Most important in the case of the relative frequency diagram is comparability to other data sets.

TABLE 3.1
Business Decision Modeling Exam 1 Grades

Exam Grade	Number receiving grade	Relative frequency	Percentage
A	10	10/51	0.1961
B	20	20/51	0.3922
C	15	15/51	0.2941
D	5	5/51	0.0980
F	1	1/51	0.0196
Total	**51**	**51/51**	**1.0000**

FIGURE 3.2
Relative Frequency Diagram for Business Decision Modeling Exam Grades

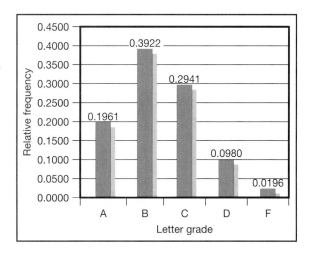

Concept *Check*
Critical Reasoning and Judgment Question

Why would a manager use a relative frequency diagram instead of a histogram? It could be because clients tend to understand and respond to percentages better. Would it be possible for a manager to use a relative frequency diagram to misrepresent data?

NUMERICAL METHODS OF DATA DESCRIPTION

Managers must employ both measures of central tendency and measures of dispersion to fully describe a problem.

For a manager to become a more effective and efficient problem solver, numerical methods of data description must be mastered. Two types of numerical methods will be detailed and include:

1. Measures of central tendency
2. Measures of dispersion

The manager who does not employ both of these measures only tells half the story.

Managers can improve their problem-solving skills greatly by learning to describe data sets in terms of central tendency and dispersion. This section provides the basic definitions and formulas behind measures of central tendency and dispersion, along with the underpinnings of probability theory and distributions covered later in the chapter.

Measures of Central Tendency

Measures of central tendency describe the data set in terms of a single number. Two of the most common measures of central tendency will be detailed:

1. Simple Mean
2. Median

Simple Mean

The simple mean is defined as the average of the data set.

The simple mean of a data set is defined as its average. It should be noted that statisticians use the terms *mean* and *average* interchangeably. The formula used to calculate simple mean is:

$$\mu = \frac{\sum_{i=1}^{n} x_i}{n}$$

where

μ = Greek lower case mu, for mean

x_i = individual data point i,

n = total number of data points

Σ = Greek capital sigma, meaning summation

Given the data set 5, 7, 12, 39, 7, the simple mean would be calculated as follows.

$$\frac{\sum_{i=1}^{n} x_i}{n} = \frac{5+7+12+39+7}{5}$$
$$= 14$$

Simple mean is seen many places in everyday life, such as a grade point average (GPA).

If you are using Excel, the formula to calculate average is: average(number1, number2, …).

We encounter and use the measure of simple mean everyday. Examples of common occurrences of the simple mean a measure of central tendency are listed in Table 3.3.

Extreme values or outliers tend to bias the simple mean.

As human beings, we overuse and at times misuse the simple mean as a measure of central tendency. This occurs when the simple mean is calculated from a sample that is biased, either by including extreme values, which we will define as outliers, or by not obtaining a large enough sample size.

The median is considered the middle value of a data set.

Look back at our example data set 5, 7, 12, 39, 7. Is there something that looks out of place? Yes, 39 is large compared to the other values. In fact, it is large enough that it could significantly bias the simple mean upward. Is there something we can do to remedy this? Yes, there is. We can use another measure of central tendency that adjusts for outliers—the median.

Median

Median is a measure of central tendency that is not biased by outliers.

The definition of the median is the middle value of the data set. The median divides the data set into two equal halves. The median is employed in areas that tend to have outliers of large magnitude or where the data set has known bias. Real-life examples of where the median is used instead of the simple mean are:

1. Housing prices
2. Professional athletes' salaries
3. National income figures

Next time you get a chance, take a look through the real estate section of your local newspaper. It should become obvious that there are some prices that are very, very high in comparison with your average price for a home. These high-priced homes tend to skew or bias the simple mean upward. Therefore, housing prices are almost always listed in terms of median and not in terms of simple mean.

Median is calculated according to the following set of rules:

1. If your data set contains an odd number of data points:
   - Order the data points from lowest to highest.
   - Starting from the left and right, count in from each side until you reach the middle data point.
   - This number is the median.
2. If your data set contains an even number of data points:
   - Order the data points from lowest to highest.
   - Starting from the left and right, count in from each side until you reach the two middle data points.
   - Take the average of these two points and this number is the median.

If we take a look back at our example data set, 5, 7, 12, 39, 7, we can calculate the median. Since the data set contains an odd number of data points, we will use the steps listed under the first set of instructions for calculating median.

TABLE 3.2
Common Uses of Simple Mean

Use	Description
Gas mileage	Average miles per gallon
Time to commute to work	Average driving time to/from work
NBA scoring leaders	Average points scored per game
Exam test scores	Determination of college GPA

Order the data points from lowest to highest: 5, 7, 7, 12, 39.

Starting from the left and the right, count in from each side until you reach the middle data point: 5, 7, **7**, 12, 39.

The middle number, 7, is the median for our example. The formula in Excel for median is: median(number1, number2, …). Now, let's compare the numbers we obtained for the simple mean and the median.

Concept *Check*
Critical Reasoning and Judgment Question

When was the last time you used a mean to explain a situation or a set of data? Have you ever used the median to describe a set of data or a situation? Look around for examples in everyday life of the use of mean and median. When would a manager want to use a mean? A median?

Comparison of Mean and Median

When we compare the mean of 14 to the median of 7, the difference may not seem significant but, in reality, it truly is. The simple mean is skewed upward because of the effect of the data point 39. This does not infer that the median is the correct measure and simple mean is the incorrect measure.

Managers must decide the most appropriate measure of central tendency to describe data sets.

A manager must decide which is the most appropriate measure of central tendency to use. If the numbers in our example were actually estimated numbers in tens of thousands of dollars representing housing prices in an area, an individual using the simple mean may be overstating the actual central tendency by relying on the simple mean. This is the reason real estate agents and the federal government use median as the measure of central tendency when relaying information on housing prices.

The Most Common Measure of Central Tendency

A manager must develop critical thinking and judgment when it comes to measures of central tendency. Basically, a manager must know where and when to use simple mean and median. However, overwhelmingly we see and use the simple mean in our everyday lives.

As was stated before, we calculate average miles per gallon, average points scored per game, and grade point averages on a daily basis. Simple mean is the most common measure of central tendency because it is the easiest to compute and the easiest to understand. There are some rules of thumb managers should remember before using the simple mean to describe a data set's central tendency. Using these rules of thumb will help managers avoid the pitfalls of overestimating or underestimating the data set's true central tendency. The rules of thumb are as follows.

The simple mean is the most common measure of central tendency.

1. Do a preliminary scan of the data to identify any outliers, i.e., very large or very small data points with respect to the overall data set.
2. If outliers are found, a couple of courses of action can be taken:
   a. Throw the data points out and use the modified data set to calculate the simple mean, making sure to note that the data points were removed somewhere in the final results.
   b. Discount the outliers by some factor and calculate the simple mean using the modified data set, making sure to note the data points that were discounted and the method used to discount them.
   c. Calculate both the mean and median and provide a comparison of the two measures for the client.

Managers must describe data sets in terms of central tendency and dispersion.

Remember that, as a manager, it is your responsibility to determine which measure of central tendency is proper for the data set; bottom line: Begin to develop your critical thinking and judgment on the issue of central tendency.

Measures of Dispersion

As mentioned earlier in this section, we all see and use measures of central tendency everyday in the real world. It is obvious at times, however, that just using central tendency to describe a data set is short sighted. If we use only the simple mean or median to describe a data set, we have only painted half the picture.

It should be noted here that measures of dispersion can be used as measures of risk. The concept of risk will be discussed in Chapter 4, but managers frequently use measures of dispersion to describe the relative risk of a data set and, in turn, the risk of possible alternatives. Overall, measures of dispersion can be used to define and quantify risk.

This section will discuss three measures of dispersion:

1. Range
2. Variance
3. Standard deviation

In addition, examples will be given to help solidify the link between measures of central tendency and measures of dispersion.

Range

Range is the simplest measure of dispersion and is the difference between the largest data point and the smallest data point.

We use range to describe data sets in our everyday lives. Terms such as "high" versus "low" or "the most" versus "the least" are common to us. The author will define the term *simple range* as the difference between high and low. The simple range is calculated as follows.

Simple range = high point of data set − low point of data set

If you are using Excel, the formula would be max(number1,number2,…) − min(number1,number2,…).

However, statisticians use the term *range* differently—or at least they use a different definition. Statisticians generally use what is called *interquartile range* (IQR) to describe the dispersion of a data set. The statistical definition of IQR will be given first and then its relationship to the simple range measurement will be discussed.

Definition of Interquartile Range (IQR)

IQR divides the data set into four equal groups and studies the extreme points.

Before the advent of handheld calculators and desktop computers, statisticians needed a quick and easy way to describe data sets with regard to dispersion. Thus the IQR was born. The following are the general rules about calculating IQR. The similarities to the calculation of median will be noted later in the section.

In essence, when calculating the IQR we wish to divide data into four equal groups and study the extreme points. To calculate the IQR we proceed as follows.

Calculation of IQR

1. Arrange the data in numerical order.
2. Divide the data into two equal groups at the median.
3. Divide these two groups again at their medians.
4. Label the median of the low group the 1st quartile (Q1) and the median of the high group the 3rd quartile (Q3)
5. The IQR = Q3 − Q1.

These calculations are fairly simple. This makes this measure of dispersion a good "back-of-the-envelope" calculation that can be used to get a quick view of the makeup of a data set. One can see the direct relation the IQR has to the median. However, managers will find that the IQR is not used all that often in real life.

Most managers find it much easier today to use spreadsheet programs to analyze data sets and calculate measures of dispersion. As a result, the use of the IQR has diminished. Other measures of dispersion have become more popular. Variance and standard deviation are two of the most common of these measures and will be detailed next.

Concept *Check* **Critical Reasoning** *and Judgment* **Question**

Many people use the term *variance* in their everyday lives. They may be using the term incorrectly. Ask yourself the following question: "How do I use the term variance in my everyday life, and am I using it correctly?"

Definition of Variance

The *variance* of a data set measures the spread from the mean. Many of us use the term variance in our everyday lives to describe data sets. Variance is calculated as follows:

$$\sigma^2 = \frac{\sum_{i=1}^{n} (x_i - \mu)^2}{n-1}$$

Variance measures the spread of the data from the mean.

From the earlier example, let's calculate the variance for the following data set:

$$5, 7, 12, 39, 7$$

Let $n = 5$ and $\mu = 14$. Therefore,

$$\sigma^2 = \frac{(5-14)^2 + (7-14)^2 + (12-14)^2 + (39-14)^2 + (7-14)^2}{5-1}$$

$$= \frac{81 + 49 + 4 + 625 + 49}{4}$$

$$= 202$$

Variance is represented by the lowercase Greek symbol sigma squared, or σ^2.

The Excel formula for variance is var(number1,number2,…). Standard statistical nomenclature labels variance as σ^2. However, statisticians use σ^2, s^2, or at times "var" to represent variance. The three labels will be used interchangeably throughout the text. It is important to note the units that correspond to variance calculated above. If the original data set units were dollars, then the variance would be in dollars squared.

This may seem strange. How can a manager compare dollars with dollars squared? This is the main difficulty with using the statistical measure of variance. The measure of dispersion used must be in the same units as the measure of central tendency. This difficulty is remedied easily and will be detailed next.

Definition of Standard Deviation

The definition of standard deviation is simple:

$$\text{Standard deviation} = \sigma = \sqrt{\sigma^2}$$

For the aforementioned example,

$$\text{Standard deviation} = \sigma = \sqrt{202} \approx 14.2$$

Measures of dispersion need to be in the same units as measures of central tendency.

Since variance is in terms of squared units, taking the square root of the variance is all that must be done to get the measure of dispersion into the proper units. The Excel formula for standard deviation is stdev(number1,number2,…).

Once again, standard statistical nomenclature labels standard deviation as σ. However, statisticians use σ, s, or at times SD to represent standard deviation. The three labels are used interchangeably throughout the text.

Standard deviation is the most common measure of dispersion. Many other industries and disciplines use standard deviation. For example,

- Stock brokers use SD in analyzing investments.
- Insurance companies utilize SD in determining rates and coverages.
- Marketing researchers use SD to describe consumer preferences.
- Economists use SD to analyze variability in markets.
- Information systems analysts use SD to describe network traffic.

Combining the use of central tendency and dispersion allows a manager to describe a data set more fully, in a sense painting the full picture.

As a manager, you must think in terms of central tendency and dispersion. In using both measures, you will become a more effective and efficient problem solver. By using both measures you gain insight into the underlying patterns of the data sets. Combining the use of central tendency and dispersion gives you the ability to describe and analyze data sets much more fully and communicate that information to your client. The following example will illustrate this point.

PAINTING THE FULL PICTURE—A CLASSROOM EXAMPLE

Let's say your business decision modeling professor tells you that, on average, the exam grades in her classes tend to be about 50 percent. Now, apart from being stunned by the low average, a student of business decision modeling may still be confused as to the makeup of the data set

TABLE 3.3
Grade Information

| | **Number of students scoring** | | | |
Score	0	49	51	100
Class 1	50	0	0	50
Class 2	0	50	50	0

Even though the simple means of two groups of data may be equal, the data sets may be very different from one another.

used to calculate the simple mean. This confusion is not uncommon. In fact, the confusion is justified because by using only the simple mean, only half the story has been told.

For illustration, let's say the professor had two different classes. The simple average for these two classes is both 50 percent. However, the professor imparts the following extra information contained in Table 3.4.

On closer look at the two data sets, it is apparent that the simple averages are the same:

$$\text{Mean of class 1} = \frac{(0 \times 50 + 100 \times 50)}{100}$$
$$= 50$$

$$\text{Mean of class 2} = \frac{(49 \times 50 + 51 \times 50)}{100}$$
$$= 50$$

However, these two classes are very different from each other. Class 1 tends to be very spread out; i.e., 1/2 of the students received 0 percent while the other half received 100 percent, a literal feast or famine when it comes to grades. Class 2, on the other hand, is very tightly packed around the mean of 50; i.e., no one really did much better or worse than 50 percent.

Concept *Check Critical Reasoning and Judgment Question*

Quickly, ask yourself which of these classes you would rather be in, everything else held constant. Keep this answer in the back of your mind and we will revisit it soon.

Many individuals use words like "variation" or "variance in the data." These individuals are not really referring to the statistical calculation of variance but are more likely talking about standard deviation. However, unless you are a statistician or around statisticians, rarely will you hear the common person use the term *standard deviation*.

With this in mind, managers must remember what the statistical definitions of variance and standard deviation are, even while individual clients or colleagues may be using layman's terms such as variation or variance to actually describe the standard deviation of a data set.

Using Central Tendency and Dispersion

To become a more effective and efficient problem solver, a manager must use measures of central tendency and measures of dispersion to analyze and describe data sets.

This is readily apparent in the class grade distribution data given in the above example. On the basis of mean alone, the two classes look identical. However, after seeing the dispersion of the data around the mean, it is obvious they are two different data sets. It is unnecessary to calculate a measure of dispersion such as the standard deviation because the simple range calculation does a good job by itself.

Chapter 3 relates mean and dispersion to the theory of probability and statistics. Chapter 4 will delve into the application of mean and dispersion to decision-making problems. In addition, Chapter 4 will begin to help the reader formulate the answer to the rhetorical question raised above: "Which group would be preferred?".

EXCEL TUTORIAL ON USING HISTOGRAM TOOL FUNCTION

The data analysis tool in Excel creates relative frequency diagrams, histograms, and cumulative frequency diagrams.

The histogram tool in the Data Analysis section of Excel has the capability to create frequency distributions, histograms, cumulative frequency diagrams, and Pareto charts. The following section will demonstrate the use of the Data Analysis menu to create graphs of these types.

Frequency Distributions

The first step in developing any of the aforementioned distributions, diagrams, or charts is to specify the classes or intervals for the distribution. The specification of the classes includes the number of classes, the width of the classes, and the beginning value for the first class. The histogram tool refers to classes as "bins."

If bins are not specified, the number of bins will be set approximately to the square root of the number of values in the data set. In addition, width will be determined as the difference between the largest data value and smallest data value divided by the number of values. Finally, the beginning value for the first class is set equal to the lowest data value. At first glance the output from the histogram tool may not be helpful.

Installing Excel's Data Analysis Add-In

If the Data Analysis command does not appear in Excel's Tools menu, choose the Add-Ins command from the Tools menu (see Figure 3.3). It should be noted that the menu in Figure 3.3 may look slightly different, depending on which version of Excel you are using.

After you choose the Add-Ins options, an Add-Ins menu will be displayed like that in Figure 3.4. In the Add-Ins available list box, check the box next to the Analysis ToolPak and then click OK. If Analysis ToolPak is not listed in the Add-Ins available list box, you may need

FIGURE 3.3
Tools Menu and Add-Ins Option

FIGURE 3.4
Add-Ins Menu

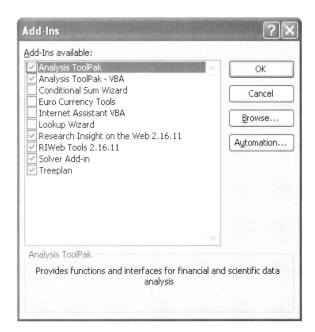

to add the Analysis ToolPak through a custom installation by using the Microsoft Excel Setup program and your original disks. Check your Microsoft Office user's guide for more information on this procedure.

EXAMPLE: USING EXCEL'S DATA ANALYSIS ADD-IN

The following example will detail the use of Excel's histogram tool. The steps in determining the number of classes/bins and the class width is discussed first, followed by an example using data from Table 3.5. Refer to the end of this chapter for a tutorial on how to install Excel's Data Analysis add-in.

Steps for Determining Classes/Bins and Class Width

It is strongly suggested that you specify the classes/bins and class width for your data set. Follow this simple process to determine the number of classes/bins and class width:

1. Identify the largest and smallest data points in your data set.
2. Round the smallest data point down to the nearest 10.
3. Round the largest data point up to the nearest 10.
4. Find the difference of these two rounded data points.
5. Divide this difference by numbers that are multiples of 2, 5, or 10, or an appropriate number of your choice that allows for easy analysis The resultant integer will be the number of classes/bins.
6. The class width is equal to the number you divided by in step 5, and the number of classes/bins is the resultant integer from step 5.

As an example, given the information in Table 3.5, let's determine the appropriate number of classes/bins and class width:

Step 1: Identify the largest and smallest data points in your data set. Smallest number in the data set = 27. Largest number in the data set = 89.

Step 2: Round the smallest data point down to the nearest 10. Round 27 down to 20.

TABLE 3.4
Weekly Sales Data for Histogram Example

Week	Sales
1	30
2	39
3	55
4	89
5	85
6	45
7	29
8	46
9	75
10	60
11	58
12	62
13	38
14	27
15	84
16	42
17	56
18	47
19	74
20	73

Step 3: Round the largest data point up to the nearest 10. Round 89 up to 90.

Step 4: Find the difference of these two rounded data points. Difference of rounded data points = 90 − 20 = 70.

Step 5: For this example, 10 is chosen as the divisor. Divide the difference in step 4 by 10. (The resultant integer will be the number of classes/bins.) 70 divided by 10 = 7.

Step 6: The class width is equal to 10 and the number of classes/bins is 7.

If the class width in step 6 is too large, too much data smoothing takes place (i.e., too few bins with too many data points). On the other hand, if the class width in step 6 is too small, too little aggregation occurs (i.e., too many bins with not enough points for data distinction). Now, using the answers developed in the steps above, let's illustrate how to create a frequency distribution, histogram, and Pareto chart with Excel's Histogram tool.

Excel's Histogram Tool

Use the following steps to create diagrams and charts with Excel's Histogram tool.

1. Open Excel and a new Excel worksheet.

2. In cell A1 type **Week** and in cell B1 type **Sales**. Proceed to enter the numbers **1** through **20** in the column under the label Week (cells A2 through A21). In addition, enter the sales data contained in Table 3.5 in the column under the label Sales (cells B2 through B21).

3. In cell C1, type **Bin**. Proceed to enter the values **20, 30, 40, 50, 60, 70, 80** in the column under the label Bin (cells C2 through C9). Your Excel worksheet should resemble Figure 3.5.

4. From the menu bar select **Tools.** In the pull-down menu, select **Data Analysis**. The Data Analysis dialog box will then be displayed (see Figure 3.6). From this dialog box, select **Histogram** and click on the command button labeled **OK**. The Histogram dialog box will appear, and you now need to input your data (see Figure 3.6).

5. Move the cursor to the text box to the right of the **Input Range** label and left-mouse click. Enter the range for the data, including the label. This may be accomplished by typing B1:B21 or clicking on cell B1 and dragging to cell B21.

6. Move the cursor to the text box to the right of the **Bin Range** label and left-mouse click. Enter the range for the Bin Ranges including the label. This may be accomplished by typing C1:C9 or clicking on cell C1 and dragging to cell C9.

7. Move the cursor to the **Labels** check box and left mouse click to check the box. This informs the Histogram program that you have included labels with your data entries.

FIGURE 3.5
Excel Worksheet for Histogram Example

FIGURE 3.6
Data Analysis Dialog Box

FIGURE 3.7
Histogram Dialog Box

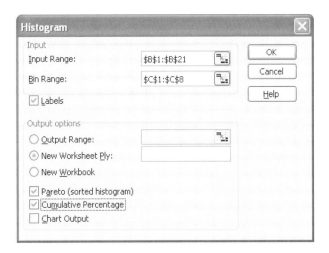

FIGURE 3.8
Final Excel Output for Histogram Example

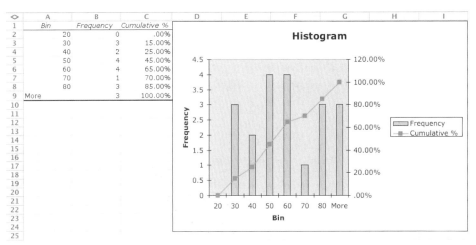

8. Move the cursor to the Output Options area and click on the appropriate output option. Generally, it is best to click on **New Worksheet Ply**. This option cuts down on the clutter of your main data sheet.

9. Sequentially, move the cursor to the last three check boxes labeled as **Pareto (sorted histogram), Cumulative Percentage,** and**Chart Output** and click to check the boxes labeled **Cumulative Percentage** and **Chart Output** (see Figure 3.7).

10. Click on the OK command button and Excel will compute and display output resembling Figure 3.8.

Figure 3.10 displays a histogram overlaid with a cumulative percentage diagram. The scale on the left depicts the frequency and the scale on the right depicts the cumulative percentile. The data table in the upper left of the spreadsheet displays the bin and frequency data.

USE OF NUMERICAL AND GRAPHICAL METHODS IN BUSINESS DECISION MODELING REPORTING

The discipline of business decision modeling is widely known for its use of graphical techniques to help solve and explain complex problems. An example executive summary using numerical as well as graphical techniques is presented next for the weekly sales data case.

Probability Concepts

A good understanding of probability and statistics is commonly considered the foundation for becoming a more effective and efficient problem solver. Therefore, the subject of probability and statistics is presented as an early chapter in this text.

Models that include uncertainty are called probabilistic techniques.

A student of business decision modeling must develop a sound foundation in probability and statistics so the physical framework associated with structuring decision making problems, modeling those problems, applying appropriate business decision modeling techniques, and interpreting the results has a solid base to rest on.

This chapter introduces the topic of uncertainty early on. The theories, rules, and formulas used will be referenced throughout the remainder of the text. As a student of business decision modeling, you should quickly become aware of the importance of probability and statistics in becoming a more effective and efficient problem solver.

Business decision modeling techniques that reflect uncertainty are called *probabilistic techniques*. The uncertainty generally applies to the information supplied to the decision maker and the resulting solutions produced with that information. In most real-world problems, uncertainty is a fact of life. What does this mean to the student of business decision modeling? It means that we should look to describe a set of solutions instead of looking for the one ultimate correct answer.

Results of probabilistic models need to be described by measures of central tendency and measures of dispersion.

The solutions produced with probabilistic models will have a probability of occurrence. These solutions tend to be described in terms of *central tendency*. A common measure of central tendency is an average. Commonly, when managers are faced with problems containing uncertainty they are inclined to describe the solutions in terms of central tendency only. This comes from a lack of understanding of the probabilistic nature of the underlying problems and the inability to integrate statistics into the description and communication of the problem solutions.

In becoming more effective and efficient problem solvers, managers must describe the solutions to problems involving uncertainty in terms of central tendency and in terms of dispersion. Dispersion can be measured by a number of statistical methods but the most common are range and standard deviation. This chapter presents the student of business decision modeling with the tools needed to begin describing problems in terms of both central tendency and dispersion. The section leads the reader through the following:

- The basic types of probability
- The fundamentals of probability and probability distributions
- The introduction of the expected value measure
- The integration of measures of central tendency and dispersion in the interpretation and communication of results

It can be said that good decision makers are good subjective probability assessors.

Business decision modeling uses two general definitions of probability. Managers loosely use these definitions when assessing the likelihood of events. This section will define the two types of probability; subjective and objective, and integrate these definitions into the decision-making process managers engage in.

Concept *Check*
Critical Reasoning and Judgment Questions

How do you assess the likelihood of events occurring? Do you or others around you use phrases such as "the chance of them scoring in the fourth quarter is a toss-up" or "I am positive the stock market will go up tomorrow"? What do these phrases have to do with probability theory and assessment?

Subjective Probability

Subjective probability assessments are estimates based on a person's knowledge or experience.

"I give it a 50/50 chance of happening."

"There will be a 75 percent chance of high surf tomorrow."

"That is guaranteed to happen!"

"There's not a chance in @#$% that could occur!"

Business managers hear and use these phrases frequently. Most of us have used these phrases to describe the occurrence of events happening or about to happen in the real world. These types of statements are called *subjective probability assessments*. A subjective probability assessment is defined as a probability estimate based on a person's knowledge or experience.

We make many subjective probability assessments every day. In many cases we are not consciously aware that we are assessing subjective probabilities. Simple decisions such as waiting for the signal at the crosswalk to change and then actually walking out into the street contain a subjective probability assessment at their core. For example, if we live in a city where drivers tend to obey traffic signals or if through experience we trust that cars will stop when the light changes, our subjective probability assessment of being struck in the cross walk is close to zero.

Managers also make many subjective probability assessments each day. They assess the probability of success of different projects or ideas. They assess the probability of events occurring or not occurring. In all, managers make decisions based on these probability assessments. If these decisions turn out to be correct or lead to favorable outcomes, the manager is said to be a good decision maker. Rarely, though, does anyone say a person is a good assessor of probability. To be a good decision maker, however, one must first think about how to become a good probability assessor.

Intuition, Luck, and Subjective Probability Assessment

Many times managers are referred to as good decision makers or bad decision makers. Other times individuals are said to have good intuition or even good luck. Intuition or luck is actually the application of experience or knowledge to a situation. If this idea is linked with the definition of subjective probability assessment, the statement could be made that good decision makers are good subjective probability assessors.

What happens when a manager doesn't have knowledge or experience in an area or does not have the time to gain the knowledge or experience needed to make a good probability assessment? Many times that knowledge or expertise is purchased. Managers may hire individuals or entire firms to make probability assessments for them. We personally do this all the time. We hire insurance agents to help us choose what policies will be the best for us and out families. We hire mortgage brokers and real estate agents to help us with the purchase of a home.

Guessing and Subjective Probability Assessment

Naïve guesses of subjective probabilities can be related to assigning equal probabilities to events.

There are situations that arise in which our best subjective probability assessment may be a guess. There are even instances where managers may refuse to assess a subjective probability or just not choose. In many of these cases, managers allow all things to be equal. The common shrug of the shoulders in response to the question "What is the probability of that event occurring?" or using the phrase "on average" are good examples of ways managers can make all things equal.

Overall, assessing subjective probabilities by guessing is not recommended unless there is no other alternative. Even if a manager chooses not to make subjective probability assessments, they are still made. Subsequently, the assessments will more than likely follow the results of a guess and end up carrying equal weight.

Objective Probabilities

Objective probability is the ratio of the number of specific outcomes to the total number of outcomes.

The flip of a coin.

The deal of a card.

The roll of a die.

We have all seen these events occur out in the real world. Each of these events has something in common. In the last section, subjective probability assessment was introduced. The concept of objective probability assessment is introduced next.

Objective probabilities differ from subjective probabilities in a dramatic way. Objective probabilities are not based on a person's experience or knowledge about a situation or event. The definition of objective probability assessment is: Given a set of outcomes of a situation, the probability of a specific outcome occurring is the ratio of the number of specific outcomes to the total number of outcomes.

For example, given a fair coin, the two outcomes for a flip of that coin are heads or tails. In turn, the probability of flipping a head is the ratio of the specific outcome (a head) to the total number of outcomes (a head and a tail), or 1/2. How about for the roll of a fair die? If the die is six sided, the total number of possible outcomes is 6 (1, 2, 3, 4, 5, or 6 dots landing face up).

INTRODUCTION AND ORIGINS OF GAMBLING

Nothing in life is certain. From listening to the weather forecaster to analyzing different business alternatives, we gauge the chances of successful outcomes in everything we do. For the greater part of human history, the study of the probability was used for only one thing: gambling. It is well documented that the ancient Egyptians used a four-sided "Astragali" to play games of chance. The Roman Emperor Claudius (10 B.C. to 54 A.D.) wrote the first known treatise on gambling, "How to Win at Dice," around the year 25 A.D.

DICE, CARDS, COINS, GAMES OF CHANCE, AND GAMBLING TODAY

Modern dice games grew popular throughout the Middle Ages. Many of the most notable mathematicians of the time developed many of the theories still used today. Renaissance period men such as Chevalier de Mere, Blaise Pascal, and Pierre de Fermat all contributed to the discipline of probability. Today, Las Vegas is one of the hottest tourist destinations in the world, and, well, people are not visiting Las Vegas for the dry heat. Modern gaming is still based on centuries-old games: coins, cards, and dice. The business of gambling involves the use of probability theory to increase profits. Next time you're in Las Vegas, take a minute and think about the probability of winning and the expected value of the games being played around you.

ORIGINS AND EQUATION OF THE NORMAL DISTRIBUTION AND FUZZY CENTRAL LIMIT THEOREM

Around the eighteenth century, Jacob Bernoulli and Abraham de Moivre developed what today is referred to as the *standard normal table*. De Moivre theorized that every normal distribution had similar characteristics. The normal distribution is referred to as the standard normal because all normal distributions can be examined with regard to two parameters, the mean (μ) and standard deviation. DeMoivre then showed that this curve is modeled by the following formula.

$$f(x) = \frac{1}{\sqrt{2\pi}} e^{-x^2/2}$$

OPTIMAL INFORMATION AREA

David, F. N. *Games, Gods, and Gambling*. New York: Hafner, 1962.

Gonick, L., and W. Smith. *A Cartoon Guide to Statistics*. New York: Harper Perennial, 1993.

Huff, D., *How to Lie with Statistics*. New York: W.W. Norton, 1954.

Jaffe, A. J., and Herbert F. Spirer. *Misused Statistics: Straight Talk for Twisted Numbers*. New York: Marcel Decker, 1987.

A priori probabilities are historically the oldest and were developed to analyze games of chance.

Therefore, the objective probability of rolling and having the 6-dot face land up would be the number of specific outcomes, which is 1 (6 dots up) divided by the total number of possible outcomes 6, or 1/6.

Cards, Coins, and Dice: Examples of Objective Probabilities

Given that we had a fair coin and a fair die, most individuals could have told us the objective probability of flipping a head or rolling a 6 before there was any explanation. The name given to this type of probability comes from that idea of knowing ahead of time, or as they say in statistics "a priori" (i.e., before) an event. Can you guess why statisticians always use coins, cards, and dice as examples in class? These types of probabilities are historically the oldest documented. These probabilities were then, and are still now, associated with gambling and games of chance. Maybe statisticians are just gamblers at heart.

Objective Probabilities Defined As Relative Frequencies

Objective probabilities can be defined in terms of relative frequencies.

Objective probabilities can also be defined as relative frequency probabilities. We see relative frequency probabilities all the time in the real world. Examples include sports teams' win-loss percentages, a baseball player's batting average, and the number of A's your business decision modeling instructor has given out compared to the total number of students that have taken the class. Relative frequency probabilities are based on the observation of past occurrences. If, for example, a baseball player has a total of 500 at bats and he gets a hit 150 of those times at bat, then his relative frequency of getting a hit (his batting average) is 150/500, or 0.30. In baseball terms the player is batting 300.

Managers use both a priori and relative frequency probabilities when solving problems.

Managers use both a priori and relative frequency probabilities when solving problems. In fact, we sometimes use a priori probabilities to make simple decisions, such as flipping a coin to see who will pay for lunch. Each day we read about relative probabilities in the paper or hear about them on television. The unemployment rate is a good example of this. Overall, people use these types of probabilities to describe situations, solve problems, and make decisions everyday.

Concept *Check*
Critical Reasoning
and Judgment
Question

Can you describe the difference between subjective probability assessments and objective probability assessments? Look around in everyday life and attempt to identify examples of both objective and subjective probability assessments and where they are used. *Hint:* Ever buy a lottery ticket? How about watching the weather forecast?

RULES OF PROBABILITY

As managers assess probabilities, a few rules regarding those probability assessments must be followed. Three rules of probability exist and are defined and displayed symbolically as follows:

1. The probability of an event must be greater than or equal to zero but less than or equal to one, i.e.,

$$0.0 \le p(x_i) \le 1.0$$

2. The sum of all the probabilities of all events in the event space must equal 1.0, i.e.,

$$\sum_{i=1}^{n} p(x_i) = 1.0$$

3. The probability of event *a* or event *b* occurring, given mutually exclusive events *a* and *b*, is

$$p(a \text{ or } b) = p(a) + p(b)$$

The three rules are discussed individually below.

$$\text{Rule 1: } 0.0 \le p(x_i) \le 1.0$$

The rules of probability are fairly self-explanatory. With regard to the first rule, it should be common sense that it is impossible to have negative probabilities or probabilities greater than 1.0. People tend not to violate probability rule 1.

$$\text{Rule 2: } \sum_{i=1}^{n} p(x_i) = 1.0$$

Managers must remember the three rules of probability when they solve problems.

As for the second rule of probability, once an event space is defined and probabilities of those events assessed, it is logical that if all the probabilities are added up, they must equal 1. Take, for example, the coin flip example. The event space is defined as heads or tails and the probabilities assessed as equal or 50/50. Adding up all the probabilities defined for the event space makes it obvious they add to 1.0.

However, rule 2 tends to be violated not because of faulty mathematics but because of user error. This error can be attributed to two main areas: inadequate event space definition and under/overassessment of event probabilities. Managers must properly define the event space they are working in and carefully assess the probabilities of those events so that the sum of the probabilities does equal 1.0.

$$\text{Rule 3: } p(a \text{ or } b) = p(a) - p(b)$$

Rule 3 speaks to a concept called mutual exclusivity. Once again the flip of a coin can be used as an example. As stated before, in the case of a fair coin, only two events exist in the event space, heads and tails. Only one of those events can occur at a time, i.e., you can not obtain both heads and tails at the same time. Hence, the coin flip is the manifestation of the third rule of probability. Written in terms of the coin flip we see rule 3 as

$$p(\text{heads or tails}) = p(\text{heads}) + p(\text{tails})$$
$$= 0.5 + 0.5$$
$$= 1.0$$

Mutual exclusivity is defined as one event occurring at a time.

It is obvious that when a coin is flipped, only one of two events can occur, heads or tails. The probability of getting either a head or a tail must be equal to the sum of the probabilities of the two events. In turn we see that for the coin flip, the two probabilities equal to 1.0 and demonstrates rule 2 in the process.

Probability rule 3, mutual exclusivity, tends to be the most commonly abused rule of probability.

Once again, user error is the main reason for violation of rule 3. Rule 3 tends to be abused by managers who have a poor grasp of the rules of probability and probability theory. Properly defining the event space and the mutually exclusive events in that space are paramount in becoming more effective and efficient problem solvers.

Analyzing an Event Space

An event space is said to be collectively exhaustive when all the possible events are included in the given event space.

Managers can analyze the data associated with an event space. Take, for example, the rating scale Standard & Poors (S&P) provides for corporate and municipal bonds. The S&P system assigns ratings from AAA to D. From a sample of bonds of 500 companies, a manager wants to know how many bonds are listed in each category. The manager has created Table 3.6 to describe the bond categories given by S&P.

From the table it can be seen in S&P's rating system, there are nine events that can occur. For what is defined as a bond, these are the only nine events that can occur. Therefore, the set of events is said to be collectively exhaustive (i.e., no other event can occur if the event space is defined as an S&P bond rating). The principle of a set of events being collectively exhaustive can be extended to other event spaces we have discussed. For example, in the coin flip example, the only two events that can occur in the flip of a fair coin are heads and tails. Therefore, we can also say the coin flipping example is collectively exhaustive. When all of the possible events that can occur are included in the event space, the set is said to be collectively exhaustive.

The table also contains information of the number of occurrences of each event, an event's relative frequency, and an event's probability of occurrence. It is clear that these three columns are related. Relative frequency is derived from the number of occurrences. In turn, the probability of an event is just the decimal representation of the relative frequency.

TABLE 3.5
Data for Standard & Poors' Bond Rating Scale

Event outcome	Number of occurrences	Relative frequency	Probability
AAA	120	120/500	0.24
AA	15	15/500	0.03
A	5	5/500	0.01
BBB	10	10/500	0.02
BB	220	220/500	0.44
B	105	110/500	0.21
CCC	15	15/500	0.03
CC	5	5/500	0.01
D	5	5/500	0.01
Totals	500		1.00

THE LANGUAGE OF PROBABILITY: UNDERSTANDING THE TERMINOLOGY

Before we proceed any further with our study of probability and statistics, the proper nomenclature must be established. This must be done so all those who study and use probability and statistics speak the same language. Overall, learning probability and statistics is a lot like learning a new language. For others to understand what we mean and for us to be able to effectively and efficiently communicate our results, we must learn to use the language and symbols of probability. Three common types of probability will be reviewed:

1. Marginal probabilities
2. Joint probabilities
3. Conditional probabilities

Marginal, joint, and conditional are commonly used probability terms.

Marginal Probability

In the previous examples, the terms event and event space have been used. Those terms are commonly used to describe occurrences out in the real world. After we define the event space, probabilities can be assigned to each of the individual events inside that space. The probability of a single event occurring is called a marginal probability. For S&P bond rating example, the probability of a AAA bond is represented by the symbol, $p(AAA)$. This is defined as the marginal probability of obtaining a AAA bond. In standard nomenclature, this is written as

$$p(AAA) = 0.24$$

Mutual Exclusivity

Mutual exclusivity is defined as the condition when events in an event space cannot happen at the same time.

The principle of mutual exclusivity will be described in this section. However, probability theory has another principle, the principle of statistical independence. This is often confused with mutual exclusivity. Therefore, students of business decision modeling need to separate these two principles into two distinct areas. These areas will center around two questions. These questions will become a guide for distinguishing between mutually exclusivity and statistical independence.

As we study sets of events, the first principle studied is that of mutual exclusivity. The first question when confronted with a set of events is: Are the events in the event space mutually exclusive? This question must be answered in order to establish the mutual exclusivity of a set of events. In turn, we must establish a definition of what mutual exclusivity is so as to answer this question.

Mutual exclusivity can be defined as follows: When events in an event space cannot happen at the same time they are considered to be mutually exclusive, e.g., obtaining a AAA and a AA bond rating at the same time. Since mutually exclusive events can only happen one at a time, it is simple to calculate the probability of one event or another event occurring, e.g.: What is the probability of obtaining a AAA or AA bond?

The simple addition rule calculates the probability of the occurrence of two or more mutually exclusive events.

The formula called the simple addition formula can be used to calculate this probability. We have seen this formula earlier in the section "Rules of Probability." The simple addition formula is

$$p(a \text{ or } b) = p(a) + p(b)$$

and for the S&P bond rating example, we see

$$p(AAA \text{ or } AA) = p(AAA) + p(AA)$$
$$= 0.24 + 0.03$$
$$= 0.27$$

The "or" in the formula is a Boolean operator and indicates union. Union is also depicted by the symbol $\cup$. Statisticians use the "or" and the $\cup$ symbol interchangeably.

Venn Diagram of Mutual Exclusivity

Venn diagrams display an event space visually.

Principles of probability can be seen visually through the use of Venn diagrams. Many understand the principles of probability better if they see them in Venn diagram form. Figure 3.9 displays a Venn diagram for events A and B.

From Figure 3.9, it can be seen that the two events, A and B, are depicted as circles. Note that these circles do not overlap. This is the visual depiction of the principle of mutual exclusivity.

A Venn diagram depicts mutual exclusivity as events in an event space that do not overlap.

The same Venn diagram can be used to illustrate mutual exclusivity for the coin flip example. In Figure 3.9, replace A and B with heads and tails and follow the same logic as presented earlier with regard to mutual exclusivity. Our S&P bond rating example can also be modeled by using a Venn diagram. See Figure 3.9 for the S&P bond rating example.

From Figure 3.10, it can be seen that the nine events, AAA, AA, A, BBB, BB, B, CCC, CC, and D are depicted as circles. Note that these circles do not overlap. Once again, this is the visual depiction of the principle of mutual exclusivity.

Joint Probability

If every event space contained events that were mutually exclusive, the study of probability and, for that matter, the real world would be fairly simplistic and possibly quite boring. For mutually exclusive events the events joint probability is zero, or it can be said $p(ab) = 0$. The joint probability of events is written as $p(ab)$.

Events in an event space that are not mutually exclusive are said to share a joint probability.

When events in an event space are not mutually exclusive, they are said to share a joint probability. The definition of joint probability is the probability of two non-mutually exclusive events occurring at the same time. A general version of the simple addition formula presented earlier can be used to express the probability of non-mutually exclusive events occurring. Therefore, the probability that two non-mutually exclusive events will occur can be expressed as

$$p(a \text{ or } b) = p(a) + p(b) - p(ab)$$

The last symbol of the formula is referred to as the joint probability and is written as $p(ab)$. At times the joint probability is also written as $p(a \text{ and } b)$. The "and" is a Boolean operator

FIGURE 3.9
Venn Diagram for Mutually Exclusive A and B

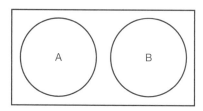

FIGURE 3.10
Venn Diagram for S&P Bond Rating Example

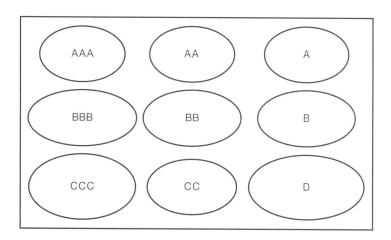

FIGURE 3.11
Venn Diagram for Non-Mutually Exclusive Events

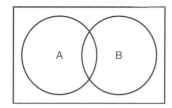

indicating intersection. Intersection is also depicted by the symbol ∩. Statisticians use the "and" and the ∩ symbol interchangeably.

A more general form of the addition formula is used to calculate the probability of two or more events in an event space. In fact, the formula is called the *general addition formula*.

Venn Diagram of Non-Mutually Exclusive Events

A Venn diagram displays joint probability by depicting events that overlap.

Principles of joint probability can also be seen visually through the use of Venn diagrams. Figure 3.11 displays a Venn diagram for non-mutually exclusive events A and B.

From Figure 3.10 it can be seen that the two circles representing events A and B overlap. This is the visual depiction of the concept of joint probability.

Putting It All Together Using the Business Decision Modeling Process

When solving probability problems, use the business decision modeling process as a guide.

At times, students of probability become frustrated in their attempt to keep track of all the symbols, formulas, and concepts presented. An easy approach to putting it all together can be developed. The business decision modeling process that was introduced in Chapter 1 will help us do this. Let's apply the first three steps of the business decision modeling process to a problem involving the concepts of simple marginal and joint probabilities, given an event space.

1. **Identifying the problem.** In dealing with marginal and joint probabilities, a simple question can be asked to identify the problem. This question is: Do we wish to calculate the probability of two or more events occurring or the probability of two or more events occurring at the same time?
2. **Defining the problem.** Once the problem has been identified, all probabilities must be defined, using the proper symbols and nomenclature.
3. **Modeling the problem.** To decide which probability model to use, ask the simple question: Are the events in the defined event space mutually exclusive? If the answer to this question is yes, the simple addition rule is be used. If the answer to the question is no, the general addition rule is used

Card examples are excellent ways to remember the principle of mutual exclusivity.

Putting It All Together Using A Deck of Cards

The probability of obtaining a red card and a queen is a joint probability.

A business decision modeling professor loves to play cards. However, she wishes to know how to figure out the probability of getting a red card or a queen. Let's illustrate this example by using the first three steps of the business decision modeling process.

Step 1: Identify the problem: calculating the probability of getting a red card or a queen.

$$p(\text{red card or queen}) = \text{probability of getting a red card or a queen}$$

Step 2: Define the problem:

$$p(\text{red card}) = \text{marginal probability of a red card}$$
$$p(\text{queen}) = \text{marginal probability of a queen}$$
$$p(\text{red card and queen}) = \text{joint probability of a red card and a queen}$$
$$p(A \text{ or } B) = p(A) + p(B) - p(A \text{ and } B) = \text{general addition formula}$$

Step 3: Model the problem. Ask the question: "Are the events red card and queen mutually exclusive?" We may not know the answer to this question up front, so the general addition formula can be used initially. It can be represented as

$$p(\text{red card or queen}) = p(\text{red card}) + p(\text{queen}) - p(\text{red card and queen})$$

Each deck of cards has a total of 52 cards. There are four suits in every deck: two colored red and two colored black. Each suits has 13 cards. The cards are made up of four face cards, jack, queen, king, ace, and nine cards numbered 2 through 10.

We can calculate the marginal probabilities defined above in step 2 as follows.

$$p(\text{red card}) = \frac{\text{number of red cards}}{\text{total number of cards}} = \frac{26}{52} = \frac{1}{2}$$

$$p(\text{queen}) = \frac{\text{number of queens}}{\text{total number of cards}} = \frac{4}{52} = \frac{1}{13}$$

The answer to the question of mutual exclusivity is now easily answered along with the form of the addition formula to use. It is possible to have a red card and a queen at the same time; therefore, we see

$$p(\text{red card and queen}) = \frac{\text{number of red queens}}{\text{total number of cards}} = \frac{2}{52} = \frac{1}{26}$$

Now we are ready to calculate the probability of getting a red card or a queen. The calculation is as follows.

$$p(\text{red card or queen}) = p(\text{red card}) + p(\text{queen}) - p(\text{red card and queen})$$
$$= \frac{1}{2} + \frac{1}{13} - \frac{1}{26}$$
$$= \frac{26}{52} + \frac{4}{52} - \frac{2}{52}$$
$$= \frac{28}{52}$$

The concept of the general addition rule has been illustrated. In sum, if the answer to the question "Are the events being studied mutually exclusive?" is yes, then the joint probability of those events is zero and the general addition formula reduces to the simple addition formula. The next section will discuss the concept of statistical independence.

Independence

Statistical independence deals with the relation of successive events.

Mutual exclusivity is the most common probability principle studied. In turn, statistical independence is the second most common principle of probability studied. It is imperative in studying probability that the principle of statistical independence is distinguished from the principle of mutual exclusivity. Statistical independence deals with the relation of successive events.

As mentioned earlier, statistical independence and mutual exclusivity are often confused. To alleviate this confusion, a set of two questions is proposed to act as a guide. The first question has to do with the mutual exclusivity of events. The second question pertains to statistical independence and is stated as follows

Are the events in the event space statistically independent?

This question must be answered in order to establish the statistical independence of a set of events. In turn, we must establish a definition of what statistical independence is in order to answer this question.

Statistically Independent Events

Statistical independence can be defined as follows: When successive events in an event space do not affect each other, they are considered to be statistically independent. For instance, for the coin flipping example consider the following:

A coin is flipped once, and we know the probability of obtaining a head is

$$p(\text{head}) = 0.5$$

Now the coin is flipped again; i.e., there are successive flips/events. We also know the probability of obtaining a head is

$$p(\text{head}) = 0.5$$

In fact, we can say the probability of flipping a head on the first flip is equal to flipping a head on the second or successive flips. In saying this, we have proved that these two events are statistically independent. This concept is represented in probabilistic nomenclature and symbols as follows:

Two successive events are considered statistically independent if the marginal probability of the first event is equal to the probability of the successive event given that the first event already occurred.

Using the correct symbolic form, we write the principle of statistical independence as

$$p(\text{head 2nd flip} \mid \text{head 1st flip}) = p(\text{head 2nd flip})$$
$$= 0.5$$

The first portion of the representation is referred to as a conditional probability. Conditional probabilities will be defined later in this chapter.

Let's get back to the coin flipping example. We all know that the event space for a coin only has two events. The fact that a head was flipped first has no effect of future flips. The probability associated with flipping a head is always 0.5, no matter how many heads have been flipped. Therefore, the answer to the question "Are successive events independent?" is yes, the marginal probability of the successive event is equal to the conditional probability of the two successive events.

In sum, when the answer is yes to the question "Are the successive events independent?" the following general relationship is true

$$p(A \mid B) = p(A)$$

This relationship will be used again in the next section to help us understand dependent events.

Dependent Events

Statistical dependence occurs when two successive events depend on each other. From the equation used above to define independent events, the following can be written for dependent events.

$$p(A \mid B) \neq p(A)$$

Why is this? What is this relationship saying? Let's begin by defining the initial term in the relationship and then move into the general rule of multiplication and the explanation why the relationship exists.

Conditional Probabilities

The initial term in the relationship above is called a *conditional probability*. Conditional probabilities are the probabilities that an event will occur, given that another event has already occurred. They take on the form

$$p(A \mid B)$$

and are read as follows: the probability of A, given that B has occurred.

General Rule of Multiplication

A general relationship for statistical independence can be formulated by using conditional probabilities. The relationship is called the *general multiplication formula* and is represented as follows:

$$p(\text{A} \mid \text{B}) = \frac{p(\text{A and B})}{p(\text{B})}$$

Statisticians commonly manipulate the formula and use the following representation also:

$$p(\text{A and B}) = p(\text{A} \mid \text{B})\, p(\text{B})$$

A very famous and widely used probabilistic principle is manifested in this relationship and is termed Bayes' rule.

Independent versus Dependent Events

In sum, statistical independence is a separate and unique probability concept. In a situation where a decision must be made regarding the dependence of a set of events, this question must be answered:

Are the events in the event space statistically independent?

For independent events it can be shown that the general rule of multiplication simplifies to

$$p(\text{A} \mid \text{B}) = \frac{p(\text{A and B})}{p(\text{B})} = \frac{p(\text{A})\, p(\text{B})}{p(\text{B})} = p(\text{A})$$

However, for dependent events the general multiplication rule cannot be simplified and stays in the following form:

$$p(\text{A} \mid \text{B}) = \frac{p(\text{A and B})}{p(\text{B})}$$

Therefore, if a decision maker can show that

$$p(\text{A} \mid \text{B}) = p(\text{A})$$

If events are independent of each other, then the following is true: $p(\text{A} \mid \text{B}) = p(\text{A})$.

then the events are said to be independent of each other. However, in many cases this cannot be shown and what statisticians call Bayes' rule must be introduced.

Given marginal and conditional probabilities, it is very easy to find joint probabilities. Use this simple rule of thumb:

$$\text{Joint probability of A and B} = (\text{marginal probability of B})$$
$$\times (\text{conditional probability of A given B})$$
$$= p(\text{A and B}) = p(\text{B})\, p(\text{A} \mid \text{B})$$

BAYES' RULE

Around 1700, a British clergyman published his probabilistic views of the world. His insight and theories on probability are still widely used today. In fact, the mathematical formula introduced above bears his name. In Bayesian analysis, marginal probabilities are altered or updated to reflect additional information.

Bayes' rule and the general multiplication rule are really one in the same. Bayes proposed that additional information can sometimes enable a decision maker to alter and possibly improve the marginal probabilities of the occurrence of an event. These altered probabilities are referred to as *revised* or *posterior probabilities*.

Business Decision Modeling Behind the Scenes

The Story of Bayes

Reverend Thomas Bayes (1702 – 1761),

BACKGROUND
Reverend Thomas Bayes (1702 – 1761) was a theologian and a mathematician who first used probability inductively and established a mathematical basis for probability inference. Bayes published his work in "Essay Towards Solving a Problem in the Doctrine of Chances," which later became the basis of a statistical technique called Bayesian estimation (a method of calculating, from the frequency with which an event has occurred in prior trials, the probability that it will occur in future trials).

EARLY LIFE
Bayes was educated privately by unknown tutors but the possibility exists that Bayes might have been tutored by Abraham de Moivre (renowned mathematician who pioneered analytic geometry and the theory of probability).

STATISTICAL WORK
Bayes' work on probability was accepted by the Royal Society of England in 1781, but later faced challenges by statisticians and mathematicians arguing different ways of assigning prior distributions of parameters and the possible sensitivity of conclusions to the choice of distributions. Since then Bayes' technique has been subject to controversy.

BAYES TODAY: THE ISBA
In 1992, The International Society for Bayesian Analysis (ISBA) was founded to promote the development of Bayesian statistical theory useful in the solution of theoretical and applied problems in science, industry, and government. By sponsoring and organizing meetings and other activities, the ISBA provides a focal point for those interested in Bayesian inference and its applications. For more information, visit the following ISBA websites:

International Society for Bayesian Analysis at http://www.bayesian.org.

St. Andrew's University MacTutor History of Mathematics Archive at http://www-history.mcs.st-andrews.ac.uk/history/Mathematicians/Bayes.html.

Bayes' rule and posterior probabilities are applied to many decision-making problems in many different fields. Bayesian analysis applications can be found in:

- Medicine
- Production operations
- Quality control
- Weather forecasting

Law of Total Probability

A different relationship exists for the events that make up the event space in many decision-making problems in the applications listed above. Bayes proposed a new mathematical relationship for successive events, since prior information now plays a role in determining the probability of successive events. The relationship is the same as the general multiplication rule with a little more detail. The following is Bayes' mathematical formulation:

If events are independent of each other, then the following is true:
$p(A \mid B) = p(A)$

$$p(A \mid B) = \frac{p(A \text{ and } B)}{p(B)}$$

The probability of A and B is generally available. However, the probability of B is not always readily available or easily obtained. Therefore, Bayes introduced the Law of Total Probability. The Law of Total Probability is:

$$p(B) = p(B \mid A)p(A) + p(B \mid \text{not } A)p(\text{not } A)$$

and therefore the modified general multiplication formula is:

$$p(A \mid B) = \frac{p(A \text{ and } B)}{p(B \mid A)p(A) + p(B \mid \text{not } A)\, p(\text{not } A)}$$

At first glance, this may seem more complicated than the original multiplication formula. But in reality a decision maker will readily have available all the probabilities listed to the right of the equation. This is something that was not true in the case of the general multiplication formula. An example of Bayes' rule applied to weather forecasting will be presented in Appendix 3A.

Probability tables and trees will be developed to aid in the process. Please read the following note regarding the difference between probability trees and decision trees. Probability trees are used to solve problems involving dependent events while decision trees are used to model and solve decision problems. In general, probability trees tend to be deductive while decision trees tend to be inductive.

NOTE: Probability trees should not be mistaken for decision trees (presented in Chapter 4). In addition, the TreePlan software is not intended to develop probability trees.

PROBABILITY DISTRIBUTIONS

When probabilities of events in an event space are grouped together, they form a probability distribution. Events in the event space that occur with no particular order or occur at random are called *random variables*. Standard statistical nomenclature generally assigns a symbol such as x to the random variable.

The concept of a probability distribution encompasses this idea of random variables. A probability distribution is characterized by two items: random variables and their associated probabilities.

Discrete Probability Distributions

A probability distribution can be constructed on the basis of a set of random variables and their associated probabilities. For example, let's take a look back at the S&P bond rating data set again.

Table 3.7 contains a discrete probability distribution. A discrete probability distribution is defined by its underlying probability mass function. A probability mass function consists of the group of individual probabilities associated with a set of random variables. Table 3.7 is an example of a probability mass function. From the table it can be seen that events in the left column are the set of random events, or x's. It should be noted that the events are considered random because the event has not occurred yet and up until the event occurs any one of the events in the event space could occur.

Many different types of discrete probability distributions exist. Some of the more notable are the binomial, the hypergeometric, and the Poisson distributions. In general, discrete probability distributions are characterized as follows:

A probability mass function consists of the group of individual probabilities associated with a set of random variables.

1. The number of random variables is finite or countable.

2. All possible values of random variables and associated probabilities can be listed.

TABLE 3.6
Probability Mass Function for S&P Bond Rating Example

Event outcome = *x*	Probability of *x* = p(*x*)
AAA	0.24
AA	0.03
A	0.01
BBB	0.02
BB	0.44
B	0.21
CCC	0.03
C	0.01
D	0.01
Totals	1.00

TABLE 3.7
Probability Distribution for Bond Return Example

Return of bond = x	Probability of x = p(return on bond)
1	0.10
2	0.20
3	0.30
4	0.40
Totals	1.00

Expected Values

In Chapter 3, the concepts of central tendency and dispersion were explored. It was concluded that managers need to investigate data sets with regard to central tendency and dispersion to fully describe the situation facing them. Managers will inevitably be confronted with data sets that contain random variables. Consequently, it is very important to describe random variables in terms of central tendency and dispersion.

The central tendency of a random variable is often referred to as the expected value of the probability of distribution.

The central tendency of a random variable is often referred to as the *expected value* of the probability distribution. Expected value is calculated by using the following formula.

$$E(x) = \sum_{i=1}^{n} x_i \, p(x_i)$$

Multiplying each random variable by its corresponding probability and then summing these products calculates the expected value. Let's take, for example, another bond scenario. Table 3.8 displays the return of investment grade bonds based on a random sample of companies from the S&P 500.

For the bond return example, the return of investment grade bonds is computed as shown in Table 3.9a. From Table 3.9a, it is seen that the expected number of investment grade bonds is 3.0.

Decision makers use the expected value calculation to compare different alternatives. The assumption that is made and will be used throughout this text is that decision makers wish to maximize expected value. Therefore, when comparing numerous alternatives, a decision maker will choose the alternative with the highest expected value.

Keep in mind that maximizing expected value is only one way to make decisions. It is a basic assumption that is made in decision theory, but it is not the only assumption one can apply to expected values. If a decision maker were dealing strictly with costs, the assumption would be that the expected value of costs should be minimized. It would not be logical for a manager to wish to maximize expected costs.

When we use the assumption of maximizing expected value, it is a single objective. Many problems in the real world do not just have one objective. On the contrary, the problems managers face may actually have numerous objectives, and those objectives will more than likely conflict with each other.

Overall, multiple objective analysis is past the scope of this text; the basic assumption followed here is maximization of a single objective, namely expected value. Expected values will be discussed further in Chapter 4.

TABLE 3.8A
Computation of Expected Bond Return

Return of bond = x	Probability of x= p(return on bond)	x × p(x)
1	0.10	0.10
2	0.20	0.40
3	0.30	0.90
4	0.40	1.60
Total	1.00	3.00

PROBABILITY DISTRIBUTIONS AND STANDARD DEVIATION

Measures of dispersion must also be calculated for probability distributions. The standard deviation (SD) of a probability distribution can be calculated as follows:

$$SD = \sqrt{\sum (x - E(x))^2 \, p(x)}$$

Take note that this formula is different than the formula for standard deviation presented earlier in this chapter. Its main difference is the inclusion of the probability of the random variables, $p(x)$. This is necessary in that the probability of the occurrence of a random variable will affect the standard deviation of the probability distribution. The simplest way to remember when it is necessary to use this method for computing the standard deviation is to ask the question "Is there a probability distribution given?"

If the answer to this question is yes, then the formula for standard deviation presented here must be used. The next section will demonstrate the use of the formula for the bond return example.

Standard Deviation Calculation for a Probability Distribution

From the bond return example given earlier, it is known that the expected value of the probability distribution or the expected bond return is 3.00. In other words, $E(x) = 3.00$. With this expected value and the probability of each random variable, $p(x)$, the standard deviation for a probability distribution is computed as shown in Table 3.9b.

Therefore, the square root of the last column sum total is the standard deviation of the bond return example, or SD = 1.00. Now we have both parameters needed to define a probability distribution. These parameters are a measure of central tendency, the expected value, and a measure of dispersion, standard deviation.

Continuous Probability Distributions

Continuous probability distributions are also defined by a function. However, continuous probability distributions differ from discrete probability distributions. Continuous probability distributions are not defined by a probability mass function but are characterized as follows:

Continuous probability distributions are usually graphed and referred to as a probability curve.

1. The number of random variable values is infinite or uncountable.
2. All possible values of random variables and associated probabilities cannot be listed.
3. The probability distribution is defined by its underlying probability density function rather than a probability mass function.

Continuous probability distributions are usually graphed and referred to as a *probability curve*.

Several standard continuous probability distributions exist and are highly applicable in the real world to model data sets. One such continuous probability distribution is the normal probability distribution. The normal distribution is a common probability distribution found numerous places.

The normal distribution is a common probability distribution found numerous places.

The normal distribution is often described as bell-shaped. In fact, it is called the bell curve at times. Students of business decision modeling may have heard of the bell curve or even been judged on a bell curve. Some professors assign grades based on a bell curve.

TABLE 3.8B
Standard Deviation Computation for Bond Return Example

Return of bond = x	Probability of x= p(return on bond)	(x−E(x))²	(x−E(x))² × p(x)
1	0.10	$(1-3)^2 = 4.00$	0.40
2	0.20	$(2-3)^2 = 1.00$	0.20
3	0.30	$(3-3)^2 = 0.00$	0.00
4	0.40	$(4-3)^2 = 1.00$	0.40
Totals	1.00		1.00

FIGURE 3.12
**Normal Probability
Distribution**

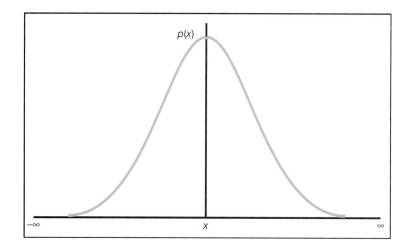

In addition, most students of business decision modeling have experienced a normal distribution when reviewing the results of college entrance exams such as the SAT or ACT. The test results are given in terms of percentiles, but the underlying curve for all test scores tends to be normal. Figure 3.12 displays an example of a normal probability distribution. It should be noted from Figure 3.12 that the *x* axis is continuous and extends left to negative infinity and right to positive infinity.

As was mentioned earlier, the normal distribution can be found and is used in numerous places in the real world. Specific examples of normal distributions, basic rules of thumb regarding normal distributions, calculation of *z* scores, and testing of two means are presented in Appendix 3A.

ALTERNATIVE DISTRIBUTIONS USED BY MANAGERS

The normal distribution works extremely well for many data sets and situations that arise out in the real world. Nevertheless, there are times that the normal distribution just is not adequate. Two areas of concern regarding the use of the normal distribution by managers are:

1. Lack of symmetry.
2. Sampling outside the given high and low values.

Lack of symmetry will be discussed first, and will be followed by a discussion of sampling outside the high and low value ranges. An alternative distribution to the normal curve is introduced that mitigates these areas of concern.

Lack of Symmetry

Lack of data set symmetry is a common problem analysts face when assessing probability distributions. For example, what happens if Jim the Client does not give high and low demand numbers that are equidistant from the mean? This does not integrate well with the requirement that normal distributions be symmetrical. In fact, the symmetry of the normal distribution that was an advantage in the past is now a hindrance.

Sampling Outside of the High and Low Value Ranges

An underlying characteristic of the normal distribution is that the tails of the distribution continue on into positive and negative infinity. This poses another real-world difficulty with the normal distribution. It is possible, although not highly probable, to obtain a demand outside the high or low given by Jim the Client. This would then nullify the previous dialog with Jim the Client. In other words, the numbers that Jim the Client gave us for his high and low demand would not actually be the high and low values for the distribution.

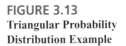

FIGURE 3.13
Triangular Probability
Distribution Example

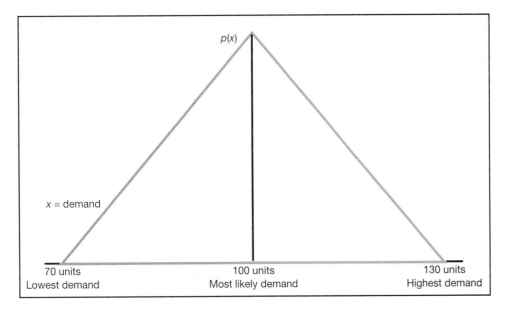

Triangular Distribution

To alleviate these areas of concern, a manager could use another type of continuous distribution, namely the triangular distribution. The triangular distribution exhibits similar characteristics to a normal distribution but is not compromised under the two areas of concern stated above.

Specifically, the triangular distribution is not required to be a symmetrical distribution. The triangular distribution lends itself easily to skewed data. In addition, the triangular distribution has a lower and upper bound. Sampling from the distribution cannot exceed the upper or lower values asserted by the manager or client.

From the conversation the manager had with Jim the Client, a triangular distribution as displayed in Figure 3.13 could be constructed.

The triangular distribution depicts a lower limit equal to 70 units, a upper limit of 130 units, and a most likely value of 100 units. The upper and lower limits are absolute. For example, in Jim the Client's case, demands less than 70 units or greater than 130 units will never occur.

In addition, the probability of obtaining a demand between the most likely value (100 units), the lowest value, or the highest value is equally likely. In other words, this triangular distribution is symmetrical. This is not and does not have to be the case for all triangular distributions.

Managers and consultants generally find it easier to elicit responses that fit a triangular distribution in the real world. More often than not, clients have the information and skill to respond to questions such as highest and lowest values. In addition, the most likely value can be identified easily and does not have to be equidistant from the lowest and highest values.

In sum, it is the job of the manager or consultant to determine which type of distribution best suits the data set or situation. Students of business decision modeling should remember that each type of distribution has its pros and cons. Linking probability theory, the assessment of probabilities, and the construction of probability distributions together is a large step in becoming a more effective and efficient problem solver.

Summary

The chapter presented the fundamental concepts of descriptive statistics, probability theory, probability distributions, and expected value. Measures of central tendency and dispersion were discussed. The laws of probability, and how to access subjective probabilities, were presented. Properties of mutual exclusivity and independence were defined and illustrated by Venn diagrams.

The concept of expectation was discussed and examples were provided on how to calculate expected value and standard deviation. The chapter also covered discrete and continuous probability distributions.

Students of business problem solving will find these topics to be of real importance as they continue to study decision theory, simulation, regression modeling, and project management.

The following example executive summary illustrates the application of the concepts discussed in this chapter.

Executive Summary for DFS Weekly Sales Data

TO: Jim Kros, Senior VP, DFS
FROM: Business Decision Modeling Consulting Group

This executive summary presents the weekly sales information you requested, covering the last 20 weeks. A numerical analysis has been done, using a simple average and standard deviation. In addition, a histogram graph detailing the number of times weekly sales fell into DFS's tracking buckets is presented.

Numerical Statistics for Weekly Sales Data

Over the 20 weeks of data, the simple average measures the center of the weekly sales data while the standard deviation measures how far the weekly sales numbers vary from this center point. Table 1 summarizes the numerical statistics for the weekly sales data.

TABLE 1
Summary of Weekly Sales Numerical Statistics

Numerical measure	Value
Simple average = mean	55.7
Standard deviation = SD*	19.3

*Denotes variation of the weekly sales data. Larger values of standard deviation mean relatively larger variations of sales from week to week.

It can be noted from the simple average that, over the last 20 weeks, sales have averaged around 56 units. If the standard deviation is compared to the average, it is seen that sales varied moderately, with a standard deviation of around 19. The term *moderately* is chosen since the magnitude of standard deviation is smaller than the average.

Weekly Sales Graph

Figure 1 displays the graph of weekly sales based on the DFS tracking buckets.

FIGURE 1 **Graph of Weekly Sales Data**

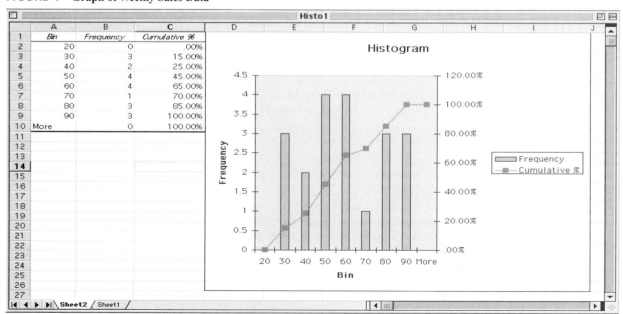

	A	B	C
1	Bin	Frequency	Cumulative %
2	20	0	.00%
3	30	3	15.00%
4	40	2	25.00%
5	50	4	45.00%
6	60	4	65.00%
7	70	1	70.00%
8	80	3	85.00%
9	90	3	100.00%
10	More	0	100.00%

The spreadsheet output also includes a tabularized version of the data and overlays a cumulative percentage graph on the DFS tracking bucket graph. The bars in the graph represent the frequency of the number of weeks in which sales are at the designated level (i.e., the *x*-axis bin). The graph also includes a cumulative line plot to indicate how weekly sales aggregate over all DFS's tracking buckets.

Conclusions

From the graph it can be noted that the DFS tracking buckets 50 and 60 represent the largest number of weekly occurring sales. It should also be noted that the lower bucket of 20 had no data points, and for this 20-week sales period there were no sales numbers higher than the 90 bucket.

Case Study: *Slicky Lube Oil Products*

BACKGROUND

John McCowski founded Slicky Lube in 1918. As the market for automobiles grew during the early and mid-1900s, the demand for specialty additives for lubricating oils also grew. Slicky Lube, in turn, expanded to meet this growth. Expansion into a range of other markets led Slicky Lube to become a market leader within the fluid sector. The company's major goal is to develop new oils and additives that are of high quality, yet environment-friendly.

The largest market segment of the fluid sector (61 percent) is the automobile market. However, this market is also the most competitive. As a result, it is crucial to Slicky Lube's continued success that the testing of new oils be highly accurate and very timely. The case study's tasks are to help Harold Scott, the Senior Chemical Engineer, analyze the data set using simple descriptive and inferential statistics and create processes for analyzing the field test data from all taxis in both New York and San Francisco in a more reasonable time frame.

THE OPERATIONAL ENVIRONMENT—TESTING AND VEHICLE SPECIFICATIONS

In 1998 Slicky Lube signed a deal with General Motors (GM). GM was to deliver 80 brand new Chevrolet automobiles to the Yellow Cab Cooperative in two different cities, New York and San Francisco. Because of their infamous reputations in regard to city driving conditions, New York and San Francisco were chosen as the test locations for new products. Each city would receive 40 new vehicles. The Chevrolet automobile utilized is a standard cab with a 4.8-liter, 140-horsepower engine.

The new oil/additive that Slicky Lube wished to test had to be used under severe operating conditions. This was necessary to find out whether it would perform better or worse in comparison to the existing products already on the market. The units operated 7 days a week, 24 hours a day ($2 \times$ 12-hour shifts). The sample oil was not replaced during the test period. Approximately every 10,000 miles, samples of the oil sludge would be taken and sent to an independent testing laboratory for testing and decomposition.

TESTING PROCESS AND PROCEDURES

The tests themselves are performed in the following manner: upon completion of the field-tests (approximately 12 months for total completion), samples of the lubricant and sludge deposits are taken from test vehicles and sent to independent laboratories for decomposition and analysis. Hard copies of the lab results are mailed via the surface mail postal system to Slicky Lube headquarters, where they analyzed by a group of 20 to 25 in-house technical specialists. Unusual or unexpected results and typographical errors in the lab reports are identified and highlighted before being sent to data entry Clerks for entry into Excel spreadsheets. These spreadsheets are returned to the technical specialists for further analysis. When the data are deemed to be free of errors, the spreadsheets are handed over to the Statistical Analysis Division of Slicky Lube for additional analysis.

PROBLEM IDENTIFICATION AND PROPOSED RESOLUTION

Slicky Lube management has identified some areas where time can be saved and reliability increased. However, no structure is set out for how to shorten the test time and increase the reliability of the measures taken. The sludge samples are then processed as described earlier.

DISCUSSION QUESTIONS

Your task is to help Harold Scott, the Senior Chemical Engineer, to create processes for analyzing the field test data from all taxis in both New York and San Francisco in a more reasonable time frame. Specifically, the following areas must be addressed:

- Conduct a thorough analysis of the data using descriptive statistics.

- Develop a statistical method to identify extreme high/low values and comment on their influence on the given data set.

- Make a comment about the strength/weakness of the oil being tested when an average value is calculated for each city and compared.

- Complete an ANOVA test to verify if all engines in the test vehicles are working properly, and a *t* test to identify differences or similarities in cylinder performance.
- Comment again on the strength/weakness of the oil being tested after the ANOVA and *t* tests have been performed.
- How can these the strength/weakness be interpreted with regard to marketing, financing, etc.? *Hint:* Averages may hide or overstate/understate how the additive performs. The ANOVA and *t* tests really are the means to address the efficacy of the additive.

The files containing the data collected can be found on the enclosed CD-ROM under the filename slicky.xls

---

Optimal Information Area

American Statistical Association (AMSTAT) home page at **http://www.amstat.org**

Gallery of Data Visualization: The Best and Worst of Statistical Graphics at **http://www.math.yorku.ca/SCS/Gallery/**

Helberg, Clay, "Statistics on the Web," at **http://www.execpc.com/~helberg/statistics.html**

Princeton University, Basic Sources of Economic Statistics, at **http://www.princeton.edu/~econlib/basic.html**

Ramseyer, Gary, "Archives of Statistics Fun," at **http://www.ilstu.edu/~gcramsey/FunArchives.html**

Grateful Med Web site at **http://igm.nlm.nih.gov**

International Society for Bayesian Analysis at **http://www.bayesian.org**

References

Bertin, Jacques. *Semiology of Graphics*, 1983.

Cohen, J. "The earth is round (p < .05)." *American Psychologist*, vol. 49 (1994), pp. 997–1003.

Corvalan, Enrique. "Evidence Based Health Care: Strategies for a New Century." Presentation at the University of Arizona College of Medicine 25th Annual Primary Care Update, March 29–April 1, 2000.

David, F. N. *Games, Gods, and Gambling*. New York: Hafner, 1962.

Gonick, L., and W. Smith. *A Cartoon Guide to Statistics*. New York: HarperPerennial, 1962.

Huff, Darrrell. *How to Lie with Statistics*. New York: W.W. Norton & Company, 1954.

Jaffe, A. J., and Herbert F. Spirer. *Misused Statistics: Straight Talk for Twisted Numbers*. New York: Marcel Decker, 1987.

King, G., "How not to lie with statistics: Avoiding common mistakes in quantitative political science." *American Journal of Political Science*, vol. 30 (1986), pp. 666–87.

McGervey, J. D. *Probabilities in Every Day Life*. New York: Ivy, 1989.

Peitetti, R. D., et al. "Evaluation of a New Rapid Antigen Detection Kit for Group A Beta-Hemolytic Streptococci." *Pediatric Emergency Care*, vol. 14, no. 6 (December 1998), pp. 396–98.

Stigler, S. M. *The History of Statistical Measurement of Uncertainty Before 1900*. Cambridge, MA: Harvard-Belknap, 1986.

Tufte, E. R. *The Visual Display of Quantitative Information*, Cheshire, CT: Graphics Press, 1983.

Tufte, E. R. *The Visual Display of Quantitative Information*. Cheshire, CT: Graphics Press, 1990.

Tufte, E. R. *The Visual Display of Quantitative Information*. Cheshire, CT: Graphics Press, 1997.

Problems

1. You are given the following data set: 2, 45, 34, 25, 6, 45, 67, 89. Using Excel's statistical functions, complete the following:

    a. Calculate the simple mean.
    b. Calculate the standard deviation.

   c. Calculate the median.

   d. Is the median equal to the mean? Why or why not?

2. You are given the following data set: 5000, 6524, 8524, 7845, 2100, 9845, 1285, 3541, 4581, 2465, 3846. Using Excel's statistical functions, complete the following:

   a. Calculate the simple mean.

   b. Calculate the standard deviation.

   c. Calculate the median.

   d. Is the median equal to the mean? Why or why not?

3. The following data on final grades were collected from a quantitative methods class at a major university. Using Excel's statistical functions, complete the following questions.

Percent grade	Letter grade and grade points	Percent grade	Letter grade & grade points
90	A− = 3.7	65	D = 1.0
85	B = 3.0	87	B+ = 3.3
82	B− = 2.7	95	A = 4.0
75	C = 2.0	78	C+ = 2.3
71	C− = 1.7	95	A = 4.0

Note: Standard grading scale is: −94 to 100 = A, 90 to 93 = A−, 87 to 89 = B+ , 84 to 86 = B, 80 to 83 = B−, 77 to 79 = C+ , 74 to 76 = C, 70 to 73 = C−, 60 to 69 = D, all else F.

   a. What is the mean percent grade for the class?

   b. What is the mean letter grade for the class?

   c. What is the median percent grade for the class?

   d. What is the median letter grade for the class?

   e. Are the mean and median percent grades equal? Why or why not?

   f. Are the mean and median letter grades equal? Why or why not?

4. The following data were collected on speeds on H1, a major highway. Using Excel's statistical functions, complete the following questions.

Speed (mph)

90	57	68	82	78 ·	71	65	69	55
75	64	60	67	57	52	63	61	55

   a. What is the mean of the data set for speed on H1?

   b. What is the standard deviation of the data set for speed on H1?

   c. Construct a histogram for the speed data set using 5 mph as your class width starting with 50 as your lowest class.

5. The following data were collected from the ECU baseball team regarding their pitcher's earned run averages (ERA) for the last 2 years. Using Excel's statistical functions, complete the following questions.

ERA

2.59	6.25	2.22	5.21	3.97	8.00	5.98	3.68	4.68
3.58	2.41	5.55	3.98	2.85	5.41	4.25	6.54	2.33

   a. What is the mean of the data set for the ECU pitcher's ERA?

   b. What is the standard deviation of the data set for the ECU pitcher's ERA?

   c. Construct a histogram for the ECU pitcher's ERA data set, using 0.5 as your class width and starting with 2.0 as your lowest class.

6. The following data were collected on scores (out of a possible 100) for a pretest in quantitative methods. Using Excel's statistical functions, complete the following questions.

Scores

99	12	94	21	11	88	10	5	10
88	2	89	18	97	5	87	100	10

    a. What is the mean of the data set for pretest scores?

    b. What is the median of the data set for the scores on the pretest? Is there a difference or similarity? Explain the similarity or difference.

    c. What is the standard deviation of the data set?

    d. Construct a histogram for the pretest score data set, using 5 as your class width and starting with 0 as your lowest class.

    e. Relate the standard deviation you calculated in part c to your histogram in part d.

7. The following are numerical statistics for five data sets. Using Excel's statistical functions, complete the following questions.

Data set	Mean	Median	Range	SD
1	50	50	6	2
2	70	100	100	47
3	25	15	92	25
4	50	44.5	60	22
5	33	0	100	41

    a. Compare the data sets with regard to measures of central tendency. Does the mean equal the median for each data set? What does it mean if they are equal? Comment on each data set.

    b. Are any data sets similar? Do some data sets appear similar with regard to measures of central tendency but different with regard to measures of dispersion? Comment on each data set.

8. The following data were collected on scores (out of a possible 100) for a pretest in quantitative methods. Using Excel's statistical functions, complete the following questions.

Arrivals

Data set 1			Data set 2		
95	75	68	45	25	18
102	67	65	62	17	15
99	87	94	49	37	54
88	120	81	48	70	31
100	71	104	50	21	54

    a. What are the means for the two data sets?

    b. What are the medians for the two data sets? Is there a difference or similarity between the mean and the median? Explain the similarity or difference.

    c. What are the standard deviations for each of the data sets?

    d. Construct a histogram for each data set, using 5 as your class width and starting with 60 as your lowest class for data set 1 and 10 for data set 2.

    e. Relate the standard deviation you calculated in part c to your histograms in part d.

9. Assume that 48 percent of all voters are men. Of those who vote, 80 percent of men and 20 percent of women think a man makes a better president.

    a. Construct a probability tree for this problem.

    b. Construct a probability table for this problem.

    c. Given a voter believes a man would make a better president, what is the probability that voter is a man?

    d. What is the probability of randomly finding a voter who does not believe a man would make a better president?

10. In a university, if a student is a business major, then there is 70 percent chance that he/she will be employed immediately after graduation. And if a student is not a business major, then there is a 35 percent chance that he/she will be employed immediately after graduation. We also know that 40 percent of students are business majors and 60 percent of students are not business majors.

    a. What is the probability that a student is employed immediately after graduation?

    b. What is the probability that a student is a business major given he or she is employed immediately after graduation?

11. Eastern Airlines knows that 20 percent of its customers fly first class, 20 percent fly business class, and the rest fly coach. Of those customers who fly first class, 70 percent are from the East Coast while 30 percent are from elsewhere. In addition, of those customers who fly business class, 50 percent are from the East Coast and 50 percent are from elsewhere. Finally, of those customers that fly coach class, 75 percent are from elsewhere and 25 percent are from the East Coast.

    a. Construct a probability tree for this problem.

    b. Construct a probability table for this problem.

    c. Determine the probability that a customer from the East Coast will fly first class.

    d. What is the probability that a customer will be from the East Coast?

12. Jim needs to find a shirt to wear to class, now. He knows that 75 percent of the shirts in his dorm room are his, while 25 percent belong to his roommate, Cyril. He also knows that 50 percent of his shirts are not clean and 75 percent of his roommate's shirts are not clean.

    a. Construct a probability tree for this problem.

    b. Construct a probability table for this problem.

    c. Given that Jim picks up a shirt from anywhere in the room, what is the probability that it is clean?

    d. What is the probability that Jim will be wearing a dirty shirt to class if he wears the first shirt he picks up?

13. Eighty percent of visitors to Honolulu go to the beach while 20 percent of visitors do not go to the beach. Forty percent of the beach goers are from the United States, while 60 percent are not from the United States. Thirty percent of the nonbeachgoers are from the United States, while 70 percent of the nonbeachgoers are not from the United States.

    a. Construct a probability tree for this problem.

    b. Construct a probability table for this problem.

    c. Given that a visitor is not from the U.S., what is the probability that the visitor does not go to the beach?

14. In 2000, the total population of Washington County was 10,525. The county is made up mostly of people of Danish ancestry. Around 62 percent of the population has a Danish background, while the rest of the population is evenly split between those of Swedish origin or those of mixed origin. Of those of Danish background, 90 percent are farmers, while only 50 percent of those with Swedish origin are farmers and only 10 percent of those with mixed origin are farmers.

    a. Construct a probability tree for this problem.

    b. Construct a probability table for this problem.

    c. If a customer walks into the local café, what is the probability that she will randomly select a person engaged in farming?

    d. Given that the customer sits down next to a person engaged in farming what is the probability that the person is not Danish or Swedish?

15. The following probabilities are for fruit boxes sold by Sam and Co. every month. From the past sales records, the company has recorded the following sales numbers and probabilities. Compute the expected number of fruit boxes that will be sold on next month.

Number of boxes	Probability
5	0.20
10	0.30
15	0.40
25	0.10

a. Using Excel, calculate the expected number of boxes.

b. Using Excel, find the standard deviation for the distribution.

16. It is the first day of pheasant season and Frank is getting ready to try his luck. This had been Frank's favorite day of the year for the past 20 years. Frank loves the first day of pheasant season and has kept records of the pheasants he has bagged. His success on opening day over the past 20 years is as shown in the table below:

Number of pheasants	Number of years
0	3
1	4
2	6
3	4
4	2
6	1

a. Using Excel, construct a histogram for Frank's pheasant distribution.

b. How many pheasants can Frank expect to bag today?

c. If Frank has guests in town, how many pheasants could he promise them with 90 percent confidence?

Appendix **3A**

Probability and Statistics Review

BAYES' RULE EXAMPLES

This appendix presents two sample problems using Bayes' rule. Probability tables and trees will be developed to aid in the process. Please keep in mind the difference between probability trees and decision trees. Probability trees are used to solve problems involving dependent events, while decision trees are used to model and solve decision problems. In general, probability trees tend to be deductive while decision trees tend to be inductive.

EXAMPLE OF BAYES' RULE AND THE GENERAL RULE OF MULTIPLICATION

A good example to help explain the relation of statistically dependent events is the TV weather report. The weather forecaster normally gives a prediction of rain or no rain; e.g., there is a 90 percent chance of rain today. It seems that the weather forecaster is providing us with a marginal probability for the chance of rain. However, much more thought went into that estimate of whether it will rain or not.

Let's put the 90 percent probability of rain in the context of what the weather forecaster might have seen prior to making the prediction. More than likely, the forecaster is constantly reviewing weather patterns and may see lightning developing or thunderclouds approaching. The occurrence of one of the two meteorological events plays a role in the probability of rain.

Armed with this prior information, the forecaster makes her probability assessment of rain. In other words, if the forecaster only saw lightning approaching, she assesses that there is a 90 percent chance of rain. On the other hand, if the weather forecaster only sees thunder clouds approaching, no lightning, she assesses that there is only a 60 percent chance of rain. Overall, there are equal chances, i.e., 50 percent/ 50 percent, of thunderclouds or lightning occurring.

SUMMARY OF PROBABILISTIC INFORMATION

The following probabilistic information can be summarized for this problem statement.

$$\text{Probability of lightning} = p(L) = 0.5$$
$$\text{Probability of thunder} = p(L) = 0.5$$
$$\text{Probability of rain given lightning} = p(R \mid L) = 0.9$$
$$\text{Probability of rain given thunder} = p(R \mid T) = 0.6$$

From these probabilities, the joint probabilities for the event space can be calculated using the general rule of multiplication. The joint probabilities are calculated as follows, where NR = no rain,

$$\text{Probability of lightning and rain} = p(L \text{ and } R)$$
$$= p(R \mid L)p(L)$$
$$= (0.9)(0.5) = 0.45$$
$$\text{Probability of lightning and no rain} = p(L \text{ and } NR)$$
$$= p(NR \mid L)p(L)$$
$$= (1 - 0.9)(0.5) = 0.05$$
$$\text{Probability of thunder and rain} = p(T \text{ and } R)$$
$$= p(R \mid T)p(T)$$
$$= (0.6)(0.5) = 0.3$$
$$\text{Probability of thunder and no rain} = p(T \text{ and } NR)$$
$$= p(NR \mid T)p(T)$$
$$= (1 - 0.6)(0.5) = 0.2$$

From this information, Table 3A.1 and Figure 3A.1 display the joint probability table and probability tree associated with the problem. The values in column 4 of the table are the marginal probabilities of rain, no rain, thunder, or lightning occurring. The values in columns 2 and 3 are the joint probabilities calculated above.

TABLE 3A.1
Joint Probability Table for Weather Forecast

	Weather phenomenon		
Weather outcome	**Thunder**	**Lightning**	**Marginal probabilities**
Rain	0.30	0.45	0.75
No rain	0.20	0.05	0.25
Marginal probabilities	0.50	0.50	1.00

FIGURE 3A.1
Probability Tree for Weather Forecast

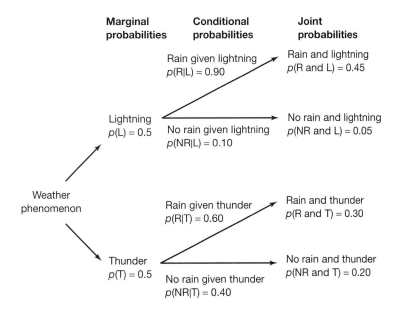

The same information displayed in the joint probability table is displayed on the probability tree. You may wish to construct a probability tree first and then create a joint probability table from the tree results.

POSTERIOR PROBABILITIES USING BAYES' RULE

The weather forecaster may wish to calculate a posterior probability. For example, given that it is raining, what is the probability that lightning was seen before the storm? This is done by using a combination of Bayes' rule and the results from the joint probability table or the Law of Total Probability.

Calculations Using Bayes' Rule and the Joint Probability Table

First, the posterior probability will be calculated by using the joint probability table. We wish to find $p(L|R)$. Given Bayes' rule we proceed as follows:

$$p(L \mid R) = \frac{p(L \text{ and } R)}{p(R)}$$

From the joint probability table, we know

$$p(L \text{ and } R) = 0.45$$
$$p(R) = 0.75$$

Using simple algebra, we therefore have

$$p(L \mid R) = \frac{0.45}{0.75}$$
$$= 0.60$$

So, the posterior probability that lightning was seen before the storm given that it is raining is 60 percent.

Calculations Using Bayes' Rule and The Law of Total Probability

The posterior probability can also be calculated by using Bayes' rule and the Law of Total Probability. We wish to find $p(L|R)$, but now we must use the following formula.

$$p(L \mid R) = \frac{p(L \text{ and } R)}{p(R \mid L)p(L) + p(R \mid T)p(T)}$$
$$= \frac{p(R \mid L)p(L)}{p(R \mid L)p(L) + p(R \mid T)p(T)}$$

We see that the denominator of the equation is the probability of rain represented by the Law of Total Probability. We also know that the joint probability $p(L \text{ and } R)$ is calculated by multiplying the conditional probability of rain given lightning by the marginal probability of lightning.

Both calculations are presented below along with the posterior probability the weather forecaster is looking for.

The joint probability of lightning and rain is

$$p(L \text{ and } R) = p(R \mid L)p(L)$$
$$= (0.90)(0.50)$$
$$= 0.45$$

and the probability of rain according to the Law of Total Probability is

$$p(R) = p(R \mid L)p(L) + p(R \mid T)p(T)$$
$$= (0.90)(0.50) + (0.60)(0.50)$$
$$= 0.75$$

Therefore, the posterior probability is

$$p(\text{L} \mid \text{R}) = \frac{p(\text{R} \mid \text{L})p(\text{L})}{p(\text{R} \mid \text{L})p(\text{L}) + p(\text{R} \mid \text{T})p(\text{T})}$$

$$= \frac{0.45}{0.75}$$

$$= 0.60$$

Once again we see that, if it is raining outside, then about 60 percent of the time lightning was seen before the storm.

Even though some statisticians tend to push students to use the Law of Total Probability, it is obvious that both methods produce the same result. Use whichever you feel most comfortable with, or use both to double-check your work.

ADDITIONAL EXAMPLE OF BAYES' RULE

A good example to help explain the relation of statistically dependent events is service processes such as those in a call center.

Calls may come into a call center from a customer with either a question or a problem; e.g., there is a 50/50 chance of a call from a customer with a question or a customer with a problem. This probability is a marginal probability of the type of call the call center is to receive. This probability could be derived from historical patterns of calls to the call center.

Now let's say that of those customers that call in with a problem, 40 percent end their call satisfied with the service provided to them. On the other hand, of those customers that call in with a question, 90 percent end their call satisfied with the service provided.

Armed with this information, we can use the same process we used earlier to identify, define, and model the problem to uncover information about the call center's process. In fact, someone could ask a question such as "Given that someone is dissatisfied with the service received, what is the probability that the customer called in with a question?" This is an important question to ask because being satisfied with the call centers service and the type of call are dependent on one another.

SUMMARY OF PROBABILISTIC INFORMATION

The following probabilistic information can be summarized for the preceding problem statement.

$$\text{Probability of problem call-in} = p(\text{P}) = 0.5$$
$$\text{Probability of question call-in} = p(\text{Q}) = 0.5$$
$$\text{Probability of satisfaction given problem call-in} = p(\text{S} \mid \text{P}) = 0.4$$
$$\text{Probability of satisfaction given question call-in} = p(\text{S} \mid \text{Q}) = 0.9$$

From these probabilities, the joint probabilities for the event space can be calculated by using the general rule of multiplication. The joint probabilities are calculated as follows, where NS = no satisfaction.

$$\text{Probability of problem call-in and satisfaction} = p(\text{P and S})$$
$$= p(\text{S} \mid \text{P})p(\text{P})$$
$$= (0.4)(0.5) = 0.20$$
$$\text{Probability of problem call-in and no satisfaction} = p(\text{P and NS})$$
$$= p(\text{NS} \mid \text{P})p(\text{P})$$
$$= (1 - 0.4)(0.5) = 0.30$$
$$\text{Probability of question call-in and satisfaction} = p(\text{Q and S})$$
$$= p(\text{S} \mid \text{Q})p(\text{Q})$$
$$= (0.9)(0.5) = 0.45$$

TABLE 3A.2
Joint Probability Table
for Call Type

	Call-In type		
Call-in outcome	Problem	Question	Marginal probabilities
Satisfaction	0.20	0.45	0.65
No satisfaction	0.30	0.05	0.35
Marginal probabilities	0.50	0.50	1.00

$$
\begin{aligned}
\text{Probability of question call-in and no satisfaction} &= p(Q \text{ and } NS) \\
&= p(NS \mid Q)p(Q) \\
&= (1 - 0.9)(0.5) = 0.05
\end{aligned}
$$

From this information, Table 3A.2 and Figure 3A.2 display the joint probability table and probability tree associated with the problem.

The values in column 4 of the table are the marginal probabilities of problem, question, satisfaction, or no satisfaction occurring. The probabilities in columns 2 and 3 are the joint probabilities calculated above.

The same information displayed in the joint probability table is displayed on the probability tree. You may wish to construct a probability tree first and then create a joint probability table from the tree results.

POSTERIOR PROBABILITIES USING BAYES' RULE

The call center manager may wish to calculate a posterior probability. For example, given that there was no satisfaction, what is the probability that a question was asked. This is done by using a combination of Bayes' rule and the results from the joint probability table or the Law of Total Probability.

Calculations Using Bayes' Rule and The Joint Probability Table

First, the posterior probability will be calculated by using the joint probability table. We wish to find $p(Q|NS)$. Given Bayes' rule, we proceed as follows.

$$
p(Q \mid NS) = \frac{p(NS \text{ and } Q)}{p(NS)}
$$

FIGURE 3A.2
Probabillity Tree for
Call Type

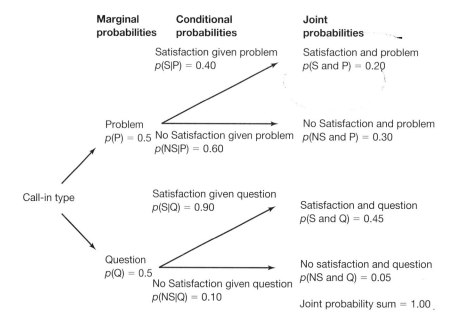

and, from the joint probability table, we know

$$p(\text{NS and Q}) = 0.05$$
$$p(\text{NS}) = 0.35$$

Using simple algebra, we therefore have

$$p(\text{Q} \mid \text{NS}) = \frac{0.05}{0.35}$$
$$= 0.143$$

So, the posterior probability that a customer asked a question, given that the customer was not satisfied with the service provided by the call center. is about 14.3 percent.

A manager would be interested in this number because being nonsatisfied depends on what kind of problem the customer presented to the call center.

Calculations Using Bayes' Rule and The Law of Total Probability

The posterior probability can also be calculated by using Bayes' rule and the Law of Total Probability. We wish to find $p(\text{Q}|\text{NS})$, but now we must use the following formula.

$$p(\text{Q} \mid \text{NS}) = \frac{p(\text{NS and Q})}{p(\text{NS} \mid \text{Q})p(\text{Q}) + p(\text{NS} \mid \text{P})p(\text{P})}$$
$$= \frac{p(\text{NS} \mid \text{Q})p(\text{Q})}{p(\text{NS} \mid \text{Q})p(\text{Q}) + p(\text{NS} \mid \text{P})p(\text{P})}$$

We see that the denominator of the equation is the probability of no satisfaction represented by the Law of Total Probability. We also know that the joint probability $p(\text{NS and Q})$ is calculated by multiplying the conditional probability of no satisfaction given a question by the marginal probability of question.

Both calculations are presented below along with the posterior probability the call center manager is looking for. The joint probability of no satisfaction and question is

$$p(\text{NS and Q}) = p(\text{NS} \mid \text{Q})p(\text{Q})$$
$$= (0.10)(0.50)$$
$$= 0.05$$

and the probability of no satisfaction, based on the Law of Total Probability, is

$$p(\text{NS}) = p(\text{NS} \mid \text{Q})p(\text{Q}) + p(\text{NS} \mid \text{P})p(\text{P})$$
$$= (0.05)(0.50) + (0.90)(0.50)$$
$$= 0.35$$

Therefore, the posterior probability is

$$p(\text{Q} \mid \text{NS}) = \frac{p(\text{NS} \mid \text{Q})p(\text{Q})}{p(\text{NS} \mid \text{Q})p(\text{Q}) + p(\text{NS} \mid \text{P})p(\text{P})}$$
$$= \frac{0.05}{0.35}$$
$$= 0.143$$

Once again we see that the posterior probability that a customer asked a question, given that the customer was not satisfied with the service provided by the call center, is about 14.3 percent.

Even though some statisticians tend to push students to use the the Law of Total Probability, it is obvious that both methods produce the same result. Use whichever you feel most comfortable with, or use both to double-check your work.

THE NORMAL DISTRIBUTION—RULES OF THUMB

As was mentioned earlier, the normal distribution can be found and is used in numerous places in the real world. Specific examples and some basic rules of thumb about normal distributions will be detailed next.

FIGURE 3A.3
Symmetry of the Normal Probability Distribution

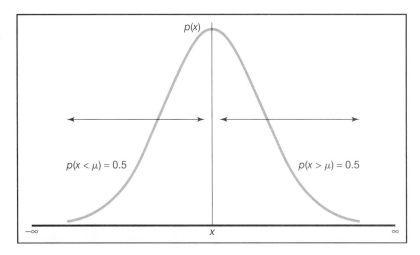

Since the normal distribution is a continuous probability distribution, it has some implicit advantages over discrete probability distributions. In general, it is much easier mathematically to deal with continuous smooth curves than it is to work with a large number of individual probabilities. In addition, the normal curve itself has some explicit advantages over many other probability distributions.

The explicit advantages that the normal curve has are detailed in the four rules of thumb below.

Normal Distribution: Rule of Thumb 1

According to the rules of probability from Chapter 2, the sum of all the probabilities under the normal curve must sum to 1.0.

Normal probability distributions are symmetric.

We know that the normal curve is considered a symmetrical distribution. A symmetrical distribution is a distribution that, when divided in two at its mean, each half has equal probability. This can be seen in Figure 3A.3. Now it must be remembered that the tails of the normal curve extend to positive and negative infinity, i.e., the tails continue to the left and to the right in Figure 3A.3 forever. Figure 3A.3 shows that if one folds the normal curve at its mean, the two halves will be identical. In other words, the distribution is symmetric.

Normal Distribution: Rule of Thumb 2

The normal distribution has tails that extend to positive infinity and negative infinity.

Now that the symmetry of the normal curve has been established, the link between the mean and the standard deviation of the distribution can be established. It takes two parameters to fully describe a distribution, the mean and standard deviation. Specific characteristics about any normal curve can be elicited by using the basic symmetry of the normal curve.

Within 1 standard deviation from the mean in the positive and negative directions, the area mapped by those boundaries contains approximately 68 percent of the curve's area.

The following statement is true about any normal curve: Within 1 standard deviation from the mean in the positive and negative directions, the area mapped by those boundaries contains approximately 68 percent of the curve's area.

Figure 3A.4 illustrates rule of thumb 2. The figure shows that the amount of probability from the mean to 1 standard deviation above the mean is equal to approximately 34 percent. Since the distribution is symmetric, the amount of probability 1 standard deviation below the mean is also approximately equal to 34 percent.

Normal Distribution: Rule of Thumb 3

Within 2 standard deviations from the mean in the positive and negative directions, the area mapped by those boundaries contains approximately 95 percent of the curve's area.

If we could describe a normal distribution by moving 1 standard deviation away from the mean, why not move 2 standard deviations away and describe the curve? Figure 3A.5 illustrates rule of thumb 3.

The following statement is true about any normal curve: Within 2 standard deviations from the mean in the positive and negative directions, the area mapped by those boundaries contains approximately 95 percent of the curve's area.

Figure 3A.5 shows that the amount of probability from the mean to 2 standard deviations above the mean is equal to approximately 47.5 percent. Since the distribution is symmetric, the amount of probability 2 standard deviations below the mean is also approximately equal to 47.5 percent. Therefore, the total probability that lies within ±2 standard deviations from the mean is approximately equal to 95 percent.

FIGURE 3A.4
Normal Probability Distrubution Rule of Thumb 2

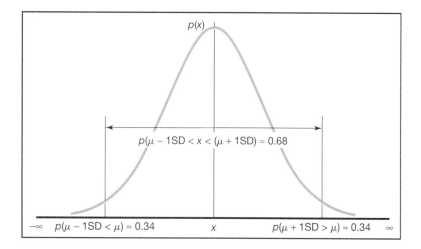

FIGURE 3A.5
Normal Probability Distrubution Rule of Thumb 3

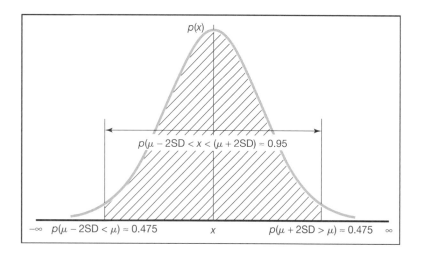

Normal Distribution: Rule of Thumb 4

Within 3 standard deviations from the mean in the positive and negative directions, the area mapped by those boundaries contains approximately 99.7 percent of the curve's area.

The following statement is true about any normal curve: Within 3 standard deviations from the mean in the positive and negative directions the area mapped by those boundaries contains approximately 99 percent of the curve's area.

Figure 3A.6 illustrates rule of thumb 4. The figure shows that the amount of probability from the mean to 3 standard deviations above the mean is equal to approximately 49.5 percent. Since the distribution is symmetric, the amount of probability 3 standard deviations below the mean is also approximately equal to 49.5 percent. Hence, the total amount of probability that lies within ±3 standard deviations from the mean is equal to approximately 99 percent.

CALCULATION OF STANDARD NORMAL PROBABILITIES

A student of business decision modeling may also ask how and where does one find the number 34 percent. Integral calculus is one way of finding this answer by calculating the area under the curve. The 34 percent is calculated by using the underlying normal distribution function to identify how much probability lies in the area bounded by the curve, the mean, and the mean plus 1 standard deviation.

Integral calculus is beyond the scope of this text and most managers would not have the time or the energy to complete such a calculation. In fact, there is no need to employ integral calculus at all because someone has already done the work for us.

From earlier work done by Bernoulli and de Moivre, the standard normal table was developed. Using the standard normal table, we can describe any normal distribution with mean μ and standard deviation σ. Table 3A.3 displays a portion of the standard normal table. The full standard normal table is in Appendix A.

FIGURE 3A.6
Normal Probability
Distribution Rule
of Thumb 4

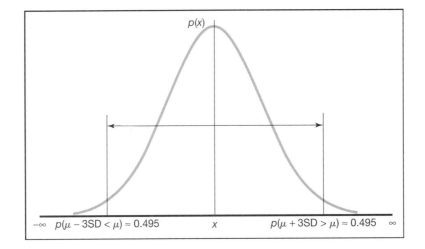

The standard normal table is used as a yardstick to explain how many standard deviations a random variable x is from the mean.

The standard normal table is used as a yardstick to explain how many standard deviations a random variable x is from the mean. For our example, we are 1 standard deviation away from the mean. This translates into what is called a z score of 1.00. The standard normal table is also referred to as the standard z table. Using the standard normal table and calculation of z scores will be covered in the next section.

STEPS FOR USING THE STANDARD NORMAL TABLE

The steps in using the standard normal table are as follows.

Step 1: First convert an x score to a z score by differencing the mean from the x score and dividing by the standard deviation. For example, given

$$\mu = 100, \sigma = 10, \text{ and } x = 110$$

$$z = \frac{x - \mu}{\sigma}$$

$$= \frac{110 - 100}{10}$$

$$= 1$$

Step 2: From Table 3A.3, refer to the far left column and identify the calculated z score. If your z score has values after the decimal point, refer to the top row of Table 3A.3 and identify them (if your z score is an integer identify zero in the top row).

Step 3: Find the intersection point of the row and column that have been identified.

Step 4: Record the value from the standard normal table at the intersection point. This value is the probability of being between the random variable x and the mean.

The steps for the example normal distribution, where we moved 1 standard deviation above the mean and the z score was given as 1.00, are as follows.

Step 1: In Table 3A.3, refer to the far left column and identify the calculated z score (see the arrow in Table 3A.4). In other words, look up the z value 1.00 in the standard normal table

Step 2: Find the intersection point of the row and column that have been identified. The number in bold italics inside Table 3A.4 denotes this intersection point.

TABLE 3A.3
Standard Normal Table
Excerpt

z	.00	.01	.02	.03	.04	.05	.06	.07	.08	.09
0.8	.2881	.2910	.2939	.2967	.2995	.3023	.3051	.3078	.3061	.3133
0.9	.3159	.3186	.3212	.3238	.3264	.3289	.3351	.3340	.3365	.3389
1.0	.3413	.3438	.3461	.3485	.3508	.3531	.3554	.3577	.3599	.3621
1.1	.3643	.3665	.3686	.3708	.3729	.3749	.3770	.3790	.3810	.3830
1.2	.3849	.3869	.3888	.3907	.3925	.3944	.3962	.3980	.3997	.4015

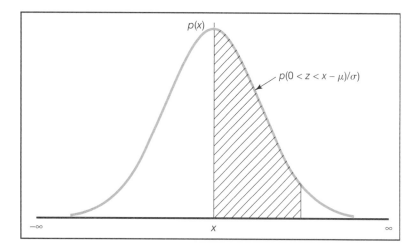

TABLE 3A.4
Standard Normal Table Excerpt

z	.00	.01	.02	.03	.04	.05	.06	.07	.08	.09
0.8	.2881	.2910	.2939	.2967	.2995	.3023	.3051	.3078	.3061	.3133
0.9	.3159	.3186	.3212	.3238	.3264	.3289	.3351	.3340	.3365	.3389
1.0	*.3413*	.3438	.3461	.3485	.3508	.3531	.3554	.3577	.3599	.3621
1.1	.3643	.3665	.3686	.3708	.3729	.3749	.3770	.3790	.3810	.3830
1.2	.3849	.3869	.3888	.3907	.3925	.3944	.3962	.3980	.3997	.4015

Step 3: Record the value from the standard normal table at the intersection point. The value indicates that the probability of being 1 standard deviation above the mean is 0.3413, or approximately 34 percent.

MANAGERIAL ASPECTS OF NORMAL DISTRIBUTIONS

Why would a manager be concerned with the normal distribution? Previously, in Chapter 2, the topic of probability assessment was introduced. It was concluded that managers who attempt to do a better job of assessing probabilities tend to become more effective and efficient problem solvers.

The basic characteristics of a normal distribution lend themselves to helping managers make better probability assessments. It would be folly for a manager to attempt to explain all the details in this chapter regarding probability distributions to a client with no training or interest in the subject. However, armed with the simple knowledge given in the rules of thumb, a manager can assess a client's distribution regarding the topic at hand.

For example, take the concept illustrated in rule of thumb 4, which states: Within 3 standard deviations from the mean in the positive and negative directions, the area mapped by those boundaries contains approximately 99 percent of the curve's area. A manager could use this principle to elicit a client's probability distribution without ever asking about the client's mean or standard deviation.

DIALOG FOR CLIENT DISTRIBUTION ASSESSMENT

A typical dialog between manager and client may go something like this:

Manager: "When we spoke yesterday on the phone you mentioned that on average you have seen demand around 100 units."

Jim the Client: "Yes, that is true. In any one month we see demand at around 100 units, give or take some."

Manager: "Jim, what would you say is the lowest demand you tend to see?"

Jim the Client: "I would have to say around 70 units we rarely see demand less than 70."

Manager: "So, Jim, 70 units would be the lowest demand you would ever see. How about the highest demand you tend to see?"

Jim the Client: "Yeah, 70 is the lowest and I would say 130 as the highest."

FIGURE 3A.7
Normal Probabillity
Distribution Example

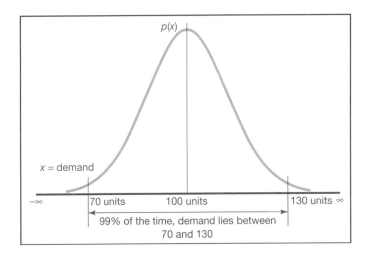

Manager: "So, Jim, would this statement be true '99 percent of the time, demand lies between 70 and 130 units with an average of 100 units'."

Jim the Client: "Yes, I would say that is a true statement."

Through this dialogue, the manager has implicitly assessed the client's probability distribution. By using the information given by the client and the third rule of thumb, the normal distribution in Figure 3A.7 can be created.

The two parameters, mean and standard deviation, that are needed to describe a normal distribution can be estimated from Figure 3A.7. Since Jim the client gave us information on the highest (130 units), lowest (70 units), and average demand (100 units), it could be inferred that those two numbers are ±3 standard deviations away from the mean.

ESTIMATION OF DISTRIBUTION STANDARD DEVIATION

This inference in the preceding paragraph can be made because over 99 percent of the values represented by a normal curve lie within ±3 standard deviations from the mean. Rule of thumb 4 states this. Since 70 and 130 are equidistant from the mean of 100 units, it can be shown that the standard deviation of the distribution must be approximately 10 units. The standard deviation is calculated by dividing the difference of the highest value minus the mean by 3.

For a manager, this is very robust information. If a manager or a consultant can elicit information as illustrated in the dialog example, a much better picture of the data and hence the situation can be drawn. It behooves managers to attempt the process of assessing client's probability distributions of upcoming or possible events. Once again, the concept of using a measure of central tendency and dispersion to fully describe a set of data is paramount.

Calculation of *z* Scores

Area under the normal curve or probability under the normal curve is measured by determining the number of standard deviations the random variable *x* is from the mean. The previous section discussed the concept of estimating a client's standard deviation using the normal distribution rules of thumb. Calculation of the *z* score calculation is somewhat the converse of this estimation procedure.

Typically, a manager uses descriptive statistics to calculate the mean and standard deviation for a data set. Then the manager makes some inferences about the data set from those statistics. For example, Jim the Client explains that average demand is equal to 100 units and the standard deviation of demand is equal to 10 units. Armed with these data set parameters, the manager can ask a question such as "How often should Jim see demand greater than 110?" This question can be answered by using what is called a *z* score. From the mean, standard deviation, and the value of a random variable included in the data set, the manager can conclude how many standard deviations away from the mean 110 units is and what the probability is that Jim the Client will see demand greater than 110 units.

z Score Formula

The formula used to compute *z* scores is as follows:

$$z = \frac{x - \mu}{\sigma}$$

For the example given above, the *z* score would be

$$\mu = 100, \sigma = 10, \text{ and } x = 110$$

$$z = \frac{x - \mu}{\sigma}$$

$$= \frac{110 - 100}{10}$$

$$= 1$$

By using the standard normal table, the probability associated with that *z* score can be found. A *z* score of 1.00 equates to a probability value of 0.3414 (this was found by using the standard normal table to look up the z score of 1.00).

The probability found in the step above identifies the probability of demand being between 100 units, the mean, and 110 units. In other words, Jim the Client can expect demand to be between 100 units and 110 units about 34 percent of the time (refer to Figure 3A.8).

This probability alone does not answer the question posed in the example problem. In order to find the probability of demand being greater than 110 units, a clue must be drawn from rule of thumb 1.

The probability being sought is actually the small area under the curve to the right of the crosshatched area in Figure 3A.8. The area labeled $p(x > 110) = ?$ can be found by using Figure 3A.8 and the following logic:

1. From rule of thumb 1, the area under the curve from the mean, 100 units, to positive infinity is 50 percent or 0.50.
2. From the calculations above, the area under the curve from the mean, 100 units, to a demand of 110 units is equal to approximately 34.14 percent or 0.3414.
3. Therefore, the area labeled $p(x > 110)$ must be equal to the area under the curve from the mean, 100 units, to infinity less the area under the curve from the mean, 100 units, to 110 units. That calculation is as follows:

$$p(x > 110) = 0.5 - 0.3414 = 0.1586$$

or approximately 15.86 percent.

Therefore, Jim the Client can expect demand to be greater than 110 units around 16 percent of the time.

Additional *z* Score Example

Let's assume Jim the Client also wishes to know how often demand will occur between 90 units and 105 units. In probability terms, Jim the Client wishes to know $p(90 < x < 105)$. Visually, Figure 3A.9 displays the area under the normal curve Jim the Client is looking for.

FIGURE 3A.8
Demand Example Distribution

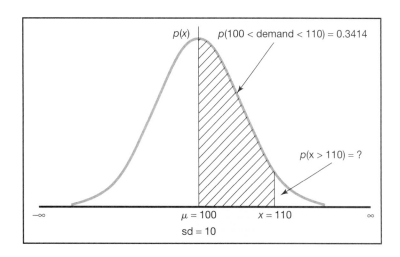

FIGURE 3A.9
Demand Example Distribution

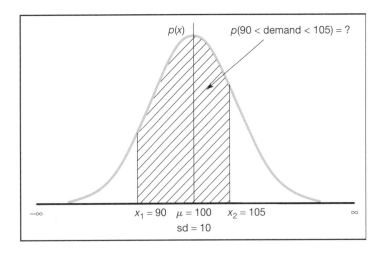

The same steps used in the earlier example are employed:

Step 1: Calculate z scores for $x_1 = 90$ units and $x_2 = 105$ units. First, $x_1 = 90$.

$$\mu = 100, \sigma = 10, \text{ and } x = 90$$

$$z = \frac{x - \mu}{\sigma}$$

$$= \frac{90 - 100}{10}$$

$$= -1$$

According to rule of thumb 1, symmetry of the normal distribution, the negative sign of the z score is unimportant. Therefore an absolute value of the z score is taken and the value of 1.00 is looked up in the standard normal. A z score of 1.00 equates to a probability value of 0.3414; i.e., $p(90 < x < 100) = 34.14\%$, or approximately 34.14 percent of the time demand falls between 90 and 100 units.

Second, $x_2 = 105$.

$$\mu = 100, \sigma = 10, \text{ and } x = 105$$

$$z = \frac{x - \mu}{\sigma}$$

$$= \frac{105 - 100}{10}$$

$$= 0.50$$

The value of 0.50 is looked up in the standard normal. A z score of 0.50 equates to a probability value of 0.1915; i.e., $p(100 < x < 105) = 19.15\%$, or approximately 19.15 percent of the time demand falls between 100 and 105 units.

Step 2: Add the probability results for $x_1 = 90$ units and $x_2 = 105$ units to determine the total probability of demand falling between 90 and 105 units.

$$p(90 < x < 105) = p(90 < x < 100) + p(100 < x < 105)$$

$$= 34.14\% + 19.15\%$$

$$= 53.29\%$$

Therefore, the manager can inform Jim the Client that the probability of demand falling between 90 and 105 units is approximately 53.29 percent.

The z scores help analyze normal distributions one at a time. What happens if a manager has two normal distributions to analyze or compare? The next section, on hypothesis testing, addresses this question.

HYPOTHESIS TESTING—ANALYZING DIFFERENCE OF TWO MEANS

This section describes a procedure for hypothesis testing. This type of hypothesis testing examines differences between two independent groups, using numerical samples. Hypothesis testing is also referred to as analyzing the difference of two means or testing two means.

Introduction to Hypothesis Testing

Before the exact procedure for testing two means is described, a short discussion of standard deviation is in order. As was presented in Chapter 2, standard deviation is one measure of dispersion. Coupled with the mean, the standard deviation describes the shape of a population and the underlying population distribution.

There are many reasons why a manager would wish to compare two populations. A manager may wish to

- Validate a claim
- Discriminate between two data sets
- Statistically prove a similarity or difference between data sets

In essence, when a manager wishes to compare two population means, a comparison of the underlying distributions is appropriate. In comparing populations or underlying data distributions, a manager is attempting to make a claim or, in statistics language, test a hypothesis.

The *Z* Test Statistic

The question at hand is how does one go about claiming two underlying distribution are the same or different from each other. A hypothesis could be established that states the following:

$$\text{Population mean 1} = \text{population mean 2}$$

The *Z* test statistic is used to test this hypothesis. However, the difference between two population means is based on the difference between two sample means $(\bar{x}_1 - \bar{x}_2)$.

Before we detail the *Z* test statistics, let's first represent the descriptive statistics of the two populations as in Table 3A.5.

The difference between the sample means, $\bar{x}_1 - \bar{x}_2$, is a test statistic that follows a standard normal distribution for samples that are large enough. The *Z* statistic itself is as follows:

$$Z = \frac{(\bar{x}_1 - \bar{x}_2) - (\mu_1 - \mu_2)}{\sqrt{\dfrac{\sigma_1^2}{n_1} + \dfrac{\sigma_2^2}{n_2}}}$$

However, as was mentioned earlier in Chapter 2, rarely does a manager know the actual standard deviation of either of the populations. Usually the only information that is obtainable is the sample means, $\bar{x}_1$ and $\bar{x}_2$, and the sample standard deviations s_1 and s_2.

Therefore, the next section will discuss another test statistic, the *t* test statistic, which will allow us to use sample means and sample standard deviations to test for differences in two means.

The *t* Test Statistic

The *t* test statistic is similar to the *Z* test statistic but uses information drawn from sample data. For the *t* test statistic, the following assumptions are made:

- Samples are drawn randomly and independently from a normally distributed population.

TABLE 3A.5
Descriptive Statistics

Population 1	Population 2
μ_1 = mean of population #1	μ_2 = mean of Population #2
σ_1 = standard deviation of population #1	σ_2 = standard deviation of population #2
n_1 = sample size of population #1	n_2 = sample size of population #2

- Population variances are equal, i.e., $\sigma_1^2 = \sigma_2^2$.
- A pooled-variance t test will be used to determine significance

These assumptions are necessary because of the lack of knowledge regarding the population standard deviations.

The t test can be performed as either a two-tailed or one-tailed test. This text will concentrate on the two-tailed t test. A two-tailed t test is used to test whether population means are similar or different. A good rule of thumb to follow is:

Two-tailed t tests use an $=$ sign in the null hypothesis

Two-tailed t tests use an $=$ sign because the test is attempting to show merely a similarity or difference in the two means.

Four Components of a Hypothesis Test for Two Means

The t test for hypothesis testing of two means, commonly referred to as the test of two means, is the most common method for comparing the means of two data sets.

The procedure for testing two means consists of four components:

1. Null hypothesis H_0
2. Alternative hypothesis H_a
3. Test statistics: t statistic and t critical
4. Rejection/acceptance region: rules of thumb to follow

The next sections will detail each of the four t test components and will be followed by an application example.

The Null Hypothesis

The null hypothesis is the claim you are trying to make or prove. For the two-tailed t test, it will consist of a statement similar to the following:

H_0: the means are from the same sample population

or

H_0 : mean 1 $=$ mean 2

or

H_0: mean male salaries $=$ mean female salaries

Standard statistical nomenclature assigns the moniker H_0 to the null hypothesis. The experimenter or decision maker is responsible for formulating and stating the null hypothesis. The null hypothesis is generally formulated and stated first.

The Alternative Hypothesis

The alternative hypothesis is the converse of the null hypothesis. For the two-tailed t test it will consist of a statement similar to the following:

H_a: the means are from different sample populations

or

H_a: mean 1 $\neq$ mean 2

or

H_0: mean male salaries $=$ mean female salaries

Standard statistical nomenclature assigns the moniker H_a to the alternative hypothesis. The experimenter or decision maker is responsible for formulating and stating the alternative hypothesis. The alternative hypothesis is generally formulated and stated second.

The Test Statistics: *t* statistic and *t* critical

Two test statistics are needed to conduct a test of two means. These statistics are as follows:

- t statistic: Calculated by using a pooled-variance t test or Excel

- *t* critical: A value based on a level of significance (usually 5 percent) and degrees of freedom (dof) and obtained from a statistical *t* table or Excel

t Statistic

The t statistic is calculated by using a pooled-variance *t* statistic. This statistic can be computed as follows:

$$t = \frac{(\bar{x}_1 - \bar{x}_2) - (\mu_1 - \mu_2)}{\sqrt{S_p^2 \left(\dfrac{1}{n_1} + \dfrac{1}{n_2} \right)}}$$

where

$$S_p^2 = \frac{(n_1 - 1)S_1^2 + (n_2 - 1)S_2^2}{(n_1 - 1) + (n_2 - 1)}$$

and

S_p^2 = pooled variance
S_1^2 = variance of the sample 1
S_2^2 = variance of the sample 2
n_1 = size of sample 1
n_1 = size of sample 2

The pooled-variance *t* test statistic follows a *t* distribution with $n_1 + n_2 - 2$ degrees of freedom. The test gets the name *pooled-variance* because the test statistic requires the pooling or combination of the sample variances.

S_1^2 and S_2^2, in addition to n_1 and n_2, are combined, or pooled (see the pooled-variance equation above), to yield a variance estimate that is common to both populations under the assumption that the population variances are equal.

t critical

The *t* critical value is a value based on a level of significance (usually 95 percent) and a number of degrees of freedom. The level of significance is also referred to as the *alpha value*.

Like the *t* statistic, the number of degrees of freedom for the *t* critical is based on $n_1 + n_2 - 2$. The actual *t* critical value can be obtained from a statistical *t* table or from a commercial statistical software package such as Excel.

Rejection/Acceptance Regions – Rules of Thumb

After the *t* statistic has been calculated and the *t* critical value obtained, a decision can be made about rejecting or accepting the null hypothesis. A few simple rules of thumb exist for rejecting or accepting the null. They are as follows:

$$\text{If} : |t \text{ stat}| > t \text{ crit, reject the null hypothesis } H_0$$

or

$$\text{If} : |t \text{ stat}| < t \text{ crit, accept the null hypothesis } H_0$$

or

$$\text{If } |t \text{ stat}| = t \text{ crit, investigate further}$$

These rules of thumb instruct a manager for a given level of significance when the null hypothesis can be rejected or accepted. The rules of thumb for rejecting or accepting the null hypothesis can also be displayed as reject and accept reasons on a normal curve as in Figure 3A.10.

t TEST APPLICATION PROBLEM

This section will present a numerical example of the pooled-variance *t* test. Novine wishes to test a hypothesis. She regularly shops at two different local grocery stores, Foodway and Safeland. Novine wishes to compare the overall average purchase prices of the groceries she bought at the two stores.

FIGURE 3A.10   **Reject/Accept Regions for Two-Tailed *t* Tests**

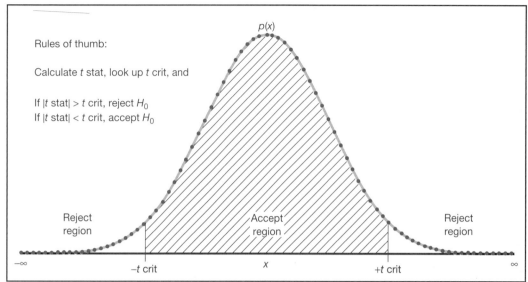

She has collected receipts for the total dollar amount of groceries she has purchased from the two different stores. Overall, the types and amounts of products she has purchased are generally the same for both stores and over time. Therefore, she believes the comparison can be made without too much bias. She has 32 receipts for Foodway and 35 receipts for Safeland. The results are presented in Table 3A.6.

Novine wishes to determine if there is a difference in the average grocery bills between the two populations of receipts. The null and alternative hypotheses are as follows:

$$H_0: \text{mean grocery receipts of Foodway} = \text{mean grocery receipts of Safeland}$$

or

$$H_0: \mu_{\text{Foodway receipts}} = \mu_{\text{Safeland receipts}}$$

or

$$H_0: \mu_{\text{Foodway receipts}} - \mu_{\text{Safeland receipts}} = 0$$

We will assume that the samples are taken from underlying normal distributions with equal variances. Therefore, a pooled-variance *t* test can be used to test the hypothesis. Novine chooses a significance level of 0.05 (a standard level in statistics), and the *t* test statistic would follow a *t* distribution with

TABLE 3A.6
Novine's Foodway and Safeland Receipt Samples

Foodway			Safeland		
$57.92	$50.35	$41.64	$77.89	$70.61	$89.18
$63.79	$76.22	$72.23	$83.99	$77.34	$35.04
$69.20	$38.57	$35.48	$52.61	$57.99	$86.96
$39.32	$45.90	$65.80	$30.82	$87.03	$85.66
$59.73	$60.17	$29.27	$103.28	$49.54	$57.58
$71.83	$30.29	$59.86	$39.92	$72.29	$31.38
$53.30	$52.36	$58.23	$70.16	$49.97	$44.62
$53.11	$33.19	$46.20	$29.42	$50.83	$51.13
$80.31	$75.84	$73.32	$65.79	$49.35	$96.12
$26.08	$37.59	$58.50	$60.76	$33.23	$55.80
$52.52	$53.98		$87.84	$77.47	$49.44
			$79.80	$104.97	

TABLE 3A.7
Summary Statistics for Novine's Grocery Receipts

	Foodway	Safeland
Sample size	$n1 = 32$	$n2 = 35$
Sample mean	$\bar{x}_1 = \$53.82$	$\bar{x}_2 = \$64.17$
Sample variance	$s12 = 227.79$	$s22 = 467.51$

$n_1 + n_2 - 2$ degrees of freedom, or $32 + 35 - 2 = 65$. Referring to an F distribution table, we find the critical value for the t test is 1.997.

Table 3A.7 displays the summary statistics for Novine's grocery t test.

The t statistic is calculated as follows:

$$t = \frac{(\bar{x}_1 - \bar{x}_2) - (\mu_1 - \mu_2)}{\sqrt{S_p^2 \left(\frac{1}{n_1} + \frac{1}{n_2} \right)}}$$

where

$$S_p^2 = \frac{(n_1 - 1)S_1^2 + (n_2 - 1)S_2^2}{(n_1 - 1) + (n_2 - 1)}$$

$$= \frac{(32 - 1)227.19 + (35 - 1)467.51}{(32 - 1) + (35 - 1)}$$

$$= 353.18$$

and therefore

$$t = \frac{53.82 - 64.17}{\sqrt{353.18 \left(\frac{1}{32} + \frac{1}{35} \right)}}$$

$$= -2.252$$

Using the rules of thumb for rejection/acceptance of the null hypothesis, we compare the t statistic to the t critical value and make recommendations, as follows:

$$|t \text{ stat}| = 2.252 \quad \text{and} \quad t \text{ crit} = 1.997$$

In turn,

$$|t \text{ stat}| > t \text{ crit}$$

$$2.252 > 1.997$$

Therefore,

The null hypothesis is rejected

or

Mean grocery receipts at Foodway $\neq$ Mean grocery receipts at Safeland

Take note that a 0.05 level of significance is used and 65 degrees of freedom. This can be interpreted as follows: If the null hypothesis were true, there would be a 5 percent probability of obtaining a t test statistic larger than ± 1.997 standard deviations from the center of the underlying distribution.

The null hypothesis is rejected because the t test statistic falls into the reject region. Novine can conclude that her average grocery bills at Foodway and Safeland are not equal.

ITEMS TO NOTE REGARDING TESTING OF TWO MEANS

A number of assumptions were made regarding the test of two means presented here. The first assumption was that the samples were drawn from normally distributed populations. The second assumption was that the two samples had equal variance. The third assumption was the level of significance that was chosen. Departures from these assumptions must be investigated.

Overall, a good rule of thumb to use when testing means by a *t* test is to have large sample sizes. Large in this sense means samples of at least 30, and the phrase "more is better" definitely does apply. Normality assumptions are met with much more ease if samples are large. If large enough samples are not available because of time, money, or other constraints, then other nonparametric tests such as the Wilcoxon rank sum test may be used to investigate the data.

If for some reason it cannot be determined that the two underlying populations have equal variances a test for unequal variances—still a *t* test—can be used. The test is similar to the pooled-variance *t* test and carries the name *unpooled-variance t test*.

Finally, a standard level of significance is 0.05, or an alpha level of 5 percent. Managers may deviate from this level, depending on their intuition or experimental design, but 5 percent is considered the statistical standard. Any commercially available data analysis software package, Excel's Data Analysis package for example, will allow you to investigate changes to the underlying *t* test assumptions. The next section will present Novine's *t* test example using Excel's Data Analysis package.

USING EXCEL'S DATA ANALYSIS ADD-IN FOR TESTING TWO MEANS

This section will show how to complete a *t* test using Excel's Data Analysis add-in. A *t* test assuming equal variances will be used here, but Excel does offer *t* tests for paired samples and for data sets with unequal variances.

Steps for Using Excel's Data Analysis Add-In

The following steps should be followed if the raw data—not just summary statistics for the data—are available.

1. Load MS Excel and enter your raw data for the two samples (see Figure 3A.11).

FIGURE 3A.11
Excel Raw Data Spreadsheet for Novine's *t* Test Problem

	A	B
1	**Foodway**	**Safeland**
2	$57.92	$77.89
3	$63.79	$83.99
4	$69.20	$52.61
5	$39.32	$30.82
6	$59.73	$103.28
7	$71.83	$39.92
8	$53.30	$70.16
9	$53.11	$29.42
10	$80.31	$65.79
11	$26.08	$60.76
12	$52.52	$87.84
13	$50.35	$79.80
14	$76.22	$70.61
15	$38.57	$77.34
16	$45.90	$57.99
17	$60.17	$87.03
18	$30.29	$49.54
19	$52.36	$72.29
20	$33.19	$49.97
21	$75.84	$50.83
22	$37.59	$49.35
23	$53.98	$33.23
24	$41.64	$77.47
25	$72.23	$104.97
26	$35.48	$89.18
27	$65.80	$35.04
28	$29.27	$86.96
29	$59.86	$85.66
30	$58.23	$57.58
31	$46.20	$31.38
32	$73.32	$44.62
33	$58.50	$51.13
34		$96.12
35		$55.80
36		$49.44
37		

FIGURE 3A.12
Tools Menu and Data Analysis Option

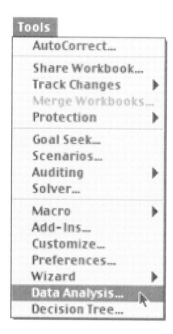

2. From the Tools menu choose Data Analysis (see Figure 3A.12). *Note:* If the Data Analysis option does not appear in the Tools menu, refer to the section at the end of Chapter 3 entitled "Installing Excel's Data Analysis Add-In."

3. In the Data Analysis menu scroll down until you locate the option t-Test: Two-Sample Assuming Equal Variances and click the OK button (see Figure 3A.13).

4. A dialog box appears prompting you to enter information concerning your data sets (see Figure 3A.14). *Note:* The t-Test dialog box in Figure 3A.14 already has information entered according to the steps detailed in step 5. When the t-Test dialog box opens initially, the edit and check boxes will be empty except for the Alpha level.

5. Follow this set of instructions for entering information in the t-Test dialog box:

- In the Variable 1 range edit box enter the range of the first data set.
- In the Variable 2 range edit box enter the range of the second data set.
- In the Hypothesized mean difference edit box either enter 0 or leave it blank.
- Select the Labels check box if you have included headers or labels in your data set.
- In the Alpha edit box enter the level of significance you have chosen (usually 5 percent).
- Select the New Worksheet Ply option and enter an appropriate name of your choice.

FIGURE 3A.13
t- **Test: Two-Sample Assuming Equal Variances Option**

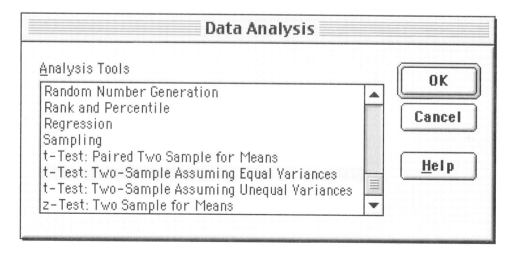

FIGURE 3A.14
t-Test Dialog Box

The resultant t-Test dialog box should now resemble Figure 3A.14. Click the OK button and Excel will generate an output worksheet that resembles Figure 3A.15.

Figure 3A.15 displays the descriptive statistics, t statistic, and t critical values for the data set. The two most important pieces of information are located in cell B10 (the *t* statistic) and cell B14 (the *t* critical two-tail value).

Other statistics of interest are in cells B4 and C4 (Foodway and Safeland mean values) and in cells B5 and C5 (Foodway and Safeland variance measurements). These additional statistics are important because they will assist us in further interpreting the test of two means.

Following the rule of thumb set down for testing of two means, we can see that

$$|t \text{ stat}| = 2.252 \text{ while } t \text{ critical two-tail} = 1.997$$

Therefore,

$$|t \text{ stat}| > t \text{ critical and the null hypothesis is rejected}$$

FIGURE 3A.15
Results for *t*-Test:
Two-Sample Assuming
Equal Variances

	A	B	C
1	t-Test: Two-Sample Assuming Equal Variances		
2			
3		Foodway	Safeland
4	Mean	53.815625	64.166
5	Variance	227.77778	467.48527
6	Observations	32	35
7	Pooled Variance	353.16323	
8	Hypothesized Mean Difference	0	
9	df	65	
10	t Stat	-2.251853	
11	P(T<=t) one-tail	0.0138585	
12	t Critical one-tail	1.6686363	
13	P(T<=t) two-tail	0.027717	
14	t Critical two-tail	1.9971367	

or

Mean grocery receipts at Foodway ≠ Mean grocery receipts at Safeland

Comparing a *t* statistic with a *t* critical value is one way to determine whether to reject or accept a null hypothesis. The next section will briefly discuss the interpretation of the *t* test via *p* values.

INTERPRETING *t* TEST RESULTS VIA *p* VALUES

The results in Figure 3A.15 can also be interpreted by using what is called the *p value*. Cell B13 contains the $p(t \leq t)$ two-tail value for the *t* test. Alternatively, the *p* value can be used to determine the reject/accept criteria. The *p* value in cell B13 is 0.027717. The *p* value must be compared to the level of significance chosen earlier. The rule of thumb is as follows:

If *p* value < level of significance, reject the null hypothesis

or

If *p* value > level of significance, accept the null hypothesis

In sum, the *p* value for Novine's *t* test is 0.027717, which is less than the level of significance, 0.05. Therefore we reject the null hypothesis that average receipts from Foodway and Safeland are equal. Note that this is the same conclusion gleaned from the *t* statistic and *t* critical analysis.

REPORTING PROBABILITY AND STATISTICS RESULTS

The reporting of probabilistic and statistical results presents a unique task to the manager. Reports that are based on probabilistic and/or statistical information are difficult to produce in a concise and effective form. Here, a report based on probability and statistics is developed from on the medical testing example in the Business Decision Modeling in Action section in Chapter 3.

Medical Testing, False Positives, and Communication of the Results

Dr. Zack Wassmuth had an interesting dilemma on his hands. He was in charge of sending out an informational memo to his resident medical students about strep throat testing. Two tests are available to a doctor when a patient complains of the symptoms of strep throat.

Dr. Wassmuth knew that one test was highly effective but took longer and cost more. However, he also knew that the quicker, cheaper test had some problems. Namely, the quicker, cheaper test gave many false readings.

He needed to inform his medical students of this problem but also give them the statistical information so they could develop their own judgment and critical reasoning on the issue of strep testing. Here is the memo Dr. Wassmuth developed.

Interoffice Memo Regarding Strep Testing

TO: All Medical Students under Dr. Wassmuth
FROM: Dr. Zack Wassmuth

This memo contains information about the streptococcus bacterium testing. Two areas of concern are raised here. The first is the relation of false readings in the rapid antigen streptococcus test to overall streptococcus diagnoses. The second is the development of judgment with regard to using the rapid antigen test and/or using the standard throat culture test.

Rapid Antigen Test Statistical Information

The rapid antigen test, while being much quicker and cheaper than the throat culture test, carries with it the risk of yielding false negative and false positive results. On average, the rapid antigen test produces a false negative result 30 percent of the time and a false positive result 15 percent of the time. In addition, of all the rapid antigen tests performed, 50 percent come back positive and 50 percent come back negative. Figure 1.1 displays a probability tree that diagrams the events and the event probabilities for the rapid antigen test.

FIGURE 1.1
Probability tree diagram
for rapid antigen testing.

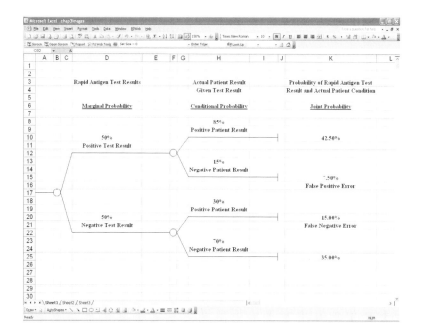

Take note in Figure 1.1 that there is an average overall error rate of 22.5 percent false positive errors plus false false negative errors (7.5% + 15% = 22.5%) when the rapid antigen strep test is used.

Probability of Positive Test Given Patient Is Positive for Streptococcus

In forming your judgment in using this test, a good question to investigate is the following: Given that a patient is positive for the streptococcus bacterium, what is the probability that the rapid antigen test will give the proper result, i.e., a positive test result. This is referred to as the posterior probability that the test will return a positive result, given that a patient is really positive with the streptococcus bacterium. The posterior probability is calculated as follows.

$$p(\text{test}+ \mid \text{patient}+) = \frac{p(\text{patient}+ \text{ and test}+)}{p(\text{patient}+)}$$

$$= \frac{42.5\%}{57.5\%} \approx 74\%$$

The numerator, 42.5%, is the percentage of patients that are positive and test positive, whereas the denominator, 57.5%, is the percentage of patients that are positive and test positive, (42.5%) plus the percentage of patients that are negative and test positive (7.5%). This result should be interpreted to mean that around 74 percent of the time when a patient is actually positive with the strep bacterium that the test will give the correct result.

Keep in mind when using the rapid antigen strep test that although quicker and less costly than the throat culture test, the rapid antigen tests fails to give an accurate result around 22.5 percent of the time. Other posterior probabilities, such as the probability that the test will return a negative result, given that a patient is really negative with the streptococcus bacterium, can also be calculated by using Figure 1.1. These calculations are left to your discretion.

**Optimal
Information Area**

Grateful Med Web site at http://igm.nlm.nih.gov.

International Society for Bayesian Analysis at http://www.bayesian.org.

Medical Matrix Web site at http://www.medmatrix.org/info/medlinetable.asp.

National Center for Biotechnology Information Web site at http://www.ncbi.nlm.nih.gov/PubMed.

St. Andrew's Mathematicians History Web site at http://www-history.mcs.st-andrews.ac.uk/history/Mathematicians/Bayes.html.

References

David, F. N. *Games, Gods, and Gambling*. New York: Hafner, 1962.

Gastwirth, J. L., *Statistical Reasoning in Law and Policy*, Vols. 1 and 2. San Diego: Academic Press, 1988.

Gonick, L., and W. Smith. *A Cartoon Guide to Statistics*. New York: HarperPerennial, 1993.

Huff, D. *How to Lie with Statistics*. New York: W. W. Norton, 1954.

Hunt, Dereck, et al. "User's Guides to the Medical Literature." *JAMA*, vol. 283, no. 14, April 12, 2000.

Jaffe, A. J., and Herbert F. Spirer. *Misused Statistics: Straight Talk for Twisted Numbers*. New York: Marcel Dekker, 1987.

Kruskal, W. "The Significance of Fisher: A Review of R. A. Fisher: The Life of a Scientist." *Journal of the American Statistical Association*, vol. 75, p. 1030.

McGervey, J. D. *Probabilities in Every Day Life*. New York: Ivy, 1989.

Peitetti, R. D., et al. "Evaluation of a New Rapid Antigen Detection Kit for Group A Beta-Hemolytic Streptococci." *Pediatric Emergency Care*, vol. 14, no. 6, December 1998, pp. 396–98.

Stigler, S. M. *The History of Statistical Measurement of Uncertainty Before 1900*. Cambridge, MA: Harvard-Belknap, 1986.

Problems

1. Nate has found out that 10 percent of the macaroni and cheese mix he buys from Loyal's Market is rancid, that 5 percent of the macaroni and cheese mix he buys from Mac's Food Mart is rancid, and that 10 percent of the macaroni and cheese mix he buys from Non-Frills is rancid. Nate buys macaroni and cheese from the three stores in the following proportions, 50 percent from Loyal's Market, 25 percent from Mac's Food Mart, and 25 percent from Non-Frills.

   a. Construct a probability tree for this problem.
   b. Construct a probability table for this problem.
   c. Find the probability that a box of macaroni and cheese Nate buys is rancid.
   d. Nate's friend Rob tells Nate that if he finds a box of rancid macaroni and cheese at Nate's house that it probably came from Loyal's Market and not from the other two stores. Is Rob correct?

2. Chris Kelling is a scratch golfer who lives on the island of Oahu. The weather on Oahu is usually sunny; however, it does rain sometimes. The probability that it is going to rain is 4 percent. Chris golfs 90 percent of the time. However, the probability of Chris golfing and it raining is 2 percent.

   a. Construct a probability table for this problem.
   b. Construct a probability tree for this problem.
   c. Given that Chris is golfing, what is the probability that it is not raining?

3. Standing at the Slots O' Fun craps table, Kathy wonders what the probability of someone rolling a certain combination of numbers is in one roll.

   a. Create a probability tree for rolling the dice.
   b. What is the probability two 1s, or "snake eyes"?
   c. What is the probability of rolling a combination of the dice totaling 2, 3, or 12?

4. Dana University has a diverse college football team. The team has many players from the Pacific Islands. Of all the players, 50 percent of the players are from mainland high schools, 20 percent of the players are from the Hawaiian Islands, 10 percent are from Tonga, 10 percent are from Samoa, 5 percent are from Fiji, and 5 percent are from Guam. Ninety percent of the players from the Pacific

Islands as a whole are offensive or defensive linemen while only 20 percent of the mainland players are offensive or defensive linemen. Specifically, 90 percent of the Hawaiians, Samoans, Tongans, Fijians, and Guamanians are offensive or defensive linemen.

   a. Construct a probability tree for this problem.
   b. Construct a probability table for this problem.
   c. What is the makeup of the team, linemen versus nonlinemen?
   d. If Clem walks into the cafeteria given that he sees an offensive or defensive lineman what is the probability that lineman will be from the Samoa?

5. Ray Henry was going to a tryout to join the Professional Bowlers Association tour. He gets one chance to qualify by bowling a single game. If he scores higher than 215, he can join the tour. John determined that his bowling average is 205 with a standard deviation of 25. His scores approximate a normal distribution curve. What are Ray's chances of qualifying for the PBA tour?

6. On January 1, the owner of Elmo's Toy Store renewed the annual lease for his store space. When the monthly sales amount from his toy store is more than $1000, Elmo has to pay 10 percent of the total sales price to his landlord in addition to the regular monthly rent of $200. During 1999, the mean of the monthly sales amount was $898 with a standard deviation of $108. In order to prepare the budget in 2000, the owner has to determine the probability that he has to pay the extra rent.

7. The average weight of a medium sized pizza at Pizza Runt is about 80 ounces. Pizza Runt knows that the standard deviation (SD) is 5 ounces.

   a. What percentage x of pizzas weigh less than 70 ounces.
   b. Recently, the company had several complaints from customers claiming that the pizzas were too sparse. Is this complaint justified?
   c. What percentage of pizzas weigh between 75 ounces and 82 ounces?.

Chapter Four

Decision Analysis: Building the Structure for Solving the Problem

Learning Objectives

After completing this chapter, students will be able to:

1. Understand the components of decision analysis.
2. Understand the types of decision environments managers face.
3. Understand how probability assessments impact the decision making process.
4. Conduct sensitivity analysis within the decision making process.
5. Develop decision trees to aid in the decision making process.
6. Use Excel to solve decision problems.

Chapter Outline

Business Decision Modeling in Action: How Legal Decision Makers Use Decision Models

Containing Litigation Costs: The Use of Decision Models in Litigation

An increasing number of companies and their lawyers have turned to decision structures such as decision trees and influence diagrams to help them make better decisions in litigation management and settlement. The results have been lower transaction costs and better outcomes.

Litigators first identify the factual and legal uncertainties in a case—the "issues"—and then proceed, through fact discovery, legal research, and the use of experts, to cope with these uncertainties. Driving this costly process is the assumption that it will culminate in a trial, at which time a judge and jury will resolve the legal and factual issues.

The reality, though, is that more than 90 percent of all cases end up being resolved through settlement rather than trial.

Decision trees and influence diagrams can be enormously helpful in allocating resources before trial. They can effectively demonstrate the cost-effectiveness of foregoing the additional research or discovery, thereby saving the client time and money. Decision trees and influence diagrams make it possible to perform the analyses needed to maximize opportunities for early settlement and reduced transaction costs while fully addressing the need to be prepared for trial.

Decision Tree for Litigation Example

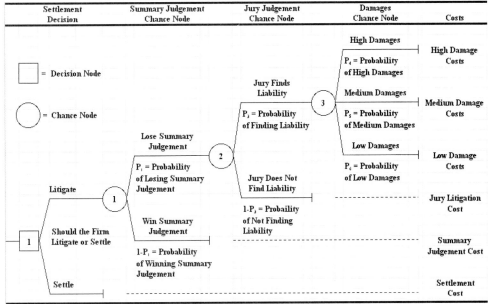

Optimal Information Area

Treeage Software Web site at
http://www.treeage.com/resources/caseStudies.html.

DECISION ANALYSIS: BUILDING THE STRUCTURE FOR SOLVING THE PROBLEM

In Chapter 2, the importance of describing data sets in terms of central tendency and measures of dispersion was discussed. Simple statistics, like mean, median, range, and standard deviation, were defined and described. Chapter 3 developed probability theory and the rules of probability along with the addition and multiplication formulas.

Importance and Relevance of Decision Analysis and Theory

Managers must link simple statistics with a mental and graphical picture of data sets.

The importance of managers' painting the full picture of data sets by using both measures of central tendency and measures of dispersion was developed. Managers do this by linking simple statistics with a mental and graphical picture of real-life data sets. This chapter will build up from the foundation that probability and statistics set down in the preceding chapters.

Linking Probability and Statistics to Decision Making

Linking probability and statistics to decision making is a goal of this chapter. Chapter 3 taught us to use the language of probability properly. A main rhetorical question was asked regarding how individuals assess probabilities as decision makers. Managers must think about how assessing probabilities will help them in becoming more effective and efficient problem solvers. Most managers do not consciously go around assessing probabilities; they just make decisions. One may ask: Where is the link between decision making and probability assessment?

A strong foundation must be formed, as we are building a decision-making and problem-solving edifice. That foundation consists of

1. Speaking in terms of central tendency and dispersion
2. Asking ourselves how we assess probabilities

Good decision makers create a link from the world of probability to the world of decision making.

3. Remembering the laws and rules of probability (addition and multiplication laws, three rules of probability) and discrete continuous probability distributions

A manager starts with this foundation and works toward the next step in the decision-making process: framing the decision problem.

Framing the Decision Problem

A manager must think about building up an edifice and putting a structure, literally a framework, around decision-making problems. Students must ask themselves an important question, "How do I make decisions and what is the process I go through?" Managers make decisions all the time, and this text is not here to tell a student of business decision modeling exactly how or what is the best way to make decisions. It would be folly to attempt to do this in one class or text.

Concept Check Critical Reasoning and Judgment Question

Take a moment and ask yourself the following question about decision making: "How do I make decisions and what is the process I go through as I choose one alternative over another?"

Managers must develop their own decision-making process or rational methodology for solving problems. All of us understand that individuals make decisions all the time: we chose to come to class, read the text, when and where to eat lunch, when to wake up, when to go to bed.

The techniques individuals use to make these decisions obviously play an important role in everyday life. Decisions made regarding situations in business and government, or choice of college and career, for example, may also deal with a tremendous amount of uncertainty.

COMPONENTS OF A DECISION-MAKING PROBLEM

A number of structures will be presented throughout the next few chapters. The next sections will discuss one basic structure to build from. Bear in mind that it is simplistic and is just one way to structure a decision-making problem.

Decision problems have three components: states, decisions, and outcomes.

Decision analysis problems generally have three distinct components:

1. States of nature
2. Decisions alternatives
3. Outcomes

States of Nature

States of nature can be defined as events that may occur in the future. As managers, we rarely have control over the states associated with a decision-making problem. In fact, the decision maker is generally uncertain which state of nature will occur.

A good example of uncertain states of nature is the weather report. The information provided by the weather forecaster may give us some insight into tomorrow's weather, but the chance of rain or no rain is uncertain. In turn, as business decision makers, we have no control over the possibility of rain and therefore must plan accordingly if that weather will adversely affect our day-to-day operations (running an amusement parks, farming, etc.).

However, as decision makers we do have control over one item. The ultimate decision that is made is the purview of the decision maker. For the rain/no rain example, the decision may be to carry an umbrella or not to carry an umbrella.

Decision Alternatives

Decision makers have ultimate control over which decision alternative they choose.

Decision alternatives are the second component in a decision analysis problem. At times decisions are also referred to as *alternatives*. As stated earlier, the decision maker has ultimate control over the decision made or the alternative chosen.

For example, the decisions a business decision maker could make regarding an outdoor promotional event could be as follows: rent and set up a tent or do not rent and set up a tent.

Renting and setting up the tent or not renting and setting up the tent incurs certain consequences. Take for example this scenario: the weather forecaster believes it will rain tomorrow; we concur and so we decide to rent and set up the tent. Remember, weather forecasters just provided advice; they are not clairvoyant. This leads directly into the definition and discussion of outcomes.

Outcomes

Outcomes are the resultant combination of a state of nature and a decision alternative.

The third component of a decision analysis problem is outcomes. An outcome is defined as the combination of a state and a decision. For our rain example, we chose to rent and set up the tent and it did happen to rain; therefore, the outcome is that the umbrella came in handy and we stayed dry. However, there exist four possible outcomes for the rain example. Table 4.1 lists the possible outcomes.

Outcomes versus Payoffs

Outcomes are generally referred to as payoffs and are given in monetary units.

It should be noted that outcomes are also referred to as *payoffs*. Pure decision analysts and economists generally refer to the combination of states and decisions as an outcome. However, managers tend to use the term payoffs.

Payoffs are typically expressed in monetary terms such as profits, revenues, or costs. The outcomes from the rain example could be turned into payoffs by equating getting wet with the cost of dry cleaning your clothes after the fact.

The term payoff is used because it directly links the combination of states and decisions to a monetary result. The authors will use the term payoff from this point on in the text.

Concept *Check Critical Reasoning and Judgment Question*

Every decision problem has states, decisions, and outcomes/payoffs. Think about a recent decision you made and try to identify the states, decisions, and outcomes/payoffs associated with the problem. Were the states easy to describe? Were the outcomes/payoffs easily quantified?

Payoff Tables

The layout of Table 4.1 allows the decision maker to see all the possible outcomes but does not organize the three components of a decision-making problem very well.

Traditional decision analysis uses what is called a *payoff table* to organize states, decision alternatives, and outcomes. Table 4.2 displays the payoff table for the rain example.

Payoff tables are a means to organize states, decisions, and payoffs.

The payoffs listed in Table 4.2 are situations rather than monetary amounts associated with the combination of a state and a decision alternative. However, one could quickly assign monetary amounts to the situations listed above.

At times these monetary amounts may be negative, or considered costs. For example, costs of not carrying the umbrella if it does not rain could be zero, while one cost of carrying the umbrella if it does rain could be the cost of the umbrella itself.

As students of business decision modeling you may be inclined to ask the question "What is the probability of it raining?" This is a good question to ask because the resulting answer to the question may help the decision maker choose a better course of action or save time and money.

TABLE 4.1
Possible Outcomes for Rain Example

Decision Alternative	State	Outcome
Rent and set up tent	Rain	Stay dry and promotional items are not adversely affected
Rent and set up tent	No rain	Incurred cost of renting and setting up tent for nothing
Do not rent and set up tent	Rain	Get wet and promotional items are spoiled
Do not rent and set up tent	No rain	No worries—dry at no additional costs

TABLE 4.2
Payoff Table for Rain Example

	States of nature	
Decision alternatives	**Rain**	**No rain**
Rent and set up tent	Stay dry and promotional items are not adversely affected	Incurred cost of renting and setting up tent for nothing
Do not rent and set up tent	Get wet and promotional items are spoiled	No worries—dry at no additional costs

Business Decision Modeling Throughout the Ages

A Brief History of Decision Making

HISTORY OF DECISION MAKING

Decision making has a long and storied history. Take a look at the progression and remember the way we make decisions today may come from decisions made in the past.

SOOTHSAYERS, ASTROLOGERS, AND FORTUNE TELLERS

- Alexander the Great consulted oracles and fortune tellers.
- The Oracle at Delphi is famous for assisting in decision making and became hugely popular.

THE ROMANS, THE BABYLONIANS, THE CHINESE AND THE USE OF HARD DATA?

- Romans also had oracles but relied heavily on "hard" data - Haruspicists examined animal entrails to predict the future (we might say they used their gut feelings).
- The Babylonians used the Talmud to deal with decisions on division of wealth–indirectly this document led to the understanding of cooperative games.
- The Chinese developed I Ching around 3000 BC – People asked I Ching for the prognosis of a given decision, an answer detailing potential risks and opportunities resulted.

THE 1700S AND 1800S

- Ben Franklin is credited with the "balance sheet" approach to decision-making.

- Playfair, in 1786, used the perspective ratios of height and width of graphs to depict skyrocketing British government debt.
- Car Gauss studies the "bell curve" and develops a structure for understanding the occurences of random events.

INFINITY AND BEYOND

- Around 1907 economist Irving Fisher introduces net present value as a decision making tool, proposing that expected cash flow be discounted at a rate that reflects an investment's risk.
- The 1960s and 1970s brought database systems & the cliche of "let's crunch the numbers."
- The 1990s introduced faster desktop and laptop computers and new software algorithms and we began to see decision analysis tools available for their personal use.

And what does the new century bring? I'll let you decide ....

OPTIMAL INFORMATION AREA

Peter L. Bernstein, *"Against the Gods: The Remarkable Story of Risk."* New York: John Wiley & Sons, 1996.

Leigh Buchanan and Andrew O'Connell (2006) *"A Brief History of Decision Making"* Harvard Business Review, 84(1), pp. 32–41.

http://www.arlingsoft.com/wp./History_Decision_Making.pdf

Concept *Check*
Critical Reasoning and Judgment Question

Managers make numerous decisions each day. However, not all those decisions are made by using probability assessments. Are there decisions you make each day without the use of probability assessments? How about where you are going for lunch?

However, the probability of a state occurring is not always readily available and decision makers may have a difficult time assigning probabilities to events. Decision making without probability assessments will be discussed next.

DECISION-MAKING CRITERIA WITHOUT PROBABILITY ASSESSMENTS

Decision making without probabilities is generally referred to as nonprobabilistic.

Decision making that does not involve uncertainty is fairly simple. Without uncertainty, we tend to have limited choices or just one choice and simple outcomes. Many of life's basic choices are this simple, or the process used in making the choice is fundamentally an unconscious one, involuntary, or a learned response.

Decision makers use decision-making criteria when determining which alternatives to choose. When information regarding the probability of a state is limited or not available, decision makers use what are referred to as *nonprobabilistic criteria*. The following sections will detail three of these criteria: the maximax, the maximin, and the minimax regret.

Spreadsheet Solution for Payoff Table Decision Problem

This section details the use of Excel spreadsheets to illustrate three nonprobabilistic criteria—a maximax, maximin, and minimax regret—and also demonstrates the Hurwicz decision criteria. A step-by-step creation of a graph to illustrate the three areas of sensitivity is developed.

TABLE 4.3
Steve's Mutual Fund
Payoff Table

Mutual Fund	States of Nature	
	Good economic conditions	Bad economic conditions
Stock fund, aggressive growth	20%	−8%
Index fund, moderate S&P 500	12%	2%
Bond fund, conservative U.S. Treasury	6%	4%
Probability of states of nature	40%	60%

FIGURE 4.1
Excel Spreadsheet for
Steve's Mutual Fund
Payoff Table

	A	B	C
1	**Steve's Mutual Fund Decision**		
2	**Payoff Table**		
3		**State of Nature**	
4		**Good**	**Bad**
5	**Mutual Fund**	**Economic Condition**	**Economic Condition**
6	**Stock Fund**	20%	-8%
7	**Aggressive Growth**		
8			
9	**Index Fund**	12%	2%
10	**Moderate S&P 500**		
11			
12	**Bond Fund**	6%	4%
13	**Conservative U.S. Treasury**		
14			

Steve's Mutual Fund Decision Problem

Steve has a decision to make. He wishes to invest in one of the three mutual funds offered in the market. Table 4.3 displays the three decisions, the states of nature, the associated payoffs, and the probability of each state of nature to occur.

The payoffs are yearly percentage returns. Take the information in Table 4.3 and input it into an Excel spreadsheet to obtain the results displayed in Figure 4.1.

Concept *Check*
Critical Reasoning
and Judgment
Question

The maximax decision criterion chooses the best of the best payoffs.

Take a moment and think to yourself, "Do I know people who make decisions regularly, using the maximax criterion?" Maybe you are the type of decision maker who uses the maximax criterion to make decisions. Can you think of professions that use this type of criterion? How about gamblers? High-risk derivatives or commodities traders?

Maximax Criterion

The maximax criterion is defined as the criterion where a decision maker selects the decision that will result in the maximum of the maximum payoffs. A decision maker who chooses to use this criterion is looking for the best of the best. It could be said that a decision maker using maximax is optimistic (believes the best will always occur). It could also be said that the decision maker using maximax is willing to accept more risk.

A spreadsheet solution using the maximax decision criterion is shown in Figure 4.2. The payoff table with appropriate headings is placed in cells A4 through cell C13. The Excel formulas that provide the calculations and an optimal solution recommendation are:

Cell D6 Compute the maximum payoff

$$= \text{MAX(B6 : C6)}$$

(Repeat formula for cells D9 and D12)

Cell E6 Determine which decision alternative is recommended

$$= \text{IF(D6} = \text{MAX(\$D\$6, \$D\$9, \$D\$12), A6, "")}$$

(Repeat formula for cells E9 and E12)

If the maximum payoff in cell D6 is equal to the best payoff in cells D6, the fund's name will be displayed in E6; otherwise, this cell will be left blank. As Figure 4.2 shows, the maximax criterion recommends the aggressive growth stock fund decision alternative with a best payoff of 20 percent.

Maximin Criterion

The maximin decision criterion chooses the best of the worst payoffs.

The maximin criterion is defined as the criterion where a decision maker selects the decision that will result in the maximum of the minimum payoffs. In other words, the decision maker is looking for the best of the worst. It could be said that a decision maker using maximin is pessimistic (believes the worst will always occur). A maximin decision maker could also be categorized as risk averse or not willing to accept more risk.

A spreadsheet solution using the maximin decision criterion is shown in Figure 4.3. The payoff table with appropriate headings is placed in cells A4 through C13. The Excel formulas that provide the calculations and optimal solution recommendation are:

FIGURE 4.2   **Excel Spreadsheet for Maximax Decision Criterion**

	A	B	C	D	E
1	**Steve's Mutual Fund Decision**				
2	**Maximax Decision Criterion**				
3		State of Nature			
4		Good	Bad	Maximum	Recommended
5	Mutual Fund	Economic Condition	Economic Condition	Payoff	Decision
6	Stock Fund	20%	-8%	20%	Stock Fund
7	Aggressive Growth				
8					
9	Index Fund	12%	2%	12%	
10	Moderate S&P 500				
11					
12	Bond Fund	6%	4%	6%	
13	Conservative U.S. Treasury				
14					

FIGURE 4.3   **Excel Spreadsheet for Maximin Decision Criterion**

	A	B	C	D	E
1	**Steve's Mutual Fund Decision**				
2	**Maximin Decision Criterion**				
3		State of Nature			
4		Good	Bad	Minimum	Recommended
5	Mutual Fund	Economic Condition	Economic Condition	Payoff	Decision
6	Stock Fund	20%	-8%	-8%	
7	Aggressive Growth				
8					
9	Index Fund	12%	2%	2%	
10	Moderate S&P 500				
11					
12	Bond Fund	6%	4%	4%	Bond Fund
13	Conservative U.S. Treasury				
14					

Cell D6 Compute the minimum payoff

$$= MIN(B6 : C6)$$

(Repeat formula for cells D9 and D12)

Cell E6 Determine which decision alternative is recommended

$$= IF(D6 = MAX(\$D\$6, \$D\$9, \$D\$12), A6, "")$$

(Repeat formula for cells E9 and E12)

The only difference between the spreadsheets in Figures 4.2 and 4.3 is that the maximin criterion finds the minimum payoff in each decision alternative.

Notice the formulas in E6, E9, and E12 remain the same. This is because Steve is still looking for the maximum result in column D. With the appropriate changes, the spreadsheet in Figure 4.3 shows that the maximin criterion recommends the Conservative U.S. Treasury Bond Fund decision alternative with the best payoff value of 4 percent.

Concept *Check*
Critical Reasoning
and Judgment
Question

Take a moment and think to yourself, "Do I know people who make decisions regularly, using the maximin criterion?" Maybe you are the type of decision maker who uses the maximin criterion to make decisions. Can you think of a group of people who use this type of criterion? How about those individuals who lived through the Great Depression in the United States?

Minimax Regret

The minimax regret criterion chooses the decision that results in the minimum regret.

The minimax regret criterion is defined as the criterion where a decision maker selects the decision that will result in the minimum regret. Before this criterion is detailed, the measure of regret must be defined.

Management Science Definition of Regret

Management science defines regret as the difference between the best decision and all other decisions for a particular state.

Management scientists define regret as the difference between the payoff from the best decision and all the other decision payoffs. Students of business decision modeling must keep in mind that management science is not the only discipline to define regret. Economics and marketing both have similar concepts of regret.

Economics Definition of Regret—Opportunity Cost

Economists refer to opportunity costs when speaking about regret.

Economists use the words *opportunity cost* to define or refer to regret. Opportunity cost is the value of the next best alternative, or opportunity, that was given up by choosing the best alternative. For example, by choosing to spend your money on beer and pizzas you give up the opportunity to invest that money in a retirement account. Your opportunity cost is the choice you gave up.

Regret, as defined by management science, is akin to the concept of opportunity cost in economics. In management science, regret is the quantifiable amount a decision maker gives up to choose a different alternative.

Marketing Definition of Regret—Buyer's Remorse

Marketers refer to regret as buyer's remorse.

The concept of regret is manifested in consumers by what marketers call buyer's remorse. Marketers describe the feeling consumers experience when they purchase an item and then feel as if they could have gotten a better deal on another item. At times this is also referred to as *postdecision doubt*.

Buyer's remorse can also manifest itself in consumers when they make a decision and then regret making that decision after the fact. Buyer's remorse occurs with some frequency in buying a home. Some homebuyers have a sense of letdown after deciding to purchase a home.

Real estate brokers attribute this feeling to the fact that a home is a very large purchase, not in terms of just dollars, but in the sense of status, ego, and commitment. A homebuyer, after making the final decision, may look around and feel a sense of regret, believing that better deals existed and were missed.

FIGURE 4.4
Excel Spreadsheet for Minimax Decision Criterion

Steve's Mutual Fund Decision
Minimax Regret Decision Criterion

	State of Nature	
	Good	Bad
Mutual Fund	Economic Condition	Economic Condition
Stock Fund Aggressive Growth	20%	-8%
Index Fund Moderate S&P 500	12%	2%
Bond Fund Conservative U.S. Treasury	6%	4%

Regret Table

	State of Nature			
	Good	Bad	Maximum	Recommended
Mutual Fund	Economic Condition	Economic Condition	Regret	Decision
Stock Fund Aggressive Growth	0%	12%	12%	
Index Fund Moderate S&P 500	8%	2%	8%	Index Fund
Bond Fund Conservative U.S. Treasury	14%	0%	14%	

Psychological Definition of Regret—Cognitive Dissonance

Psychologists refer to regret as cognitive dissonance.

According to cognitive dissonance theory, there is a tendency for individuals to seek consistency among their beliefs and choices. Cognitive dissonance theory applies to all situations involving attitude formation and change. It is especially relevant to managers in the decision-making and problem solving process.

Consider someone who is going to purchase an expensive car but discovers that it is not comfortable on long drives. The driver believes that an expensive car should be comfortable. Cognitive dissonance exists, since the belief that an expensive car should be a comfortable car on long drives is violated.

In general, decision makers will alter their beliefs instead of removing the conflicting attitude or behavior. The buyers of the expensive but uncomfortable car may convince themselves that the car will be used only for short trips, thereby eliminating the conflict in beliefs.

The term cognitive dissonance has also been adopted by the marketing discipline. Many advertising campaigns attempt to eliminate cognitive dissonance or buyer's remorse by focusing on product strengths or developing new nonconflicting attitudes toward the product.

Concept Check *Critical Reasoning and Judgment Question*

As a decision maker have you ever felt regret? Have you ever thought about the opportunity costs of choosing one item over another? As a consumer have you ever felt buyer's remorse? Should decision makers rely on minimizing regret as the criterion to make decisions or solve problems? Do you make choices based on minimizing regret, opportunity costs, or buyer's remorse?

Minimax Regret Criterion Process

A decision maker who chooses to use this criterion is looking to minimize the measure of regret. Regret has been defined as the difference between the payoff from the best decision and all the other decision payoffs. Therefore, the first step in the minimax regret criterion is to determine regret.

A spreadsheet solution using the minimax regret decision criterion is shown in Figure 4.4. The payoff table with appropriate headings is placed in cells A4 through C13. The Excel formulas that provide the calculations and optimal solution recommendation are:.

Cell B19 Compute the amount of regret
= MAX($B$6, $B$9, $B$12) – B6
(Repeat formula for cell B22 and B25)

Cell C19 Compute the amount of regret

$$= MAX(\$C\$6, \$C\$9, \$C\$12) - C6$$

(Repeat formula for cell C22 and C25)

Cell D19 Compute the maximum regret

$$= MAX(B19 : C19)$$

(Repeat formula for cell D22 and D25)

Cell E19 Determine which decision alternative is recommended

$$= IF(D19 = MIN(\$D\$19, \$D\$22, \$D\$25), A19, "\ ")$$

In Figure 4.4, Steve first calculates the amount of regret under each economic condition by subtracting each return figure from the largest figure in the appropriate economic condition. Steve then finds the maximum regret for each fund in column D. Continuing, Steve then finds the minimum regret in the Maximum Regret column, and thus accomplished the minimax regret decision. We can see from Figure 4.4 that the moderate S&P 500 index fund offers the least amount of regret.

Regret As a Measure of Risk

Measures of dispersion were linked to measures of risk earlier in Chapter 2. Regret can also be used as a means to define and quantify risk. The definition of regret has been established in the minimax regret example. Regret is usually presented in terms of units.

It is important to remember that regret is not something tangible. In the previous crop-planting example, the farmer did not lose $11 by choosing oats. He will experience the least amount of regret by choosing oats. As was detailed in the sections preceding the minimax regret example, regret can be thought of as an opportunity cost, or a feeling of buyer's remorse, or a psychological feeling of cognitive dissonance.

Regret is used as a measure of risk to give decision makers a sense of what the other alternatives have to offer. Sometimes regret is called upside or downside risk. The concept of upside and downside risk will be detailed in the section "Sensitivity Analysis," below.

Equal Likelihood Criterion—LaPlace and Simple Weighted Averages

The equal likelihood criterion is akin to an expected value when all states are weighted equally, i.e., are a simple mean.

The concept of expected values was introduced in Chapter 3. Expected values are commonly referred to as *weighted averages*. In other words, each event has a weight or a probability assessment associated with it. The equal likelihood criterion also weights each state of nature. As the name implies, all events are weighted equally.

Concept *Check Critical Reasoning and Judgment Question*

Have you ever used a weighted average before? More than likely you have. At times information on the likelihood of states is not available or time is limited to assess state probabilities, so in many cases a simple weighted average, or simple mean, is used. When managers use a simple mean, they are assigning equal probabilities to all states. When do you use a simple mean to calculate central tendency?

The equal likelihood criterion is also referred to as the LaPlace criterion, named for the mathematician Pierre Simon LaPlace. By assigning equal weights to the events in the event space, the decision maker is assuming that the states of nature are also equally likely to occur. This approach is akin to summing the payoffs for each decision and dividing by the number of payoffs summed. In other words, taking a simple mean or an expected value where all the $p(x)$'s are equal. For Steve's mutual fund example, we find the equal likelihood payoffs to be 6 percent for aggressive stock, 7 percent for the index fund, and 5 percent for the bond fund, therefore the index fund is chosen.

FIGURE 4.5
Excel Spreadsheet for the Hurwicz Decision Criterion

	A	B	C	D	E
1	Steve's Mutual Fund Decision				
2	Hurwicz Decision Criterion: Alpha = .40				
3		State of Nature			
4		Good	Bad		Recommended
5	Mutual Fund	Economic Condition	Economic Condition	Payoff	Decision
6	Stock Fund	20%	-8%	3.2%	
7	Aggressive Growth				
8					
9	Index Fund	12%	2%	6.0%	Index Fund
10	Moderate S&P 500				
11					
12	Bond Fund	6%	4%	4.8%	
13	Conservative U.S. Treasury				
14	*Probability of States*	*40%*	*60%*		
15					

Hurwicz Criterion

The Hurwicz criterion weights the best and worst payoffs according to the decision maker's optimism about that state occurring.

The Hurwicz criterion is said to be a compromise of the maximax and maximin criterion. The three criteria combined complete the entire spectrum of expected outcomes. The maximax criterion relays the best of the best outcomes, the maximin criterion details the best of the worst outcomes, while the Hurwicz criterion covers every outcome in between.

The Hurwicz criterion uses a coefficient of optimism to weight the best and worst payoff for each decision. This coefficient of optimism is referred to as *alpha* in standard decision analysis nomenclature. The idea of payoffs is not a new one. Chapter 3 introduced the concept of expected value.

The Hurwicz criterion is the same concept as expected value but referred to by a different name. The general equation for expected value is a weighted average or the sum of a set of unique probabilities (or weights) multiplied by the corresponding payoffs. The equal likelihood criterion is a specific case of the expected value where all the alphas, or weights, are equal.

The payoff table with appropriate headings is placed in cells A3 through C14. The Excel formulas that provide the calculations and optimal solution recommendation are:

Cell D6 Compute the payoff

$$= B6*\$B\$14 + C6*\$C\$14$$

(Repeat formula for cells D9 and D12)

Cell E6 Determine which decision alternative is recommended

$$= IF(D6 = Max(\$D\$6, \$D\$9, \$D\$12), A6, \text{""})$$

(Repeat formula for cells E9 and E12)

Given alpha equal to 0.4, Figure 4.5 displays, for the mutual fund example, the Hurwicz criterion. For example, in the mutual fund scenario, alpha = 0.4 would be applied to the good economic conditions state. In this example, good economic conditions and bad economic conditions are mutually exclusive events and, consequently, according to the rules of probability, the coefficient or weight applied to the bad economic conditions state is 1−alpha, or 0.6. For situations with more than two states of nature, the same procedure is followed by using just the best and worst payoffs for each decision alternative.

In Figure 4.5, we first calculated the payoff by multiplying the return figures of each fund under both economic conditions against their appropriate probabilities of occurrence. Furthermore, if the maximum payoff in column D is equal to the best payoff of a fund, the fund's name will appear in column E indicating that fund is the optimal recommended decision. In using the Hurwicz decision criterion, we can see that the moderate S&P 500 index fund offers the optimal payoff of 6.0 percent.

Concept *Check*
Critical Reasoning and Judgment Question

As a decision maker, ask yourself "How do I assess probabilities of the occurrence of certain states?" Do you see the similarity when a manager guesses and applies the same probability to all states and uses the equal likelihood criterion? Can we apply the same principles of central tendency and dispersion to the Hurwicz criterion and decision-making processes?

TABLE 4.4
Summary of Final
Mutual Fund Example
Choices

Decision criterion	Maximax	Maximin	Minimax regret	Equal likelihood	Hurwicz alpha = 0.40
Fund to choose	Stock fund	Bond fund	Index fund	Index fund	Index fund

Summary of Decision Criteria Results

Table 4.4 displays the final mutual fund example decision choices for each decision criterion. It can be seen from Table 4.4 that no one mutual fund alternative dominates the decision criteria. Depending on the decision criteria, the stock, index, or bond fund could be the best choice.

Strict dominance cannot be established for the mutual fund example. Dominance is the first area a manager should analyze in the decision making process. The principle of dominance will be defined and discussed later in this chapter.

Concept *Check*
Critical Reasoning
and Judgment
Question

Faced with numerous optimal or "good" choices how does a manager make the right choice? Is there a process that a person uses when faced with multiple conflicting "good" choices? Are there a set of standard analyses that a manager can follow that will assist in the decision making process?

From on these results, it seems that a manager has a dilemma. Unless a manager can assess the probability of the states exactly (i.e., predict the future) or has a very optimistic or pessimistic risk profile, there will be multiple optimal crop choices. In fact, there seems to be some sort of interactions or trade-offs between the three choices.

DECISION-MAKING CRITERIA WITH PROBABILITY ASSESSMENTS

A more common occurrence in business decision modeling problems is decision making under uncertainty or decision making relying on probability assessments. Given Steve's payoff table with probability assessments for all states of nature, the expected value of his decision alternatives can be calculated. From Chapter 3, recall that the expected value calculation is

$$E(x) = \sum_{i=1}^{n} x_i p(x_i)$$

For Steve's mutual fund example problem, let's attach a probability of the good economic conditions happening as 0.6, and therefore the probability of the bad economic conditions happening would be 0.4. The expected value of each decision alternative is then calculated as follows:

$$E(\text{stock fund}) = 20\% \times 0.6 + (-8\%) \times 0.4 = 8.8\%$$

$$E(\text{index fund}) = 12\% \times 0.6 + 2\% \times 0.4 = 8.0\%$$

$$E(\text{bond fund}) = 6\% \times 0.6 + 4\% \times 0.4 = 5.2\%$$

Thus, according to the expected value criterion, Steve would chose the stock fund, since it garners the maximum expected value.

Expected Value of Perfect Information

Now let's suppose that Steve has a good friend who is a prominent economist and has given Steve some insight into the future state of the economy. Steve's economist friend claims that he can tell with certainty whether the future economic conditions will be good or bad. This information would change Steve's decision problem from one under uncertainty to one under certainty. This information would help Steve make a better choice and garner a better return.

However, Steve's friend wants a cut of the action. Specifically, he wants a couple of percentage points, 2 points, of return for his efforts. In other words, if Steve would garner an 8 percent return, 2 of those percentage points would go to Steve's friend, leaving Steve with a net 6 percent return. Is it worth it to Steve to pay this fee? Is 2 percentage points fair, or what do you think it might be worth to Steve? To answer these questions we need to calculate the expected value of perfect information (EVPI).

If Steve's friend were able to determine which state of nature would occur, then they would know exactly what alternative to choose to maximize returns. Since the payoffs under this perfect information will increase, this knowledge has value. Therefore, we need to determine the value of this information. The expected value of perfect information is defined as the difference between the payoff under certainty and the payoff under risk.

$$EVPI = \text{expected value under certainty} - \text{maximum expected value}$$

To find the EVPI we must compute the expected value under certainty. The expected value under certainty is the expected return if the decision maker has perfect information before each decision has to be made.

In calculating this value, the decision maker chooses the best alternative for each state of nature and multiplies its payoff by the probability of occurrence of that state of nature. For Steve's example, we will use 0.6 as the probability of good economic conditions (the same probabilities used to calculate expected value earlier), and expected value under certainty is then calculated as follows:

$$\text{Expected value under certainty} = 20\% \times 0.6 + 4\% \times 0.4 = 13.6\%$$

The 20 percent is the best payoff under the good economic conditions and the 4 percent is the best payoff under bad economic conditions. Therefore, the expected value of perfect information is, for the expected value under certainty and maximum expected value calculations,

$$EVPI = \text{expected value under certainty} - \text{maximum expected value}$$
$$= 13.6\% - 8.8\% = 4.8\%$$

In other words, the most Steve would be willing to pay for the perfect information is 4.8 percentage points.

If Steve's friend is asking for 2 percentage points then Steve would come out ahead by at least 2.8 percentage points. So it appears that taking his friend's advice is worth it. This conclusion is based on the assumption that the probability of good economic conditions occurring will be 0.6. If the probability assessment of good economic conditions changes, then the expected value of information will change.

Confusion over Multiple "Good" Choices

Sensitivity analysis assists managers when faced with multiple conflicting choices.

Obtaining multiple conflicting "good" choices is often confusing to students of business decision modeling as well as real-world managers. This confusion over choices is actually common when people are attempting to solve complex problems. Part of the confusion is linked to the belief that the decision analysis process will lead managers and/or students to one ultimate correct choice.

The decision analysis process should lead a decision maker to a set of "good" choices and subsequently produce a more robust picture of the entire problem. The tool to assist decision makers to produce a more robust picture is sensitivity analysis.

Three Areas of Sensitivity Analysis

The principles of dominance, trade-offs, and risks are commonly used in solving decision problems. If dominance cannot be established, multiple optimal choices arise. Multiple optimal choices lead to trade-offs between those choices and a need to analyze the risk involved with one choice compared to another. In sum, when faced with multiple optimal choices, managers must complete analysis with regard to three areas:

Sensitivity analysis is characterized by three areas: dominance, trade-offs, and risk.

* Dominance
* Trade-offs
* Risks

The principles of dominance, trade-off analysis, and risk analysis can be grouped together into a standard set of analyses. This standard set of analyses is referred to as *sensitivity analysis*. Sensitivity analysis and the three areas of analysis are detailed next.

SENSITIVITY ANALYSIS

Managers can sort out all possible scenarios and make a more effective and efficient decision by using sensitivity analysis.

The sensitivity analysis process assists managers faced with multiple conflicting "good" choices. Sensitivity analysis includes analysis in three areas: dominance, trade-offs, and risks. The three areas could be referred to as a three-step approach to building a more robust understanding of the decision-making problem. The three areas, or steps, are detailed next, followed by an application to the crop payoff table example.

Step 1: Establish a Dominant Decision

In general, dominance is established on the basis of maximizing expected value.

Given that a decision maker wishes to maximize expected value, an alternative that always returns the highest expected value would be considered the dominant choice. However, in many problems there is not one dominant decision. In other words, the decision that maximizes expected value, may change, depending on the decision maker's probability assessments of the states.

When strict dominance cannot be established, trade-offs among the alternatives will occur. Trade-off analysis is the second step of analyzing a decision problem.

Step 2: Examine the Trade-offs between Dominant Decisions

Trade-off analysis gives the decision maker a means to judge how much will be given up by choosing one alternative over another.

If strict dominance can not be established, trade-offs between the alternatives must exist. Trade-offs are akin to the break-even analysis detailed in Chapter 1. A trade-off is defined as the point where the expected value of two or more alternatives is equal. On the leading edge of this trade-off point, one alternative dominates, while on the lagging edge of the trade-off point another alternative dominates.

In break-even analysis, the trade-off is the point where costs are equal to revenues. On the leading edge of the break-even point, costs dominate revenues (i.e., revenues are not covering fixed costs, resulting in losses). In turn, on the lagging edge of the break-even point, revenues dominate costs (i.e., revenues cover fixed costs, resulting in profits).

Trade-off analysis gives the decision maker a means to judge how much will be given up by choosing one alternative over another.

Step 3: Define and Quantify the Risk

Risk can be defined and quantified by a number of criteria: range, regret, and/or standard deviation.

The author believes that, as managers assess probabilities of states occurring, they are actually assessing a measure of risk.

Risk must be defined and then quantified for each decision-making problem. Risk can be defined in a number of different way. Table 4.5 lists the ways in which this text has defined risk. A manager may employ all of these definitions and methods of quantification when making complex decisions.

Each method carries with it certain advantages and inadequacies. However, a manager must define and quantify risk in order to fully analyze a decision-making problem.

TABLE 4.5

Definitions and Quantifications of Risk

Risk measurement	Relation of measurement	Definition of measurement
Range	Larger ranges relate to higher relative risk	Difference of high versus low of a data set
Regret	Regret is not a monetary amount, but a feeling of loss	Buyer's remorse or opportunity costs (i.e., minimax regret criterion)
Standard deviation	Relatively higher standard deviations mean relatively higher risk	$SD^* = \sqrt{\dfrac{\sum(x-\mu)^2}{n-1}}$
		$SD^\dagger = \sqrt{\sum(x-E(x))^2\, p(x)}$

*Use with raw data.
† Use when a probability distribution is given.

FIGURE 4.6
Sensitivity Analysis Data Calculations

◇	A	B	C	D
1	Steve's Mutual Fund Decision Problem			
2	Payoff Table			
3		State of Nature		
4		Good	Bad	
5	Mutual Fund	Economic Conditions	Economic Conditions	
6	Stock Fund	20%	-8%	
7	Aggressive Growth			
8				
9	Index Fund	12%	2%	
10	Moderate S&P 500			
11				
12	Bond und			
13	Conservative U.S. Treasury	6%	4%	
14				
15	Expected Value Criterion			
16		Expected Payoff Values		
17		Aggressive Growth	Moderate S&P 500	Conservative U.S. Treasury
18	p(Good Economic Conditions)	Stock Fund	Index Fund	Bond Fund
19	0	-8.00%	2.00%	4.00%
20	0.1	-5.20%	3.00%	4.20%
21	0.2	-2.40%	4.00%	4.40%
22	0.3	0.40%	5.00%	4.60%
23	0.4	3.20%	6.00%	4.80%
24	0.5	6.00%	7.00%	5.00%
25	0.6	8.80%	8.00%	5.20%
26	0.7	11.60%	9.00%	5.40%
27	0.8	14.40%	10.00%	5.60%
28	0.9	17.20%	11.00%	5.80%
29	1	20.00%	12.00%	6.00%
30				

Importance of Sensitivity Analysis

It is the manager's job, when solving complex problems, to complete the three steps of sensitivity analysis before coming to a conclusion. Some refer to sensitivity analysis as *what if analysis* or *scenario analysis*. These terms are synonymous with sensitivity analysis.

It is important to note that, while sensitivity analysis may be the most critical and meaningful aspect of the decision making process, it often tends to be the most underutilized. It could be said that a problem is only half-solved if a manager does not include a formal sensitivity analysis. The next section will detail the three steps of sensitivity analysis with regard to the mutual fund investment example.

Concept *Check Critical Reasoning and Judgment Question*

At times sensitivity analysis is referred to as "what if" analysis. In fact, the term what if analysis has become the standard nomenclature with the proliferation of the spreadsheet as a decision support tool. Have you ever conducted a what if or sensitivity analysis on a decision problem? I would bet you have, especially when final exam time rolls around.

Sensitivity Analysis: Steve's Mutual Fund Example

Now that Steve has computed the results of the maximax, maximin, minimax regret, and Hurwicz decision criteria, he is faced with a difficult decision because there is not one dominant decision.

This section will detail a sensitivity analysis, which offers Steve a deeper understanding and will assist him in making a better decision on which mutual fund to invest in.

"What If" Analysis

At times sensitivity analysis is referred to as what if analysis. In other words, "What if something changes, does our recommended decision change?" Figure 4.6 shows an adequate method to analyze the outcomes for the expected value criterion. In addition, the information contained in Figure 4.6 can be graphed to reveal a much clearer picture of what is really happening as alpha changes.

Figure 4.6 uses different alphas, ranging from 0.0 to 1.0 and shows the payoff potential for each fund. The following Excel commands produce the information in Figure 4.6.

Cell B19 Compute the payoff figure for the aggressive growth stock fund

$$= \$B\$6*A19 + \$C\$6*(1-A19)$$

(Repeat formula for cells B20 through B29)

Cell C19 Compute the payoff figure for the moderate S & P 500 index fund

$$=\$B\$9*A19 + \$C\$9*(1-A19)$$

(Repeat formula for cells C20 through C29)

Cell D19 Compute the payoff figure for the aggressive growth stock fund

$$= \$B\$12*A19 + \$C\$12*(1-A19)$$

(Repeat formula for cells C20 through C29)

The essence of sensitivity analysis is to paint a more robust picture of the dominance, trade-offs, and risks among the alternatives.

Steve has now computed all the possible combinations on the occurrence of the state of nature. Since Steve is more visual than mathematical, he decides to convert the tabular display into a graphical display. A detailed walk-through on creating a sensitivity graph in Excel is next.

How to Construct a Sensitivity Graph in Excel

This section is a step-by-step tutorial on converting tabular data into a graphical form. This should prove useful to any student who is unfamiliar with Excel. Figure 4.7 shows the steps in construction a graph from the data in Figure 4.6. The steps are:

1. Highlight cells B18 through D29.
2. Click on **Chart Wizard** on the standard toolbar.
3. Click on the tab **Custom Types**.
4. Scroll down and click **Smooth Lines** for chart type.
5. Click Next at the bottom.

FIGURE 4.7   **Graphing in Excel**

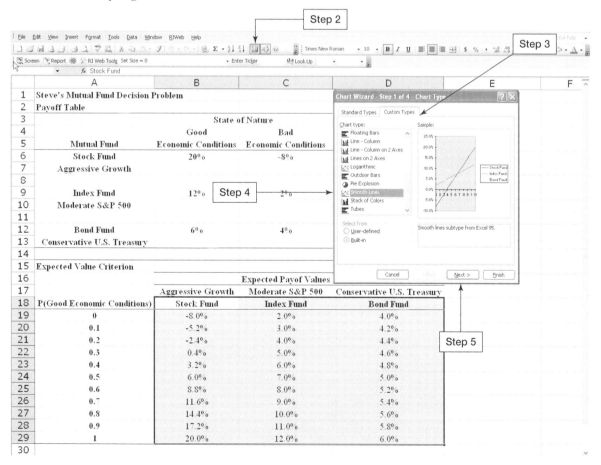

6. Now the top of the dialog box should indicate **Chart Wizard – Step 2 of 4 – Chart Source Data**.

7. Click on the **Series** tab.

8. You should now see from the sample graph that the X axis label ranges from 1 to 11. This is *not* the correct label.

9. Click on **Category (X) Axis Label** (the red and blue button on the right of the dialog box; see Figure 4.8).

10. Highlight cells A19 through A29 to designate the values for the X axis. Cells A19 though A29 should be surrounded by a moving dashed line (Figure 4.9).

11. Once again, click the blue and red button to accept the data range for X axis labels.

12. The X axis labels in the sample graph should now take on the values between 0.0 and 1.0.

FIGURE 4.8
Sensitivity
Graphing in Excel

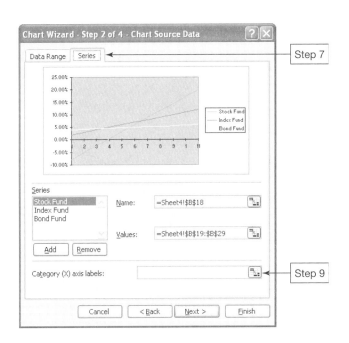

Figure 4.9   Sensitivity Graphing in Excel

15	Expected Value Criterion			
16		Expected Payoff Values		
17		Aggressive Growth	Moderate S&P 500	Conservative U.S. Treasury
18	p(Good Economic Conditions)	Stock Fund	Index Fund	Bond Fund
19	0	-8.00%	2.00%	4.00%
20	0.1	-5.20%	3.00%	4.20%
21	0.2	-2.40%	4.00%	4.40%
22	0.3	0.40%	5.00%	4.60%
23	0.4	3.20%	6.00%	4.80%
24	0.5	6.00%	7.00%	5.00%
25	0.6	8.80%	8.00%	5.20%
26	0.7	11.60%	9.00%	5.40%
27	0.8	14.40%	10.00%	5.60%
28	0.9	17.20%	11.00%	5.80%
29	1	20.00%	12.00%	6.00%
30				
31	=Sheet4!$A$19:$A$29			
32				

13. Click on **Next**.

14. Now you should see another dialog box, **Chart Wizard – Step 3 of 4 – Chart Options**. Click on the Title tab.

15. Enter "Mutual Funds" for Chart Title, "Probability Level" for Category (X) axis, and "Returns (%)" for Value (Y) axis (Figure 4.10).

16. You can play around with the formatting in this dialog box simply by clicking the different tabs at the top. For our purposes, click on **Legend**, and then click **Bottom** to move the legend to below the graph.

17. Click **Next**.

18. Now you should see the dialog box **Chart Wizard – Step 4 of 4 – Chart Location**.

19. Click the desired placement in either a new sheet or as an object in an existing sheet (Figure 4.11).

20. Click Finish and you should see the finished product, an Excel graph.

FIGURE 4.10
Sensitivity Graphing in Excel

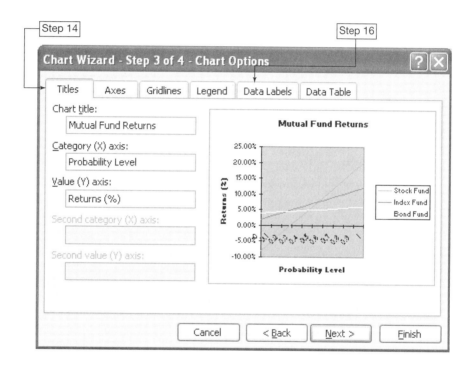

FIGURE 4.11   **Excel Chart Wizard Dialog Box**

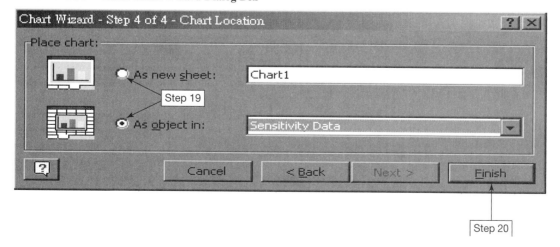

21. Now you may format the graph as you want by clicking the items on the chart where changes are desired (Figure 4.12)

Analyzing the Sensitivity Graph

Figure 4.12 reveals some very interesting information about the mutual fund example. The sensitivity graph in itself illustrates the three areas of sensitivity analysis: dominance, trade-offs, and risk. Let's review the three steps of sensitivity analysis with regard to Figure 4.12.

Establish Dominance

The dark lines juxtaposed on the graph represent the dominant decisions for Steve's mutual fund example. The graph is telling the decision maker the following:

1. If your assessment of the probability of good economic conditions is less than about 25 percent, then the bond fund is the best fund alternative.
2. If your assessment of the probability of good economic conditions is greater than about 25 percent but not greater then 55 percent, then the index fund is the best fund alternative.
3. If your assessment of the probability of good economic conditions is greater than about 55 percent, then the stock fund is the best fund alternative.

Strict Dominance

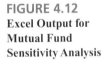

If strict dominance can be established, there is one decision that is better than all others.

Overall, a dominance structure has been established. However, this dominance is not strict dominance. Strict dominance is established when there is one decision that dominates in all situations. In the mutual fund example, there are three decision alternatives that dominate at different probability levels of good economic conditions. Since strict dominance cannot be established, the decision problem will contain trade-offs between the conflicting choices.

Trade-Off Analysis

Let's assume a manager is clairvoyant and knows whether or not enough rain will fall. The decision, then, would be very simple. A manager with this clairvoyant edge would only look at the right hand or left hand side of the graph to make a decision. As we all know, no manager is clairvoyant. Therefore, the point at which the two dominant choices cross is very important.

The point at which the two dominant choices intersect is referred to as the *trade-off point*. The exact value of the trade-off point can be calculated, but is not of overall importance to the manager. The most important issue is the identification and acknowledgment of the trade-off point.

There are several tradeoffs involved with the three mutual funds. It is Steve's understanding that, should he yearn for a more profitable return, he would have to take on more risk from

FIGURE 4.12
Excel Output for Mutual Fund Sensitivity Analysis

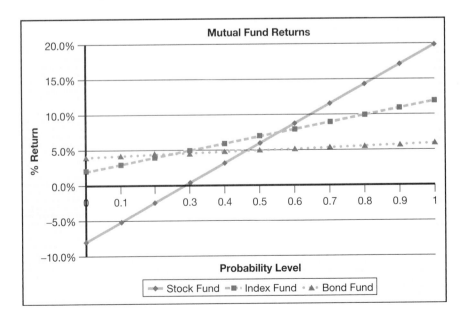

the aggressive growth stock fund (represented by the steep slope of the line), moderate risk with the moderate S&P 500 index fund, and the least risk with the conservative U.S. Treasury Bond fund. Thus, in order for Steve to make his decision, Steve should really think about his risk tolerance level.

Defining and Quantifying Risk

Risk must be defined by the decision maker and used to evaluate the choices in comparison to each other.

Risk must be defined and quantified when a manager is faced with trade-offs associated with numerous "good" alternatives. At the trade-off point, the alternatives look equally desirable. Subsequently, the risk associated with each of the alternatives may be the only way to differentiate the alternatives.

For the mutual fund example, risk is defined by using the measures of range and regret. Risk will not be defined by standard deviation, because of the small payoff sample size. Standard deviation will be used to define and quantify risk in Chapter 5, Simulation Modeling.

Risk Defined and Quantified by Range

From Figure 4.12 it can be seen that the lines associated with the different fund alternatives have different slopes. The stock fund tends to have a much steeper slope than the index and bond funds do. In this case, the slope of the line is related directly to range.

Range is defined as the difference between the highest value and the lowest value in the data set. Larger measurements of range mean the highest and lowest values in the data set are further apart. As a line becomes steeper, the difference between the high and low values is greater. Hence, steeper slope, like larger values of range, translates into higher relative risk.

Table 4.6 contains the range calculations for the mutual fund example. From the table it is seen that the stock fund has the highest range and could be considered to have the highest relative risk. Refer back to Figure 4.12 and relate the range measurements to the slope of each line.

If Steve has assessed the probability of good economic conditions to be around the trade-off point, 0.55, the range definition of risk could assist the decision-making process. An investor who is optimistic or who is more risky may choose the stock fund because of the higher payoff in the best scenario. Conversely, an investor who is less optimistic or less risky may choose one of the other two fund alternatives.

Risk Defined and Quantified by Regret

If Steve chooses to invest in the index fund, the payoff received will be moderate compared to the Stock Fund but greater than the Bond Fund most of the time. Steve could say he might have less regret by investing in the index fund when comparing it to the highs and lows of the other funds. In fact, it has been shown that the index fund is the choice that minimizes regret. Table 4.7 contains the minimax regret calculations for the mutual fund example.

However, if Steve chooses the index fund in order to minimize regret, something is given up. Steve may actually feel some measure of regret by choosing the index fund. Specifically, he will lose the ability to receive higher payoffs from the stock fund or more stable payoffs from the bond fund.

TABLE 4.6
Range calculations for Mutual fund Example

Fund	Range
Stock	28
Index	10
Bond	2

TABLE 4.7
Minimax Regret Calculations for Mutual fund Example

Fund	Minimax regret
Stock	12
Index	8
Bond	14

The Risk-Return Trade-off

A manager must analyze a problem with regard to measures of central tendency and dispersion in order to make an informed decision. In the words of decision analysis, a manager must analyze each decision problem with regard to return (i.e., expected values) and risk (i.e., range or regret). Only after analyzing the risk-return trade-offs can a decision be made.

Each of us must analyze complex decision problems in terms of return and risk. As students of business decision modeling and future managers, we must integrate sensitivity analysis into the problem-solving process while developing critical reasoning and judgement skills with regard to the risk/return trade-off.

In sum, this book cannot tell decision makers exactly what decisions will be the best when they are faced with complex problems. It is a guide to assist in developing a rational methodology for solving problems. Overall, the text provides a process for becoming a more effective and efficient problem solver.

MODELING, DECISION TREES, AND INFLUENCE DIAGRAMS

Definition of Modeling

A decision model can be defined as any quantitative or logical abstraction of reality that is created and used to help decision makers solve a problem. A model consists of states, decisions, payoffs, a structure to frame those decision components, and the definition and quantification of objectives the decision maker wishes to investigate.

Why Model?

Models are created to assist in the decision-making process.

A manager creates a model to assist in the decision-making process. Models assist managers in two ways. First, in building a model and structuring a decision problem, a manager can respond to increased levels of complexity that cannot be grasped and/or resolved by analyzing the individual pieces of a problem.

Second, a model, with computer support, can keep track of many details and rapidly perform all necessary computations and sensitivity analysis. This allows a manager to devote attention to judgments about the individual details and composite results produced by the model.

Five Main Reasons for Modeling

Five main reasons are detailed in this chapter. They encompass the major themes of modeling.

Necessity

There are numerous advantages to modeling, but five reasons—necessity, better decisions, insight, intuition, and aiding in the presentation—are central to the theme of modeling.

Models are built from necessity. They are done when simpler approaches are not adequate. Models are not a goal in themselves even though they can be engaging and, at times, almost supplant the decision at hand in our attention. However, managers require the assistance that models can efficiently give. Learning to model requires adapting one's language in order to communicate the model and its results effectively.

Better Decisions

It could be said that a model has helped a decision maker if a better decision is reached. In general, the decision is better because the model has allowed a sensitivity analysis. Sensitivity analysis, as presented in Chapter 4, allows for the study of the outcomes of interest as different assumptions are methodically varied, the effect of uncertain factors on the surety of results, and which assumptions affect the outcomes the most. The decision can include the interaction of influences over a much longer period of time so that the decision does not just respond to the most obvious short-term considerations.

Insight

A model gives the decision maker insight into a subject. The model allows a manager to explore the dominance of alternatives, the trade-offs among the factors that enter into those alternatives, and the risk associated with one alternative compared to another. Modeling equips a manager with the ability to break a problem into pieces and put it back together, offering insight along the way, that otherwise might have been overlooked.

Intuition

Overall, complex systems behave nonintuitively. Modeling gives a manager insight into these nonintuitive behaviors that come from time lags between actions and responses, from interactions, and from the damping of one influence by another. The model provides intuition about the whole, starting with intuition about the parts.

The model tells you which uncertainties in your knowledge matter. In general, a decision maker may be working with incomplete understanding and incomplete data. Some of this uncertainty may not affect the decision choice; however, the model analysis reveals which pieces of information are of the most importance. If time and money allow, a manager will know which areas to study more to improve the quality of the decision; i.e., intuition has been achieved.

Aid to Presentations

A model is an aid to the final presentation of the results. The presentation to the client uses the structure inherent in the model to explain those final results. The model illustrates the problem as compactly as possible. In general, clients need to see a physical structure in order to fully understand the problem and the alternatives presented.

STRUCTURING DECISION PROBLEMS

Payoff tables are an example of a very simple model.

Earlier in this chapter the components of a decision problem were identified and defined. In addition, a simple structure, called a payoff table, was presented to aid in the decision-making process. As a student of business decision modeling, you will quickly find out that payoff tables, although straightforward and helpful, are inadequate for more complex problems.

Payoff tables are just one way to structure problems. What kind of structure is needed for these more complex problems? How should one proceed in modeling complex decision problems? The decision modeling process consists of three fundamental steps:

1. Identifying and defining the variables and outcomes of interest.
2. Organizing the variables and outcomes into a logical framework.
3. Verification and refinement of the framework.

Each of these steps will be detailed next.

Identifying and Defining Variables and Outcomes of Interest

Identifying the variables that impact the decision is the first step in modeling.

The decision maker must first identify the variables that affect the decision. Once these variables are identified, they must be defined and the initial parameters, or bounds, set on their values. Outcomes of interest may be identified at the same time or after variables are established. Let's turn back to Chapter 1 and use a break-even example.

- A manager must define the variables that affect the decision problem. For example, how many units do I need to produce to break even.
- The variables that are needed are fixed costs, variable costs, and price charged.
- The outcome of interest for the manager is the break-even point.
- The links between fixed cost, variable cost, and price charged are fairly straightforward and a basic mathematical equation or framework already exists for this decision problem.

Organizing Variables and Outcomes into a Logical Framework

Modeling gives a decision maker a means to structure a decision problem.

Payoff tables were introduced as a means to organize states, decisions, and payoffs. Payoff tables are one means to structure or put a physical framework around a decision problem. However, as was mentioned earlier, payoff tables become inadequate fairly quickly when a manager is faced with complex problems. Two additional means of framing a decision problem are introduced here: decision trees and influence diagrams.

Each of the approaches has different advantages for framing complex decision problems. Decision trees work extremely well for multistage decision problems while influence diagrams structure problems needing additional interactions and/or feedback. In fact, the two structures complement each other.

Verification and Refinement of the Framework

Models must be refined and the structure verified in order to proceed with further analysis.

Once a manager has identified and defined the variables and outcomes of interest and framed the problem, verification and refinement of the model or framework must be completed. This follows closely the review and iterate step in the business decision modeling process from Chapter 1.

A manager must be clear on what variables affect the outcomes of interest, what the basic parameters of those variables and outcomes are, and how to measure the outcomes. In addition, the overall structure should be analyzed. A manager need not lose sight the forest for the trees by choosing a framework that accommodates all the details but is too unruly or complex as a whole. One goal of putting structure to decision problems is to provide the client with a visual package to aid in the understanding and analysis of the situation.

Take, for example, the mutual fund decision problem. A payoff table appeared to work well for Steve's simple decision regarding mutual fund to choose. However, the payoff table framework soon becomes inadequate when additional variables are introduced. A review and refinement of the decision structure would be in order. The next section presents the concepts of decision trees and influence diagrams.

DECISION TREES

Decision trees contain three types of symbols: square decision nodes, round chance nodes, and straight-line branches.

A decision tree is a graphical representation of a decision problem. Decision trees are another method to structure a problem. The decision tree framework consists of nodes and branches.

Decision Nodes, Chance Nodes, and Decision Trees

A decision tree contains two types of nodes, decision nodes and chance nodes, and brancks, defined as follows:

A **decision node**, defined by a square, denotes when a decision maker must make a choice or a decision.

A **chance node**, defined by a circle, represents an event or state of nature that can occur in the future.

A **branch**, defined by a line, represents decision alternatives and/or states of nature, and links decisions and/or states.

A decision maker can use a decision tree to structure a problem and compute expected values.

In using a decision tree, a manager computes expected values at each chance node and makes a choice or decision on the basis of those expected values at decision nodes.

Decision trees provide a visual representation of the states, decisions, and outcomes of a sequential decision problem. Decision trees provide a framework for problems that payoff tables are unable to illustrate.

Building Decision Trees

To frame a problem by using a decision tree, the components of the problem must be identified and defined. Recall that the components of any decision-making problem are as follows: states, decisions, and payoffs. Let's use Steve's mutual fund problem example as the decision problem of interest. Figure 4.13 displays the payoff table for the mutual fund example.

From any payoff table, a decision tree can be built.

From the information given in the payoff table, a decision tree can be built. First, let's relate the components of the decision problem to the graphical components of decision trees.

Obviously, the three decisions match up with the decision node component. A common starting place for most decision trees is a decision node. For the mutual fund payoff table, three decisions emanate from the initial decision node as decision branches.

At the end of each of the decision branches, a chance node is placed. From each chance node two branches depicting the two states—good economic conditions and bad economic conditions—emerge. At the end of these chance branches the payoffs associated with each decision, state combination are listed. Figure 4.14 displays the corresponding decision tree.

FIGURE 4.13   **Payoff Table for Steve's Mutual Fund Example**

	A	B	C
1	**Steve's Mutual Fund Decision**		
2	**Payoff Table**		
3		State of Nature	
4		Good	Bad
5	Mutual Fund	Economic Condition	Economic Condition
6	Stock Fund	20%	-8%
7	Aggressive Growth		
8			
9	Index Fund	12%	2%
10	Moderate S&P 500		
11			
12	Bond Fund	6%	4%
13	Conservative U.S. Treasury		
14			

FIGURE 4.14   **Decision Tree for Mutual Fund Example**

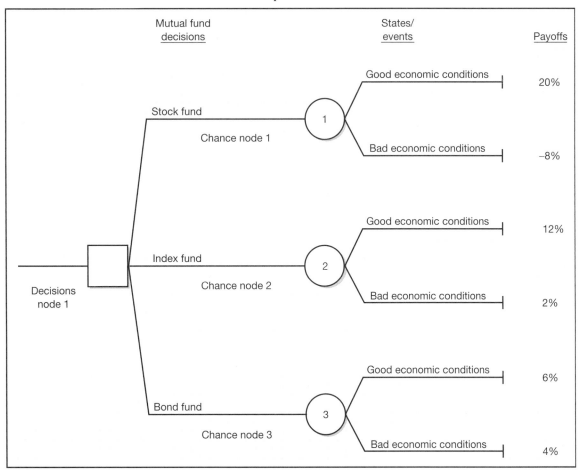

For the mutual fund example, only one decision and one set of chance nodes are needed. The decision tree structure allows for any combination of decision and chance nodes. The next section will briefly discuss the concept of folding back the tree. The application of decision trees to multiple sequential decision making will be detailed later in this chapter.

Folding Back the Tree: Calculating Expected Values

Folding back the tree refers to the process of calculating expected values at chance nodes.

One goal of a decision tree is to calculate the expected value of the tree, or perform a process called *folding back the tree*. This process is based on a set of rules for decision trees. When analyzing a decision tree a decision maker may encounter decision nodes or chance nodes. Two rules govern decision trees regarding these nodes:

1. At a chance node, a decision maker computes an expected value based on the payoffs and probabilities given.
2. When faced with a decision node, a decision maker must make a decision. The criterion used to make the decision is to maximize the expected value of the various alternatives in question.

When a decision maker encounters a chance node an expected value calculation is performed. Accordingly, when faced with a decision node, a decision maker must make a decision and chooses based on maximizing expected value.

In general, when faced with a decision tree, a decision analyst begins at the far right of the tree with the payoffs, at chance nodes calculates expected values, and at decision nodes chooses the decision that maximizes expected value. This process is followed until the decision analyst reaches the far left of the tree. This process is referred to as folding back the tree.

Example of Folding Back a Decision Tree

Figure 4.15 displays the tree for the mutual fund example under the equal likelihood scenario. Expected values for the chance nodes are shown on the tree and will be calculated; in addition, a final recommendation is displayed on the tree at the final decision node.

According to the rules set down in the previous section, expected values are calculated at chance nodes 1, 2, and 3. The calculations are as follows:

$$\text{Chance node 1:} \quad E(1) = 20\% \times 0.5 + (-8\%) \times 0.5 = 6\%$$

$$\text{Chance node 2:} \quad E(2) = 12\% \times 0.5 + 2\% \times 0.5 = 7\%$$

$$\text{Chance node 3:} \quad E(3) = 6\% \times 0.5 + 4\% \times 0.5 = 5\%$$

Folding back the tree is akin to finding the weighted average of the branches at each chance node of a decision tree.

Subsequently, at the far-left decision node, the expected values are compared and the mutual fund with the highest expected value is chosen. Table 4.8 displays the three expected values and highlights the index fund as the final recommendation made at the far-left decision node.

In summary, the process of folding back a decision tree consists of calculating expected values at chance nodes and making decisions at decision nodes based on maximizing expected values. Therefore, in the mutual fund example, when the decision maker's assessment of the occurrence of good economic conditions state is 0.5, the index fund will be the recommendation.

In sum, when a decision maker is confronted with a chance node an expected value must be calculated; subsequently, when confronted with a decision node, the decision maker must make a choice based on maximizing expected value.

Multistage Decision Trees

Decision trees generally begin with a decision node, but a decision maker does not always have to follow this rule.

In general, decision trees begin with a decision node. However, it is possible to begin a decision tree with a chance node. In addition, the decision tree structure allows for any number and combination of decision nodes and chance nodes.

FIGURE 4.15 **Mutual Fund Example Decision Tree**

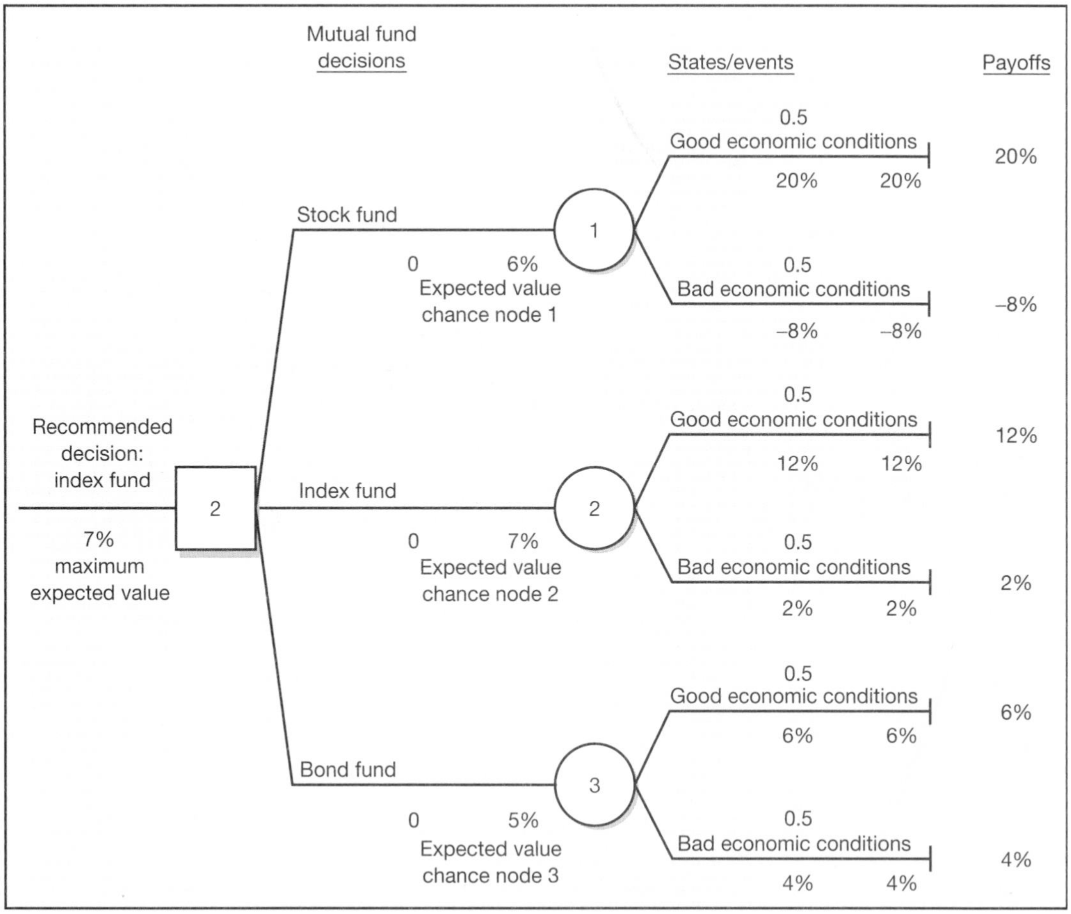

TABLE 4.8
Mutual fund Decision Tree Expected Values

Mutual fund	Expected value. $\alpha = 0.5$
Stock fund	6%
Index fund	**7%**
Bond fund	5%

For example, if Steve wishes to make another decision after witnessing bad economic conditions, he may want to switch to Fund B; the decision tree structure allows this very easily. In addition, Steve knows that there is a chance of a corporate scandal if he is invested in the stock fund.

Multistage decision trees depict events and decisions that occur one after another or in a sequential manner.

To accommodate these additional decisions and states, the original decision tree must be augmented. Figure 4.16 displays the modified decision tree including these added decisions and states.

From Figure 4.16 it is obvious that any order, combination, and/or number of decision and chance nodes is possible. This makes the decision tree framework very robust for structuring decision problems with multistage decisions and states.

One inadequacy of decision trees is the lack of a feedback loop.

Inadequacies of Decision Tree Structures

Although decision trees provide a more robust structure for framing decision problems, there may be times when a decision maker is faced with a problem that does not exactly fit the tree format. In fact, the basic tree format does not incorporate feedback well. In addition, the tree structure becomes large as the number of decision and chance nodes grows. To ameliorate these inadequacies, another decision structure is introduced—the influence diagram.

FIGURE 4.16   **Multistage Decision Tree Example**

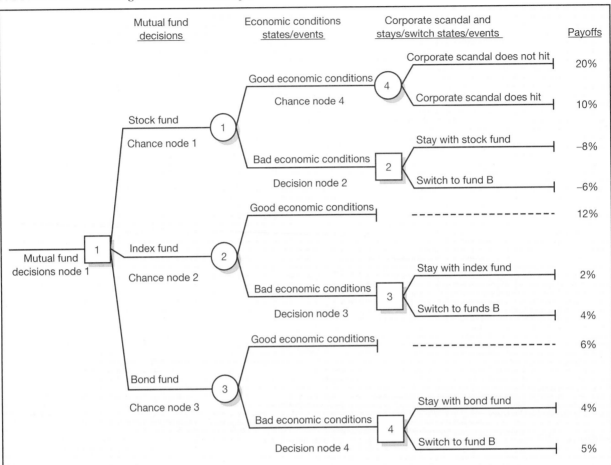

INFLUENCE DIAGRAMS

Influence diagrams are tools for structuring a model design from a set of defined variables. Having identified and defined the variables of a model, we next decide how these variables relate to one another.

An influence diagram displays all the model variables and indicates the direction and type of influence from one variable to another.

Influence Diagram Symbols

Influence diagrams consist of three types of symbols: square decision variables, round intermediate variables, and oval attribute or outcome variables.

A rectangle in an influence diagram represents a decision variable, a circle is an intermediate variable, and an oval (or ellipse) signifies an attribute or an outcome of interest. Figure 14.17 depicts these symbols.

Figure 14.18 depicts a number of simple influence diagrams characterizing the different types of variables, influence, and random or nonrandom nature.

Influence Diagrams and Depicting Influence

Arrows connect related variables in an influence diagram. An arrow indicates the direction of influence. The arrow indicates that the value of the influencing variable is set first and is used in determining the level of any variable that it influences.

Three types of influence arrows are used in an influence diagram. A single straight arrow, as displayed in Figure 4.18 Example A, indicates certain influence. An arrow that resembles a lightening bolt, as displayed in Figure 4.18 Example B, stands for an uncertain influence.

FIGURE 4.17
Influence Diagram Symbols

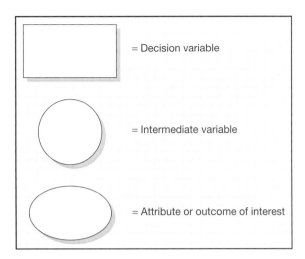

FIGURE 4.18
Examples of Simple Influence Diagrams

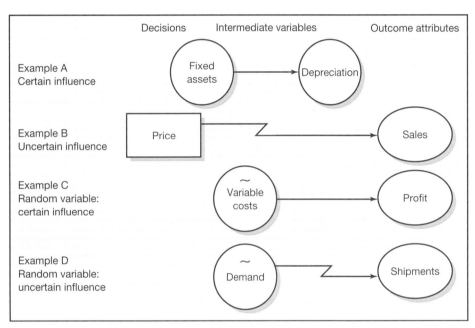

Three types of influence are used in influence diagrams: a single straight arrow, a single kinked arrow, or a double arrow.

Looking at Example A, we see the level of fixed assets has certain influence on the amount of depreciation. If fixed assets increase, then without question, depreciation will increase. This is indicated by the single straight arrow.

In contrast, Example B of Figure 4.18, price, a decision variable, will affect sales, in this case an outcome attribute. But the influence is uncertain. That is, if price is changed upward, we would expect sales to be lower (recall economics and simple supply and demand), but we are unsure by how much. Actually, if we did know this we would have a measure of the price elasticity of the item being sold. This uncertainty is represented by an arrow with a lightening bolt look to it.

Arrows connect related variables and indicate direction of influence.

Random Variables

A variable and its influence may also be exogenous, or random, as displayed in Figure 4.18 Examples C and D. Random variables can impart certain or uncertain influence. However, by definition, random variables have no decision variables as direct or indirect predecessors in the influence diagram structure. In this case, *predecessor* refers to the influence relationship, not necessarily in time.

Variables that are random are represented by a tilde (~) above the respective variable.

Any variable influenced by a random variable is also a random variable. Any random variable will be noted with a tilde (~) above the variable. Figure 4.19 displays an influence diagram for a simple borrowing decision.

Figure 4.19 shows a decision variable at the left. This decision variable indicates which loan is taken. This choice influences the down payment needed, which, in turn, influences the buyer's cash position. The decision also influences the actual percentage rate on the loan. This example has two outcome attributes: the applicant's cash remaining and the actual percentage rate on the loan.

Order, Precedence, and/or Influence Diagram Structure

Variables in an influence diagram can appear in virtually any order.

Influence relationships have been described that relate decision variables to intermediate variables or to outcome attributes. Influence relationships may also relate intermediate variables to outcome attributes or they may simply relate one intermediate variable to another.

Variables may appear in virtually any precedence order in the influence diagram. This is in contrast to a decision tree, where the structure of the problem tends to flow from left to right. In fact, outcome attributes or intermediate variables resulting from one set of decision variables may themselves influence other decisions.

Figure 4.20 displays an influence diagram having two decisions. First, an undergraduate student decides on the level of effort to put into an academic career. An outcome of this level of effort is the grades the student receives. But grades may in turn influence the decision made by a graduate admissions committee whether to admit the student into a particular graduate program. This decision in turn influences the career path that the student pursues.

Two-Way and Loop Influence

Influence diagrams differ from decision trees in that they allow two-way and loop influence.

Relationships that contain two-way influence are also possible. However, it should be cautioned that if the variables are treated as random variables, two-way influences become so complex that the solution goes beyond the scope of this text. Two-way relationships between random variables do appear in econometric models and are treated in texts on econometric model building.

The following example using interest expense and debt levels illustrates a two-way dependency. This relationship would be expressed in a line model by two simultaneous equations.

FIGURE 4.19 **Influence Diagram for Simple Borrowing Decision**

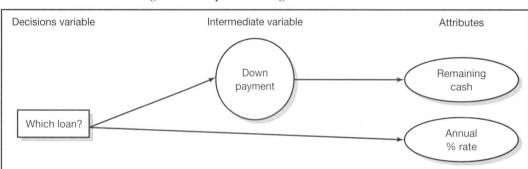

FIGURE 4.20 **Student's Influence Diagram**

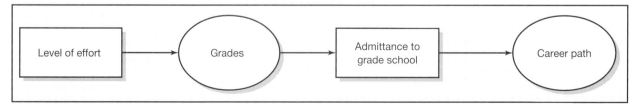

The equations might be as follows:

$$\text{Interest expense} = 0.08(\text{debt level})$$

$$\text{Debt level} = \$10,000 + \text{interest expense}$$

Figure 4.21a displays the influence diagram associated with the debt level and interest expense example.

An influence loop is created when influence arrows go in both directions between variables.

The concept of an influence loop is created when the arrows go in both directions. A loop involving many variables without using two-way influences can also be created. Figure 4.21b depicts an example where both income and expenses affect the deficit, which, in turn, affects borrowings. This, in turn, affects expenses through interest expense.

One reason for drawing an influence diagram prior to constructing the mathematical model is to detect loops such as this. Any time such a loop exists, simultaneous equations are needed in the model and special instructions may be required to enable the model to run.

Influence Diagrams to Measure Time

Influence diagrams can also be constructed to measure the effect of variables in different time periods.

Influence diagrams can also be constructed to measure the effect of variables in different time periods. Figure 4.22a illustrates an influence diagram of the relationships between assets and depreciation in different time periods. The assets in year n determine the depreciation in year n, which in turn affects the assets in year $n + 1$. This case does not involve a loop, since assets in year n and year $n + 1$ are really separate variables.

Rather than create separate variables for each time period, which may result in a large, cluttered influence diagram, the modeler may instead use subscript notation to show time variation. If a variable, e.g., assets, is influenced by the previous value of another variable, e.g., depreciation, this may be indicated by using a notation system, such as the subscript "Previous," on the arrow. Figure 4.22b is such a way of writing the general relationship in Figure 4.22 (a).

FIGURE 4.21 **(a) Two-Way Influence Diagram and (b) Loop Influence Diagram**

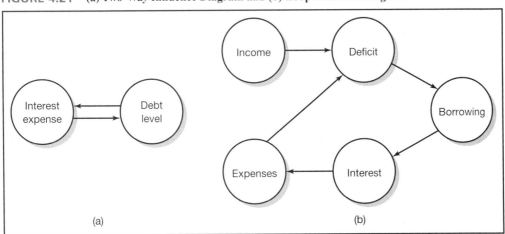

(a)   (b)

FIGURE 4.22 **(a) Influence Diagram Measuring Time; (b) The Same Relationship with Subscript Notation to Show Time Variation**

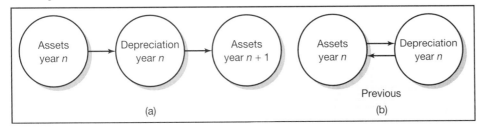

(a)   (b)

FIGURE 4.23

**Sales Erosion
Influence Diagram**

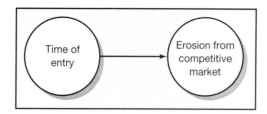

To show the effects of time in an influence diagram, a modeler may use subscript variables.

At times modelers use a separate variable to depict the effects of time. For example, Figure 4.23 depicts the effects of the introduction of a new product into a market. One of the variables is sales erosion of the new product that would result from the future entry of a competitive product. The magnitude of that erosion may depend on when competitors introduce their product.

Building the Influence Diagram Structure

Managers are faced with large, complex problems that require large complex models.

As a manager, you will be faced with large, complex problems that require large, complex models. In designing large models, it is not advisable to attempt to write down the entire model in one step. Outline the parts of the model first, then proceed to flesh out the details. Begin with the two ends of the problem and the simplest decisions and outcomes, then work to fill in the linkage between them.

Coyle (1977) proposes six possible justifications for an influence between variables: conservation considerations (mass balance), direction observation, instructions (or policy statements) of a system, accepted theory, hypothesis or assumption, and statistical evidence. A manager should think of the justification that may be appropriate when documenting influence, not only to avoid modeling erroneous influences but also to be able to understand what the influence is.

PUTTING IT ALL TOGETHER: A REAL ESTATE INFLUENCE DIAGRAM

The rental price on apartment units is a variable that a manager decides on. Profits are the final outcome of interest. The development of a complete set of relationships is necessary to link the price decision to the profit outcome.

It is easy to see that the decision variable, price, will affect occupancy. In turn, occupancy affects revenue, and finally profit. Or working in reverse, profit is influenced by cash flow from the rental units and the amount of money invested. Linking the appropriate variables with influence arrows, e.g., connecting revenue and cash flow, completes the influence diagram. Figure 4.24 represents a decision tree and the corresponding influence diagram for the real estate management example.

Converting a Decision Tree to an Influence Diagram

It is possible to structure a problem by using a decision tree and then converting the tree to an influence diagram. However, the converse may not be true.

It is possible to structure the problem using a decision tree and then convert the tree to an influence diagram. It is always possible to convert a decision tree into an influence diagram. This is accomplished by including the variables at the nodes of the decision tree in the diagram and by adding arrows flowing between them in the same direction as the tree opens up.

Even though an influence diagram can be created for any decision tree, the converse is not true. Not every influence diagram created can be turned into a decision tree. Decision trees cannot accommodate feedback loops in their structure. There are a number of differences between influence diagrams and decision trees. A comparison of the two decision structures is next.

Influence Diagrams and Decision Trees: A Comparison

Influence diagrams have flexibility, which decision trees do not. Decision trees are sequential in nature. Variables to the right are implicitly influenced by variables to their left. This is seen in Figure 4.24a, where the fixed cost node must be inserted before or after variable cost. The

FIGURE 4.24 **Real Estate Management (a) Decision Tree and (b) Influence Diagram**

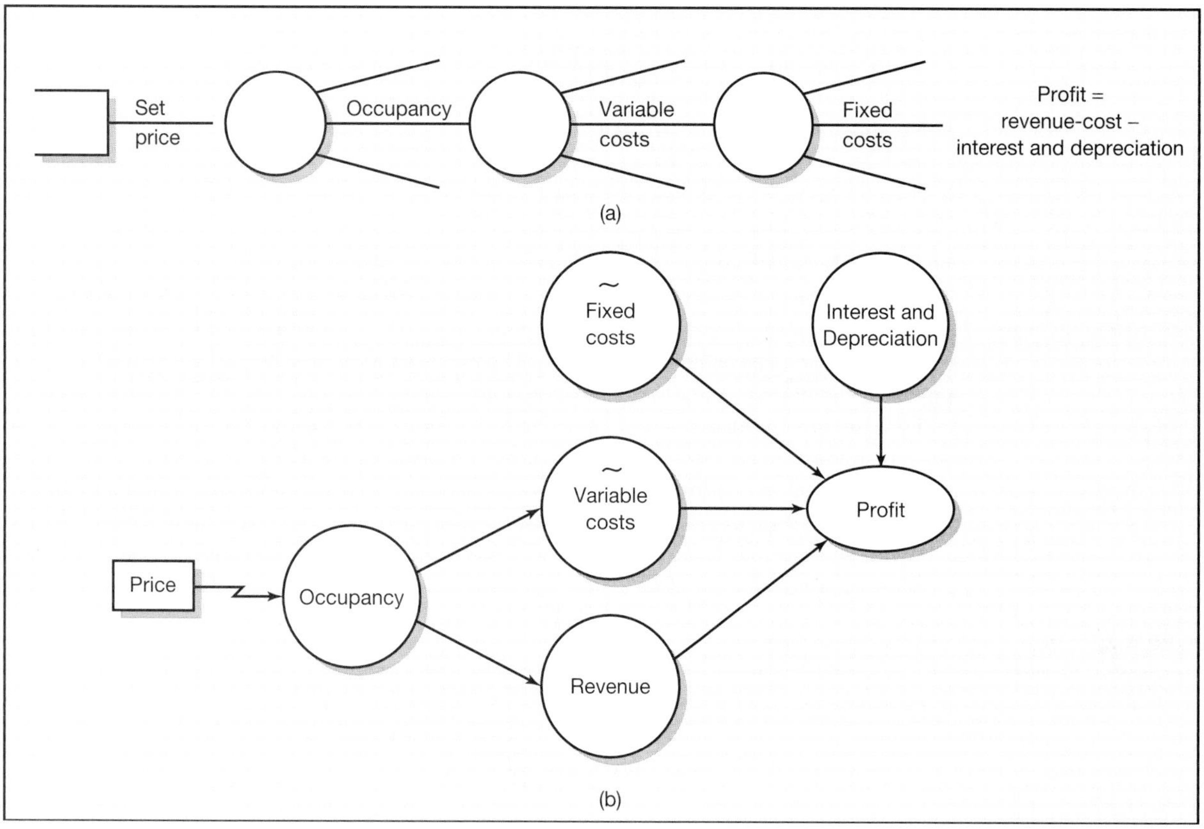

placement of the fixed cost node may suggest influence over variable cost or vice versa. However, as is explicit in simple financial models, fixed cost generally does not influence variable cost nor does variable cost influence fixed cost.

Influence diagrams show relationships more concisely and accurately than decision trees and indicate a wider range of intricate relationships. These points are demonstrated in the subsequent influence diagram in Figure 4.24b. The influence diagram clearly illustrates that variable and fixed costs are unrelated.

In addition, the influence diagram reveals that revenue is influenced directly by price and also indirectly influenced by price through occupancy. Decision trees do not have the ability to portray these links. Numerous predecessors having any structure of relationships among them may influence variables in an influence diagram.

Advantages of Influence Diagrams and Areas of Consideration

Advantages of influence diagrams: They are a general decision structuring device, expandable, and simple to build and use.

In general, influence diagrams accommodate and accomplish a number of items more effectively and efficiently than decision trees. These areas are summarized as follows:

1. Influence diagrams are more general tools for structuring models than decision trees.
2. Influence diagrams are expandable; variables can be broken down into finer points or variables.
3. Influence diagrams are simple to initiate and easy to modify.

Although influence diagrams appear to be simple enough tools, first-time modelers often encounter pitfalls during development. The following areas should be noted to prevent misuse and overuse:

Influence diagrams are not: flow charts, precedence charts, or hierarchical structures.

1. An influence diagram is not:

   a. A flow chart; it does not indicate things such as "units shipped from point A to point B."
   b. A precedence chart, such as might be used in PERT planning. An arrow does not mean "must be followed by."

c. A representation of hierarchical structure, as in an organizational chart. An arrow does not mean "is an element of."

2. Think of variables as levels of some quantity and arrows as effects of variables on each other, but make it clear what higher or lower levels mean.
3. Divide variables into two or more variables only when more detailed expression is needed for clarity.
4. If (and only if) an influence arrow needs more explanation, insert another variable.

The Completed Real Estate Influence Diagram

Figure 4.25 displays the completed influence diagram of a real estate investment model that is to be used in evaluating new apartment-building projects. The company faces three decisions in any new project: (1) whether to take it on, (2) how big a building to build (or whether to expand a purchased building), and (3) what to charge for rent.

Two uncertain influences are included in the diagram: the price-occupancy relationship and market demand. Fixed costs and variable costs are treated as random variables. Two attributes, amount invested and net present value (NPV), are the outcomes of interest. Amount invested is linked to NPV by the fact that larger investments should bring larger returns, or NPV. The general model for the real estate investment problem is described adequately by the influence diagram. However, two additional steps are necessary to generate the model from the diagram.

FIGURE 4.25   **Real Estate Influence Diagram**

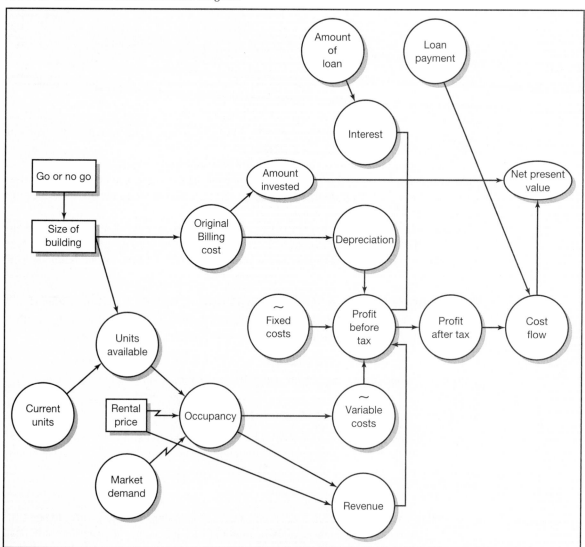

After the basic influence diagram structure is in place, the mathematical forms or functions of the relationships must be derived or constructed.

1. Mathematical forms of relationship (functions) that apply to each arrow in the diagram must be constructed. The functions for most of the arrows would be the same for all projects considered (for example, the same form of depreciation rule would be applied to each project). A quick perusal of a real estate investment text would supply most of the answers to the functional relationships depicted in the influence diagram.

2. Specific numbers must be supplied to these functions, e.g., the prevailing interest rate. Specific numbers may vary from case to case or project to project. The influence diagram is flexible enough to handle these variations.

USING TREEPLAN TO DEVELOP DECISION TREES IN EXCEL

TreePlan is an add-in to Excel spreadsheets that greatly simplifies the process of constructing decision trees. Excel does have sufficient resources to develop decision trees without using an add-in software package like TreePlan, but the process is difficult and slow. This section describes and explains how to access, install, and use TreePlan in conjunction with Excel.

Loading and Accessing TreePlan

Since TreePlan is an add-in for Excel, the first step in using TreePlan is loading the software via Excel's Add-Ins menu. You must copy the Excel add-in file, TreePlan.xla, onto your hard disk drive. In turn, use the Tools and Add-Ins menus to locate and load the TreePlan program. Follow these steps to install the TreePlan.xla file.

1. Choose the Tools menu in Excel.
2. Choose the Add-Ins option from the tools menu.
3. From the Add-Ins option, choose Browse and locate the TreePlan.xla file you saved earlier.
4. Once you have found the path name for the TreePlan program, click OK and Excel will instruct you what to do next.

At this point, the TreePlan program should be loaded and available via the Tools menu. Figure 4.26 displays the Tools menu with TreePlan added in.

Creating an Initial Decision Tree in TreePlan

To use TreePlan, open Excel, choose the Tools menu, and click on Decision Tree... menu. The menu displayed should resemble Figure 4.27. TreePlan defines decision nodes in the same manner as the text, but refers to chance nodes as event nodes. The two terms will be used synonymously throughout the rest of the text.

FIGURE 4.26
Tools Menu Including TreePlan

Note: If you have just opened Excel to load TreePlan, it is advisable to open a new workbook before attempting to use TreePlan. This avoids any potential errors.

FIGURE 4.27 **Initial TreePlan Menu**

FIGURE 4.28 **Initial Decision Tree**

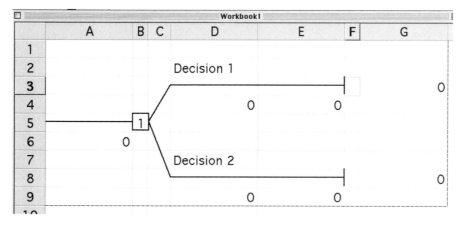

FIGURE 4.29 **Treeplan Formula Example**

	A	B	C	D	E	F	G
1							
2				Decision 1			
3							=SUM(D4)
4				0	=G3		
5		=IF(A6=E4,1,IF(A6=E9,2))					
6	=MAX(E4,E9)						
7				Decision 2			
8							=SUM(D9)
9				0	=G8		

Note: Do not type cells that contain formulas. This invalidates the tree and consequent tree calculations.

Click the New Tree button and a decision tree will appear in the active Excel worksheet. The decision tree generated should resemble Figure 4.28.

Adding, Changing, and/or Modifying a Decision Tree in TreePlan

Once the initial tree has been created in Excel, the user can modify it by adding branches, chance nodes, or additional decision nodes. Please read the following note regarding data input into TreePlan and refer to Figure 4.29 for a visual display of the concept.

The next section details the instructions for modifying a decision tree in TreePlan.

Adding Chance Nodes

1. To add a chance node in TreePlan, place the cursor at the end of a branch at the T intersection, orterminal node. The placement of the cursor should resemble that in Figure 4.30.

2. After placing the cursor, click on the Tools menu and chose the Decision Tree option.
3. A dialog box resembling Figure 4.31 will appear.
4. Chose the option you wish to perform. For example, in Figure 4.30 the cursor is at the end of a terminal node and an event node is to be added. Therefore, click on the Change to event node button and click OK.
5. The tree in your workbook should resemble Figure 4.32 after this procedure is finished.

Modifying Decision Nodes

1. To modify a decision node in TreePlan, place the cursor on the decision node you wish tomodify.
2. Chose the Decision Tree ... option from the Tools menu. A menu resembling Figure 4.33 should appear.

FIGURE 4.30
Cursor Placement for Modifying Trees in TreePlan

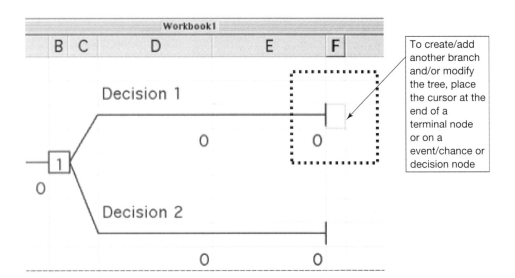

FIGURE 4.31
TreePlan Add/Change/ Modify Dialog Box

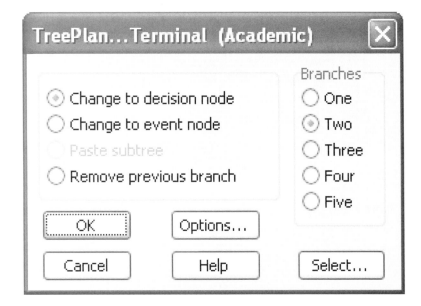

3. From the menu in Figure 4.33, chose the instruction you wish to have TreePlan perform.

4. The same procedure can be used to modify chance nodes.

These commands for adding chance nodes and/or modifying decision nodes can be combined to create detailed sequential decision trees. A few items must be taken note of whenever you are developing a decision trees in TreePlan:

•   As a previous note cautions, **do not type in the cells** that contain formulas in TreePlan. Figure 4.34 displays a generic two-decision, two-state, decision tree. Dashed boxes mark the cells where data should be entered and asterisks mark the cells where probabilities should be entered.

•   It is acceptable to enter data into any of the cells containing a probability (refer to the asterisked numbers in Figure 4.34). However, the user must keep in mind the rules of probability. **If the sum of the event probabilities does not add to 1.0, TreePlan will return an error**.

•   **It is easier to go forward building a tree than to undo hastily made branches or nodes.** Draw the tree on paper first and then proceed in TreePlan.

FIGURE 4.32   **Decision Tree with Chance Node Added**

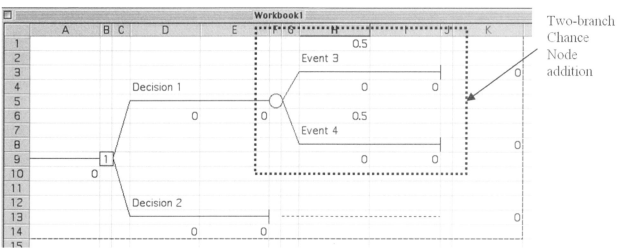

FIGURE 4.33
TreePlan Menu for Modifying an Existing Node

Business Decision Modeling Behind the Scenes

The Story of John von Neumann

THE FATHER OF DECISION ANALYSIS

John von Neumann (1903–1957), often considered to be the father of decision analysis, was a child prodigy born into a banking family in Budapest, Hungary. At the age of 6, von Neumann was able to divide eight-digit numbers in his head. From the age of 13 he showed a pronounced interest in mathematics, which was fostered by his teachers at the Lutheran High School of Budapest. After graduation from high school, von Neumann studied chemistry for 2 years in Berlin and for 2 years in Zurich, but spent much of his time with mathematicians, taking a Ph.D. in mathematics at the University of Budapest not long after receiving his chemistry diploma at Zurich.

MATHEMATICIAN, ECONOMIST, AND PHYSICIST

Von Neumann lectured at Berlin from 1926 to 1929 and at Hamburg from 1929 to 1930. In 1930 von Neumann became a visiting lecturer at Princeton University, being appointed professor there in 1931. He became one of the original six mathematics professors in 1933 at the newly founded Institute for Advanced Study in Princeton, a position he kept for the remainder of his life.

Von Neumann's brilliant work in mathematics also carried him into theoretical economics and technology as well as theoretical physics—areas where he was able to make vital contributions not only to science but also to the welfare of his adopted country. His work in quantum mechanics gave him a profound knowledge concerning the application of nuclear energy to military and peacetime uses, enabling him to occupy an important place in the scientific councils of the nation.

DEVELOPER OF ATOMIC BOMB AND ADVISOR TO THE ATOMIC ENERGY COMMISSION

During the Second World War, he played a major role among the Los Alamos group of scientists who developed the atomic bomb. After the war he served on the advisory committee of the Atomic Energy Commission and on the commission itself from 1954 until his death.

OPTIMAL INFORMATION AREA

http://mondrian.princeton.edu/CampusWWW/Companion/von_neumann_john.html

http://ei.cs.vt.edu/~history/VonNeumann.html

FIGURE 4.34 **Example Tree Depicting Data Entry Areas**

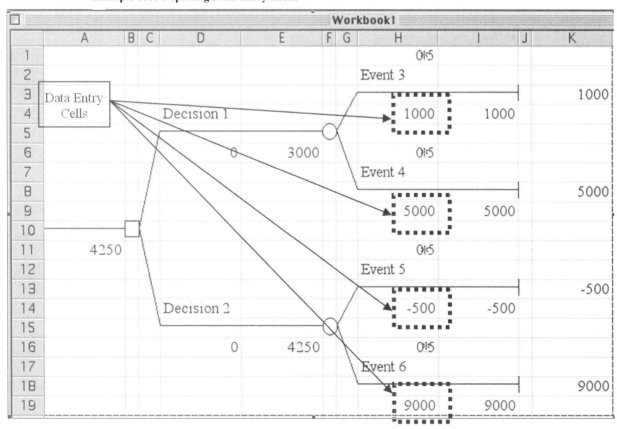

Summary

This chapter illustrates how decision analysis can be used to structure and analyze decisions involving numerous and conflicting alternatives. A rational methodology has been put forth for a manager to become a more effective and efficient problem solver. The goal of decision analysis is to identify the best alternative in the face of uncertain or risky future conditions.

Three types of criteria were presented for making decisions not based on probability assessments: the maximax, the maximin, and the minimax regret. The concept of expected values and the Hurwicz criterion were linked with the issue of probability assessment and decision analysis. Three areas of sensitivity analysis were explored and the idea was presented that the decision analysis framework and sensitivity analysis provide a manager with a rational method to compare and ultimately make a choice.

A completed decision tree and/or influence diagram expresses the structure of a formal model. They provide participants in the modeling process a means of communication. They also serve as the framework for expressing more specifically the exact nature of relationships.

The following example executive summary illustrates the application of the concepts discussed in this chapter.

Executive Summary for Steve's Mutual Fund Decision

TO: Steve Puryear

FROM: Steve's Consulting Group

Problem Identification

Steve is faced with a dilemma in deciding which mutual fund to invest his money in. Each of the three funds' potential return is forecasted according to two possible future economic conditions, good and bad at 40 percent and 60 percent respectively. Steve assumes that the forecasted returns for the funds are accurate and he base his decision on the figures given.

Modeling the Problem

To avoid rash decision making, Steve decides to conduct a series of quantitative method decision analyses to resolve his dilemma. The methods that Steve employs are the maximax, maximin, minimax regret, and Hurwicz decision criteria.

By simply using the different decision criteria analysis, Steve simply cannot make a decisive decision since all three funds appear superior in one criterion to another. Thus, Steve decides to conduct a sensitivity analysis using the Hurwicz criterion by using a range of possible alpha level ranging from 0.00 to 1.00. The results are shown in graphical format below. This section details three areas of sensitivity analysis for Steve's decision problem.

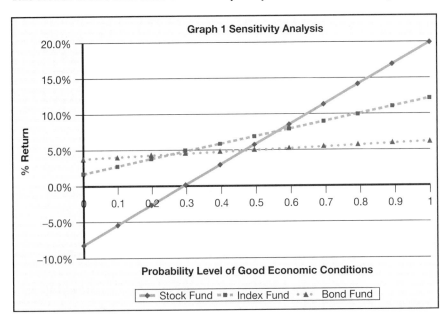

Dominance

No dominant solution was identified by the previous analysis. Therefore, Graph 1 displays a sensitivity analysis for Steve's decision. It is apparent from the graph that each of the decisions

TABLE 1.1
Payoff Table Decision Criteria

Fund	Maximax	Maximin	Minimax regret	Hurwicz
Stock fund	20.00%			
Index fund			6.00%	6.00%
Bond index		4.00%		

dominant at some level of economic conditions. The Bond Fund is dominant for approximately the first quarter of the graph, while the Index Fund is dominant over approximately the second quarter of the graph. The Stock Fund then dominates roughly the second half of the graph.

Tradeoffs

After conducting the sensitivity analysis, Steve can see that there are several tradeoffs. Tradeoffs occur between each of Steve's decisions, specifically where the various funds cross each other on the sensitivity graph (e.g., at around 25% and 55%).

Sensitivity Analysis: Dominance, Trade-offs, and Risks

Graph 1 shows where the various funds cross each other (i.e., at around 25% and 55%).

Risk

Considering the difficulty in accurately predicting future economic conditions, we recommend that Steve consider the risk of each investment. Risk can be defined and quantified by range (i.e., high value–low value). The stock fund exhibits the largest risk (range = 28) followed by the index fund (range = 10), with the bond fund having the lowest risk (range = 2).

Conclusions and Action Items

With Steve being a very conservative investor, we recommend he invest in the bond fund where return will range between 4.00 and 6.00%. For Steve, the other two funds are simply too volatile; their return fluctuates too much and they are more risky.

Case Study: *Ibanez Produce*

BACKGROUND

Mike Ibanez had a big decision to make. He had inherited his family's vegetable business. Ibanez Produce grew, harvested, packaged, and sold produce. Mike was concerned because a large storm was approaching and he had to make a decision regarding his lettuce crop.

Ibanez Produce had around 10,000 acres in cultivation and lettuce made up around 25% of the total crop value. Mike's concern was that the storm may bring severe winds and dust. Rain was not a major concern, but high winds and blowing dust wreaked havoc on the lettuce crop. The high winds generally tear apart the lettuce and the dust renders the crop almost unsalvageable.

THE SOLUTION

From his Father's records, he had read that if he applied water combined with standard wax a residue would form on the lettuce and the crop could be saved. He knew that if the storm did come he could lose the whole crop if it was not protected. However, he didn't know how much the solution would cost him or how much he should pay.

THE OUTCOMES

Mike knew that the storm had about a 50/50 chance of hitting. He also knew that if the storm did not hit and he did protect his crops the residue left might cause problems during harvest. After

conversing with his Co-op Extension officer, he had surmised that the probability of the residue causing problems was around 30 percent. If this problem did occur, Mike would get only 80 percent of his normal crop.

Mike usually sold his lettuce with a $0.15 margin per pound. Normally the crop was around 800,000 pounds. If he did not protect his crop and the storm hit, he maybe could salvage 10 percent of the lettuce. However, if he did protect and the storm did hit, there was no guarantee that 100 percent of the crop would be saved.

In fact, from the information the Co-op Extension officer had provided there was around a 60 percent chance that he would lose part of his crop even if he did take protective measures and the storm hit. He surmised that three scenarios could occur in this case: a 90 percent salvage rate, a 75 percent salvage rate, and a 50 percent salvage rate. Mike thought these three scenarios had equal probability.

MIKE'S DECISION PROBLEM

Mike also knew that if he harvested right now he could make $0.05 margin per pound on the total crop of lettuce. Overall operating costs were about the same in any situation. Mike needs to know if he should protect his crop and a starting point on what he should pay. Help Mike with his dilemma.

DISCUSSION QUESTIONS

1. What is Mike's expected gross revenue if he harvests now? What is his gross expected revenue if he does nothing and

waits out the storm? What are the risks in choosing to harvest now or in waiting out the storm?

2. Is it a good idea for Mike to protect his crop? Why? What is the maximum that Mike should pay for the protection?

Optimal Information Area

Lexicon of Decision Analysis, at **http://faculty.fuqua.duke.edu/daweb/lexicon.htm**.

References

Bayes, T. "An Essay towards solving a problem in the doctrine of chances." *Phil. Trans. Royal Society*, vol. 53 (1763), pp. 370–418.

Bazerman, Max, and Margaret Neale. *Negotiating Rationally*. New York: Free Press, 1992.

French, Simon. *Decision Theory: An Introduction to the Mathematics of Rationality*. London: John Wiley & Sons, 1986.

Hogarth, Robin M. *Judgment and Choice*, 2nd ed. New York: John Wiley & Sons, 1987.

Howard, Ronald A., and James Matheson, (eds.) *The Principles and Applications of Decision Analysis* (2 volumes). Palo Alto, CA: Strategic Decisions Group, 1983.

Daniel Kahneman, Paul Slovic, and Amos Tversky. *Judgment under Uncertainty: Heuristics and Biases*. Cambridge: Cambridge University Press, 1982.

Keeney, Ralph. *Value-Focused Thinking: A Path to Creative Decision Making*. Cambridge, MA: Harvard University Press, 1992.

Lindley, Dennis V. *Making Decisions*, 2nd ed. New York: John Wiley & Sons, 1985. (This is a classic by a founder in the field. Professor Lindley explains difficult concepts well. The problems tend to be somewhat abstract.)

Miller, G. A. "The Magical Number Seven Plus or Minus Two: Some Limits on Our Capacity for Processing Information." *Psychological Review*, vol. 63 (1956), pp. 81–97.

Morgan, M. Granger, and Max Henrion. *Uncertainty: A Guide to Dealing with Uncertainty in Quantitative Risk and Policy Analysis*. Cambridge: Cambridge University Press.

von Neuman, J., and O. Morgenstern. *Theory of Games and Economic Behaviour*. Princeton, NJ: Princeton University Press, 1944.

Raiffa, Howard. *Decision Analysis*. Reading, MA: Addison-Wesley, 1968.

Problems

1. Mr. Merrill Lynch is planning on investing in stocks. He is considering three different types stocks, ABC, DEF, and XYZ to choose from under two possible states, good and bad. As a result of favorable stock market conditions, there is a 0.75 probability of good and 0.25 probability of bad state. The table below indicates the profits and losses of investing in the following three stocks under the given states—good and bad.

Stocks	Good (0.75)	Bad (0.25)
ABC	$75,000	$45,000
DEF	$90,000	−$30,000
XYZ	$35,000	$15,000

Using Excel, set up a spreadsheet to find the best decision using:

a. Maximax

b. Maximin

c. Equal likelihood

d. Expected value

2. Etsuko needs to decide between two choices stock investments—IBN and Microsopht. The return for each investment given two future economic conditions is shown in the following payoff table. Set up an Excel spreadsheet to determine what probability for each market condition would make her investment choice even between IBN and Microsopht?

Decision	Boom	Steady
IBN	$ 6,000	$ 1,500
Microsopht	$100,000	−$40,000

3. SellsLotsOfStuff.com, a small online retailer, is considering buying a firewall for its website. The cost of the firewall is $10,000. There is an 85percent chance of that the site will not be hacker-attacked during the life of the firewall, a 10 percent chance of a minor attack occurring resulting in $25,000 in damage, and a 5 percent chance of a major attack occurring resulting in $125,000 in damage. Construct an Excel spreadsheet to:

    a. Compute the expected cost for each decision and select the best one strictly on the basis of expected cost.

    b. Discuss the risks involved with basing the decision strictly on expected cost.

4. A company is planning to start a manufacturing unit. The success of the manufacturing unit depends on the ability of the company to obtain patent approval on a product. The company can invest to receive patents from the U.S. government. If the company is successful in its patent application, it can make $60,000. If it doesn't receive the patent, the company will make $5,000. Or the company can fund a caucus for election 2000; if it is accepted then the company can make $50,000, or else it loses $20,000. Or if the company goes for an awareness campaign, it can make $25,000, but if it is not successful, then the return will be only $10,000. Probability of success is 0.6 and of failure is 0.4. Construct an Excel spreadsheet to find the best decision using the following:

    a. Maximax

    b. Maximin

    c. Equal likelihood

    d. Expected value

    e. Create a sensitivity graph comparing the different alternatives as the probability of success changes.

5. John has to determine which stock he should invest in: stock A or stock B. The economic conditions, good and poor, will determine the profit and loss from his investment. Construct an Excel spreadsheet to compute the expected value for each decision and select the best one.

Decision	Good (0.6)	Poor (0.4)
Stock A	$12,000	−$3,000
Stock B	$ 3,500	$3,000

Using the spreadsheet find the best decision for the following:

    a. Maximax

    b. Maximin

    c. Equal likelihood

    d. Expected value

    e. What does the probability of good have to be to make the two decisions equally attractive with regard to expected value?

6. Etsuko, who is an HPU student, is wondering whether she should purchase HMSA health insurance or not for next year. Construct an Excel spreadsheet to compute the expected value to determine whether she should purchase HMSA or not. Is one option riskier than the other? Explain.

Decision	No Accident (0.99)	Accident (0.01)
Purchase HMSA	$416	$ 416
Do not purchase HMSA	$ 0	$50,000

7. A machine shop owner is attempting to decide whether to purchase a new drill press, a lathe, or a grinder. The return from each will be determined by whether the company succeeds in getting a government

military contract. The profit or loss from each purchase and the probabilities associated with each contract outcomes are shown in the following payoff table. Construct an Excel spreadsheet to:

a. Compute the expected value for each purchase and select the best one.

b. Decide if one purchase more risky than another. Explain.

Purchase	Contract (0.7)	No Contract (0.3)
Drill press	$40,000	−$ 8,000
Lathe	$20,000	$ 4,000
Grinder	$12,000	$10,000

8. A farmer needs to decide which crops to grow this year. According to his Farmer's Almanac, there is a 0.45 probability that the weather will be good this year and a 0.55 probability that it will be bad. The following table is given. Construct an Excel spreadsheet to:

Purchase	Good (0.45)	Bad (0.55)
Soy	$100,000	−$30,000
Corn	$ 80,000	−$10,000
Potatoes	$ 90,000	−$ 2,000

a. Determine which crop he should grow this year if he wants to maximize expected value.

b. Create a sensitivity graph comparing the different alternatives as the probability of good changes.

9. ABC can sell surfboards or body boards. The revenues of selling and producing surfboards or body boards depend on how the waves are during this season. If the waves, on average, are bigger than 5 feet, producing and selling surfboards will result in sales of $4,000,000, while producing and selling body boards will lead to sales of $1,500,000. If the waves are smaller than 5 feet, surfboards will result in sales of $1,000,000 and body boards will result in sales of $3,500,000. According to the latest forecast for the 3-month period, there is a 60 percent chance of getting waves bigger than 5 feet on average.

Create a payoff table in Excel and use it to find the following:

a. Maximax

b. Maximin

c. Equal likelihood

d. Expected value

e. Create a sensitivity graph comparing the different alternatives as the probability of success changes.

10. Rob's three brothers offer to buy his mint-condition Yugo. They each offer different payment plans. Each brother has an interesting situation that might make him completely default on the payment plan.

Ryan will buy the Yugo outright for $1,500 cash. There is a 0.20 probability that his cash is counterfeit and worthless.

Ronald will pay $1,000 outright in noncounterfeit money and pay $500 at the end of the year for the next 2 years. There is a 0.30 probability that Ronald will go bankrupt by the end of the year and never pay Rob any more than the original $1,000.

Ray will pay no money down but will pay $500 at the end of the year for 5 years. There is a 0.40 probability that Ray will flee the country to Mexico at the end of the third year.

Construct an Excel spreadsheet to analyze Rob's offers. On the basis of expected value what is the best choice for Rob? What is the risk associated with this choice?

11. A computer company is contemplating whether to buy a new server, router, or phone system. The return from each will be determined by whether the company gets picked for a contract. The probability that the company will get the contract is 70 percent, and the probability that the company

doesn't get the contract is 30 percent. Construct an Excel spreadsheet to determine the equipment that will give the best-expected returns.

Purchase	Contract (0.7)	No contract (0.3)
Server	$70,000	−$10,000
Router	$90,000	−$15,000
Phone system	$60,000	−$ 2,000

12. Kristine is helping her cousin Logan (5 years old) develop his business spirit. He can sell either lemonade or coffee at his corner stand. If it is a sunny day, Logan will sell 55 glasses of lemonade and 12 cups of coffee. If it is an overcast day, Logan will sell 10 glasses of lemonade and 12 cups of coffee. If it is a rainy day, Logan will sell 0 glasses of lemonade and 40 cups of coffee. Both of the beverages sell for $0.50. The weather forecast calls for 40 percent chance of rain, 40 percent chance of sun, and 20 percent chance of overcast.

   a. In Excel, develop a payoff table for the above situation.

   b. Using the spreadsheet, find the following:

      i. Maximax

      ii. Maximin

      iii. Equal likelihood

   c. Using the spreadsheet, create a sensitivity graph comparing the different alternatives as the probability of having a sunny day changes.

13. Ricardo and sons are planning to invest in advertising to sell three of their products. There are three different outcomes: A sells the most, B sells the most, or C sells the most. Two possible states exist, good and bad. The table below indicates the profits and losses of investing in the advertising of the three products under given states—good and bad. Construct an Excel spreadsheet to answer the following:

Product	Good (0.6)	Bad (0.4)
A	$5.0 million	$ 0 million
B	$2.5 million	$2.5 million
C	$7.5 million	−$2.5 million

   a. Determine which product they should invest in this year based on maximizing expected value.

   b. Create a sensitivity graph comparing the different alternatives as the probability of Good changes.

14. A new small manufacturing company, which produces toys, has to decide whether it want to distribute its product through a wholesale distributor, go directly to department stores, or open its own store. The table below shows the revenue results for each decision. Construct an Excel spreadsheet to answer the following:

Distribution network	Good economic conditions	Not-so-good economic conditions
Wholesale	$ 75.0 million	$ 60 million
Direct	$ 82.5 million	$ 12.5 million
Own store	$177.5 million	−$112.5 million

   a. What is the probability value of good economic conditions that will make distributing through a wholesaler or direct equal? What is the probability value to equate wholesaler and own store?

   b. Create a sensitivity graph comparing the different alternatives as the probability of good economic conditions changes.

15. Tech and A&M are in the fourth quarter of their annual football game. A&M has the ball, and it is third down and 10 yards to go on their own 30. A&M's offensive coordinator is trying to determine what play to call to get the necessary 10 yards. A screen pass has an 85 percent chance of being completed, and if completed, has a 20 percent chance of gaining 20 yards, a 30 percent chance of gaining 10 yards, and a 50 percent chance of gaining 5 yards. A slant pass has a 60 percent chance of being completed, and if completed has a 30 percent chance of gaining 20 yards, a 40 percent chance of gaining 12 yards, and a 30 percent chance of gaining 8 yards. A bomb has a 20 percent chance of being completed, and if completed has a 20 percent chance of gaining 40 yards, a 20 percent chance of gaining 50 yards, and a 60 percent chance of gaining 70 yards. A&M receives no yards if the pass is incomplete.

    a. Using TreePlan, create a decision tree for this problem, computing the expected yardage under each scenario.

    b. Which decision should A&M make if they want to maximize expected total yards?

    c. Which decision should they make if they want to maximize their chance for a first down (>10 yards)?

16. The profit level for a router manufacturer using three different plants 1, 2, and 3 and the demand level A, B, and C, is given by the following table ($000). Construct an Excel spreadsheet to answer the following:

	Demand		
Plant	**A**	**B**	**C**
1	200	350	600
2	250	350	540
3	300	375	490

    a. For the information in the table, what decision would be made by using the maximax criterion?

    b. For the information in the table, what decision would be made by using the maximin criterion?

    c. For the information in the table, what decision would be made using the minimum regret criterion?

    d. Using the information in the table and TreePlan, draw a decision tree for the problem. Be sure to carefully label the branches of the tree and provide the value at each node.

17. A couple has just purchased a second home to remodel into a bed and breakfast. The table below contains their expected profit ($000s) the first year, depending on how many rooms they choose to remodel and demand. Construct an Excel spreadsheet to answer the following:

	Demand		
Alternative	**Low (0.30)**	**Moderate (0.50)**	**Heavy (0.20)**
5 rooms	15	20	25
10 rooms	10	35	50
15 rooms	5	50	75

    a. For the information in the table, what decision would be made if the maximax criterion is used?

    b. For the information in the table, what decision would be made if the maximin criterion is used?

    c. For the information in the table, what decision would be made if the minimax regret criterion is used?

    d. For the information in the table, what decision would be made if the equal likelihood criterion is used?

    e. For the information in the table, what decision would be made if the Hurwicz criterion is used with alpha = 0.75?

    f. For the information in the table, what is the expected value of each alternative? What is the best decision?

g. Using the information in the table and TreePlan, draw a decision tree for the problem. Be sure to carefully label the branches of the tree and provide the value at each node.

18. Legal Services of Kinston is going to increase its capacity to provide free legal advice but must decide whether to do so by hiring another full-time attorney or by using part-time attorneys. The table below shows the expected costs of the two options for three possible demand levels.

	States of nature		
Alternative	Low demand	Medium demand	High demand
Hire full time	$300	$500	$ 700
Hire part time	$ 0	$350	$1,000
Probabilities	0.25	0.45	0.30

a. Using Excel, calculate the expected value of each alternative,
b. What should Legal Services do?

19. Chad Holmes has been thinking about starting his own independent gasoline station. Chad's problem is to decide how large his station should be. The annual returns will depend on both the size of the station and a number of marketing factors related to the oil industry and demand for gasoline. After a careful analysis, Chad developed the following table:

Size of first station	Good market ($)	Moderate market ($)	Poor market ($)
Small	55,000	25,000	10,000
Medium	85,000	35,000	−20,000
Large	150,000	35,000	−40,000
Very large	350,000	25,000	−160,000

a. Using Excel, determine the maximax decision.
b. Using Excel, determine the maximin decision.
c. Using Excel, determine the equally likely decision.

20. The following table displays the sales levels for different scenarios for a bakery. Construct an Excel spreadsheet to answer the following:

	Sales level			
	10 dozen	11 dozen	12 dozen	13 dozen
Inventory Level	Probability			
	0.10	0.20	0.40	0.30
10 dozen	$3,000	$3,000	$3,000	$3,000
11 dozen	$2,970	$3,300	$3,300	$3,300
12 dozen	$2,940	$3,270	$3,600	$3,600
13 dozen	$2,910	$3,240	$3,570	$3,900

a. For the data in the table, what is the expected value of sales level for each level of inventory (i.e., 10, 11, 12, and 13 dozen)?
b. For the data in the table, what decision would be made using the Hurwicz criterion (with alpha = 0.3)?
c. On the basis of expected value, what level of inventory would you tell the bakery to hold and why? How does this differ from your recommendation in part b?

21. A T-shirt salesperson at a Lynyrd Skynyrd concert tour created a table of conditional values for the various alternatives (stocking decision) and states of nature (size of crowd):

Decision alternatives	States of nature (demand)		
	Heavy	Average	Light
Larger stock	$24,000	$10,000	−$2,000
Average stock	$16,000	$ 8,000	$6,000
Smaller stock	$ 8,000	$ 6,000	$4,000

The probabilities associated with the states of nature are 0.35 for a heavy demand, 0.45 for an average demand, and 0.20 for a light demand.

   a. Using Excel, determine the alternative that provides the greatest expected value.
   b. Using Excel, compute the expected value of perfect information (EVPI).

22. The Dandy Don Specialty Co. is considering a new consumer product. Managers believe that there is a probability of 0.45 that the Jim Dandy Co. will come out with a competitive product. If Dandy Don adds an assembly line for the product and Jim Dandy Co. does not follow with a competitive product, Dandy Don's expected profit is $60,000; if Dandy Don adds an assembly line and Jim Dandy follows suit, Dandy Don still expects $12,000 profit. If Dandy Don builds a new plant addition and Jim Dandy does not produce a competitive product, Dandy Don expects a profit of $650,000; if Jim Dandy does compete for this market, Dandy Don expects a loss of $200,000.

   a. Using Excel, develop a payoff table for Dandy Don's decision problem.
   b. Using Excel, determine the expected value of each decision.
   c. Using Excel, compute the expected value of perfect information.

23. James Bernard, head of leasing at New Braunfels Inc., has to decide whether to build a new state-of-the-art processing facility. If the new facility works, the company could realize a profit of $200,000. If it fails, New Braunfels could lose $150,000. At this time, Reid estimates a 60 percent chance that the new process will fail. The other option is to build a pilot plant and then decide whether to build a company-wide facility. The pilot plant would cost $10,000 to build. James estimates a fifty-fifty chance that the pilot plant will work. If the pilot plant works, there is a 90 percent probability that the complete plant, if it is built, will also work. If the pilot plant does not work, there is only a 20 percent chance that the complete project (if it is constructed) will work. James faces a dilemma. Should he build the plant? Should he build the pilot project and then make a decision? Help James by analyzing this problem:

   a. Create a decision tree, using TreePlan.
   b. What recommendation, based on expected value, would you give James?

24. Daryll Miller, president of Seacresst Industries, is considering whether to build a manufacturing plant in the Ozarks. Her prospective revenues for the plant are summarized in the following table:

Alternatives	Favorable market	Unfavorable market
Build large plant	$400,000	$300,000
Build small plant	$ 80,000	$ 80,000
Don't build	$ 0	$ 0
Market probabilities	0.33	0.67

   a. Construct a decision tree using TreePlan.
   b. Determine the best strategy, using expected value.
   c. What is the expected value of perfect information (EVPI) and how would it help Daryll make a decision?

25. Jennifer Coggburn buys forms from two suppliers. Supplier A's overall nondefect rate is 90 percent (i.e., 90 percent of the time no forms are defective, whereas 10 percent of the time there are defects). Supplier B's overall nondefect rate is 85 percent (i.e., 85 percent of the time no forms are defective,

whereas 15 percent of the time there are defects). The quality of the forms, when forms are defective, from each of the suppliers is indicated in the following table:

Percent defective	Probability for supplier A	Probability for supplier B
1%	0.70	0.30
2%	0.15	0.45
3%	0.15	0.25

For example, if a batch of forms is defective, the probability that the batch is 1percent defective from supplier A is 0.70. Because Jennifer orders 10,000 forms per order, this would mean that there is a 0.7 probability of getting 100 defective forms out of the 10,000 forms if supplier A is used to fill the order. A defective form can be used for other purposes within Jennifer's own department, but it costs her $0.50 per form in internal handling charges to do so. Although the quality of supplier B is lower, it will sell an order of 10,000 forms for $37 less than supplier A.

a. Develop a decision tree, using TreePlan.
b. Which supplier should Jennifer use if she bases her choice on the expected value criterion? (*Hint:* Jennifer is looking for the least expensive solution.)

Chapter **Five**

Simulation Modeling

Learning Objectives

After completing this chapter, students will be able to:

1. Understand what basic simulation and spreadsheet simulation is.

2. Understand how simulation can affect and how it can benefit managers.

3. Develop random number intervals and use them to generate outcomes.

4. Explain the advantages and disadvantages of simulation.

5. Develop spreadsheet simulation models for a wide variety of business problems, such as profit/loss generation, queuing, and waiting lines.

6. Use a commercially available simulation package, such as @Risk.

Chapter Outline

Business Decision Modeling in Action: The Super Flush Simulation

Simulation at a Major American Football Stadium

A very interesting simulation took place in the summer of 1998 at the Baltimore Ravens' new football stadium in Northern Maryland. The simulation consisted of 600 football fans flushing the stadium's toilets.

Flushing Toilets? Simulation? Is This For Real?

Hundreds of Baltimore Raven fans requested passes to participate in a choreographed "Super Flush." The idea behind the test was to simulate half-time conditions in games when fans race for the restrooms. Although rigorous design and planning had gone into the plumbing systems for the stadium, and the system's designers had simulated peak usage conditions with a computer simulation model, the engineers staged the practice run to help detect any major overflows or underflows.

Emcee of the Super Flush

The Baltimore Ravens invited VIPs and even hired an emcee to preside over the simulated plumbing event. The flushes were conducted in waves, with groups of 300 people trying the toilets on the east side of the stadium first, followed by another test on the west side 40 minutes later.

Super Flush Results

It was concluded that the plumbing system at the stadium was ready to go. as everything went smoothly at the Super Flush. The question that needs to be asked with regard to the principles of simulation is: "Were there enough flushes and were those flushes randomly generated?" The author will leave the students of business to decide, but just think to yourself next time you are at the game: Have these restrooms passed the Super Flush simulation test?

Reference

" 'Super Flush' passes test," *USA Today*, July 16, 1998.

SIMULATION MODELING

This chapter focuses on a different business decision modeling technique than has been studied so far in the text. All the previous concepts and techniques presented do play a role in simulation. Some of the earlier topics presented solution approaches that were more or less analytical and were based on mathematical models. However, problems arise that cannot be fully examined by using only these analytical methods.

Background

Simulation modeling can be used to analyze problems in a different light. Simulation has been a technique used by scientists for many years. Much of the training done in the military or in the development of industrial age inventions is simulation. Modern day simulation is a technique that allows inputs to a model to vary and measures the outcomes of various model outputs. Computer simulation allows for numerous replications of inputs to develop a broad idea of what the output characteristics are.

Computer Spreadsheet Simulation

Simulation allows a problem solver to manipulate a process or system and observe how the process or system reacts to changes in the underlyingassumptions.

Why replicate a current process or system with an off-line or outside-of-real-life process or system? There are many processes in everyday life that we are interested in replicating. For example, all of society would benefit from the replication of certain surgical processes to hone surgeons' skills without the risk of actually cutting into a person, or military leaders might gain insight from replicating troop movements before an operation took place.

Simulators do exist, and they operate on the same principle as replication. We use simulators to train pilots and even surgeons. Simulations are used to predict weather characteristics. Simulation models of worldwide weather patterns exist for which much hope is expressed but which can't be utilized yet because of the inadequacies of the current generation of computers. However, with the advent of desktop computers and advanced software, much of the simulation effort has turned to computer spreadsheet models.

This text focuses on computer spreadsheet simulation. The chapter covers the concept of random number generation, use of spreadsheets in simulation modeling, and Monte Carlo simulation, and presents a tutorial on simulation model building and the use of the software package @Risk.

What Is Simulation? And Why Are We Using It?

Simulation is a powerful tool to help managers make better decisions.

Simulation is a powerful business decision modeling tool to help managers make better decisions. Many studies have revealed that simulation is one of the most often used tools in academia, business decision modeling, and the business world. Simulation is also in use in much of the real world around us.

It is used in the design process, for example. Automobiles, airplanes, ships, hair dryers, etc. can be designed on a computer, and then, using simulations, one can predict what the performance characteristics will be and how the product will really work and react under simulated real-life conditions.

Real-World Simulation Examples

We see the effect of simulation in the auto industry, where sedans tend to look alike, the jellybean look some say, because simulations show this shape saves the most fuel as a car moves through air. Today we see airplanes with unusual wing and tail configurations because simulations show advantages to these. It is much more efficient and effective to try given configurations out through simulation without actually building a prototype until one is confident of the design.

An especially talented group of experts over a period of years has developed a highly promising simulated model of the human heart. When in use, it will allow surgeons to simulate different operations to repair defects and predict the results. Artificial heart design should also make quantum leaps. A group of brilliant scientists is spending years of hard work in New Mexico trying to simulate the process of evolution. In the military, simulation is used to model combat strategies in exercises called *war games*.

SIMULATION AFFECTING MANAGERS

Simulation is widely used in the business world to model waiting lines, inventory, stock and commodity pricing, consumer behavior and marketing, and election results. You must look very hard to find a more universally applicable technique. Simulation has considerable utility in modeling both highly complex phenomena and phenomena that are less complex.

Types of Data

This chapter will discuss two types of data important to simulation models: categorical and numerical. Categorical data is sometimes referred to as *qualitative* data whereas; numerical data is referred to as *quantitative*. The basic distinction between the two is whether any arithmetic will be done on the data. It makes sense to do arithmetic on numerical data. Although we are interested in categorical data, this chapter focuses on the analysis of numerical data from simulation models.

Numerical Data—Discrete versus Continuous

Discrete data arise from observations that can take only certain numerical values, usually counts such as number of quarterly earnings reports submitted or the number of machines on an assembly line. Continuous data are numerical data that can theoretically be measured in infinitely small units. For example, although profit and loss is usually analyzed to two decimal places, it is considered continuous since profit or loss can be any positive or negative number. The interval measurement scale is intended for continuous data. Sometimes continuous data are given discrete values at certain thresholds; for example, growth rate of quarterly gross domestic product (GDP) is a discrete value, but GDP itself is a continuous quantity; in these situations it is reasonable to treat discrete values as continuous. Remember that information is lost when continuous data are recorded only in ranges, and the statistical analysis of continuous data is more powerful than that of categorical data.

Simulation and the Link to Earlier Chapters

In becoming more effective and efficient problem solvers, managers must remember what was set forth in the earlier chapters of the text. The concepts of central tendency, dispersion, probability theory, decision structures and criteria, and spreadsheet modeling will all be incorporated in simulation modeling.

Simulation, Spreadsheet Modeling, and Model Verification and Validity

Chapters 2 and 4 spoke about the concept of modeling, especially the concept of spreadsheet modeling. The major payoff of modeling and building decision structures such as decision trees and influence diagrams is the sensitivity analysis that results. Simulation modeling leads to the same end. Asking "what if" questions and interpreting the outcome after your model has run is one of the main strengths of simulation. It is also very important to make sure your model can be verified and that it is valid.

Simulation Verification

By verification we mean making sure the computer or spreadsheet program used in the model is not flawed. This requires checking and rechecking the work, perhaps writing it in different languages to see if similar results occur and perhaps asking independent experts to review the work.

Model Validity

A simulation is valid when it models what it is supposed to model. After working long hours on a simulation and viewing results that are aesthetically pleasing, it is easy to be seduced into believing the results while losing sight of the fact that the model misses the point.

A few years ago, an American city was just about to invest nearly 2 billion dollars on a limited rapid transit system that simulations indicated would be cost-effective. An astute member

Business Decision Modeling Throughout the Ages

Monte Carlo Simulation

WHAT IS MONTE CARLO SIMULATION?

The term *Monte Carlo* refers to a group of methods in which physical or mathematical problems are simulated by using randomly generated numbers. Monte Carlo methods have been used for centuries, but only in the past several decades has the technique gained the status of a full-fledged numerical method capable of addressing the most complex applications.

Some of the application of Monte Carlo Simulation statistical technique can be found in nuclear reactor design, radiation cancer therapy, econometrics, stock index forecasting, and oil well exploration. As is evident, the range of application varies enormously.

BACKGROUND OF MONTE CARLO TERMINOLOGY

The term Monte Carlo was not coined until 1944 during the development of the atomic bomb under the Manhattan Project. The work involved a direct simulation of the probabilistic problems concerned with random neutron diffusion in fissile material.

The term Monte Carlo was used because of the simulations technique's similarity to the statistical simulation to a game of chance and also because the capital of Monaco, at that time, was the center for gambling and similar pursuits.

USE OF MONTE CARLO SIMULATION METHOD

In the early 1970s, the newly developing theory of computational complexity provided a more precise and persuasive rationale for employing the Monte Carlo method. The theory identified a class of problems for which the time to evaluate the exact solution to a problem within the class grew at an exponential rate, and the results of several studies conducted by mathematicians and scientists make it evident that the Monte Carlo method has lived up to its potential by being able to solve complex problems.

OPTIMAL INFORMATION AREA

Sabri Pllana's History of Monte Carlo Method Web site at http://www.geocities.com/CollegePark/Quad/2435/.

Contingency Analysis Monte Carlo Simulation Glossary Web site at http://www.contingencyanalysis.com/glossarymontecarlosimulation.htm.

Computational Science Education Project Introduction to Monte Carlo Methods Web site at http://csep1.phy.ornl.gov/mc/node1.html.

---

of the city council insisted on talking to other cities that had experience with such systems and discovered many systems to be less than cost–effective, and the plans were scrapped.

In building and validating a simulation model it is important to talk to workers closest to the action, to contrast and compare other models and the experience of other experts, utilize whatever data is available to identify trends for what if analysis, and keep an open mind.

RANDOM NUMBER GENERATION

Random number generation is an integral step in the simulation process.

Before any computer spreadsheet models are considered, the concept of random number generation must be developed. Random number generation is an integral step in the simulation process. As a preliminary step we need to gain some understanding of random numbers and how to assign them to a probability distribution before a simulation model can be built.

Random Number Example

Suppose you are asked to fill 100 blanks with a random sequence of integers. Figure 5.1 displays 100 blanks filled in with 100 random numbers from 0 to 1.

Random Number Generation Techniques

Generating random numbers is not a trivial exercise, but is essential to creating and running simulation models.

Could you free-associate and produce a stream of random numbers? Could anybody? You are invited to try to do this and to find objective tests to see if you succeed. The fact is that humans are not good at this. We tend to favor some numbers at the expense of others and most people fail to adequately represent successions of the same number.

Think of techniques you might use to fill in the blanks in a manner that would produce a true random set of numbers. What we mean by *random* is that each of the 10 integers is equally

FIGURE 5.1
Random Number
Example

0.9942	0.0496	0.3057	0.6575	0.9925	0.2069	0.9823	0.9806	0.6048	0.4372
0.8404	0.7913	0.5677	0.8781	0.8946	0.8086	0.8491	0.7477	0.1354	0.3631
0.5802	0.5688	0.4429	0.2226	0.4355	0.5429	0.5921	0.8076	0.6965	0.9331
0.0990	0.9123	0.5915	0.2238	0.2096	0.6906	0.8170	0.2597	0.8688	0.1824
0.9465	0.0369	0.0687	0.3290	0.1670	0.6268	0.6186	0.2945	0.7551	0.6961
0.1406	0.7184	0.7062	0.0430	0.4858	0.0296	0.2596	0.7634	0.0849	0.6920
0.7281	0.6495	0.7857	0.8361	0.1568	0.3220	0.7856	0.2879	0.4204	0.8502
0.5849	0.8281	0.1902	0.6128	0.0653	0.1296	0.5037	0.2226	0.5428	0.8857
0.9117	0.2474	0.1067	0.4460	0.4225	0.0012	0.1263	0.8703	0.4066	0.1990
0.6702	0.2026	0.7418	0.4543	0.0579	0.7455	0.5190	0.8237	0.6961	0.3235

likely to appear on each of the blanks. What occurs before or after a given blank must have no bearing on that blank, and the method of choice must make it equally likely that any of the 10 possible integers appear.

Developing Random Number Generation Techniques

Developing random number generators is not a trivial exercise. As you read these words, some of the world's greatest mathematicians are trying to find better ways to generate random numbers. (One promising technique is to measure the radiation emanating from a "lava lamp" type device.)

Although random number generation from lava lamps is interesting, for our purposes, random numbers can be found in tables or by using calculators or computer spreadsheets that have algorithms built into them that produce number streams sufficiently random for all but the most sophisticated research.

Generating Random Numbers by Spreadsheets

Random numbers can be generated via a spreadsheet program such as Excel or with a spreadsheet add-in such as @Risk.

The "=rand()" function in Excel generates random numbers.

At this point you should make sure you can generate such numbers with a spreadsheet. This section explains how it is done.

To generate random numbers in an Excel spreadsheet, go to a cell and type

$$=rand( )$$

in the formula bar for the cell and move to another cell. If you want a column or row of random numbers, highlight the cell with a random number, place the crosshair of the cursor on the lower right corner of that cell, and drag the cursor across the cells you want to show random numbers. A detailed section on how to generate random numbers in an Excel spreadsheet is provided later in this chapter.

SIMULATION AND CURRENCY EXCHANGE RATES

Imagine you are planning to start selling some of your products abroad in the near future. You are interested in exchanging your U.S. dollars for the currency of the country you are trading with (e.g., country X). You could take a look on the Internet and find what the current exchange rate is and base your calculations for U.S. dollar conversion on that rate. However, if you exchange your dollars now for the other currency, the rate of exchange may be different by the time you finish the deal. If the currency value (X/$) appreciates you will have lost out on some extra money, but if the currency value (X/$) depreciates you will have protected yourself against a drop in how much your dollar could buy. No one knows exactly what the future rate will be but history gives some clue. In all, you would like to know on average what your outcome would be. Consider Table 5.1 as an example.

Table 5.1 describes what can happen to the currency value (column 1), the historical frequency over the last 200 days of the event (second column), and finally the historical frequencies converted to a probability distribution (column 3).

Event (X/$)	Historical frequency over last 200 days (days)	Probability of occurrence
Currency value stays neutral	24	24/200 = 0.12
Currency value of $ appreciates (i.e., X/$ rate rises)	90	90/200 = 0.45
Currency value of $ depreciates (i.e., X/$ rate falls)	86	86/200 = 0.43

Cumulative Probability Distributions and Random Number Intervals

For the sake of simplicity, let's define the outcomes of the events as follows: You get even money for neutral currency value (i.e., you get 1X for every $1), you get 1.5X for every $1 for appreciating currency value, and you get 0.75X for every $1 for depreciating currency value.

Table 5.2 displays these outcomes as well as the probability of occurrence, the cumulative probability distribution for each event, and the interval of random numbers assigned to each event. The *expected* outcome (i.e., currency valuation) can be computed as follows (*Note:* Remember the expected value calculations from Chapter 3):

$$E(\text{currency valuation}) = (0.12)(1) + (0.45)(1.5) + (0.43)(0.75) = 1.1175$$

Therefore, in the long run, one could expect to have currency valuation of around 1.1175X/$1, or some currency appreciation.

Generating Random Numbers and Simulating Currency Values

Random numbers may be generated for simulation problems in different ways. A table of random digits could be used or the spin of a numbered wheel. We will use the RAND function in Excel to generate the random numbers for this example and to simulate the currency values.

Excel Spreadsheet Simulation of Currency Value Example

Figure 5.2 contains an Excel spreadsheet program that simulates the currency value situation for 10 trials. Once operational, numerous trials with associated results can be repeated at nearly the speed of light by *refreshing* the random numbers with the F9 key.

Refreshing means to replace each random number in the simulation with a new random number. You are urged to study the codes for this spreadsheet and modify and extend them to try other strategies. The code for this program is illustrated in Figure 5.3. To modify an Excel program to show the codes click Tools, Options, and View then check the Formulas box and click OK.

It should be noted that the average currency valuation of 0.95X to $1 in this 10-trial simulation differs from the *expected* currency valuation, 1.1175X to $1, which was computed earlier. If this simulation were repeated hundreds of thousands of times, it is much more likely that the *simulated* currency valuation would be very close to the *expected* currency valuation.

Figure 5.3 contains the spreadsheet formulas for the currency valuation example. Cumulative probabilities are calculated via Excel formulas in column D to avoid mathematical errors

Event X/$	Outcome	Probability of occurrence	Cumulative probability	Lower range of random numbers
Currency value neutral	1X to $1	24/200 = 0.12	0.12	0.00
Currency value appreciation	1.5X to $1	90/200 = 0.45	0.57	0.12
Currency value depreciation	0.75X to $1	86/200 = 0.43	1.00	0.57

FIGURE 5.2
Excel Spreadsheet for Currency Valuation Example

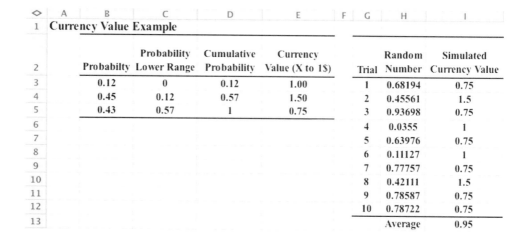

	Probabilty	Probability Lower Range	Cumulative Probability	Currency Value (X to 1$)	Trial	Random Number	Simulated Currency Value
	0.12	0	0.12	1.00	1	0.68194	0.75
	0.45	0.12	0.57	1.50	2	0.45561	1.5
	0.43	0.57	1	0.75	3	0.93698	0.75
					4	0.0355	1
					5	0.63976	0.75
					6	0.11127	1
					7	0.77757	0.75
					8	0.42111	1.5
					9	0.78587	0.75
					10	0.78722	0.75
						Average	0.95

Figure 5.3 **Excel Spreadsheet Formulas for Currency Valuation Example**

A	B	C	D	E	F	G	H	I
Currency Value Example								
	Probabilty	Probability Lower Range	Cumulative Probability	Currency Value (X to 1$)		Trial	Random Number	Simulated Currency Value
	0.12	0	=B3	1		1	=RAND()	=VLOOKUP(H3,$C$3:$E$5,3,TRUE)
	0.45	=D3	=D3+B4	1.5		2	=RAND()	=VLOOKUP(H4,$C$3:$E$5,3,TRUE)
	0.43	=D4	=D4+B5	0.75		3	=RAND()	=VLOOKUP(H5,$C$3:$E$5,3,TRUE)
						4	=RAND()	=VLOOKUP(H6,$C$3:$E$5,3,TRUE)
						5	=RAND()	=VLOOKUP(H7,$C$3:$E$5,3,TRUE)
						6	=RAND()	=VLOOKUP(H8,$C$3:$E$5,3,TRUE)
						7	=RAND()	=VLOOKUP(H9,$C$3:$E$5,3,TRUE)
						8	=RAND()	=VLOOKUP(H10,$C$3:$E$5,3,TRUE)
						9	=RAND()	=VLOOKUP(H11,$C$3:$E$5,3,TRUE)
						10	=RAND()	=VLOOKUP(H12,$C$3:$E$5,3,TRUE)
							Average	=AVERAGE(I3:I12)

that may occur through hand calculations. The = VLOOKUP function is used in column I to "look up" the random numbers generated in column H. Cell I13 calculates the average currency value (X to $1) for the 10 trials by averaging cells I3 through I12. This is the number that is compared to the *expected* currency valuation calculation.

SIMULATION OF A QUEUING SYSTEM

Waiting in a line or a queue is one of the most common occurrences in everyday life. Not only do people spend time waiting in line or in queue but so do products in a manufacturing facility, so do planes waiting for takeoff, and so on. As students of business we know that time is a valuable resource and that the reduction of waiting time or time in the queue is a very important topic for discussion. This section will study what is called the single-server waiting line system.

Single Server Waiting Line System

The single-server waiting line system is the simplest form of queuing system. It will be used to illustrate the fundamentals of a queuing system. As a practical example of this type of queuing system, think of the line at the fast-food drive-through or the line at the cashier at a smaller convenience mart.

The most important factors to consider in analyzing a queuing system are the following:

1. Where the customers come from, or what is referred to as the *calling population*.
2. The order in which the customers are served, or the *queue discipline*.
3. How often customers arrive, or the *arrival rate*.
4. How fast the customers are served, or the *service time*.

Each of these items will be discussed next.

Where Customers Come from—The Calling Population

The calling population is the source of the customers to the marketplace. Many queuing systems have an assumed infinite calling population. In other words, there exist such a large number of possible customers in the area where the queue is located that the number of potential customers is assumed to be infinite. However, there do exist queuing systems that have finite calling populations. An example is the repair facility for a distribution and logistics company that has 30 trucks in service at any one time. The finite calling population then is 30, the number of trucks in service at that point.

The Order in which Customers Are Served—The Queuing Discipline

The queue discipline refers to the order in which customers are served. For many waiting lines this is as simple as first-come, first-served. Think of the line at the convenience store cashier. The first person in line is the first to be served. At times the queue discipline may be random. For example a machine operator may reach into a full box of parts and select one completely at random. There are numerous queuing disciplines that exist, but the most frequent in waiting line examples is first-come, first-served. For this reason the first-come, first-served discipline will be employed in this chapter.

How Often Customers Arrive at the Queue—The Arrival Rate

The specific rate at which the customers arrive at the service facility during a specified time period is called the arrival rate. Arrival rates can be estimated empirically by watching a queue or can be calculated as the average of data over time.

For example, if 200 customers are served in 10 hours at a fast-food drive-through window, then it could be said that the arrival rate averages 20 customers per hour. This rate is an average, and in actuality no customers could arrive the first 30 minutes and then 200 customers could arrive in the second 30 minutes. It is also assumed that these arrivals are independent of each other and vary randomly over time.

It is also commonly assumed that the arrivals at a service facility conform to some probability distribution, namely the Poisson distribution. Although, the Poisson distribution has been determined as the most likely distribution for modeling arrivals, any distribution that a business decision modeler deems necessary can be used.

How Fast Customers Are Served—The Service Time

The specific rate at which customers can be served during a specified time period is referred to as the service rate. The service rate is similar to the arrival rate in that it is a random variable. For example, at a certain fast-food drive-through, 60 customers can be served in an hour. Standard nomenclature in the queuing world is to refer to arrivals in terms of a rate but to refer to service in terms of time.

It is also assumed that the service time can be defined by a probability distribution. Service times are most commonly represented by the exponential distribution. However, as before, business decision modelers can use whatever distribution they deem necessary.

LUNCH WAGON SIMULATION EXAMPLE: ARRIVALS AND PROFIT DETERMINATION

For a more practically oriented problem, let's consider a simple lunch wagon where we are interested in the profit derived from customer arrival. This is not exactly a single-server queuing problem, but it sets the scene for such a problem a little later in this section.

During lunch hour potential customers arrive at a rate per minute determined by a uniform distribution, with a maximum of four customers in any given minute. (If more than four per minute show up they go somewhere else out of frustration.) For this example, we are interested only in the profit determination from the given arrival information. It is assumed that there are no congestion problems, service deterioration, or balking as more folks wait in line.

Using the scheme we have learned, we can use random numbers to simulate arrivals any given minute by utilizing Table 5.3. Although the method presented in Table 5.3 works, for this example we will simplify the spreadsheet by using a nested IF statement (see Table 5.4, cell C4). This bypasses the need to input the entire set of information from Table 5.3.

Customer Spending Habits

The amount of money spent by customers is known to be normally distributed with a mean of $6.30 and a standard deviation of $1.56. How could these numbers be determined from

TABLE 5.3
Lunch Wagon Arrival Distribution

Event—Number of customers arriving	Probability of arrival	Cumulative probability	Lower range of random numbers
0	0.20	0.20	0.0
1	0.20	0.40	0.2
2	0.20	0.60	0.4
3	0.20	0.80	0.6
4	0.20	1.00	0.8

TABLE 5.4
Excel Formulas for Lunch Wagon Simulation

Cell	Formulas	Action
B4 (hidden cell)	=rand()	Copy to cells B5:B13
C4	=IF(B4 < 0.2,0,IF(AND(B4 >= 0.2,B4 < 0.4),1, IF(AND(B4 >= 0.4,B4 < 0.6),2,IF(AND(B4 >= 0.6,B4 < 0.8),3,4))))	Copy to cells C5:C13
D4	=IF(C4 >= 1,NORMINV(RAND(),6.3,1.56),0)	Copy to cells D5:D13
E4	=IF(C4 >= 2,NORMINV(RAND(),6.3,1.56),0)	Copy to cells E5:E13
F4	=IF(C4 >= 3,NORMINV(RAND(),6.3,1.56),0)	Copy to cells F5:F13
G4	=IF(C4 >= 4,NORMINV(RAND(),6.3,1.56),0)	Copy to cells G5:G13
H4	=SUM(D4:G4)	Copy to cells H5:H13
H14	=SUM(H4:H13)	-----

cash register records? We want to simulate the cash flow at this lunch wagon over a period of time—say 10 minutes, to keep it simple.

Origination of Probability Distributions

The probability distribution determining the amount spent on a given order is formula driven, in this case the normal probability distribution with a particular mean and standard deviation.

Actually, we will use its *inverse* to determine how much is spent by a particular customer. A spreadsheet program like Excel makes this easy to accomplish. The reason we must use the inverse normal distribution is because the usual normal distribution pairs dollars spent by the customer (x, or independent variable) with probabilities ($P(x)$, or dependent variable) in that order.

We will reverse this order and use random numbers to identify the probability of a particular expenditure associated with a given order and use the inverse function to determine, as output, the dollar amount of the order. Examine the format given in Table 5.4 for this simulation. Table 5.4 displays the Excel formulas that create the simulation numbers in Figure 5.4.

Random Number and Normal Probability Generation

You can fill in the second column by using a stream of random numbers and the table above. The dollar amount of each order can be determined by using a different random number for each appropriate cell and the inverse normal distribution with a mean of $6.30 and a standard

FIGURE 5.4
Lunch Wagon Example
Excel Spreadsheet

◇	A	C	D	E	F	G	H
1							
2							
3	Minute	Arrivals	First Order $	Second Order $	Third Order $	Fourth Order $	Total $
4	1	2	$6.94	$6.31	$0.00	$0.00	$13.25
5	2	0	$0.00	$0.00	$0.00	$0.00	$0.00
6	3	4	$6.07	$4.46	$4.25	$6.36	$21.15
7	4	3	$6.50	$3.61	$8.09	$0.00	$18.20
8	5	0	$0.00	$0.00	$0.00	$0.00	$0.00
9	6	1	$5.91	$0.00	$0.00	$0.00	$5.91
10	7	2	$4.38	$5.03	$0.00	$0.00	$9.41
11	8	4	$4.85	$5.96	$6.99	$8.21	$26.00
12	9	1	$5.54	$0.00	$0.00	$0.00	$5.54
13	10	0	$0.00	$0.00	$0.00	$0.00	$0.00
14							$99.47

deviation of $1.56. Of course, if the number of arrivals is less than four, some number of orders will not exist and one or more cells on the right should remain blank.

Computing Relevant Simulation Statistics and Distributions

After completing the simulation you can use the last column to find relevant statistics like the mean and standard deviation and the maximum and minimum. Your accuracy will improve if you do the simulation more than 10 times. Using an Excel spreadsheet, you can quickly do this for 10,000 or more minutes.

Lunch Wagon Waiting Line Simulation

From Figure 5.4 it appears that the lunch wagon is generating a sufficient amount of revenues. However, the lunch wagon has heard some complaints regarding waiting times. The simulation run earlier gave an idea about revenue generation given that all groups of customers could be served. This is great information for the lunch wagon staff, but it does not assist them in getting a handle on waiting times during lunchtime. In situations where customer arrivals and service times are considered events that occur at discrete points in time, the simulation model that should be employed is called a *discrete-event simulation model*. This type of problem is considered a classical single server–queuing, or waiting line, problem.

Interarrival Times

The lunch wagon knows how arrivals and service times are distributed. In a waiting line simulation model, arrival times are determined by randomly generating the time between two successive arrivals. This is referred to as the *interarrival time*. The lunch Wagon knows that customer group interarrival times are uniformly distributed between 0 and 3 minutes. As was stated in the previous simulation model, the lunch wagon can service a group of customers of one to four equally well, but groups of five or more balk and go to another establishment. So interarrival times are for groups of customers instead of just one customer.

If we allow r to denote a random number between 0 and 1, an interarrival time for two successive customer groups can be simulated by using the formula:

$$\text{Interarrival time} = a + r(b - a)$$

where a is the minimum interarrival time and b is the maximum interarrival time. For the lunch wagon, the minimum interarrival time is $a = 0$ minutes and the maximum interarrival time is $b = 3$ minutes. In turn, the formula for interarrival time is

$$\text{Interarrival time} = 0 + r(3 - 0) = 3r$$

Customer group interarrival times can be calculated as:

Customer group	Random number r	Interarrival time, minutes	Arrival time, minutes, from initial start time = 0
1	0.5364	1.6092	1.6092
2	0.3562	1.0686	2.6778
3	0.1987	0.5961	3.2739

Customer Service Times

The lunch wagon also knows what customer service times are. Customer service time is the time it takes for the lunch wagon staff to take a group's order, calculate the final bill, collect the group's payment, and send them to the pick-up station (i.e., the back of the wagon). The lunch wagon estimates that service times are normally distributed with a mean of 1 minute and a standard deviation of 0.1 minute.

Overall the lunch wagon waiting line simulation proceeds as follows:

1. An interarrival time for a new customer group is created.

2. That interarrival time is then added to the arrival time of the preceding customer group to determine the new customer group's arrival time.

3. The new customer group's arrival time is compared to the completion time of the preceding customer to determine whether the lunch wagon is idle or busy.

4. If the new customer group's arrival time is greater than the completion time of the preceding customer, the lunch wagon is done taking the preceding customer group's order and is idle and the new customer group can be waited on immediately.

5. The service start time for the new customer group is then calculated as the group's arrival time.

6. If the arrival time of the new customer group is not greater than the completion time of the preceding customer group, then the new customer group must wait until the preceding customer group is finished. In this case the lunch wagon is busy.

7. The service start time for the new customer group is equal to the completion time of the preceding customer group.

8. A customer group's completion time is the service start time plus the service time itself.

9. A customer group's total time in the system is the difference between the completion time and the group's arrival time.

On an Excel spreadsheet, the lunch wagon operations are simulated for 500 customer groups. The worksheet treats the first 100 customer groups as the start-up period and the summary statistics are calculated for the 400 remaining customer groups. Figure 5.5a displays the spreadsheet for the lunch wagon waiting line simulation.

The summary statistics show that 164 out of 400 lunch wagon customers had to wait. Thus, there is a 164/400 = 41% probability that a customer will have to wait for service. This appears to be a large number of people and a high probability of waiting at the lunch wagon. However, before one concludes that the lunch wagon's process is out of control, the average wait time and maximum wait time should be examined.

The average wait time from the summary statistics area is 0.2976 minutes, or about 18 seconds. The maximum wait time is approximately 3.3 minutes. From these waiting times, it does not appear that the lunch wagon's process is drastically out of control. In fact, think to yourself how you would feel if on average you waited 18 seconds at a fast-food restaurant on average and the longest you ever waited was about 3.3 minutes. In addition, it appears at least 90 percent of customer groups are being served in 1 minute or less. So the line must move

Figure 5.5a   Lunch Wagon Waiting Line Spreadsheet Model

◇	A	B	C	D	E	F	G	H	I	J
1	Lunch Wagon Waiting Simulation									
2										
3	Interarrival Times (Uniform Distribution)									
4	Lower Value	0								
5	Upper Value	3								
6										
7	Service Times (Normal Distribution)									
8	Mean	1								
9	Standard Deviation	0.1								
10										
11			Waiting Line Model							
12										
13		Customer Group	Interarrival Time	Arrival Time	Service Start Time	Wait Time	Service Time	Completion Time	Time in System	Idle Time
14		1	1.8202	1.8202	1.8202	0.0000	0.9172	2.7374	0.9172	0.0000
15		2	2.2927	4.1129	4.1129	0.0000	1.0817	5.1946	1.0817	1.3755
16		3	0.4089	4.5218	5.1946	0.6728	0.9739	6.1685	1.6467	0.0000
17		4	0.9293	5.4511	6.1685	0.7175	1.0763	7.2448	1.7937	0.0000
18		5	2.0662	7.5173	7.5173	0.0000	1.0757	8.5929	1.0757	0.2725
513		500	2.0380	766.1888	766.1888	0.0000	1.0382	767.2270	1.0382	0.3428
514										
515										
516				Summary Statistics						
517				Number that Have a Wait		164				
518				Probability of Waiting		0.4100				
519				Average Wait Time		0.2976				
520				Maximum Wait Time		3.3078				
521				% of Time Lunch Wagon Busy		0.7199				
522				Number Waiting > 1 Minute		38				
523				Probability of Waiting >1 Minute		0.0950				
524				Average # in Line		0.1936				

Figure 5.5b **Lunch Wagon Waiting Line Spreadsheet Model Formulas**

	A	B	C	D	E	F	G	H	I	J
1	Lunch Wagon Waiting Simulation									
2										
3	Interarrival Times (Uniform Distribution)									
4	Lower Value	0								
5	Upper Value	3								
6										
7	Service Times (Normal Distribution)									
8	Mean	1								
9	Standard Deviation	0.1								
10										
11		Waiting Line Model								
12										
13	Customer Group	Interarrival Time		Arrival Time	Service Start Time	Wait Time	Service Time	Completion Time	Time in System	Idle Time
14	1	=$B$4+RAND()*($B$5-$B$4)		=0+C14	=D14	=E14-D14	=ABS(NORMINV(RAND(),$B$8,$B$9))	=E14+G14	=H14-D14	=0
15	=B14+1	=$B$4+RAND()*($B$5-$B$4)		=D14+C15	=IF(D15>H14,D15,H14)	=E15-D15	=ABS(NORMINV(RAND(),$B$8,$B$9))	=E15+G15	=H15-D15	=E15-H14
16	=B15+1	=$B$4+RAND()*($B$5-$B$4)		=D15+C16	=IF(D16>H15,D16,H15)	=E16-D16	=ABS(NORMINV(RAND(),$B$8,$B$9))	=E16+G16	=H16-D16	=E16-H15
17	=B16+1	=$B$4+RAND()*($B$5-$B$4)		=D16+C17	=IF(D17>H16,D17,H16)	=E17-D17	=ABS(NORMINV(RAND(),$B$8,$B$9))	=E17+G17	=H17-D17	=E17-H16
18	=B17+1	=$B$4+RAND()*($B$5-$B$4)		=D17+C18	=IF(D18>H17,D18,H17)	=E18-D18	=ABS(NORMINV(RAND(),$B$8,$B$9))	=E18+G18	=H18-D18	=E18-H17
513	=B512+1	=$B$4+RAND()*($B$5-$B$4)		=D512+C51	=IF(D513>H512,D513,H512)	=E513-D513	=ABS(NORMINV(RAND(),$B$8,$B$9))	=E513+G513	=H513-D513	=E513-H512
514										
515										
516		Summary Statistics								
517		Number that Have a Wait				=COUNTIF(F114:F513,">0")				
518		Probability of Waiting				=F517/COUNT(F114:F513)				
519		Average Wait Time				=AVERAGE(F114:F513)				
520		Maximum Wait Time				=MAX(F114:F513)				
521		% of Time Lunch Wagon Busy				=1-(SUM(J114:J513)/H513)				
522		Number Waiting > 1 Minute				=COUNTIF(F114:F513,">1")				
523		Probability of Waiting >1 Minute				=F522/COUNT(F114:F513)				
524		Average # in Line				=SUM(F114:F513)/(H513-H113)				
525										

quickly even when it is full. Figure 5.5b displays the formulas for the Excel spreadsheet in Figure 5.5a.

Simulation's Real Payoff—The Sensitivity/What if Analysis

Simulation allows managers to take a look at complex processes or events and analyze them without actually building the product or waiting for theprocess to complete itself.

The real payoff from a simulation of this type comes when we start to ask what if questions. For example, because of anticipated changes in the economy or the demographics of where we have our lunch wagon parked, the uniform distribution for anticipated arrivals of customers might change.

Maybe we are considering investing in an advertising campaign. For the same or different reasons we may anticipate the mean and standard deviation of the distribution determining the amount to be spent on each order will change also. By modifying the distributions appropriately, we can anticipate what the difference will be in our conclusions. For a lunch wagon, we might want to compare different estimates for different places we can park the wagon about the city. It is important to note that asking what if questions often maximizes the usefulness of simulation.

@RISK TUTORIAL

Running @Risk in Excel

This section will detail how to get @Risk up and running in Excel after @Risk is installed on your computer.

1. Click on the Start menu in Windows.

FIGURE 5.6
**@Risk Program File
Menu**

2. Click on Program Files and find the Program Folder for Palisade Decision Tools and click on the @Risk application. The application menu should read something like "@Risk for Excel (32 bit)" (see Figure 5.6)

After @Risk has been loaded, Excel will automatically be loaded and the user may begin using @Risk to develop a simulation model.

What @Risk Will Do for the Modeler

@Risk is an add-in for Excel that runs simulation models. It is the responsibility of the modeler/ user to construct a simulation model in Excel and to instruct @Risk what functions to perform. @Risk performs two main functions:

1. Allows users to input stochastic variables or uncertainty into their models.
2. Allows users to keep track of and analyze models that are linked to these input variables.

User Responsibilities

Once the modeler/user has built the simulation model, three main decisions areas must be made regarding:

- Inputs
- Outputs
- Settings

These areas *must* be covered and decisions made regarding their makeup in order to use @Risk and have it produce simulation data for analysis. Specifically, these main areas and decisions are:

1. Identify input variables that contain uncertainty—i.e., identify the stochastic variables in the model.
2. Identify the output variables of interest—i.e., identify what outputs from your model you wish to monitor (e.g., expected profits, average time in the queue, expected costs, NPV)
3. Inform @Risk of the following simulation **settings**:
   a. The type of simulation to run—Monte Carlo.
   b. How many iterations to run—e.g., 100,000.

Getting Started

@RISK is an add-in for spreadsheets such as Microsoft Excel that performs risk analysis. Risk analysis is any method, quantitative or qualitative, for assessing the impacts of risk on decision situations. @RISK uses Monte Carlo simulation to perform risk analysis.

Figure 5.7
Income Statement

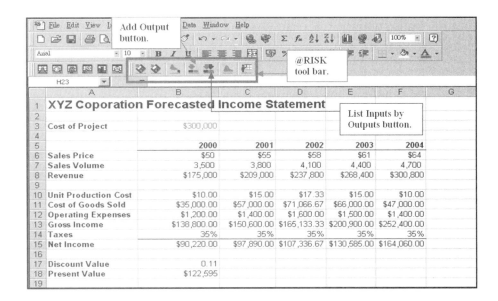

In the following example, XYZ Corporation is faced with a critical decision on whether or not to launch a new product to the market. The initial cost of the project is calculated by the accounting department at $300,000 (cell B3); the content of the income statement, including individual cell formulas, will be discussed in detail later in this tutorial. At the bottom of the income statement (Figure 5.7), XYZ has also calculated net present value (cell B18) of the project, using a discount value (cell B17). The spreadsheet file for the XYZ Corporation example can be found on the CD ROM that accompanies the text and is entitled xyzcorp.xls.

Upon loading of @Risk, a new toolbar is created in your spreadsheet. This toolbar is visible whenever @RISK is running. The toolbar buttons run many of the commands you need to perform a risk analysis. If you are unfamiliar with the @RISK toolbar button, holding the cursor over a button will allow a ToolTip to appear.

Input Cells

The spreadsheet in Figure 5.7 may look like a typical spreadsheet model, but looks can be deceiving. Let's take a look at the contents of the cells:

Cells B6 through F6 contain the formula =RiskTriang(#1,#2,#3), where #1, #2, and #3 represent the three triangular distribution values starting with #1 at the lowest value, #2 the most likely value, and #3 the highest value.

This can be interpreted as follows: XYZ has determined that for every year, sales price can range between three values. For example, in year 2000, sales price (cell B6) ranges from 20, 50, to 80. Thus the formula for cell B6 is =RiskTriang(20,50,80). For years 2001 through 2004, the same formula is used, but with different triangular distribution values. Use the following triangular distributions for 2001 through 2004: =RiskTriang(25,55,85), =RiskTriang(28,58,88), =RiskTriang(31,61,91), and =RiskTriang(34,64,94), respectively.

The Triangular Distribution

Figure 5.8 displays the triangular distribution presented in cell B6. Turn back to Chapter 3 for more information on distributions, especially the triangular distribution.

When a simulation is not running, @RISK will display the most likely value for the triangular distribution; thus in year 2000, 50 is displayed. During a simulation run, @RISK will sample values for cells B6 through F6 across the range of the triangular distribution. For each iteration (or recalculation of the spreadsheet) a new, randomly generated value will be placed in the worksheet cell.

Cells B10 through F10 (Unit Production Cost) and cell B17 (Discount Value) also contain the triangular distribution formula with exactly the same triangular distribution interpretation, but different high, most likely, and low parameters.

Cells B7 through F7 contain the formula =RiskNormal(#1,#2), where #1 represents a mean value and #2 represents the standard deviation value. The interpretation is that XYZ has

FIGURE 5.8
Triangular Distribution for Sales Price

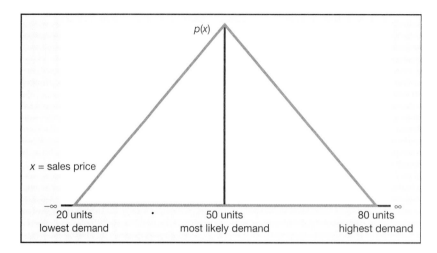

FIGURE 5.9
Normal Distribution for Sales

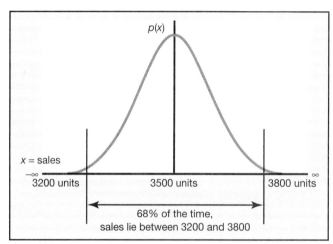

determined that the volume of sales will have a normal distribution with a mean value and will fluctuate in respect to its standard deviation value.

The Normal Distribution

Figure 5.9 displays the normal distribution presented in cells B7 through F6. Turn back to Chapter 3 for more information on distributions, especially the normal distribution.

Thus the formula in cell B7 is =RiskNormal(3500,300). This means that, in year 2000, there is a 68.26 percent chance that sales volume will fall between 3200 and 3800. For years 2001 through 2004, the same formula is used but with different normal distribution values. Use the following normal distributions for 2001 through 2004: =RiskNormal(3800,300), =Risk-Normal(4100,300), =RiskNormal(4400,300), and =RiskNormal(4700,300), respectively.

When a simulation is not running, @RISK will display the mean value for the normal distribution, thus in year 2000, 3500 is displayed. During a simulation run, @RISK will sample values for those cells that fall along the normal distribution defined by their formulas.

Cells B12 through F12 (Operating Expense) also contain the normal distribution formula with exactly the same normal distribution interpretation, but different mean and standard deviation.

Note that the above-mentioned cells are called input cells, which @RISK will calculate and recalculate during a simulation run. Use the following normal distributions for 2000 through 2004: =RiskNormal(1200,200), =RiskNormal(1400,200), =RiskNormal(1600,200), =Risk-Normal(1500,200), and =RiskNormal(1400,200), respectively.

Output Cells

Let's take a look at the *output* cells. In @RISK, an output is a cell whose value we are interested in studying, a bottom-line value. Output cells contain formulas that reference input cells; their calculations use values from the cells containing @RISK functions you have entered. In the XYZ model, we are interested in the net Present Value, calculated in cell B18, and the Net Income value for all 5 years, calculated from cells B15 through F15. Cell B18 is calculated using the following Excel formula: =NPV(B17, B15:F15)−B3.

To add cell B18 as an output, select it in the spreadsheet and click the Add Output button on the @RISK toolbar. During a simulation, each time the spreadsheet is recalculated, the value of cell B18 will be recorded. The result will be a range of possible outcome values.

XYZ is also interested in the Net Income for each year, calculated in cells B15 through F15. You can highlight the entire range from B15 through F15 and then click the Add output" button to define these cells as outputs. By defining a group or range of cells as an output, you can study the impact of each cell individually or the impact of the whole range at once.

Summary of Inputs and Outputs

Now that we have defined uncertainty in our model and selected output cells, let's take a look at our inputs and outputs by clicking the List Inputs by Outputs button on the @RISK toolbar.

@Risk Window

Figure 5.10 shows that we are in the @RISK window. In addition to information on the selected inputs and outputs, simulation results and graphs are displayed here. This is discussed later in the tutorial.

You can return to Excel by clicking the Hide button in the larger @RISK toolbar above the input and output display windows. The Input by Outputs window lists all @RISK inputs on the right and outputs on the left.

Notice that @RISK automatically assigned names to the inputs and outputs from the spreadsheet. You can highlight and type in a new one if you so desire. The inputs list also shows the @RISK function contained in the cell. Now that our model is set up, we are ready to run a risk analysis.

Running a Risk Analysis

In this section, a risk analysis is run and the results studied. We will discuss the following topics associated with the risk analysis: simulation settings, running a simulation, and analyzing the results.

Simulation Settings

Let's first discuss the settings for running a simulation, click the Simulation Setting button at the top of the toolbar (refer back to Figure 5.10). You will see another dialog box displayed as in Figure 5.11.

FIGURE 5.10
List Inputs by Outputs

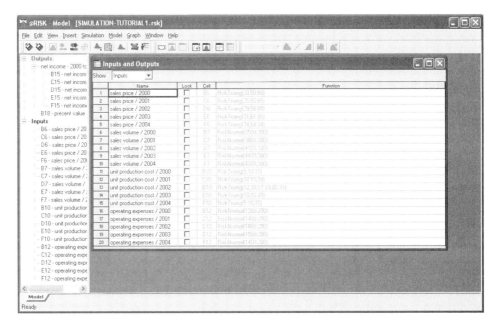

FIGURE 5.11
Simulation Settings

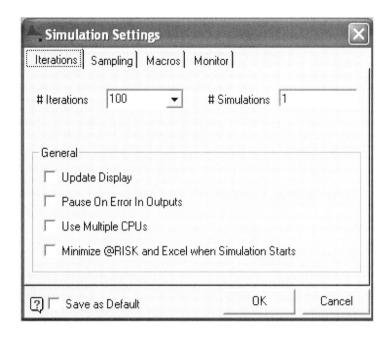

FIGURE 5.12
Sampling Tab

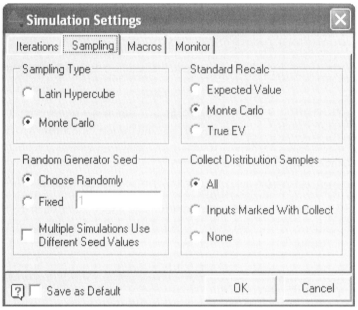

The Iteration tab defines the number of iterations to run during a simulation. At each iteration, a new set of random numbers that is generated and the worksheet is recalculated. We are currently set to run 10,000 iterations. For most simulations, you will want to run a larger number of iterations, say 100,000. However, we will use 10,000 iterations for the purpose of this tutorial.

Sampling Tab

The Sampling tab controls how each distribution in your worksheet will be sampled. We will be using the Monte Carlo sampling type, which achieves more accurate results with a larger amount of iterations. Should you be running the simulation with lesser iterations, it is recommended that you should use the default sampling type, Latin Hypercube. Figure 5.12 displays the Sampling tab. If you wish to complete sensitivity analysis at the end of the simulation run be sure the 'All' button is engaged in the 'Collect Distribution Sample' menu.

Monitor Tab

The monitor tab allows you to monitor your outputs while the simulation is running to see when they become stable or converge. The AutoStop setting allows your simulation to run

FIGURE 5.13
Convergence Tab

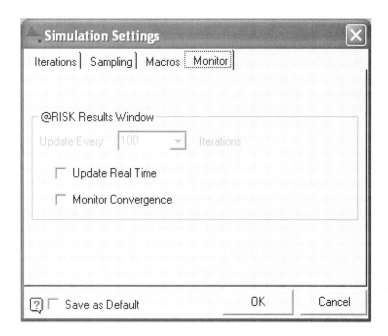

until all outputs have reached the level of convergence you specify. For the purpose of this tutorial, we will let the simulation run completely. Figure 5.13 displays the Monitor tab.

Macro Tab

You may continue on the Macro tab, which allows advanced users to run Excel macro commands before, during, or after a simulation. Use this feature if your model requires calculations that must be defined by macro functions.

Running the Simulation

You are now ready to run the simulation. Click the Start Simulation button at the top of the toolbar and the simulation will begin running all by itself. (Refer back to Figure 5.10 if you are unable to find the Simulation button)

Analyze the Results

After the computer has completed running the simulation, the results will be displayed automatically, and we should now take a look at how to interpret these results so XYZ may determine whether or not to conduct this product launch. The results are displayed in Figure 5.14.

The Results window (top window) displays a summary of the simulation results, including minimum, mean, and maximum values calculated for each output cell and input distribution. We can see that NPV has a minimum value of -63939.94, a mean value of 122789.60, and a maximum value of 328501.30. That's quite a large range of results, and depending on XYZ's tolerance for risk, it might consider this a very risky project.

Simulation Statistics

When the simulation is done running, the summary statistics window automatically appears. To obtain detailed statistics click on the Detailed Statistics Window in the @Risk toolbar. Look around in this window and obtain a better sense of the statistics calculated by the simulation.

Data Window and @Risk Report Command

Referring back to Figure 5.14, it is seen that summary and detailed statistics are displayed. However, a user may wish to see all the data @Risk collected during the simulation runs.

FIGURE 5.14
Simulation Results

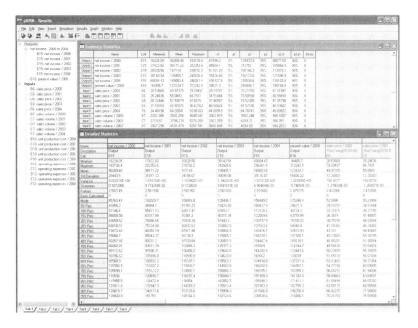

FIGURE 5.15
Reports to Worksheet

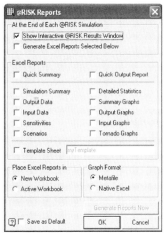

Note: Selecting the Output Data button in the @
Risk Reports window is not recommended. This
option tends to crash most computer systems
because of the large file size.

Since statistics are already displayed in the bottom window, click on the Data Window button in the toolbar. The Data Window button allows you to display all the data collected and generated during each simulation for each iteration. You can transfer data and results to an Excel spreadsheet with the @Risk Reports menu command under the Results menu on the toolbar (see Figure 5.15 for the @Risk Reports menu). Use this commend to export simulation data into and Excel spreadsheet using the options listed in the @Risk Reports menu.

Click on the space that represents the data that you would like to have transferred to your Excel worksheet. Once your results have been transferred to Excel, you can format, print, or run further analyses on them.

Sensitivity Command

In the "Sensitivity" window, Figure 5.16, the outputs are listed on the left. On the right, the inputs are ranked in order of their effect of the selected output. Here we see that Sales Price is the most important input affecting the NPV.

@RISK uses two methods to measure sensitivity: multivariate stepwise regression measures the change in the selected output due to a unit change in the input variable (in units of standard deviations from the output mean), and rank-order correlation measures the rank-order correlation between the input and output data sets.

Figure 5.16   Sensitivity Command

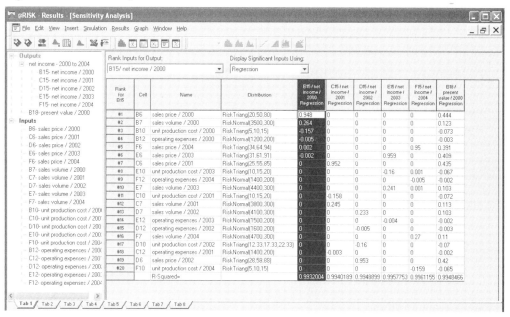

Figure 5.17   Scenario Command

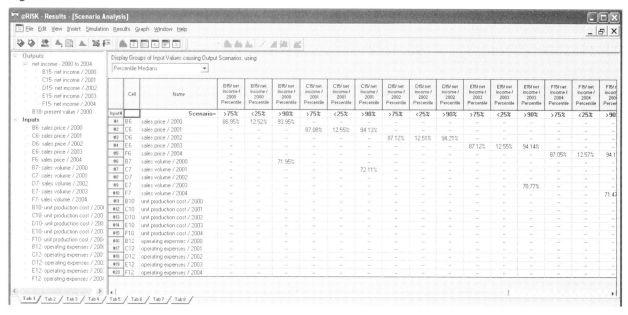

For either measurement, a value of 0 indicates that changes in the input variable have no effect on the output. The greater the magnitude of the value, the bigger the effect the input has on the output.

Scenario Command

Scenario analysis allows you to determine which input values contribute significantly toward reaching a goal. For example, scenario analysis can be used to determine which variable contributes to an exceptionally high or low NPV. In Figure 5.17, we see the results of a scenario analysis when the NPV is greater than 75 percent (that is, when the NPV is at or above its 75th percentile value).

Scenario target values are entered in the Simulation Statistics window. According to the simulation, Sales Price is the most significant input variable when the NPV is at or above the 75th percentile value.

Graphing the Results

In this section, we will take a look at the different techniques in graphing the results from the simulation and how to interpret these graphs. We will examine the topics of histograms, graph format commands, summary graphs, tornado graphs, and graphs in the Excel spreadsheet.

Graphing: Understanding the Data More Clearly

The whole idea of graphing statistical results is to offer a method of better understanding the enormous amount of data that you have generated thus far. It is a way to put everything together and manipulate your data to make it more understandable.

Although @RISK will generate graphs for you, they may be difficult to understand; thus you can always choose to transfer your data to the Excel spreadsheet and graph it in a way both you and your audience can easily comprehend.

Using @Risk to Create a Histogram of NPV

We will first take a look at the graph for the NPV value generated from the simulation. Simply click on the Graph Selected Item(s) in the Explorer List menu in the toolbar and then click on Histogram and you will generate your first graph in @RISK.

Figure 5.18 is called a *histogram.* It shows the distribution of possible values for cell B18 (NPV). The height of each bar represents the number of samples that fell in the range, defined by the width of the bar. In short, the histogram is a graphic representation of the uncertainty inherent in the output variable.

Using @Risk to Create a Smooth Bell-Shaped Curve of NPV

Let's view this graph in a different format. Right-click on the graph, click Format Graph, click on the Style tab, click on the Format menu in the Curve Style area, and set the choice to Line, and then click OK.

Now we can see that the NPV statistics calculated from the simulation is simply a bell curve. This should make interpretation of the graph easier and not so esoteric.

Using @Risk to Create a Cumulative Distribution Graph of NPV

Let's view the graph in a cumulative distribution format. Right click on the graph and click on the Format Graph menu. A figure resembling Figure 5.20 will appear, click on the Cumulative Ascending option in the Display As menu, and then click on the Style tab and in the Format option of the Curve Style menu choose Solid.

The graph is now displayed as a cumulative probability curve (Figure 5.21). The graph shows the probability of a result less than or equal to any value in the range. For example, there is a 20 percent probability that the NPV will be less than approximately $75,000.

FIGURE 5.18
NPV Graph—
Histogram.

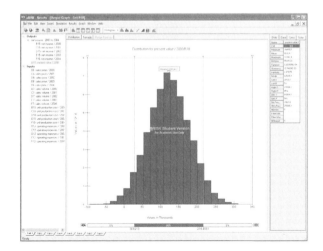

FIGURE 5.19
**Smooth Bell-Shaped
Curve of NPV**

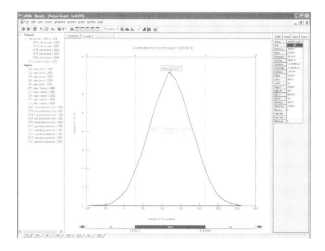

FIGURE 5.20
**Cumulative Distribution
Graph Setting**

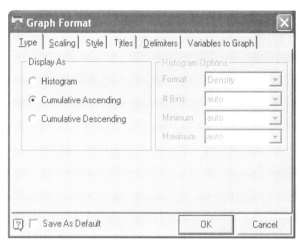

FIGURE 5.21
**Cumulative Distribution
Graph**

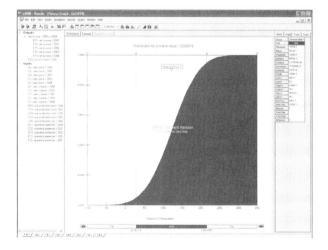

Cumulative Distribution Outline Graph

Let's change the format once again to see if we can better understand this graph. Right-click on the graph, click on the Format Graph menu, click on the Style tab, and in the Format option of the Curve Style menu choose Line. A new graph resembling Figure 5.22 will appear.

You may notice that this is the same graph, except it is simply an outline of the previous graph. This graph may be more visually pleasing, since we can now see how the value of the

FIGURE 5.22
Cumulative Distribution
Graph—Outline

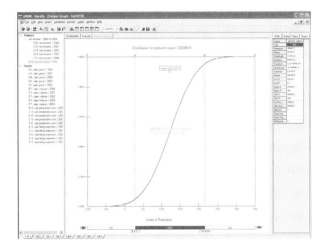

Figure 5.23   **Selecting a Cell in the Range**

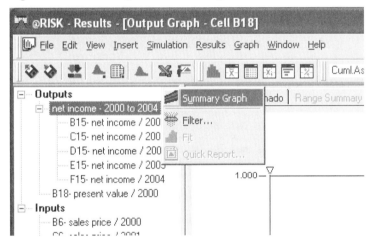

NPV starts low, climbs steeply, and then levels off at the top. This graph presents the same idea as the normal distribution graph (bell curve).

Summary Output Graphs

What about the output range we selected in our model, the Net Income? We mentioned earlier that one advantage of selecting a range of cells as an output is that you can study changes of the whole group at once. Select the range output from the Outputs list and right-click, then choose the Summary Graph option from the menu (see Figure 5.23).

The Summary Graph (Figure 5.24) summarizes the distributions generated for the cells in the selected output range—in this case for the five Net Income cells (B15 through F15).

The lighter line in Figure 5.24 represents the trend in the mean of the distribution over 5 years, as described in the model. The darker band extends for one standard deviation about the mean. The outer medium color band extends to the 5th and 95th percentiles. The Summary Graph is useful for looking at how values change across an output range.

Interpretation of the Summary Graph

In this example, the graph demonstrates a steady upward trend for the first 2 years and then the trend picks up rapidly after the third year. This is atypical in a product life cycle, from a marketing perspective. As a product first becomes available to the public, it takes 1 to 2 years to gain recognition. As the product becomes accepted and management becomes more competent, sales volume increases and costs decrease, thus net income increases.

FIGURE 5.24
Summary Graph

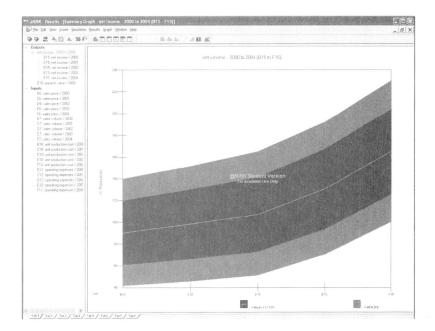

FIGURE 5.25
Tornado Graph

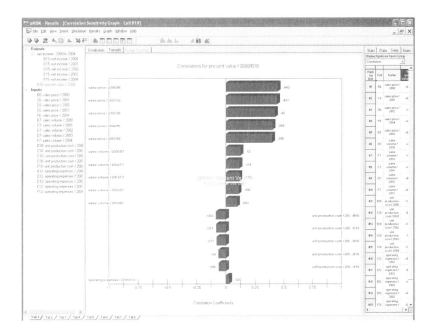

Sensitivity Analysis and the Tornado Diagram

Now let's look at the sensitivity analysis data in a graphical format. Click on the Sensitivity Window on the @Risk toolbar and then choose from the Display Significant Inputs Using menu between a Correlation or a Regression tornado graph. For the purpose of this tutorial, click Correlation and then click OK.

As you can see from the tornado graph in Figure 5.25, Sales Price for year 2000 is the most significant input, which is drawn at the top of the graph with the longest bar. The correlation coefficients are represented along the *x* axis, and each input variable is charted on the *y* axis.

The tornado graph summarizes the effect of variables in a neat, simple graph. We can easily compare the magnitude of the effect of each input by the size of the bar and whether the effect is positive or negative in the direction of the bar (right or left, respectively).

Graphing in Excel

There may be times when you want to take data into an Excel spreadsheet or a different program for graphing. @RISK makes it easy to convert any graph to the native chart format of your spreadsheet via the Graph in Excel command.

Referring back to Figure 5.14, right-click on the graph, click Graph in Excel, and the graph will automatically be created in your Excel spreadsheet. Not only does @RISK create a histogram as an Excel chart, it will also copy all the data points to the same worksheet. You can use Excel's Chart Wizard to customize the graph as you would any other chart.

The End

Now that you have just completed a basic tutorial for @RISK, it is up to you to make a decision for XYZ Corporation. It will take a few rounds of practice and some playing around to become proficient at @RISK and interpreting the results. Do you think XYZ should launch this new product? On what basis are you making your recommendation? Remember, your decision has to be based on the data and statistics you have generated, hence the name of this course, business decision modeling. Enjoy!

Summary

Overall, some very important points must be remembered when building, running, and interpreting simulation models. The most points are:

- **Randomness and random number generation.** Simulation models must sample from distributions that exhibit random properties—i.e., correct random number generation.
- **Run enough trials.** Enough trials must be run when implementing simulation models—i.e., enough is usually 100,000 trials.
- **Verify the model.** Models must be verified with regard to inputs, outputs, and uncertainty—link uncertainty to probability distributions (Chapters 1 to 3).
- **Validate the model.** Models must be validated—link validation to decision structuring (Chapters 4 and 5).
- **Conduct sensitivity analysis.** Sensitivity analysis generally tends to be the most robust area for interpreting simulation results—link sensitivity analysis to Chapters 4 and 5.

The major payoffs of simulation modeling are often the result of asking what if questions when the model is running. It is also very important to make sure your model is *valid* and that it has been *verified*. By verify we mean to make sure the computer or spreadsheet program used in the model is not flawed. This requires checking and rechecking the work, perhaps writing it in different languages to see if similar results occur and perhaps asking independent experts to review the work.

Conducting sensitivity analysis is the real payoff in modeling and running simulations.

A simulation is valid when it models what it is supposed to model. After working long hours on a simulation and viewing results that are aesthetically pleasing it is easy to be seduced into believing the results while losing sight of the fact that the model misses the point. To have a valid simulation model, it is important to talk to workers closest to the action, to contrast and compare other models and the experience of other experts, to utilize whatever data are available to identify trends for what if analysis, and to keep an open mind.

BUSINESS DECISION MODELING COMMUNICATION: EXECUTIVE SUMMARY FOR SIMULATION MODELING

The next section displays an executive summary example for the XYZ Corporation simulation modeling example detailed in the @Risk tutorial section.

Executive Summary for XYZ Corporation

To: Delta Investing Corporation
From: Alan Fang, President Fang Consulting

Problem Identification

XYZ Corporation is seeking a net present value (NPV) analysis on a potential project launch. Items such as the forecasted sales price, unit production costs, and discount factor are triangularly distributed with three possible values, whereas sales volume and operating expenses are normally distributed with a mean and a standard deviation (SD). The criterion for XYZ Corporation to accept this project is positive NPV after discounting the future cash flows (Net Income) from year '00 to '04. The alternative for XYZ is not launching the project, which has a net NPV of zero.

Modeling the Problem

A spreadsheet model is constructed by utilizing basic accounting principles to calculate net income. NPV is then calculated by discounting the five forecasted net income figures, using a current discount value and subtracting the original cost of the project. To obtain a full analysis on the upside potential and the downside risk of the project, XYZ Corporation decided to employ a Monte Carlo simulation comprising 100,000 iterations. The simulation offers XYZ Corporation a detailed perspective on a range of possible NPVs for the project and the probability of the NPV to occur above $0.

Results: Sensitivity Analysis

From the simulation, the result of all possible NPVs is graphed in Figure 1.

Dominance

As we can see from the graph, the NPV has a mean value around $125,000, a low value around –$60,000, and a high value of $310,000. The project's NPV is positive approximately 95 percent of the time. By not launching the project, XYZ would have zero NPV and would avoid this downside loss. It appears that launching dominates not launching the project around 95 percent of the time.

Tradeoffs

The points are read off the graph by finding the percentile of interest on the *x* axis (NPV percentile), let's say 50 percent, proceeding vertically from the 50 percent point until the graph is reached, and then horizontally proceeding to the *y* axis and reading the corresponding NPV. The tradeoff point between launching or not launching the project occurs around the 5th NPV percentile (i.e., 5 percent on the *x* axis).

FIGURE 1

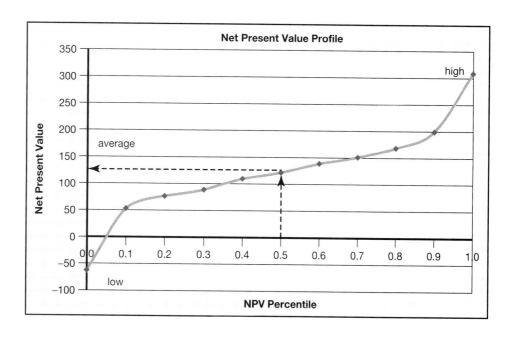

Case Study: *Steve's Solar System*

BACKGROUND AND HISTORICAL ELECTRICITY INFORMATION

Steve is considering installing a solar hot water system (SHH2OS) in his business to transfer some of his power consumption off the grid. Steve knows that the up-front costs of the SHH2OS including materials and labor are $11,600. Future operating and maintenance costs are negligible. Obviously, SHH2OSs work best and are most efficient when it is sunny outside. However, it is not always sunny outside where Steve's business currently resides. Therefore, Steve knows the SHH2OS will save him at most 80 percent but at least 50 percent with a most likely number around 70 percent of the electricity he normally would use for hot water heating each month.

From past records, Steve has estimated that the business' electricity bills run about $450 a month. However, some months they could be as high as $575 or as low as $290. Steve also estimated that hot water heating in general makes up anywhere from 30 percent to 50 percent of the electricity bill with a most likely number of 40 percent.

SOLAR INCENTIVES

Currently, there are no discounts for installing an SHH2OS. However, Steve is expecting new legislation to be passed on the federal and state levels that will allow some discounts on the cost

of a system. The federal legislation would allow for a 35 percent discount off the total price on the SHH2OS. The state legislation would allow for a flat $1400 discount on any SHH2OS originally priced above $5000.

PAYBACK PERIOD CALCULATIONS AND CONCERNS

Steve would like to know his expected payback period from the installation of the SHH2OS with and without the discounts. The payback period for an investment or project is the number of periods it takes before the investment's or project's initial investment is paid back.

SIMULATION MODELING AND DISCUSSION QUESTIONS

Using Excel, create a simulation model to help Steve. Given the following assumptions, run the simulation model for 100,000 trials and interpret the results. Help Steve understand:

1. What his expected monthly and annual saving could be with the new unit with and without the discounts.

2. The payback period for the SHH2OS with and without the discounts.

Distribution Assumptions	Variable	Distribution
	Monthly electricity saving from the SHH2OS	Triangular: 50% as the low, 70% as the most likely, and 80% as the high
	Monthly electricity bills	Triangular: $290 as the low, $450 as the most likely, and $575 as the high
	Percent of electricity from hot water heating	Triangular: 30% as the low, 40% as the most likely, and 50% as the high

Risks

Risk for this decision can be defined and quantified in two ways, by range and by SD. The average, high, and low values are listed on the graph. Range (high–low) for launching the project is around $370,000. The range for not launching the project is $0. Although informative, range is not the best measure of risk here. SD should also be analyzed. Risk can be interpreted by declaring that out of all NPVs calculated from the simulation, few fall below $0, and overall NPV climbs steadily from around a value of $50,000 to a value of $200,000. This in essence is the SD for the NPV of launching the project and has an actual value of $56,616.

Conclusion and Recommendations

Based on the criteria on whether to accept a project on NPV, XYZ Corporation has decided to accept this particular project because there is a 95 percent (100% to 5%) probability that NPV will be greater than $0. With mean value of around $125,000 and an SD value of around $57,000, thus there is a 66.68 percent chance that the NPV will fall between $68,000 and $182,000 and a 95 percent chance that the NPV will fall between $11,000 and $239,000. XYZ would be wise to accept this project.

Interactive Case: *Serving the Customers at Schenck's*

Visit www.mhhe.com/krosj1e to analyze the problem using the Waiting Line Module.

BACKGROUND

Steve Schenck has run his family delicatessen for 10 years. The delicatessen serves food all day long from 7 A.M. until 9 P.M. and also provides customers with packaged meat and other products for take-home use. Business has always been busy, even when his father ran the business. However, two new office buildings and a new subdivision have been built nearby over the last 5 years. These additions have brought many new customers, and Steve has been hearing complaints about the wait. Specifically, the complaints have been about the wait to check out.

CURRENT SETUP

Currently Steve has one cash register to serve his customers. In general, customers place their orders at the order window and employees process the orders (e.g., make a sandwich, cut some corned beef, pack up some dill pickles). This process usually isn't the bottleneck, since the behind-the-counter employees are well seasoned, know the layout well, and manage the work easily (i.e., there are enough workers, since all can do each others' jobs).

The bottleneck comes when the customers go to check out. Steve knows that customers have complained about the wait and he has heard that some have mentioned to the cashier that they might go elsewhere in the future because of the long waits to check out. In fact, Steve stood outside the store just the other day and watched as some customers looked in the window, saw the long line at the cashier, and decided not to go into the delicatessen. Steve knows the word is getting out and wants to improve the situation before he starts losing current customers as well as future customers.

Steve is contemplating adding another cashier to the process to alleviate the long line that builds. However, his brother is telling him that it will cost too much money and overall won't solve the problem. Steve's brother believes that the cashier just needs to work faster and the problem will take care of itself.

DATA ANALYSIS AND SIMULATION

Steve believes adding another cashier will help and he wishes to test his theory versus his brother's theory. From data that his son collected for a college business decision modeling course, Steve knows the arrival rate and service rate for his customers. The data tell Steve that his customer arrival rate is 5 customers per hour and his customer service rate is 3 customers per hour.

Steve knows that he could send his cashier to some training classes at the local business college and his service rate would improve. He estimates that after training the cashier could process customers faster and that the service rate would go up to 4 customers per hour but no higher. However, these classes would cost Steve money, around $2000. Steve's brother speculates that training the cashier and in turn improving the service rate would cut the number of customers waiting in line by 80 percent and cut the time they wait by more than half. These metrics, cutting customers in line by 80 percent and cutting waiting time by more than half are definitely two of Steve's goals and, if they are realized, he could justify the $2000 spent.

Steve asked his son about his brother's speculation and his son didn't agree. His son does not think just by training the cashier and improving service rates that they will see these dramatic improvements. Therefore, Steve's son has suggested that they add another cashier (i.e., add another server to the queue). His son estimates that if they add another cashier in the process they will at least cut the average number of customers waiting in the line by 80 percent and cut the time customers wait in the line by half. However, adding another cashier will cost money too, about $400 a week in pay and benefits. Overall, Steve is willing to pay the money if his goals of cutting the number of customers in line and the waiting time could be met.

WAITING LINE SIMULATION SETTINGS

Three waiting line simulations (Current Setup, Training Option, Extra Cashier Option) have been suggested by Steve's son for comparison. Table 5.5 contains the parameters that should be entered in the interactive waiting line simulation menus.

Run the simulation, observing the system, until 50 customers have been served. Then record for each simulation (Current Setup, Training Option, Extra Cashier Option) the performance measures (Lq, Ls, Wq, and Ws).

DISCUSSION QUESTIONS

1. How does the Training Option compare to the Current Setup? Are Steve's goals of cutting the number of customers waiting in line by 80 percent and cutting customer waiting time by more than half realized?

2. How does the Extra Cashier Option compare with both the Current Setup and Training Options? Does the Extra Cashier Option meet Steve's goals?

3. What would you advise Steve to do?

TABLE 5.5
Parameters for interactive waiting time simulation

Parameter	Current Setup	Training Option	Extra cashier Option
Phases	One	One	One
Speed	Fast	Fast	Fast
Arrival rate	5	5	5
Service rate	3	4	3
Number of servers in phase 1	1	1	2
Server breakdown severity	N	N	N

Optimal Information Area

Computational Science Education Project Introduction to Monte Carlo Methods Web site at **http://csep1.phy.ornl.gov/mc/node1.html.**

History of Monte Carlo Method Web site at **http://stud2.tuwien.ac.at/~e9527412/history.html.**

Glossary: Monte Carlo Simulation Web site at **http://www.contingencyanalysis.com/glossarymontecarlosimulation.htm.**

Sabri Pllana's History of Monte Carlo Method Web site at **http://www.geocities.com/CollegePark/Quad/2435/.**

Palisade Incorporated simulation software Web site at **http://www.palisade.com.**

References

Camm, J. D., and J. R. Evans. *Management Science: Modeling, Analysis, and Interpretation.* Cincinnati, OH: South-Western Publishing Co., 1996.

Evans, J. R., and D. Olson. *Introduction to Simulation and Risk Analysis.* Upper Saddle River, NJ: Prentice-Hall, 1998.

Law, A. M., and W. D. Kelton. *Simulation Modeling and Analysis*, 2nd ed. New York: McGraw-Hill, 1991.

Leon, L., Z. Przasnyski, and K. C. Seal. "Spreadsheets and OR/MS models: An End-User Perspective." *Interfaces*, vol. 26, no. 2 (1996), pp. 92–104.

Ragsdale, C. T. *Spreadsheet Modeling and Decision Analysis, A Practical Introduction to Management Science*, 2nd ed., Cincinnati, OH: South-Western Educational Publishing.

Sheel, Atul. "Monte Carlo Simulations and Scenario Analysis: Decision-Making Tools for Hoteliers. *Cornell Hotel and Restaurant Administration Quarterly*, "vol. 36, no. 5 (1995), pp. 18–26.

"'Super Flush' passes test," *USAToday*, July 16, 1998.

Uyeno, D. "Monte Carlo Simulation on Microcomputers." *Simulation*, vol. 58, vol. 6 (1992), pp. 418–423.

Problems

1. A basic skill needed to do simulation is to be able to correctly assign random numbers to a probability distribution. Do this for the circumstances described below. In each instance identify all possible outcomes and the probabilities associated with those outcomes before assigning random numbers according to the scheme described in this chapter.

   a. Rolling a die.
   b. Flipping a coin.
   c. Having a birthday in a month that begins with J. Ignore leap years and assume it is equally likely a person is born on any given day.

2. Simulate flipping two coins and rolling a die at the same time. Do 100 simulations. From your results estimate:

   a. The probability of having at least one head.
   b. The probability of the coins having the same faces and the face of the die being greater than four.
   c. The probability the face of the die is an even number and the faces of the coins do not match.

3. Use the mathematics of probability to calculate the theoretical result for each part of Problem 2 and compare your results. Why are they different from the results of the simulation? How could you improve on the simulated results?

4. The following information was found about a credit card processing facility: a uniform maximum arrival rate of 3 units per minute and a minimum arrival rate of 0, a normally distributed average service rate of 1.2 units per minute, a standard deviation of 0.75 units per minute. Develop a simulation model in Excel to determine;

a. What is the average number of customers in the waiting line?

b. What is the probability of waiting?

c. What is the average customer waiting time?

d What is the number waiting more than 1 minute?

e. What is the percentage of time the credit card processing facility is busy?

f. What is the maximum wait time?

5. To create a probability distribution from historical data, one first needs to create a frequency distribution and then a relative frequency distribution. Suppose you track the weekly change in price for 1 year (52 weeks) of a particular stock with the results indicated in the following table. Using Excel, re-create the table and fill in the blanks.

Weekly change in price (nearest $)	Number of Weeks	Relative frequency	Assigned random numbers
+4	5	5/52 = 0.0962	
+3	5		
+2	6		
+1	4		
0	12		
−1	11		
−2	5		
−3	4		

6. In macho frontier times a game called Gambler's Ruin was played. In such a contest, two opponents document all their assets, obtain a supply of good whiskey and proceed to play cards, generally with a crowd watching, until one has lost all he has to the other. To simulate this as a game of pure chance is probably not accurate because in a game like poker, chance and skill combine to determine the winner. Nevertheless we can gain insights into such a set of circumstances by simulating a game of chance by flipping a coin where the assets of each player are identified by an appropriate integer. One student may start with five assets and another with two and each student is identified with either "heads" or "tails" as his or her winning circumstance. Play the game until one is ruined. Try starting with different divisions of assets and see if you can discover an underlying relationship that will predict the probability of being ruined for each player on the basis of the player's original assets. Is it to the advantage of the player with the most assets or least assets to play such a game?

7. Historical data indicate that a student's income for any month of school from work, parents, scholarships, and loans is consistent with the following probability distribution:

Income	Probability
$750	0.20
$950	0.36
$1150	0.30
$1350	0.14

Expenses for the same student are believed to be consistent with the following probability distribution:

Expense	Probability
$900	0.40
$1000	0.25
$1100	0.20
$1200	0.15

Assuming the student begins the school year with a balance of $1200, use Excel and @Risk to simulate 9 months of activity and to predict the position of the student at the end of the year.

8. Redo Problem 7 if expenses are believed to be normally distributed with a mean of $1026 and a standard deviation of $191.36. How does this change the average cash position of the student compared to what you found in Problem 7?

9. Pick a stock or commodity and establish a probability distribution like the one in Problem 7. Identify your trading strategy and, using Excel and @Risk, simulate the activity of a year.

10. A particular stock has been tracked for the past year with note being made of the change in price from the beginning of the week to the end of the week. Relative frequency considerations produce the following probability distribution for the performance over the past year.

Change in price, $	Relative frequency
+4	0.09
+3	0.11
+2	0.11
+1	0.10
0	0.20
−1	0.20
−2	0.19

Assume you own 1000 shares of the stock, for which you paid $150 per share, and that you adopt a trading strategy of selling 100 shares each week the stock goes up and buying 100 shares each week the stock goes down. On the assumption that the probability distribution for next year will be the same as for this year, simulate your position a year hence. Set up a simulation model in Excel and use @Risk to simulate the stock price and to track your trading strategy. Try asking "what if" the distribution changes in some way when you invent or try changing the trading strategy, or both, and contrast and compare your results.

11. A one-person-operated food stand finds that on a Monday morning its customers arrive at the maximum rate of 12 per hour (i.e., a lower interarrival time of 5 minutes) and a minimum rate of 2 per hour (i.e., an upper interarrival time of 30 minutes). The average time to serve a customer is normally distributed and is 7 minutes with a standard deviation of 1 minute. Develop a simulation model in Excel to determine the following:

    a. What is the average number of customers in the waiting line?
    b. What is the probability of waiting?
    c. What is the average customer waiting time?
    d. What is the number waiting more than 1 minute?
    e. What is the percentage of time the food stand is busy?
    f. What is the maximum wait time?

12. The daily demand for newspapers at a particular vending machine is either 20, 21, 22, or 23, with probabilities 0.4, 0.3, 0.2, or 0.1, respectively. Assume the following random numbers have been generated: 08, 54, 74, 66, 52, 58, 03, 22, 89, and 85. Using these numbers, set up an Excel spreadsheet that generates daily newspaper sales for 10 days.

13. The number of machine breakdowns per day at ASQ's factory is either 0, 1, or 2, with probabilities 0.5, 0.3, or 0.2, respectively. Using Excel and the @Risk add-in simulate 100 days of business for the factory. What proportion of these days had at least 1 breakdown?

14. The number of cars arriving at Nathan Hunt's self-service gasoline station during the last 50 hours of operation is as follows:

Number of cars arriving	Probability
6	0.25
7	0.45
8	0.15
9	0.15

Using Excel and the @Risk add-in, simulate 100 days of business for the station. What is the average number of arrivals during this period? What is the range of arrivals (i.e., the difference between the high and the low)?

15. The time between arrivals at the drive-through window of Hugh Leach's fast-food restaurant follows a uniform distribution with a lower bound of 0 minutes and an upper bound of 5 minutes. The service-time distribution is also uniform with a lower bound of 0.5 minutes and an upper bound of 3.0 minutes. Simulate the utilization of the drive-through over 500 minutes. Use Excel to construct the model and @Risk to simulate the 500 minutes. What is the average wait at the drive-through? What is the longest someone will wait in line? On average, how many people are in line at the drive-thru?

16. J. J. Stakem sells papers at a newspaper stand for $0.75. The papers cost $0.15 each, giving her a $0.60 profit on each one she sells. From past experience J. J. knows that

    20 percent of the time she sells 100 papers

    20 percent of the time she sells 150 papers

    30 percent of the time he sells 200 papers

    30 percent of the time he sells 250 papers

    Assuming that J. J. believes the cost of a lost sale to be $0.15 and any unsold papers cost her $0.35, simulate her profit outlook over 100 days if she orders 200 papers for each of the 100 days. Use Excel to construct the model and @Risk to simulate the 100 days.

17. Billy O'Boyle's liquor store has noted the following figures with regard to the number of people who arrive at the store's checkout stand and the time it takes to check them out. Interarrival times tend to be uniformly distributed with a lower bound of 0 minutes and an upper bound of 4 minute, and service times tend to be uniformly distributed with a lower bound of 1 minute and an upper bound of 2 minutes.

    Simulate the utilization of the checkout stand over 500 minutes. Use Excel to construct the model and @Risk to simulate the 500 minutes. What is the average wait at Billy's liquor store? What is the longest someone will wait in line? On average, how many people are in line at Billy's store?

Chapter **Six**

Linear Regression Modeling

Learning Objectives

After completing this chapter, students will be able to:

1. Understand and identify dependent and independent variables and use them in a regression model.
2. Develop simple linear regression equations from sample data, using Excel, and interpret the slope and intercept.
3. Develop a multiple regression model with Excel's Data Analysis package and use it to predict.
4. Interpret the output from Excel's Data Analysis Regression package, including the coefficient of determination R, the coefficient of correlation R^2, the F test, and the t tests/p values.
5. List the assumptions used in regression and use tests for multicollinearity, autocorrelation, and heteroscedasticity to identify problems.
6. Understand and avoid common mistakes made in using regression analysis.

Chapter Outline

Business Decision Modeling in Action—Linear Regression Analysis at General Motors

Linear Regression Modeling
> *Forecasting Technique*
> *Areas of Statistics*
> *Data Sources*
> *Statistical Software*
> *Population versus Sample*
> *Sample Size*
> *Scatter Plots*

Business Decision Modeling throughout the Ages: History of Regression

Hypothesis Testing

Simple Linear Regression Equation

Business Decision Modeling behind the Scenes: The Scientists of Regression

Multiple Regression Model

Performance Measures

t Statistic

F Statistic

p Value

Confidence Level

Multicollinearity

Autocorrelation

Alternative Method for Computing the Durbin-Watson Statistic

Heteroscedasticity

Measuring Accuracy

Lagged Variables

MS Excel Tutorial: Using Add-ins
> *Installing Excel's Data Analysis ToolPak*
> *Excel Tutorial: Regression*
> *Excel Tutorial: Correlation*
> *Excel Tutorial: Scatter Plot*

The Leading Causes of Job Creation in Information Technology: A Regression Analysis
> *Background*
> *Determining the Relationship: Dependent and Independent Variables*
> *Data*
> *Model Selection*
> *Relative Effectiveness of Models*
> *The Regression Line Equation*
> *Dependent Variable versus Independent Variable*

Business Decision Modeling in Action—Linear Regression Analysis at General Motors

Linear Regression: Identifying Support and Resistance

Linear regression is one of the accepted standards for identifying major trends. This statistical model, based on volatility, produces a center- line, or equilibrium price, around which prices will fluctuate; and buy and sell lines that define the range of projected price fluctuation. In theory, 90 percent of all prices will fall between the buy and sell lines. Long-term investors can buy with a minimum of risk when the price approaches the buy line and sell with maximum reward at the sell line.

A daily bar chart for General Motors with linear regression lines and color-coded volume bars.

Optimal Information Area

MacChart Market Analysis Software Web site at http://www.macchart.com/tasc/lsqr.htm.

LINEAR REGRESSION MODELING

Forecasting Technique

Linear regression is a forecasting technique used in business to predict companies' futures.

Regression is one of many forecasting techniques used in the business world to predict companies' futures. The purpose of forecasting is to reduce the level of uncertainty. Some methods are better at predicting short term while others predict better in the long-term range. Regression is one of the most popular methods. The regression analysis helps determine the relationship between the dependent variable (y) and one or more independent variables (x).

You might have tried to purchase or sell a car. In a regression model, sales price would be the dependent variable and the model, year, and mileage could be the independent variables. Many managers use the regression model to predict company sales. Sales would be the dependent variable and advertising might be the independent variable. In reality, it might not be this simple as there are many factors influencing the outcome. However, regression analysis provides the tools for making such predictions. There are many reasons why forecasters choose a linear relationship:

- Simple representation.
- Ease of use.
- Ease of calculations.
- Many relationships in the real world are linear.

Many management scientists use regression because it is better to start with a simple relationship and eliminate relationships that do not work.

The clue is to start simple and eliminate relationships that do not work. This chapter is designed to introduce regression analysis to the reader. Some basic information such as where to look for statistical data will be given, ideal sample size will be introduced, examples of where regression is being used will be presented, and regression modeling steps, scatterplots, and hypotheseies testing will be looked at to make sure all readers have the same statistical background before going on to analyze the data.

Areas of Statistics

Three areas of statistics are studied in this text: descriptive statistics, probabilistic relationships, and inferential statistics.

The most common areas of statistics these days are descriptive, probability, and inferential statistics. **Descriptive statistics** is a procedure for summarizing, organizing, and presenting information graphically to describe quantitative information. It developed when there was a need for collecting data on a nationwide basis. **Probability statistics** is said to be a causal relationship where a change in one variable increases or decreases another. However, that is not the primary cause behind the change. The word *probability* refers to the likelihood that an event will occur. **Inferential statistics** allows a researcher to draw a conclusion from the information as to how likely it is that the result could have been produced by chance. This is also referred to as *statistical induction* and is based on the need for sampling.

Data Sources

Collecting data is a big problem for many. Data refers to primary data or secondary data in statistics. There are several ways to gather data:

- Conduct a survey.
- Conduct a meta study.
- Conduct an observational study.
- Design an experimental study.

Primary data are the original data collected by a researcher. Secondary data are data received literally second hand from someone else.

Primary data are original data collected by the researcher for the first time. These data are collected through surveys, experiments, or interviews. We will not focus on how to conduct a primary research in this textbook. **Secondary data** are data already collected by others. It is difficult and time-consuming to find where to look for many years of data. In conducting a study, it is important to collect data from reliable sources, otherwise the study will be of no importance and false indications will be made. For the data to be useful, they need to be reliable, accurate, relevant, and consistent.

The list below gives an indication of where to look for secondary data and what types of data can be found. Thanks to technology, we are able to gather data in a timely manner and keep ourselves updated.

- *Economic Indicators*, published monthly for the Joint Economic Committee by the Council of Economic Advisers. It includes data on total output, income, spending, employment, unemployment, wages, production, business activities, prices, money, credit, security markets, federal finance, and international statistics.

- *Economic Indicators Handbook,* written by Arsen Darnay, covers a wide range of statistical data from the economy, income, production, GDP, etc.

- *Statistical Abstract of the United States* is published by the U.S. Department of Commerce, Bureau of the Census, annually. The abstract has been published since 1878 and is a summary of statistics on the social, political, and economic organization of the United States.

- *Almanac of the 50 States* presents a general overview of every state. It includes information on population, demographics, geography, environment, health, education, social insurance, welfare programs, housing, construction, government, elections, government finance, crime, law enforcement, courts, labor, income, business trends, etc.

- *Business Statistics of the United States* covers the recent or historical information about the U.S. economy. The book contains information on 2000 economic time series, predominantly from federal government sources for economic trends and patterns.

- *Digest of Education Statistics*, published by the U.S. Department of Education since 1962. It covers information on American education from kindergarten through graduate school.

- *U.S. Industrial Outlook* is published by McGraw Hill and the U.S. Department of Commerce. The book covers statistical information on natural resources and energy, construction and related industries, industrial materials and components, production and manufacturing equipment, information and communication, consumer economy, transportation, health care, financial, business, and educational services.

- *Statistical Yearbook* by Unesco covers statistical data on education, science and technology, culture, and communication. The first issue was published in 1963.

- *International Marketing Data and Statistics* first came out in 1975. A statistical yearbook of business and marketing information, the book covers marketing statistics on 24 principal subject areas.

- *Gale Country & World Rankings Report* covers 3000 countries and world area rankings on a variety of topics including arts, leisure, demographics, education, governmental expenditures, and taxes.

- *The World Almanac* has been published since 1868. It is a book of facts covering economy and business, states of the United States, travel, health, consumer information, sports, etc.

- *The Internet* offers many sites with a wealth of statistical data. Good places to look include government or corporate websites. A book, *Finding Statistics Online*, explains how to search the Internet. This is a good reference when you want to search the Web for the first time for statistical data.

In an observational setting, a researcher is attempting to record what the subject does. No manipulation of the subject is conducted.

In an **observational setting,** the researcher is not trying to influence or manipulate the variables. The researcher inspects the subject being studied and records the data as it is. An observational study involves collecting data visually, listening, reading, smelling, and touching. A positive aspect of an observational study is that information can be collected and recorded as it is found. One does not need to rely on others. In addition, the observation is captured in its natural setting. A negative aspect of an observational study is that it can be a slow process and can be expensive because researchers researchers are needed to monitor the study or purchase surveillance equipment to monitor the event. This again can lead to a limited study because it can become hard to learn about the past.

In an **experimental setting**, the data are generated by setting up an experimental study. The independent variables are chosen before the dependent variable is decided on. Experiments involve interventions by the researcher. The researcher usually manipulates the variables and observes how it affects the dependent variable, which is the subject being studied. A positive aspect of an experiment is that the study can be repeated with other subjects. In addition, the subject can be controlled more easily when studied. A negative aspect is that a laboratory does not make the setting natural and can affect the outcome. It is also not possible to conduct an experiment of the past and it can be difficult to conduct a study based on predictions or intentions.

In an experimental setting, the researcher is manipulating the subject and subsequently observing how the subject behaves.

Statistical Software

There are many statistical software programs on the market that can help the researcher with the regression analysis. The one we find the most useful is Microsoft Excel. The statistical tool pack by Microsoft has advanced greatly over the years and has a wide variety of analysis tools to offer its customers. Advantages are that the analysis tools are very user-friendly and most people have Excel installed on their computers. Other excellent software includes SPSS, SAS, and Minitab. If you are searching for other statistical software, refer to this Web page: *http://www.statistics.com/vendors/Azlisting.html.*

Statistical software packages such as the Data Analysis tool for MS Excel, SPSS, SAS, and Minitab aid in the regression analysis process.

Population versus Sample

A study can be conducted either on a true population or on a sample. A **population** is the collection of all items or entire group. It is the entire item under consideration. In a **sample,** a subgroup is selected to represent the entire population. It is most common to select a sample, for reasons of time and cost limitations. In addition, not all elements in a population can be tested. The most common type of sampling procedure is simple random sampling. The items in the sample are selected so that each possible sample (n) is equally likely to be chosen. The reasons for choosing a sample are that sampling:

Population refers to the collection of all the items in a group. Sample refers to a smaller subgroup. This text will investigate samples only.

- Takes less time.
- Is less costly.
- Is more practical to handle.

Sample Size

It is important to collect enough data for a study to be considered valid. A rule of thumb is to collect n greater than or equal to 10 times the number of β parameters. If there are 3 independent variables in the model, 30 years of data should be collected ($10 \times 3 = 30$). However, in collecting a sample it is important to be sure that the sample represents the true population. Therefore, if more observations are needed to explain the population. then more need to be collected.

Scatter Plots

In a spreadsheet there are two variables, x and y. These variables are plotted in a pair (coordinates). The variable x is plotted horizontally, and the variable y is plotted vertically. These coordinates are the points in the scatter plot. When the slope is large, the line is steep. When the slope is small, the line is almost flat. The relationship can be positive, negative, or curved—or there can be no relationship at all. However, if the line is perfect, one should be suspicious. A person interested in the future would want to determine if the variable y would increase, decrease, or stay the same when x changes. It is important to find out whether the relationship forms a straight or curved line and how steep the line is. The scatter plot patterns (x-y data plots) that one can encounter are illustrated in Figures 6.1 to 6.4.

A scatter plot is a two-dimensional graph in x and y.

From Figure 6.1, it can be seen that when x increases, so does y in a perfect linear relationship. A straight line can easily be drawn between the data points.

In Figure 6.2, the data points form a perfect negative relationship. When x increases, the variable y decreases in a perfect relationship. A straight line can also be drawn between these data points.

Figure 6.3 shows a curved relationship. It is not possible to draw a straight line though these data points.

Finally, Figure 6.4 shows no linear relationship between the x and y data pairs.

Scatter plots that depict a group of data points rising from left to right are said to be positive linear relationship.

Scatter plots that depict data points falling from left to right are said to have a negative linear relationship.

FIGURE 6.1
Scatter Plot of a
Perfect Positive Linear
Relationship

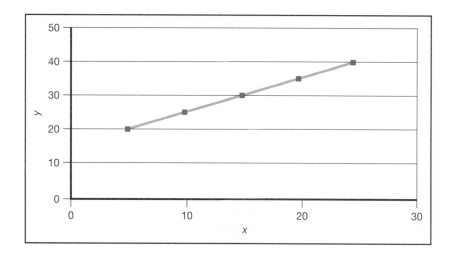

FIGURE 6.2
Scatter Plot of a
Perfect Negative Linear
Relationship

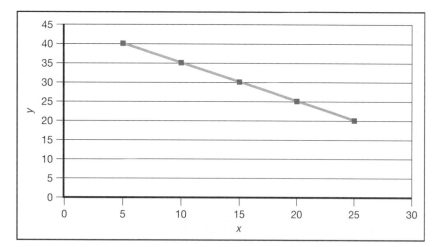

FIGURE 6.3
Scatter Plot Depicting a
Curvilinear Relationship

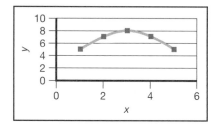

FIGURE 6.4
Scatter Plot Depicting
No Linear Relationship

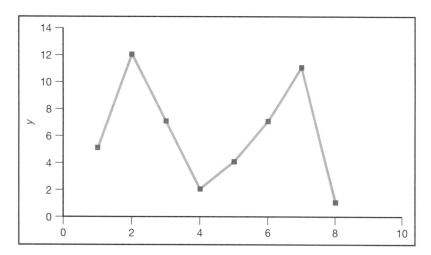

EGYPTIANS, GREEKS, AND ROMANS AND STATISTICS

Statistics can be traced back to the early years of the Egyptians, Greeks, and Romans. Until 1850 the word *statistics* was used in a different sense than it is used today. It meant information about political states, the kind of material that is nowadays to be found assembled in the *Statesman's Yearbook*.

PEARSON, GALTON, GAUSS? WHERE DID IT ALL START?

The technique of regression analysis is not new; it's a standard statistical tool for comparing the relative behavior of two or more variables. Regression analysis originated in Great Britain in the late 19th century, and it has been revised and reconstructed since then to take the present form of $y = a + bx$.

The origin of regression first stemmed from the "Theory of Errors," or Gaussian model (named after K. F. Gauss), which was devised for a measurement problem in astronomy and took the form $\mu = X\beta$. This model was later revised by J. Neyman in 1934 and A. C. Aitken in 1935 and became known as the linear model. The most prominent scientists in developing the regression model were Franc Galton, Francis Ysidro Edgeworth, George Udny Yule, and K. F. Gauss.

PEARSON, GAUSS, AND THE THEORY OF CORRELATION

In 1896, Karl Pearson presented regression and correlation as aspects of the multinormal distribution, hence the entrance of the Theory of Correlation. Pearson's formulas for the multinormal regression were exactly identical to those developed by Gauss for the "least squares" technique, except that the variables *x* and *y* in the Gaussian model were not correlated. To further enhance the technique of regression analysis, G. U. Yule in 1897 extended the linear regression specifications to cases of skew correlation and least squares.

FISHER AND THE STANDARD REGRESSION MODEL

Eventually, in 1922, R. A. Fisher synthesized the regression theory of Pearson and Yule with the least squares theory of Gauss to introduce the fixed *x* regression model. As time passed, mathematicians and scientists have debated over the intricacies of the regression model. It is up to you to decide whether regression analysis will best suit your statistical needs.

OPTIMAL INFORMATION AREA

http://www.processbuilder.com/applications/strategy/help/STRATEGYRunning_a_Regression_Analysis.html

HYPOTHESIS TESTING

Hypothesis testing is used to statistically prove or disprove a hypothesis.

Hypothesis testing is all about testing some kind of claim where the null hypothesis is assumed to be true. There are two kinds of error that can occur; Type I error and Type II error (Table 6.1). The hypothesis is designed so that the correct decision will be made. However, there is always a chance of accepting the null hypotheses when it should not have been done. If the null hypothesis H_0 is considered false, there has to be a second hypothesis H_1 that is true. The H_1 is the alternative hypothesis.

Hypothesis testing is designed so that our rejection of the null hypothesis is based on evidence from the sample that our alternative hypothesis is far more likely to be true. Failure to reject the null hypothesis is not proof that it is true.

We can never prove that the null hypothesis is correct because our decision is based only on the sample information and not on the entire population. Therefore, if we fail to reject the null hypothesis we can only conclude that there is insufficient evidence to warrant its rejection.

There are four steps to hypothesis testing.

There are four steps we should follow when conducting a hypothesis test when we want to make a statistical decision:

- State the null hypothesis.
- State the alternative hypothesis.

TABLE 6.1
Type I and Type II Error

	H_0 true	H_0 false
Accept H_0	Correct decision probability = $1 - \alpha$	Type II error probability = α
Reject H_0	Type I error probability = α	Correct decision probability = $1 - \alpha$

- Choose the level of significance and sample size.
- Find the rejection regions.

Concept *Check*
Example

One of Aironet Inc.'s product lines is the Cisco Aironet 340 series, a local wireless area network technology. This product allows people to move around and still be connected to the network. The system offers 11-Mbps bandwidth and guarantees that at a 1-Mbps range the system can connect at a distance up to 1800 ft in open air and 350 ft inside the office.

- H_0 = 11-Mbps bandwidth
- $H_1 \neq$ 11-Mbps bandwidth

Assume that we want to test the inside range of the product at a 95 percent confidence level. The α value can be found in a t table to be equal 1.960.

- Reject H_0 if $t > +1.96$
- Reject H_0 if $t < -1.96$
- Accept H_0 if the t value is within the range

If the calculated t statistic is less than the t critical value, one must accept the null hypothesis.

Further, assume a total of 50 wireless local-area networks (WLANs) have been monitored and average a total range of 357 ft (mean = 357) and a standard deviation of 30. By using the t-test statistic, the t value can be found.

$$t = \frac{\bar{X} - \mu}{\frac{S}{\sqrt{n}}}$$

Since $t = +1.6499$, we can see that $-1.96 < +1.65 < +1.97$. The decision is therefore to not reject H_0. It can be concluded that the Cisco Aironet 340 can cover a range of 357 ft on average. It can further be concluded that there is no evidence that the average range of Cisco Aironet 340 is different from 350 ft.

$$t = \frac{357 - 350}{\frac{30}{\sqrt{50}}} = 1.65$$

SIMPLE LINEAR REGRESSION EQUATION

A linear regression consists of one dependent and one independent variable. The independent variable predicts the dependent variable. The dependent variable, on the other hand, is the variable being predicted and is referred to as the *criterion variable*. The regression equation of a sample, which is the equation of a straight line, is expressed as:

$$\hat{Y} = b_0 + b_1 X_1 + \varepsilon$$

where

$\hat{Y}$ = the dependent variable
X_1 = the independent variable
b_0 = intercept
b_1 = individual independent variable contributions
ε = error term

The dependent variable is also referred to as the *predictor*. The slope is defined as the change in y for every one-unit change in x. When data are tested with the regression model, the slope is expected to change in response when the predictor increases by one unit (Figure 6.5):

$$\hat{y} = b_0 + b_1 x$$

FIGURE 6.5
Simple Linear
Representation

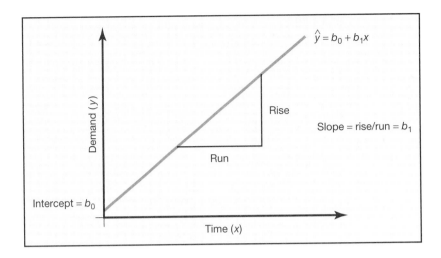

Simple linear regression attempts to fit a line to a set of data.

The intercept is defined as the value of the response, y, expected when the predictor, x, equals zero:.

The symbol b is referred to as the *population parameter*. Looking at the graph, we see that b_0 represents the point where the line crosses the vertical y-axis. The symbol b_1 represents the slope of the line. Figure 6.5 displays a simple linear relationship and the equation for a line in slope intercept form.

Concept *Check*
Example

Suppose the data in Table 6.2 have been found for sales and selling price, where y = sales per day, and x = the selling price. The calculations necessary to find b_0 and b_1 are shown in the table.

The slope of the linear regression curve is therefore

$$b_1 = \frac{\sum_{i=1}^{n} x_i y_i - n\overline{x}\overline{y}}{\sum_{i=1}^{n} x_i^2 - n\overline{x}^2} = \frac{145 - (1/6)(30)(32)}{164 - (1/6)(30)^2} = \frac{-15.00}{14.06} = -1.0669$$

The intercept can be calculated as follows:

$$\overline{x} = \frac{30}{6} = 5 \quad \text{and} \quad \overline{y} = \frac{32}{6} = 5.33$$

$$b_0 = \overline{y} - b_1\overline{x} = 5.33 - (-1.0669)(5.00) = 10.6645$$

The least squares regression line for the data above is found to be:

$$\hat{y} = 10.6645 - 1.0669x$$

TABLE 6.2
Linear Regression
Computation

i	x_i	y_i	$x_i y_i$	x_i^2
1	5	5	25	25
2	8	3	24	64
3	3	8	24	9
4	4	6	24	16
5	4	6	24	14
6	6	4	24	36
Sum	30	32	145	164

FRANC GALTON (1822–1911)

Galton showed early signs of intellectual prowess. His major contributions to statistics were in connection with genetics and psychology. The fact that the regression of y on x differed from that of x on y made him worry. In 1877 he discovered a solution. By normalizing x and y in terms of their own variability, he solved the problem. The regression coefficient he then called the *correlation coefficient*. Since it was a regression, Galton called it simple r, hence the modern one-word name.

GEORGE UDNY YULE (1871–1951)

Yule was born in Beech Hill near Haddington, Scotland, and at the age of 16 he began engineering studies at University College, London. Yule laid the foundations for the autoregressive series and invented the correlogram. The terms *Yule process* and *Yule distribution* are well known in the statistical literature.

KARL PEARSON (1857–1936)

Pearson was educated at University College School and at Kings College, Cambridge. Through his many papers, Pearson studied the likelihood function, χ^2 goodness-of-fit test, frequency curves, and the errors of movements. Pearson expressed the goal of the statistician in this way: "The imagination of man has always run riot, but to imagine a thing is not meritorious unless we demonstrate its reasonableness by the laborious process of studying how it fits experience."

RONALD AYLMER FISHER (1890–1962)

In 1912, Fisher published a paper on the maximum likelihood theory. He was able to prove that using the sample mean instead of the population mean was equivalent to reducing the dimensionality of the sample space by one. This concept became known as the degrees of freedom concept.

FRANCIS YSIDRO EDGEWORTH (1845–1926)

Edgeworth's original contributions to mathematical, or analytical, economics include the indifference curve, the contract curve, the law of diminishing returns, and the determination of economic equilibria. His statistical contributions included work on index numbers, the law of error, the theory of estimation, correlation, goodness of fit, and probability theory.

MULTIPLE REGRESSION MODEL

In a multiple regression, the linear equation is the same as in simple linear regression except more than one independent variable is present.

$$\hat{y} = b_0 + b_1 x_1 + b_2 x_2 + \ldots + \varepsilon$$

where

Multiple linear regression is a more powerful extension of simple linear regression, where the model now contains multiple independent variables.

$\hat{y}$ = the dependent variable
x_i = the independent variable(s)
b_0 = intercept
b_i = individual independent variable contributions
ε = error term

This is a more realistic model, as real-life situations are not as easy and simple as a simple linear regression. Usually more than one independent variable is necessary to explain the dependent variable. To determine the multiple regression equation the values of b_0, b_1, and b_2 are found by using the following equations.

$$\sum y = nb_0 + b_1 \sum x_1 + b_2 \sum x_2$$

$$\sum x_1 y = b_0 \sum x_1 + b_1 \sum x_1^2 + b_2 \sum x_1 x_2$$

$$\sum x_2 y = b_0 \sum x_2 + b_1 \sum x_1 x_2 + b_2 \sum x_2^2$$

These equations are referred to as *normal equations*. To solve these equations the matrix method is used.

Concept *Check*
Example

A store owner wants to determine if consumer confidence is affected by gross domestic product (GDP) and the unemployment rate. This example involves two variables. A total of 15 years of data have been found. This problem is solved by using Excel.

The following computations for the linear multiple regression analysis are necessary to determine the values of b_0, b_1, and b_2:

$$1480 = 15b_0 + 50.2b_1 + 96.4b_2$$
$$5186 = 50.2b_0 + 201.28b_1 + 317.21b_2$$
$$9222.4 = 96.4b_0 + 317.21b_1 + 640.24b_2$$

Table 6.3 displays the data for the example problem and Table 6.4 shows the computation results.

The regression output created by Excel is presented in Figure 6.6. From this output, the regression equation is found to be:

$$\hat{y} = 163.54 + 4.94x_1 - 12.67x_2$$

TABLE 6.3
Linear Regression
Example Data

t	Year	y	x_1	x_2
1	1984	102	7	7.4
2	1985	100	3.6	7.1
3	1986	95	3.1	7.9
4	1987	103	2.9	7.1
5	1988	115	3.8	5.4
6	1989	117	3.4	5.2
7	1990	92	1.7	5.6
8	1991	69	−0.2	7.8
9	1992	62	3.3	7.5
10	1993	66	2.4	7.9
11	1994	91	4.0	7.1
12	1995	100	2.7	5.6
13	1996	105	3.7	5.4
14	1997	125	4.5	4.9
15	1998	138	4.3	4.5

Note: y = consumer confidence, x_1 = GDP, and x_2 = unemployment rate.

TABLE 6.4
Multiple Regression
Example Computations

t	y	x_1	x_2	x_1y	x_2y	x_1x_2	y^2	x_1^2	x_2^2
1	102	7	7.4	714	754.8	51.8	10404	49	54.76
2	100	3.6	7.1	360	710	25.56	10000	12.96	50.41
3	95	3.1	7.9	294.5	750.5	24.49	9025	9.61	62.41
4	103	2.9	7.1	298.7	731.3	20.59	10609	8.41	50.41
5	115	3.8	5.4	437	621	20.52	13225	14.44	29.16
6	117	3.4	5.2	397.8	608.4	17.68	13689	11.56	27.04
7	92	1.7	5.6	156.4	515.2	9.52	8464	2.89	31.36
8	69	−0.2	7.8	−13.8	538.2	−1.56	4761	0.04	60.84
9	62	3.3	7.5	204.6	465	24.75	3844	10.89	56.25
10	66	2.4	7.9	158.4	521.4	18.96	4356	5.76	62.41
11	91	4	7.1	364	646.1	28.4	8281	16	50.41
12	100	2.7	5.6	270	560	15.12	10000	7.29	31.36
13	105	3.7	5.4	388.5	567	19.98	11025	13.69	29.16
14	125	4.5	4.9	562.5	612.5	22.05	15625	20.25	24.01
15	138	4.3	4.5	593.4	621	19.35	19044	18.49	20.25
Total	1480	50.2	96.4	5186	9222.4	317.21	152352	201.28	640.24
Mean	98.667	3.347	6.423						

Performance Measures

A number of statistical performance measures must be analyzed to decide if the regression model is an adequate or "good" model. The following sections investigate the *R, F,* and *t* statistics.

R Square

R square is a measure of correlation and indicates the percentage of variation that results from the independent variable(s).

Output from a software package such as Excel contains almost all the information needed to analyze and develop a linear regression model.

R square is referred to as the *coefficient of determination. R* square is also another measure of correlation. This value should be close to 1.0. The scale ranges from 0.0 to 1.0. R^2 indicates the percentage of variation in the dependent variable that results from the independent variable. It is basically a measure of how well the independent variables explain the dependent variable. It is referred to as the measure of *goodness of fit.* R^2 can never decrease when a new independent variables is introduced to the model. The reason is that the method of least squares minimizes the explained sum of squares. This basically means we could increase R^2 regardless of whether the independent variable relates to the dependent variable. The formula for R^2 is:

$$R^2 = \frac{\sum_{i=1}^{n}(\hat{y}_i - \bar{y})^2}{\sum_{i=1}^{n}(y_i - \bar{y})^2}$$

Concept *Check Example*

Going back to the example of consumer confidence, we find that R^2 equals 76.08 percent. This means that 76.08 percent of the total variance in the dependent variable around the mean has been accounted for by the two independent variables in the estimated regression function. This means the independent variables are doing a good job of explaining the dependent variable.

Multiple R

Multiple *R* is a measure of the strength of a linear relationship.

Multiple *R* represents the strength of the linear relationship between actual and estimated values. The scale ranges from 0.0 to 1.0. It is preferable to have a value close to 1.0 because this indicates a good fit.

Figure 6.6   Excel Output for Multiple Regression Example

	A	B	C	D	E	F	G	H	I
1	SUMMARY OUTPUT								
2									
3	*Regression Statistics*								
4	Multiple R	0.872277395							
5	R Square	0.760867854							
6	Adjusted R Square	0.721012497							
7	Standard Error	11.22716398							
8	Observations	15							
9									
10	ANOVA								
11		*df*	*SS*	*MS*	*F*	*Significance F*			
12	Regression	2	4812.742801	2406.371	19.09073	0.000186994			
13	Residual	12	1512.590532	126.0492					
14	Total	14	6325.333333						
15									
16		*Coefficients*	*Standard Error*	*t Stat*	*P-value*	*Lower 95%*	*Upper 95%*	*Lower 95.0%*	*Upper 95.0%*
17	Intercept	163.543706	18.96528608	8.623319	1.73E-06	122.2218974	204.8655145	122.2218974	204.8655145
18	X1	4.940809362	1.988908544	2.484181	0.028737	0.607349915	9.274268809	0.607349915	9.274268809
19	X2	-12.66788609	2.521192535	-5.02456	0.000297	-18.16109273	-7.174679459	-18.1610927	-7.17467946

Our model presented a value of 87.23 percent, which is good, and now we can continue on to the next test.

Concept *Check*
Example

Adjusted *R* square adjusts the *R* measurement on the basis of the sample size of the data set.

Adjusted R

This value is supposed to give the researcher a clearer estimate of how much the independent variable in a regression analysis explains the dependent variable. Again, this estimate is a measure of strength.

Concept *Check*
Example

Looking at Figure 6.6, we find the adjusted *R* square is 72.10 percent, which is within the boundaries as well.

t Statistic

The *t* statistic looks at individual variables and shows how they affect *y* singularly. The *t* statistic is the value that is compared to the critical region. A critical region is an area in a sampling distribution representing values that are critical to a particular study. They are critical because, when a sample statistic falls in that region, the null hypothesis can be rejected. The null hypothesis, in general for any independent variable that is being tested, is

The *t* statistic measures the significance of each individual independent variable.

$$H_0 : b_i = 0$$

In words, we are testing to see if a particular coefficient of contribution (b_i) is actually different from zero. If the *t* statistic is deemed significant, we reject this hypothesis. Acceptance or rejection of the underlying hypothesis is next.

The rule of thumb says the *t* statistic should be greater than 2. However, to be more accurate, the *t* table can be used to find the real value. It is possible to conduct a one-tail test or a two-tail test.

Concept *Check*
Example

Looking up the t distribution in a table, we find the number of degrees of freedom is 12. When the critical value of *t* is at the 5 percent level of significance, it shows a value of 2.179. This is the value for a two-tailed test. Our *t* values, from Figure 6.6, are 2.48 for x_1 and -5.02 for x_2. The null hypothesis is therefore rejected because both the values fall within the rejected regions.

F Statistic

The *F* statistic measures how well the independent variables as a whole are predicting the dependent variable.

The *F* statistic measures the significance of statistical joint relationships among independent variables, and it looks at the model as a whole. For the most part, the *F* statistic is associated with the analysis of variance (ANOVA).

The null hypothesis that is being tested is as follows:

$$H_0 : b_0 = b_1 = b_2 = \cdots b_n = 0$$

In words, we are testing to see if any of thecoefficients of contribution (*b*'s) actually are different from zero. If *F* is deemed significant we reject this hypothesis. Acceptance or rejection of the underlying hypothesis is next.

F is automatically calculated a regression analysis is run. In earlier years, one had to refer to an *F* distribution table to look up the value. The rule of thumb is that the *F* statistic should be greater than 4 to be considered significant. The equation for the *F* test is:

Concept *Check*
Example

$$F = \frac{\text{mean square of regression}}{\text{mean square of error}} = \frac{\text{variance of regression}}{\text{variance of error}}$$

Figure 6.6 shows an *F* value of 19.09, which is greater than 4. This means the *F* value meets the criterion. Looking up the exact value of *F*, find it to be 3.88. The result is that the null hypothesis is accepted.

p values are another way to interpret t statistics. The rule of thumb is: If the *p* value is less than the level of significance, the variable is statistically significant.

p Value

The *p* value should be less than 0.05, which means there would be less than a 0.05 chance that the data have been produced by chance. In addition, the *p* value goes hand in hand with the *t* statistic. This value is often viewed as the minimum level of significance.

Referring back to Figure 6.6, the *p* value for *x*1 is 0.028 and for *x*2 is 0.0003, which means the criterion has been satisfied.

Confidence Level

The confidence level is set to be 95 percent. A confidence level is a desired percentage of the scores. It is usually set at 95 or 99 percent, meaning that 95 or 99 percent would fall within a certain range of confidence limits. It is calculated by subtracting the alpha level from 1 and multiplying the result times 100; for example, $100(1 - 0.05) = 95\%$.

A confidence interval is a range of values of a sample statistic that is likely to contain a population parameter. It is the interval that will include the population parameter a certain percentage of the time. The wider the confidence interval, the higher the confidence level. Basically an alpha level of 0.05 results in a confidence coefficient of 0.95. Figure 6.7 displays the dialog box that prompts the user to input the confidence level.

Consider a sample size of 30 in which the average age is found to be 25, and the sample standard deviation equals 10. The interval is 1.96; this value can be found in a *t* table. This interval is found by forming an interval around the sample mean. Basically, there are 1.96 standard deviations on each side of the mean of any normal curve, and this interval will include approximately 95 percent of the values. The formula used to calculate the range is:

$$\text{Range} = X + \frac{ZS}{\sqrt{n}}$$

$$= 25 + \frac{(1.96)(10)}{\sqrt{30}}$$

$$= 25 \pm 3.579$$

$$= 21.421 \text{ to } 28.579$$

From this it can be concluded that there is a 95 percent chance the sample mean was chosen from the sampling distribution and that the population mean lies in the interval range of 21.421 to 28.578. The formula for calculating the interval for a population is:

$$\bar{p} \pm Z \frac{\sqrt{p(1-p)}}{n}$$

Consider the scenario of predicting consumer confidence. When conducting a regression analysis, Excel creates the interval when the user specifies the level of confidence desired (Figure 6.8).

FIGURE 6.7
Excel Data Tools
Regression Dialog Box

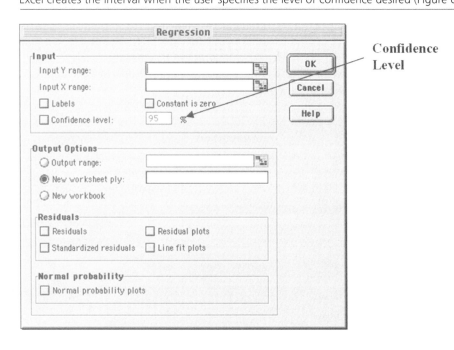

Figure 6.8 **Excel Output for Example Regression Analysis**

	A	B	C	D	E	F	G	H	I
1	SUMMARY OUTPUT								
2									
3	*Regression Statistics*								
4	Multiple R	0.872277395							
5	R Square	0.760867854							
6	Adjusted R Square	0.721012497							
7	Standard Error	11.22716398							
8	Observations	15							
9									
10	ANOVA								
11		*df*	*SS*	*MS*	*F*	*Significance F*			
12	Regression	2	4812.742801	2406.371	19.09073	0.000186994			
13	Residual	12	1512.590532	126.0492					
14	Total	14	6325.333333						
15									
16		*Coefficients*	*Standard Error*	*t Stat*	*P-value*	*Lower 95%*	*Upper 95%*	*Lower 95.0%*	*Upper 95.0%*
17	Intercept	163.543706	18.96528608	8.623319	1.73E-06	122.2218974	204.8655145	122.2218974	204.8655145
18	X1	4.940809362	1.988908544	2.484181	0.028737	0.607349915	9.274268809	0.607349915	9.274268809
19	X2	-12.66788609	2.521192535	-5.02456	0.000297	-18.16109273	-7.174679459	-18.1610927	-7.17467946

In this example the confidence interval was set at 99 percent. Therefore the result will come up with an upper and lower percentile range for both the 95 and 99 percent confidence interval.

Multicollinearity

Multicollinearity exists when two or more variables are highly correlated.

Multicollinearity increases the uncertainty of the parameter estimates. This makes it difficult, if not impossible, to determine the parameters' separate effects on the dependent variable. Multicollinearity is something that should be avoided if possible. Excel can help test for collinearity. In trying to solve the problem, one can:

* Rethink the impetus of linear regression.
* Drop one of the correlated variables.
* Use stepwise regression to screen variables (SPSS is a software program that can help eliminate factors).
* Look for new variables that can better explain the model.

Variables are said to be correlated if the absolute value of R is high.

The correlation coefficient can range from -0.1 to $+1.0$. A relationship of $+1$ indicates a perfect positive correlation. A relationship of -1 indicates a perfect negative correlation. The value of 0 indicates no correlation at all. The interpretation is summarized in Table 6.5.

Further, a correlation matrix can be created to analyze the relationship between the independent variables (Table 6.6). From this matrix one can compare any of the combinations of two variables.

TABLE 6.5
Interpretation of Correlation and *R*

|R|	Interpretation
0.90	Very strong linear relationship/correlation
0.70 to 0.90	Strong linear relationship/correlation
0.50 to 0.70	Suspect linear relationship/or moderate correlation
0.50	Most likely not a linear relationship/ or weak correlation

TABLE 6.6
Correlation Matrix

Variable	x_1	x_2	x_3
x_1	1		
x_2	r_{21}	1	
x_3	r_{31}	r_{32}	1

FIGURE 6.9
Example of Excel Data Analysis Dialogue Box

Excel's Data Analysis tool performs correlation analysis.

A negative number has no effect on the correlation between the variables. All numbers are looked at without the sign in front. If a correlation above 0.80 should occur, multicollinearity is taking place. It is preferable that the correlation be less than 0.50, as one does not want the variables to measure the same thing. Multicollinearity increases the likelihood of rounding errors in calculating the parameter estimates. In addition, it increases the level of uncertainty. Figure 6.9 displays the Excel Data Analysis dialog box.

Concept *Check* *Example*

Consider the scenario of predicting consumer confidence. By highlighting the independent variables x_1 and x_2, using the correlation test, the correlation matrix in Table 6.7 is created.

Looking at the data, we find the correlation to be -0.04256, which means a linear relationship is most likely not taking place. This means the two independent variables do not explain the same thing and can successfully be used together in a multiple regression test to predict the dependent variable. The negative sign has no effect on the decision and interpretation. It can also be concluded that no multicollinearity is taking place.

Autocorrelation

A Durbin-Watson statistic is used to detect residual autocorrelation.

A Durbin-Watson statistic must to be calculated to measure autocorrelation. It measures the correlation of each residual and the residual for the time period immediately preceding the one of interest. It is desirable that the Durbin-Watson statistic be above 2 and greater than the upper range found in a statistical table for the values given. As the autocorrelation increases, the Durbin-Watson statistic goes down.

Basically, the larger the autocorrelation, the less reliable the results of the regression analysis will be. Calculate the Durbin-Watson statistic (d) and find upper and lower d limits, d_U and d_L. The rule of thumb is that if $d = 2$, residuals are uncorrelated. The criteria are

If the Durbin-Watson statistic is equal to 2, then the residuals are uncorrelated. Otherwise, the Durbin Watson test statistic must be compared to a high and low range table.

If $d > d_U$ residuals are uncorrelated (do not reject H_0)

If $d < d_L$ residuals are uncorrelated (reject H_0)

If $d_L < d < d_U$ test is inconclusive

If the residuals are correlated, one must rethink the model. When conducting a Durbin-Watson test, the following hypothesis needs to be tested:

$$H_0 : p = 0$$

$$H_1 : p > 0$$

TABLE 6.7
Example Data Correlation Matrix

	x_1	x_2
x_1	1	
x_2	-0.04256	1

The symbol p is the autocorrelation parameter. When the Durbin-Watson statistic is larger than the upper range, the autocorrelation coefficient is equal to zero. When the Durbin-Watson statistic is less than the lower range, the autocorrelation coefficient is greater than zero. Finally, when the Durbin-Watson statistic lies between the upper and lower range, the test is inconclusive. Therefore, it can be concluded that more tests are needed to come to a conclusion. There are three steps to calculate the Durbin-Watson statistic:

1. The least squares regression line needs to be fitted to the data.
2. The residuals need to be calculated.
3. The Durbin-Watson statistic is computed.

Autocorrelation leads to spurious regression results.

The formulas for the Durbin-Watson calculation are:

$$\text{DW} = \frac{\sum_{t=2}^{n} (e_t - e_{t-1})^2}{\sum_{t-1}^{n} e_t^2}$$

e_t = error or difference between point and line

e_{t-1} = error or difference between and line for previous time period

$\sum_{t=2}^{n} (e_t - e_{t-1})^2$ = difference between present residual and previous residual, squared and

summed for all observations

$\sum_{t=1}^{n} e_t^2$ = each of residuals squared and then summed

Concept *Check* *Example*

Let us go back to the example of predicting the consumer confidence index and determining the effect the independent variables has on the dependent variable. The Durbin-Watson (DW) computation is demonstrated below and results are shown in Figure 6.10.

$$e_t - e_{t-1} = 8.661 - (-2.387) = 10.998$$

$$(e_t - e_{t-1})^2 = 10.998^2 = 120.964$$

$$e_t^2 = 8.611^2 = 74.156$$

$$\text{DW} = \frac{\sum_{t=2}^{n} (e_t - e_{t-1})^2}{\sum_{t=1}^{n} e_t^2} = \frac{1927.14}{1512.59} = 1.27$$

In Figure 6.10, columns A, B, and C were created automatically by Excel when the regression was run. The rest has to be calculated either by hand or by using formulas. The Excel formulas for the Durbin-Watson calculation are shown in Table 6.8.

95 percent level of significance. Analyzing the Durbin-Watson at the 0.05 level of significance, we find from a statistical table that the lower range is 0.95 and the upper range is 1.54. Therefore we can conclude that, at the 95 percent level of significance, the test is inconclusive and more analysis would be needed.

99 percent level of significance. Looking at the values for Durbin-Watson at the 0.01 level of significance, we find from a statistical table that the lower range is 0.70 and the upper range is 1.25. Therefore, we can conclude that, at the 99 percent level of significance, the test shows there is no autocorrelation.

It is important to be aware of the difference between the 95 and 99 percent levels of confidence, as it can have a big effect on the model being tested.

FIGURE 6.10
Excel Spreadsheet for Durbin-Watson Calculation

	A	B	C	D	E	F	G
						C7-LR1.xls	
23	RESIDUAL OUTPUT						
24							
25	*Observation*	*Predicted Y*	*Residuals*	*et-1*	*et - (et-1)*	*(et - (et-1))2*	*et2*
26	1	104.387014	-2.3870144				5.69783776
27	2	91.3886284	8.6113716	-2.3870144	10.998386	120.9644947	74.1557208
28	3	78.7839148	16.2160852	8.6113716	7.60471356	57.83166828	262.961418
29	4	87.9300618	15.0699382	16.2160852	-1.146147	1.313652953	227.103036
30	5	113.912197	1.08780337	15.0699382	-13.9821348	195.5000932	1.18331616
31	6	114.46945	2.53054989	1.08780337	1.44274653	2.081517538	6.40368275
32	7	101.00292	-9.00291976	2.53054989	-11.5334696	133.0209221	81.0525641
33	8	63.7460326	5.25396744	-9.00291976	14.2568872	203.2588325	27.6041739
34	9	84.8392312	-22.8392312	5.25396744	-28.0931986	789.2278073	521.63048
35	10	75.3253483	-9.32534829	-22.8392312	13.5138829	182.6250301	86.9621208
36	11	93.3649521	-2.36495215	-9.32534829	6.96039615	48.4471145	5.59299865
37	12	105.943729	-5.94372912	-2.36495215	-3.57877697	12.80764461	35.3279158
38	13	113.418116	-8.4181157	-5.94372912	-2.47438658	6.122588952	70.8646719
39	14	123.704706	1.29529376	-8.4181157	9.71340946	94.3503234	1.67778594
40	15	127.783699	10.2163012	1.29529376	8.92100743	79.58437365	104.37281
41						1927.136064	1512.59053
42							
43	DW:	1.2740633					

TABLE 6.8
Excel Formulas for Calculating the Durbin-Watson Statistic

Cell	Formula
D27	=C26
E27	=C27−D27
F27	=E27^2
G26	=G26^2
F41	=SUM(F27:F40)
G41	=SUM(G27:G40)
B22	=F41/H41

Alternative Method for Computing the Durbin-Watson Statistic

The Durbin-Watson statistic can also be computed by using some simple Excel formulas. Figures 6.11 and 6.12 display the mechanics of computing the Durbin-Watson statistic in this manner.

Figure 6.11 displays just the residuals (column B) and the final Durbin-Watson statistics (cells F4 to F6). Figure 6.12 displays the formulas behind the calculations. Note in Figure 6.11 that the residuals have not been rounded as they are in Figure 6.12. This is a result of formatting and has no effect on the calculations.

As would be expected, the two calculation methods produce the same Durbin-Watson statistic and the same final conclusions as stated earlier.

Heteroscedasticity

Heteroscedasticity exists when the residuals of a linear regression model do not have constant variance.

Heteroscedasticity exists when the errors or residuals do not have a constant variance across an entire range of values. This also needs to be looked into by plotting the residuals in a graph. From the graph it can be determined if a pattern exists or not.

FIGURE 6.11
Alternative Method for Computing the Durbin-Watson Statistic

	C7-LR1.xls					
	A	B	C	D	E	F
1	RESIDUAL OUTPUT					
2				Durbin Watson Calculations		
3	*Observation*	*Residuals*				
4	1	-2.38701		Squared Difference of Residuals		1927.136064
5	2	8.61137		Squared Residuals		1512.590532
6	3	16.21609		Durbin-Watson Statistic		1.274063286
7	4	15.06994				
8	5	1.08780				
9	6	2.53055				
10	7	-9.00292				
11	8	5.25397				
12	9	-22.83923				
13	10	-9.32535				
14	11	-2.36495				
15	12	-5.94373				
16	13	-8.41812				
17	14	1.29529				
18	15	10.21630				

FIGURE 6.12
Excel Formulas for Durbin-Watson Statistic Calculations

	C7-LR1.xls					
	A	B	C	D	E	F
1	RESIDUAL OUTPUT					
2				Durbin Watson Calculations		
3	*Observation*	*Residuals*				
4	1	-2.3870144		Squared Difference of Residuals		=SUMXMY2(B5:B18,B4:B17)
5	2	8.61137159		Squared Residuals		=SUMSQ(B4:B18)
6	3	16.2160851		Durbin-Watson Statistic		=F4/F5
7	4	15.0699381				
8	5	1.08780336				
9	6	2.53054989				
10	7	-9.0029197				
11	8	5.25396744				
12	9	-22.839231				
13	10	-9.3253482				
14	11	-2.3649521				
15	12	-5.9437291				
16	13	-8.4181156				
17	14	1.29529376				
18	15	10.2163011				

Concept *Check* *Example*

Consider the scenario of predicting consumer confidence. Figure 6.13 displays the square values of the residuals from the original regression. It can be concluded that there is a tendency of heteroscedasticity, as there seems to be continuous growth from 1994 to 1999.

MEASURING ACCURACY

Error measurements are important for proving the validity and comparing linear regression models.

The R, F, and t statistics are used to determine if the underlying regression model is a good fit. However, when different forecasting models, including regression models, are compared to each other, a set of accuracy measures must be looked at.

This is an important process for the researcher because this strategy will lead to valid and useful results for the industry, future students, degree holders in this field, universities, investors, etc. The example below will illustrate how the computations are completed for the error measurements by using formulas in an MS Excel spreadsheet.

To evaluate and compare multiple regression models, four forecasting error techniques will be used to evaluate the forecasting method. These are mean square error (MSE), mean absolute error or mean absolute deviation (MAD), mean percentage error (MPE), and mean absolute percentage error (MAPE). These methods measure the accuracy of the models and tell the researchers which method is the best. They are used for model comparison.

FIGURE 6.13
Plot of Residuals Depicting Heteroscedasticity

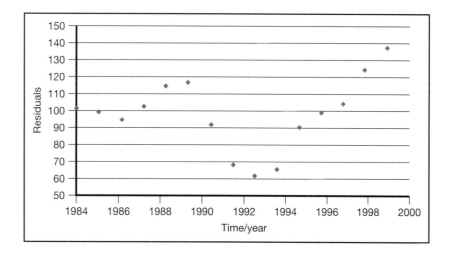

MSE measures the mean square error of the model.

MSE is a method that provides a penalty for large forecasting errors because it squares each error or residual. The formula is:

$$MSE = \frac{\sum\limits_{t=1}^{n} (y_t - \hat{y}_t)^2}{n}$$

MAD measures the mean absolute deviation of a model.

MAD measures the forecast accuracy by averaging the magnitudes of the forecast errors. This technique is most useful when you want to measure forecast error in the same units as the original series. The formula is:

$$MAD = \frac{\sum\limits_{t=1}^{n} |y_t - \hat{y}_t|}{n}$$

MAPE measures the mean absolute percentage error of a model.

MAPE is a method that tries to find the absolute error in each period. MAPE provides an indication of how large the forecast errors are in comparison to the actual values of the series. In addition, MAPE can be used to compare the accuracy of the same or different techniques on two entirely different series. The formula is:

$$MAPE = \frac{\sum\limits_{t=1}^{n} \frac{|y_t - \hat{y}_t|}{y_t}}{n}$$

MPE measures the mean percentage error of a model.

MPE is an excellent method to determine if a bias exists. This tells us if the method is consistently forecasting too low or too high. The formula is:

$$MPE = \frac{\sum\limits_{t=1}^{n} \frac{(y_t - \hat{y}_t)}{y_t}}{n}$$

Concept *Check*
Example

Consider the scenario of predicting consumer confidence. The four error estimates to test the model have been used. The result of the residual printouts and calculations will be shown. The predicted *y* and residuals columns are created by Excel when it runs a regression. The other columns have to be created manually. Other parts of this example will later be expanded on. The results of the Excel calculations are:

$$MSE = \frac{\sum\limits_{t=1}^{n}(y_t - \hat{y}_t)^2}{n} = \frac{1513.58}{15} = 100.8394$$

It is important to calculate many different error measurements and compare them, as each measures error in a different manner.

$$MAD = \frac{\sum_{t=1}^{n} |y_t - \hat{y}_t|}{n} = \frac{120.56}{15} = 8.0375$$

$$MAPE = \frac{\sum_{t-1}^{n} \frac{|y_t - \hat{y}_t|}{y_t}}{n} = \frac{1.39}{15} = 0.927$$

$$MPE = \frac{\sum_{t=1}^{n} \frac{(y_t - \hat{y}_t)}{y_t}}{n} = \frac{-0.301}{15} = -0.020$$

The formulas in Figure 6.14 show how the error measurements are calculated and Table 6.9 displays the Excel formulas used in the calculations.

Looking at the results, we can conclude that there is no bias taking place because MPE has a value close to zero.

LAGGED VARIABLES

In some instances it is necessary to lag one or more of the variables to create a more appropriate data set and a more useful result. A very realistic example in the business world is sales and advertising expenditures. In a scenario like this, it is more useful to compare previous advertisement to current sales than current advertisement to current sales. The reason is that one always wants to look at previous years when predicting the future. For example, a student would look at earlier years as a student when predicting the financial needs to continue the education. To avoid any possible problems with the regression model, the data can be incorporated into a time-series regression. The regression model would be written as:

$$\hat{y} = \beta_0 + \beta_1 x_t + \beta_2 x_{t-1} + \epsilon_t$$

Figure 6.14 **Excel Output for Error Calculations**

	A	B	C	D	E	F	G	H	I	J	K
1	RESIDUAL OUTPUT										
2											
3	Observation	Actual Y	Predicted Y	Residuals	et-1	et - (et-1)	(et - (et-1))2	et2	|et|	et/Y	|et|/Y
4	1	102	104.387014	-2.3870144				5.69783776	2.3870144	-0.0234021	0.0234021
5	2	100	91.3886284	8.6113716	-2.3870144	10.998386	120.964495	74.1557208	8.6113716	0.08611372	0.08611372
6	3	95	78.7839148	16.2160852	8.6113716	7.60471356	57.8316683	262.961418	16.2160852	0.17069563	0.17069563
7	4	103	87.9300618	15.0699382	16.2160852	-1.146147	1.31365295	227.103036	15.0699382	0.14631008	0.14631008
8	5	115	113.912197	1.08780337	15.0699382	-13.982135	195.500093	1.18331616	1.08780337	0.00945916	0.00945916
9	6	117	114.46945	2.53054989	1.08780337	1.44274653	2.08151754	6.40368275	2.53054989	0.02162863	0.02162863
10	7	92	101.00292	-9.0029198	2.53054989	-11.53347	133.020922	81.0525641	9.00291976	-0.0978578	0.09785782
11	8	69	63.7460326	5.25396744	-9.0029198	14.2568872	203.258833	27.6041739	5.25396744	0.07614446	0.07614446
12	9	62	84.8392312	-22.839231	5.25396744	-28.093199	789.227807	521.63048	22.8392312	-0.3683747	0.3683747
13	10	66	75.3253483	-9.3253483	-22.839231	13.5138829	182.62503	86.9621208	9.32534829	-0.1412932	0.14129316
14	11	91	93.3649521	-2.3649521	-9.3253483	6.96039615	48.4471145	5.59299865	2.36495215	-0.0259885	0.02598849
15	12	100	105.943729	-5.9437291	-2.3649521	-3.578777	12.8076446	35.3279158	5.94372912	-0.0594373	0.05943729
16	13	105	113.418116	-8.4181157	-5.9437291	-2.4743866	6.12258895	70.8646719	8.4181157	-0.0801725	0.08017253
17	14	125	123.704706	1.29529376	-8.4181157	9.71340946	94.3503234	1.67778594	1.29529376	0.01036235	0.01036235
18	15	138	127.783699	10.2163012	1.29529376	8.92100743	79.5843736	104.37281	10.2163012	0.07403117	0.07403117
19							1927.13606	1512.59053	120.562621	-0.2017809	1.39127128
20											
21	MAD:	8.03750808									
22	MSE:	100.839369									
23	MAPE:	0.09275142									
24	MPE:	-0.0134521									

TABLE 6.9
Excel Formulas for Error Calculations

Cell	Formula
H4	=D4^2
I4	=abs(D4)
J4	=D4/B4
K4	=I4/B4
B21	=I19/ count(A4:A18)
B22	=H19/count(A4:A18)
B23	=K19/ count(A4:A18)
B24	=J19/count(A4:A18)

At times it is necessary to lag variables to create a more appropriate data set and model.

In Table 6.10, 6 years of data have been collected. The first column, y, illustrates the sales in time period t. The sales are also considered the dependent variable. The second column shows the advertisement expenditures in time period t, and the last column is advertisement expenditures in time period $t-1$. A variable can also be lagged more than one period.

When a variable is lagged, the first time period will get lost. There is no value to compute in this time period. This would leave our example with five observations rather than six.

Lagging variables does not always result in a better model because sometimes multicollinearity is created. In addition, vital information could get lost. The regression output for the one period lagged advertisement expenditures is found in Table 6.11.

To determine whether lagging the variables is appropriate, the following hypothesis should be tested:

$$H_0 : B_1 = 0$$

$$H_1 : B_1 \neq 0$$

The hypothesis is usually tested at the 95 percent or 99 percent confidence level. At the 95 percent level the value is 3.182 at the 99 percent level the value is 5.841. This is found by looking at the degrees of freedom from the regression result output. In this example df = 3.

If $t > 3.182$ or $t < 3.182$ reject the H_0
If $t > 3.182$ or $t < 3.182$ accept the H_0

In this example the t statistic equals 10.387. The null hypothesis in this example is to be rejected. It can be concluded that the lagging in this example is useful and will result in a better regression equation for forecasting.

MS EXCEL TUTORIAL: USING ADD-INS

Microsoft Excel contains add-in statistical functions that help the researcher with the analysis of data. These add-ins are preprogrammed functions that simplify the job. Data analysis is still left up to the researcher, however, since no statistical programs can perform this function.

TABLE 6.10
Example of Lagged Variables

y	x_t	x_{t-1}
$ 3,500	$ 700	
$ 7,000	$1,500	$ 700
$10,000	$2,000	$1,500
$12,400	$2,200	$2,000
$12,400	$2,500	$2,200
$15,000	$3,000	$2,500

TABLE 6.11 Excel Regression Example Output

SUMMARY OUTPUT

Regression statistics

Multiple R	0.98637
R square	0.97293
Adjusted R square	0.96391
Standard error	572.0050
Observations	5

ANOVA

	Degrees of freedom (df)	SS	MS	F	Significance F
Regression	1	35290431	35290430	107.8592	0.001904
Residual	3	981569	327189		
Total	4	36272000			

	Coefficients	Standard error	t statistic	p value	Lower 95%	Upper 95%
Intercept	3860.36	767.0945	5.0390	0.0151	1422.31	6298.42
x	4.2132	0.4057	10.3856	0.0019	2.9222	5.5044

Installing Excel's Data Analysis ToolPak

This section details the procedure for installation and use of Excel's Data Analysis ToolPak. The procedure is as follows:

1. In Excel, click on Tools and select Add-Ins (Figure 6.15).
2. Select Analysis ToolPak and Analysis ToolPak – VBA (Figure 6.16)
3. Click OK. The statistical methods are now ready to be used.

Excel Tutorial: Regression

In this example, grades are the dependent variable, whereas age and number of hours studied per week are the independent variables influencing the dependent one. A total of 8 observations have been gathered. We will use Excel to create the regression result.

1. Enter the data into Excel (Figure 6.17 shows data for an analysis of grades versus age versus study hours).
2. On the main menu bar in Excel, click on Tools and Data Analysis (Figure 6.18).
3. Select Regression from the list and click OK (Figure 6.19).

A total of 8 observations have been gathered. In this example, grades are the dependent variable whereas; age and number of hours studied per week are the independent variables influencing the dependent one. We will use MS Excel to create the regression result. The next section illustrates the use of Excel's regression tool.

The input and output options available are explained below, with reference to Figure 6.20.

Input Options

- *Input Y Range.* Highlight the *Y* range; this is the dependent variable in your example (Grades).
- *Input X Range.* Highlight the *X* range; these are the independent variables in your example (Age and Study hours). Note that the independent variables can span multiple rows.
- *Labels.* This is optional; however, it will make it easier to identify the variables later when analyzing the data.
- *Confidence Level.* This is set at 95 percent; however, it can be changed. Note if the data will be tested at the 95 percent level, in the ANOVA result the boundaries are reported twice with the same values.

FIGURE 6.15

FIGURE 6.16

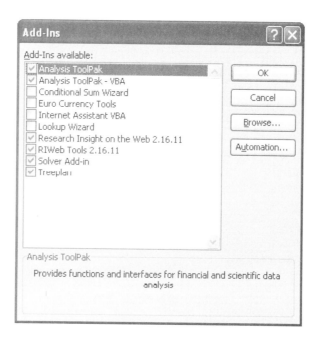

FIGURE 6.17

	A	B	C	D
1		Grades	Age	Study (hrs per week)
2	1	4.0	20	30
3	2	2.8	20	20
4	3	3.2	18	20
5	4	3.0	19	16
6	5	3.0	21	15
7	6	1.8	18	5
8	7	2.5	18	10
9	8	3.6	19	25

FIGURE 6.18

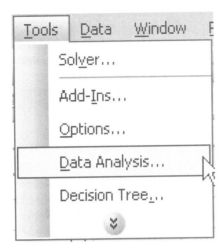

FIGURE 6.19

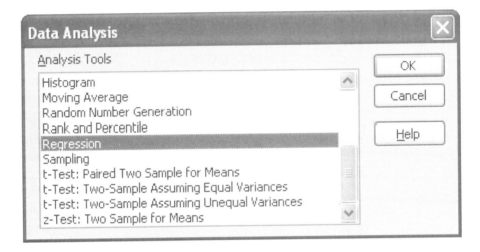

FIGURE 6.20

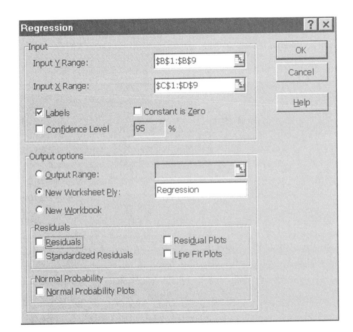

- *Constant is Zero.* This should not be checked, as it would force a regression line through the origin.

Output Options

- *Output Range.* Select this box if you would like the regression result to be placed in the same worksheet as the raw data.
- *New Worksheet Ply.* Selecting this box will move the result into a new worksheet. Remember to name the sheet if you are going to create many of them.
- *New Workbook.* This box will place the regression result in a new workbook.

Residuals

- *Residuals.* A residual is the difference between the actual *Y* and the predicted *Y* value.
- *Residual Plots.* These graphs compare the actual *Y* with the predicted *Y* for each of the predictors.
- *Standardized Residuals.* Combines the residuals into a unit normal distribution with the mean of 0 and standard deviation of 1.
- *Line Fit Plots.* These graphs show the difference between the actual and predicted values of *Y*.

Normal Probability

Selecting Normal Probability Plots -will generate a chart of normal probabilities. When you have selected all the options you want, click OK, the regression result will be generated (Figure 6.21). An explanation of the Summary Output follows.

Multiple R

Multiple *R* represents the strength of the linear relationship between the actual and the estimated values for the dependent variables. The scale ranges from -1.0 to 1.0, where 1.0 indicates a good direct relationship and -1 indicates a good inverse relationship. Multiple *R* is found to be 95.78 percent, which means there is a strong linear relationship.

R Square

R^2 is a symbol for a coefficient of multiple determination between a dependent variable and the independent variables. It tells how much of the variability in the dependent variable is

FIGURE 6.21

◇	A	B	C	D	E	F	G	H	I
1	SUMMARY OUTPUT								
2									
3	*Regression Statistics*								
4	Multiple R	0.957810149							
5	R Square	0.917400281							
6	Adjusted R Square	0.884360393							
7	Standard Error	0.227347255							
8	Observations	8							
9									
10	ANOVA								
11		*df*	*SS*	*MS*	*F*	*Significance F*			
12	Regression	2	2.870316129	1.435158064	27.76644676	0.001960859			
13	Residual	5	0.258433871	0.051686774					
14	Total	7	3.12875						
15									
16		Coefficients	Standard Error	t Stat	P-value	Lower 95%	Upper 95%	Lower 95.0%	Upper 95.0%
17	Intercept	1.280862754	1.543156462	0.830027794	0.44433322	-2.685947215	5.247672723	-2.685947215	5.247672723
18	Age	0.016238017	0.08476099	0.191574183	0.855612586	-0.201647043	0.234123078	-0.201647043	0.234123078
19	Study (hrs per week)	0.079210506	0.011958415	6.623829548	0.001180729	0.04847042	0.109950591	0.04847042	0.109950591

explained by the independent variables. R^2 is a goodness-of-fit measure, and the scale ranges from 0.0 to 1.0.

This study shows R^2 is equal to 0.9174. This means that 91.74 percent of the total variance in the dependent variable around its mean has been accounted for by the independent variables in the estimated regression function.

Adjusted R square

In the adjusted R square, R^2 is adjusted to give a truer estimate of how much the independent variables in a regression analysis explain the dependent variable. Taking into account the number of independent variables makes the adjustment. The adjusted R square is found to be 88.44 percent, and is a measure of strength.

Standard Error of Estimates

The standard error of estimates is a regression line. The error is how much the research is off when the regression line is used to predict particular scores. The standard error is the standard deviation of those errors from the regression line. The standard error of estimate is thus a measure of the variability of the errors. It measures the average error over the entire scatter plot.

The lower the standard error of estimate, the higher the degree of linear relationship between the two variables in the regression. The larger the standard error, the less confidence can be put in the estimate. For this data set, the standard error of estimates equals to 0.2273. This indicates that the Y value falls 0.2273 units away from the regression line.

t test

The rule of thumb says the absolute of t should be greater than 2. To be more accurate, the t table has been used. When the critical value of t is at the 5 percent level of significance, it shows a value of 2.364, since this example is a one-tailed test.

The critical values can be found in the back of most statistical textbooks. The critical value is the value that determines the critical regions in a sampling distribution. The critical values separate the obtained values that will and will not result in rejecting the null hypothesis.

Referring back to the regression results, it needs to be determined if the coefficients are significantly different from zero at the 5 percent significance level. From the data, it can be seen that the Age variable's t statistic equals 0.1916 and for Study equals 6.6238.

It can be concluded that the null hypothesis can be rejected for the Study variable. However, the null hypothesis for the Age variable is not rejected. The researcher may conclude that this variable can be discarded or that more study is needed to determine the variable's true impact in the model.

In all, it appears the study has been successful and the theory is true. We are able to reject the null hypothesis by showing that chance variation is not a reasonable explanation for the result. This is a classical approach of assessing the statistical significance of findings, which involves comparing empirically observed sample findings with theoretically expected findings. This means the variable X_2 is doing a good job of explaining the model and that one of the independent variables are valid.

F Statistic

The F distribution shows 2 and 5 degrees of freedom. Looking at the F distribution table at the 5 percent level of significance, we find the value 5.786. In the results, it can be seen that the critical value equals 27.7664 and is greater than the F statistic of 5.7861.

The result is that H_0: $B_1 = B_2 = 0$ is to be rejected. This implies in this study that the explanatory variables in the regression equation are doing a good job of explaining the variation in the dependent variable Y.

p Value

The p value should be less than 0.05, which would mean there would be less than a 0.05 chance that the data have been produced by chance. In this case, variable X_2 meets the criterion, as its p value is 0.0012. The p value can be viewed as the minimum level of significance that can be chosen for the test and result in rejection of the null hypothesis.

The *p* value for the variable X_1 equals 0.8556 and is larger than the rule of thumb says it should be. Therefore it indicates a higher chance the data are created by coincidence.

Overall, it could be said from the regression analysis that hours studied do a very good job of predicting grades, but age does not seem to be a good predictor.

Excel Tutorial: Correlation

To run a correlation analysis, follow these steps:

1. Enter the data into Microsoft Excel or use the data entered for the regression, as in Figure 6.17.
2. On the main menu bar in Excel, click on Tools and select Data Analysis, as in Figure 6.18.
3. Select Correlation from the Data Analysis list and click OK (Figure 6.22). A Correlation menu will appear (Figure 6.23).
4. Insert the Input Range, which consists of the independent variables (*X*).
5. The data should be grouped by Columns.
6. Check the Labels in First Row box; this it will make it easier when you are interpreting the results.
7. Check the New Worksheet Ply box; this will create a separate sheet for your correlation matrix.
8. Click OK when you are done.

Excel Tutorial: Scatter Plot

To generate a scatter plot, follow these steps:

1. Highlight columns B and C, as in Figure 6.24.
2. Click on the Chart Wizard in the Tools menu. The screen shown in Figure 6.25 will appear.
3. Select XY Scatter from the list Chart Types.
4. Click the Next button. The Chart Source Data Screen will appear (Figure 6.26).
5. You have the option to enter titles for the X axis, Y axis, and chart.
6. Press Next when you are done. The Chart Options screen will appear (Figure 6.27).
7. Choose to either paste the graph in the existing worksheet or create a new one.
8. Click Finish to create the graph. You may choose a location for the chart on the Chart Location screen (Figure 6.28).
9. Font size, color, shape of graph can later be edited if a different style is desired by clicking on the object.

FIGURE 6.22

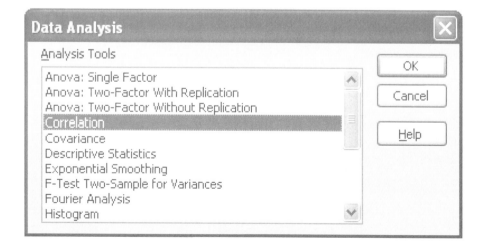

FIGURE 6.23

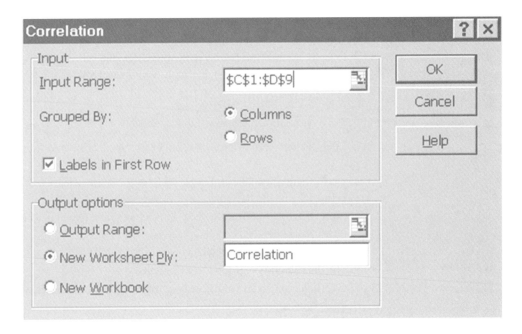

FIGURE 6.24

	A	B	C
1		Y	X2
2	1	4.0	30
3	2	2.8	20
4	3	3.2	20
5	4	3.0	16
6	5	3.0	15
7	6	1.8	5
8	7	2.5	10
9	8	3.6	25

FIGURE 6.25

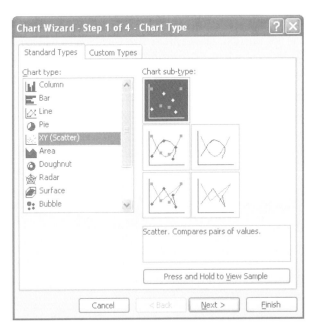

THE LEADING CAUSES OF JOB CREATION IN INFORMATION TECHNOLOGY: A REGRESSION ANALYSIS

This section presents a walk-through scenario with actual data to familiarize students and professionals with how to construct a linear regression in Excel, run the linear regression model, and read the Excel linear regression statistical outputs.

FIGURE 6.26

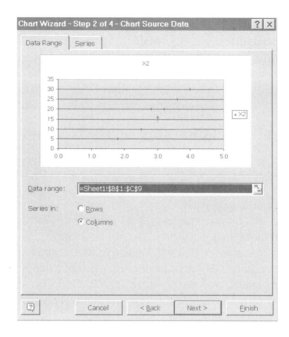

FIGURE 6.27

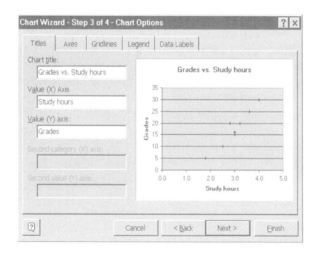

FIGURE 6.28

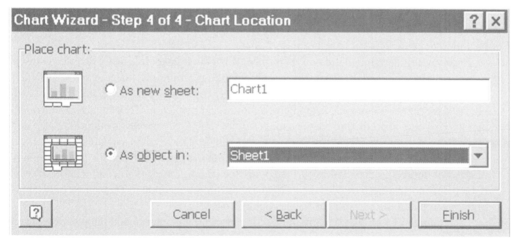

Background

As the global marketplace becomes smaller and smaller, companies must look overseas to generate more profit. Competition has toughened when it comes to capturing highly qualified employees, increasing market share, and offering competitive salaries. In addition, computers have become a necessity in the daily work routine. Governmental agencies and private companies invest heavily in new technology that can help them get an advantage.

Determining the Relationship: Dependent and Independent Variables

The following data set has been collected to determine what the future holds for students graduating from a university with a master of science in information systems degree in the coming years. From this example, it is possible to see how the independent variables relate to the dependent one. A person needs to study the independent variables to be able to predict future job opportunities in this industry.

For this case, consumer confidence, value of exports, and number of degree holders are the independent variables. To determine the relationship, a multiple regression model will be utilized. With this model, we will be able to see the effect the independent variables have on the dependent variable. Throughout this case, the multiple regression model will be expanded on and its results will be explained in detail.

Data

The data have been gathered for a total of 29 years. This represents a fairly large sample size. Furthermore, for this study, only data for the United States are utilized, as the United States is one of the largest nations and is a major player in this industry. The data used for this research are collected from secondary sources. The value of exports can be found in the book *U.S. Industrial Outlook*. The degrees earned in computer and information sciences can be found in the book *Digest of Education Statistics*. This makes the data set highly reliable, as the U.S. Bureau of Census has conducted the studies. Lastly, the consumer confidence index can be found in *The Almanac* by the *Wall Street Journal* from data gathered by the Conference Board, a private research organization. The data are listed in Table 6.12, where Y = employment in thousands, X_1 = number of degree holders (actual numbers), X_2 = consumer confidence index, and X_3 = export in millions of dollars.

Model Selection

With the regression model selected as a means of analyzing the data, it is important to select the correct combination of the selected variables. Usually there are many variables influencing the dependent variable. It is not always appropriate to select them all. The selection process is completed by running a single regression on each of the possible combinations. To select the most appropriate combination, R square, F statistic, t statistic, and p value will be compared.

After running all possible combinations, we find that export (X_3) alone in a single regression is the only model that satisfies the regression rules for model selection, where R^2 needs to be above 70 percent, F stat > 4, $|t$ stat$| > 2$, and p value < 0.05.

However, this decision to use only X_3 may be a bit shortsighted. It is better practice to investigate a number of models that look "good", including a multiple linear regression model. Rarely are real life situations ever explained or influenced by just one factor or variable. Overall, multiple regression models tend to give a more accurate picture. To see if any other combinations are better at predicting the dependent variable employment rate (Y), the value of export (X_3), which is the independent variable, has been lagged. The result is shown in Table 6.14.

The level of export accounts for 98.24 percent of the variance in Y and the combination of number of degree holders and export accounts for 98.34 percent. The combination with all three independent variables does the best job of explaining the model. This leaves only a total of 0.75 percent of the variation in Y unaccounted for.

Even though export does explain most of the model, it is better to add the two other independent variables; that way, fewer errors are produced. Looking at the errors, we clearly see

TABLE 6.12
Data Set for Information Technology Example

t	Year	Y	X_1	X_2	X_3
1	1970	76	4,104	90	932
2	1971	82	5,546	80	965
3	1972	107	6,613	103	1,341
4	1973	120	7,230	98	1,717
5	1974	135	7,545	71	2,198
6	1975	143	8,499	75	2,229
7	1976	159	9,421	94	2,588
8	1977	187	10,435	98	3,264
9	1978	224	12,010	106	4,194
10	1979	271	15,041	92	5,500
11	1980	304	19,591	74	7,606
12	1981	337	25,453	77	8,493
13	1982	365	30,093	59	8,957
14	1983	416	38,613	86	10,300
15	1984	474	46,227	102	13,511
16	1985	542	50,303	100	13,964
17	1986	588	48,444	95	13,266
18	1987	629	44,148	103	13,929
19	1988	673	40,419	115	18,137
20	1989	736	37,561	117	22,345
21	1990	772	35,083	92	24,111
22	1991	797	34,859	69	25,872
23	1992	836	35,168	62	24,879
24	1993	893	35,426	66	25,276
25	1994	959	35,614	91	28,956
26	1995	1,090	35,802	100	34,294
27	1996	1,208	35,990	105	37,621
28	1997	1,411	36,178	125	41,380
29	1998	1,599	36,366	138	44,100

TABLE 6.13
Model Selection

Independent variables	R^2	F statistic	t statistic	p value
X_1	No	Yes	Yes	Yes
X_2	No	Yes	Yes	Yes
X_3	Yes	Yes	Yes	Yes
X_1 and X_2	No	Yes	Yes	Yes
X_1 and X_2	Yes	Yes	No	No
X_2 and X_3	Yes	Yes	No	No
X_1 and X_2 and X_3	Yes	Yes	No	No

that this model presents the least amount of errors and the highest R_2. This means that the confidence intervals around any predictions made with this model will be more precise and reliable.

Relative Effectiveness of Models

To check the models' relative effectiveness, we change the representation of the models by dividing the dependent variable and independent variables by 1,000 and running all tests separately to see if the changes have an effect on the model. When the independent variables were changed, all the errors remained the same. When the dependent variable was changed, the errors became smaller, but the relationship still remained the same.

TABLE 6.14
*R*2 **Comparison for Information Technology Example**

Independent variables	R^2	Standard error
X_1	0.4419	317.1392
X_2	0.1870	381.5622
X_3	0.9824	57.1320
X_1 and X_2	0.5265	297.9499
X_1 and X	0.9834	55.5906
X_1, X_2, and X_2	0.9925	38.0540

The Regression Line Equation

The term b_0 is called the Y intercept because it is the value Y takes on when X is equal to zero. Further, the net regression coefficient (b_1, b_2, b_3) measures the average change in the dependent variable per unit change in the relevant independent variable, holding the other independent variable constant. X_1, X_2, and X_3 represent the independent variables, and Y is the dependent variable. The letter t represents the time or year for the chosen data set. The equation used in the multiple regression and its explanations can be found in Table 6.15.

Dependent Variable versus Independent Variable

To explain the variables more in detail, we can say that the dependent variable is the variable whose values are predicted by the independent variable, whether or not caused by it. It is the presumed effect in a study, because it depends on another variable. In this case it is the number of people employed in the information system field.

The independent variable is the presumed cause in a study, because it can be used to predict or explain the values of other variables—for this research, the number of degrees earned in computer and information science at a higher level, the amount of exported goods in dollars in the information system field, and consumer confidence.

In predicting a variable, two important characteristics exist: A good predictor variable is related to the dependent variable and is not highly related to any other independent variables.

Type of Data

There are two types of data which are of interests to a forecaster; single point in time data and time series data. The data for this study are time series data, as the data has been collected every year. Time series data are a chronologically arranged sequence of observations on a particular variable.

The data found are annual data, therefore a seasonal component does not need to be considered. Further, one needs to determine if the data selected are linear or if the data show a trend. To determine these factors, we use Microsoft Excel to analyze the data. The results are presented in Figure 6.29.

The data show a clear trend. A trend is a long-term component that underlies the growth or decline in a time series. It can further be described by a straight line or a curve. To determine if the data are linear, one assumes that a variable is increasing by a constant amount each time period. Looking at Figure 6.29, we can see that the data are in a growing stage and its values are steadily increasing.

TABLE 6.15
Regression Equation Details for Information Technology Example

Formula	$\hat{Y}_t = b_0 + b_1 X_1 + b_2 X_2 + b_3 X_3$
B_0	Intercept
b_1, b_2, b_3	Coefficients of contribution
X_1	Degrees earned in information science
X_2	Consumer confidence index
X	Value of exports in U.S. dollars
$\hat{Y}$	Employment
t	Time (years)

Regression Results

To be able to receive the regression results, data are entered into a Microsoft Excel spreadsheet and a regression is run. The multiple regression result is shown in Table 6.16.

Regression Line Equation

Looking at the results from the regression analysis, the regression coefficient shows a value of 0.0012 for the number of degrees earned, 2.1939 for the consumer confidence index, and 0.0318 for the value of export. A regression coefficient is a number indicating the value of a dependent variable associated with the values of the independent variables.

This means that Y increases by an average of 0.0012, 2.1939, and 0.0318, respectively, when the independent variables increase by 1. These data make up the best linear regression function. From this information the regression equation can be created:

$$\hat{Y} = -114.5713 + 0.0012X_1 + 2.1939X_2 + 0.0318X_3$$

Multiple *R*

Multiple R represents the strength of the linear relationship between the actual and the estimated values for the dependent variables. The scale ranges from -1.0 to 1.0, where 1.0 indicates a good direct relationship and -1 indicates a good inverse relationship. Multiple R is found to be 99.63 percent, which means there is a strong linear relationship.

R Square

R^2 is a symbol for the coefficient of multiple determination between a dependent variable and the independent variables. It tells how much of the variability in the dependent variable is explained by the independent variable. R^2 is a goodness-of-fit measure, and the scale ranges from 0.0 to 1.0.

This study shows R^2 is equal to 0.9925. This means that 99.25 percent of the total variance in the dependent variable around its mean has been accounted for by the independent variables in the estimated regression function.

Adjusted *R* Square

The adjusted R square is R^2 adjusted to give a truer estimate of how much the independent variables in a regression analysis explain the dependent variable. Taking into account the number of independent variables makes the adjustment. The adjusted R square is found to be 99.16 percent. It is a measure of strength.

Standard Error of Estimates

The standard error of estimates is a regression line. The error indicates how much the research is off when the regression line is used to predict particular scores. The standard error is the

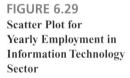

FIGURE 6.29
Scatter Plot for Yearly Employment in Information Technology Sector

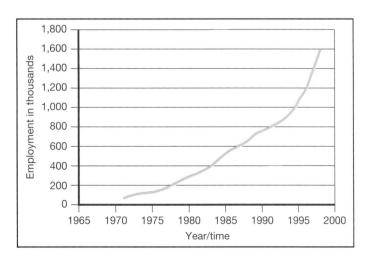

TABLE 6.16 **Excel Regression Output for Information Technology**

SUMMARY OUTPUT

Regression statistics	
Multiple R	0.9963
Rsquare	0.9925
Adjusted R square	0.9916
Standard error	38.0539
Observations	28

ANOVA

	df	SS	MS	F	Significance F
Regression	3	4621264	1540421	1063.74	1.201E−25
Residual	24	34754	1448		
Total	27	4656018			

	Coefficients	Standard error	t statistic	p value	Lower 95%	Upper 95%
Intercept	−114.57	37.7730	−3.0331	0.005734	−192.53	−37.61
X_1	0.0011786	0.0006582	1.7907	0.085967	−0.0001798	0.00253
X_2	2.1939	0.4050	5.4177	1.45E-05	1.36	3.02972
X_3	0.0318134	0.0008218	38.7081	3.83E-23	0.0301171	0.03350

standard deviation of those errors from the regression line. The standard error of estimate is thus a measure of the variability of the errors. It measures the average error over the entire scatter plot.

The lower the standard error of estimate, the higher the degree of linear relationship between the two variables in the regression. The larger the standard error, the less confidence can be put in the estimate. For this data set, the standard error of estimates equals 38.0540. This indicates that the Y value falls 38.0540 units away from the regression line.

t Test

The rule of thumb says the absolute of t should be greater than 2. To be more accurate, we have used the t table. When the critical value of t is at the 5 percent level of significance, it shows a value of 2.064, since this example is a one-tailed test.

The critical values can be found in the back of most statistical textbooks. The critical value is the value that determines the critical regions in a sampling distribution. The critical values separate the obtained values that will and will not result in rejecting the null hypothesis.

Referring back to the regression results, it needs to be determined if the coefficients are significantly different from zero at the 5 percent significance level. From the data, it can be seen that the t statistic for the number of degree holders equal 1.7907, for consumer confidence it equals 5.4177, and for the value of export it equals 38.7081.

It can be concluded that the null hypothesis can be rejected for the consumer confidence and value of exports variables. However, the null hypothesis for the number of degree holders variable is not rejected. The researcher may conclude that this variable can be discarded or that more study is needed to determine the variables' true impact in the model.

In all, it appears the study has been successful and the theory is true. We are able to reject the null hypothesis by showing that chance variation is not a reasonable explanation for the result. This is a classical approach of assessing the statistical significance of findings, which involves comparing empirically observed sample findings with theoretically expected findings. This means the variables X_2 and X_3 do a good job explaining the model and that two of the independent variables are valid.

F Statistic

The *F* statistic should be greater than 4, which it is. The *F* distribution shows 3 and 24 degrees of freedom. Looking at the *F* distribution table at the 5 percent level of significance, the value 3.01 can be found. In the results, it can be seen that the critical value equals 1063.7490 and is greater than the *F*-statistic of 3.01.

The result is that H_0: $b_1 = b_2 = b_3 = 0$ is to be rejected. This implies in this study that the explanatory variables in the regression equation are doing a good job explaining the variation in the dependent variable *Y*.

p Value

The *p*-value should be less than 0.05, which means there would be less than a 0.05 chance that the data have been produced by chance. In this case variables X_2 and X_3 meet the criteria. The *p* value can be viewed as the minimum level of significance that can be chosen for the test and result in rejection of the null hypothesis.

The *p* value for the variable X_1 equals 0.0859 and is larger than the rule of thumb says it should be. Therefore there is a higher chance that the data were created by coincidence.

Multicollinearity

In addition, it needs to be determined if multicollinearity exists. For this problem, a correlation matrix is created by computing the simple correlation coefficient, which indicates the relationship between the variables, using Excel. Using the correlation matrix as a way of analyzing the data is important, because it is a crucial step in detecting any problems involving multiple independent variables.

From Table 6.17, we can see how the independent variables are interrelated with each other. Further, from this table we can see that a problem of heavy multicollinearity does not exists, because the correlation coefficient is less than 0.80. However, variables X_1 and X_3 do appear to be moderately correlated.

Autocorrelation

Serial correlation needs to be tested. This is the correlation between members of a series of observations. This question arises when the residuals are dependent from one observation to another. To determine if serial correlation is a problem, the Durbin-Watson (DW) test is used. According to the DW table found in the back of any statistical book, the DW lower equals 1.18 and the DW upper equals 1.65, at the 0.05 level of significance. The rule of thumb is:

- If DW > *U*, conclude H_0
- If DW < *L*, conclude H_1
- If DW lies within the upper and lower limits, conclude the test is inconclusive

Going back to the data, it can be found that the Durbin-Watson statistic equals 1.20. This value falls within the upper and lower limits. It can therefore be concluded that the data are inconclusive. This means that, at this point, it cannot be concluded whether there is a positive autocorrelation. Therefore, more observations will need to be made.

Heteroscedasticity

Last, the model needs to be checked for heteroscedasticity. Heteroscedasticity occurs when there is considerably unequal variance in the dependent variable for the same values of the independent variable in the different populations being sampled and compared in a regression analysis.

Heteroscedasticity comes from hetero, meaning other or different, and scedasticity, meaning tendency to scatter. An example of heteroscedasticity is when the error term gets larger

TABLE 6.17
Excel Correlation Matrix Output for Information Technology Example

	X_1	X_2	X_3
X_1	1		
X_2	0.224	1	
X_3	0.646	0.346	1

because the variable or variables involved tend to grow at a constant rate instead of by a constant amount.

To find out if heteroscedasticity exists, we examine a printout of the errors. Figure 6.30 displays the square values of the residuals from the original regression.

From the diagram, it can be concluded there is no continuous growth. Therefore, no heteroscedasticity exists in this regression model. As a result, the variance of the residuals does not increase steadily over time. Instead the residuals oscillate up and down from year to year and contain no visible structure.

Residual Plots

These graphs are produced with Excel. They compare the actual *Y* with predicted *Y* for each of the three predictors (Figures 6.31, 6.32, and 6.33). Regression residuals are the vertical deviations about the fitted line. These are the deviations that are squared, summed, and then minimized in the defining least squares.

The residuals are simply the residuals divided by their standard deviation. No funneling or trend pattern can be seen within Figures 6.31, 6.32, or 6.33. In all the graphs the residuals are randomly scattered. From the residual plots, it can be concluded that the assumptions underlying this fitted model are reasonable.

Line Fit Plots

When three independent variables are involved, three line fit plots get developed (Figures 6.34, 6.35, and 6.37). Each plot takes one view of the plane that is generated by the regression equation. The difference between the actual and predicted values of *Y* is shown. From the figures, it can be seen that the predictions are very accurate.

Normal Probability Plot

A normal probability plot (Figure 6.37) is an easy way to evaluate whether the sample values on the dependent variable are consistent with the normality assumption. This plot supports the assumption of normality.

Measuring Forecasting Errors

Measuring the forecasting error is a technique used to compare and evaluate forecasting techniques. Four common methods for evaluating these forecasting techniques, mean absolute deviation (MAD), mean squared error (MSE), mean absolute percentage error (MAPE) and

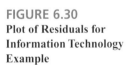

FIGURE 6.30
Plot of Residuals for Information Technology Example

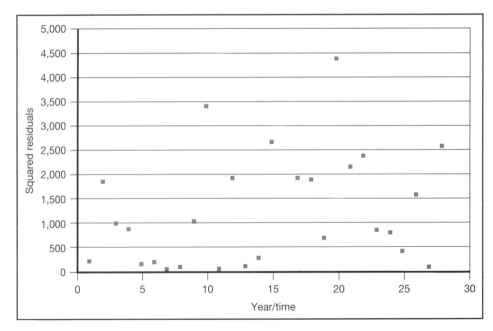

Figure 6.31 **Residual Plot for Number of Degree Holders**

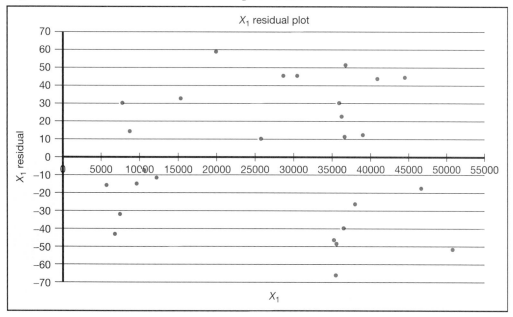

FIGURE 6.32
**Residual Plot for
Consumer Confidence
Index**

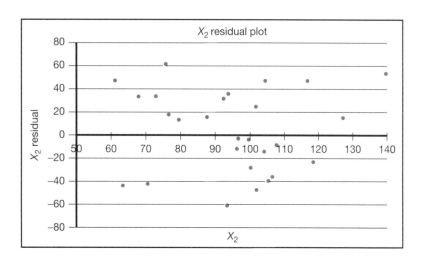

FIGURE 6.33
**Residual Plot for
Number of Exports**

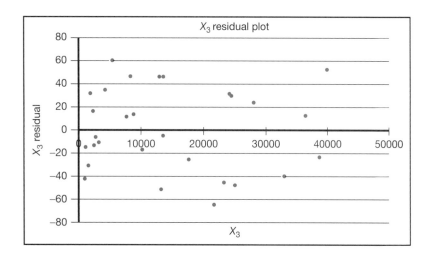

FIGURE 6.34
**Line Fit Plot for Number
of Degree Holders**

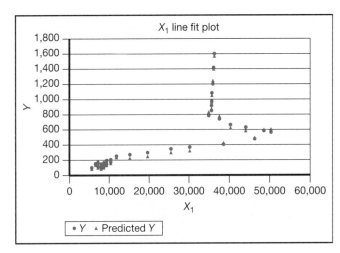

FIGURE 6.35
**Line Fit Plot for
Consumer Confidence
Index**

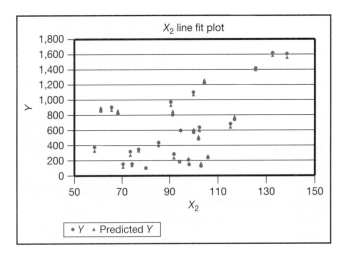

FIGURE 6.36
Line Fit Plot for Exports

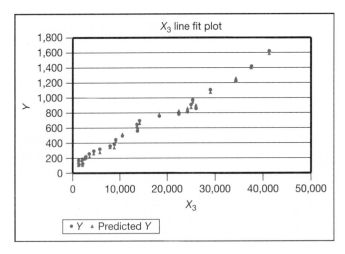

mean percentage error (MPE) are presented here. The errors are calculated from the residuals, and can be seen in Table 6.18.

Looking at the four measurements, we can conclude that the MPE and MAPE create the smallest errors. It is further found that no bias exists in the models since the MPE is close to zero. The MAPE indicates an appropriate size has been chosen to test the relationship with.

In addition, with the values close to zero, it can be concluded that the methods do not over- or underestimate the number of future jobs in information technology. The reason for getting such large error on the MSE is the data chosen. The Y and X_1 variables are presented in actual

FIGURE 6.37
Normal Probability Plot

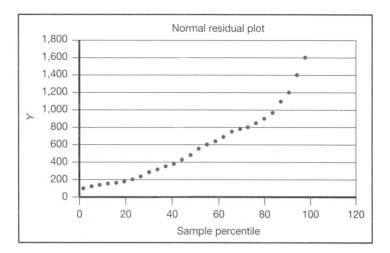

numbers, the export in dollars, and the consumer confidence as an index. Therefore, MSE will result in large errors on certain tests.

Forecasting

To forecast 1 year ahead, the regression equation is utilized to create a forecast. For example, using 1998 data for x_1, x_2, and x_3

$$\hat{Y} = -114.571 + 0.0012 X_1 + 2.1939 X_2 + 0.0318 X_3$$

$$\hat{Y} = -114.571 + 0.0012 (36366) + 2.1939 (138) + 0.0318 (44100)$$

$$\hat{Y} = 1634.21$$

That is, the number of future jobs in information technology will continue to increase. Therefore, when for $x_1 = 36{,}366$, $x_2 = 138$, and $x_3 = 44{,}100$, the number of new jobs the linear regression model predicts is 1634.21.

Conclusion

From this case, it can be concluded that the independent variables can be used to predict the number of future jobs in the information system field. The regression equation created from the model can be used to determine the number of jobs in the future.

The independent variables chosen for this example do a good job of explaining the dependent variable. In addition, the fact that the sample size is fairly large makes the study and its results valid. It is very useful to be able to predict the future, as organizations can use the information as a guideline for what the future holds for them regarding employment.

Further, being able to understand which variables have an effect on the subject being studied, students can use the information to determine future work situations and decide if other areas are of more interest. All the important findings have been discussed in the regression results section such as multicollinearity, heteroscedasticity, and serial correlation.

In addition, we discussed such factors as the number of observations, degrees of freedom, critical value of F and the t test, hypotheses, R^2, adjusted R^2, and the standard error of estimates.

TABLE 6.18
Forecast Error Measurements

Method	Value
MAD	30.368
MSE	1232.082
MAPE	0.083
MPE	0.006

Presented below is a sample executive summary for the information technology example.

Executive Summary

Objective: Run a multiple linear regression model and interpret the results.
Alternative: The data can be examined statistically by using the regression model.
Assumptions: Data are normally distributed and represent the true population.
Methodology: The multiple regression model is based on one dependent variable, which is employment (Y). The independent variables are number of degree holders (X_1), consumer confidence index (X_2), and exports (X_3).

Results

The multiple R is found to be 99.63 percent, which means there is a strong linear relationship. R^2 is equal to 0.9925. This means that 99.25 percent of the total variance in the dependent variable around its mean has been accounted for by the independent variables in the estimated regression function.

In regard to the t statistic, it was found that for the number of degree holders, it equals 1.7907; for consumer confidence, it equals 5.4177; and for value of exports, it equals 38.7081. The hypotheses $H_0:b_2 = 0$ and $b_3 = 0$ can be rejected. The t statistic for the number of degree holders is 1.7907, which is less than the critical value of 2.048 and is not considered to be significant at the 5 percent level. However, the t statistic is significant at the 10 percent level and therefore we will include it in our final model. The F statistic equals 1063.75 and is greater than the F statistic criterion of 3.01. The result is that $H_0:b_1 = b_2 = b_3 = 0$ is to be rejected. Further, from Table 1.1 it can be seen that a problem of heavy multicollinearity does not exist, because the correlation coefficient is less than 0.80. However, variables X_1 and X_3 do possess moderate correlation.

Serial Correlation

To determine if serial correlation is a problem, the Durbin-Watson (DW) test is used. According to the DW table found in the back of any statistical book, the DW lower limit equals 1.18 and the DW upper limit equals 1.65, at the 0.05 level of significance.

It can be found that the Durbin-Watson statistic equals 1.20. This value falls within the upper and lower limits. It can therefore be concluded that the data is inconclusive.

Heteroscedasticity

From a residual plot, it can be concluded there is no continuous growth. Therefore, heteroscedasticity does not exist in this regression model. The variance of the residuals shows no structure and exhibits a random pattern of ups and downs.

Final Linear Regression Model and Use

The final regression model is $\hat{Y} = -114.571 + 0.0012X_1 + 2.1939X_2 + 0.0318X_3$. If we allow $X_1 = 36,366, X_2 = 138$, and $X_3 = 44,100$, the model produces a predicted employment value of $\hat{Y} = 1634.21$.

Recommendation and Conclusion:

From the various tests, the model is found to be good and can be used to predict number of future jobs in information technology. It can be concluded the independent variables do a good job of explaining the dependent one.

TABLE 1.1
Multicollinearity

	X_1	X_2	X_3
X_1	1		
X_2	0.224	1	
X_3	0.646	0.346	1

Case Study: *Kealoha's Labor Lobby Regression*

Maile Kealoha works for a labor lobbyist group in Washington, D.C. She has a theory. She believes that strike activity in a state (the percentage of total hours lost due to strikes, Y) can be described by using one or more of the following three variables: X_1 = percentage of union members in nonagricultural establish-ments, X_2 = percentage of all nonagricultural employment that is manufacturing, and X_3 = average hourly earnings of workers on manufacturing payrolls. Table 6.19 contains the data for all 50 states.

TABLE 6.19
Labor Data for the 50 United States

State	Y	X_1	X_2	X_3	State	Y	X_{1s}	X_2	X_3
AK	0.11	32.2	8.9	18.54	LA	0.10	17.1	17.8	17.49
AL	0.14	18.0	30.5	17.17	MA	0.07	29.1	33.0	17.37
AR	0.10	26.2	29.2	16.78	MD	0.25	23.4	32.9	17.84
AZ	0.09	20.1	15.3	17.72	ME	0.15	20.3	36.6	17.00
CA	0.16	33.8	24.9	17.96	MI	0.83	38.9	40.7	18.11
CO	0.04	21.6	15.8	17.74	MN	0.02	33.0	24.0	17.64
CT	0.08	24.6	42.5	17.62	MO	0.14	39.8	28.5	17.53
DE	0.41	21.5	36.1	17.65	MS	0.14	11.6	30.5	16.76
FL	0.20	13.1	15.5	17.11	MT	0.28	36.2	12.2	17.71
GA	0.13	12.7	31.8	16.92	NC	0.01	6.7	41.6	16.75
HI	0.02	24.2	12.1	17.14	ND	0.03	14.8	5.8	17.28
IA	0.16	20.8	25.4	17.71	NE	0.05	19.3	16.6	17.36
ID	0.11	19.2	18.8	17.50	NH	0.03	20.9	40.9	17.00
IL	0.18	37.9	33.5	17.76	NJ	0.27	37.7	37.1	17.67
IN	0.16	34.1	40.8	17.81	NM	0.09	13.4	6.8	17.29
KS	0.11	18.8	20.6	17.65	NV	0.36	32.8	4.6	18.16
KY	0.17	25.7	26.6	17.43					

NOTE: United States Postal abbrevbviations are used to denote each state.

DISCUSSION QUESTIONS

1. After quickly looking at the data, Maile thinks she sees a difference in strike activity for states that pay higher than $17.50 per hour compared to those states that pay $17.50 per hour or less. Help her test this hypothesis and interpret the results.

2. Maile also believes she can develop a single linear regression model using just Y = percentage of total hours lost due to strikes and X_1 = percentage of union members in nonagricultural establishments. Help her develop this model.

3. However, she also knows that a single regression model may be too simplistic. She needs help in developing a multiple linear regression model and interpreting its adequacy. In addition, she wants a discussion of the basic linear regression tests, plots, and pitfalls.

Interactive Case: *Plotting Linear Trend for Ellis' DVD Service Demand*

Please go to www.mhhe.com/kros1e to access the Interactive Linear Trend Model.

BACKGROUND

Michelle Ellis runs a small business that designs, creates, and burns DVDs for customers. The content of the DVDs comes from many different sources (the client, Michelle's files, etc.) and medium types (VCR tape, old 8-mm tape, pictures, electronic files, etc.). Michelle listens to what her customers wish to create and then puts it all together for them on DVDs.

BUSINESS CLIMATE

Starting out, business was slow, but as time has passed business has picked up. In fact, along the way Michelle has had to add more staff and more equipment. Specifically, in the sixth month (period) of business Michelle added one new staff member and two new computers with DVD editing software and DVD burners, and in the twelfth month (period) of business she added another new staff member and two more computers with the same DVD software and hardware as before.

MICHELLE'S DEMAND NUMBERS

The following table illustrates Michelle's demand (number of DVD projects completed) over the last 14 months (periods) of business.

Month (period)	Demand	Month (period)	Demand
1	5	8	37
2	7	9	41
3	9	10	48
4	15	11	54
5	25	12	60
6	30	13	65
7	33	14	72

Michelle wishes to know, on the basis of the past demand data, if there is a way to predict future demand for her DVD service. In fact, she believes that there is a linear relationship underlying the demand for her services. She believes this because at each of the last 6-month intervals she added staff and equipment.

TREND MODELING

Using the linear trend equation model, input the demand data and create a linear trend equation. Then use the equation to answer the following questions:

1. What is the linear trend equation for the demand for Michelle's DVD services? Interpret the equation (i.e., what does the intercept infer and what does the slope infer).

2. Since Michelle believes that about every 6 months she will need to add staff and equipment, what is the demand forecast for period 18? What managerial implications does this forecast carry with it?

Optimal Information Area

Regression Tutorial URLs:

http://et.nmsu.edu/~etti/fall96/computer/sra/sra.html

http://barney.sbe.csuhayward.edu/~acassuto/mgmt6110/REGSUM.html

http://www.processbuilder.com/applications/strategy/help/STRATEGYRunning_ a _RegressionAnalysis.html

GraphPad Instat software ordering and tutorial:
http://www.graphpad.com/instatman/instat3.htm

MacChart Market Analysis Software Web site:
http://www.macchart.com/tasc/lsqr.htm

References

Dielman, T. E. *Applied Regression Analysis for Business and Economics*, 2nd ed. Pacific Grove California: Duxbury Press, 1996.

Hanke, J. E., and A. G. Reitsch. *Business Forecasting*, 6th ed. Englewood Cliffs, NJ: Prentice Hall, 1998.

Mendenhall, W., and T. Sincich. *A Second Course in Statistics: Regression Analysis*, 5th ed. Englewood Cliffs, NJ: Prentice Hall, 1996.

Montgomery, D. C., and E. A. Peck. *Introduction to Linear Regression Analysis*, 2nd ed. New York: Wiley Interscience, 1992.

Ragsdale, C. T. *Spreadsheet Modeling and Decision Analysis, A Practical Introduction to Management Science*, 2nd ed., Cincinnati, OH: South-Western Educational Publishing.

Vogt, P. W. *Dictionary of Statistics & Methodology*, 2nd ed. Thousand Oaks California: Sage, 1998.

Problems

1. Linear trend is calculated as $\hat{y} = 18.6 + 0.65t$. What is the trend projection for period 12?

2. A trend line for the attendance at a restaurant's Sunday brunch is given by $\hat{y} = 246 + 0.72t$, with t in weeks. How many guests would you expect in week 30?

3. The trend line of new contributors to a public radio station's annual fund drive over the last 10 years is: $\hat{y} = 24 + 15.345t$, where t is in years. What would the forecast for $t = 10$ be?

4. The trend line for average SAT verbal score for students from one high school over the last 10 exams is $\hat{y} = 500.933 - 0.352t$, where t is the time period. What would the forecast for $t = 7$ be?

5. The number of cans of soft drinks sold in a machine each week is recorded below:

Weekly period	1	2	3	4	5	6	7	8
Soft drinks sold	122	85	92	98	110	108	115	102
Weekly period	9	10	11	12	13	14	15	16
Soft drinks sold	95	98	105	125	85	106	140	84
Weekly period	17	18	19	20	21	22	23	24
Soft drinks sold	92	85	78	105	111	152	140	108

   a. Using Excel, develop forecasts for periods 1 to 24, using a trend line.

   b. Calculate the MSE and MAD for your model.

   c. Calculate an R statistic and interpret it.

6. Attendance at the IceBats Hockey games is listed below.

   2863, 2481, 3239, 3519, 3349, 3637, 3501, 3892, 3732, 3526, 3652, 2584, 3849, 2458, 3598, 4001, 3999, 3145, 2895, 2958.

   a. Using Excel, develop forecasts for periods 1 to 20, using a trend line.

   b. Calculate the MSE and MAD for your model.

   c. Calculate an R statistic and interpret it.

7. A hospital records the number of floral deliveries its patients receive each day. For a 2-week period, the records show:

   36, 33, 29, 25, 30, 32, 38, 42, 37, 39, 34, 31, 36, 33, 29, 31, 28, 36, 37, 39, 34, 33, 19.

   a. Using Excel, develop forecasts for periods 1 to 23, using a trend line.

   b. Calculate the MSE and MAPE for your model.

   c. Calculate an R statistic and interpret it.

8. The number of girls who attend a summer basketball camp has been recorded for the 7 years the camp has been offered. The numbers of girls attending camp in each year are:

   95, 110, 163, 147, 172, 175, 183

   a. Using Excel, develop forecasts for periods 1 to 11, using a trend line.

   b. Calculate the MSE and MAD for your model.

   c. Calculate an R statistic and interpret it.

9. The numbers of new contributors to a public radio station's annual fund drive over the last 10 years are:

   63, 58, 61, 72, 98, 103, 121, 147, 163, 198

   a. Using Excel, develop a trend equation for this information, and use it to predict next year's number of new contributors.

   b. What is the mean square error for the linear trend forecasts?

10. The average SAT verbal score for students from one high school over the last 10 exams is:

$$508, 490, 502, 505, 493, 506, 492, 490, 503, 501$$

   a. Using Excel, develop a trend equation for this information.
   b. Do the scores support an increasing or a decreasing trend?
   c. Calculate MSE, MAD, MAPE, and MPE. Compare the results.

11. An accountant at the firm Bragg and Bragg believed that several traveling executives were submitting unusually high travel vouchers when they returned from business trips. First, she took a sample of 300 vouchers submitted from the past year. Then she developed the following multiple regression equation relating expected travel cost (y) to number of days on the road (x_1) and distance traveled (x_2) in miles:

$$\hat{y} = \$90.00 + \$48.50x_1 + \$0.40x_2$$

The coefficient of correlation computed was .68.

   a. If Bill Tomlinson returns from a 300-mile trip that took him out of town for 5 days, what is the expected amount he should claim as expenses (use the regression equation to predict this value)?
   b. Tomlinson submitted a reimbursement request for $685. What should the accountant do?
   c. Should any other variables be included? Which ones? Why?

12. The graduate assistant for the Santa Clara Broncos football team has compiled the following statistics:

Year	Wins	Average offensive yards	Average interceptions
1	10	500	2
2	8	450	4
3	5	250	10
4	10	485	1
5	7	399	4
6	11	521	2
7	4	158	15
8	11	525	0
9	8	485	4
10	4	300	9
11	5	350	9
12	7	375	9
13	2	150	15
14	5	380	5

   a. Using Excel, develop a linear regression model for wins, employing average offensive yards and average interceptions.
   b. Calculate the MAD for your model.
   c. Calculate R, F, and t statistics and interpret them.
   d. Run tests for multicollinearity, autocorrrelation, and heteroscedasticity. Comment on the outcomes.

13. Novine knows that over the last 10 years average computer prices have fallen. She believes that average computer prices can be predicted by time, computing speed (number of instructions processed per second), memory (RAM), storage (hard drive space), and processor chip price.

   a. Using Excel, develop a linear regression model for the average computer price using the variables above.

b. Calculate the MAD for your model.

c. Calculate R, F, and t statistics and interpret them.

d. What is the best regression model to use to predict average computer price? Is there a problem with using linear regression on this data?

e. Run tests for multicollinearity, autocorrelation, and heteroscedasticity. Comment on the outcomes.

Average computer price, $	Year	Computer speed, bits per second	RAM	Storage, megabits	Processor chip price, $
3,000	1990	2	4	40	870
2,850	1991	4	8	80	800
2,750	1992	4	8	80	790
2,250	1993	8	16	100	700
2,100	1994	8	24	200	500
1,900	1995	16	32	500	450
1,850	1996	16	64	500	400
1,700	1997	32	64	1,000	375
1,500	1998	64	128	2,000	350
1,100	1999	64	128	4,000	300

14. Summer-month METRO ridership in Washington, D.C., is believed to be tied heavily to the number of tourists visiting the city and has changed over the years as the population in DC has fluctuated. During the past 12 years, the following data have been obtained:

Year	Number of tourists, millions	Ridership, millions	Year	Number of tourists, in millions	Ridership, in millions
1	7	1.5	7	16	2.4
2	2	1.0	8	12	2.0
3	6	1.3	9	14	2.7
4	4	1.5	10	20	4.4
5	14	2.5	11	15	3.4
6	15	2.7	12	7	1.7

a. Develop a regression relationship using Excel's Data Analysis package, using year and number of tourists as independent variables. What is the regression equation?

b. What is expected ridership if 10 million tourists visit the city in year 13?

c. Explain the predicted ridership if there are no tourists at all in year 13.

d. What are the model's correlation coefficient and coefficient of determination? Interpret and discuss these values.

e. Run tests for multicollinearity, autocorrelation, and heteroscedasticity. Comment on the outcomes.

15. Given the following data, use Excel to construct a least squares regression model that develops a relation between the number of games lost, the rainy days, and the team payroll of the Winterville Indians baseball team. The model should predict future lost games.

a. What is the regression equation?

b. What are expected games lost if Winterville experiences 15 rainy days and has a payroll of $200?

c. What is the model's correlation coefficient and coefficient of determination? Interpret and discuss these values.

d. What are the model's R, F, and t statistics? Comment on their outcomes.

Year	Games lost	Rainy days	Payroll ($000)
1993	25	26	175
1994	20	30	178
1995	10	3	240
1996	15	6	235
1997	22	17	180
1998	12	10	241
1999	25	22	173
2000	8	2	255
2001	4	2	267
2002	28	38	160
2003	29	34	147

Chapter **Seven**

Introduction to Forecasting

Learning Objectives

After completing this chapter, students will be able to:

1. Understand and know appropriate usage of various time series forecasting models.

2. Construct moving averages and exponential smoothing models, using Excel.

3. Understand what autocorrelation is and its link to seasonality.

4. Adjust data for seasonality.

5. Develop a seasonal forecasting model using linear regression.

Chapter outline

Business Decision Modeling in Action: Using Forecasting and Time Series in Stock Market Technical Analysis

What is Technical Analysis?

Technical analysis is the examination of past stock price movements to forecast future stock price movements. Technical analysts rely almost exclusively on charts and some fairly simple forecasting techniques in their analysis of stocks. Technical analysts are sometimes referred to as *chartists* because of this.

Technical analysis is applicable to really any tradable instrument whose price is influenced by the forces of supply and demand. Technical analysts refer to price as any combination of the open, high, low, or close price for a given security over a specific time frame. The time frame can be based on intraday (tick, 5-minute, 15-minute, or hourly), daily, weekly, or monthly data and last a short time, few hours, or a long time, many years.

The Basis of Technical Analysis

Overall, the Dow theory laid the foundations for what was later to become modern technical analysis. Dow theory was not presented as one complete amalgamation, but rather pieced together from the writings of Charles Dow over several years. Three theorems put forth by Dow stand out:

- Price discounts everything.
- Price movements are not totally random.
- *What* is more important than *why*.

Technical analysis utilizes the information captured by the price to interpret what the market is saying with the purpose of forming a view on the future. Price movements are not totally random; most technicians agree that prices trend. In his book, *Schwager on Futures: Technical Analysis*, Jack Schwager states:

> One way of viewing it is that markets may witness extended periods of random fluctuation, interspersed with shorter periods of nonrandom behavior. The goal of the chartist is to identify those periods (i.e., major trends).

A technician believes that it is possible to identify a trend, invest or trade on the basis of the trend, and make money as the trend unfolds. Because technical analysis can be applied to many different time frames, it is possible to spot both short-term and long-term trends. Technicians, as technical analysts are called, are concerned with only two things:

1. What is the current price?
2. What is the history of the price movement?

The objective of analysis is to forecast the direction of the future price.

Basics of Chart Analysis

Technical analysis can be as complex or as simple as you want it. The example in the figure on page 261 represents a simplified version explaining a few areas of technical analysis, such as overall trend and momentum:

Overall Trend: The first step is to identify the overall trend. This can be accomplished with trend lines, moving averages or peak/trough analysis. See the lines for MA(50) and MA(200) on the chart for Intuit.

Momentum: Momentum is usually measured with an oscillator such as moving average convergence/divergence (MACD). To see an example of an MACD in action refer to the lower part of the Intuit chart.

Technical Evaluation Overall: Pros and Cons

Many technical analysts comment that a person does not need an economics degree to analyze a market index chart. Charts are charts. The technical principles can be applied to any chart. However, there is a large group of stock analysts who do not put any worth in technical analysis and generally debunk much of what technical analysts do.

Optimal Information Area

International Federation of Technical Analysts Web site at www.ifta.org.

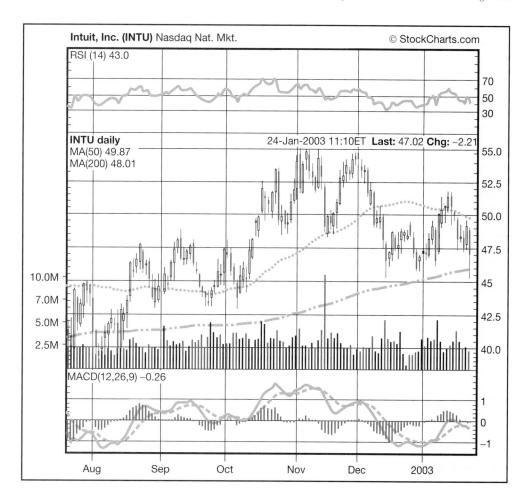

ANALYZING TIME SERIES DATA

This chapter will review techniques for identifying patterns in time series data and introduce models to represent time series data and generate forecasts. Time series analysis is based on the assumption that successive data points represent consecutive measurements taken at equally spaced time intervals.

Two Goals: Identify and Forecast

Two main goals of this chapter are to identify the nature of time series and to forecast future values.

This chapter has two main goals: identifying the nature of the situation represented by the time series data and forecasting future values of the time series data. Determining the pattern of the observed time series and formally describing that pattern are conditions of these goals. Once the pattern of the time series is established, a mathematical model can be used to describe the time series and in turn the model can be used to predict future time series data points or events.

Identifying Patterns in Time Series Data

Patterns in time series data tend to fall into four distinct components: trend, seasonal, cyclical, and irregular. Chapter 6, "Linear Regression Modeling," introduced the concept of linear trend, but it will be reviewed again here and followed by discussions on seasonal, cyclical, and irregular components.

Linear Time Series

Linear trend is the systematic increase or decrease in time series data.

Linear trend is the simple systematic increase or decrease in time series data over a given time range. In addition, simple trend patterns do not repeat themselves. Figure 7.1 displays a trend time series pattern.

FIGURE 7.1   **Linear Trend Time Series Pattern Example**

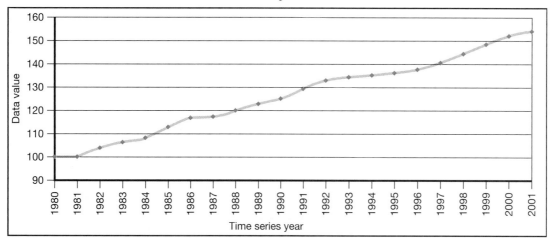

FIGURE 7.2   **Nonlinear Trend Time Series Pattern Example**

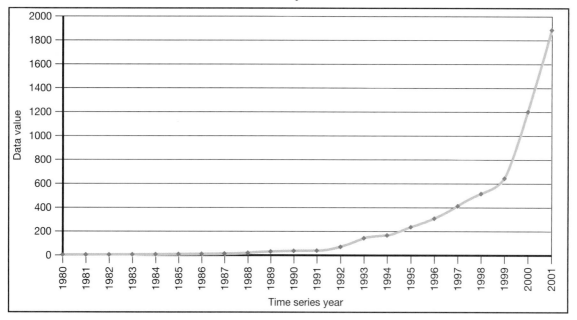

It is obvious that the line plotted in Figure 7.1 is relatively straight and rises from left to right. The TREND( ) function in Excel can be used to model a data set such as the one in Figure 7.1 as a linear relationship. However, trend can also be nonlinear in nature. In other words, a nonlinear trend must be modeled by using a nonlinear mathematical model.

Nonlinear Time Series

Nonlinear data is characterized by dramatic upward or downward curves.

Let's say, for example, the data have a dramatic upward or downward curve or the data seem to oscillate up and then down again. There are many kinds of data that exhibit these characteristics and change over time in a nonlinear fashion. Excel's GROWTH( ) function allows for simple nonlinear modeling. Figure 7.2 displays an example of a nonlinear data set.

Nonlinear tend modeling is not discussed further as the topic is beyond the scope of this text. Please consult the references at the end of this chapter for information on nonlinear modeling.

Seasonal Time Series

The repetition of the time series is the essence of seasonal patterns

The essence of seasonal patterns in time series data is the repetition of the time series in systematic intervals over a given time range. Seasonal patterns may also contain a trend component. Figure 7.3 displays a seasonal time series pattern.

FIGURE 7.3   **Seasonal Time Series Pattern Example**

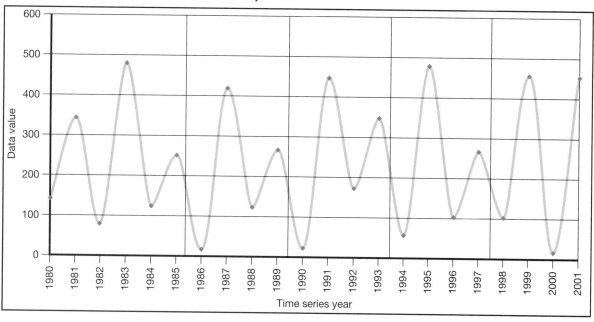

FIGURE 7.4   **Combined Trend and Seasonal Time Series Pattern Example**

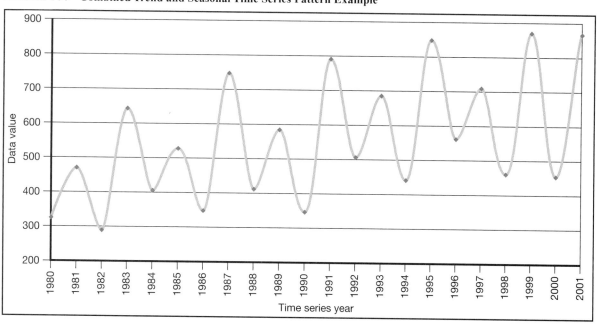

From Figure 7.3 one can see a pattern. The vertical black lines split the time series at its seasonality. In other words, the time series repeats itself every four periods. In actuality, the two categories of patterns in time series do coexist in real-life data.

Figure 7.4 displays a combined trend and seasonal time series data set. From Figure 7.4 one can see two patterns. The time series has a seasonal component and trend component. The data repeats itself every four periods and tends to rise from left to right. In sum, Figure 7.4 displays a combined seasonal and trend time series.

Cyclical Time Series

Although time series data may exhibit seasonal and/or trend patterns over the long term, there may exist recurring sequences of points at shorter intervals of time within the data. Any sequence of points that recurs, falling above or below the data's trend, and lasts more than 1 year can be attributed to the cyclical component of the time series.

Many time series contain or exhibit cyclical behavior. Cyclical behavior is most often characterized by regular runs of data points above and/or below the data's trend line. In most cases, the cyclical component of time series data is attributed to multiperiod economic movements. For example, nonfarm payrolls often have a cyclical component to them. Periods of rapid job growth (i.e., expansion) can be followed by periods of rather slow or even negative Job growth (i.e., contraction or recession). These individual time series data points alternate above and below the generally increasing trend.

Irregular Time Series

At times the irregular component is referred to as the *random component*. It encompasses the residual or random variability in the time series. Irregular variations do not follow any discernible pattern. They can be caused by short-term, unanticipated, and/or nonrecurring factors that effect the time series data. Since the nature of this time series component is random, we do not attempt to predict its impact.

General Forms of Time Series Models

In general, two forms of time series models exist: multiplicative and additive. The multiplicative model is the most widely used, and it assumes that demand is the product of the four time series components. It is expressed as follows:

$$\text{Demand} = T \times S \times C \times I$$

The additive model simply adds the components together:

$$\text{Demand} = T + S + C + I$$

It should be noted that most real-world forecasters assume the irregular component will average itself out over time and they concentrate only on the trend, seasonal, and cyclical components.

ANALYZING PATTERNS IN TIME SERIES DATA

There are no automated techniques for analyzing time series data. In fact, many of the techniques that exist to analyze time series data require substantial computational effort and statistical insight. Effort is expended in building and choosing the proper models and insight is applied in interpreting the output from the models.

Latest Period or Naïve Method

This method may be the simplest method available. In this method a forecaster uses the value of the latest period to forecast the next period. This method is sometimes referred to as the naïve method because it uses just one piece of data when other relevant data is available.

Trend Analysis

If the time series has a pattern akin to Figure 7.1 or 7.2, the analysis is typically not difficult. These time series exhibit a trend component that is consistently increasing. Excel's TREND ( ) function can be used to easily model these types of time series (see the chapter on linear regression). However, if the trend is not as distinct as those in Figure 7.1 and 7.2, or contains considerable noise, then the time series may need to be adjusted to help identify the trend. This adjustment process is generally referred to as *smoothing*.

Smoothing

Smoothing always incorporates some form of averaging.

Smoothing always incorporates some form of averaging of the time series data. The most common smoothing techniques are the moving average and exponential smoothing. The moving average technique will be presented first followed by exponential smoothing.

Moving Averages

Moving averages calculate a forecast at any period of the date set by averaging several observations in the time series.

Moving averages tend to be the easiest technique to use. The technique calculates a forecast at any period of the data set by averaging several observations in the time series. For example, if one wanted to smooth the data for the months of February, March, and April (referred to as a 3-month moving average), a forecast for May could be developed. This forecast would be calculated by averaging the data points from February, March, and April.

A 4-month moving average could be developed by using the months of January, February, March, and April. The longer a moving average is, the smoother the data set becomes. In fact, one can control the effect of smoothing on the time series data by using a longer or shorter averaging period. The formula for calculating a moving average is as follows:

$$MA_n = \frac{\sum_{i=1}^{n} D_i}{n}$$

(7.1)

where

n = number of periods in moving average
D_i = data in period i

Excel's Data Analysis add-in can be used to calculate moving averages

We will demonstrate 3-year and 5-year moving averages on the data set provided in Table 7.1, using Excel's Moving Average tool. The following steps should be completed to create a moving average in Excel:

TABLE 7.1
Moving Average Example Sales Data Set

Year	Sales ($000)	Year	Sales ($000)
1980	52.04	1991	83.18
1981	59.42	1992	87.05
1982	55.66	1993	84.79
1983	53.86	1994	73.49
1984	64.59	1995	76.23
1985	75.28	1996	96.54
1986	61.89	1997	95.08
1987	73.74	1998	87.05
1988	81.19	1999	96.02
1989	97.52	2000	98.90
1990	86.50	2001	83.23

Concept *Check*
Moving Average
Example Using
Excel

To illustrate the concept of smoothing using moving averages, let's analyze the data set listed in Table 7.1.

1. Be sure to have Excel's Data Analysis package loaded (see Microsoft Help menu).
2. Choose the Tools menu in Excel and then the Data Analysis option.
3. From the dialog box displayed in Figure 7.5, choose Moving Average and click OK.
4. Excel displays a dialog box that prompts you for an Input range, Interval, and Output range. This dialog box. accompanied by the time series data, is shown in Figure 7.6.
5. Enter the sales data range in the Input range edit box by highlighting the data or typing in its reference.
6. Click on the Labels in the first row box if the data set contains a label in the first row.
7. Enter the number of periods to be included in the moving average in the Interval edit box.
8. Click on the Output range edit box and enter the address of the cell or click on the cell where you want the output to start. The author suggests juxtaposing your forecasted values with your actual values.
9. Click OK.

FIGURE 7.5
Data Analysis Dialog Box

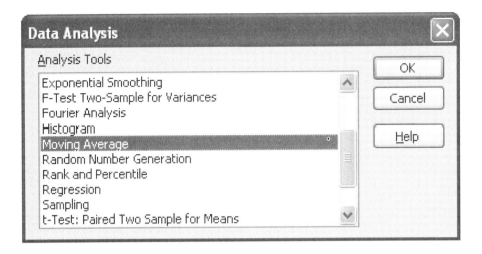

FIGURE 7.6   **Excel's Moving Average Dialog Box**

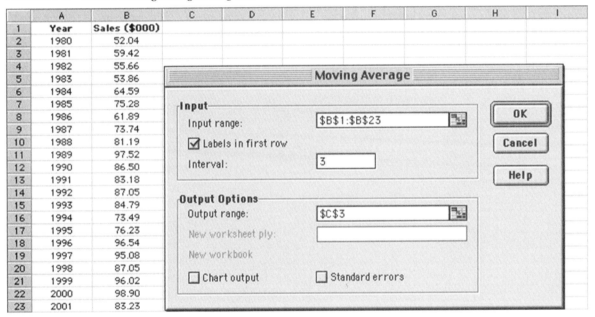

	A	B
1	Year	Sales ($000)
2	1980	52.04
3	1981	59.42
4	1982	55.66
5	1983	53.86
6	1984	64.59
7	1985	75.28
8	1986	61.89
9	1987	73.74
10	1988	81.19
11	1989	97.52
12	1990	86.50
13	1991	83.18
14	1992	87.05
15	1993	84.79
16	1994	73.49
17	1995	76.23
18	1996	96.54
19	1997	95.08
20	1998	87.05
21	1999	96.02
22	2000	98.90
23	2001	83.23

Excel will fill in the formulas for the moving average. The moving average will begin with the term #N/A. There will be as many #N/A terms as the number of intervals you specified, minus one. Excel does this because there is not enough data to calculate an average for those observations that number less than the interval. Figure 7.7 displays the results of the 3- and 5-year moving averages on the sales time series data (see Table 7.1).

Using Excel's charting feature, it is very simple to create a graph of the sales baseline data, the 3-year moving average, and the 5-year moving average all on one graph. Figure 7.8 displays such a graph.

It is easy to see from Figure 7.8 that the longer the moving average interval is, 5-year versus 3-year, the smoother the forecast is. In addition, it can be seen that the moving averages lag behind movements in the baseline. This is because the moving averages is based on prior data points. In other words, longer moving averages tend to smooth data more and also tend to lag behind movements in the underlying baseline more.

Overall, moving average techniques tend to work best on stable time series. However, this is a bit ironic, in that if a time series is more stable, smoothing techniques may not have to be used at all. Weighted moving averages will be covered next followed by exponential smoothing.

FIGURE 7.7
Three- and Five-year Moving Averages for Sales Time Series Data

	A	B	C	D
	Year	**Sales ($000)**	**3-Month MA**	**5-Month MA**
1				
2	1980	52.04		
3	1981	59.42	#N/A	#N/A
4	1982	55.66	#N/A	#N/A
5	1983	53.86	55.71	#N/A
6	1984	64.59	56.31	#N/A
7	1985	75.28	58.04	57.11
8	1986	61.89	64.58	61.76
9	1987	73.74	67.25	62.26
10	1988	81.19	70.30	65.87
11	1989	97.52	72.27	71.34
12	1990	86.50	84.15	77.92
13	1991	83.18	88.40	80.17
14	1992	87.05	89.07	84.43
15	1993	84.79	85.58	87.09
16	1994	73.49	85.01	87.81
17	1995	76.23	81.78	83.00
18	1996	96.54	78.17	80.95
19	1997	95.08	82.09	83.62
20	1998	87.05	89.28	85.23
21	1999	96.02	92.89	85.68
22	2000	98.90	92.72	90.18
23	2001	83.23	93.99	94.72
24			92.72	92.06

FIGURE 7.8   **Graph of Base Line, 3-year, and 5-year Moving Averages**

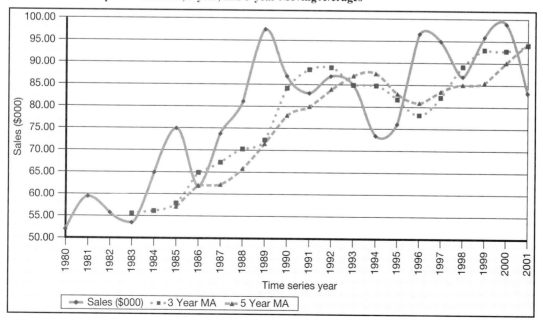

Weighted Moving Averages

In using a simple moving average, all weights assigned to the data points are equal. Weighted moving averages are a variation on simple moving averages that allow the forecaster to choose the weights assigned to the data points. A weighted moving average (WMA) can be expressed as follows

$$\text{WMA} = \frac{\sum (\text{weight for period } n)(\text{demand in period } n)}{\sum \text{weights}}$$

Weights can be used to place more emphasis on recent data or more emphasis on older data. The weighting scheme chosen makes the technique more responsive. In general, more weight is applied to the recent data. Let's use the sales data from Figure 7.7 to calculate a weighted 3-year moving average with the most recent data point receiving 3 times as much weight as the oldest data point while the middle data point receives twice as much weight as the oldest data point. The forecast for 2002 would be as follows

$$\text{WMA 2002 sales} = \frac{3}{6}(83.23) + \frac{2}{6}(90.90) + \frac{1}{6}(96.02) = 90.59$$

Note that for the weighted moving average the sum of the weights is equal to 1.0. This is also true for a 3-year simple moving average where each weight was 1/3. Recall that the forecast using a 3-year simple moving average was 92.72.

Exponential Smoothing

Exponential smoothing calculates a forecast by combining a prior forecast with a weighted error measurement.

In general, exponential smoothing is another smoothing technique, one that calculates a forecast at any period by using past observations. Specifically, exponential smoothing combines a prior forecast with a weighted error measurement. This error measurement comes from the difference between the prior forecast and the actual observation at the time of the prior forecast. The basic equation is as follows:

$$F_{T+1} = F_T + \alpha e_T \qquad \textbf{(7.2)}$$

Given that T is time, F_T is the forecast at time T, α is a smoothing constant (a value between 0.0 and 1.0 inclusive), and $e_T = A_T - F_T$, where A_T denotes the actual observation at time T, Equation 1.2 can be rewritten as follows:

$$F_{T+1} = F_T + \alpha(A_T - F_T) \qquad \textbf{(7.3)}$$

With some mathematical manipulation, Equation 1.3 can be rearranged to yield Equation 1.4:

$$F_{T+1} = (1 - \alpha)F_T + \alpha A_T \qquad \textbf{(7.4)}$$

Using α of 1.0 will result in a forecast incorporating just the actual observation from the past period.

Equation 1.4 describes the forecast at period $T + 1$ as a proportion of the forecast at period T plus a proportion of the actual observation at period T. If α is 1.0, the forecast at period $T + 1$ is the actual observation from period T. Conversely, if α is 0.0, the forecast at period $T + 1$ is the forecast from period T.

Concept *Check*
Exponential Smoothing Example Using Excel

Excel's Data Analysis add-in, located in the Tools menu, performs exponential smoothing in a spreadsheet.

To illustrate the concept of exponential smoothing, let's analyze the same data set previously listed in Table 7.1. We will use $\alpha = 0.1$ and $\alpha = 0.3$. Take note that Excel uses what is called a *damping factor*. The damping factor is equal to 1 minus the smoothing constant. See step 6 below for further discussion. The following steps should be completed to create an exponentially smoothed model in Excel:

1. Be sure to have Excel's Data Analysis package loaded (see Excel Help Menu).
2. Choose the Tools menu in Excel and then the Data Analysis option.
3. From the dialog box displayed in Figure 7.9, choose Exponential Smoothing and click OK.
4. Excel displays a dialog box that prompts you for an Input range, Damping factor, and Output range. This dialog box accompanied by the time series data is shown in Figure 7.10.

FIGURE 7.9
Data Analysis Dialog Box

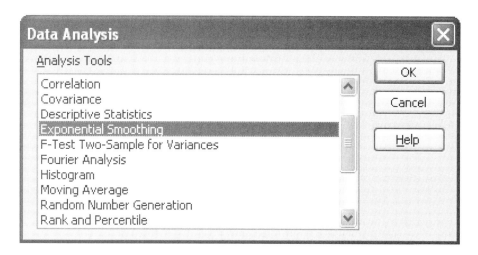

FIGURE 7.10
Excel's Exponential Smoothing Dialog Box

	A	B	C	D	E
1	Year	Sales ($000)			
2	1980	52.04			
3	1981	59.42			
4	1982	55.66			
5	1983	53.86			
6	1984	64.59			
7	1985	75.28			
8	1986	61.89			
9	1987	73.74			
10	1988	81.19			
11	1989	97.52			
12	1990	86.50			
13	1991	83.18			
14	1992	87.05			
15	1993	84.79			
16	1994	73.49			
17	1995	76.23			
18	1996	96.54			
19	1997	95.08			
20	1998	87.05			
21	1999	96.02			
22	2000	98.90			
23	2001	83.23			

5. Enter the sales data range in the Input range edit box by highlighting the data or typing in its reference.

Excel's Exponential Smoothing analysis tool refers to a Damping factor; this factor is equal to 1 minus the smoothing constant discussed earlier.

6. Enter the value of $1 - \alpha$ in the Damping factor edit box. Excel requests a damping factor instead of a smoothing constant. The damping factor is equal to 1 minus the smoothing constant (i.e., 1 − smoothing constant = damping factor).

7. Click on Labels in the first row box if the data set contains a label in the first row.

8. Click on the Output range edit box and enter the address of the cell or click on the cell where you want the output to start. Refer to the help menu in MS Excel for more details regarding Output range selection.

9. Click OK.

Excel will fill in the formulas for the exponentially smoothed model. The exponentially smoothed forecasts will begin with the term #N/A. There will be one #N/A term. Excel does this because there is not enough data to calculate an exponentially smoothed forecast for the first observation. Figure 7.11 displays the results of the exponentially smoothed models for $\alpha = 0.1$ and $\alpha = 0.3$.

We see from Figure 7.11 that the higher the smoothing constant α is, the smoother the forecast is. In addition, we can be seen that the exponentially smoothed forecasts lag behind movements in the baseline. This is because the exponentially smoothed data is based on a weighted average of prior data points and the present data point.

FIGURE 7.11 **Graph of Base Line and Exponentially Smoothed Sales Data**

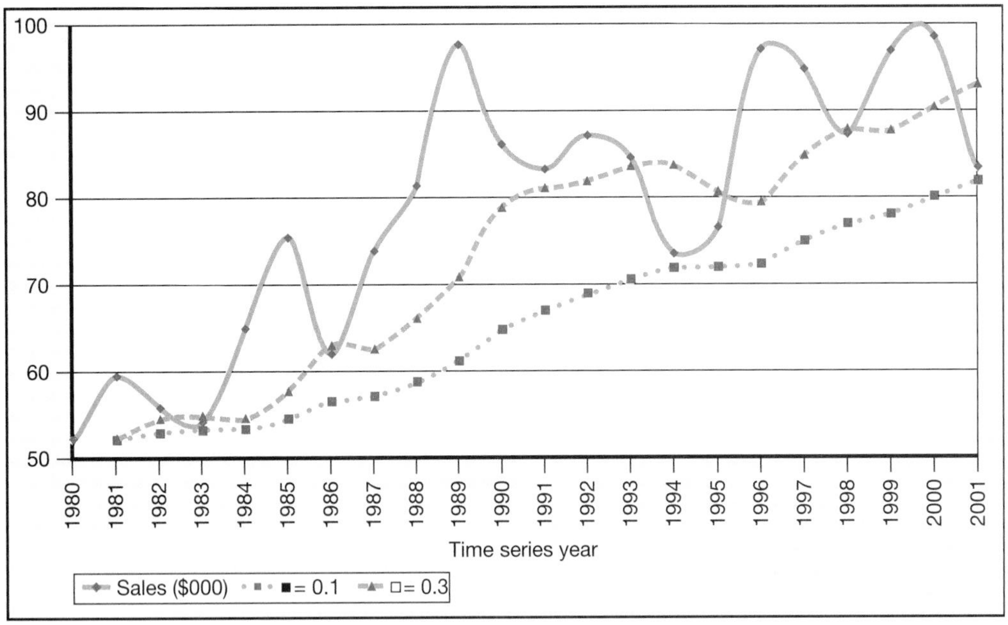

Choosing a Smoothing Constant

In general, the higher the smoothing constant, the smoother the forecast.

In general, the higher the smoothing constant α, the smoother the forecast will be. Standard forecasting nomenclature states that the smoothing constant should be between 0.1 and 0.3. This recommendation is based on the following: If exponential smoothing appears to work significantly better when a larger smoothing constant is chosen, the improved results are likely to due a substantial amount of autocorrelation in the time series data.

AUTOCORRELATION

Autocorrelation occurs when there is dependency between time series data points.

Autocorrelation occurs when there is dependency between time series data points. For example, a current time series data point could be dependent on a time series data point or points a number of time periods earlier. This type of dependency describes the essence of a seasonal time series. Autocorrelation is key to forecasting seasonal time series.

Autocorrelation can be calculated by lagging a data set against itself (refer to Figure 7.12).

Identifying Autocorrelation

Autocorrelation can be calculated by lagging a data set against itself. If the data points in a time series are paired with the data points that immediately precede them, you can calculate the correlation ρ between the two data sets. If the correlation is strong, $\rho > 0.5$, then there is a substantial amount of autocorrelation in the time series. The Excel function CORREL( ) calculates the correlation between a set of time series data. Figure 7.12 displays an example of a lagging time series data set and the corresponding correlation coefficient, ρ.

If the lagged time series correlation ρ is strong, then there is a substantial amount of autocorrelation with the data.

It is seen from Figure 7.12 that the correlation is relatively high for the lagged variables. This leads us to believe there is dependency between the time series data points. In turn, this may lead one to believe there is a seasonal component to the time series.

Measuring autocorrelation can identify seasonality in a time series.

Autocorrelation and Seasonality

Measuring autocorrelation can identify seasonality in a set of time series data. Figure 7.13 displays a time series that has a pronounced seasonal component. From Figure 7.13 one notices peaks and valleys at regular intervals.

Seasonal periods may be long term, such as yearly, or shorter term, such as monthly or weekly.

Seasonal time series data can be adjusted by using a simple weighting method to develop seasonal factors.

If one wishes to forecast future sales, then seasonal variations in the time series must be identified. For example, sales data tend to be seasonal in nature. Sales of fireworks tend to peak around the end of June preceding the Fourth of July and may peak again around the New Year holiday (January 1 or the Chinese celebration).

FIGURE 7.12
Lagged Time Series Example and Correlation Estimate

	A	B	C
1	Year	Sales ($000)	Lagged Sales ($000)
2			52.04
3	1980	52.04	59.42
4	1981	59.42	55.66
5	1982	55.66	53.86
6	1983	53.86	64.59
7	1984	64.59	75.28
8	1985	75.28	61.89
9	1986	61.89	73.74
10	1987	73.74	81.19
11	1988	81.19	97.52
12	1989	97.52	86.50
13	1990	86.50	83.18
14	1991	83.18	87.05
15	1992	87.05	84.79
16	1993	84.79	73.49
17	1994	73.49	76.23
18	1995	76.23	96.54
19	1996	96.54	95.08
20	1997	95.08	87.05
21	1998	87.05	96.02
22	1999	96.02	98.90
23	2000	98.90	83.23
24	2001	83.23	
25			
26	Correlation = ρ =	0.77	

FIGURE 7.13   **Seasonal Time Series Data Example**

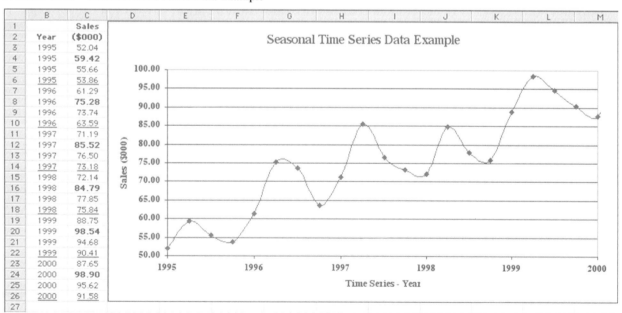

Figure 7.13 notes the seasonality of the time series to be at regular intervals of 4 years. The underlined data points denote this. The data points in bold are the highest sales for the respective 4-year seasonal period. A trend can also be seen in the time series as the data points rise from left to right.

SEASONAL ADJUSTMENTS

A seasonal factor is basically the portion of the total demand assigned to each seasonal period.

A number of methods for adjusting seasonal time series exist. The author suggests a simple weighting method for developing seasonal factors of a time series. The method consists of dividing the actual demand for a single period by the total demand over the entire seasonal period. The basic equation for this calculation is as follows:

$$SF_i = \frac{D_i}{\sum_{i=1}^{n} D_i} \qquad (7.5)$$

where
SF_i = seasonal factor for period i
D_i = demand for period i

Basically, Equation 7.5 calculates the portion of total demand assigned to each seasonal period. These seasonal factors are then multiplied by the forecasted demand to yield seasonally adjusted forecasts. The forecasted demand is obtained by using a linear regression model on the original data. An example using the data starting in 1995 from Figure 7.13 is presented next.

Concept *Check*
Seasonal Adjustment Example

Figure 7.14 depicts the data starting in 1995, sorted by seasonal period. The sum of each column and the total sum have been computed. The seasonal factors are computed by dividing each seasonal period (columns) demand total by the overall total demand.

The following calculations exhibit the seasonal factors.

$$SF_1 = \frac{D_1}{\sum_{i=1}^{n} D_i} = \frac{433.06}{1858.02} \approx 0.233$$

$$SF_2 = \frac{D_2}{\sum_{i=1}^{n} D_i} = \frac{502.45}{1858.02} \approx 0.270$$

$$SF_3 = \frac{D_3}{\sum_{i=1}^{n} D_i} = \frac{474.05}{1858.02} \approx 0.255$$

$$SF_4 = \frac{D_4}{\sum_{i=1}^{n} D_i} = \frac{448.46}{1858.02} \approx 0.241$$

To obtain a deseasonalized forecast, the seasonal factors must be multiplied by the forecast itself.

These seasonal factors then must be multiplied by the forecast for the upcoming period. Overall, there seems to be an upward trend in the amount of sales each year. This can be seen in the last column of Figure 7.14, as sales steadily rise from around 246 to around 373 ($000). Therefore, it would be reasonable to use linear regression to predict the trend component of the time series and adjust it for seasonality.

Linear Regression Forecast and Seasonal Adjustment

A linear trend line is calculated to forecast sales for 2001. The trend equation for the time series, where x_1 is in years, is as follows:

$$\hat{y} = -51,479 + 25.93x_1$$

Therefore, the forecast for 2001 is

$$\hat{y} = -51,479 + 25.93(2001) = 406.93 \qquad (7.6)$$

FIGURE 7.14 Seasonally Sorted Demand Data

	A	B	C	D	E	F
1						
2				Demand ($000)		
3				Seasonal Period		
4		1	2	3	4	Totals
5	1995	52.04	59.42	55.66	53.86	220.98
6	1996	61.29	75.28	73.74	63.59	273.90
7	1997	71.19	85.52	76.50	73.18	306.39
8	1998	72.14	84.79	77.85	75.84	310.62
9	1999	88.75	98.54	94.68	90.41	372.38
10	2000	87.65	98.90	95.62	91.58	373.75
11		433.06	502.45	474.05	448.46	1858.02

Using this forecast for sales demand for 2001, the seasonally adjusted forecasts SF_i for the four quarters of 2001 are as follows

$$SF_1 = (0.233)(406.93) = 94.85$$
$$SF_2 = (0.271)(406.93) = 110.04$$
$$SF_3 = (0.255)(406.93) = 103.82$$
$$SF_4 = (0.241)(406.93) = 98.22$$

Figure 7.15 displays the combined graph of the original time series and the new forecasts. It is apparent that these forecasts reflect both the seasonal variation and upward trend in the sales time series.

FIGURE 7.15 Combined Graph of Original Time Series and Forecasted Data

	B	C
1		Sales
2	Year	($000)
3	1995	52.04
4	1995	59.42
5	1995	55.66
6	1995	53.86
7	1996	61.29
8	1996	75.28
9	1996	73.74
10	1996	63.59
11	1997	71.19
12	1997	85.52
13	1997	76.50
14	1997	73.18
15	1998	72.14
16	1998	84.79
17	1998	77.85
18	1998	75.84
19	1999	88.75
20	1999	98.54
21	1999	94.68
22	1999	90.41
23	2000	87.65
24	2000	98.90
25	2000	95.62
26	2000	91.58
27	2001	98.88
28	2001	113.94
29	2001	99.7
30	2001	94.41
31		

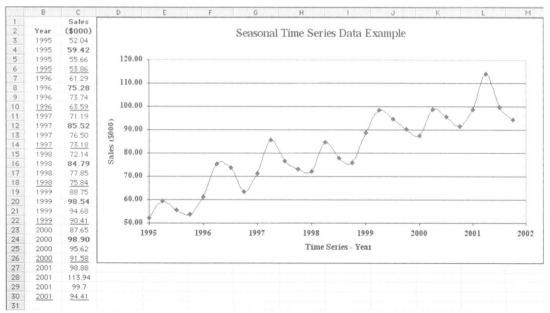

Business Decision Modeling Behind the Scenes

Business Forecasting—More Art Than Science?

FANCY MODELS VERSUS COMMON SENSE

There are no magic forecasting methods that always work or computer programs that forecast by themselves. The heart of forecasting is "good" guessing and the best guess is an educated guess. Business managers use common sense and judgment and as much information as possible. They look at as many angles as they can and consider past trends, new developments, anticipated cycles, and anything else that can give a hint at what is to come. Statistical models and computers can assist a business manager in constructing models to analyze these trends, cycles, and new developments.

FORECASTING: SCIENCE OR ART

Business forecasting is not a pure science. However, some firms never attempt to forecast at all. A business manager does not have to be an expert in statistics or mathematics to create a basic forecasting model. More than mathematics and statistics, you need patience and a little bit of confidence mixed together with common sense. Computers, mathematical formulas, and models store knowledge, but they can't do it all alone. Business managers not only build forecasting models but they also must interpret their output. They do use computerized econometric or simulation models or trends analysis, but they also must exercise good judgment when it comes time

to interpret the outputs. Hence, a good business manager must master both the science and art of forecasting.

WHAT TO DO ABOUT FORECASTING NEW PRODUCTS?

Business managers have historically had a number of tools (like focus groups and surveys—qualitative forecasting techniques) to gather data on product acceptance. However, what does a manager do if large volumes of data do not exist or if the product is so new no data exists at all. One solution is the development of a process based upon diffusion theory and the product life cycle. Diffusion theory employs the use of a number of equations that produce an S-shaped curve resembling a product life cycle (Bass, 1969). Overall, the Bass model has shown very good results for many companies in many industries.

OPTIMAL INFORMATION AREA

Mahajan, Vijay, Eitan Muller, and Frank M. Bass. "*New Product Diffusion Models in Marketing: A Review and Direction for Research.*" *Journal of Marketing*, vol. 54 (January 1990), pp. 1–26.

Thomas, Robert J. *New Product Development: Managing and Forecasting for Strategic Success.* New York: John Wiley & Sons, 1993, pp. 189–195.

Summary

Moving average and exponential smoothing techniques can be effective tools to identify and confirm trend. However, managers should learn to identify situations that are suitable for analysis with moving averages and how this analysis should be applied.

The advantages of using these techniques must be weighed against the disadvantages. Both techniques are trend following, or lagging, indicators that will always be a step behind. This is not necessarily a bad thing. Once in a trend, moving averages and exponential smoothing techniques inform you about that trend, but also give late signals. Moving averages and exponential smoothing are simple but effective tools for basic forecasting, but must be coupled with sound business acumen to achieve superior forecasting results.

An executive summary that illustrates the principles discussed in this chapter follows.

Executive Summary for Seasonal Decomposition of Demand for Futura Company

TO: Senior Vice President Futura
FROM: Forecast Incorporated
SUBJECT: Seasonal Decomposition of Demand and Forecast
DATE: April 13, 2003

Introduction

Table 1a depicts the demand data for the Futura Company starting in 1995, sorted by seasonal period (quarter). The sum of each column and the total sum have been computed to facilitate seasonal decomposition. The seasonal factors are computed by dividing each seasonal period (columns) demand total by the overall total demand. The calculations in Figure 1 exhibit the seasonal factors.

TABLE 1A
Seasonally Sorted Demand Data

$$SF_1 = \frac{D_1}{\sum_{i=1}^{n} D_i} = \frac{433.06}{1858.02} \approx 0.233$$

$$SF_2 = \frac{D_2}{\sum_{i=1}^{n} D_i} = \frac{502.45}{1858.02} \approx 0.270$$

$$SF_3 = \frac{D_3}{\sum_{i=1}^{n} D_i} = \frac{474.05}{1858.02} \approx 0.255$$

$$SF_4 = \frac{D_4}{\sum_{i=1}^{n} D_i} = \frac{448.46}{1858.02} \approx 0.241$$

TABLE 1B

	A	B	C	D	E	F
1						
2			**Demand ($000)**			
3			**Seasonal Period**			
4		**1**	**2**	**3**	**4**	**Totals**
5	**1995**	52.04	59.42	55.66	53.86	220.98
6	**1996**	61.29	75.28	73.74	63.59	273.90
7	**1997**	71.19	85.52	76.50	73.18	306.39
8	**1998**	72.14	84.79	77.85	75.84	310.62
9	**1999**	88.75	98.54	94.68	90.41	372.38
10	**2000**	87.65	98.90	95.62	91.58	373.75
11		433.06	502.45	474.05	448.46	1858.02

These seasonal factors then must be multiplied by the forecast for the upcoming period. Overall, there seems to be an upward trend in the amount of sales each year. This can be seen in the last column of Table 1b as demand steadily rises from around 246 to around 373 ($000). Therefore, it would be reasonable to use linear regression to predict the trend component of the time series and adjust it for seasonality.

Linear Regression Forecast and Seasonal Adjustment

A linear trend line is calculated to forecast sales for 2001. The trend equation for the time series, where x_1 is in years, is as follows: $\hat{y} = -51,479 + 25.93x_1$. Therefore, the forecast for 2001 is $\hat{y} = -51,479 + 25.93(2001) = 406.93$. On the basis of this forecast for sales demand for 2001, the seasonally adjusted forecasts SF_i for the four quarters of 2001 are listed in Table 3.

From the seasonal factors, the Futura Company can expect about 23 percent of its sales to come in the first quarter, 24 percent of annual sales in the fourth quarter, 27 percent of

TABLE 2
Seasonally Adjusted Forecasts for 2001

$$SF_1 = (0.243)(406.93) = 98.88$$
$$SF_2 = (0.280)(406.93) = 113.94$$
$$SF_3 = (0.245)(406.93) = 99.70$$
$$SF_4 = (0.232)(406.93) = 94.41$$

annual demand in the second quarter and about 26 percent of annual sales in the third quarter. These seasonal factors are multiplied by the forecasted annual demand to yield the forecasted demand for each quarter. Those forecasts are presented next.

Conclusion

Therefore, the Futura Company could expect an annual sales forecast for 2001 of approximately 407 units with first quarter demand of approximately 99 units, second quarter demand of approximately 114 units, third quarter demand of approximately 100 units, and fourth quarter demand of approximately 94 units.

Case Study: *Jaqui's Import Beers Sales Seasonality*

BACKGROUND

Jaqui was the owner of a beer and wine distributorship. She had been in the business for a number of years and thought she knew the trends in beer sales fairly well. However, over the last 4 years or so she thought she saw a run-up in import beer sales within the United States. In fact, she also believed that in addition to an upward trend in import beer sales there existed a seasonal component.

SEASONAL HYPOTHESIS

Her hypothesis was as follows: Import beer sales follow a bimonthly seasonal pattern. She deduced through her experience that January and February commonly were down months for import beer sales because of the after-holiday lag. Therefore, she would group sales in bimonthly units starting with January and February, then March and April, and so on for the rest of the year. Her groupings would resemble the following table.

Month	Seasonal group
January	S1
February	S1
March	S2
April	S2
May	S3
June	S3

Month	Seasonal group
July	S4
August	S4
September	S5
October	S5
November	S6
December	S6

Jaqui knew of a technique called linear regression, but she also knew that if a data set contains seasonal variation a standard linear regression model does not provide very good results. With seasonal effects, the data tend to drop well below the trend lines or ascend sharply above the trend lines in noticeable patterns. Forecasts for future time periods would be much more accurate if the regression model reflected these drops and ascents in the data.

PROBLEM AT HAND AND DISCUSSION QUESTIONS

Therefore Jaqui had decided to develop a seasonally adjusted regression model for the import beer sales data. Jaqui's data set

can be found on the CD-ROM that accompanies the text under the filename BEER1.xls.

1. She needs your help to construct a simple weighting method for developing the seasonal factors, to create a linear trend line for the import beer sales over time, and then combine the two in order to forecast sales for 2005.

2. How is Jaqui's model doing? Is it predicting import beer sales over time accurately? Interpret the R_2, F, and t statistics when answering this question.

Interactive Case: *Forecasting Using Exponential Smoothing for Bill's Brew Threw*

Please goto www.mhhe.com/kros1e to access the Interactive Forecasting Model.

BACKGROUND

Bill Fredericks runs a minimart that sells basic convenience goods like soda, beer, ice, chips, and snacks. Bill's business is good and relatively stable over time (i.e., no large trends upward or downward over time). However, he has noticed changes in the amount of soda he has been selling. Bill wishes he had a forecasting method that took into account past data but allowed him to chose which data he thought the most important (i.e., apply a weighting scheme).

BILL'S DEMAND NUMBERS

Bill had put together data on his business' soda sales each month over the past 12 months (periods). The following table illustrates Bill's demand (number of sodas sold) over the last 12 months (periods) of business.

Bill wishes to know, on the basis of past demand data, if there is a way to predict future demand for monthly soda sales. Bill has heard of a forecasting technique called exponential smoothing. Although the technique is exactly what Bill wants, a method that incorporates all past data and allows for weighting, he does not know what weight to use or how to determine if one weighting scheme is better than another.

Month (periods)	Soda sales (units)
1	3,591
2	3,703
3	3,952
4	3,882
5	3,677
6	3,659

Month (periods)	Soda sales (units)
7	3,935
8	3,615
9	3,879
10	3,653
11	3,768
12	3,754

EXPONENTIAL SMOOTHING MODELS

Using the exponential smoothing model and Excel's Exponential Smoothing option, input the demand data into the demand column, set the init = value at 359, and press Forecast. Then, analyzing the model output, answer the following questions:

1. Set the alpha slider bar to alpha = 0.1 and note the value of MAD. Now increment the alpha slider bar in 0.1 increments, noting the value of the MAD at every increment. How does the forecast change as alpha is incremented upward? Why does the forecast change in this manner when alpha is changed?

2. What value of alpha outputs the lowest MAD value?

3. What is the forecast value for Bill's soda sales for the 13th month (period) at the best alpha value (i.e., the alpha value that produces the lowest MAD value)?

Optimal Information Area

Stockcharts Web site at **www.stockcharts.com.**

International Federation of Technical Analysts Web site at URL **www.ifta.org.**

Mahajan, Vijay, Eitan Muller, and Frank M. Bass. "New Product Diffusion Models in Marketing: A Review and Direction for Research." Journal of Marketing, vol. 54 (January 1990), pp. 1–26.

Thomas, Robert J. *New Product Development: Managing and Forecasting for Strategic Success.* New York: John Wiley & Sons, 1993, pp. 189–195.

Financial Sense Web site at **http://financialsense.com/stormwatch/oldupdates/2003/0111.htm.**

American Management Association Web site at **http://amanet.org/seminars/cmd2/outlines/1276_outline.htm.**

Economic Forecasting at **http://gbr.pepperdine.edu/001/forecast.html.**

Problems

1. The number of cans of soft drinks sold in a machine each week is recorded: 122, 85, 92, 98, 110, 108 115, 102, 95, 98. Using Excel's Data Analysis add-in, forecast the sales for all periods using a three-period moving average?

2. For the number of cans of soft drinks sold in a machine each week in Problem 1, what is the MAD for a three-period moving average.

3. Using Excel's Data Analysis add-in, find the four period moving average for the data in Table 7.2. Historical records show 2863, 2481, 3239, 3519, 3349, 3637, 3501, 3892, 3732, 3526.

4. Given the following data,

   a. Compute a 3-month moving forecast of demand through December and for the next month, January.

   b. Compute the MAD for the forecast.

Month	Demand	Month	Demand
January	808	July	794
February	1135	August	1155
March	704	September	987
April	919	October	1282
May	1051	November	857
June	1283	December	1154

5. Given the following data,

   a. Compute a 6-month moving average forecast of demand through December and for the next month, January.

   b. Compute the MAD for the forecast.

Month	Demand	Month	Demand
January	808	July	794
February	1135	August	1155
March	704	September	987
April	919	October	1282
May	1051	November	857
June	1283	December	1154

6. Given the following data,

   a. Compute a weighted 3-month moving average forecast of demand through December, using weights of 0.50 (most recent data), 0.30, and 0.20 (most distant data).

   b. Compute the MAD for the forecast.

   c. Compute the forecast for the next month (January).

Month	Demand	Month	Demand
January	808	July	794
February	1135	August	1155
March	704	September	987
April	919	October	1282
May	1051	November	857
June	1283	December	1154

7. Given the following data,

   a. Compute an exponentially smoothed forecast with alpha = 0.20 through May.

   b. Compute the forecast for the next month (June).

Month	Demand
January	160
February	268
March	170
April	275
May	180

8. Given the following data,

   a. Compute an exponentially smoothed forecast with alpha = 0.60 through May and create a forecast for the next month, June.

Month	Demand
January	160
February	268
March	170
April	275
May	180

   b. Compare the forecasts you computed in this Problem to the forecasts you computed in Problem 7. Which forecasting model does a better job?

9. A hospital records the number of floral deliveries its patients receive each day. For a 2-week period, the records show 25, 30, 32, 38, 42, 37, 39, 34, 31, 36, 33, 29, 31, 28. Using Excel's Data Analysis add-in for exponential smoothing with a smoothing constant of 0.1, forecast the number of deliveries in period 15.

10. Quarterly billing for water usage is shown below.

Seasonal Irregular Component Values:

Winter   0.971, 0.918. 0.908

Spring   0.840, 0.839, 0.834

Summer   1.096, 1.075, 1.109

Fall   1.133, 1.156, 1.141

What is the seasonal index for the Winter season? What is the seasonal index for the Fall season?

11. A claims form processing center uses exponential smoothing to forecast the number of incoming checks each month. The number of checks received in June was 39 million, while the forecast was 37 million. A smoothing constant of 0.3 is used. What is the forecast for July?

12. Daily high temperatures in degrees Fahrenheit in the city of Lubbock for the last week have been as follows: 93, 94, 93, 95, 96, 88, 90. Using Excel's Data Analysis add-in,

    a. Forecast the high temperature today, using a 3-day moving average.

    b. Forecast the high temperature today, using a 2-day moving average.

    c. Calculate the mean absolute deviation (MAD) based on a 2-day and a 3-day moving average. Compare the two MAD results. Which forecasting method provides a lower MAD?

13. You are given the following data on truck sales:

Month	Sales (000)	Month	Sales (000)
Jan	15	July	17
Feb	13	Aug	14
Mar	17	Sept	12
Apr	12	Oct	14
May	20	Nov	19
June	14	Dec	16

Using Excel's Data Analysis add-in, construct a moving average with 3 periods and determine the demand for trucks for next January.

Using a weighted moving average with three periods, determine the sales demand for February. Use 1/2, 1/3, and 1/6 for the weights of the most recent, second most recent, and third most recent periods, respectively. Compare the two forecasting methods, using MAD.

14. Data collected on the yearly demand, in thousands, for 50-lb bags of potting soil at Jim's Seed and Supply Store are shown in the following table.

Year	1	2	3	4	5	6	7	8	9	10	11
Demand (000)	4	6	4	5	10	8	7	9	12	14	15

Using Excel's Data Analysis add-in, develop a 3-year moving average to forecast sales from year 4 to year 12.

Estimate demand again for years 4 to 12 with a weighted moving average in which sales in the most recent year are given a weight of 1/2 and sales in the other 2 years are each given a weight of 1/4.

Graph the original data and the two forecasts. Which of the two forecasting methods seems better?

15. Passenger miles, in thousands flown, on Commuter West Airlines, a commuter firm serving the Salt Lake hub, are shown for the past 12 weeks.

Week	1	2	3	4	5	6
Actual passenger miles (000)	13	26	13	23	15	19

Week	7	8	9	10	11	12
Actual passenger miles (000)	24	19	22	22	16	25

Assuming an initial forecast for week 1 of 13,000 miles, use Excel's Data Analysis add-in for exponential smoothing to compute miles for weeks 2 through 12. Use $\alpha = 0.7$.

What is the MAD for this model?

16. Joe Sonar, owner of Blair Boot and Supply, has used time series extrapolation to forecast retail sales for the next four quarters. The sales estimates are $150,000, $110,000, $190,000, and $130,000 for the respective quarters. Seasonal indices for the four quarters have been found to be 1.25, .90, .75, and 1.10, respectively. Compute a seasonalized or adjusted sales forecast.

17. Attendance at Buckfield's newest Disney-like attraction, Vacation Land, has been as follows:

Quarter	Guests	Quarter	Guests
Winter `98	73	Summer `99	124
Spring `98	104	Fall `99	52
Summer `98	168	Winter `00	89
Fall `98	74	Spring `00	146
Winter `99	65	Summer `00	205
Spring `99	82	Fall `00	98

Compute seasonal indices using all of the data.

Chapter **Eight**

Introduction to Optimization Models

Learning Objectives

After completing this chapter, students will be able to:

1. Understand the basic assumptions and properties of optimization and linear programming (LP).
2. Use Excel spreadsheets to construct and solve optimization models, especially LP problems.
3. Understand the role of sensitivity analysis.
4. Understand major optimization application areas, including production, labor scheduling, transportation, and finance.
5. Gain experience in solving LP problems with Excel Solver software.

Chapter Outline

Business Decision Modeling in Action: Spreadsheet Optimization Models in Use, or Why Use Spreadsheets to Optimize?

Weighing the Pros and Cons of Optimization Modeling Using Spreadsheets

It was once stated that, in spite of the drawbacks spreadsheets have, 30 million users favor using spreadsheets as the analytical vernacular of management. In a sense, can that many business folks be completely wrong?

Spreadsheets: Today's Modeling Tool of Choice

The spreadsheet has become the modeling tool of choice for today's business problems. Custom linear optimization packages did exist before the first copies of Lotus 1-2-3 or Excel had ever shipped. However, as any business decision modeling student today can testify, everyone knows how to use spreadsheets. In addition, in most cases "the computer already comes loaded with a spreadsheet program."

Around 1985, linear optimization packages were being released for Lotus 1-2-3. These early optimization packages were highly acclaimed and won numerous awards including *PC Magazine*'s prestigious Technical Excellence Award. Soon after this, mainstream business and computer publications such as *The Wall Street Journal* and *The New York Times* began to bring widespread attention to these packages and their unique abilities.

Solving Larger-Scale Optimization Problems

Many of the current spreadsheet optimization packages have their roots in tackling large-scale, real-world problems. As early as 1991, a utility company in England was using an optimization package to solve spreadsheet models in excess of 100,000 variables. By 1994, spreadsheet add-ins capable of solving large-scale nonlinear models had been developed. Today, graduate as well as undergraduate business and engineering students use spreadsheets to assist in solving constrained optimization problems in many different areas.

Optimal Information Area

@RISK, Palisade Corp., Newfield, NY, http://www.palisade.com.

Crystal Ball, Decisioneering Inc., Boulder, Co, http://www.decisioneering.com.

Excel Solver, Frontline Systems, http://www.frontsys.com.

What'sBest!, Lindo Systems, http://www.lindo.com.

INTRODUCTION TO OPTIMIZATION MODELS

An optimization model is a decision model that seeks to optimize a given performance measure while meeting some set of given constraints.

This chapter investigates a powerful area of business decision modeling, spreadsheet optimization. Many situations arise in business activities that call for optimal decisions. Models called optimization models generate these optimal decisions. The definition of an optimization model is:

> A deterministic decision model consisting of a single performance measure (an objective function) to be optimized subject to satisfaction of a given set of constraints

Specific techniques are used to identify the optimal solution to this objective function. The technique, which will be described in this chapter, is known as *mathematical programming*. Hence, the author refers to models that use mathematical programming to identify the optimal solution as an optimization model.

It is important to note the difference between a descriptive model, a model that merely describes alternatives or outcomes, and an optimization model, a model that actually finds the "optimal" alternative or outcome. In addition, this chapter will discuss using spreadsheets in a manner to develop, construct, and solve optimization models.

How Does an Optimization Model Find an Optimal Solution?

A good question for the reader to ask is "How does an optimization model find this optimal solution?" In fact, there are a number of good questions to be asked right about now, such as:

- How is an optimization model constructed?
- Can descriptive models be transformed into optimization models?
- What is an objective function?
- What are constraints?
- Do I need to understand complex mathematics to construct and solve optimization models?

Actually, let's answer the last question first. With the advent of readily available computing power and user-friendly software, it is feasible to construct and solve optimization models without an explicit understanding of higher-order mathematics. However, it is important to familiarize the reader with a basic set of core components that make up optimization models. This chapter introduces these components and uses spreadsheets to illustrate how these components fit together and result in a final optimal solution.

The chapter also defines the classic constrained resource problem and describes a specific type of mathematical programming called linear programming (LP). In addition, LP formulation, and two LP solution approaches, LP sensitivity analysis and general LP problem types, are presented. Spreadsheets are used throughout to illustrate LP concepts.

Descriptive Models: The Foundation for Optimization Models

A good descriptive model is the cornerstone to the development of an optimization model.

Building the framework for an optimization model is critical to solution success. A good descriptive model is cornerstone to the development of an optimization model. The descriptive model is the foundation from where an optimization model directs its search for a solution.

Therefore, a working descriptive model is a necessity for constructing, solving, and analyzing an optimization model.

Transforming a Descriptive Model into an Optimization Model

Descriptive models get their name from their function; they describe a situation or circumstance. Models that describe a situation or circumstance are very valuable but lack a basic necessity for business decision making, the ability to provide a recommendation that is "best" or "optimal." To do so, descriptive models must be transformed into what the author refers to as *optimization models*. The next section provides an example of a descriptive model and its transformation into an optimization model.

Classic Descriptive Economic Order Quantity Model

A classic example of a descriptive model is the economic order quantity (EOQ) model used in many economics and operations management courses. The EOQ model is derived from the total annual cost formula for a unique product. The term EOQ refers to the quantity that should be ordered so setup costs are balanced with carrying costs, resulting in the lowest possible overall annual cost of purchasing and carrying inventory of a product.

The EOQ model is a classic descriptive model because it describes what the components of total annual costs are and how they are aggregated. However, the basic total annual cost and EOQ descriptive model provide a business decision maker with only the means to describe costs. They do not provide a true optimal cost or EOQ value.

By using basic algebra to construct the total annual cost equation and some elementary calculus to minimize total annual costs with regard to order quantity, an optimal answer can be found. Thereby, one transforms the descriptive model into an optimization model. This can be done with paper and pen, as has been the case for decades. However, with the advent of spreadsheets, the process of finding the optimal solution to the EOQ model has not only changed, it has also improved. The next section details a unique example of an EOQ problem and illustrates its solution by using a spreadsheet optimization model.

A classic example of a descriptive model is the economic order quantity model.

EOQ models provide an optimal order number by balancing holding and setup costs.

Concept *Check*
EOQ Example:
Kaye's Floral
Optimal Order
Quantity Problem

Kaye's design studio purchases glass vases for floral arrangements. Each vase is then hand painted and sent to the distributor for resale through a number of outlets. Each vase's purchase cost is $15. Annual demand for the vases is 15,000 units and is evenly distributed throughout the year. Kaye's holding costs or costs to carry inventory are 10 percent of the purchase cost per year. Each order has a fixed setup cost of $200 per order, no matter how many units are purchased.

Kaye wishes to know the number of vases to order so to minimize total annual costs. She thinks she can figure out how to calculate total annual costs associated with the ordering of the vases but is having trouble finding the optimal number of vases to order so as to minimize the cost.

Kaye has listed all the variables associated with total annual costs below and set up a preliminary descriptive model. In addition, Kaye is currently ordering 1,100 units per order.

Purchase cost $= P = \$15$

Annual demand $= D = 15{,}000 \text{ units/year}$

Carrying costs $= C = 10\%$ of the purchase price/year

Setup costs $= S = \$200$

Order quantity $= Q$

Orders per year $= \dfrac{D}{Q}$

Average annual inventory $= \dfrac{Q}{2}$

Therefore,

$$\text{Annual purchase cost (APC)} = P \times D = \$15 \times 15{,}000 = \$225{,}000$$

$$\text{Annual carrying costs (ACC)} = P \times C \times \frac{Q}{2} = \$15 \times 0.10 \times \frac{1{,}100}{2} = \$825.00$$

$$\text{Annual setup costs (ASC)} = S \times \frac{D}{Q} = \$200 \times \frac{15{,}000}{1{,}100} = \$2{,}727.27$$

and

$$\text{Total annual costs} = APC + ACC + ASC$$

or, in functional form,

$$\text{Total annual costs} = (P \times D) + \left(P \times C \times \frac{Q}{2} \right) + \left(S \times \frac{D}{Q} \right) = \$228{,}552.27$$

The descriptive model for Kaye's EOQ provides measures for the different costs associated with purchasing vases and holding vases in inventory. It also gives Kaye a total annual cost number, in this case $228,552.27. However, the descriptive model does not inform Kaye if she is ordering the optimal amount of vases so to minimize total annual costs.

In order to find the optimal number of vases to order to minimize total annual total costs, Kaye's descriptive model must be transformed into an optimization model. Specifically, a spreadsheet optimization model can assist Kaye in determining her optimal order quantity or EOQ. The next section develops a spreadsheet optimization model and describes how to use Excel's Solver tool to optimize the model, i.e., find Kaye's optimal order quantity or EOQ.

EOQ Spreadsheet Optimization Model

Figure 8.1 displays the spreadsheet optimization model for Kaye's floral EOQ problem. At an order quantity of 1,100, Kaye's annual carrying cost is $825.00, while the annual setup cost is $2,727.27. In an EOQ model that is optimal, the carrying cost is equal to the setup cost. Therefore, we know Kaye's order quantity of 1,100 is not the optimal order quantity because carrying cost and setup cost are not equal. Figure 8.2 displays the formulas associated with Kaye's EOQ spreadsheet.

Finding the Optimal EOQ

A better method in approaching the solution to the EOQ problem is to use a tool in Excel called Solver.

Using the spreadsheet model presented in Figures 8.1 and 8.2, an optimal order quantity could be found by trial and error. However, this method is very tedious and inefficient. A much better approach is to employ a built-in Excel tool, called Solver. The next section will discuss how to use solver to find the optimal order quantity for Kaye's Floral problem.

FIGURE 8.1
EOQ Spreadsheet Model for Kaye's Floral Problem

	A	B	C
			Kaye's Floral EOQ
1			
2	Purchase Price	P	$15.00
3			
4	Annual Demand	D	15,000
5			
6	Carrying Cost	C	10%
7			
8	Setup Cost	S	$200
9			
10	Order Quantity	Q	1,100
11			
12	Annual Purchase Cost	APC	$225,000.00
13			
14	Annual Carrying Cost	ACC	$825.00
15			
16	Annual Setup Cost	ASC	$2,727.27
17			
18	Total Annual Cost	TAC	$228,552.27

FIGURE 8.2
Spreadsheet Formulas for Kaye's Floral EOQ Problem

	A	B	C
1			
2	Purchase Price	P	15
3			
4	Annual Demand	D	15000
5			
6	Carrying Cost	C	0.1
7			
8	Setup Cost	S	200
9			
10	Order Quantity	Q	1100
11			
12	Annual Purchase Cost	APC	=C2*C4
13			
14	Annual Carrying Cost	ACC	=C2*C6*C10/2
15			
16	Annual Setup Cost	ASC	=C8*C4/C10
17			
18	Total Annual Cost	TAC	=C12+C14+C16

FIGURE 8.3
Excel Tools Menu Highlighting Solver

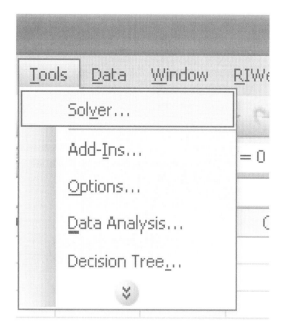

Excel's Solver

The Solver add-in is located in the Excel Tools menu.

Solver is an add-in to Excel that allows users to find an optimal value for a formula in one cell, called the target cell, on a worksheet. Solver works with related group of cells, either directly or indirectly, to solve the target cell formula. To produce the result you specify from the target cell formula, Solver adjusts the values in the changing cells you specify, called the adjustable cells. You can apply constraints to restrict the values Solver can use in the model, and the constraints can refer to other cells that affect the target cell formula. The next section describes how to setup Solver in Excel. The terms *target cell*, *adjustable cells*, and *constraints* will be used from this point forward.

Setting Up Solver in Excel

The following steps should be followed to setup Solver in an Excel spreadsheet.

1. On the Tools menu, click Solver. Figure 8.3 displays the Tools menu.

FIGURE 8.4
Excel Solver Dialogue Box

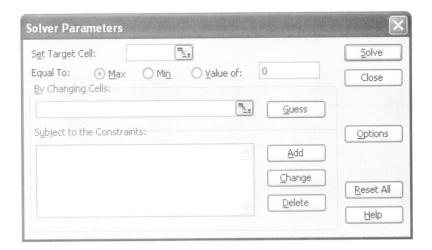

2. If the Solver command is not on the Tools menu, you need to install the Solver add-in. Click on the Add-Ins option under the tools menu and click on the box marked Solver.

If the Solver command is not on the Add-Ins option in the Tools menu, run the ValuePack installer from your original Microsoft Office CD and install Solver.

Using Solver to Find Solutions to a Spreadsheet Optimization Model

This section discusses how to use solver to optimize a spreadsheet model in Excel. It is assumed that the user has already built a spreadsheet optimization model in Excel (refer to Figures 8.1 and 8.2).

After you click on Solver in the Tools menu, the Solver dialog box, shown in Figure 8.4, will appear. The following steps enable Solver to find solutions to optimization spreadsheets.

The Set Target Cell box in Excel's Solver contains the objective you wish to accomplish (i.e., maximize profits or minimize costs).

1. In the Set Target Cell box, enter a cell reference or name for the target cell. The target cell must contain a formula.
2. To have the value of the target cell be as large as possible, click Max. To have the value of the target cell be as small as possible, click Min. To have the target cell be a certain value, click Value of, and then type the value in the box.
3. In the By Changing Cells box, enter a name or reference for each adjustable cell, separating nonadjacent references with commas. The adjustable cells must be related directly or indirectly to the target cell. You can specify up to 200 adjustable cells. To have Solver automatically propose the adjustable cells based on the target cell, click Guess.
4. In the Subject to the Constraints box, enter any constraints you want to apply.
5. Click Solve.

Applying these steps to Kaye's Floral spreadsheet problem defines a target cell, adjustable cells, and constraints as shown in Table 8.1 (refer to Figures 8.1 and 8.2):

The solver menu will resemble Figure 8.5 after the values from Table 8.1 have been entered into the Solver dialog boxes.

TABLE 8.1
Solver Cell Definitions

Set Target Cell	$C$18
Equal To	Min
Adjustable Cells	$C$10
Constraints*	$C$10 >= 0

*Specifying a constraint is a must, as order quantity must be a positive number. This can also be accomplished via the Options menu in Solver by clicking the Assume Non-negativity check box (refer to Figure 8.26).

FIGURE 8.5

Final Solver Parameters for Kaye's Floral EOQ Model

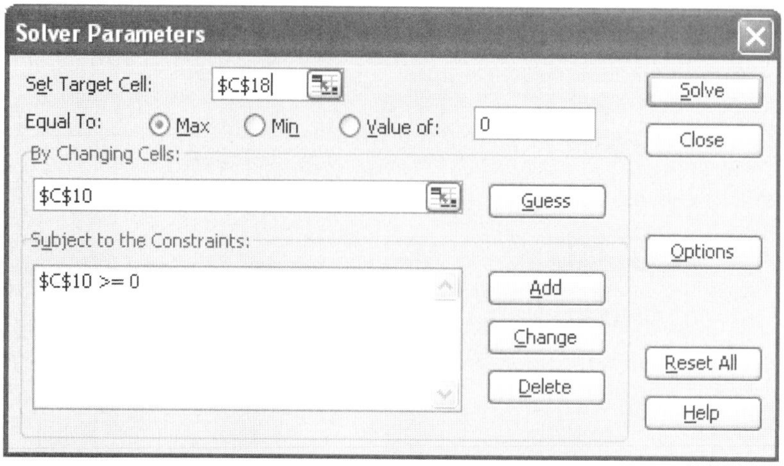

FIGURE 8.6

Optimized EOQ Spreadsheet Model for Kaye's Floral Problem

	A	B	C
2	Purchase Price	P	$15.00
4	Annual Demand	D	15,000
6	Carrying Cost	C	10%
8	Setup Cost	S	$200
10	Order Quantity	Q	2,000
12	Annual Purchase Cost	APC	$225,000.00
14	Annual Carrying Cost	ACC	$1,500.00
16	Annual Setup Cost	ASC	$1,500.00
18	Total Annual Cost	TAC	$228,000.00

Figure 8.6 displays the final EOQ spreadsheet model for Kaye's Floral problem with the optimal order quantity, 2,000 (refer to cell C10). Cell C10 is of special interest, as it contains the optimal order quantity, which minimizes Total Annual Cost (cell C18). If the value in cell C18 ($228,000) from Figure 8.6 is compared to cell C18 ($228,552.27) in Figure 8.2, Total Annual Costs for the order quantity of 2,000 (cell C10, Figure 8.6) are less by approximately $553.

Thus, by ordering in quantities of 2,000 instead of 1,100, Kaye will save $553 annually in carrying and setup costs. Kaye's EOQ problem could have been solved via the age-old EOQ formula

$$EOQ = \sqrt{\frac{2DS}{C}} = \sqrt{\frac{2 \times 15,000 \times 200}{1.50}} = 2000$$

A spreadsheet model allows a manager to perform "what if" analysis and test changes in underlying assumptions.

The descriptive model for EOQ can always be solved without a spreadsheet or an optimization model. So why would a manager waste time and resources building a complicated spreadsheet for a problem that can be solved by hand?

The answer lies in the underlying assumptions of the descriptive model. A number of assumptions are implicit to the descriptive EOQ model, such as enough capacity to hold the optimal order quantity. What happens if Kaye's facility can only hold a maximum of 1500 units at any one time (i.e., an upper bound constraint on the EOQ model)? Also, how does the model change if the supplier requires customers to purchase a minimum number of units with each order, i.e., a lower bound constraint on the EOQ model.

If these underlying assumptions change, or constraints added, then the descriptive model is fairly impotent to adjust and find an optimal answer. However, this is exactly what a spreadsheet optimization model is used for. The next section introduces two constraints to Kaye's Floral EOQ problem and discusses the implementation in the spreadsheet optimization model and impact on the "optimal" order quantity.

Concept *Check EOQ Example: Kaye's Floral Optimal Order Quantity Problem with Constraints*

Kaye has just thought of two new pieces of information regarding her optimal order quantity problem. She has realized that her facility can not hold 2,000 units because of space constraints. In fact, the largest amount of units she can hold at one time is 1,500. This is an upper limit placed on the optimal order quantity, in other words, an upper constraint.

Kaye has also heard that the company supplying her with vases will not take orders for less than 1,000 units without increasing the setup cost, in other words, a lower constraint. This seems to negate the earlier answer for the optimal order quantity of 2,000, as a result of Kaye's inability to hold 2,000 units because of space constraints. What is Kaye to do?

Kaye could attempt to approximate the optimal order quantity by enumerating various order quantities, but that would be tedious and it may not deliver the true optimal answer. To assist Kaye, let's refer back to the spreadsheet optimization model constructed earlier (see Figures 8.1 and 8.2).

In order for Kaye to use the spreadsheet optimization model presented in Figures 8.1 and 8.2 in light of the two new constraints introduced, a few modifications of the original model must be made. Specifically, the upper and lower constraints on order quantity must be added into the spreadsheet and into the Solver menu. Figure 8.7 displays an example of what the new spreadsheet may look like after adding the two constraints.

The two modifications to the original spreadsheet are rows 12 and 13 in Figure 8.7. These two rows contain the upper and lower order quantity limits for Kaye's EOQ problem. The second area that must be modified is within Solver. The following steps must be taken to inform Solver that the spreadsheet model now contains additional constraints on the variable cell C10.

The Solver add-in allows for constraints to be added to any optimization model by using the Add Constraint feature.

1. Open Solver inside the EOQ spreadsheet and click on the Add button in the Subject to the Constraints area (refer to Figure 8.5).
2. A dialog box resembling Figure 8.8 will appear. This dialog box is used to inform Solver that the variable cell order quantity has an upper limit.

FIGURE 8.7
EOQ Spreadsheet Model for Kaye's Floral Problem with Constraints

	A	B	C
			Kaye's Floral EOQ
1			
2	Purchase Price	P	$15.00
3			
4	Annual Demand	D	15,000
5			
6	Carrying Cost	C	10%
7			
8	Setup Cost	S	$200
9			
10	Order Quantity	Q	2,000
11			
12	Order Quantity Upper Limit	Q_u	1,500
13	Order Quantity Lower Limit	Q_l	1,000
14			
15	Annual Purchase Cost	APC	$225,000.00
16			
17	Annual Carrying Cost	ACC	$1,500.00
18			
19	Annual Setup Cost	ASC	$1,500.00
20			
21	Total Annual Cost	TAC	$228,000.00

Note: The order quantity listed here is the optimal order quantity without the upper and lower constraints. As the constraints are taken into account, this number will be adjusted.

FIGURE 8.8 Solver Add Constraint Dialogue Box

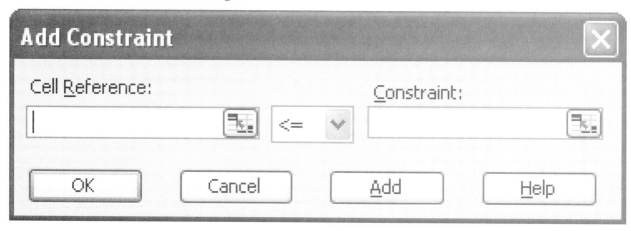

FIGURE 8.9 Solver Add Constraint Dialog Box for Upper Constraint

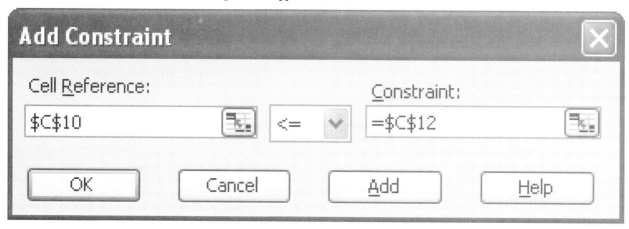

3. In the Cell Reference: box, identify or type in the variable cell, cell C10.

4. In the Constraint: box identify or type in the cell reference for the upper bound, cell C12.

5. The Add Constraint dialog box should resemble Figure 8.9 after you have completed these entries.

6. Repeat steps 1 to 5 for the lower constraint, using cell C10 again as the Cell Reference and C13 as the Constraint cell. Figure 8.10 displays what the Add Constraint dialog box should resemble after these entries have been completed.

After these two constraints have been added into the model, the solver menu will resemble Figure 8.11.

Figure 8.12 displays the final EOQ spreadsheet model for Kaye's Floral problem including constraints. It should be noted the optimal order quantity is 1,500 (refer to cell C10). Cell C10 is of special interest, as it contains the optimal order quantity, which minimizes Total Annual Cost (cell C21 in Figure 8.12). If the value in cell C21 ($228,125) from Figure 8.12 is compared to cell C18 ($228,000) in Figure 8.6, Total Annual Costs for the order quantity of 1,500 (cell C10, Figure 8.12) are more by approximately $125.

Thus, by having to order in quantities no greater than 1,500 and no less than 1,000 (the upper and lower order quantity limits—see cell C12 and C13 in Figure 8.12) instead of the optimal EOQ of 2,000 found earlier (see Figure 8.6), Kaye incurs $125 extra in total annual cost.

It should be noted that the total annual cost given in cell C21 in Figure 8.12 is optimal with regard to the constraints imposed on Kaye's ordering amount (refer to cells C12 and C13 in Figure 8.12). The issue of constraints is very important to optimization and spreadsheet

FIGURE 8.10 Solver Add Constraint Dialog Box for Lower Constraint

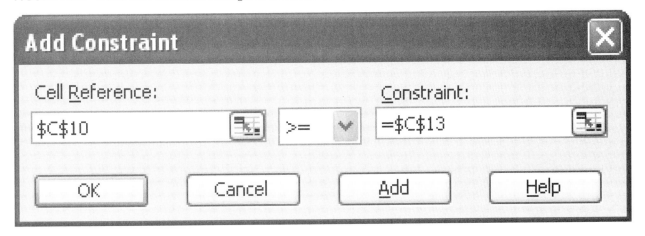

FIGURE 8.11
Final Solver Parameters
for Kaye's Floral EOQ
Model with Constraints

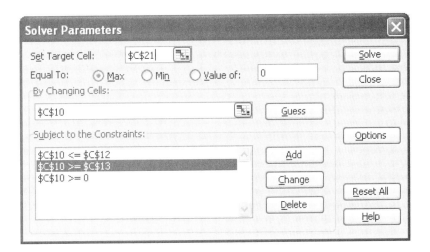

FIGURE 8.12
Optimized EOQ
Spreadsheet Model for
Kaye's Floral Problem

	A	B	C
2	Purchase Price	P	$15.00
4	Annual Demand	D	15,000
6	Carrying Cost	C	10%
8	Setup Cost	S	$200
10	Order Quantity	Q	1,500
12	Order Quantity Upper Limit	Q_u	1,500
13	Order Quantity Lower Limit	Q_l	1,000
15	Annual Purchase Cost	APC	$225,000.00
17	Annual Carrying Cost	ACC	$1,125.00
19	Annual Setup Cost	ASC	$2,000.00
21	Total Annual Cost	TAC	$228,125.00

modeling. In fact, constraints are really what brings us to the concept of mathematical programming, or what many refer to as *constrained resource planning*.

MATHEMATICAL PROGRAMMING

The term *mathematical programming* refers to a class of models that contain a general objective statement subject to a set of constraints.

The term mathematical programming refers to a class of models in which levels of various activities are selected, subject to a set of constraints, to maximize or minimize an objective such as total profit or total cost. In Kaye's Floral example with constraints, the activity is the order quantity, and the purpose of the model is to find the order quantity that minimizes total annual cost subject to the upper and lower bounds on order quantity itself.

The word programming used here does not mean a computer program which must be written or developed, but originates from the British term *programme*, which can be defined as a plan or a schedule of operations.

Linear Programming Models

A special subset of mathematical programming problems is linear programming problems.

A special subset of mathematical programming models exists called linear programming models. Linear programming models are commonly referred to as LP models. In fact, the word linear really gives away the uniqueness of LP. All objectives and constraints must be linear in order for an optimization model to be considered an LP model.

Properties of LP Models

Linear programming problems a unique in three properties: proportionality, additivity, and divisibility.

More specifically, linear programming models are a unique subset of mathematical programming models because of three important properties: proportionality, additivity, and divisibility. The next sections will briefly discuss these properties.

Proportionality

Proportionality deals with the relation of any activity to another activity.

Proportionality deals with the relation of the level of any activity to another activity. An assumption of proportionality is made when an LP model is used. This proportionality is said to be met when the following is true: When the level of any activity is multiplied by a constant factor, then the contribution of this activity to the objective, or to any of the constraints in which the activity is involved, is multiplied by the same factor. For example, if the optimal value of an activity is cut in half, then the amounts of resources it uses should also be cut in half.

Proportionality deals directly with the linear concept of linear programming. If the last statement was not true, let's say if the optimal value of an activity were cut in half and the amounts of resources used decreased by an amount larger than one-half, then the proportionality assumption is violated. In fact, a relationship such as the one just described would be considered a nonlinear relationship.

Additivity

Additivity refers to the sum of contributions from the various activities of a particular constraint.

Additivity refers to the sum of contributions from the various activities to a particular constraint. The additivity assumption is said to hold when the sum of the contributions from the various activities to a particular constraint equals the total contribution to that constraint. In addition, additivity applies to the objective as well.

An example of the additivity is as follows: four separate activities each take 100, 200, 300, and 400 units of constraint 1 to complete, therefore the total units used is the sum of these amounts, 1,000 units. In regard to the objective, the sum of the contributions from the various activities is the value of the objective itself. Additivity implies that the contribution of any activity to the objective or to any constraint is independent of the levels of the other activities.

Divisibility

Divisibility encompasses the concept of integer and noninteger levels of activities.

Divisibility encompasses the concept of integer and noninteger levels of activities. We assume that activities can take on all values greater than zero, integer and noninteger included. However, there are many instances in reality where noninteger activity values do not make sense. For example, if the optimal order quantity of vases for Kaye's Floral shop were 1501.98, Kaye could not order 0.98 of a vase. Kaye must order in integer quantities, as vases do not come in fractional quantities. Conversely, there are activities, such as water measured in gallons, where a noninteger value like 1501.98 gallons makes sense.

When activities need to be integer values, there are two approaches: (1) solve the linear model without an integer constraint, and if the solution turns out to contain noninteger values, an attempt to round them to integer values may be successful, or (2) the LP can be explicitly constrained so certain activities are required to be integer values. This latter approach is considered integer programming, a more difficult subset of LP problems that is studied at the end of this chapter.

Activity Scaling and LP Models

There are times when all three properties have been met and a true linear model has been formulated, but an error still occurs in the Solver. For some reason, Solver is not convinced that the model that has been defined has met all the LP assumptions. This is typically due to round-off error within Solver.

Round-off error can occur when activities have vastly different scales. For example, if activity A is in thousands of units, whereas activity B is in hundredths of units (a factor of five difference), the model is poorly scaled. Poorly scaled models lead to increases in round-off error and may result in error messages regarding the linearity of the LP model. Employing the automatic scaling feature in Solver and/or redefining all activities units to a similar magnitude can ameliorate round-off error.

> Errors that occur in Solver even when all three properties of LP problems have been met are typically attributed to round-off error.

Modeling a Real Problem and the LP Assumptions

In general, whenever a manager creates a model for a real-life problem, some simplifying assumptions are made. The three properties discussed above may or may not all be satisfied for every model. In fact, models are many times simplified to meet the three properties and therefore provide solutions more quickly.

Overall, real-life problems are frequently nonlinear. However, LP models have been successfully applied in the real world, in applications such as shipping, personnel scheduling, food processing, and petroleum processing. LP models are useful even when the solutions are only approximations of reality. Much of the insight gained by managers from LP models is in the formulation and sensitivity analysis that occurs after a solution is obtained. Unless one suspects major violations of the three properties discussed earlier—proportionality, additivity, and divisibility— LP models can be used effectively to describe and solve constrained resource problems.

Three Parts of an LP Model

Every LP model has three distinctive parts:

- The objective function
- Constraints
- Non-negativity assumptions

> Every LP model has three distinct parts: objective function, constraints, and non-negativity assumptions.

As a modeler, you are required to define each of these parts. A short introductory section defining some terms is next followed by a section defining and describing the three parts of an LP model.

Definition of LP Terminology

Before the three parts of an LP are defined and described, a few terms must be defined. The following are the appropriate terms and definitions:

Decision variables. Symbols used to represent an item of interest to the user that can take on any value (e.g., x_1 = labor hours, x_2 = number of workers).

Parameters. Known constant values that are defined for each problem (e.g., price of a unit, production capacity).

Modified standard form. A standard form that LP models are converted into that allows the solution process to proceed and provides easy understanding of the overall problem formulation.

> Decision variables are items of interest to the user, such as how much labor to use or how much raw material A to use.

Students should take note that formal LP nomenclature makes reference to the term *standard form* instead of modified standard form. The latter teminology is due to the authors use of spreadsheet models, and its import will become apparent later in this chapter. Do not let this confuse you as you attempt to build LP models. It should also be noted that decision variables and parameters must be defined for each unique LP model, and the responsibility of defining these decision variables and parameters falls upon the modeler.

The Objective Function

The objective function of an LP problem always consists of a maximize or minimize statement.

The objective function of an LP model is always defined as a linear relationship of decision variables describing the problem objective. In other words, the objective function is what you are trying to accomplish, such as maximizing profit or minimizing costs.

By definition, the objective function always consists of maximizing or minimizing some value (e.g., maximize profit, minimize cost) and is customarily given the designation Z. Examples of typical objective functions are

$$\text{Maximize profit} = Z = 3x_1 + 5x_2$$
$$\text{Minimize cost} = Z = 6x_1 + 15x_2$$

where x_1 and x_2 would be decision variables defined for the LP model and the coefficients would be profits or costs associated with each of the decision variables.

For example, in the first objective function, Maximize profit $= Z = 3x_1 + 5x_2$, the coefficient of x_1, 3, is interpreted as follows: If x_1 increases by one unit (all things held constant) then the objective function will increase by 3 units ($3 \times 1 = 3$). This same logic holds for each decision variable and coefficient pair.

It should be noted that in this text the author works within the realm of single objective optimization and single objective spreadsheet models. Multiple objective optimization and multiple optimization models do exist in the real world but are not covered here.

The Constraints

Constraints are defined as physical limitations or restrictions on the LP problem.

Constraints are defined as physical limitations or restrictions on the LP problem. Constraints are constructed as linear relationships of decision variables representing these physical limitations or restrictions. Physical limitations or restrictions could include limited resources such as labor or capital, hours in the workday, or amount of a commodity such as corn or wheat that can be purchased or stored.

It is the responsibility of the LP modeler to construct the constraint functions. Constraints come from knowledge about an activity or a set of activities. LP modelers are confronted with phrases such as
"Total labor hours must be less than or equal to 50"or
"x_1 must use at least 20 pounds of corn"These phrases are actually statements of restrictions of the LP model and must be defined as linear relationships of decision variables. For the aforementioned phrases, the following linear relationships can be developed, assuming two decision variables x_1 and x_2:
"Total labor hours must be less than or equal to 50" is transformed into

$$x_1 + x_2 \leq 50$$

and

"x_1 must used at least 20 pounds of corn" is transformed into

$$x_1 \geq 20$$

A fully formulated LP model may contain tens, even hundreds, of constraints.

A fully formulated LP model may have tens, even hundreds, of constraints, involving all or any combination of decision variables. Constraints can consist of greater than or equal to ($\geq$), less than or equal to ($\leq$), and/or strictly equal to ($=$) operators. Constraints can also contain additive ($+$) and/or subtractive ($-$) operators within their construction.

The Non-Negativity Assumptions

The third and final part of an LP model is the non-negativity assumptions.

The third and final part of an LP model is one of the simplest and most logical parts of the LP formulation. Non-negativity assumptions basically define the decision variables as always being positive in quantity. This is logical because negative decision variables are inconceivable in most LP problems For example, minus 10 units of production, a negative consumption, or scheduling less than zero employees make no sense Non-negativity assumptions are written as follows, assuming two decision variables x_1 and x_2:

$$x_1, x_2 \geq 0$$

Although non-negativity assumptions are the simplest part of the LP formulation, they are easy to forget. Solver attempts to remedy this problem by providing a menu option in Solver automatically defining all decision variables as non-negative. However, the LP modeler still needs to remember to check the menu box for this option in Solver.

Putting It All Together—Steps in Formulating an LP Model

LP formulation steps: (1) Define decision variable, (2) determine objective function, (3) formulate constraints.

1. **Define the decision variables**—identify the key variables whose values we wish to determine.
2. **Determine the objective function**—determine what we are trying to do (i.e., Maximize profit, Minimize total cost).
3. **Formulate the constraints**—determine the limitations of the decision variables.

The steps listed above must be completed for each LP model developed. In addition, it is the responsibility of the modeler to perform the steps. Many times the completion of the steps is a tedious process. The next section addresses ways to formulate LP problems.

Putting It all Together—Modified Standard Form

The preceding sections discussed definitions and nomenclature associated with LP models. As with any discipline, mastering the nomenclature or jargon for any technique is part of the learning process. LP modeling combines the aforementioned nomenclature using what is called modified standard form.

Modified standard form combines decision variables, the objective function, and non-negativity assumptions together in one place.

Modified standard form combines decision variables, the objective function, the constraints, and non-negativity assumptions. LP modelers use modified standard form to communicate the structure of the LP problem. Overall, each LP model should be transformed into modified standard form. Transforming each LP model into standard form accomplishes two main goals: (1) provides a common form to communicate the structure of LP models and (2) provides an easy form for spreadsheet entry and solution using Solver.

In general, modified standard form for an LP model is as follows where the three parts of the LP model are numbered as follows: Equation (8.1) objective function, Equation (8.2) constraints, and Equation (8.3) non-negativity assumptions:

$$\text{Maximize } Z = c_1 x_1 + c_2 x_2 + \cdots + c_n x_n \tag{8.1}$$

$$\text{subject to } a_{11} x_1 + a_{12} x_2 + \cdots + a_{1n} x_n \leq b_1 \tag{8.2}$$

$$a_{m1} x_1 + a_{m2} x_2 + \cdots + a_{mn} x_n \leq b_m$$

$$x_1, x_2, x_n \geq 0 \tag{8.3}$$

where

x_i = decision variable i

c_i = coefficient of contribution for decision variable i

a_{ni} = coefficient of contribution for constraint n, decision variable i

b_m = total amount of constraint m

Business Decision Modeling Throughout the Ages

The History of Mathematical Programming

DEFINITION AND ESSENCE OF MATHEMATICAL PROGRAMMING

Mathematical programming, or constrained optimization, or math programming for short, is a mathematical procedure for determining optimal allocation of scarce resources. Math programming, and its most popular special form, linear programming (LP), has found practical application in almost all facets of business, from advertising to production planning. Transportation and aggregate production planning problems are the most typical objects of LP analysis.

LIMITED RESOURCES AND ACTIVITIES

For most optimization problems, one can think of two important classes of objects. The first of these is limited resources, such as land, plant capacity, and sales force size. Second are activities, such as "produce low carbon steel," "produce stainless steel," and "produce high carbon steel". Each activity consumes or possibly contributes additional amounts of the resources. The problem is to determine the best combination of activity levels that does not use more resources than are actually available. Many managers are faced with this task everyday, and hence the birth of the field of mathematical programming.

THE DIET PROBLEM

The diet problem is one of the first optimization problems to be studied dating back to the 1930s and '40s. It was first motivated by the Army's desire to meet the nutritional requirements of the field GIs while minimizing the cost. One of the early researchers to study this problem was George Stigler. He made an educated guess of the optimal solution to linear program by using a heuristic method. His guess for the cost of an optimal diet was $39.93 per year (1939 prices).

In the fall of 1947, Jack Laderman of the Mathematical Tables Project of the National Bureau of Standards undertook solving Stigler's model with the new simplex method. It was the first "large scale" computation in optimization. The linear program consisted of nine equations in 77 unknowns. It took nine clerks using hand-operated desk calculators 120 worker-days to solve for the optimal solution of $39.69. Stigler's guess for the optimal solution was off by only 24 cents per year.

GOAL OF THE DIET PROBLEM

The goal of the diet problem is to find the cheapest combination of foods that will satisfy all the daily nutritional requirements of a person. The problem is formulated as a linear program where the objective is to minimize cost and meet constraints that satisfy nutritional needs. Constraints that regulate the number of calories and amounts of vitamins, minerals, fats, sodium and cholesterol in the diet are also included. The mathematical formulation is simple, but you will find out by running the model that people do not actually choose their menus by solving this model. Humans' nutritional requirements can be met, yet their concerns for taste and variety go unheeded. No one would drink gallons of vinegar or include a few bouillon cubes in meals; however, such "optimal" menus have been created by using this model.

PRACTICAL COMPUTING METHODS AND LINEAR PROGRAMMING MODELS

The systematic development of practical computing methods for linear programming began in 1952 at the Rand Corporation in Santa Monica, under the direction of George B. Dantzig. After 1956, the work continued at CEIR, Inc., in Washington for some years and later in many places by many individuals and firms. By the late 1960s, elaborate systems of programs known as mathematical programming systems (MPS) had become a standard part of the available software for a number of mainframe computers. Work still continues and substantial improvements have been made in speed, reliability, supporting data management and control systems, and application techniques including the use of desktop PCs and spreadsheets to design and solve LP models.

GEORGE DANTZIG'S TAKE ON THE HISTORY OF LINEAR PROGRAMMING MODELS

"In retrospect," Dantzig wrote in a 1991 history book, "it is interesting to note that the original problem that started my research is still outstanding—namely the problem of planning or scheduling dynamically over time, particularly planning dynamically under uncertainty. If such a problem could be successfully solved it could eventually through better planning contribute to the well-being and stability of the world."

The nature of that original problem is also detailed in the book. Dantzig's contributions, he explained, grew out of his experience in the Pentagon during World War II, when he had become an expert on programming—that is, planning methods done with desk calculators. In 1946, as mathematical adviser to the U.S. Air Force Comptroller, he was challenged by his Pentagon colleagues to see what he could do to mechanize the planning process, "to more rapidly compute a time-staged deployment, training and logistical supply program.." In those pre–electronic computer days, mechanization meant using analog devices or punch-card machines. "Program" at that time was a military term that referred not to the instructions used by a computer to solve problems, which were then called "codes," but rather to plans or proposed schedules for training, logistical supply, or deployment of combat units. The somewhat confusing name "linear programming," Dantzig explained in the book, is based on this military definition of "program."

OPTIMAL INFORMATION AREA

Abstracted primarily from "A History of Mathematical Programming in the Petroleum Industry" by C. E. Bodington and T. E. Baker, *Interfaces*, vol. 20, no. 4 (1990), pp. 117–127.

Lenstra, J.K., A.H.G. Rinnoy, and A. Schrijver. *History of Mathematical Programming: A Collection of Personal Reminiscences.* Amsterdam, The Netherlands: Elsevier Science Publishers B.V., 1991

The equations presented for modified general form may look somewhat daunting. However, modified standard form contains all parts of an LP model in compact form, which allows for easy spreadsheet entry and solution. To aid in the understanding of modified standard form and the process of formulating LP models, an example is given next.

MARK'S BATS LP EXAMPLE—THE STORY

Mark's firm produces two types of baseball bats, the Wooden Wonder and the Aluminum Ally. Mark's firm makes $7 profit for each Wooden Wonder and $10 profit for each Aluminum Ally it produces. The bats go through three processes before they are ready to be shipped: shaping, stamping, and packing.

The first process is shaping. Each type of bat is shaped on a different machine. The machine used to shape the Wooden Wonder has a finite capacity of 100 hours per week, whereas the machine used to shape the Aluminum Ally has a finite capacity of 120 hours per week. Each Wooden Wonder bat uses 1.5 hours of shaping machine capacity, while each Aluminum Ally uses 2 hours of shaping machine capacity.

The second process is stamping, and both bats can be stamped on the same machine. The stamping machine has 60 hours of capacity a week. The Wooden Wonder bats take 15 minutes to stamp whereas the Aluminum Ally takes 30 minutes to stamp because of the metal exterior.

Both styles of bats are packed on the same machine and each requires the same amount of time, 15 minutes. The packing machine has a finite capacity of 25 hours a week. Finally, Mark's firm has already agreed to produce 30 Wooden Wonders for a preferred customer.

Mark's firm needs assistance in figuring out how many Wooden Wonders and how many Aluminum Ally bats to produce to maximize total profits. Mark believes an LP model will aid in solving this problem.

LP Example—The Formulation Process

The problem that Mark is faced with is a typical problem that can be solved by using an LP model. This type of problem is referred to as a *product mix problem* and occurs in many industries, including furniture, automobile, and electronics manufacturing.

Identifying Decision Variables

The best way to identify decision variables is to ask "What are the activities that I must decide on?"

The first step in formulating Mark's bat production problem is to identify the decision variables. The best way to identify the decision variables is to ask the question "What are the activities that Mark must decide on?"

In the bat production problem, it is clear that Mark wishes to know how many of each bat to produce. The entire problem would be moot if Mark could just produce an infinite amount of both bats and in turn make an infinite amount of profit. However, as has been stated earlier and as reality dictates, Mark's firm has constraints on its capacity and therefore cannot produce an infinite amount of bats.

The decision variables for Mark's bat production problem are then defined as :

$$\text{Decision variable } 1 = x_1 = \text{number of Wooden Wonders}$$
$$\text{Decision variable } 2 = x_2 = \text{number of Aluminum Allys}$$

Take note that each of the above decision variables is in number produced per week. This per week measure must be followed throughout the LP formulation for proper scaling.

Objective Function Formulation

The next step in Mark's bat production LP model is the formulation of the objective function. We know that, for each Wooden Wonder produced, $7 of profit is realized and, for each

Aluminum Ally produced, $10 of profit is realized. It is also known that Mark's firm wishes to maximize profits. The objective function is formed from the profit gained from each style of bat being multiplied by the appropriate decision variable and added together.

Therefore, the objective function takes on the form

$$\text{Maximize } Z = \$7x_1 + \$10x_2$$

An objective function always contains a maximize or minimize statement.

Constraint Formulation

Formulation of the constraints restricting the production of each style of bat is the next step in developing the LP model. From the earlier narrative about Mark's bat production process, we know that three capacity limits exist. These limits translate into three constraints: one constraint for shaping, a constraint for stamping, and a constraint for packing.

In addition, Mark's firm has promised one of its clients 30 Wooden Wonders. This means that there must be at least 30 Wooden Wonders produced. This may not seem like a constraint limiting production at the outset. However, one must keep in mind that constraints not only limit but also may define minimum levels of activity.

Shaping Constraints

To formulate the constraints, the words from the narrative must be transformed into linear equations. Let's first look at the shaping process. The Wooden Wonder requires 1.5 hours to shape and the machine used in shaping the Wooden Wonder has a maximum of 100 hours. Therefore, the total hours used to shape Wooden Wonders cannot exceed 100 hours per week. The constraint takes on the form

$$1.5x_1 \leq 100 \text{ Wooden Wonder shaping constraint}$$

Constraints can be formulated as $\geq$, $\leq$, or $=$ relationships.

The constraint is formed by taking the amount of hours required for a single Wooden Wonder multiplied by the respective decision variable, x_1, and setting the result less than or equal to the maximum amount of Wooden Wonder shaping hours available.

The same logic then applies to the Aluminum Ally constraint. Each Aluminum Ally requires 2 hours of shaping, and the machine used to shape the Aluminum Ally has a maximum of 120 hours. Therefore, the constraint takes on the form

$$2.0x_2 \leq 120 \text{ Aluminum Ally shaping constraint}$$

Stamping Constraint

The constraint for the stamping process is based on similar logic but takes on a slightly different form. First, only one machine is used in the stamping process. Therefore, both the hours used to stamp the Wooden Wonder and the Aluminum Ally must be related to the total stamping hours available. According to the clues given in the narrative, the stamping constraint takes on the form

$$0.25x_1 + 0.5x_2 \leq 60 \text{ Stamping constraint}$$

The constraint is constructed from the two decision variables, the stamping time associated with each decision variable, and the total stamping time available.

The same logic used in the shaping constraints is employed here also. However, the coefficients for each decision variable must be discussed. It should be noted in the stamping constraint that the coefficient of x_1 is 0.25. This is because 15 minutes is a quarter of an hour and the coefficient for x_1 must be in the same units as the total number of stamping hours available. Thereby the units of the coefficients and the total constraint amount match. Overall, for any constraint, the constraint coefficients and the total constraint amount must be in the same units.

Packing Constraint

The constraint for the packing process follows the same construction as the stamping constraint. According to the information given in Mark's bat production narrative, the packing constraint takes on the form

$$0.25x_1 + 0.25x_2 \leq 25 \text{ Packing constraint}$$

The issue of unit matching of the coefficients and the total packing time is also relevant here. Take note of the constraint coefficients for x_1 and x_2.

Minimum Wooden Wonder Production Constraint

Since Mark has agreed to produce 30 Wooden Wonders for a client, there must be a constraint formulated for this information. Basically, no matter how many Aluminum Ally bats Mark's firm produces, 30 Wooden Wonders must be produced to meet the preferred customer demand. Therefore, a minimum Wooden Wonder constraint must be formulated. According to the clues given in the narrative, the minimum Wooden Wonder production constraint takes on the form

$$x_1 \geq 30 \text{ Minimum Wooden Wonder production constraint}$$

Take note that this constraint contains a greater than or equal to operator. Relate this to the discussion regarding the preferred customer's order. This completes the formulation of the constraints associated with Mark's production problem. The next section provides the final part of the LP model to be constructed, the non-negativity assumptions.

Non-Negativity Assumptions

Non-negativity assumptions state that all decision variables must be equal to or greater than zero.

Since there are two decision variables, x_1 and x_2, the non-negativity assumptions are basic and take on the following form:

$$x_1, x_2 \geq 0$$

Remember that, even though the non-negativity assumptions are the simplest part of the LP model, they must be included. The next section combines all three parts of the LP model together into modified standard form.

Modified Standard Form—Mark's Bat Production Problem

Modified standard form for Mark's bat production LP model is as follows where the three parts of the LP model are numbered as follows: Equation (8.4) objective function, Equations (8.5a) to (8.5e) constraints, and Equation (8.6) non-negativity assumptions.

When an LP model is formulated and transformed into modified standard form, a method for solving the LP model can be employed. The next section details two methods for solving LP models and provides both solution types for Mark's Bat Production problem.

$$\text{Maximize } Z = \$7x_1 + \$10x_2 \qquad \textbf{(8.4)}$$

$$\text{subject to } 1.5x_1 \leq 100 \text{ Wooden Wonder shaping constraint} \qquad \textbf{(8.5a)}$$

$$2.0x_2 \leq 120 \text{ Aluminum Ally shaping constraint} \qquad \textbf{(8.5b)}$$

$$0.25x_1 + 0.5x_2 \leq 60 \text{ Stamping constraint} \qquad \textbf{(8.5c)}$$

$$0.25x_1 + 0.25x_2 \leq 25 \text{ Packing constraint} \qquad \textbf{(8.5d)}$$

$$x_1 \geq 30 \text{ Minimum Wooden Wonder production constraint} \qquad \textbf{(8.5e)}$$

$$x_1, x_2 \geq 0 \qquad \textbf{(8.6)}$$

METHODS OF SOLVING LP PROBLEMS

Two methods of solving LP problems exist: the graphical method and the simplex method.

Once the LP model is in modified standard form, two basic approaches to solving the LP model exist. The first method is the graphical method, and the second is called the simplex method. The next section describes the graphical method and the subsequent solution to Mark's bat production LP model. A section describing the simplex method follows the description of the graphical method and the solution generated by Solver for Mark's bat production LP model.

THE GRAPHICAL METHOD

The graphical method is simple, but is limited to smaller LP models (i.e., two or three decision variables). The limitation on decision variables is due to the nature of the graphical method. When presented with an LP model with two decision variables, the graphical method produces a two-dimensional graph. In turn, when presented with an LP model with three decision variables, the graphical method produces a three-dimensional graph.

This logic makes it clear that when an LP model contains four or more decision variables, it is impossible to use the graphical method of solution, as no n-dimensional graph can be developed for n greater than 3. The next section provides a set of steps to follow when the graphical method is to solve LP models.

Steps to Implementing the Graphical Method

The following set of steps is used for implementing the graphical method of solving LP models. Before the steps are detailed, however, a few terms must be defined.

The feasible region is defined as the region mapped by the constraints containing values of decision variables that are allowed by the constraint set.

Feasible region. The region mapped by the constraints containing values of the decision variables that are allowed by the constraint set.

Corner point. A point where a set of constraints intersect.

Corner point feasible solution. A point where a set of constraints intersect that is on the edge of the feasible region.

The steps are presented next. Their application to Mark's bat production problem can be found in Appendix 8A.

1. Construct an x-y coordinate plane/graph.
2. Plot all constraints on the plane/graph.
3. Identify the feasible region dictated by the constraints.
4. Identify all corner point feasible solutions of the feasible region.
5. Identify the optimum solution by plotting a series of objective functions over the feasible region.

A six-step process can be followed to solve LP problems graphically.

6. Determine the exact solution values of the decision variables and the objective function at the optimum solution.

Using Spreadsheets to Model LP Problems

As was demonstrated earlier in this chapter, spreadsheets can be used to model optimization problems. This is also true for LP problems. The next section details how to create and solve an LP spreadsheet model for Mark's bat production LP problem.

Creating the LP Spreadsheet Model

This section describes how to create the underlying spreadsheet LP model for Mark's bat production problem. Figure 8.13 displays the basic spreadsheet model in Excel. Figure 8.14 displays the spreadsheet formulas associated with the LP model. The decision variables are defined in words in cells C3 and C4 and then defined as variables in cells D3 and D4. The objective function is defined in row 8 and specifically represented in words in cell C8 and as a mathematical function in cell D8.

FIGURE 8.13
Spreadsheet LP Model for Mark's Bat Production Problem

◇	A B	C	D	E
1	Decision Variables			
2				
3		x_1 = # of Wooden Wonders to Produce	0	
4		x_2 = # of Aluminum Allys to Produce	0	
5				
6	Objective Function			
7				
8		Max $Z = \$7x_1 + \$10x_2$	0	
9				
10	Constraints		LHS	RHS
11		Wooden Wonder Shaping		
12		$1.5x_1 \leq 100$	0	100
13		Aluminum Ally Shaping		
14		$2.0x_2 \leq 120$	0	120
15		Stamping		
16		$0.25x_1 + 0.5x_2 \leq 60$	0	60
17		Packing		
18		$0.25x_1 + 0.25x_2 \leq 25$	0	25
19		Minimum Wooden Wonder Production		
20		$x_1 \geq 30$	0	30

The terms LHS and RHS are used in Figure 8.13 to denote left-hand side of a constraint and right-hand side of a constraint, respectively. It should be noted that, since the decision variables are currently set at zero, the objective function and all LHS constraints are zero.

Figure 8.14 displays the spreadsheet formulas associated with the LP model. Specific formulas for the objective function and individual LHS constraints are found in column D.

FIGURE 8.14
Spreadsheet Formulas Associated with Mark's Bat Production Problem

◇	A	B	C	D	E
1	Decision Variables				
2					
3			x_1 = # of Wooden Wonders to Produce	0	
4			x_2 = # of Aluminum Allys to Produce	0	
5					
6	Objective Function				
7					
8			Max $Z = \$7x_1 + \$10x_2$	=7*D3+10*D4	
9					
10	Constraints			LHS	RHS
11			Wooden Wonder Shaping		
12			$1.5x_1 \leq 100$	=1.5*D3	100
13			Aluminum Ally Shaping		
14			$2.0x_2 \leq 120$	=2*D4	120
15			Stamping		
16			$0.25x_1 + 0.5x_2 \leq 60$	=0.25*D3+0.5*D4	60
17			Packing		
18			$0.25x_1 + 0.25x_2 \leq 25$	=0.25*D3+0.25*D4	25
19			Minimum Wooden Wonder Production		
20			$x_1 \geq 30$	=D3	30

FIGURE 8.15
Excel Solver Dialog Box

Using Solver to Find Solutions to a Spreadsheet Optimization Model

Solver allows you to input an objective function, a set of constraints, and non-negativity assumptions within a spreadsheet.

This section discusses how to use Solver to optimize a spreadsheet LP model in Excel. It is assumed that the user has already built a spreadsheet optimization model in Excel (refer to Figures 8.13 and 8.14). After clicking on Solver in the Tools menu, the Solver dialog box (Figure 8.15) will appear.

The following steps enable Solver to find solutions to optimization spreadsheets.

1. In the Set Target Cell box, enter a cell reference or name for the target cell. The target cell must contain a formula.
2. To have the value of the target cell be as large as possible, click Max. To have the value of the target cell be as small as possible, click Min. To have the target cell be a certain value, click Value of and then type the value in the box.
3. In the By Changing Cells box, enter a name or reference for each adjustable cell, separating nonadjacent references with commas. The adjustable cells must be related directly or indirectly to the target cell. You can specify up to 200 adjustable cells. To have Solver automatically propose the adjustable cells based on the target cell, click Guess.
4. In the Subject to the Constraints box, enter any constraints you want to apply. Click on the Add button and add your constraints as follows:

   a. Click in the Cell Reference box and add the cell reference for the LHS portion of the constraint in the spreadsheet.
   b. Adjust the operator menu to match the constraint's operator (e.g., $\leq$, $=$, or $\geq$).
   c. Click on the Constraint box and add the cell reference for the RHS portion of the constraint in the spreadsheet.
   d. Click OK when finished adding the constraint. You will be taken back to a screen that resembles Figure 8.15

5. Click Solve.

   Applying these steps to Mark's bat production spreadsheet LP problem, a target cell (the objective function), adjustable cells (the decision variables), and constraints are defined as shown in Table 8.2 (refer to Figures 8.13 and 8.14):

   In entering the solver cell definitions for the constraints, follow the same procedure as detailed in Figures 8.8, 8.9, and 8.10, using the constraints for Mark's LP model. The solver menu will resemble Figure 8.16 after you have entered the values from Table 8.2 into the Solver dialog boxes.

   Since Mark's bat production problem contains only linear constraints, Solver must be notified. This is in most cases a formality, but it is good form to follow. Notifying Solver of a linear model is simple:

1. Press the options button in the Solver menu.

TABLE 8.2
Solver Cell Definitions

Set Target Cell	$D$8
Equal To:	Max
By Changing Cells:	$D$3:$D$4
Subject to the Constraints:	
Wooden Wonder shaping	$D$12 <= $E$12
Aluminum Ally shaping	$D$14 <= $E$14
Stamping	$D$16 <= $E$16
Packing	$D$18 <= $E$18
Minimum Wooden Wonder production	$D$20 >= $E$20

FIGURE 8.16
Final Solver Parameters for Mark's Bat Production Problem

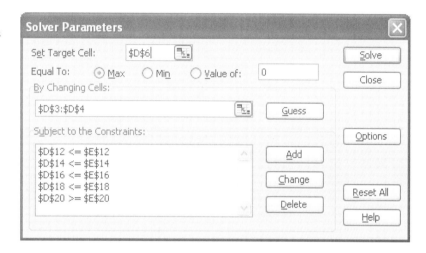

2. A menu like the one displayed in Figure 8.17 will appear.
3. Check the boxes next to Assume Linear Model and next to Assume Non-Negative.
4. Click the OK button and return to the screen shown in Figure 8.16.

After the linear assumption and non-negativity assumption have been enabled, Solver is ready to be employed to solve Mark's bat production LP problem. From the Solver menu (refer to Figure 8.16), click the Solve button to commence the solution process.

FIGURE 8.17
Solver Options Menu

To define the LP properly the Assume Non-Negativity and the Assume Linear Model check boxes must be checked inside the Solver Options menu.

FIGURE 8.18
**Optimized Spreadsheet
Model for Mark's Bat
Production LP Problem**

◇	A	B	C	D	E
1	Decision Variables				
2					
3			x_1 = # of Wooden Wonders to Produce	40	
4			x_2 = # of Aluminum Allys to Produce	60	
5					
6	Objective Function				
7					
8			Max Z = $\$7x_1 + \$10x_2$	880	
9					
10	Constraints			LHS	RHS
11			Wooden Wonder Shaping		
12			$1.5x_1 \leq 100$	60	100
13			Aluminum Ally Shaping		
14			$2.0x_2 \leq 120$	120	120
15			Stamping		
16			$0.25x_1 + 0.5x_2 \leq 60$	40	60
17			Packing		
18			$0.25x_1 + 0.25x_2 \leq 25$	25	25
19			Minimum Wooden Wonder Production		
20			$x_1 \geq 30$	40	30

Figure 8.18 displays the final spreadsheet model for Mark's bat production LP problem. The optimal production quantities of 40 Wooden Wonders and 60 Aluminum Allys and the maximum objective function value of $880 are shown (refer to cells D3, D4, and D8 respectively).

Cell D8 is of special interest as it contains the optimal value of the objective function. If Mark produces 40 Wooden Wonders and 60 Aluminum Allys he will maximize his profit. The maximum profit generated, $880, is identical to the maximum objective function calculated by the graphical method (refer to Appendix 8A).

Comparison of Constraints and Sensitivity Analysis

The optimal solution to an LP model will generally lie at the intersection of a set of constraints.

Another area of interest is comparison of LHS and RHS cells (refer to columns D and E). In comparing the cells, it can be seen that some cells labeled LHS are equal to the cells labeled RHS. This occurs because an LP model contains only linear relationships and the corner point feasible solutions must be found on the perimeter of the feasible region. As discussed earlier, the optimal solution will lie at the intersection of a set of constraints that make up the perimeter of the feasible region. The constraints that intersect to form the optimal solution are indicated when LHS cells equal the RHS cells. The next section will discuss the implications when the LHS and RHS are equal and when they are not equal.

Binding and Nonbinding Constraints

A binding constraint is considered to be used up or have no slack.

Information about the relationship between the optimal solution and the constraints is contained in the LHS and RHS cells. From the LHS and RHS cells, it can be determined which constraints are "binding" and which constraints contain "slack." A binding constraint can be defined as a constraint that is "used up"; in our example, the LHS cell would equal the RHS cell. A constraint that has slack is not used up, and, in our example, the LHS would not be equal to the RHS cell. This information is important as it tells the user on which constraints the optimal solution lies. It must be noted that word slack is used in a different sense from what is defined as a slack variable and/or a surplus variable in the simplex method. The term slack is used in the present context to characterize constraints.

A constraint that has slack is not fully used up.

From Figure 8.18, it is seen that the LHS and RHS for the Aluminum Ally shaping constraint and for the packing constraint are equal (see cells D14, E14, D18, and E18). The intersection of the Aluminum Ally shaping constraint and the packing constraint defines a feasible corner point solution and the optimal solution (40, 60). In turn, since the optimal solution lies at the intersection of these two constraints, they are completely used up. In being used up, all resources for Aluminum Ally shaping and packing are consumed. In turn, the constraints where the LHS is not equal to the RHS (Wooden Wonder shaping, stamping, and minimum Wooden Wonder production) are not used up and contain slack. In other words, there is left-over Wooden Wonder shaping time, stamping time, and more than enough Wooden Wonders produced to meet the minimum requirement.

RESULTS AND SENSITIVITY ANALYSIS IN EXCEL

Solver will generate answer and sensitivity reports for an LP solution.

Excel has the capability to produce reports containing information about LP results and constraint sensitivity analysis. To generate the answer and sensitivity reports, follow these steps:

1. After solver has completed its solution process, a screen like that in Figure 8.19 will appear.
2. In the Solver Results window, select the Answer and Sensitivity options in the Reports menu.
3. Two new worksheets will be generated, one for the answer report and one for the sensitivity report

The answer report is the first report discussed, followed by the sensitivity report.

Answer Report in Excel

The answer report generated within Solver details three areas: target cells, adjustable cells, and constraints. Figure 8.20 displays the answer report generated for Mark's bat production LP problem.

Target Cell Section

The Target Cell section in Solver's answer report contains information about the objective function.

The first section of interest is the Target Cell section. The Target Cell section contains information regarding the objective function. Cell C8 contains the objective function defined in the original spreadsheet LP model, whereas cell D8 contains the original value of the objective function. The original value for Mark's bat production problem is zero, since the decision variables were set to zero (see the Adjustable Cell section).

FIGURE 8.19 **Excel Solver Results Window**

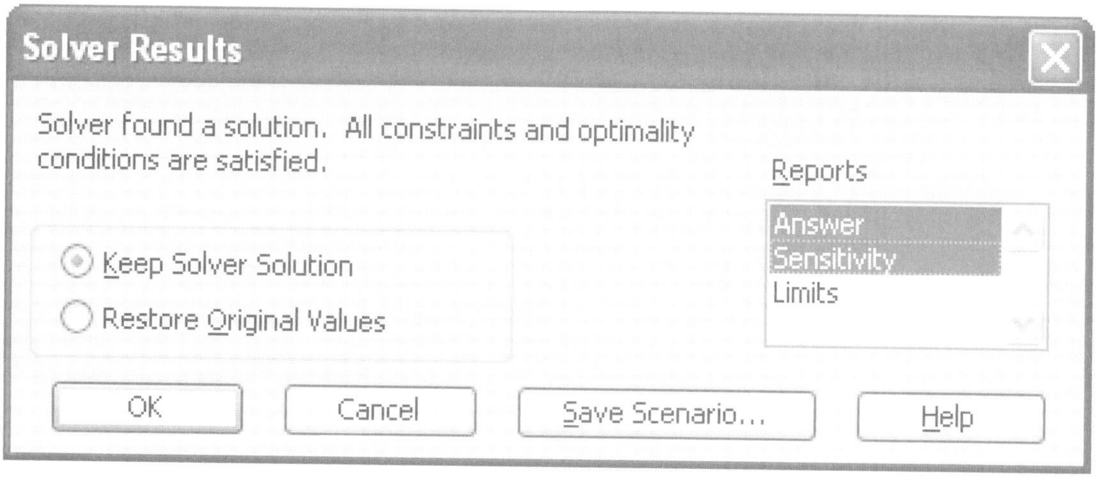

FIGURE 8.20

Excel Answer Report for Mark's Bat Production LP Problem

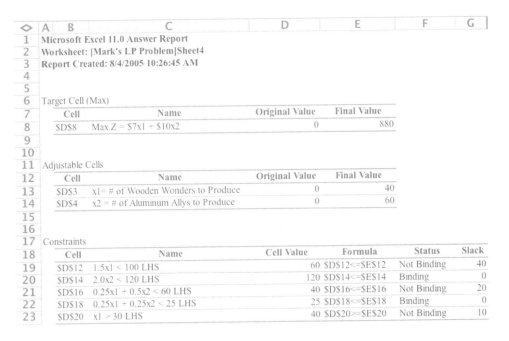

Cell E8 contains the final value of the objective function. In this LP model the final value of the objective function is 880. This value is the same as the value calculated by the graphical method detailed in the Appendix 8A. Overall, the Target Cell section provides information about the objective function, specifically its final and optimal value.

Adjustable Cells Section

The Adjustable Cells section in Solver's answer report contains information about the decision variables.

The Adjustable Cells section provides information about the decision variables x_1, the number of Wooden Wonders to produce, and x_2, the number of Aluminum Allys to produce. Cells D13 and D14 contain the original values of the decision variables. The values in the cells are zero, as the decision variables were set to zero originally. Cells E13 and E14 contain the final values of the decision variables, 40 Wooden Wonders and 60 Aluminum Allys. In sum, the Adjustable Cells section informs the decision maker of the optimal number of bats to produce.

Constraints Section

The Constraints section in Solver's Answer Report contains information about the constraints or limitations on the decision variables.

The Constraints section contains information about the constraints or limitations on the decision variables. This section should be linked to the earlier discussion involving the LHS and RHS columns in Figure 8.18. The Constraints section contains the same information as the LHS and RHS columns in Figure 8.18. However, the Constraints section organizes constraint information more efficiently and provides information on slack. As defined earlier, slack is defined as an amount of a constraint that is not used up.

The Constraint section in Figure 8.20 contains the constraint formulas, cells C19 to C23; the final constraint value, labeled Cell Value and contained in cells D19 to D23; and the Excel constraint formulas labeled "Formula" in cells E19 to E23. In addition, the Constraint section contains information about whether the constraint is binding or not binding in cells F19 to F23, labeled Status.

The cells labeled Slack, cells G19 to G23, contain information about how much of a constraint is left over and are related to cells F19 to F23. If a cell in the Status section is labeled Binding, the corresponding Slack cell will be zero. Likewise, if a cell in the Status column is labeled Not Binding, the corresponding Slack cell will contain a positive value.

Slack values correspond to the amount of a constraint that is not used up.

Slack values correspond to the amount of the respective constraint that is not used up. When the slack value is zero, the Status label will always read, Binding. A connection should be made, in that when a constraint is Binding, the optimal solution lies on that constraint and that constraint is in turn used up (i.e., slack equals zero). Refer back to the discussion "Binding and Nonbinding Constraints," above, to make this connection.

FIGURE 8.21 **Excel Sensitivity Report for Mark's Bat Production LP Problem**

	A B	C	D	E	F	G	H
1	Microsoft Excel 11.0 Sensitivity Report						
2	Worksheet: [Mark's LP Problem]Sheet4						
3	Report Created: 8/4/2005 10:26:47 AM						
4							
5							
6	Adjustable Cells						
7			Final	Reduced	Objective	Allowable	Allowable
8	Cell	Name	Value	Cost	Coefficient	Increase	Decrease
9	$D$3	x1= # of Wooden Wonders to Produce	40	0	7	3	7
10	$D$4	x2 = # of Aluminum Allys to Produce	60	0	10	1E+30	3
11							
12	Constraints						
13			Final	Shadow	Constraint	Allowable	Allowable
14	Cell	Name	Value	Price	R.H. Side	Increase	Decrease
15	$D$12	1.5x1 < 100 LHS	60	0	100	1E+30	40
16	$D$14	2.0x2 < 120 LHS	120	1.5	120	20	53.33333333
17	$D$16	0.25x1 + 0.5x2 < 60 LHS	40	0	60	1E+30	20
18	$D$18	0.25x1 + 0.25x2 < 25 LHS	25	28	25	6.666666667	2.5
19	$D$20	x1 > 30 LHS	40	0	30	10	1E+30

Sensitivity Report in Excel

The Sensitivity report generated within Solver details two areas: adjustable cells and constraints.

The Sensitivity report generated within Solver details two areas: adjustable cells and constraints. Figure 8.21 displays the sensitivity report generated for Mark's bat production LP problem.

The report displayed in Figure 8.21 summarizes information on how sensitive the optimal solution is to changes in various coefficients in the underlying LP model. The Adjustable Cells section is detailed first, followed by the Constraints section.

Adjustable Cells Section

The Adjustable Cells section in Solver's answer report contains information about the sensitivity of changes to the decision variables.

The adjustable cells section of the sensitivity report provides information about the sensitivity of changes to the decision variables. The column labeled Final Value contains the optimal values for the number of Wooden Wonders and Aluminum Allys to produce. For Mark's bat production LP, the optimal number of Wooden Wonders to produce is 40, while 60 Aluminum Allys should be produced. These are the same values presented in the answer report (see Figure 8.20). However, the sensitivity report gives additional information on changes to the adjustable cells in the LP. The Reduced Cost area is discussed next.

Reduced Cost

The Reduced Cost column indicates how much the objective coefficient of a decision variable must improve before that decision variable assumes a positive value in the optimal solution.

Specifically, the Reduced Cost column indicates how much the objective coefficient of a decision variable must improve before that decision variable could assume a positive value in the optimal solution. In the case of Excel Solver, the absolute value of the Reduced Cost column is always taken and interpreted. In Mark's bat production LP problem, both values in the Reduced Cost column are zero. This occurs since each decision variable is already a positive value (40 Wooden Wonders and 60 Aluminum Allys respectively) in the objective function.

Objective Coefficient, Allowable Increase, and Allowable Decrease

The Allowable Increase and Allowable Decrease columns describe the range an objective coefficient must stay within for the optimal decision variables to be valid.

The column labeled Objective Coefficient corresponds to the coefficients that accompany each decision variable in the objective function.

The next columns in the adjustable cell section are labeled Allowable Increase and Allowable Decrease. These columns are linked to the Objective Coefficient column. For Mark's bat production LP, the Wooden Wonder objective coefficient is 7, the allowable increase value is 3, and the allowable decrease is 7. If one adds 3 to or subtracts 7 from the current Wooden

Wonder objective coefficient of 7, a range of optimality for the objective coefficient is obtained. The range for the Wooden Wonder decision variable, C_{ww}, would then be

$$0 \leq C_{ww} \leq 10$$

This range informs us that, as long as the objective coefficient (profit contribution) from Wooden Wonders remains between $0 and $10 inclusive, the optimal production numbers, 40 Wooden Wonders and 60 Aluminum Allys, remain optimal. The same analysis can be performed for the Aluminum Ally objective coefficient.

Constraints Section

The Constraints section gives the user insight into how the constrained resources are being utilized.

The information provided in the Constraints section gives the user insight into how the constrained resources are being utilized. For example, the entries in the Final Value column display the exact units of a constraint needed to produce the optimal combination of 40 Wooden Wonders and 60 Aluminum Allys. Therefore, producing 40 Wooden Wonders and 60 Aluminum Allys takes 60 hours of Wooden Wonder shaping (refer to row 15 in the Constraints section), 120 hours of Aluminum Ally shaping (refer to row 16 in the Constraints section), 40 hours of stamping (refer to row 17 in the Constraints section), 25 hours of packing (refer to row 18 in the Constraints section), and 40 units of Wooden Wonder production (refer to row 19 in the Constraints section).

The Constraint R.H. Side Column

The values in the R.H. Side column are the original RHS values for each constraint: 100 hours of Wooden Wonder shaping, 120 hours of Aluminum Ally shaping, 60 hours of stamping, 25 hours of packing, and 30 units minimum of Wooden Wonder production. One should notice that the slack variables discussed in the section describing the answer report are just the absolute value of the Constraint R.H. Side column less the Final Value column. Keep in mind that the Wooden Wonder production constraint is a minimum constraint; therefore, producing more than the minimum value of 30 is logical and the slack is the extra units produced (i.e., $10 = |30 - 40|$).

Shadow Price Column

The Shadow Price column assists in determining what additional amounts of constrained resources would be worth.

For constraints with a shadow price of zero, it can be determined that changing the RHS of a constraint would have no effect on the objective function.

The Shadow Price column assists the user in determining what additional amounts of constrained resources would be worth. A Shadow Price is defined as the amount by which the objective function value changes given a unit increase/decrease in the RHS value of the constraint, assuming all other coefficients remain the same.

Given that a shadow price is positive, a subsequent increase in the RHS value of the associated constraint would result in an improvement in the objective function value. Likewise, given that a shadow price is negative, a subsequent increase in the RHS value of the associated constraint would result in a declination in the objective function value. For constraints that have a shadow price of zero, it can be determined that changing the RHS of the constraint would have no effect on the objective function value, and it can be inferred that the constraint is also nonbinding (i.e., has slack).

However, one must keep in mind that increases or decreases in the RHS value of a constraint must be within certain limits or else the shadow price commentary is invalid. In other words, if you change the RHS value of a constraint outside of a given increase/decrease range, the entire LP problem changes and the shadow prices are not valid anymore.

Allowable Increase and Decrease Columns

The Allowable Increase and Allowable Decrease columns describe the range a RHS constraint must stay within for the shadow price to be valid.

For Mark's Bat Production LP problem, it can be seen in Figure 8.21 that the shadow price for the first constraint (refer to row 15 in the Constraints section) is zero. Note that the allowable increase is listed as 1E+30 (scientific notation for a very, very large number) and the allowable decrease is 40. Since the constraint is nonbinding, the RHS of the constraint could be increased infinitely with no change occurring in the objective function (i.e., a shadow price of zero). In turn, the RHS of the constraint could be decreased a maximum of 40 without changing the objective function. This logic is true for each of the constraints that have shadow prices of zero (refer to rows 15, 17, and 19 in Figure 8.21).

However, for constraints where the shadow price is nonzero, increases or decreases in the RHS of the constraints will change the value of the objective function. For example, the shadow price for the second constraint, the Aluminum Ally shaping constraint (refer to row 16 in the Constraints section of Figure 8.21) is 1.5.

Therefore, if the number of available shaping hours increased by any amount in the range from 0 to 20 hours (this is the amount of the allowable increase), the optimal objective function would increase by $1.50 per hour of increase in Aluminum Ally shaping time. Consequently, if the number of Aluminum Ally shaping hours decreased by any amount in the range 0 to 53.3333 (this is the amount of the allowable decrease), the optimal objective function would decrease by $1.50 per hour of decrease in the Aluminum Ally shaping time.

Comment on Shadow Prices

It is important to note that if the constraint's RHS values are altered (increased or decreased), then either more or less of a key resource is available. In keeping with this logic, the optimal values of the decision variables may also change. In reality, this makes perfect sense. For example, if a user can somehow acquire more hours for shaping, stamping, or packing bats in Mark's bat production LP, it should be possible to produce more bats (all other things held constant).

Shadow price is akin to marginal value and equates to the marginal value of a resource being used with the marginal benefit of the goods being produced.

This description of shadow prices is unique to Solver in Excel. Regrettably, there does not seem to be a standard method of reporting shadow prices. When compared to Solver in Excel, different LP software packages may report shadow prices with opposite signs.

In sum, shadow price information is extremely valuable to users, as it opens up the question of efficient use of resources and cost-benefit analysis. For example, in the case of Mark's bat production LP problem, what if Mark could somehow obtain an additional amount of Aluminum Ally shaping hours? From the sensitivity report we know that for each hour of Aluminum Ally shaping resource added, Mark will see his objective function (and overall profit) increase by $1.50.

Resources that have slack will have shadow prices that are zero.

However, the real question at hand is "How much would Mark be willing to pay for those additional hours of Aluminum Ally shaping?" Some would say it definitely would not be more than the gain in increased profits (the increase in the objective function) by adding the extra resource. Numerous discussion topics could be developed here regarding evaluation based on fixed cost or variable cost assumptions. These discussions are not investigated here, and students are referred to any text detailing linear program applications for further inquiry. However, significant points regarding shadow prices to remember are:

- Shadow prices are akin to marginal value.
- Shadow prices equate the marginal value of a resource being used with the marginal benefit of the goods being produced.
- Resources that have excess supply or slack (i.e., nonbinding resources) will have shadow prices of zero.
- Resources that do not have excess supply or slack (i.e., binding resources) will have shadow prices.

A BRIEF DISCUSSION OF THE SIMPLEX METHOD

The simplex method was developed by George B. Dantzig around 1952.

As was discussed earlier, the systematic development of practical computing methods for linear programming (LP) began in 1952 at the Rand Corporation in Santa Monica, under the direction of George B. Dantzig. Dantzig developed what is referred to as the *simplex method* of solving LP problems. The next section gives a brief overview of the simplex method and provides references for those interested in further study.

Simplex and Slack Variables

Solver was able to solve Mark's bat production problem because of the simplex algorithm. The simplex algorithm requires that all constraints in the LP be expressed as equalities. Take a look back at the step 4 under "Steps to Implementing the Graphical Method," as this step refers to corner point solutions. Relate the idea of corner point feasible solutions to equality constraints.

In turning inequality constraints into equality constraints, the simplex algorithm adds one new variable to each less than or equal to constraint and subtracts one new variable from each greater than or equal to constraint. These new variables are called slack and surplus variables. A slack variable is added to the LHS of a ≤ constraint to convert it to an equality constraint. Likewise, a surplus variable is subtracted from the LHS of a ≥ constraint to convert it to an equality constraint.

With Solver there is no need to set up slack variables, as Solver automatically completes this step. In fact, we have discussed the concept of slack in the section on Solver's answer report. It must be noted that the term *slack*" used within this text is different from the term *slack variable* or *surplus variable* used in the simplex method. The values we spoke about in the answer report section provided by Solver correspond to the optimal values of the slack variables in the simplex algorithm.

How the Simplex Method Finds the Optimal Solution

In adding slack or surplus variables to the LP problem, all inequalities are converted to equalities. The simplex algorithm uses this fact to its advantage. Simplex first identifies any of the corner point feasible solutions for the LP, using the relationships between equality constraints—think about how the corner point feasible solutions were found in Mark's bat problem. The algorithm then moves to an adjacent corner point feasible solution if that move improves the objective function. When no movement to an adjacent corner feasible solution improves the objective function, the current corner point feasible solution is considered optimal and the algorithm halts.

Summary

Overall, the simplex algorithm considers only the corner point feasible solutions and is a very efficient way to solve linear constrained problems. Slack variables are introduced to convert inequality constraints to equality constraints, so the simplex method can move systematically from corner point feasible solution to corner point feasible solution in the attempt to improve the objective function. When no improvement can be achieved by this systematic movement, the algorithm stops and the last identified corner point feasible solution is then the optimal solution to the LP problem.

CLASSIC LINEAR OPTIMIZATION PROBLEMS

In the area of business decision making, LP models have been one of the most successful quantitative approaches over the last few decades. Applications of LP modeling are widespread in almost every industry from production operations to financial services and planning to marketing. We have already uncovered a classic problem type where LP models prove extremely valuable: Mark's bat production problem successfully illustrated the use of an LP model to determine the mix of bats Mark should produce and sell. This type of LP model is referred to as a *product mix* or *blending* LP formulation. This is a classic linear optimization application area. The next section details another classic linear optimization application area: the network flow/transportation model.

Network Flow/Transportation Problems

Many network flow problems are common in business. Network flow problems have similar common characteristics and in general can be described via a network flow diagram or graph. Network flow problems are also at times referred to as transportation problems, shortest path problems, or assignment problems. The next section details a common network flow or transportation problem.

THE TRANSPORTATION PROBLEM: PIRATE LOGISTICS

The transportation problem appears in many places in real life. Shipping companies, freight forwarding companies, the U.S. Postal Service, and the railways all have transportation problems to solve. In general, a network of supply nodes and demand nodes characterizes the transportation problem. Figure 8.22 displays an example of a network of supplying nodes and receiving nodes for the Pirate Logistics Company. The Pirate Logistics Company example is used to illustrate the transportation problem and LP formulation. The company has three supply locations: Wilmington, New Bern, and Lynchburg. In turn, Pirate Logistics ships goods to three demand locations: Grand Island, Omaha, and Sioux Falls.

Characteristics of the Transportation LP

The one-way flow of goods makes network problems unique LP problems.

What makes the transportation problem a unique network problem is the one-way flow of goods. From the direction of the arrows in Figure 8.22, it can be seen that goods flow from the supply locations to three demand locations. Other unique characteristics of the basic transportation problem are:

- A unique shipping cost is associated with each supply locale.
- Limited supply amounts are provided at any supply locale.
- Each demand locale must meet a required demand amount.
- Amount supplied must equal amount demanded.
- Cost minimization is the objective.

Transportation LP problems appear regularly in shipping companies.

These characteristics are common in real-life transportation problems. Each locale a firm ships to has its own cost structure, depending on distance, geographic region, highway accessibility, etc. Also, a firm can ship only a limited amount of goods, usually based on what it has in stock (i.e., the limited supply caveat). In turn, when a company orders goods to be delivered, it wants delivered only what it ordered, no more or no less (i.e., the required demand amount). The idea of equating amount supplied and amount demanded links the supply amount directly to the demand amount. Finally, it is just common sense that a business would wish to ship all goods at the lowest cost possible, hence the cost minimization objective.

FIGURE 8.22
Network for Pirate Logistics Company

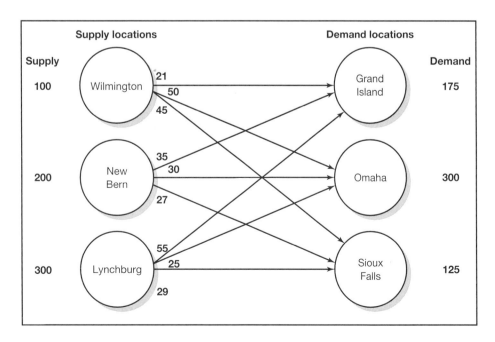

The General LP Formulation for the Transportation Problem

The following notation details the general linear programming formulation for the transportation model.

i = index for supply locations, i = 1 to m

j = index for demand locations, j = 1to n

x_{ij} = number of units shipped from supply location i to demand location j

c_{ij} = cost per unit shipped from supply location i to demand location j

s_i = supply or capacity in units at location i

d_j = demand in units at location j

The general transportation LP model for m-supply locations and n-demand destinations is

Most transportation LP models contain a minimize cost objective function.

$$\text{Min} \sum_{i=1}^{m} \sum_{j=1}^{n} c_{ij} x_{ij}$$

s.t.

$$\sum_{i=1}^{n} x_{ij} = s_i \quad \text{for } i = 1 \text{ to } m \quad \text{Supply constraint}$$

$$\sum_{i=1}^{m} x_{ij} = d_j \quad \text{for } j = 1 \text{ to } n \quad \text{Demand constraint}$$

$$x_{ij} \geq 0 \quad \text{for all } i \text{ and } j$$

Setting Up the Transportation LP in a Spreadsheet

The basic transportation LP can be formulated, solved, and analyzed very easily in a spreadsheet. Figure 8.23 displays the spreadsheet formulation for the Pirate Logistics transportation LP problem.

FIGURE 8.23 Spreadsheet Formulation for Pirate Logistics

Pirate Logistics.xls

	A	B	C	D	E	F	G
1							
2				**Shipping Cost per Unit**			
3				Demand Location			
4		Supply Location	Grand Island	Omaha	Sioux Falls		
5		Wilmington	21	50	45		
6		New Bern	35	30	27		
7		Lynchburg	55	25	29		
8							
9				**Supply and Demand Requirements**			
10				Demand Locations to Ship to			
11		Supply Location	Grand Island	Omaha	Sioux Falls	Total Shipped	Supply Available
12		Wilmington	0	0	0	0	100
13		New Bern	0	0	0	0	200
14		Lynchburg	0	0	0	0	300
15		Total Received	0	0	0		
16		Demand Required	175	300	125		
17							
18		**Objective Function - Minimize Shipping Costs from Supply Locations to Demand Locations**					
19		**Cost =**	0				
20							

LP Formulation / Formulae

Ready NUM

Description of the Spreadsheet

In the spreadsheet, the shipping costs per unit for each supply and demand location are summarized first (cells C5 through E7, Figure 8.23). Supply and demand requirements are summarized next in cells C16 to E16 and G12 to G16, respectively.

Decision Variables

In most transportation LP models, the decision variables are defined as the amount to ship from one locale to another.

The actual amounts to be shipped from supply locations to demand locations are defined by cells C12 to E14. These nine cells correspond to the nine decisions that must be made in the original problem "How much should be shippped from each supply locale to each demand locale?"

Supply and Demand Constraints

Three supply locales multiplied by three demand locales gives nine decision variables. To see this, take a look back at Figure 8.22 and you will notice nine lines connecting the six nodes. Figure 8.23 displays how the spreadsheet will look when you are finished. However, there are a number of formulas throughout the spreadsheet itself. Figure 8.24 displays the formulas behind the spreadsheet in Figure 8.23.

In terms of RHS and LHS variables, which were used earlier to describe LP model constraints, cells C12 to E14 would be considered LHS variables, whereas cells C16 to E16 and G12 to G14 would be considered RHS variables.

The Objective Function

Cell C19 contains the objective function. The objective in the Pirate Logistics problem is to meet shipping requirements at the lowest cost. The formula in cell C19, Figure 8.24, is

$$\text{Formula for cell C19} := \text{SUMPRODUCT(C5:C7,C12:E14)}$$

A transportation LP's objective function is usually a cross product of shipping costs and amounts shipped.

The SUMPRODUCT() function in Excel multiplies the elements of two ranges and sums those products. In the Pirate Logistics case, it is the range of supply and demand shipping costs (cells C5 to C7) multiplied by the actual amounts to be shipped from supply to demand locations, i.e., the decision variables (cells C12 to E14), and summed.

Non-Negativity Assumptions

Simply put, it does not make sense to have negative amounts shipped from one locale to another. Therefore, it is implicit in the model that the nine decision variables (cells C12 to E14) will always be greater than or equal to zero. However, we must inform Excel of this when Solver is set-up.

FIGURE 8.24 **Spreadsheet Formulas Associated with Pirate Logistics' LP Problem**

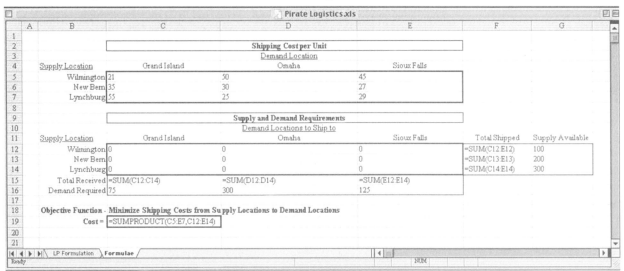

SETTING UP SOLVER TO FIND SOLUTIONS TO THE PIRATE LOGISTICS LP PROBLEM

This section discusses how to use solver to optimize the spreadsheet LP model for Pirate Logistics. It is assumed that the user has already built a spreadsheet optimization model in Excel (refer to Figures 8.23 and 8.24). After clicking on Solver in the Tools menu, the Solver dialog box resembling (Figure 8.25) will appear. The following steps enable Solver to find solutions to optimization spreadsheets.

1. In the Set Target Cell box, enter a cell reference or name for the target cell. The target cell must contain a formula.
2. To have the value of the target cell be as large as possible, click Max. To have the value of the target cell be as small as possible, click Min. To have the target cell be a certain value, click Value of, and then type the value in the box.
3. In the By Changing Cells box, enter a name or reference for each adjustable cell, separating nonadjacent references with commas. The adjustable cells must be related directly or indirectly to the target cell. You can specify up to 200 adjustable cells. To have Solver automatically propose the adjustable cells based on the target cell, click Guess.
4. In the Subject to the Constraints box, enter any constraints you want to apply.
5. Click Solve.

In the Pirate Logistics spreadsheet LP problem, a target cell (the objective function), adjustable cells (the decision variables), and constraints are defined as shown in Table 8.3 (refer to Figures 8.23 and 8.24):

In entering the solver cell definitions for the constraints, follow the same procedure as detailed in Figures 8.8, 8.9, and 8.10 for Mark's bat production problem, using the constraints for Pirate Logistics supply and demand requirements. The solver menu will resemble Figure 8.26 after you have entered the values from Table 8.3 into the Solver dialog boxes.

The Pirate Logistics LP model contains only linear constraints; therefore, Solver must be notified. This is in most cases a formality, but it is good form to follow. Notifying Solver of a linear model is simple:

FIGURE 8.25
Excel Solver Dialog Box

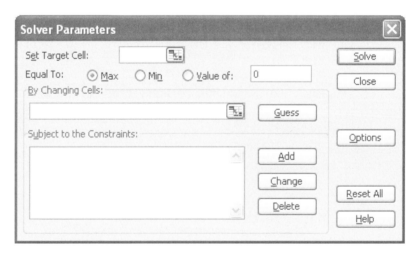

TABLE 8.3
Solver Cell Definitions

Set Target Cell	$C$19
Equal To:	Min
By Changing Cells:	$C$12:$E$14
Subject to the Constraints:	
Demand required	$C$15:$E$15 <= $C$16:$E$16
Supply available	$F$12:$F$14 = $G$12:$G$14

FIGURE 8.26
Final Solver Parameters for Pirate Logistics LP Problem

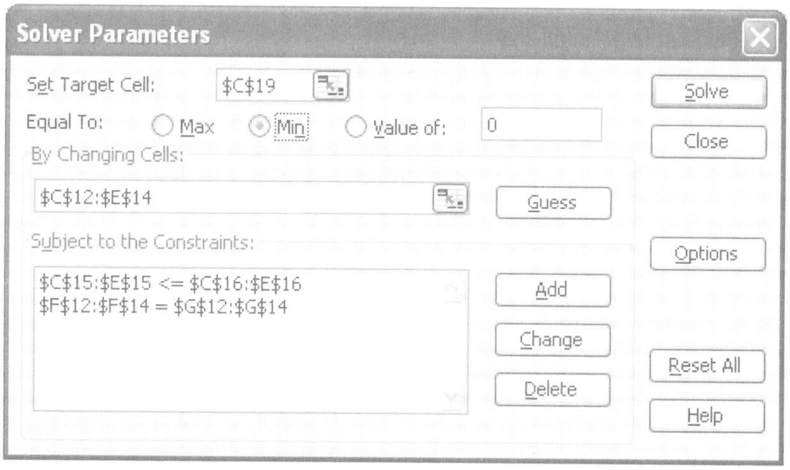

FIGURE 8.27
Solver Options Menu

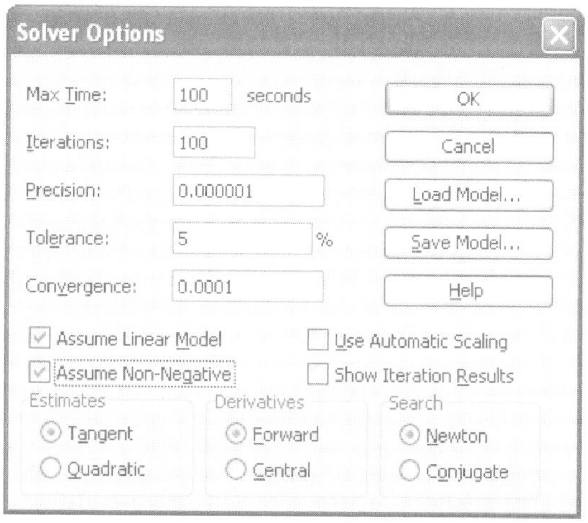

1. Press the Options button in the Solver menu.
2. A menu such as the one in Figure 8.27 will appear.
3. Check the boxes next to Assume Non-Negative and Assume Linear Model.
4. Click the OK button and return to the screen in Figure 8.26.

After the non-negativity and linear assumptions have been enabled (refer to Figure 8.27), Solver is ready to be employed to solve Pirate Logistics' LP problem. From the Solver menu, refer to Figure 8.26, click the Solver button to commence the solution process.

Figure 8.28 displays the final spreadsheet model for the Pirate Logistics LP problem. The optimal shipping quantities are shown in Table 8.4, and Figure 8.28 shows the minimum objective function value of $15,600 (refer to cell C19).

TABLE 8.4
Optimal Shipping Quantities

Shipping locale to receiving locale	Cells	Optimal shipping amount
Wilmington to Grand Island	C12	100
New Bern to Grand Island	C13	75
Lynchburg to Grand Island	C14	0
Wilmington to Omaha	D12	0
New Bern to Omaha	D13	0
Lynchburg to Omaha	D14	300
Wilmington to Sioux Falls	E12	0
New Bern to Sioux Falls	E13	125
Lynchburg to Sioux Falls	E14	0

FIGURE 8.28
Optimized Spreadsheet Model for the Pirate Logistics LP Problem

Pirate Logistics.xls

Shipping Cost per Unit

Supply Location	Grand Island	Omaha	Sioux Falls
	Demand Location		
Wilmington	21	50	45
New Bern	35	30	27
Lynchburg	55	25	29

Supply and Demand Requirements

Supply Location	Grand Island	Omaha	Sioux Falls	Total Shipped	Supply Available
	Demand Locations to Ship to				
Wilmington	100	0	0	100	100
New Bern	75	0	125	200	200
Lynchburg	0	300	0	300	300
Total Received	175	300	125		
Demand Required	175	300	125		

Objective Function - **Minimize Shipping Costs from Supply Locations to Demand Locations**

Cost = 15600

LP Formulation / Formulae

Answer Report in Excel

The answer report generated in Solver details three areas: target cells, adjustable cells, and constraints.

The answer report generated within Solver details three areas: target cells, adjustable cells, and constraints. Figure 8.29 displays the answer report generated for the Pirate Logistics LP problem.

Target Cell Section

The Target Cell section of the answer report contains information about the objective function.

The first section of interest is the Target Cell section. The Target Cell section contains information about the objective function. Cell D8 contains the original value of the objective function. The original value for the Pirate Logistics LP problem is zero since the decision variables were set to zero (see the Adjustable Cell section).

Cell E8 contains the final value of the objective function. In this LP model, the final value of the objective function is 15600. Overall, the Target Cell section provides information regarding the objective function, specifically its final and optimal value.

Adjustable Cells Section

The Adjustable Cells section provides information about the decision variables x_1 through x_9. Cells D13 to D21 contain the original values of the decision variables. The values in the cells are zero, as the decision variables were set to zero originally. Cells E13 to E21 contain the final values of the decision variables (100, 0, 0, 75, 0, 125, 0, 300, and 0 respectively). In sum, the Adjustable Cells section informs the decision maker on the optimal number of units to ship from a supply locale to a demand locale.

Constraints Section

The Constraints section contains information about the constraints or limitations on the decision variables. This section should be linked to the earlier discussion involving the LHS and RHS columns. The Constraints section contains the same information as the LHS and RHS columns. However, the Constraints section organizes constraint information more efficiently and provides information about slack. As defined earlier, slack is the amount of a constraint that is not used up.

The Constraint section in Figure 8.29 contains the final constraint value, labeled Cell Value contained in cells D26 to D31, and the Excel constraint formulas labeled Formula in cells E26 to E31. In addition, the Constraint section contains information as to whether the constraint is binding or not binding. Cells F26 to F31, labeled Status, detail whether a constraint is binding or not binding.

FIGURE 8.29 **Excel Answer Report for Pirate Logistics LP Problem**

			Pirate Logistics.xls				
A	B	C	D	E	F	G	H

1 Microsoft Excel 9.0 Answer Report
2 Worksheet: [Pirate Logistics.xls]LP Formulation
3 Report Created: 10/25/2002 12:21:50 PM
4
5
6 Target Cell (Min)

	Cell	Name	Original Value	Final Value
7				
8	$C$19	Cost = Grand Island	0	15600

9
10
11 Adjustable Cells

	Cell	Name	Original Value	Final Value
12				
13	$C$12	Wilmington Grand Island	0	100
14	$D$12	Wilmington Omaha	0	0
15	$E$12	Wilmington Sioux Falls	0	0
16	$C$13	New Bern Grand Island	0	75
17	$D$13	New Bern Omaha	0	0
18	$E$13	New Bern Sioux Falls	0	125
19	$C$14	Lynchburg Grand Island	0	0
20	$D$14	Lynchburg Omaha	0	300
21	$E$14	Lynchburg Sioux Falls	0	0

22
23
24 Constraints

	Cell	Name	Cell Value	Formula	Status	Slack
25						
26	$C$15	Total Received Grand Island	175	$C$15<=$C$16	Binding	0
27	$D$15	Total Received Omaha	300	$D$15<=$D$16	Binding	0
28	$E$15	Total Received Sioux Falls	125	$E$15<=$E$16	Binding	0
29	$F$12	Wilmington Total Shipped	100	$F$12=$G$12	Binding	0
30	$F$13	New Bern Total Shipped	200	$F$13=$G$13	Binding	0
31	$F$14	Lynchburg Total Shipped	300	$F$14=$G$14	Binding	0

Answer Report 1 / Sensitivity Report 1 / LP Formulation / Formulae /

The cells labeled Slack, cells G26 to G31, contain information about how much of a constraint is left over and are related to cells F26 to F31. If a cell in the Status section is labeled Binding the corresponding Slack cell will be zero. Likewise, if a cell in the "Status" column is labeled "Not Binding" the corresponding Slack cell will contain a positive value.

Slack values correspond to the amount of the respective constraint that is not used up. When the slack value is zero, the Status label will always read Binding. A connection should be made in that, when a constraint is Binding, the optimal solution lies on that constraint and that constraint is in turn used up (i.e., slack equals zero). Refer to "Binding and Nonbinding Constraints," above, to make this connection. For the Pirate Logistics LP, we stated that supply must equal demand; therefore, all constraints are binding and there is no leftover units to be supplied or extra units to be demanded.

Sensitivity Report in Excel

The sensitivity report generated within Solver details two areas: adjustable cells and constraints. Figure 8.30 displays the sensitivity report generated for the Pirate Logistics LP problem.

The report in Figure 8.30 summarizes information on how sensitive the optimal solution is to changes in various coefficients in the underlying LP model. The Adjustable Cells section is detailed first, followed by the Constraints section.

Adjustable Cells Section

The adjustable cells section of the sensitivity report provides information about the sensitivity of changes to the decision variables. The column labeled Final Value contains the optimal values for the number of units to ship from a supply locale to a demand locale. For the Pirate

FIGURE 8.30 Excel Sensitivity Report for Pirate Logistics LP Problem

	A	B	C	D	E	F	G	H
				Pirate Logistics.xls				
	A	B	C	D	E	F	G	H
1	Microsoft Excel 9.0 Sensitivity Report							
2	Worksheet: [Pirate Logistics.xls]LP Formulation							
3	Report Created: 10/25/2002 12:21:51 PM							
4								
5								
6	Adjustable Cells							
7				Final	Reduced	Objective	Allowable	Allowable
8		Cell	Name	Value	Cost	Coefficient	Increase	Decrease
9		$C$12	Wilmington Grand Island	100	0	21	32	1E+30
10		$D$12	Wilmington Omaha	0	34	50	1E+30	34
11		$E$12	Wilmington Sioux Falls	0	32	45	1E+30	32
12		$C$13	New Bern Grand Island	75	0	35	25	5
13		$D$13	New Bern Omaha	0	0	30	5	7
14		$E$13	New Bern Sioux Falls	125	0	27	7	1E+30
15		$C$14	Lynchburg Grand Island	0	25	55	1E+30	25
16		$D$14	Lynchburg Omaha	300	0	25	7	1E+30
17		$E$14	Lynchburg Sioux Falls	0	7	29	1E+30	7
18								
19	Constraints							
20				Final	Shadow	Constraint	Allowable	Allowable
21		Cell	Name	Value	Price	R.H. Side	Increase	Decrease
22		$C$15	Total Received Grand Island	175	0	175	1E+30	0
23		$D$15	Total Received Omaha	300	-5	300	75	0
24		$E$15	Total Received Sioux Falls	125	-8	125	75	0
25		$F$12	Wilmington Total Shipped	100	21	100	0	100
26		$F$13	New Bern Total Shipped	200	35	200	0	75
27		$F$14	Lynchburg Total Shipped	300	30	300	0	75

Answer Report 1 \ Sensitivity Report 1 / LP Formulation / Formulae /

Logistics LP, the optimal number of units to ship from Wilmington to Grand Island is 100, from New Bern to Grand Island is 75, from New Bern to Sioux Falls is 125, and Lynchburg to Omaha is 300 (all the other supply-to-demand locales are zero). These are the same values presented in the answer report (see Figure 8.29). However, the sensitivity report gives additional information regarding changes to the adjustable cells in the LP. The Reduced Cost area is discussed next.

Reduced Cost

Specifically, the Reduced Cost column indicates how much the objective coefficient of a decision variable must improve before that decision variable could assume a positive value in the optimal solution. In the case of Excel Solver, the absolute value of the Reduced Cost column is always taken and interpreted. In the Pirate Logistics LP problem, four decision variables have nonzero numbers in the Reduced Cost column whereas the others are zero. We can interpret the Reduced Cost column as follows. To become a positive value in the optimal solution, the following objective coefficients must improve: Wilmington to Omaha must fall by 34, Wilmington to Sioux Falls must fall by 32, Lynchburg to Grand Island must fall by 25, and Lynchburg to Sioux Falls must fall by 7.

Objective Coefficient, Allowable Increase, and Allowable Decrease

The column labeled Objective Coefficient corresponds to the coefficients that accompany each decision variable in the objective function. The next columns in the adjustable cell section are labeled Allowable Increase and Allowable Decrease. These columns are linked to the Objective Coefficient column.

For the Pirate Logistics LP, the Wilmington to Grand Island objective coefficient is 21, the allowable increase value is 32 while the allowable decrease is 1E+10 (scientific notation for a very large number). If one adds 32 to the current objective coefficient of 21, the upper range of optimality for the objective coefficient is obtained. The lower range of optimality is unbounded, meaning you can decrease the coefficient infinitely and the decision variables will still be optimal. The range for the Wilmington to Grand Island decision variable, C_{W-GI}, would then be

$$\infty \leq C_{W\text{-}GI} \leq \$53$$

This range informs us that as long as the objective coefficient (cost contribution) from Wilmington to Grand Island remains below $53, the optimal shipping numbers remain optimal. The same analysis can be performed for the other objective coefficients.

Constraints Section

The information provided in the Constraints section gives the user insight into how the constrained resources are being utilized. For example, the entries in the Final Value column display the exact units of a constraint needed for shipping the optimal combination units. Since we assumed supply must equal demand in the Pirate Logistics problem, the values found in the Final Value column all match the R. H. Side column. In the prior LP problem we did not see this (i.e., there were nonbinding variables or there were constraints that had slack or units left over).

The Constraint R.H. Side Column

The values in the R.H. Side column are the original RHS values for each constraint. One should notice that the Slack variables discussed in "Answer Report in Excel," above, are just the absolute value of the Constraint R.H. Side column less the Final Value column (zero for the Pirate Logistics problem).

Shadow Price Column

The Shadow Price column assists the user in determining what additional amounts of constrained resources would be worth. A Shadow Price is defined as the amount by which the objective function value changes, given a unit increase/decrease in the RHS value of the constraint, assuming all other coefficients remain the same.

Given that a shadow price is positive, a subsequent increase in the RHS value of the associated constraint would result in an increase in the objective function. Likewise, given that a shadow price is negative, a subsequent increase in the RHS value of the associated constraint would result in a decrease in the objective function. For constraints that have a shadow price of zero, it can be determined that changing the RHS of the constraint would have no effect of the objective function value and it can be inferred that the constraint is also nonbinding (i.e., has slack).

However, one must keep in mind that increases or decreases in the RHS value of a constraint must be within certain limits or else the shadow price commentary is invalid. In other words, if you change the RHS value of a constraint outside of a given increase/decrease range, the entire LP problem changes and the shadow prices are not valid anymore.

Allowable Increase and Decrease Columns

For the Pirate Logistics LP problem, it can be seen in Figure 8.30 that the shadow price for the first constraint (refer to row 22 in the Constraints section) is zero. Note that the allowable increase is listed as 1E+10 (scientific notation for a very, very large number) and the allowable decrease is 0. The RHS of the constraint could be increased infinitely with no change occurring in the objective function (i.e., a shadow price of zero). In turn, the RHS of the constraint could not be decreased without changing the objective function.

However, for constraints where the shadow price is nonzero, increases or decreases in the RHS of the constraints will change the value of the objective function. For example, the shadow price for the second constraint, the Total Received Omaha (refer to row 23 in the

Constraints section, Figure 8.30) is −5. Therefore, if the number of available units Omaha demands increases by any amount in the range from 0 to 75 units (this is the amount of the allowable increase), the optimal objective function would decrease by $5 per unit of increase in demand. Consequently, since the allowable decrease is zero, no decrease in Omaha demand can be allowed for the current shadow price to be valid.

For an additional example, let's take a look at the Lynchburg Total Shipped constraint (refer to row 27 in the Constraints section, Figure 8.30). The shadow price for this constraint is 30. The allowable increase is zero, while the allowable decrease is 75. Therefore, if we were somehow able to decrease the amount shipped out of Lynchburg, up to 75 units, the objective function would increase by $30 for every unit increase. Keep in mind that we have stated that supply must equal demand; consequently, if we increase or decrease supply or demand in one area, a similar increase or decrease must occur elsewhere to keep the balance.

Summary of the Pirate Logistics LP Problem

In sum, Pirate Logistics should ship 100 units from Wilmington to Grand Island, 75 units from New Bern to Grand Island, 125 units from New Bern to Sioux Falls, and 300 units from Lynchburg to Omaha. The total amount shipped equals the amount received; therefore, the Supply Available and Demand Required constraints are both met. The total shipping cost Pirate Logistics incurs is $15,600.

INTEGER LINEAR PROGRAMMING

Integer linear programming (ILP) is characterized by some or all of the decision variables in a linear program being restricted to only integer values. Many practical business problems are restricted to solutions that contain only integer values. Problems dealing with the scheduling of employees, allocating assets, and/or producing items that cannot be broken into fractional units are all examples. This section discusses how to construct and solve optimization problems that contain integer variables.

Stating Integer Properties and Solving ILPs

Although it is fairly simple to state variables as integers, often it makes finding solutions to the subsequent optimization problem much more difficult. In fact, Excel's Solver is at times unable to solve some ILP problems even when an optimal solution exists. A specific type of ILP, the binary ILP, will be examined in this section.

Basics of Binary ILP Problems

Some problems naturally are suited for ILP modeling (e.g., the employee scheduling problem). However, at times business managers have only two options they can choose from. This type of decision problem is at times referred to as a "go, no-go" decision problem and is characterized as a binary ILP. In a binary ILP, the decision variables can take on only two integer values: 0 or 1.

The Capital Budgeting Problem

A common binary ILP is the capital budgeting problem, where a decision maker is presented with several potential investment types of projects to choose from. The investments or projects typically require different levels of capital, labor, or other resource and produce different levels of cash flow. The objective of ensuing optimization problem is to select the investments or projects that maximize the net present value (NPV) of these cash flows.

The Basic Information

In general, a capital budgeting binary ILP begins as a regular capital budgeting problem. Consider the following example:

Clem Gathman is a director of research and development for iTech Consulting and is responsible for evaluating and ultimately choosing among numerous and competing R&D investments/projects. Clem has just finished looking at the seven investments/projects that

TABLE 8.5

NPV and Capital Requirements for iTech's R&D Investments/ Projects

Investment/project	Expected NPV ($000)	Capital (in $000) required per year				
		Year 1	Year 2	Year 3	Year 4	Year 5
1	$ 74	$ 22	$ 20	$18	$16	$14
2	$233	$100	$ 20	$20	$20	$20
3	$177	$ 50	$ 25	$12.5	$ 6.25	$ 3.125
4	$190	$ 40	$ 30	$20	$10	$ 0
5	$287	$ 90	$ 90	$45	$45	$45
6	$107	$ 30	$ 15	$15	$15	$15
7	$301	$120	$120	$60	$60	$60

made it past the engineers and accountants. Although all the investments/projects look good (positive NPV), Clem knows he cannot pick all of them, since there is not enough money (i.e., capital) to go around. Clem must determine which of the investments/projects to accept to maximize potential NPV but yet stay within company capital budgets. The expected NPV and capital requirements for each of the seven investments/projects are listed in Table 8.5.

iTech Consulting has $300,000 in capital to invest right now and has budgeted $150,000 for continued operational expenses for years 2–3 and $90,000 for years 4–5. Surplus funds in any year cannot be carried over from year to year. The next sections will define the parts of the ILP and construct the final ILP model in Excel.

Identifying and Defining the Decision Variables

There are seven investments/projects from which Clem may choose. In turn, seven decision variables can be defined to represent the seven alternative investments/projects. $X_1, X_2,..., X_7$ therefore represent the seven decision variables for the problem and operate as follows:

$$X_i = \begin{cases} 1, & \text{if project is accepted} \\ 0, & \text{otherwise} \end{cases} \quad i = 1, 2, ..., 7$$

A binary value is assigned to each decision variable in the problem. A value of 1 is assigned if the investment/project is accepted, whereas a value of 0 is assigned if the investment/project is not accepted.

Defining the Objective Function

Clem's objective is to choose the set of investments/projects that maximize NPV. This is stated mathematically as follows:

$$\text{Maximize } Z = \$74X_1 + \$233X_2 + \$177X_3 + \$190X_4 + \$287X_5 + \$107X_6 + \$301X_7$$

Simply put, the objective function sums the NPV numbers together for the selected investments/projects.

Defining the Constraints

Since iTech Consulting has capital limitations for years 1 to 5, one capital constraint must be constructed for each year to ensure that the accepted investments/projects do not exceed the available capital. The capital constraints (cc) are as follows:

$$\$22X_1 + \$100X_2 + \$50X_3 + \$40X_4 + \$90X_5 + \$30X_6 + \$120X_7 \leq 300 \text{ year 1 cc}$$

$$\$20X_1 + \$20X_2 + \$25X_3 + \$30X_4 + \$90X_5 + \$15X_6 + \$120X_7 \leq 150 \text{ year 2 cc}$$

$$\$18X_1 + \$20X_2 + \$12.5X_3 + \$20X_4 + \$45X_5 + \$15X_6 + \$60X_7 \leq 150 \text{ year 3 cc}$$

$$\$16X_1 + \$20X_2 + \$6.25X_3 + \$10X_4 + \$45X_5 + \$15X_6 + \$60X_7 \leq 90 \text{ year 4 cc}$$

$$\$14X_1 + \$20X_2 + \$3.125X_3 + \$0X_4 + \$45X_5 + \$15X_6 + \$60X_7 \leq 90 \text{ year 5 cc}$$

Defining the Binary Assumptions

Each decision variable is assumed to be a binary variable. A formal statement of this assumption must be included in the ILP model. The binary assumption is stated as follows:

$$\text{All } X_i \text{ must be binary for all } i$$

Binary ILP in Modified Standard Form

The binary ILP for Clem's problem is as follows:

$$\text{Maximize } Z = \$74X_1 + \$233X_2 + \$177X_3 + \$190X_4 + \$287X_5 + \$107X_6 + \$301X_7$$

Subject to:

$$\$22X_1 + \$100X_2 + \$50X_3 + \$40X_4 + \$90X_5 + \$30X_6 + \$120X_7 \le 300$$
$$\$20X_1 + \$20X_2 + \$25X_3 + \$30X_4 + \$90X_5 + \$15X_6 + \$120X_7 \le 150$$
$$\$18X_1 + \$20X_2 + \$12.5X_3 + \$20X_4 + \$45X_5 + \$15X_6 + \$60X_7 \le 150$$
$$\$16X_1 + \$20X_2 + \$6.25X_3 + \$10X_4 + \$45X_5 + \$15X_6 + \$60X_7 \le 90$$
$$\$14X_1 + \$20X_2 + \$3.125X_3 + \$0X_4 + \$45X_5 + \$15X_6 + \$60X_7 \le 90$$

All X_i must be binary for all i.

Developing the Spreadsheet Model

The binary ILP for Clem's problem is shown in Figure 8.31.

Cells B6 to B12 contain a value of zero to indicate that they are decision variables from the binary ILP model we constructed. The capital constraint LHS formula is entered in cell D13 and then copied to cells E13 to H13. The RHS values for the capital constraints are listed in cells D14 to H14 as:

Formula for cell D13 : = sumproduct(D6:D12,$B$6:$B$12)

FIGURE 8.31 **Spreadsheet Model for Clem's Binary ILP Selection Problem**

	A	B	C	D	E	F	G	H
1	**Clem Gathman's Capital Investment Problem**							
2								
3								
4	**Investment/**	**Select?**			**Capital per Investment/Project Required in**			
5	**Project**	**(0=No, 1=Yes)**	**NPV**	**Year 1**	**Year 2**	**Year 3**	**Year 4**	**Year 5**
6	1	0	$74	$22	$20	$18	$16	$14
7	2	0	$233	$100	$20	$20	$20	$20
8	3	0	$177	$50	$25	$12.50	$6.25	$3.125
9	4	0	$190	$40	$30	$20	$10	$0
10	5	0	$287	$90	$90	$45	$45	$45
11	6	0	$107	$30	$15	$15	$15	$15
12	7	0	$301	$120	$120	$60	$60	$60
13			**Capital Required**	$ -	$ -	$ -	$ -	$ -
14			**Capital Available**	$ 300	$ 150	$ 150	$ 90	$ 90
15								
16			**Total NPV**	$ -				

Figure 8.32 **Spreadsheet Formulas for Clem's Binary ILP Selection Problem**

	A	B	C	D	E	F	G	H
1	Clem Gathman's Capital Investment Problem							
2								
3								
4	Investment/	Select?				Capital per Investment/Project Required in		
5	Project	(0=No, 1=Yes)	NPV	Year 1	Year 2	Year 3	Year 4	Year 5
6	1	0	74	22	20	18	16	14
7	2	0	233	100	20	20	20	20
8	3	0	177	50	25	12.5	6.25	3.125
9	4	0	190	40	30	20	10	0
10	5	0	207	90	90	45	45	45
11	6	0	107	30	15	15	15	15
12	7	0	301	120	120	60	60	60
13		Capital Required		=SUMPRODUCT(D6:D12,$B$6:$B12)	=SUMPRODUCT(E6:E12,$B$6:$B12)	=SUMPRODUCT(F6:F12,$B$6:$B12)	=SUMPRODUCT(G6:G12,$B$6:$B12)	=SUMPRODUCT(H6:H12,$B$6:$B12)
14		Capital Available	300		150	150	90	90
15								
16		Total NPV	=SUMPRODUCT(C6:C12,B6:B12)					

FIGURE 8.33
Solver Parameter Dialog Box for Clem's Binary ILP Model

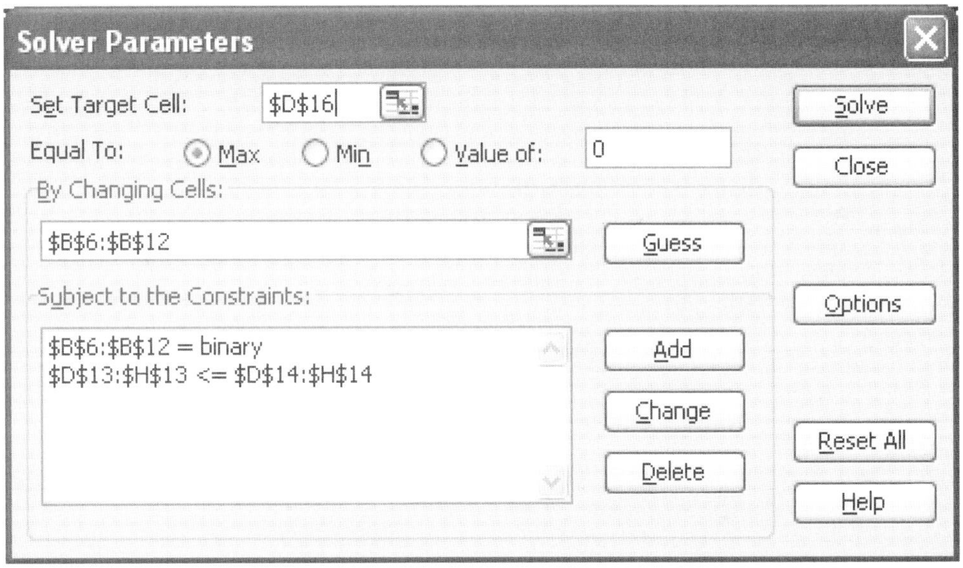

The objective function is contained in cell D16 and is represented as:

Formula for cell D16 : = sumproduct(C6:C12, $B$6:$B$12)

Each of the formulas for the constraints and objective function are displayed in Figure 8.32.

Solving the Binary ILP Model

We will employ the Solver Add-In that accompanies Excel to solve Clem's binary ILP model. In order to do this, we must tell Solver where the objective function, the decision variables, and constraints are located within the spreadsheet.

The Solver Parameters dialog box in Figure 8.33 indicates the following:

Objective function (Set Target Cell): Cell $D$16

Decision variables (By Changing Cells): Cells $B$6:$B$12

Constraints (Subject to the Constraints): $B$6:$B$12 = binary

$D$13:$H$13 <= $D$14:$H$14

The objective function is located in cell D16, the decision variables in cells B6 to B12, and the constraints are located in cells B6 to B12 and D13 to H13. The first set of constraints ensures the binary condition and the second set of constraints ensures we meet the maximum capital

Business Decision Modeling Behind the Scenes

The Development of Spreadsheet Optimization Programs

INTRODUCTION

There have been many optimization packages marketed over the years. In fact, many a graduate engineering, mathematics, or computer science student has been tasked with "coding" up a simple linear optimization algorithm based on the simplex method. However, it wasn't until the early 1990s that an optimization package for spreadsheets was marketed on a large scale.

VISICALC, VINO, AND WHAT'SBEST!

However, before the first copies of spreadsheet applications such as 1-2-3 or Excel had shipped, a company called LINDO Systems debuted VINO. VINO was the predecessor to their popular program called What'sBest!, and could be designated the first spreadsheet solver. The program was written for the first popular spreadsheet, VisiCalc.

In 1985, LINDO Systems and General Optimization jointly completed development on the first release of What'sBest! for Lotus 1-2-3 Release 1a. What'sBest! soon became recognized by *PC Magazine*'s prestigious Technical Excellence Award and received attention from other computer publications and such mainstream publications as *The Wall Street Journal* and *The New York Times*. What'sBest! specializes in tackling large-scale, real-world spreadsheet models with more than 100,000 variables and with nonlinear constraints.

WHAT-IF SOLVER

In 1990, a company called Frontline introduced What-If Solver, an add-in for Lotus 1-2-3 and Symphony. What-If Solver was the precursor of the modern spreadsheet solver add-ins. The advent of the desktop PC and the proliferation of the spreadsheet drove this new software innovation and led to what many now know as simple Solver in Microsoft Excel.

What-If Solver solved both linear and nonlinear problems, at speeds much greater than competitors. In 1991, What-If Solver won the Editor's Choice in its category in *PC Magazine*'s roundup of spreadsheet add-ins. As the popularity of the spreadsheet add-in increased, it became well known among MBA students wishing to solve complex mathematical programming problems within spreadsheets in less time.

THE EXCEL SOLVER

The introduction of Lotus's spreadsheet solver in 1-2-3/G motivated other spreadsheet vendors to develop or acquire solvers of their own. In 1990—well before the launch of Windows 3.0—Frontline became the developers for creating a solver on an OEM basis for Microsoft Excel 3.0. In the next year, with the introduction of Windows 3.0 and Excel 3.0, a period of rapid adoption and growth for the Microsoft products began.

In fact, the Solver program now is the optimization program of choice by the main spreadsheet programs, Microsoft's Excel, Corel's Quattro, and Lotus's 1-2-3, as well as Mathsoft's Mathcad, which provides visual display, editing, and computational power for technical mathematics.

EVOLUTIONARY SOLVER

In 1997 and 1998, other vendors developed "solver" products for Microsoft Excel that were based on genetic algorithms. Although slower than the standard optimization add-in, which used classical optimization methods, they did have an advantage. These genetic algorithms could handle arbitrary Excel functions, such as IF and CHOOSE, and could obtain a more precise global optimum than classical methods.

INCLUSION IN TEXTS AND STUDENT VERSIONS

By the early 1990s, Frontline developed the Student Edition of What-If Solver, distributed by Addison-Wesley Publishing Company for colleges and universities. The Student Edition of What-If Solver is the parent of the Excel Solver add-in used today by numerous business decision modeling students, spreadsheet users, and practitioners across the world.

Also by 1995, educational licenses for the What's Best! Solver Suite were made available at a price students could afford. As more and more students today have their own computers, the spreadsheet optimization add-in has allowed many of them to run the software on their own machine rather than having to visit the universities computer lab or "code-up" up their own.

THE FUTURE

The spreadsheet has become the modeling tool of choice for today's business problems. Overall, optimization add-ins for spreadsheets have become commonplace. Almost all new textbooks being published include a version of a solver-type program or an upgraded Solver add-in program. Look for the optimization package in this text and other texts you use in your course work.

OPTIMAL INFORMATION AREA

History of Lindo page, http://www.mpassociates.gr/software/distrib/science/lindo/history.html.
http://www.solver.com/presshist.htm.

FIGURE 8.34 **Optimal Integer Solution to Clem's Selection Problem**

	A	B	C	D	E	F	G	H
1	**Clem Gathman's Capital Investment Problem**							
2								
3								
4	Investment/	Select?			**Capital per Investment/Project Required in**			
5	Project	(0=No, 1=Yes)	NPV	Year 1	Year 2	Year 3	Year 4	Year 5
6	1	0	$74	$22	$20	$18	$16	$14
7	2	1	$233	$100	$20	$20	$20	$20
8	3	1	$177	$50	$25	$12.50	$6.25	$3.125
9	4	0	$190	$40	$30	$20	$10	$0
10	5	1	$287	$90	$90	$45	$45	$45
11	6	1	$107	$30	$15	$15	$15	$15
12	7	0	$301	$120	$120	$60	$60	$60
13			Capital Required	$ 270	$ 150	$ 93	$ 86	$ 83
14			Capital Available	$ 300	$ 150	$ 150	$ 90	$ 90
15								
16			Total NPV	$ 804				

expenditure limits. To obtain the identical results shown in Figure 8.34, do not check the Assume Linear Model in the options dialog box.

Figure 8.34 displays the optimal solution for Clem's binary ILP problem. The optimal solution indicates that if Clem selects investments/projects 2, 3, 5, and 6 (cells B7, B8, B10, B11), iTech Consulting can achieve a total NPV of $804 (cell D16). Take note that this solution set does not use up all the capital iTech has available (compare cells D13 through H13 to cells D14 through H14).

EXECUTIVE SUMMARY

Executive Summary Example for Pirate Logistics

TO: Braxton "Pitbull" Davis
FROM: Business Decision Modeling Consulting Group

This executive summary presents the suggested distribution schedule of Pirate Logistics. A transportation network was constructed and a linear programming (LP) model developed to minimize distribution costs while maintaining required supply and demand constraints. The basic LP, a shipping schedule, and expected costs are presented next.

Basic Transportation Network and LP

Pirate Logistics wishes to minimize the costs of distribution. The Pirate Logistics Company has three supply locations: Wilmington, New Bern, and Lynchburg. In turn, Pirate Logistics ships goods to three demand locations, Grand Island, Omaha, and Sioux Falls. Specific supply and demand constraints on Pirate Logistics exist. The distribution network including the supply and demand constraint is displayed in Figure 1.1.

In Figure 1.1, the shipping costs per unit for each supply and demand location are juxtaposed on the lines connecting supply and demand locales (e.g., to ship from Wilmington to Grand Island it costs Pirate Logistics $21 per unit. Supply and demand requirements are listed on the far left and far right of Figure 1.1, respectively.

FIGURE 1.1

Distribution Network for Pirate Logistics

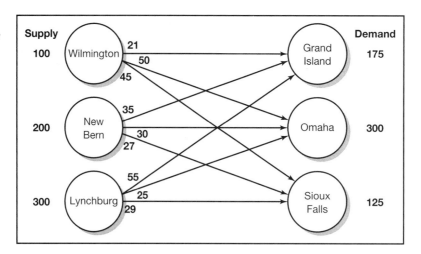

Pirate Logistics is interested in learning how much to ship from each supply locale to each demand locale. The LP model answers this question while providing the least costly solution. Table 1.1 displays the lowest cost shipping schedule for Pirate Logistics.

Shipping Schedule and LP Model Solution

Table 1.1 contains the optimal shipping amount for Pirate Logistics to ship from each supply locale to each demand locale (nonzero shipping amounts are in bold). For example, the amount to ship from Wilmington to Grand Island is 100 units. Likewise, no units are shipped from Lynchburg to Sioux Falls.

This shipping schedule results in a cost to Pirate Logistics of $15,600. Take note that total supply equals demand (i.e., total amount shipped equals 600) and that all individual supply and demand constraints are met (e.g., Wilmington has the ability to supply only 100 units and exactly 100 units are shipped, whereas Grand Island demands 175 units and exactly 175 units are shipped).

TABLE 1.1

Pirate Logistics Shipping Schedule

Shipping locale to receiving locale	Optimal shipping amount
Wilmington to Grand Island	**100**
New Bern to Grand Island	**75**
Lynchburg to Grand Island	0
Wilmington to Omaha	0
New Bern to Omaha	0
Lynchburg to Omaha	**300**
Wilmington to Sioux Falls	0
New Bern to Sioux Falls	**125**
Lynchburg to Sioux Falls	0

Shipping Schedule Sensitivity and What if Scenario

The shadow price assists in performing what if analysis. For the Pirate Logistics distribution problem, a shadow price is defined as the amount by which the total cost changes, given a unit increase/decrease in the supply or demand amounts. Shadow prices associated with supply are of most concern to Pirate Logistics, since amount shipped and shipping locale are more readily under its control than demand amount or location. Table 1.2 displays the shadow prices for the three shipping locales; take note that Lynchburg has the largest Shadow Price.

As Pirate Logistics main objective is to maintain low shipping costs, it would be beneficial if units shipped could be transferred from the higher costs Lynchburg locale to a lower cost locale, such as Wilmington or New Bern. The logic here is as follows: As units are shifted from Lynchburg to Wilmington, overall shipping costs will decrease by $9 per unit (i.e., from

$30 to $21). However, before this can occur, Pirate Logistics must verify that Wilmington can accommodate the extra units to be shipped and that overall supply equals overall demand.

TABLE 1.2
Shipping Locale Shadow Prices

Shipping locale	Shadow price
Wilmington	21
New Bern	31
Lynchburg	30

Case Study: *Chris's Capital Budgeting Ballyhoo*

BACKGROUND

Chris' firm, Tennessee Oil Ventures Inc. (TOVI), has $12,400,000 to invest in oil drilling exploration in the Gulf of Mexico over the next 5 years. Six investment opportunities have arisen since the latest round of hurricanes took out some production capacity in the Gulf. Table 8.6 displays the details of the six investments.

TABLE 8.6
Investment Details

Investment/ Project	Expected NPV ($000)	Capital (in $000) required per year				
		Year 1	Year 2	Year 3	Year 4	Year 5
1	$2700	$ 975	$ 350	$200	$ 100	$50
2	$3330	$1200	$ 200	$200	$ 200	$200
3	$7010	$2500	$1200	$850	$ 400	$400
4	$5770	$1550	$1350	$675	$ 337.5	$168.75
5	$2900	$1400	$ 350	$ 87.5	$ 21.875	$0
6	$4870	$1900	$1900	$350	$ 350	$350

The $14,400,000 in investment capital is spread over the 5 years as follows:

Capital (in $000) allocated per year				
Year 1	Year 2	Year 3	Year 4	Year 5
$5800	$3500	$1300	$900	$900

PROBLEM AT HAND

Chris had just finished looking at the six investment/projects that made it past the engineers and accountants. Although all the investments/projects look good (positive NPV), Chris knows TOVI cannot pick all of them since there is not enough money (i.e., capital) to go around. Chris and in turn TOVI must determine which of the investments/projects to accept to maximize potential NPV but yet stay within company capital budgets. However, a few caveats have cropped up regarding some federal and state laws regarding these projects.

1. Surplus capital funds in any year cannot be carried over from year to year.

2. If TOVI decides to invest in the second investment/project, it must also invest in the fourth.

3. If TOVI decides to invest in the first investment/project, it cannot invest in the fifth investment/project.

DISCUSSION QUESTIONS

1. Help Chris and his firm, TOVI, solve this problem by defining the parts of an ILP, constructing an ILP model in Excel, and using Excel's Solver to find a solution.

2. What projects should Chris and his firm invest in? How much capital do they use? Why are certain projects being left out?

Optimal Information Area

@RISK, Palisade Corp., Newfield, N.Y.; http://www.palisade.com.

Bodington, C. E., and T. E. Baker. "A History of Mathematical Programming in the Petroleum Industry.", *Interfaces*, vol. 20, no. 4 (1990), pp. 117–127.

Crystal Ball, Decisioneering Inc., Boulder, COolo.; http://www.decisioneering.com.

Essbase, Arbor Software, http://www.arborsoft.com.

Excel Solver, Frontline Systems, http://www.frontsys.com.

Frontline Systems, Solver history page, http://www.solver.com/presshist.htm.

History of Lindo, http://www.mpassociates.gr/software/distrib/science/lindo/history.html.

Neuwirth, Erich, Web page on Spreadsheets in Education, http://sunsite.univie.ac.at/Spreadsite/.

Savage, Sam L. *Fundamental Analytic Spreadsheet Tools for Quantitative Management*. New York: McGraw-Hill, 1993.

Savage, Sam L., Web home page with downloadable software, http://www.stanford.edu/~savage/faculty/savage/.

What'sBest!, Lindo Systems, http://www.lindo.com.

Problems

1. The Waikiki Enterprise Corporation produces two types of computers at its manufacturing plant in Torrance, California. Profit on computer A is $900 per unit and for computer B is $600. The manufacturing plant can produce not more than 50 of computer A and 100 of computer B a day. The following table displays the capacity for the manufacturing plant.

Plant	Capacity of computer A	Capacity of computer B	Maximum available capacity
A Riverview Plant	51	101	18,000
Unit profit	$900	$600	

   a. What are the decision variables?
   b. What is the objective function?
   c. What are the constraints?
   d. What are the non-negativity assumptions?

2. Firebridge's new radial tires come in two styles. The Fire Hawk uses 20 pounds of rubber and 6 pounds of steel. The Tiger Claw requires 15 pounds of rubber and 1 pound of steel. They currently have 3000 pounds of rubber and 300 pounds of steel. Firebridge is obligated to provide these tires to the government in the following minimum quantities: at least 20 Tiger Claws and at least 10 Fire Hawks. However, the government stipulates that of all the tires provided, twice as many must be Tiger Claws than Fire Hawks. In addition, Firebridge must provide at least 100 tires total. There is a cost of $10 for the Fire Hawk and $10 for a Tiger Claw.

	Units per Fire Hawk	Units per Tiger Claw	Available products
Steel	6	1	300
Rubber	20	15	3000
Cost	$10	$10	

   a. What are the decision variables?
   b. What is the objective function?
   c. What are the constraints?
   d. What are the non-negativity assumptions?
   e. Solve the LP via Excel's Solver.

3. The Backpack Corporation makes two types of backpacks for students, regular and deluxe. The company has a prior pricing agreement with the distributor, who is willing to buy as much of each kind of bag as Backpack could conceivably make. There are two steps in making a bag, first

assembling it and then packaging it. Each regular bag requires 3 hours of assembling and 1 hour of packaging. On the other hand, the deluxe requires 4 hours in assembling and 2 hours in packaging. The profit obtained for each regular bag is of $15, while that for each deluxe bag is $25. In order to maximize the profit for the company, how many bags of each type should Backpack manufacture? The data are summarized in the table below.

	Making Bag	Packaging Bag	Profit
Regular	3 hours	1 hour	$15
Deluxe	4 hours	2 hours	$25
Total Available Hours	300	200	

    a. What are the decision variables?

    b. What is the objective function?

    c. What are the constraints?

    d. What are the non-negativity assumptions?

    e. Solve the LP via Excel's Solver.

4. A senior class of 420 students will rent buses and vans for a class trip. Each bus can transport 50 students plus 3 chaperones, and costs $1200 to rent. Each van can transport 10 students and 1 chaperone, and costs $100 to rent. There are only 36 chaperones available (so they can't all go in vans). How many vehicles of each type should be rented in order to minimize the cost?

	Student	Chaperones	Cost
Bus	50	3	$1200
Van	10	1	$ 100
Totals	420	36	

    a. What are the decision variables?

    b. What is the objective function?

    c. What are the constraints?

    d. What are the non-negativity assumptions?

    e. Solve the LP via Excel's Solver.

5. Solve the following linear programming problem via Excel's Solver

$$\text{Maximize } 30X + 10Y$$

$$\text{Subject to } 4X + 10Y \leq 28$$

$$1X + 5Y \leq 50$$

$$Y \geq 1$$

$$X, Y \geq 0$$

6. Solve the following linear programming problem via Excel's Solver.

$$\text{Maximize } 4X + 4Y$$

$$\text{Subject to } 3X + 3Y \leq 85$$

$$X - 4Y \leq 40$$

$$Y \geq 5$$

$$X, Y \geq 0$$

7. Tire World produces two different series, the 50 series and the 65 series, at two plants. The profit for sale of a 50 series is $20 per tire and the profit from the sale of a 65 series is $30 no matter what plant they are produced at. The 50 series uses 800 units of capacity per tire while the 65 series uses 1000 units of capacity per day at plant 1. At the second plant the 50 series uses 600 units of capacity while the 65 series uses 400 units of capacity per tire at plant 2. Maximum daily capacity for each

plant is listed in the table below. Tire World must produce at least fifty 50 series tires overall. How many of each series should Tire World produce to at each plant to maximize profit? The following table displays the capacity of Tire World plant.

Plant	Capacity per 50 series	Capacity per 65 series	Maximum daily available capacity
1	800	1000	70,000
2	600	400	32,000
Profit per tire	$ 20	$ 30	

    a. What are the decision variables?

    b. What is the objective function?

    c. What are the constraints?

    d. What are the non-negativity assumptions?

    e. Solve the linear programming problem via Excel's Solver.

8. Polaski Petro Chemical Corp. produces two types of jet fuel: JP-2 and JP-3. For each gallon of JP-2 produced, a profit of $4.20 is earned; for each gallon of JP-3, a profit of $3.18 is earned. In its diffraction separator, Polaski has the capacity to produce a total of 62,000 gallons a week. A gallon of JP-2 takes 15 gallons of crude oil, and a gallon of JP-3 takes 12 gallons of crude oil. Polaski Petro Chemical receives 700,000 gallons of crude oil a week. Because of border disputes with the Hungarian Peoples Front, the Romanian Air Force has requested that JP-2 production be increased to fuel its MIG-29 fighter aircraft for the upcoming war. The government responded by limiting JP-3 production to 30,000 gallons a week. Which mix of fuels produced will maximize profits for the Polaski Petro Chemical Corporation? The table below lists the relevant data.

Plant	Capacity used per gallon of JP-2	Capacity used per gallon of JP-3	Maximum gallon capacity
1	8	6.5	62,000
Unit profit	$4.20	$3.18	

    a. What are the decision variables?

    b. What is the objective function?

    c. What are the constraints?

    d. What are the non-negativity assumptions?

    e. Solve the LP via Excel Solver.

9. Digitex is a small computer start-up company. At present it has an opportunity to enter the market by providing two types of server computers, one powered by Windows NT and the other backed by the up-and-coming Linux OS. The profits from these products are $1,000 from a single Windows NT server and $999 from one Linux server. Digitex has 2,000 units of capacity, with 88 units used per Windows NT servers and 96 units used per Linux server. How much of each server should Digitex produce to maximize profit?

Plant	Capacity use per Windows NT server	Capacity used per Linux server	Maximum available capacity
A	88	96	2000
Unit profit	$1000	$999	

    a. What are the decision variables?

    b. What is the objective function?

    c. What are the constraints?

d. What are the non-negativity assumptions?

e. Solve the LP via Excel Solver.

10. The local bakery sells three different kinds of bread mixes by the sack: Whiteness, Wheatness, and Multiness. The bakery has 5,000 lb of flour and 3,010 lb of sugar available. The white bread needs 2 lb of flour and 1.75 lb of sugar per sack, and the profit is $2.50 per sack. The wheat bread takes 3 lb of flour and 0.75 lb of sugar and garners $7.00 in profit per sack. Finally, the Multiness bread takes 2.5 lb of flour and 2 lb of sugar but gets $9.00 in profit per sack. However, the marketing department has informed the operations manager that no more than 50 sacks total of Wheatness and Multiness combined will be sold and warned not to overproduce the two types. In addition, the marketing department has promised a customer 10 sacks of Wheatness mix. Partial sacks of mix can be produced. Help the bakery to find the best combination to maximize profit.

	Whiteness	Wheatness	Multiness	Availability
Flour	2.0	3.0	2.5	5000
Sugar	1.75	0.75	2.0	3010
Profit	$2.5	$7.0	$9.0	

a. What are the decision variables and what is the objective function?

b. What are the constraints and what are the non-negativity assumptions?

c. Solve the LP via Excel Solver.

11. A firm services different types of computerized equipment (items 1, 2, 3, 4, 5), choosing from components A, B, C, D, and E to service the equipment. The firm determines that some components in service inventory will not be used in the process during the upcoming year. However, the firm wants certain components to be used in the current year since this will increase profitability. If not, then these service components must be sent to an auxiliary production location and no profit will be gained. The level of components in the inventory is as follows;

Component item	Units in inventory
A	20,000
B	18,000
C	7,500
D	5,000
E	22,300

The level of each component that is used per each service process is as follows:

	Computerized equipment				
Component	1	2	3	4	5
	Number used in service process				
A	30	40	0	30	50
B	20	30	20	20	60
C	10	10	10	10	20
D	10	10	10	0	20
E	20	30	20	40	80

The maximum service process forecasts for each service process is 2,000, 1,500, 500, 4,000, 5,000 for items 1, 2, 3, 4, 5, respectively. The profitability per unit (items 1, 2, 3, 4,) is $20, $40, $80, $60, $20. The objective is to maximize profit. The question is how many of each of the five items should be used. Thus, the maximum possible number can be used for inventory to meet current service needs.

 a. What are the decision variables and what is the objective function?

 b. What are the constraints and what are the non-negativity assumptions?

 c. Solve the LP via Excel Solver.

12. The following report has been generated in Excel by using Solver.

Microsoft Excel 10.0 Answer Report

Worksheet: [Book1]Sheet1

Report Created: 7/27/2003 11:38:10 AM

Target Cell (Max)

Cell	Name	Original Value	Final Value
$A$5	Objective Function	410	410

Adjustable Cells

Cell	Name	Original Value	Final Value
$C$5	CD Player Solution	30	30
$C$6	Receiver Solution	40	40

Constraints

Cell	Name	Cell Value	Formula	Status	Slack
$D$5	CD Player Constraints	240	$D$5 <= $E$5	Binding	0
$D$6	Receiver Constraints	100	$D$6 <= $E$6	Binding	0
$D$7	Constraints	30	$D$7 >= $E$7	Not Binding	30
$D$8	Constraints	40	$D$8 >= $E$8	Not Binding	40

Microsoft Excel 10.0 Sensitivity Report

Worksheet: [Book1]Sheet1

Report Created: 7/27/2003 11:38:10 AM

Adjustable Cells

Cell	Name	Final Value	Reduced Cost	Objective Coefficient	Allowable Increase	Allowable Decrease
$C$5	CD Player Solution	30	0	7	3	0.333333333
$C$6	Receiver Solution	40	0	5	0.25	1.5

Constraints

Cell	Name	Final Value	Shadow Price	Constraint R.H. Side	Allowable Increase	Allowable Decrease
$D$5	CD Player Constraints	240	1.5	240	60	40
$D$6	Receiver Constraints	100	0.5	100	20	20
$D$7	Constraints	30	0	0	30	1E + 30
$D$8	Constraints	40	0	0	40	1E + 30

Answer the following questions from the output above:

 a. What is the objective function optimal value?

 b. What are the final values of the decision variables at this optimal value?

 c. Explain which constraints are binding and not binding and what that means.

 d. What is the maximum increase in the objective coefficient of the first variable that can occur without changing the optimal product mix?

13. The following report has been generated in Excel by using Solver. Answer the following questions from the output above:

Microsoft Excel 10.1 Answer Report
Worksheet: [LPPROBS.XLS]Sheet1
Report Created: 5/4/2004 8:51:20 AM

Target Cell (Max)

Cell	Name	Original Value	Final Value
$F$7	max profit	0	4605

Adjustable Cells

Cell	Name	Original Value	Final Value
$F$2	x1	0	1670
$F$3	x2	0	10
$F$4	x3	0	40

Constraints

Cell	Name	Cell Value	Formula	Status	Slack
$F$11	multiness	50	$F$11<=$G$11	Binding	0
$F$9	flour	3465	$F$9<=$G$9	Not Binding	1535
$F$10	sugar	3010	$F$10<=$G$10	Binding	0
$F$12	wheatness	10	$F$12>=$G$12	Binding	0

Microsoft Excel 10.1 Sensitivity Report
Worksheet: [LPPROBS.XLS]Sheet1
Report Created: 5/4/2004 8:51:22 AM

Adjustable Cells

Cell	Name	Final Value	Reduced Cost	Objective Coefficient	Allowable Increase	Allowable Decrease
$F$2	x1	1670	0	2.5	0.3	2.5
$F$3	x2	10	0	7	0.214285714	1E+30
$F$4	x3	40	0	9	1E+30	0.214285714

Constraints

Cell	Name	Final Value	Shadow Price	Constraint R.H. Side	Allowable Increase	Allowable Decrease
$F$11	multiness	50	6.142857143	50	1461.25	40
$F$9	flour	3465	0	5000	1E+30	1535
$F$10	sugar	3010	1.428571429	3010	1343.125	2922.5
$F$12	wheatness	10	-0.214285714	10	40	10

a. What is the objective function optimal value?

b. What are the final values of the decision variables at this optimal value?

c. Explain which constraints are binding and not binding their meaning.

d. What is the shadow price for the flour constraint? Explain its meaning.

e. What would happen to the objective function if you could increase the flour constraint from 5,000 to 5,500?

Appendix **8A**

Review of Graphical Solutions to Optimization Problems

MODIFIED STANDARD FORM—MARK'S BAT PRODUCTION PROBLEM

Modified standard form for Mark's bat production LP model is as follows, where the three parts of the LP model are numbered as follows: Equation (8A.1) objective function, Equations (8A.2a) to (8A.2e) constraints, and Equation (8A.3) non-negativity assumptions.

When an LP model is formulated and transformed into modified standard form, a method for solving the LP model can be employed   The next section details two methods for solving LP models and provides both solution types for Mark's Bat Production problem.

$$\text{Maximize} \qquad Z = \$7x_1 + \$10x_2 \qquad \textbf{(8A.1)}$$

subject to $\qquad 1.5x_1 \leq 100 \quad$ Wooden Wonder shaping constraint $\qquad$ **(8A.2a)**

$2.0_2 \leq 120 \quad$ Aluminum Ally shaping constraint $\qquad$ **(8A.2b)**

$0.25x_1 + 0.5x_2 \leq 60 \quad$ Stamping constraint $\qquad$ **(8A.2c)**

$0.25x_1 + 0.25x_2 \leq 25 \quad$ Packing constraint $\qquad$ **(8A.2d)**

$x_1 \geq 30 \quad$ Minimum Wooden Wonder production constraint $\qquad$ **(8A.2e)**

$x_1, x_2 \geq 0 \qquad$ **(8A.3)**

METHODS OF SOLVING LP PROBLEMS

Two methods of solving LP problems exist: the graphical method and the simplex method.

Once the LP model is in modified standard form, two basic solution approaches to solving the LP model exist: the graphical method and the simplex method. This appendix describes the graphical method and the subsequent solution to Mark's bat production LP model. The main text of Chapter 8 describes the simplex method.

THE GRAPHICAL METHOD

The graphical method is simple, but is limited to smaller LP models (i.e., two or three decision variables). The limitation on two to three decision variables is due to the nature of the graphical method. When presented with an LP model with two decision variables the graphical method produces a two-dimensional graph. In turn, when presented with an LP model with three decision variables the graphical method produces a three-dimensional graph.

This logic makes it clear that, when an LP model contains four or more decision variables, it is impossible to use the graphical method of solution, as no *n*-dimensional graph can be developed for *n* greater than three. The next section provides a set of steps to follow when using the graphical method to solve LP models.

STEPS TO IMPLEMENTING THE GRAPHICAL METHOD

The feasible region is defined as the region mapped by the constraints containing values of decision variables that are allowed by the constraint set.

The following steps are used for implementing the graphical method of solving LP models. Before the steps are detailed a few terms must be defined.

> **Feasible region.** The region mapped by the constraints containing values of the decision variables that are allowed by the constraint set.

> **Corner point.** A point where a set of constraints intersect.

> **Corner point feasible solution.** A point where a set of constraints intersect that is on the edge of the feasible region.

The steps are presented next and their application to Mark's Bat Production problem follows.

A six-step process can be followed to solve LP problems graphically.

1. Construct an *x-y* coordinate plane/graph.
2. Plot all constraints on the plane/graph.
3. Identify the feasible region dictated by the constraints.
4. Identify all corner point feasible solutions of the feasible region.
5. Identify the optimum solution by plotting a series of objective functions over the feasible region.
4. Determine the exact solution values of the decision variables and the objective function at the optimum solution.

APPLICATION TO MARK'S BAT PRODUCTION PROBLEM

The following section details the application of the LP graphical solution method to Mark's Bat Production Problem.

Step 1: Construct an *x-y* Coordinate Plane/Graph

Drawing an *x-y* coordinate plane is the first step in solving an LP problem graphically.

This step is by far the easiest and involves constructing a simple *x-y* coordinate plane. This should be familiar from past algebra or geometry courses. Figure 8A.1 displays an example of an *x-y* coordinate plane.

Step 2: Plot All Constraints on the Plane/Graph

Plotting the constraints on the *x-y* coordinate plane is the second step in solving an LP problem graphically.

The second step to solving an LP model graphically is to plot all constraints on the *x-y* coordinate plane. This is accomplished by calculating where each constraint crosses the coordinate axis. From this point forward the *y* axis is referred to and labeled x_2, whereas the *x* axis is referred to and labeled x_1. This is done to coincide with standard LP modeling nomenclature and the two constraints defined earlier in Mark's bat production problem.

Constraint 1

Let's begin with the first constraint. Constraint 1 in functional form is

$$1.5x_1 \leq 100$$

One should take note that constraint 1 contains only decision variable x_1. Therefore, constraint 1 never intersects the x_2 axis. In addition, the decision variable x_2 can take on any value with regard to constraint 1.

Constraint 1 actually has an upper boundary, since the constraint contains a less than or equal to sign. This upper bound is found by dividing both sides of the constraint by 1.5 (the coefficient of x_1 in the constraint). The resulting equation is $x_1 \leq 66.67$ and is graphed in Figure 8A.2.

Constraint 2

Constraint 2 in functional form is

$$2.0x_2 \leq 120$$

FIGURE 8A.1 *x-y* **Coordinate Plane**

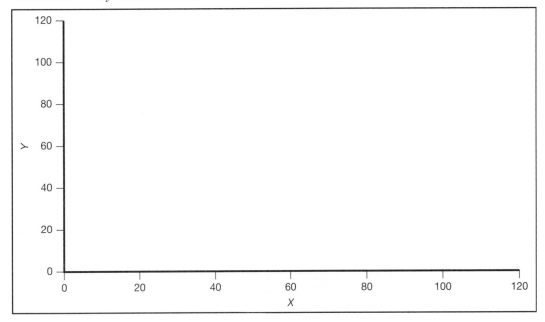

FIGURE 8A.2
Mark's Bat Production
Problem with
Constraint 1

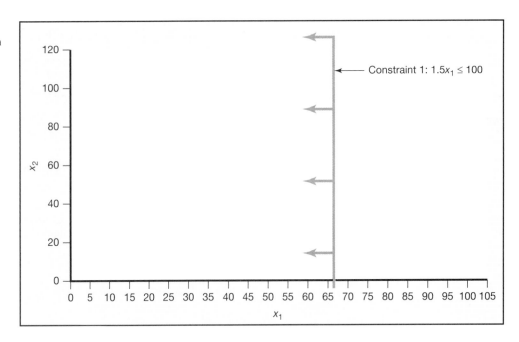

One should take note that constraint 2 contains only decision variable x_2. Therefore, constraint 2 never intersects the x_1 axis. In addition, the decision variable x_1 can take on any value with regard to constraint 2.

Constraint 2 actually has an upper boundary, since the constraint contains a less than or equal to sign. This upper bound is found by dividing both sides of the constraint by 2.0 (the coefficient of x_2 in the constraint). The resulting equation is

$$x_2 \leq 60.00$$

It is graphed, along with constraint 1, in Figure 8A.3.

FIGURE 8A.3

Mark's Bat Production Problem with Constraints 1 and 2

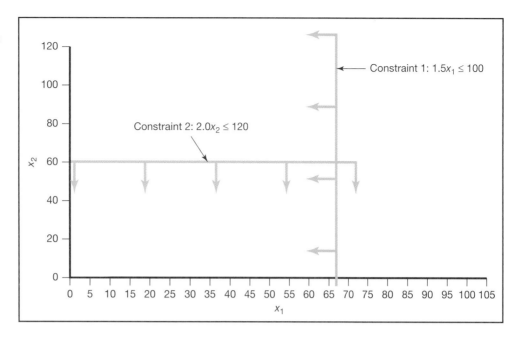

Constraint 3

Constraint 3 in functional form is

$$0.25x_1 + 0.5x_2 \leq 60$$

Constraint 3 has an upper boundary, since the constraint contains a less than or equal to sign. In addition, this upper bound is a line with a certain slope. The equation of this line is found easily by finding where the constraint crosses the x_1 and x_2 axes. These intercepts are found by setting one decision variable equal to zero and dividing both sides of the constraint by the coefficient of the other constraint and then performing the same operation for the other decision variable.

For example, let's allow decision variable x_1 to equal zero; the resulting equation becomes $x_2 \leq$ 120.00. Continuing with the same logic and allowing decision variable x_2 to equal zero, we find the resulting equation becomes

$$x_1 \leq 240.00$$

Therefore, the two points where constraint 3 intersects the $x1$ and $x2$ axes are (240, 0) and (0, 120). The equation for the line of the upper bound is then found by using these two numbers and simple algebra.

$$x_2 \leq 240 - 0.5x_1$$

It is graphed, along with constraints 1 and 2, in Figure 8A.4.

Constraint 4

Constraint 4 in functional form is

$$0.25x_1 + 0.25x_2 \leq 25$$

Constraint 4 has an upper boundary, since the constraint contains a less than or equal to sign. In addition, this upper bound is a line with a certain slope. The equation of this line is found easily by finding where the constraint crosses the x_1 and x_2 axes. These intercepts are found by setting one decision variable equal to zero and dividing both sides of the constraint by the coefficient of the other decision variable and then performing the same operation for the other decision variable.

For example, let's allow decision variable x_1 to equal zero, the resulting equation becomes $x_2 \leq$ 100.00. Continuing with the same logic and allowing decision variable x_2 to equal zero, the resulting

FIGURE 8A.4
Mark's Bat Production Problem with Constraints 1, 2, and 3

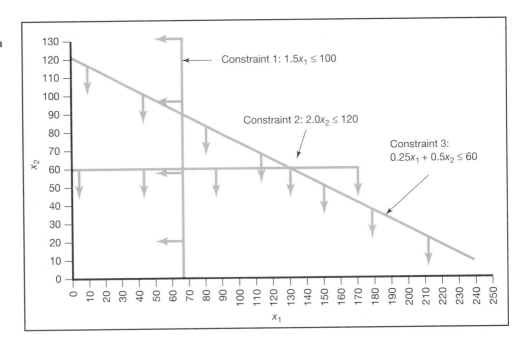

FIGURE 8A.5
Mark's Bat Production Problem with Constraints 1, 2, 3, and 4

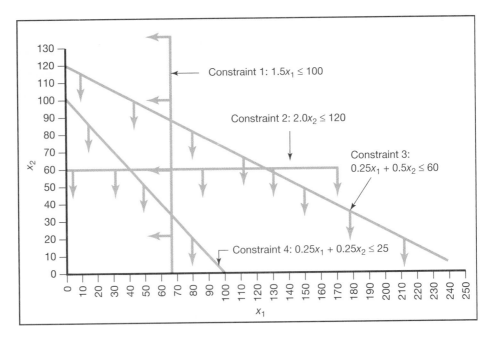

equation becomes $x_2 \leq 100.00$; therefore, the two points where constraint 3 intersects the x_1 and x_2 axes are (100, 0) and (0, 100). The equation for the line of the upper bound is then found by using these two numbers and simple algebra.

$$x_2 \leq 100 - 1.0x_1$$

It is graphed, along with constraints 1, 2, and 3, in Figure 8A.5.

Constraint 5

Constraint 5 in functional form is

$$x_1 \geq 30$$

One should take note that constraint 5 contains only decision variable x_1. Therefore, constraint 5 never intersects the x_2 axis. In addition, the decision variable x_2 can take on any value with regard to constraint 5.

Constraint 5 has a lower boundary, since the constraint contains a greater than or equal to sign. Since constraint 5 is in its simplest form, the constraint is graphed as in Figure 8A.6.

Step 3: Identify the Feasible Region Dictated by the Constraints

The next step in finding the LP model solution graphically is to identify the feasible region that is dictated by the constraints. The arrows on any of the constraint graphs (Figures 8A.2 through 8A.6) guide us in identifying the feasible region.

In Figure 8A.6, which figure contains all constraints for Mark's bat production problem, the feasible region is identified by following the arrows on each constraint and narrowing down the region of the graph where feasible solution points exist. This is the area bordered by constraints 1, 2, 4, and 5. This region is shaded in Figure 8A.7.

Identifying the feasible region dictated by the constraints is the third step in solving an LP problem graphically.

FIGURE 8A.6
Mark's Bat Production Problem with All Constraints

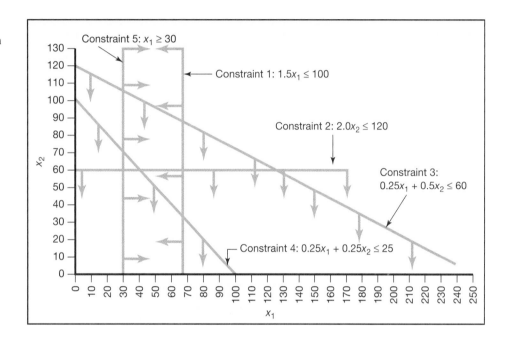

FIGURE 8A.7
Feasible Region Identification for Mark's Bat Production Problem

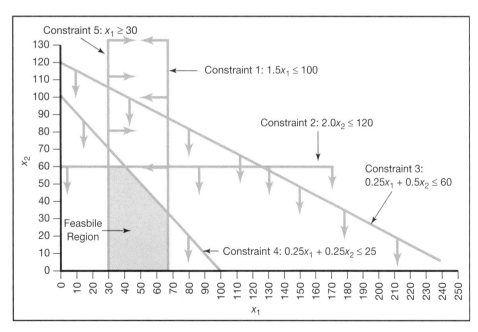

Step 4: Identify All Corner Point Feasible Solutions of the Feasible Region

Identifying the corner point feasible solutions of the feasible region is the fourth step in solving an LP problem graphically.

The next step in finding the LP model solution graphically is to identify the corner point feasible solutions. Since an LP model contains only linear relationships, the corner point feasible solutions must be found on the perimeter of the feasible region. Take a look at the shaded region of Figure 8A.7. This shaded region is referred to as the *feasible region*. The points where any two constraints intersect within the feasible region reveal a corner point feasible solution.

This text does not delve deeply into why only these corner points are part of the feasible solution set. However, since we are attempting to optimize by using linear relationships, the feasible region identified is considered a convex set. Therefore, mathematically speaking, the optimal solution to any convex set must lie on the solution set's boundary and most likely at a unique corner point. This text chooses to explain how each of the corner point feasible solutions is found to aid in the underlying geometric and algebraic layout of an LP problem. However, it is well known that this process is not necessary to obtain the optimum. For those wishing to omit this section, please skip to Figure 8A.9 and read the discussion on passing the objective function through the feasible region to obtain the optimum.

To find the exact corner points of the feasible region in Figure 8A.7, some basic algebra must be employed. In short, we need to find the coordinates (x_1, x_2) of where each constraint intersects another

FIGURE 8A.8
Corner Point Feasible Solutions to Mark's Bat Production Problem. Constraint 3 is not graphed, as it is not part of the feasible region

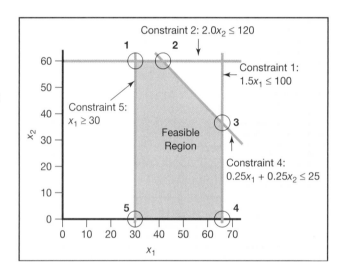

FIGURE 8A.9
Successive Objective Function Plots

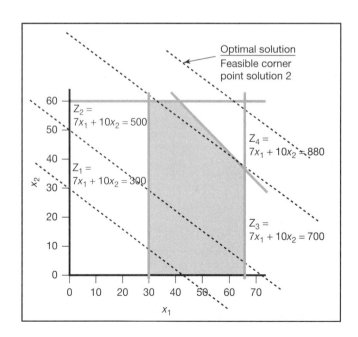

constraint over the feasible region. To accomplish this, let's first identify all corner point feasible solutions on a graph. Figure 8A.8 displays an enlarged view of the feasible region from Figure 8A.7.

The corner point feasible solutions are denoted by circles in Figure 8A.8. The coordinates of each of these corner points must be identified. The next section details how to determine the coordinates of the five corner point feasible solutions.

Determining Exact Corner Point Feasible Solutions

To find the exact corner points of the feasible region, the coordinates where each constraint intersects must be found.

In general, exact corner point feasible solution points are where constraints intersect on the boundary of the feasible region.

To find the exact corner points of the feasible region in Figure 8A.8, some basic algebra must be employed. In short, we need to find the coordinates (x_1, x_2) of where each constraint intersects another constraint over the feasible region.

Corner Point Feasible Solutions 4 and 5

Let's start with the obvious intersection points from Figure 8A.8. Corner point 5 intersects the x_1 axis at 30 and the x_2 axis at 0. Therefore, the coordinates for corner point feasible solution 5 are (30, 0). In turn, corner point 4 intersects the x_1 axis at $66.6\overline{6}$ and the x_2 axis at 0. Therefore, the coordinates for corner point feasible solution 4 are ($66.6\overline{6}$, 0). Mathematically speaking, this corner point feasible solution is allowed. With regard to Mark's bat production problem, one-third of a wooden bat would not be a feasible production amount. However, or this example and the entirety of this problem, fractions of bat production are allowed.

Corner Point Feasible Solution 1

Finding the coordinates of corner point feasible solution 1 is also simple. The coordinates are the intersection of two constraints. From Figure 8A.8, follow the two constraints that make up corner point feasible solution 1 (constraints 2 and 5) from the corner point to the respective axis. For example, follow constraint 5 down toward the x_1 axis and note the value at the intersection point of the constraint and the x_1 axis. This value is 30. Therefore, the x_1 coordinate of corner point feasible solution 1 is 30.

In turn, follow constraint 1 to the left towards the x_2 axis and note the value at the intersection point of the constraint and the x_2 axis. This value is 60. Therefore, the x_2 coordinate of corner point feasible solution 1 is 60. The coordinates for corner point feasible solution 1 are (30, 60).

Corner Point Feasible Solution 2

In order to find the coordinates for corner point feasible solution 2, the equations for the two intersecting constraints must be identified. It can be seen from Figure 8A.8 that constraint 2 and constraint 4 intersect at corner point feasible solution 2. The equations of constraints 2 and 4 are respectively as follows:

$$2.0x_2 \leq 120$$

$$0.25x_1 + 0.25x_2 \leq 25$$

To find the point at which these two equations intersect, the equations must be simultaneously solved. This can be accomplished in a number of ways. The author uses the method of substitution and solving for the intersection point. The following algebra and mathematical manipulations solve for the intersection point.

1: Replace each inequality with an equality sign:

$$2.0x_2 = 120$$

$$0.25x_1 + 0.25x_2 = 25$$

2: Solve for x_2 in constraint 2:

$$2.0x_2 = 120$$

$$x_2 = 60$$

3: Substitute the value of x_2 found in step 2 into constraint 4:

$$0.25x_1 + 0.25(60) = 25$$

and solve for x_1

$$0.25x_1 + 15 = 25$$

$$0.25x_1 = 10$$
$$x_1 = 40$$

Therefore, the coordinates for corner point feasible solution 2 are (40, 60).

Corner Point Feasible Solution 3

The process for finding the coordinates for corner point feasible solution 3 is the same as for corner point feasible solution 2. In order to find the coordinates, the equations for the two intersecting constraints must be identified. It can be seen from Figure 8A.8 that constraint 1 and constraint 4 intersect at corner point feasible solution 3. The equations of constraint 1 and 4 are respectively as follows:

$$1.5x_1 \leq 100$$
$$0.25x_1 + 0.25x_2 \leq 25$$

To find the point at which these two equations intersect, the equations must be simultaneously solved. This can be accomplished in a number of ways. The author uses the method of substitution and solving for the intersection point. The following algebra and mathematical manipulations solve for the intersection point.

1: Replace each inequality with an equality sign:

$$1.5x_1 = 100$$
$$0.25x_1 + 0.25x_2 = 25$$

2: Solve for x_2 in constraint 1.

$$1.5x_1 = 100$$
$$x_1 = 66.6\overline{6}$$

3: Substitute the value of x_1 found in step 2 into constraint 4:

$$0.25(66.6\overline{6}) + 0.25x_2 = 25$$

and solve for x_1:

$$16.6\overline{6} + 0.25x_2 = 25$$
$$0.25x_2 = 8.3\overline{3}$$
$$x_2 = 33.3\overline{3}$$

Therefore, the coordinates for corner point feasible solution 3 are $(66.6\overline{6}, 33.3\overline{3})$. Mathematically speaking, this corner point feasible solution is allowed. With regard to Mark's bat production problem, one-third of a wooden or aluminum bat would not be a feasible production amount. However, for this example and the entirety of this problem, fractions of bat production are allowed.

Summary of Corner Point Feasible Solution Coordinates

Table 8A.1 displays the coordinates of the five corner point feasible solutions. It should be noted from Table 8A.1 that all corner point feasible solutions are listed for this example.

Now that all the corner point feasible solutions are identified, an optimum solution can be found. Step 4 identifies the optimum solution by plotting a series of objective functions over the feasible region.

TABLE 8A.1
Corner Point Feasible Solution Coordinates

Corner point feasible solution	Coordinates (x_1, x_2)
Corner point 1	(30, 60)
Corner point 2	(40, 60)
Corner point 3	$(66.6\overline{6}, 33.3\overline{3})$.
Corner point 4	$(66.6\overline{6}, 0)$.
Corner point 5	(40, 0)

Step 5: Identify the Optimum Solution

This step calls for plotting a series of objective functions over the feasible region in order to identify the optimum solution. This means physically plotting successive objective functions starting at or near the origin and moving away from the origin on both axes until an optimum solution is identified. The optimal solution will be the last corner point feasible solution that the objective function intersects with before leaving the feasible region altogether.

It is not necessary to calculate the profit for each feasible solution. Instead we can select an arbitrary value for profit and identify all the feasible solutions (x_1, x_2) that yield the selected value. For example, what feasible solutions provide a profit of $300? The solution is given by the value of (x_1, x_2) in the feasible region that will make the objective function

$$7x_1 + 10x_2 = 300$$

This expression is simply the equation of the profit line where profit equals $300. Thus all feasible solution points (x_1, x_2) yielding a profit of $300 must be on the line. From "Determining Exact Corner Point Feasible Solutions," above, we learned how to graph a line such as the profit equation. We let $x_1 = 0$ and solve for x_2, with the resultant solution point at $(x_1 = 0, x_2 = 30)$. Similarly, by setting $x_2 = 0$ and solving for x_1, we find the resultant solution point is ($x_1 \approx 42.86, x_2 = 0$). The graph of this line is represented by Z_1 in Figure 8A.9.

Figure 8A.9 displays what step 4 produces. The dashed lines (labeled Z_1, Z_2, Z_3, Z_4) represent the successive objective function plots and the arrow identifies the optimum solution at different levels of profit. Z_1 represents the profit line at $300, Z_2 represents the profit line at $500, Z_3 represents the profit line at $700, and Z_4 represents the profit line at $880. The heart of this method lies in understanding the relationship between the feasible region, the corner point feasible solutions, and the objective function.

Objective Function Slope

Looking at Figure 8A.9 one notices that the profit lines are all parallel to each other and that profit increases the farther one moves away from the origin. These observations can be expressed algebraically as a line in *slope-intercept form*. If π represents profit, then the objective function is

$$\pi = 7x_1 + 10x_2$$

Solving for x_2 in terms of x_1 and π, we obtain

$$x_2 = \frac{-7}{10}x_1 + \frac{\pi}{10}$$

This equation is in *slope-intercept form* for a linear equation relating x_1 to x_2. The coefficient of x_1, $-7/10$, is the slope of the line, and the term $\pi/10$ is the intercept.

Although the objective function plotting method is effective, it is obtuse in its actual manifestation. A far easier method for solving smaller LP problems once the corner point feasible solutions have been identified is available. This method consists of calculating the objective function value by plugging in each of the corner point feasible solutions (see Step 6, below).

In this example, the number of feasible corner point solutions is small enough that we can enumerate the profit generated from each pair of feasible corner points. Let's begin with the maximization case and at the origin, i.e. (0, 0). In short, as the objective function passes through the feasible region, the objective function's value increases until the objective function entirely leaves the feasible region. The arrow in Figure 8A.9 demarcates this point and the solution to the LP problem.

In sum, Figure 8A.9 displays the essence of the graphical method of solving an LP model. The relationship between the objective function, the constraints, the feasible region, the corner point feasible solutions, and the optimal solution itself is manifested in Figure 8A.9.

Step 6: An Alternative to Passing the Objective Function through the Feasible Region

In the case of a maximization LP, the corner point feasible solution that produces the largest objective function value is defined as the LP optimum.

Enumeration of the feasible corner point solutions to find profit works well when the LP has a small number (i.e., five to ten) of feasible corner point solutions. We will find profit for one feasible corner point solution now. Given $x_1 = 30$ and $x_2 = 60$, the objective function value is

$$Z = \$7x_1 + \$10x_2 = (\$7 \times 30) + (\$10 \times 60) = \$810$$

The same method is used to calculate the value of the objective function for each of the corner point feasible solutions. Table 8A.2 displays the objective values for each corner point feasible solution.

TABLE 8A.2
Objective Function Values

Corner point feasible solution	Coordinates (x_1, x_2)	Objective function value
Corner point 1	(30, 60)	$810
Corner point 2	(40, 60)	$880
Corner point 3	(66.6̄6̄, 33.3̄3̄)	$800
Corner point 4	(66.6̄6̄, 0)	$466.6̄6̄
Corner point 5	(40, 0)	$280

As in step 4, the largest value from the last column in Table 8.2, $880, denotes the optimal solution to the LP problem objective function. The coordinates $x_1 = 40$ and $x_2 = 60$ produce the objective value of $880 and are the true answers to Mark's bat production problem. In other words, based on the LP formulation given, Mark should produce 40 Wooden Wonder bats and 60 Aluminum Ally bats. Mark would garner a profit off $880 at these production levels and is the maximum profit attainable, given the profit per bat amounts and constraints.

Looking back at the section of Results & Sensitivity Analysis in Excel & Figure 8.20 it should be noted that the results presented here are the same as those calculated and presented by Excel's Solver.

Chapter **Nine**

Project Management: PERT/CPM

Learning Objectives

After completing this chapter, students will be able to:

1. Understand how to plan, monitor, and control projects with the use of PERT.
2. Determine earliest start, earliest finish, latest start, latest finish, and slack times

for each activity along with the total project completion time.

3. Reduce total project time at the least total cost by crashing the network, using manual or linear programming techniques.
4. Understand the important role of software in project management.

Chapter Outline

Business Decision Modeling in Action—CPM, Project Scheduling, and Claims Litigation

Basis for Using CPM in Construction Claims Litigation

The critical path method (CPM) scheduling requirements of federal government agencies, the growing use of CPM scheduling on large projects, and the general recognition of the usefulness of CPM scheduling in project management and planning elevated it to an accepted standard in the construction industry. Consequently, courts and contract dispute boards have become willing to accept CPM scheduling as a tool for identifying the existence and causes of disruption and delays on projects.

Court Recognition of CPM Techniques

The courts have recognized and accepted CPM scheduling as a tool in construction claims litigation since the mid-1970s. Around 1974, significant advancements have been made in all phases of CPM analysis on contract disputes.1 For example, in *Haney v. United States*, 676 F.2d 584 (1982), the court found that:

> The Government welcomed Haney's use of CPM as a planning and management tool …
>
> At trial, plaintiff [Haney] presented expert testimony which established, by CPM analysis,
>
> the cumulative effect of each delay that occurred on the project.

Thus, CPM scheduling became a tool that could help establish the effect of delays on a project. CPM's ability to establish a baseline in measuring the acceleration or delay of a project is key to its use in litigation proceedings. Courts generally accept a planned completion date that is provided by a CPM schedule and agreed on by both parties to a construction contract as the basis for the determination of delay or acceleration.

Bar Charts versus CPM

Over time, the use of CPM in litigation proceedings has become more sophisticated. The use of CPM scheduling has become the preferred method of proving and assessing delays, as demonstrated by several state court decisions.

For example, in *Al Johnson Constr. Co. v. United States*, 854 F.2d 467, 470 (Fed. Cir. 1988), the Court of Appeals for the Federal Circuit supported the Board of Contract Appeal's decision that had criticized

> … the "bar chart" appellant [Al Johnson Construction Co.] provided … lacked a "critical
>
> path," a favorite device with present day fact finders in contract disputes.

Again, in *H. W. Detwiler Co.*, ASBCA No. 35,327, 89-2 BCA ¶ 21,612 (1989), the Board provided similar criticism of the inability of a contractor's bar chart schedule to provide the necessary support for its claim:

> Detwiler opted to schedule work on a bar graph through which it reported both its
>
> scheduled and actual progress. Because Detwiler chose to use a bar graph to assess
>
> its progress, its proposed schedule was necessarily general and somewhat vague with
>
> respect to planning discrete construction activities.

Establishing Cause and Effect and the Dynamic Nature of CPM Networks

By 1985, CPM was accepted in the courts as a tool for establishing the cause-and-effect relationship necessary for proving damages. In several cases, the courts imposed requirements on the maintenance of the CPM network in order for damages to be proved.[2,3] This requirement, of course, implies that a well-maintained CPM network may be sufficient to prove damages, providing that liability is established for delay.

Also in 1985, the courts recognized the dynamic nature of CPM. The United States Claims Court recognized that control of a project and the time extension process were lost if the parties to a contract did not update and maintain the CPM network to reflect delays and time extensions.[4]

Types of Claims Where CPM is Used

Other litigation issues related to CPM, such as ownership of float, concurrent delay, buy-back time, sequence changes, and automatic time extension, became recognized by courts as issues to be debated in claims cases. These issues are built on the foundational acceptance of CPM as a tool in construction claims in the 1970s and 1980s.

Without the basic recognition of CPM in the courts, these derivative issues may never have been considered. Presently, the use of CPM in construction litigation is firmly in place in the legal system. Three general claim categories, which utilize and rely on CPM scheduling, are delay, disruption, and acceleration claims. The advent of personal computers and CPM software programs has made the CPM scheduling technique economically feasible for projects of even the smallest nature.

Endnotes

Wickwire, Jon M., Thomas Driscoll, and Stephen B. Hurlbut. *Construction Scheduling: Preparation, Liability, and Claims*. New York: John Wiley & Sons, 1991, p. 224.

Preston-Brady Co., VABCA Nos. 1892, 1991, 2555, 87-1 BCA ¶ 19,649 (1987).

Titan Mountain States Construction Corp., ASBCA Nos. 22,617, 22,930, 23,095, 23,188, 85-1 BCA ¶ 17,931 (1985).

In *Fortec Constructors v. United States*, 9 Cl. Ct. 490, 504-08 (1985).

Optimal Information Area

The Associated General Contractors of America. *The Use of CPM in Construction: A Manual for General Contractors and the Construction Industry*. Washington, DC: The Associated General Contractors of America, 1976.

Barba, Evans M,. and Judah Lifschitz, Esq. "Schedule Delay Analysis: Linking Liability to Damages." 8th Annual Construction SuperConference, 1993.

"Contractor Entitled to Compensation for Government-Caused Delays, Less Time Spent on Contractor-Caused, Concurrent Delays." *Construction Litigation Reporter*, vol. 12, no. 2 (February 1991), pp. 41–43.

Gavin, Donald G., Esq., and Robert J. Smith, Esq. "Targeting Construction Claims by Contractors Against Owners." 5th Annual Construction SuperConference, New York, March 1990.

Jervis, Bruce, Esq., ed. "As-Built Schedule Fails to Prove Delay Claim." Construction Claims Monthly, 14, no. 9 (September, 1992), p. 4–5.

Jervis, Bruce, Esq., ed., "As-Planned CPM Schedule Not Conclusive on Delay Impact." *Construction Claims Monthly*, vol. 11, no. 12 (December, 1989), p. 2.

Jervis, Bruce, Esq., ed. "Contractor Must Prove Feasibility of Intended Early Completion." *Construction Claims Monthly*, vol. 14, no. 11 (November 1992), p. 4.

Jervis, Bruce, Esq., ed. "CPM Schedule Fails to Prove Entitlement to Extension." *Construction Claims Monthly*, vol. 11, no. 5 (May 1989), p. 4.

Jervis, Bruce, Esq., ed. "Delayed Work Was Off the Critical Path." *Construction Claims Monthly*, vol. 11, no. 7 (July 1992), p. 4–5.

Jervis, Bruce, Esq., ed. "Establishing the Cause and Effect of Delay." *Construction Claims Monthly*, vol. 13, no. 7 (July 1991), p. 1, 7.

Jervis, Bruce, Esq., ed. "Flawed CPM Schedules Lacked Credibility." *Construction Claims Monthly*, vol. 15, no. 6 (June 1993), p. 2.

Wickwire, Jon M., Thomas J. Driscoll, and Stephen B. Hurlbut. *Construction Scheduling: Preparation, Liability, and Claims*. New York: John Wiley & Sons, 1991.

PROJECT MANAGEMENT: PERT/CPM

Introduction

This chapter investigates the area of project management. Two project management techniques are presented, the critical path method (CPM) and the program evaluation and review technique (PERT). Spreadsheets are used to develop the two concepts.

Definition of a Project

A project can be defined
as a coordinated effort to
achieve a goal within a
fixed period of time.

A project can be defined as a coordinated effort to achieve a goal within a fixed period of time. In addition, projects have recognizable attributes, such as

- A goal.
- A fixed time frame.
- Required resources.
- Requires monitoring and coordination.

Almost all of us have assumed the responsibility for the completion of some type of project. Whether that project is complex, like planning a remodeling project for your home, or as simple as producing a research paper for a college course, successful completion of any project requires organization, planning, control, and leadership.

Large projects, such as software development or electronics prototyping, tend to use project management software such as Microsoft Project to analyze tasks. However, even small projects present managers with an abundance of details, which must be kept track of.

Use of Spreadsheets for Project Management

Two common project
management techniques are
critical path method (CPM)
and program evaluation and
review technique (PERT).

Although large companies almost exclusively use some type of project management software, smaller companies may not have the resources to purchase and train employees to use such software. To ameliorate this situation, spreadsheets have been employed as an alternative to expensive complicated project management software.

This chapter describes the use of spreadsheets for project management, specifically, the critical path method (CPM) and the program evaluation and review technique (PERT).

PLANNING, SCHEDULING, AND CONTROL

PERT/CPM allows any
project to be broken down
into component activities
requiring varying amounts
of time and a sequential
completion order.

Planning, scheduling, and control are considered to be basic managerial functions. These functions may be called basic, but on a large-scale project the coordination of these functions is very complex. PERT/CPM allows any project to be broken down into component activities requiring varying amounts of time and a sequential completion order. The technique provides a framework for project planning, scheduling, and control in the face of uncertainty.

Far more than the technical benefits, PERT/CPM provides a focus around which managers can brainstorm. It is a great communication medium by which thinkers and planners at one level

DEVELOPMENT OF PERT/CPM

CPM/PERT, or network analysis, as the technique is sometimes called, developed along two parallel streams, one industrial and the other military.

CPM

CPM was developed in the late 1950s by M. Walker of E. I. du Pont de Nemours & Co. and J. Kelly of Remington Rand. The method was first applied to the construction of a new DuPont chemical plant. The method was further tested during a maintenance shutdown at a DuPont plant in Louisville, Kentucky. CPM reduced unproductive time during the maintenance shutdown by around 25 percent—a significant reduction at the time.

PERT

The Special Projects Office of the U.S. Navy, in conjunction with Lockheed Missile Systems and business consultants Booz, Allen, and Hamilton, devised PERT during the Polaris missile program. Many of the tasks required for the development of the missile system had never been attempted before and the time to complete the tasks was uncertain.

PERT was designed to aid in estimating the probability of completing a project by a given deadline. The times to perform individual activities of a project are actually random variables and affect the final project completion date in different ways.

PERT/CPM AND GANTT CHARTS

Many times, PERT and CPM are referred to as the same concept or technique. Over time, PERT and CPM have become one term, PERT/CPM or CPM/PERT. The basic concept of PERT/CPM is the brains behind most of the commercially available project management software.

Henry Gantt, during World War I, developed Gantt charts as a graphical display for production control. These charts are usually coupled with PERT/CPM techniques as a visual way to manage projects.

OPTIMAL INFORMATION AREA

Jewell, Thomas. *A Systems Approach to Civil Engineering Planning and Design*. New York: Harper and Row, 1986.

Antill, James M., and Ronald W. Woodhead (contributor). *Critical Path Methods in Construction Practice*, 4th ed. New York: John Wiley & Sons, 1990.

---

of managers can communicate their ideas, doubts, and uncertainty to another level of managers. In addition, it is a useful tool for evaluating the performance of individuals and teams.

Project Management Questions and PERT/CPM

PERT/CPM answers questions regarding how long a project will take to be completed, what risks are involved, which are the critical activities, andwhether the project is on schedule, behind schedule, or ahead of schedule.

Although there are many variations of PERT/CPM, all are useful in planning costs, scheduling manpower, and organizing tasks. Whichever variation is used, PERT/CPM techniques can answer the following important questions:

How long will the entire project take to be completed?

What are the risks involved?

Which are the critical activities or tasks in the project that could delay the entire project if they were not completed on time?

Is the project on schedule, behind schedule, or ahead of schedule?

If the project has to be finished earlier than planned, what is the best way to do this at the least cost?

Any manager who has worked on any type of project has faced these questions or questions similar to them. The next section presents a framework for answering these questions and develops the PERT/CPM technique.

A Framework for PERT and CPM

A key concept in CPM/PERT is that a project can be broken down into a small set of activities or components that must be accomplished in a particular order. This particular order, referred to as the critical path, is made up of a set of tasks that make up the longest path through the activity network and control the entire project.

PERT/CPM generally consists of five steps.

There are five steps that make up the framework for conducting PERT/CPM analysis:

1. Identify all significant activities and/or tasks.
2. Develop precedence relationships among the activities.
3. Create the project network connecting all the activities and assigning time and/or cost estimates to each activity.
4. Find the critical path of the network, i.e., the longest time path through the network.
5. Analyze the critical path and the resulting project schedule to help plan, schedule, monitor, and control the project.

A goal of any project manager is a project's smooth completion. The critical path identified by PERT/CPM can aid in this smooth completion.

A goal of any project manager is a project's smooth completion. The critical path identified by PERT/CPM can aid in this smooth completion. A manager has a distinct advantage, as the "critical" activities can be identified and assigned to responsible persons. By concentrating on the few activities that determine the fate of the entire project, management resources can then be optimally employed.

Noncritical activities can be replanned and/or rescheduled and resources for them can be reallocated flexibly, without affecting the whole project.

A PERT/CPM EXAMPLE

A senior business decision modeling case study project team has developed a schedule of activities for their project, using their best estimate of completion times. The schedule is listed in Table 9.1. The Business Decision Modeling Group has a number of other different class projects they are working on concurrently. The group need a formal procedure for planning, monitoring, and controlling this project.

The Business Decision Modeling Group wish to use PERT/CPM to assist them in organizing and completing the project.

Defining the Network and Developing Precedence Relationships

When nodes represent project activities, the network design is referred to as an activity-on-node (AON) network.

The author represents project activities as nodes. Directed arcs connect the nodes. This type of network design is referred to as an activity-on-node (AON) network. Arcs in this type of network indicate precedence relationships between the activities or nodes. The following set of questions is very useful for a manager to ask when preparing a network.

Is this a start activity?
Is this a finish activity?
What activity precedes this?
What activity follows this?
What activity is concurrent with this?

Table 9.1 summarizes a set of activities and the precedence relationships between the activities. In most cases, managers must create an activity table themselves. The aforementioned questions will assist a manager in creating an activity table of the type shown in Table 9.1.

Activity predecessors are defined as activities that must be completed before the successor activity can start.

In Figure 9.1, activity A is an immediate predecessor of activity B. Activities F and G are immediate successors of activity E. The terms *predecessor* and *successor* will be used throughout the rest of this chapter.

TABLE 9.1
Activities for Business Decision Modeling Group Project

No.	Activity	Activity description	Time, days	Immediate predecessors
1	A	Contact client	4	
2	B	Write proposal	2	A
3	C	Obtain approval	3	B
4	D	Complete computer programming	12	C
5	E	Complete industry literature review	10	
6	F	Write final draft	6	D, E
7	G	Complete oral report	5	D, E

FIGURE 9.1
Activity-on-node Network for Business Decision Modeling Group Project

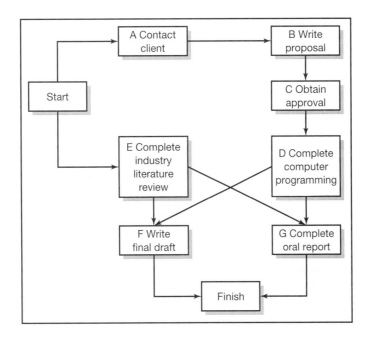

Take note of the start and finish nodes. Table 9.1 does not list start and finish nodes. PERT/CPM techniques require that all projects have a unique start and finish activity. That is why the network diagram includes a unique start and finish point. Otherwise, the Business Decision Modeling project would contain two starting points and two ending points. In this example, the start and finish nodes are actually artificial to the problem to facilitate PERT/CPM criteria.

Finding the Critical Path

Finding the critical path through the network is one of the main goals of PERT/CPM. To find the critical path, we make a forward pass through the network to determine each activity's earliest start and finish time. Overall, the forward pass will result in the earliest time the project can be finished.

> Finding the critical path through the network is one of the main goals of PERT/CPM.

Subsequently, a backward pass through the network is completed to determine the latest time that each activity can start and finish without delaying the completion of the project.

The critical path is the longest path through the project network. This longest path directly corresponds to the earliest finish time of the project. The critical path contains the activities that must be completed to finish the project by the earliest finish time. This may result in certain activities in the network that then can be sped up or slowed down in coordination with the start and finish of these critical path activities.

> The critical path is the longest path through the project network.

One of the largest benefits of PERT/CPM is the ability to identify this critical path. Managers must make themselves aware of the critical path and plan accordingly so delays can be avoided, activities can be coordinated, and resources allocated in an efficient manner.

The Forward Pass

The first step in determining the critical path is to determine the earliest time an activity can begin. This is referred to as the *earliest start time* and will be denoted ES. The earliest time an activity can finish, the *earliest finish time*, is also needed to determine the critical path and will be denoted EF. The earliest time an activity can finish is the earliest start time of the activity plus the time it takes the activity to be completed.

> Completing the forward pass is the first step in determining the critical path.

Earliest Start and Earliest Finish Times

The following relationship can be established between earliest start times and earliest finish times:

> The earliest time an activity can begin is referred to as the *earliest start time* and is denoted ES.

$$EF_i = ES_i + t_i$$

For start activities, the following is true, since $ES_i = 0$:

$$EF_{start} = 0 + t_{start}$$

The earliest time an activity can finish is referred to as the *earliest finish time* and is denoted EF.

By following this logic, a table of activities, earliest start times, and earliest finish times can be created. Subsequently, the earliest finish time for the entire project can then be determined from the EF times. Figure 9.2 displays this type of table for the Business Decision Modeling Group project in spreadsheet form.

Figure 9.2 contains the individual activity ES and EF times as well as the overall earliest finish time for the project. Columns F and G contain the ES and EF times, while cell G11 contains the earliest finish time for the project, 27 days.

The formulas used to create the ES and EF are patterned after the equations set up earlier. However, it should be noted that precedence activities for each activity and each unique project must be taken into account in calculating ES and EF times. This issue will be discussed next along with an example of the Excel formulas used in the Business Decision Modeling Group project PERT/CPM problem.

Figure 9.3 displays the formulas used to create the ES and EF times for the Business Decision Modeling Group project PERT/CPM network.

Take note that the ES times for activities 1 and 5 are zero (cells F4 and F8, Figure 9.3). These activities have no immediate predecessors; therefore, their ES times are 0. Also, take note that if an activity has more than one predecessor, a maximum of those predecessors' EF times is used as the ES time for the activity. Refer to cells F9 and F10 in Figure 9.3.

In addition, if there happens to be more than one activity preceding the finish activity, the maximum of the EF times of those preceding activities must be used as the EF time for the entire project (refer to cell G11, Figure 9.3).

The Backward Pass

Completing the backward pass is the second step in determining the critical path.

The next step in determining the critical path is to determine the latest time an activity can begin. This is referred to as the latest start time and will be denoted LS. The latest time an activity can finish is also needed to determine the critical path and will be denoted LF. The latest time an activity can start is the latest finish time of the activity minus the time it takes the activity to be completed.

Latest Start and Latest Finish Times

The latest time an activity can begin is referred to as the *latest start time* and is denoted LS.

The following relationship can be established for latest start times and latest finish times:

$$LS_i = LF_i - t_i$$

For start activities, the following is true, since LF_i = project completion time

$$LS_{start} = \text{project completion time} - t_{start}$$

FIGURE 9.2 Forward Pass Table for Business Decision Modeling Project

	A	B	C	D	E	F	G
1				Precedence	Time		
2	No.	Activity	Activity Description	Activities	in Days	ES	EF
3			Start	--	--	--	--
4	1	A	Contact Client	--	4	0	4
5	2	B	Write Proposal	A	2	4	6
6	3	C	Obtain Approval	B	3	6	9
7	4	D	Complete Computer Programming	C	12	9	21
8	5	E	Complete Industry Literature Review	--	10	0	10
9	6	F	Write Final Draft	D, E	6	21	27
10	7	G	Complete Oral Report	D, E	5	21	26
11			Finish	F, G	----	----	27

FIGURE 9.3 Forward Pass Excel Formulas for Business Decision Modeling Project

PERT_CPM.xls

	A	B	C	D	E	F	G
1				Precedence	Time		
2	No.	Activity	Activity Description	Activities	in Days	ES	EF
3			Start	--	--	--	--
4	1	A	Contact Client	--	4	0	=F4+E4
5	2	B	Write Proposal	A	2	=G4	=F5+E5
6	3	C	Obtain Approval	B	3	=G5	=F6+E6
7	4	D	Complete Computer Programming	C	12	=G6	=F7+E7
8	5	E	Complete Industry Literature Review	--	10	0	=F8+E8
9	6	F	Write Final Draft	D, E	6	=MAX(G7:G8)	=F9+E9
10	7	G	Complete Oral Report	D, E	5	=MAX(G7:G8)	=F10+E10
11			Finish	F, G	---	---	=MAX(G9:G10)

The latest time an activity can finish is referred to as the *latest finish time* and is denoted LF.

For the final activity (or activities), the LF time is the project completion time computed from the forward pass. The LF time for an earlier activity is the minimum of the LS times for all activities in the precedence structure that follow that activity.

By following this logic, a table of activities, ES, EF, LS, LF, and slack times can be created. Slack is defined as the difference between the LS and ES times. Figure 9.4 displays this type of table for the Business Decision Modeling Group project in spreadsheet form.

Figure 9.4 contains the individual activity ES, EF, LS, LF, and slack times for the project. Slack is computed as follows:

Slack is the amount of time an activity can be delayed without affecting the completion time of the project.

$$\text{Slack} = LF_i - EF_i \quad \text{or} \quad \text{Slack} = LS_i - ES_i$$

Either method gives the same slack number. This is a good way to check if your starting and finishing times are correct. Slack is the amount of time an activity can be delayed without affecting the completion time of the project.

The formulas used to create the LS and LF are patterned after the equations set up earlier. However, it should be noted that precedence activities for each activity and each unique project must be taken into account in calculating LS and LF times. This issue will be discussed next along with an example of the Excel formulas used in the Business Decision Modeling Group project PERT/CPM problem.

Figure 9.5 displays the formulas used to create all variables of interest in the Business Decision Modeling Group project PERT/CPM network.

The Critical Path and Slack

As mentioned earlier, the critical path is the longest path through the project network. It consists of the set of activities that, if delayed, would delay the completion of the entire project. The results of the forward and backward pass identify the critical path, specifically, those

FIGURE 9.4 Forward and Backward Pass Table for Business Decision Modeling Project

PERT_CPM.xls

	A	B	C	D	E	F	G	H	I	J
1				Precedence	Time					
2	No.	Activity	Activity Description	Activities	in Days	ES	EF	LS	LF	Slack
3			Start	--	--	--	--			
4	1	A	Contact Client	--	4	0	4	0	4	0
5	2	B	Write Proposal	A	2	4	6	4	6	0
6	3	C	Obtain Approval	B	3	6	9	6	9	0
7	4	D	Complete Computer Programming	C	12	9	21	9	21	0
8	5	E	Complete Industry Literature Review	--	10	0	10	11	21	11
9	6	F	Write Final Draft	D, E	6	21	27	21	27	0
10	7	G	Complete Oral Report	D, E	5	21	26	22	27	1
11			Finish	F, G	---	---	27	---	---	---

FIGURE 9.5 **Forward/Backward Pass Excel Formulas for Business Decision Modeling Project**

No.	Activity	Activity Description	Precedence Activities	Time in Days	ES	EF	LS	LF	Slack
		Start	--	--	--	--			
1	A	Contact Client	--	4	0	=F4+E4	=I4-E4	=H5	=H4-F4
2	B	Write Proposal	A	2	=G4	=F5+E5	=I5-E5	=H6	=H5-F5
3	C	Obtain Approval	B	3	=G5	=F6+E6	=I6-E6	=H7	=H6-F6
4	D	Complete Computer Programming	C	12	=G6	=F7+E7	=I7-E7	=MIN(H9,H10)	=H7-F7
5	E	Complete Industry Literature Review	--	10	0	=F8+E8	=I8-E8	=MIN(H9,H10)	=H8-F8
6	F	Write Final Draft	D, E	6	=MAX(G7:G8)	=F9+E9	=I9-E9	=G11	=H9-F9
7	G	Complete Oral Report	D, E	5	=MAX(G7:G8)	=F10+E10	=I10-E10	=G11	=H10-F10
		Finish	F, G	---	---	=MAX(G9:G10)	---	---	---

activities that do not have any slack. This is equivalent to saying the critical activities have equal latest start and earliest start times (or equal latest finish and earliest finish times).

Figure 9.6 displays the critical path as bold lines in the network. The critical path for the Business Decision Modeling Group project is as follows:

$$A \rightarrow B \rightarrow C \rightarrow D \rightarrow F$$

If any of these activities do not start by their earliest start time, the project will not finish in the estimated time frame. Even though the example presented here has only one critical path, it should be noted that it is possible for a network to have more than one critical path.

Noncritical activities in the project can be identified by the presence of slack. Slack is the amount of time by which the start of an activity can be delayed without delaying the entire project. For the Business Decision Modeling Group project, it can be seen that activities E and G have 11 days and 1 day of slack, respectively. A manager could delay the start of activity E by up to 11 days and activity G by 1 day and still keep the entire project on schedule.

It must be noted that when any activity is delayed, the delay changes the nature of the future activities in the network. Specifically, there is a domino effect; as activities are delayed, future activities will be delayed and overall any slack in the system will be reduced.

GANTT CHARTS AND EXCEL

The spreadsheet methodology presented here works very well for smaller projects. However, the process becomes unwieldy when individual formulas must be built for each unique project and/or activity. For large projects, commercial software packages, such as Microsoft Project,

FIGURE 9.6
Critical Path for Business Decision Modeling Group Project

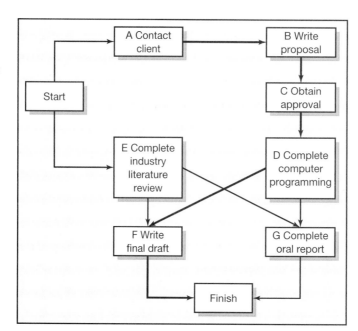

are a must. One of the benefits of using commercial project management software is the graphical output the software produces. One type of graphical output common to these software packages is a Gantt chart.

Gantt charts are a popular means for displaying a project's scheduled activities.

Gantt charts are a popular means for displaying a project's scheduled activities. Project managers find Gantt charts very useful for visualizing activity start times, activity end times, and the length of the project. Figure 9.7 displays the Gantt chart for the Business Decision Modeling Group project.

From Figure 9.7, it is very obvious, if all start times are met, that the project will be completed in 27 days. It is also very easy to see which activities constitute the critical path. The critical path is seen as any activity whose bar on the bar chart is bounded or covered at both ends. For example, notice that the activity Write Proposal is bounded on the left by the activity Contact Client and on the right by the activity Obtain Agreement.

Note that the activity Complete Industry Literature Review is not bounded on either the left or right by any activity. In addition, this is not the case for the first activity and last activity, as only one end of the bar will be bounded or covered.

Drawbacks to Gantt Charts

Although very useful as a visual aid, Gantt charts do not show interdependencies between activities.

Although very useful as a visual aid, Gantt charts do have some drawbacks. Gantt charts do not show interdependencies between activities. Questions regarding delay of activities are not answered easily by Gantt charts, as a result of their inability to show interdependencies.

Creating Gantt Charts in Excel

The Gantt chart in Figure 9.7 is fairly simple to create in a spreadsheet program such as Excel. The chart is a stacked horizontal bar chart. These are the steps for creating a Gantt chart in Excel:

1. From the forward and backward pass table, select the columns corresponding to activity name, time to complete, and earliest start time (columns B, D, and E in Figure 9.4). *Note:* You may wish to select only the actual activity names and raw data at first and format the chart later.

2. Select the Insert menu and click on Chart. The menu in Figure 9.8 will appear.

3. Figure 9.8 is the first menu in a number of menus that Excel's Chart Wizard will prompt you with. Take note that the Bar Chart type from the left-hand dialog box and the Chart sub-type of stacked horizontal (see arrows in the figure) must be chosen by the creator.

4. Click on the Next button three times, following the instructions in each dialog box. Take note that the creator can customize the chart, as appropriate, by using the menu options in each dialog box.

5. After clicking the Next button three times, the menu in Figure 9.9 will appear. Click on the "As new sheet" button and name the chart accordingly, e.g., Gantt Chart.

6. The chart that Chart Wizard has created will not look exactly like a Gantt chart yet. To create a true Gantt chart, the order in which the bars in the bar graph are listed must be

FIGURE 9.7
Gantt Chart for the Business Decision Modeling Group Project

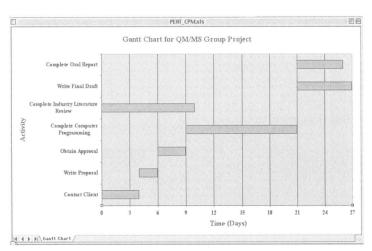

FIGURE 9.8
Chart Wizard Menu 1,
Chart Type

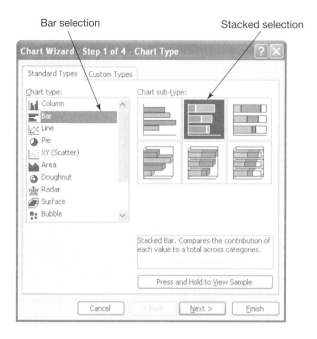

FIGURE 9.9 **Chart Wizard Menu 2, Chart Location**

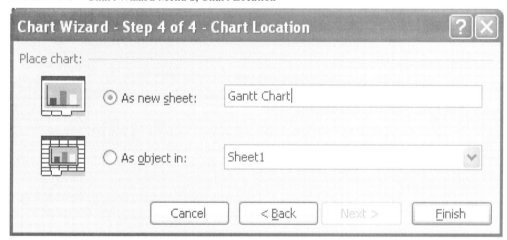

reversed and the bar patterns must be changed. To reverse the bars and change the bar patterns use the following steps:

a. In the bar chart, click on the bars representing the ES times (usually denoted as Series 2). A formula resembling the formula in Figure 9.10 will appear.

b. In the formula bar, change the very last number to a 1 (see arrow, Figure 9.10).

c. In the bar chart, double-click on the bars representing the ES times and select the Patterns option (see Figure 9.11). Click the None button under both the Border and Area options.

The Gantt chart can now be customized, as the creator deems appropriate, using standard Excel charting commands.

DEVELOPING A PROBABILISTIC PERT NETWORK

One goal of PERT is to incorporate probabilities of completing activities into the network. PERT was essentially developed for projects where the time to perform each individual activity is a random variable. In turn, these individual random variables combine to make the final completion of the project a random variable.

FIGURE 9.10 **Chart Formula Bar**

FIGURE 9.11
Format Data Series Menu

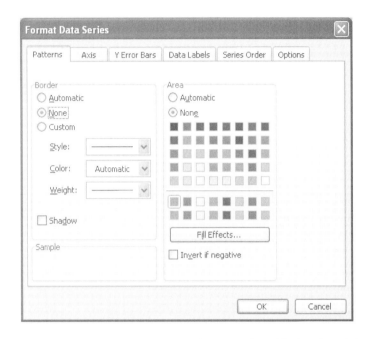

One goal of PERT is to incorporate probabilities of completing activities into the network.

From the forward and backward passes, the critical path and the total completion time for the project was determined. However, this final completion time is a static or point estimate. To develop a probabilistic network, probability estimates of completion times for each activity must be estimated.

Estimating Activity Completion Times and Distributions

In reality, probabilities of completion times most likely will not be available. However, a manager can estimate a distribution of completion times. By combining these individual completion time distributions, a distribution can be estimated for the final project completion time. Two parameters are needed to estimate a distribution: a measure for the center of the distribution and a measure of the variability of the distribution.

In many cases, we will not know accurately how long each activity will take. Therefore, a variant of PERT, the PERT 3 Estimate Approach, can be used in these cases. We assume that three estimates are available for the time taken by each activity: an optimistic approach, a most likely approach, and a pessimistic approach.

PERT and the Beta Distribution

The probability distribution for the time taken by each activity is a beta distribution.

We further assume that the probability distribution for the time taken by each activity is a beta distribution. (The beta distribution has a long right tail, reflecting the fact that there are more ways for an activity to be delayed than for it to be sped up). From these three estimates, we can calculate the mean and variance of the corresponding beta distribution as follows:

Activity Variance Calculations

Statistically the variance for each activity can be estimated by using the following formula:

$$\text{Activity variance} = \left(\frac{\text{most pessimistic} - \text{most optimistic}}{6} \right)^2$$

The variance of the final project completion time is computed by adding the variances of all the activities along the critical path.

To be more statistically accurate, the expected completion time for each activity should be used instead of the most likely value.

The variance of the final project completion time is computed by adding the variances of all the activities along the critical path. The standard deviation is then found by taking a square root of the variance number along the critical path.

Expected Activity Completion Time Calculations

To be more statistically accurate, the expected completion time for each activity should be used instead of the most likely value. Expected completion time is calculated as follows:

$$\text{Expected completion time} = \frac{\text{most pessimistic} + [(4) \times (\text{most likely})] + \text{most optimistic}}{6}$$

Figure 9.12 displays a modified forward and backward pass Excel spreadsheet with estimated activity completion times, including measurements for optimistic, pessimistic, activity variance, and final project variance.

On the basis of these values, PERT will use an activity network to calculate a mean finishing time along with a variance about that finishing time. Once these values have been calculated, the final completion time is the sum of each of the individual activity expected completion times. Figure 9.13 displays the formulas associated with the probabilistic PERT problem presented earlier.

Critical Assumptions about PERT

Two critical assumptions behind probabilistic PERT problems are (1) activity times are independent of each other and (2) a critical path is always the longest path in the network.

There are two critical assumptions behind probabilistic PERT problems:

1. Activity times are independent of each other.
2. A critical path is always the longest path in the network, no matter how the activity lengths turn out.

Unfortunately, these assumptions are very stringent. A manager must be careful when using any canned software package, for it hides these assumptions very well.

Statistical Questions about Expected Completion Times

From the normal distribution, quantiles of the finishing time can be calculated.

The overall expected completion time is assumed to be normally distributed. From the normal distribution, quantiles of the finishing time can be calculated. These calculations allow a manager to answer such questions as:

- What is the probability the total time is less than 20 days?
- What is the probability the total time is more than 30 days?

FIGURE 9.12

Modified Forward and Backward Pass Excel Spreadsheet

	No.	Activity	Activity	Precedence Activities	Most Optimistic	Most Likely	Most Pessimistic	Expected Time	ES	EF	LS	LF	Slack
			Start	--				--	--	--	--	--	--
	1	A	Contact Client	--	3	4	5	4	0	4	0	4	0
	2	B	Write Proposal	A	0.5	2	3	1.9167	4	5.92	4	5.92	0
	3	C	Obtain Approval	B	0.5	3	4	2.75	5.92	8.67	5.92	8.67	0
	4	D	Complete Computer Programming	C	4	12	15	11.1667	8.67	19.8	8.67	19.8	0
	5	E	Complete Industry Literature Review		8	10	14	10.3333	0	10.3	9.5	19.8	9.5
	6	F	Write Final Draft	D, E	5	6	7	6	19.8	25.8	19.8	25.8	0
	7	G	Complete Oral Report	D, E	4	5	8	5.3333	19.8	25.2	20.5	25.8	0.6667
			Finish	F, G				---	---	25.8	---	---	---

	No.	Activity	Activity	Precedence Activities	Critical Path	Project Completion	Variance	Project Variance
			Start	--				
	1	A	Contact Client	--	1	4	0.1111	0.1111
	2	B	Write Proposal	A	1	5.9167	0.1736	0.1736
	3	C	Obtain Approval	B	1	8.6667	0.3403	0.3403
	4	D	Complete Computer Programming	C	1	19.8333	3.3611	3.3611
	5	E	Complete Industry Literature Review	--	0	0	1	0
	6	F	Write Final Draft	D, E	1	25.8333	0.1111	0.1111
	7	G	Complete Oral Report	D, E	0	0	0.4444	0
			Finish	F, G		25.83		4.10

		Expected Project Completion Time	25.83	
		Project Standard Deviation	2.02	

FIGURE 9.13   Excel Formulas for Probabilistic PERT Problem

No.	Activity	Activity	Precedence Activities	Most Optimistic	Most Likely	Most Pessimistic	Expected Time	ES	EF	LS	LF	Slack
		Start	--				--	--				--
1	A	Contact Client	--	3	4	5	=(G4+4*F4+E4)/6	0	=I4+H4	=L4-H4	=K5	=K4-I4
2	B	Write Proposal	A	0.5	2	3	=(G5+4*F5+E5)/6	=J4	=I5+H5	=L5-H5	=K6	=K5-I5
3	C	Obtain Approval	B	0.5	3	4	=(G6+4*F6+E6)/6	=J5	=I6+H6	=L6-H6	=K7	=K6-I6
4	D	Complete Computer Programming	C	4	12	15	=(G7+4*F7+E7)/6	=J6	=I7+H7	=L7-H7	=MIN(K9:K10)	=K7-I7
5	E	Complete Industry Literature Review	--	8	10	14	=(G8+4*F8+E8)/6	0	=I8+H8	=L8-H8	=MIN(K9:K10)	=K8-I8
6	F	Write Final Draft	D, E	5	6	7	=(G9+4*F9+E9)/6	=MAX(J7:J8)	=I9+H9	=L9-H9	=J11	=K9-I9
7	G	Complete Oral Report	D, E	4	5	8	=(G10+4*F10+E10)/6	=MAX(J7:J8)	=I10+H10	=L10-H10	=J11	=K10-I10
		Finish	F, G				--	--	=MAX(J9:J10)	--	--	--

No.	Activity	Activity	Precedence Activities	Critical Path	Project Completion	Variance	Project Variance
		Start	--				
1	A	Contact Client	--	=IF(M4=0,1,0)	=IF(E16=1,I4,0)	=((G4-E4)/6)^2	=IF(E16=1,G16,0)
2	B	Write Proposal	A	=IF(M5=0,1,0)	=IF(E17=1,I5,0)	=((G5-E5)/6)^2	=IF(E17=1,G17,0)
3	C	Obtain Approval	B	=IF(M6=0,1,0)	=IF(E18=1,I6,0)	=((G6-E6)/6)^2	=IF(E18=1,G18,0)
4	D	Complete Computer Programming	C	=IF(M7=0,1,0)	=IF(E19=1,I7,0)	=((G7-E7)/6)^2	=IF(E19=1,G19,0)
5	E	Complete Industry Literature Review	--	=IF(M8=0,1,0)	=IF(E20=1,I8,0)	=((G8-E8)/6)^2	=IF(E20=1,G20,0)
6	F	Write Final Draft	D, E	=IF(M9=0,1,0)	=IF(E21=1,I9,0)	=((G9-E9)/6)^2	=IF(E21=1,G21,0)
7	G	Complete Oral Report	D, E	=IF(M10=0,1,0)	=IF(E22=1,I10,0)	=((G10-E10)/6)^2	=IF(E22=1,G22,0)
		Finish	F, G		=MAX(F21:F22)		=SUM(H16:H22)

| | | Expected Project Completion Time | =F23 |
| | | Project Standard Deviation | =(H23)^0.5 |

- How much should the project budget be increased in order to ensure 99 percent probability that the project will finish within 20 days?

Since we have the mean, μ_{CT}, and standard deviation, SD_{CT}, of the completion time's underlying distribution, questions such as those posed above can be answered and several statistically significant conclusions can be made.

As was demonstrated in Chapter 3, a random variable drawn from a normal distribution has 0.68 probability of falling within 1 standard deviation of the distribution average. Therefore, there is a 68 percent chance that the actual project duration will be within 1 SD of the estimated average length of the project.

For the example presented in Figure 9.12, there is a 68 percent chance that the project will be completed within 25.83 ± 2.02 days, which is to say, between 23.81 and 27.85 days.

In turn, as was presented in Chapter 3 also, it is known that just over 95 percent (0.954) of the area under a normal distribution falls within two standard deviations of the mean. Therefore, it can be stated that the probability that the project will be completed within 25.83 ± 4.04 days is very high, or approximately 95 percent.

TRADE-OFFS WITHIN CPM: PROJECT CRASHING

Project completion times and costs are rarely certain.

Activity completion times and activity costs are treated as certain quantities in basic CPM analysis. However, completion times and costs are rarely certain. In fact, in most cases the time to complete an activity can be shortened by adding more resources (e.g., labor or capital) to the activity. In turn, adding resources to an activity most likely adds costs.

Therefore, the decision to shorten activity times must take into consideration the additional cost involved. In reality, a project manager has to make a decision about a trade-off, specifically, a decision regarding the trade-off between shortening activity times and additional project cost.

Project Crashing within CPM

Project crashing analyzes changes in activity times.

Project crashing involves four steps:

1. Find the critical path for the regular network and identify the critical activities.
2. Compute the crash cost per time period for all activities in the network. Crash costs per time period can be calculated by the formula:

$$\text{Crash cost/time period} = \frac{\text{crash cost} - \text{normal cost}}{\text{normal time} - \text{crash time}}$$

3. Select the activity on the critical path with the smallest crash cost per time period. Crash this activity (shorten its completion time) to the maximum extent possible or to the point where your desired deadline will be met.

4. Check the critical path to assure it is still critical. Often a reduction in activity time along the critical path leads to a noncritical path or to other paths becoming critical. If the critical path is still the longest path through the network, return to step 3. If not, find the new critical path and return to step 3.

Let's go back to the Business Decision Modeling Group project (see Figure 9.6) and apply these rules of project crashing. Table 9.2 displays the normal and crash times and normal and crash costs for the case study project problem.

Note that activity A's normal time is 4 days and its crash time is 2 days. This means that the activity can be shorted by 2 days if extra resources are provided. The normal cost of activity A is $4000 while the crash cost is $6000. This implies that if activity A is crashed, it will cost an additional $2000. The CPM technique assumes that crashing costs are linear.

Figure 9.14 displays the time-cost relationship for activity A. Crash costs for all other activities can be computed in a similar fashion. Then steps 3 and 4 can be applied to reduce the project's completion time.

Following step 3, we locate the activity that is on the critical path and has the lowest crash cost per time period. Activities A, B, C, D, and F are on the critical path. From Table 9.2, activity C has the smallest crash cost per time period of the activities that are on the critical path. The group can crash activity C by 2 days to reduce the project completion time to 25 days. The cost is an additional $100 and the critical path remains the same: A, B, C, D, and F. Since the path being crashed is still critical, step 3 can be repeated for the next activity that is critical and has the smallest crash cost per time period.

The goal of crashing is to reduce overall project duration at minimum cost.

Overall, the goal of project crashing is to reduce the duration of the project at minimum cost. Since only crashing activities on the critical path can shorten the project's completion time, it may turn out that not all activities have to be crashed for improvements to be seen. However, as activities are crashed, the critical path may change, requiring additional crashing of noncritical activities to reduce the project's completion time further.

FIGURE 9.14
Time-cost Relationship for Activity A

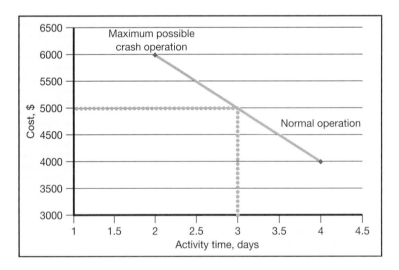

TABLE 9.2
Normal and Crash Data for Business Decision Modeling Group Project

No.	Activity-predecessors	Time, days		Cost		Crash cost per day	Critical path?
		Normal	Crash	Normal	Crash		
1	A–none	4	2	$4000	$6000	$1000	Yes
2	B–A	2	1	$1000	$1800	$ 800	Yes
3	C–B	3	1	$ 200	$ 300	$ 50	Yes
4	D–C	12	6	$1000	$8000	$1167	Yes
5	E–none	10	5	$ 500	$ 600	$ 20	No
6	F–D, E	6	4	$ 400	$ 600	$ 100	Yes
7	G–D, E	5	4	$ 500	$ 700	$ 200	No

Business Decision Modeling Behind the Scenes

PERT, Production Scheduling, and Filmmaking (No Pun Intended)

FILM MAKING AND PROJECT MANAGEMENT

Lights, camera, action! Filmmaking is not as easy as these three words portray it to be. Film production managers have deadlines to meet, extras to schedule, and sets to be built. In order to meet these deadlines and, of course, stay within budget, filmmakers need schedules. More than one producer has said "We live or die by the schedule" and meant it. Not only that, studios find written schedules reassuring—a sign that the production team has everything under control.

PRODUCTION SCHEDULING AND PERT

The following figure is an example of a PERT chart for a film production project.

The production project is broken up into activities and events. Activities are on the arcs and events are depicted as the nodes.

It should be noted that the PERT chart contains a distinct starting and ending point. Most filmmaking projects will have a distinct starting and ending point. However, at times it may be necessary to create dummy starting and ending points. In addition, these types of PERT charts usually contain best, worst, and average activity duration times. Probabilistic PERT is then used to assist production managers with approximating probabilities of finishing.

Filmmakers generally use PERT charts coupled with Gantt charts to visually display film production projects.

The Gantt chart is a time line chart. It clearly shows when each task is to begin, the time it will take to complete each task, and which tasks will be going on simultaneously. You may want to use more than one level of Gantt chart. One chart may show the whole production phase from beginning to end. Another may show 2 or 3 weeks' activities. Another might show the current week's tasks.

OPTIMAL INFORMATION AREA

http://www.smartdraw.com/drawing/gantt/resources.htm.

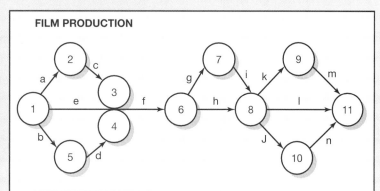

FILM PRODUCTION

ACTIVITIES	
CODE	**MEANING**
a	Obtain funds, loans, investors
b	Solicit director interest
c	Drawn up staff contracts, agree on salaries
d	Pick and hire production staff
e	Advertise, contact agents
f	Scout locations
g	Build sets
h, i	Film scenes
j	Pick a conductor, choose songs
k	Edit film
l	Write press releases, buy ads, create preview
m	Prescreen with audiences
n	Create soundtrack CD

EVENTS	
CODE	**MEANING**
1	Obtain script
2	Budget acquired
3	Talent hired
4	Production staff hired
5	Director signed contract
6	Locations picked
7	All sets final
8	Filming completed
9	Film edited
10	Soundtrack complete
11	Film released

PERT CHART

PERT charts are typically used for projects that involve numerous contractors, departments, and organizations where the duration times are hard to define and the relationships between tasks are complex. Each PERT chart starts with an initial point from which all tasks originate. Each subsequent task is connected to other tasks and is either coded or annotated with its name, the people assigned to it, and its best, worst, and average duration time. The chart is completed when all networked tasks come together to a completion point.

SAMPLE EXECUTIVE SUMMARY

Executive Summary

TO: Dr. Schlapfer
FROM: Senior Business Decision Modeling Group

Introduction

The Senior Business Decision Modeling Group has conducted an analysis of the group project requirements. Proper scheduling of the tasks is crucial to ensure the project is completed on time. To aid in this process, data on optimistic times, most likely times, and pessimistic times are incorporated into the final recommendations.

PERT - Program Evaluation and Review Technique

A schedule for the project has been developed by using a standard planning technique known as PERT. On the basis of the precedence relationships and time estimates for each individual activity, the project's expected completion time is 25.83 days. In addition, it can be said that the project should be completed with 95 percent certainty within 30 days. Therefore, if the project begins on April 10, the project should be finished with 95 percent certainty on May 10. The exact optimistic, most likely, and pessimistic completion times are listed below.

The Schedule

Table 1.1 displays the Business Decision Modeling Group's PERT schedule. Each activity is listed with its respective precedence activity, optimistic, most likely, and pessimistic activity time estimates.

TABLE 1.1
Business Decision Modeling Project PERT Schedule

No.	Activity	Precedence Activities	Most Optimistic	Most Likely	Most Pessimistic	Expected Time	Expected Start Time	Expected Finish Time
	Start							
1	Contact Client	--	3	4	5	4	April 10th	April 14th
2	Write Proposal	1	0.5	2	3	1.91667	April 14th	April 16th
3	Obtain Approval	2	0.5	3	4	2.75	April 16th	April 19th
4	Complete Computer Programming	3	4	12	15	11.1667	April 19th	April 30th
5	Complete Industry Literature Review	--	8	10	14	10.3333	April 10th	April 21st
6	Write Final Draft	4, 5	5	6	7	6	April 30th	May 6th
7	Complete Oral Report	4, 5	4	5	8	5.33333	April 30th	May 6th
	Finish	6, 7				---		

Expected Project Completion Time	25.83333	
Project Standard Deviation	2.02416	

From these estimates, the projects expected completion time is 25.83 days after the start date. Incorporating the optimistic and pessimistic estimates, the project has a 95 percent chance of being completed within 30 days. This completion time is found by using the expected completion time plus two times the project standard deviation.

Gantt Chart for Business Decision Modeling Project

Figure 1.1 displays the Gantt chart for the Business Decision Modeling Group project. Each activity is denoted on the vertical axis, while time in days is denoted on the horizontal axis.

FIGURE 1.1 **Business Decision Modeling Group's Gantt Chart**

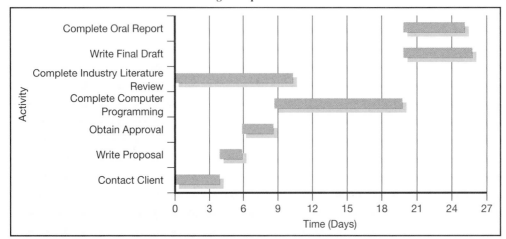

The Gantt chart displays the individual expected start and completion times with blue bars. Deviations due to activities finishing ahead or behind expected dates are not listed on the chart but are easily computed by using Table 1.1.

Recommendations

In summary, the expected project completion time is 25.83 days. If the project commences on April 10, the project should be completed by May 10 with 95 percent certainty. However, if the project starting date changes, the expected completion date must be adjusted accordingly. Should any of the estimated activity times change, a revised PERT schedule and Gantt chart can be supplied.

Case Study: *Jennifer's Prototype Palpitations*

BACKGROUND

Jennifer is the project manager on the prototyping team for the JBK handheld electronic digital assistant. The digital assistant is being designed for executives who want cell phone access and high-speed Internet access and also the capability to directly interface with a laptop or desktop computer via USB or Firewire ports.

Prototype Activities, Duration Times, and Precedence Structure

Jennifer has been told that the JBK prototype needs to be completed in time for the net big trade show on May 10. All the key buyers and purchasing agents in the industry would be there to preview the product. Jennifer has heard that their competitors have been discussing a similar device but most likely could not make the May 10 deadline for the trade show. As of today, November 11, Jen's team has collected the following information regarding the activities, duration times (in days), and precedence requirements for each area within the prototyping plan. Table 9.3 contains this information.

TABLE 9.3 **Prototype Project Information**

Activity	Description	Duration	Predecessor	Activity	Description	Duration	Predecessor
1	Electrical schematics	10	None	9	Testing socumentation	20	8
2	All specifications	48	1	10	I/O sssembly procurement	27	1
3	Plastic procurement	28	1	11	Surface mount electronics	5	8,10
4	Chip procurement	56	1	12	Power/battery supply procurement	23	1
5	SW development	23	2	13	Assemble prototypes	75	1,3,4,7,11,12
6	Firmware development	12	5	14	Lab test prototypes	2	9,13
7	Firmware programming	2	6	15	Field test prototypes	3	14
8	Test SW/firmware interface	2	6	16	Document prototype working instructions	5	14

PROJECT SCHEDULE, CRITICAL ACTIVITIES, AND DISCUSSION QUESTIONS

Jennifer needs to establish a schedule for these activities that includes a precedence diagram and notes earliest and latest start and finish times, that identifies the activities on the critical path, and thatcalculates the estimated completion for the project itself. Help Jennifer by answering these important questions:

1. Will the project as planned meet the May 10 deadline?
2. Is the project sensitive to changes in duration times?
3. What activities should Jennifer be concerned with?

Interactive Case: *Critical Path Scheduling for Samantha's Custom Ceramics*

Please goto www.mhhe.com/kros1e to access the Interactive Project Managment Model.

BACKGROUND

Samantha Taylor runs a small business that develops, creates, fires, and paints custom ceramic products (housewares, tile, decorative ornaments, etc.). The process she uses has a number of steps, some of which are sequential and some not sequential. Lately she has had a tough time deciding which steps in the process are really the most important to get accomplished and which steps may have some wiggle room in the schedule.

SAMANTHA'S PROCESS

Samantha's process has six steps: (A) designing a pattern, (B) mixing clay, (C) obtaining the proper paint, (D) molding clay, (E) firing clay and applying first paint, (F) finish and decorative painting. The process is about the same for all of her products. However, she has a big order for some decorative ornaments that was just signed. From past experience she generally knows the time each activity takes in the ornament-making process. Table 9.4 contains Samantha's estimates of activity times (in days) and precedence relationship for each of the six steps in the process:

TABLE 9.4

Activity	Time	Precedence
A: designing pattern	2	—
B: mixing clay	3	A
C: obtaining paint	10	A
D: molding clay	2	B
E: firing clay and applying first paint	3	B, D
F: finish and decorative painting	2	E

PROBLEM AT HAND

Lately her staff has been informing her that clients have noted that their orders took a long time from initial consultation to final product. Help Samantha learn how to speed up the process. Using the interactive critical path model, set the Select a problem menu to 1, input the activity times given in Table 9.4 into the column labeled TIME, and press the Auto button. From your results, give Samantha answers to the following questions about the next big order:

1. How long will the entire process take?
2. What are the critical activities (i.e., the activities on the critical path)?

3. If the initial consultation was on May 10, can she guarantee completion by May 25?
4. Sabrina, the employee responsible for buying paint, has informed Samantha that she might be able to convince the paint supplier to reduce the time it takes to obtain paint. She has negotiated a reduction of 5 days in obtaining paint (i.e., activity C, obtaining paint, now takes 5 days instead of 10). Press the Reset button and enter 5 in the TIME column for activity C and then press the Auto button. Analyze the new results. How does this reduction in activity time affect the process?

Problems

1. A project network diagram is shown below. The time, in weeks, for each activity is listed in the table below. Construct an Excel spreadsheet and use a forward pass and a backward pass to determine the critical path.

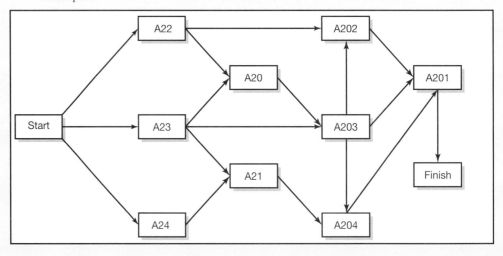

Activity	Precedence activities	Time, weeks
A22		55
A23		40
A24		80
A20	A22, A23	44
A21	A23, A24	120
A203	A23, A20	110
A202	A22, A203	30
A204	A21, A203	10
A201	A203, A202 ,A204	55
Finish	A201	

2. A project network diagram is shown below. The time, in weeks, for each activity is listed in the table below.

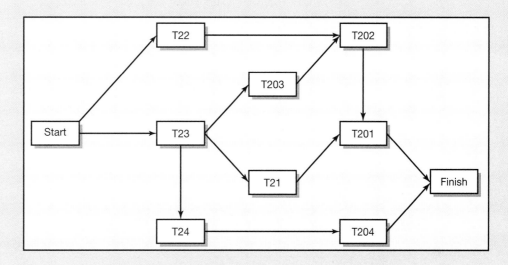

Activity	Precedence activities	Time, weeks
T22		18
T23		12
T24	T23	15
T21	T23	13
T203	T23	17
T202	T22, T203	16
T204	T24	22
T201	T202, T21	20
Finish	T204, T201	

   a. Construct an Excel spreadsheet and use a forward and a backward pass to determine the critical path.

   b. What happens to the critical path if activity T201 takes 10 weeks instead of 20 weeks?

3. Refer back to the problem presented earlier on the Business Decision Modeling Group project (see Table 9.1 and Figure 9.1). One of the members of the group hears that if they purchase an upgrade for their programming software package, they can complete the final draft in just 3 days and complete the programming in just 8 days.

   By saving this time, the group can cash in on the deal offered by Binko's Copies and save $10 on the printing for each day earlier the project is completed. One of the group members says they will save $70 total (7 days × $10day). Is this correct? How does this reduction in time for writing the final draft affect the overall network diagram, critical path, and project completion?

4. The following activity times and precedence are given.

Activity	Precedence	Time, weeks
A23		101
A22	A23	41
A20	A22	21
A202	A22	21
A24	A23	66
A21	A23, A20	33
A201	A202	41
A203	A21, A201	67
A205	A202	55
A204	A24	44

a. Create a network diagram and construct an Excel spreadsheet, then use a forward and a backward pass to determine the critical path.

b. What activities are on the critical path.

5. For the previous problem, what happens to the critical path when activity A24 takes only 26 weeks instead of 66 weeks? How long does it take to complete the project now?

6. The following network, with activities and times estimated in days, is given.

Activity	Optimistic	Most probable	Pessimistic	Precedence
A	2	5	6	
B	1	3	7	
C	6	7	10	A,B
D	5	12	14	C
E	3	4	5	C
F	8	9	12	D,E

a. Create a network diagram that follows the precedence above.

b. Construct an Excel spreadsheet and use a forward and a backward pass to determine the critical path.

7. The following network, with activities and times estimated in days, is given.

Activity	Optimistic	Most probable	Pessimistic	Precedence
A	1	5	3	—
B	0.5	3	3.5	—
C	3	7	5	A,B
D	2.5	12	7	C
E	1.5	4	2.5	C
F	4	9	6	D,E

a. Using the estimated activity times, calculate the expected times and variances for the activities.

b. Construct an Excel spreadsheet and use a forward pass and a backward pass to determine the critical path.

c. What is the expected time to complete the project?

8. A CD-ROM manufacturing guide gives the following numbered steps.

1. Print CD labels: Printed one at a time

2. Print CD case labels: Printed one at a time

3. Transfer files to CD software: Individual transfer one at a time

4. Burn one CD: One at a time

5. Stuff CD case labels: One at a time

6. Attach CD labels: One at a time

7. Return finished CD into CD case: One at a time

Although the steps are numbered, they do not always reflect immediate precedence relationships. The following table lists the immediate predecessors for each activity. Each CD is unique in its CD label, CD case label, and files to be transferred.

Activity	Immediate Precedence	Time, minutes
Print CD labels		1
Print CD case labels	Print CD labels	2.5
Stuff CD case labels	Print CD case labels	0.5
Attach CD labels	Print CD labels	1
Transfer files to CD software		10.5
Burn a labeled CD	Transfer files to CD software	22
Return finished CD into a labeled CD case	Begin burning a labeled CD	0.5

a. Create a network diagram.

b. Construct an Excel spreadsheet and use a forward pass and a backward pass to determine the critical path.

9. For the previous problem, what happens to the critical path when burning the labeled CD takes only 8 minutes instead of 22 minutes? How long does it take to complete the project now?

10. The following arrival and assembly times for electronic parts are given. All times are in weeks. The precedence structures for assembly are included.

Number	Parts	Optimistic	Most probable	Pessimistic	Assembly precedence
1	Metal boxes	14	15	16	5, 8
2	Resistors	21	23	27	
3	Circuit boards	6	7	10	2, 4
4	Capacitors	15	17	19	
5	Cabling	13	14	15	3
6	Self-locking screws	16	19	21	5, 8
7	Simple screws	3	4	5	1
8	Transformers	12	19	21	

a. Create a network diagram that follows the precedence above.

b. Construct an Excel spreadsheet and use a forward pass and a backward pass to determine the critical path.

c. What is the expected time to complete the project?

11. Given the data in the network diagram below, construct an Excel spreadsheet and use a forward pass and a backward pass to determine the earliest start, earliest finish, latest start, latest finish, and slack for each activity. Indicate the critical path. Labels for nodes 1–9 are located within each node,

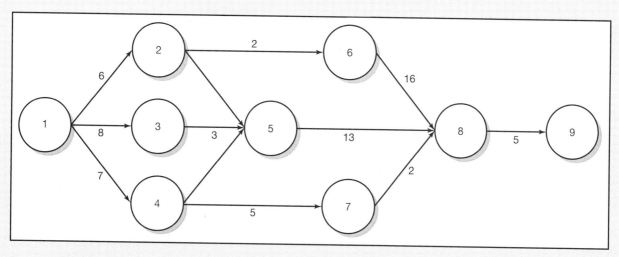

whereas the time to complete each activity is located on the arc leading into the node. For example, once activity 8 is completed it takes 5 periods to complete activity 9 and arrive at node 9.

12. The following network, with activities and times estimated in days, is given.

Activity	Optimistic	Most probable	Pessimistic	Precedence
ZZ	200	255	266	—
BB	10	30	70	ZZ
SS	68	79	100	ZZ
HH	50	120	140	BB
II	31	41	51	BB
PP	89	91	122	HH
RR	150	170	190	II
GG	38	48	54	RR, SS
WW	81	98	112	GG, PP

a. Using the estimated activity times, calculate the expected times and variances for the activities.

b. Construct an Excel spreadsheet and use a forward pass and a backward pass to determine the critical path. Is it the same as in Problem 8?

c. What is the expected time to complete the project?

13. Given the data in the network diagram and table below, construct an Excel spreadsheet and use a forward pass and a backward pass to determine the earliest start, earliest finish, latest start, latest finish, and slack for each node. Indicate the critical path and project completion time.

Activity	Time estimates, weeks
1–2	2
2–3	8
2–4	6
3–6	7
3–5	3
4–5	5
5–7	7
6–7	4
7–8	6

Chapter Ten

Introduction to Visual Basic Programming

Learning Objectives

After completing this chapter, students will be able to:

1. Understand the basic capabilities of Excel's Macro Recorder.

2. Understand how to managing macros with the Visual Basic (VB) Editor.

3. Work with elementary VB code and understand what a procedure is.

4. Understand the basics of how to manage modules and projects (i.e., sharing macros with others).

Chapter Outline

Introduction: What is Visual Basic Programming?

Why Visual Basic? Why Excel?

What is a Macro?

Excel's Macro Recorder

Excel Macro Recorder Example

How to Record a Macro for Formatting Cells

Use the Macro You Created

Creating a Toolbar or Assigning a Keystroke for a Macro

Recording a Macro by Using Relative References.

Managing Macros with the Visual Basic Editor

What is the Visual Basic Editor?

Viewing and Editing Excel Visual Basic Macros

Creating a Simple Macro in Visual Basic Editor

Working with VB Code: An Introduction to Procedures

What is a Subroutine?

What Does the Code Mean?

How Does the Code Work?

Business Decision Modeling Throughout the Ages: The Chronology of Visual Basic

Managing Modules and Projects

Sharing Macros with Others

Business Decision Modeling Behind the Scenes: The History and Origin of VB

Technical Writing for the VB Programmer

Summary

Optimal Information Area

Problems

Business Decision Modeling in Action: Real-World VBA Project

Shell Chemical Company Makes Sales Proactively Using Microsoft ® Excel & VBA

The marketing staff for Shell Chemical had a random method of soliciting sales orders. In the past, the routine was to work through an alphabetical list of customers and make some phone calls to those who had not ordered any product yet that month.

Overall, in Shell's business there is minimal difference in either the price or quality of chemical products from one producer to another. So, often the determining factor between whether Shell got the business or a competitor did was simply who got there first when a customer had demand. If the sales agents called a customer too early, they didn't get an order. If they waited for a customer to call, then they risked losing the sale to a competing supplier. If they could anticipate customers' needs they would be secure the orders.

Microsoft Excel Visual Basic for Applications [VBA] Software Solution

Using a database of past order history, Shell Chemical's sales staff developed a method to forecast customers' needs. They employed Microsoft Excel and Microsoft Visual Basic for Applications to automatically process thousands of records each week. The tool was designed by using past order frequency and volume to provide sales agents with an ability to predict individual customers' product requirements, often even before the customer had. Every Sunday night the operation would run automatically, so on Monday morning the sales staff would be able to call just the customers most likely to be due to reorder products.

Effect of VBA Programming

Customers were amazed that their sales representative for Shell Chemical Company had known when they would need more products. The the sales calls were highly effective. In addition to realizing sales increases, the company saved hundreds of hours of employee time each month by proactively focusing on customers likely to have a need at the time.

Optimal Information Area

Real world VBA projects at http://www.beyondtechnology.com.

INTRODUCTION: WHAT IS VISUAL BASIC PROGRAMMING?

A common question that business spreadsheet users have is

> I keep doing a particular series of actions over and over again in Excel. Can I record these actions and play them back at the push of a button?

For instance, do you often apply the same combination of formats, or do you receive data every week or month that you organize and analyze the same way every time? It is possible to use an Excel macro to combine all of the steps in a task into a single command.

So far Excel has been employed to model and solve many different types of problems. Excel itself contains powerful routines that can solve many problems with relatively little effort (e.g., Goal Seek and Solver). However, there are many circumstances where the built-in functions are insufficient to solve a problem and a custom program needs to be written. Excel provides a solution to this need, a programming language called Visual Basic.

> Visual Basic for Applications is a programming language to build custom functions.

This section introduces some basic areas of Microsoft Visual Basic for Applications and a simple process for automating tasks in Excel by using macros. The section introduces the concept of macros and illustrates how to use a tool called the Macro Recorder that helps you create and manage macros to speed up your work.

Why Visual Basic? Why Excel?

In the past, most computer programs were written almost exclusively by using programming languages such as BASIC, FORTRAN, COBOL, or C. All of these languages are still commonly used, especially by engineers, software developers, and where computational speed is required. However, it is also possible to write computer programs within Excel. Programs written in Microsoft Excel are referred to as macros and are written in a language called Visual Basic for Applications, or VBA.

In fact, all of the Microsoft Office applications (Word, Excel, PowerPoint, and Access) can execute programs by using macros written in VBA. These are all derived from the Microsoft Visual Basic (VB) language, which is used to write a large number of Windows applications. The Visual Basic editor used in Office applications is exactly the same as that found in Visual

Basic itself. The main difference between VBA and Visual Basic itself is that it cannot be compiled into a distinct application but must be run from within the Office application itself. The other difference is that each of the different Office applications has its own set of Visual Basic subroutines that are specific to the application itself (e.g., Excel).

VBA is an extremely complex and powerful language. Here, we just scratch the surface of what its capabilities are. This section details some basic VB programming in Excel, programs called macros, and does not attempt to teach the user to program complex operations in Excel. The online help files provided by Microsoft are comprehensive and should be perused at your leisure. In addition, there are many books written about Visual Basic that also serve as good references. A few of these references are listed at the end of the chapter in the "Optimal Information Area."

What is a Macro?

A macro is a set of computer instructions written to perform a specific task or function.

A macro is a set of computer instructions that you can write or record and associate with a shortcut key combination or a macro name. Then, when you press the shortcut key combination or click the macro name, your computer program carries out the instructions of the macro. This saves you time by replacing an often-used, sometimes lengthy series of actions with a shorter action. For example, instead of clicking several menus and buttons to add or modify cells or cell ranges in Excel documents, you can record those modifications in a macro and then run the macro to perform all the changes/additions in just one step.

EXCEL'S MACRO RECORDER

The macro recorder records a user's mouse clicks and then allows for playback at a later time.

The macro recorder records your mouse clicks and keystrokes while you work and lets you play them back later. You can use the macro recorder to record the sequence of commands you use to perform a certain task. When you run the macro, it plays those exact commands back in the same order, causing Excel to behave just as if you had entered the commands yourself.

Macros are easy to create: You tell Excel to start recording, perform actions as you normally do, and then tell Excel when you're done. Behind the scenes, Excel uses Visual Basic for Applications (VBA) to record your instructions. You don't have to know anything about programming or VBA to create and use the macro recorder. The next section describes how to create and use a simple macro that formats a cell, then changes the macro to add functionality. It also explains your options for storing macros so that you can use them from any workbook.

Excel Macro Recorder Example

Applying formats is a fairly simple macro example, but you can record macros to do more complex tasks like retrieving and filtering external data, creating and customizing charts, and more.

Let's say you work in a group that uses Excel to track accounts payable. Every week you and your coworkers each submit a report in which your manager expects to see overdue amounts formatted so that they're easy to see: the numbers are bold, outlined, and the cells have borders.

How to Record a Macro for Formatting Cells

1. In the workbook where you track your accounts payable (or any workbook you are interested in formatting), click one of the cells you're going to format.

To find the macro recorder in Excel, go to the Tools menu and click on Macro.

2. Point to Macro on the Tools menu, and then click Record New Macro (refer to Figure 10.1).

3. In the Record Macro dialog box, type a name for the macro in the Macro name box (refer to Figure 10.2). Macro names must start with a letter and can include letters, numbers, and underscore characters, but can't include spaces. You don't need to change the other boxes.

Once you have turned on the macro recorder, every operation you carry out (e.g., any mouse clicks) will be stored as a macro.

4. When you click OK, the Stop Recording toolbar appears (refer to Figure 10.3), and you're ready to record. Until you stop the recording, every Excel command and keystroke will be recorded in the macro, in the order in which they are entered. **Caution!** Every

FIGURE 10.1
Macro Recorder Menu

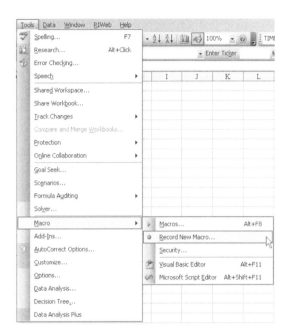

FIGURE 10.2
Record Macro Dialogue Box

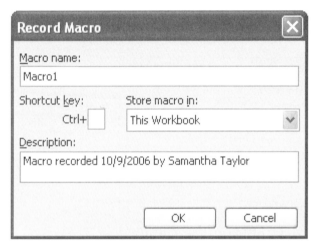

FIGURE 10.3
Stop Recording Toolbar

operation you carry out will now be stored as a macro until you click on the Stop Recording button.

5. Now format the cell the way your boss wants it flagged: click Cells on the Format menu, click the Font tab, click Bold under Font style, click Embossed for Color, click the Border tab and the border thickness you want, click Outline, and then click OK (refer to Figure 10.4).

6. To finish recording the macro, click the Stop Recording button (refer to Figure 10.3 – the blue square is the Stop Recording button).

Now you have a macro that can perform in a single operation all the mouse clicks that it took to format the cell.

FIGURE 10.4
Format Cells Menu with Font Tab Displayed

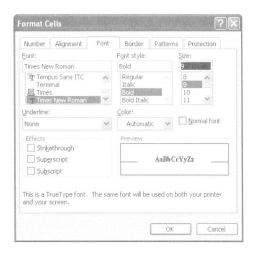

Use the Macro You Created

To run a recorded macro, go to the Tools menu, click on Macro, then click on Macros, and finally click on the name of the macro you wish to run.

The next time you need to flag a cell, you can run the macro:

1. Click the cell you want to format.
2. On the Tools menu, point to Macro, and then click Macros (refer to Figure 10.1).
3. Click the name of your macro (refer to Figure 10.5), and then click Run.

If you're going to use the macro frequently, you can create a toolbar button for it, or assign a keystroke for it, or both.

If you are using a macro frequently, create a toolbar button for it.

Creating a Toolbar or Assigning a Keystroke for a Macro

To create a toolbar button that runs your macro:

1. On the Tools menu, click Customize, and then click the Commands tab.
2. Under Categories, click Macros.
3. Drag the Custom button to the toolbar where you want it.
4. On the Customize dialog box, click Modify Selection, and then click Assign Macro.
5. In the Assign Macro dialog box, click the name of your macro, and then click OK.
6. To change the appearance of the button, click Modify Selection again, point to Change Button Image, and click one of the available images; or click Edit Button Image and use the Button Editor to create your own image.
7. Click Close.

To assign a keystroke to run your macro:

FIGURE 10.5
Macro Menu Dialog Box

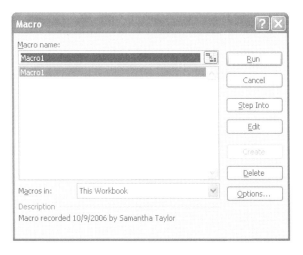

1. On the Tools menu, point to Macro, and then click Macros.
2. Click the name of your macro, and then click Options.
3. In the Shortcut key box, type the key to use along with CTRL to run your macro.

Note: Avoid using a keystroke that's already used for other Excel operations, such as CTRL+C for copy.

Recording a Macro by Using Relative References

Relative referencing refers to cells offset from an active cell rather than to an absolute position.

Some spreadsheet users wish to record a macro that uses relative references (i.e., one that always refers to cells offset from your active cell in the spreadsheet rather than an absolute position in the spreadsheet). Recording a relative reference macro is simple. You need to instruct the macro recorder before you start recording any commands. This is done by displaying the Stop Macro toolbar (refer to Figure 10.3). The icon on the right toggles the recorder between absolute and relative referencing. When it has been clicked, the recorder will use relative referencing. You can switch between referencing modes whenever the need occurs.

MANAGING MACROS WITH THE VISUAL BASIC EDITOR

The Visual Basic editor displays VB code.

Up to this point, we created a Visual Basic Macro using the Macro recorder. However, we have yet to see any VB code. Before we are able to view any VB code, we must ensure that the VBA editor toolbar is active. To do so, activate the VBA editor toolbar by selecting View from the main menu and click on the Toolbars submenu. Ensure that the Visual Basic option is checked (refer to Figure 10.6).

What is the Visual Basic Editor?

The Visual Basic editor, included with most Office applications, including Excel, is the environment you use to create, modify, and manage Office macros. A macro commonly consists of code starting with the keyword Sub and ending with the keywords End Sub (these words are abbreviations for the word subroutine). A module contains one or more macros or subroutines, while a project contains one or more modules.

The Visual Basic editor can be found on the Visual Basic toolbar.

The Visual Basic editor is used to manage projects and their associated modules. To look at the Visual Basic code that corresponds to a macro, we need to select the Visual Basic editor from the Visual Basic toolbar (refer to Figure 10.7) by clicking on the Visual Basic Editor button.

FIGURE 10.6
Activating the VBA Editor Toolbar

Figure 10.7   **Visual Basic Toolbar**

Visual Basic
Editor Button

This action invokes the Visual Basic editor. This is the same editor used by the stand-alone version of Visual Basic and by all the other Office applications. Once you become familiar with it in Excel, you will have no trouble using it in any other application. After clicking the Visual Basic editor button, menus resembling those in Figure 10.8a will appear in your Excel worksheet.

Viewing and Editing Excel Visual Basic Macros

The top window (labeled Project – VBAProject) is the most important at this stage. It displays the locations of the Visual Basic code in our spreadsheet. As for now, do not concern yourself with the window marked Properties, as it is more relevant to building larger applications.

We are interested in the file folder labeled Modules in the top window. This file folder contains the VB code for the current spreadsheet. To see the Visual Basic code associated with your macro, double-click on the icon Module. A drop-down menu under Modules should appear (Figure 10.8b).

From this new menu, double-click on the file marked Module1. A new menu resembling Figure 10.9 will appear with the VB code that was recorded earlier (refer to "Excel Macro Recorder Example," above).

Note that the name is preceded by the keyword Sub (this will be colored blue on the Excel screen) and has a corresponding End Sub (located at the end of the code). These define the start and finish of our macro. This block of code is known as a *subroutine* in Visual Basic, as noted, hence the words Sub and End Sub.

Within the editor, it is possible to directly change the Visual Basic code. Visual Basic key-words are normally colored blue and comments green. A comment is designated by a ' at the beginning of the line. The other Visual Basic instructions are associated with the operations we carried out when we recorded the macro.

The Visual Basic Project Manager displays the locations of the Visual Basic code.

The Visual Basic Project Manager displays the locations of the Visual Basic code.

FIGURE 10.8A
Visual Basic Project Manager Window

Top
Window

FIGURE 10.8B
VB Project Manager Window

FIGURE 10.9
VB Code for Macro 1

```
Sub Macro1()
'
' Macro1 Macro
' Macro recorded 10/1/2002 by Samantha Taylor
'
'
    With Selection.Font
        .Name = "Times New Roman"
        .FontStyle = "Bold"
        .Size = 9
        .Strikethrough = False
        .Superscript = False
        .Subscript = False
        .OutlineFont = True
        .Shadow = False
        .Underline = xlUnderlineStyleNone
        .ColorIndex = xlAutomatic
    End With
    Selection.Borders(xlDiagonalDown).LineStyle = xlNone
    Selection.Borders(xlDiagonalUp).LineStyle = xlNone
    With Selection.Borders(xlEdgeLeft)
        .LineStyle = xlContinuous
        .Weight = xlMedium
        .ColorIndex = xlAutomatic
    End With
    With Selection.Borders(xlEdgeTop)
        .LineStyle = xlContinuous
        .Weight = xlMedium
        .ColorIndex = xlAutomatic
    End With
    With Selection.Borders(xlEdgeBottom)
        .LineStyle = xlContinuous
        .Weight = xlMedium
        .ColorIndex = xlAutomatic
    End With
    With Selection.Borders(xlEdgeRight)
        .LineStyle = xlContinuous
        .Weight = xlMedium
        .ColorIndex = xlAutomatic
    End With
End Sub
```

When you use the Visual Basic editor, modifications to a macro can be made by simply editing text.

Modifications to the macro are performed by simply editing the text. You should edit with caution, as incorrect modifications to the text can result in errors and, in turn, your macro may no longer run. It is also possible to correct any errors you may have made when recording the macro within the editor itself. It is also possible to directly create macros in the editor without recording anything to begin with. To exit the editor, first select File and then Close and Return to Microsoft Excel. The next section details the use of the Visual Basic editor to create and run a macro. Contrast the section with the section "Creating a Simple Macro in Visual Basic Editor," above, which detailed how to use the macro recorder to create a macro.

Creating a Simple Macro in Visual Basic Editor

Using the Visual Basic editor, we can create any macro. In fact, this is how most "programmers" create macros. The simple macro we will create changes the background color of a Microsoft Excel spreadsheet according to the color values you specify. This exercise gives the user a look at:

- How to **declare object variables** using a **Dim** statement. Dim is an abbreviation for dimension, a leftover from the old Basic language days.
- How to **define variable types** as integer values in a range using the **Integer** command.
- How to use the **InputBox** command to create an **input box** to accept data from a user.
- How to use and create a **message box** using the **MsgBox** command to display a message back to a user.
- How to change the color of an entire Excel spreadsheet according to a user's preferences—i.e., allowing a user to input values for red, green, and blue to physically change the worksheet's color using the **RGB** command

The following is the process to create and run the macro:

1. Start Microsoft Excel.
2. Create a new blank worksheet.
3. On the Tools menu, point to Macro and then click Macros.
4. In the Macros in box, click on This Workbook.
5. In the Macro name box, type ChangeColor and then click Create. Figure 10.10 displays what the Visual Basic editor window should resemble.
6. Next, edit (physically go click in the editor box and type) the code so that it resembles that in Figure 10.11. *Note:* The actual VB code is listed in Table 10.11 for a clearer view. *Note:* Type the VB code in exactly in the manner presented in the figure and table. Remember that each character has a purpose, and if the code is not entered properly the macro will not perform as expected.
7. On the View menu, click Microsoft Excel.
8. Type some text in the spreadsheet to give some contrast between the document's background and the text.
9. On the Tools menu, point to Macro, and click Macros.
10. Click ChangeColor, and click Run. *Note:* If a message appears stating that the macros in the project are disabled, refer to the Microsoft Excel Help menu and the topic area of Changing Macro Security Settings in Office XP.
11. In the dialog box that appears, enter a whole number between 0 and 255 three times (for each value of red, green, and blue), and click OK each time.

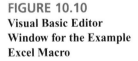
FIGURE 10.10
Visual Basic Editor Window for the Example Excel Macro

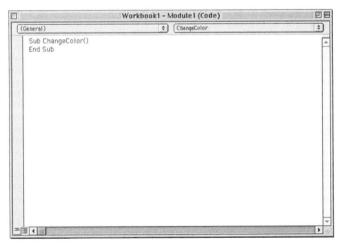

FIGURE 10.11
Visual Basic Editor
Window for the Example
Excel Macro, with Code

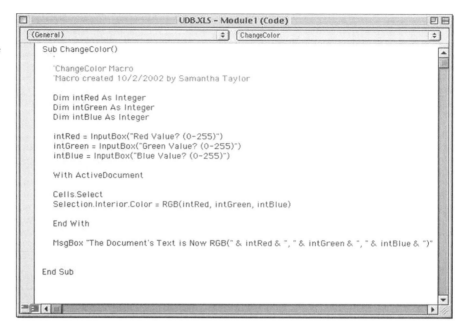

TABLE 10.1
Visual Basic Code for
ChangeColor Subroutine

```
Sub ChangeColor()
'
'ChangeColor Macro
'Macro created 10/2/2002 by Samantha Taylor

Dim intRed As Integer
Dim intGreen As Integer
Dim intBlue As Integer

intRed = InputBox("Red Value? (0-255)")
intGreen = InputBox("Green Value? (0-255)")
intBlue = InputBox("Blue Value? (0-255)")

With ActiveDocument

Cells.Select
Selection.Interior.Color = RGB(intRed, intGreen, intBlue)

End With
MsgBox "The Document's Text is Now RGB(" & intRed & ", " & intGreen & ",
" & intBlue & ")"

End Sub
```

The document's background color changes to match the combined red-green-blue (RGB) value you provided in the previous step.

WORKING WITH VB CODE: AN INTRODUCTION TO PROCEDURES

Macros are stored in blocks of code called *procedures*.

Microsoft Excel macros are stored in blocks of code called *procedures*. By learning the skills described in this article, you will learn how to interpret procedures created by Excel when recording macros.

As explained earlier, a macro is a set of computer instructions that you can record and associate with a shortcut key combination or a macro name. Consequently, when you press the shortcut key combination or click the macro name, Excel carries out the instructions of the macro. Macros can be written in Excel to extend features or automate tasks in spreadsheet documents and applications (refer back to "Creating a Simple Macro in Visual Basic Editor").

What is a Subroutine?

Each macro begins with one subroutine. When you instruct Excel to run a macro, Excel begins with the first line of code contained within the macro's corresponding subroutine. This section explains and demonstrates how to work with code in subroutines.

If you're unsure what a subroutine is, pick up a handheld calculator (or, on a Microsoft Windows computer, click the Start button, point to Programs, point to Accessories, and then click Calculator), and do the following:

1. Press or click the button with the number 2 on it.
2. Press or click the button with the addition symbol ($+$) on it.
3. Press or click the button with the number 3 on it.
4. Press or click the button with the equals symbol ($=$) on it.

As expected, the calculator displays the number 5. By following these steps, you execute, or run, the subroutine $2 + 3 = 5$. This can also be expressed in symbolic terms as intFirstNumber + intSecondNumber = AdditionResult2, where intFirstNumber represents the integer (a number without fractions) value 2, intSecondNumber represents the integer value 3, and AdditionResult2 represents the integer value 5. This can also be expressed in VBA code as follows:

```
Sub AdditionResult1()
AdditionResult2 = intFirstNumber + intSecondNumber
End Sub
```

What Does the Code Mean?

In VBA terms, the Sub keyword signifies a subroutine and is the moniker signifying the start of the code for the task to be performed. In the world of VB, subroutines are also referred to as macros and are also called procedures. To avoid confusion, from this point on, the author will refer only to subroutines.

The AdditionResult1 portion following the Sub keyword signifies the subroutine's name. From now on, the subroutine (or this block of code) is referred to as the AdditionResult1 subroutine.

The values intFirstNumber and intSecondNumber are referred to as the subroutine's *arguments* or *input parameters*. The AdditionResult2 value just before the keywords End Sub is the procedure's return value.

Now that you understand how subroutines work, let's create a simple subroutine that calls the AdditionResult1 subroutine.

1. Start Microsoft Excel.
2. Create a new blank worksheet.
3. On the Tools menu, point to Macro and then click Macros.
4. In the Macros in box, click on This Workbook.
5. In the Macro name box, type AdditionResult and then click Create. *Note:* A screen resembling Figure 10.10 should now be in view.
6. Next, edit (physically go click in the editor box and type) the code so that it resembles Figure 10.12: *Note:* The actual VB code is listed in Table 10.2 for a clearer view. Type the VB code in exactly in the manner presented in the figure and table. Remember each character has a purpose, and if the code is not entered properly the macro will not perform as expected.
7. On the View menu, click Microsoft Excel.
8. On the Tools menu, point to Macro, and click Macros.
9. Click AdditionResult, and click Run. *Note:* If a message appears stating that the macros

FIGURE 10.12
Visual Basic Editor Window for the Example Excel Macro

TABLE 10.2
Visual Basic Code for AdditionResult Subroutine

```
Dim intFirstNumber As Integer
Dim intSecondNumber As Integer
Dim AdditionResult2 As Integer

Sub AdditionResult()

    '
    ' CallAdditionResult Macro
    ' Macro created {date} by {name}
    '

    intFirstNumber = InputBox(Prompt: = "Type the first integer.")
    intSecondNumber = InputBox(Prompt: = "Type the second integer.")

    Call AdditionResult1

    MsgBox intFirstNumber & " + " & intSecondNumber & " = " & AdditionResult2 & "."

End Sub

Sub AdditionResult1()

    AdditionResult2 = intFirstNumber + intSecondNumber

End Sub
```

in the project are disabled, refer to the Microsoft Excel Help menu and the topic area of Changing Macro Security Settings in Office XP.

10. In the dialog boxes that appear, enter integers when prompted, and click OK each time.

The final message box you see displays an algebraic formula containing the two integers entered and their sum.

How Does the Code Work?

Each line of VB code carries a meaning. This section explains what each line of code means in Figure 10.12.

1. Three Dim statements are given initially.

   - These Dim statements define the three variables that are to be used in the Addition Subroutine.
   - The Dim statements instruct VBA to create three locations in your computer memory to store values.
   - The first memory location will be called intFirstNumber; the second memory location will be called intSecondNumber, and the third memory location will be called AdditionResult2.
   - The three memory locations will be sized big enough to hold integer values, hence the "As Integer" code at the end of the Dim statements.

2. VBA starts running the macro at the line Sub CallAdditionResult(). The Sub command is the way to tell VB a subroutine is coming.

3. The next three lines of code are comments and begin with a comment marker ('). Comments are similar to notes; they are for our personal use and are ignored by VBA. However, as a programmer you absolutely should use comments to give yourself and future users notes about your code. *Note*: You can type anything you want after a comment marker, or you can delete comments entirely, and it won't affect the running of your code.

4. The lines intFirstNumber = InputBox(Prompt: = "Type the first integer.") and intSecondNumber = InputBox(Prompt: = "Type the second integer.") are interpreted by VBA as follows:

   a. Display an input box with the label Type the first integer.
   b. After the user has clicked OK, store in the memory location called intFirstNumber, whatever the user has typed in the box.
   c. Display an input box with the label Type the second integer.
   d. After the user has clicked OK, store in the memory location called intSecondNumber whatever the user has typed in the box.

5. The line Call AdditionResult1 is telling VB to call a subroutine named AdditionResult1. VB literally goes and finds the subroutine named AdditionResult1".

6. When VB locates the block of code named SubAdditionResult1(), the input parameters infirstNumber and intSecondNumber are in memory.

   a. The subroutine then performs the required addition calculation and defines the addition of the two input parameters as AdditionResult2.
   b. The subroutine is then completed and closed with the End Sub command, which tells VB to finish and go back to the main subroutine—in this case the SubAdditionResult.

7. As VB moves back into the SubAdditionResult subroutine, the next line, MsgBox Prompt: = intFirstNumber & " + " & intSecondNumber &" = " & AdditionResult(int First: = intFirstNumber,intSecond: = intSecondNumber), shows a message box with a label that is constructed as follows:

   a. Display the value that is stored in the memory location called intFirstNumber.
   b. Display the symbol +.
   c. Display the value that is stored in the memory location called intSecondNumber.
   d. Display the symbol =.
   e. Display the return value of the AdditionResult2 parameter defined in the AdditionResult1 subroutine.

8. The AdditionResult1 subroutine performs the addition of the values stored in the memory locations intFirstNumber and intSecondNumber (in this case, 2 and 3), and stores the answer (in this case, 5) in a location called AdditionResult2.

9. The value of the AdditionResult2 parameter is determined by passing the value that is stored in the memory location called intFirstNumber, followed by passing the value that is stored in the memory location called intSecondNumber to the AdditionResult1 subroutine.

10. The entire AdditionResult subroutine is closed with the End Sub command.

Overall, calling subroutines and passing values between subroutines enables users to create very powerful and useful VB programs.

Dim statements define variables and instruct VBA to create a location in computer memory to store values.

VB's real power comes from the ability to call subroutines and pass values between subroutines.

Business Decision Modeling Throughout the Ages

The Chronology of Visual Basic

The following time line is paraphrased from *Visual Basic Programmer's Journal*, February 2000.

March 1988: Microsoft Buys Tripod
Alan Cooper, the father of Visual Basic, shows a drag-and-drop shell prototype called Tripod to Bill Gates. Microsoft negotiates to buy the concept, now code-named Ruby. The tool includes a widget control box, the ability to add widgets dynamically, and a small language engine.

March 20, 1991: VB1 Debuts at Windows World
Microsoft marries QuickBasic to Ruby shell app and gives it a new code name: Thunder. The result is the first tool that lets you create Windows applications quickly, easily, and visually. Features include a drag-and-drop control toolbox, codeless UI creation, and an event-oriented programming model.

May 1991: Third Party Market Born
Several standard-setting add-ons become available at or slightly after VB1's introduction, including MicroHelp's VBTools.

May 1991: Sheridan Software's VBAssist Debuts
First add-on to integrate directly into the IDE.

March 1992: VB 2.0 Toolkit (Rawhide) Released
This toolkit integrated several third-party tools into a single package, putting controls in the hands of many VB developers for the first time. It provided instrumental in achieving third-party critical mass.

November 1992: VB2 Debuts
Adds ODBC Level 1 support, MDI forms, and object variables. First version to feature the Professional Edition.

November 1992: Microsoft Access Ships
It brings VB's combination of extensibility, ease of use, and visual point-and-click emphasis to a relational database. It also includes a macro language called Access BASIC that contains a subset of VB 2.0's core syntax.

June 1993: VB3 Debuts
Integrates the Access Engine (Jet), OLE automation, and reporting.

May 1995: Borland's Delphi Debuts
The perennial preview for the features you'll find in the next VB release.

Fall 1996: Internet Explorer 3.0 Ships
Features include VBScript, which contains a subset of VB. It lets developers leverage their existing VB skills in Web programming.

October 1996: VB4 Debuts
Permits you to create your own add-ins. Also introduces classes and OCXs.

January 1997: Microsoft Office 97 Debuts
Developer Edition integrates VBA into all Office apps (except Outlook, which uses VBScript).

April 1997: VB5 Debuts
Incorporates compiler, WithEvents, and the ability to create ActiveX controls.

October 1998: VB6 Debuts
Introduces WebClasses, windowless controls, data designers, new reporting designers, and the ability to create data sources.

OPTIMAL INFORMATION AREA

History of Visual Basic Web site at http://www.johnsmiley.com/visualbasic/vbhistory.htm.

IN THE BEGINNING

Many people do not remember when Microsoft did not write applications, but was just a language and OS company. Around 1982 Apple came to Microsoft with an offer, Apple was making a new computer (called the Macintosh) and wanted some applications for it. If Microsoft was going to try to break into the application market, then the Mac was the perfect opportunity to do so. Microsoft created Word, Excel, and File originally for the Mac.

MACBASIC

Apple (specifically Donn Denman) had been working on a basic language for the Mac, appropriately named MacBasic. The Mac was designed with object-oriented design concepts and Pascal. The Lisa (the forerunner to the Mac) was designed around Pascal and had an object-oriented framework called Clascal that later grew and migrated into Object Pascal and MacApp framework. Apple was so inspired that the company worked with Nicholas Wirth (the creator of Pascal) to create Object Pascal. So it was no surprise that Apple's Basic also had many object-oriented concepts.

HYPERCARD

A Mac programmer, Bill Atkinson, was annoyed with the lack of a basic programming language. After many months of hard work, he later created Hypercard. It was visual and object-oriented, easy to use, and more graphically oriented than most other languages. Hypertext is now the primary concept of the World Wide Web and HTML (the file format of the Web. Atkinson (and Apple) used Hypertext concepts 10 years before the Web took off.

VISUALBASIC = MACBASIC + HYPERCARD

Hypercard may not have had Apple's full attention, but it certainly got the attention of Microsoft. Lots of animators and people creating multimedia content could do so on the Mac and script something up in a hurry. So Microsoft created VisualBasic. It was quick to make, since MS already had the code for its Basic.

Apple at this time was creating AppleEvents and Apple-Script so that Mac users could script any application by using a universal scripting language on the Mac. Microsoft, about 5 years later, developed what is now called VB for Applications.

OPTIMAL INFORMATION AREA

David K. Every Web site at URL

http://www.mackido.com/History/History_VB.html

MANAGING MODULES AND PROJECTS

The main code-management tool in VB is called the Project Explorer.

The main code-management tool used in the Visual Basic editor to work with modules and projects is called the Project Explorer. The Project window is usually visible when you open the Visual Basic Editor. If the Project Explorer window is not visible, clicking Project Explorer on the View menu in the Visual Basic Editor can display it. The Project window displays the contents of all stored macro code associated with the active Office application and/or Office document.

Sharing Macros with Others

When you distribute databases, spreadsheets, presentations, and documents containing macros to others, they can start running the attached macros immediately. You can also distribute individual modules containing macros, separate from Office documents and projects, to other Office users.

To distribute individual modules separately from Office documents and projects

1. Right-click the module containing your macro in the Project window.

When code is distributed individually as modules, separately from Office documents, it must be imported into an Office application to run.

2. Click Export File and follow the directions to save the exported code to a stand-alone file.

Notethat the code in this type of file will not run on its own, however; it must be imported into an existing Office document or project, depending on the Office application.

To import a code file:

1. On the File menu in the Visual Basic Editor, click Import File.

2. Follow the directions to bring the file's code into your document or project.

TECHNICAL WRITING FOR THE VB PROGRAMMER

The way to produce better technical writing about VB or any other documentation is a three-part process:

- Recognizing that the "customer is king."
- Recognizing (on the part of corporate resource management) that good documentation is as important as good code, and that good documentation demands a full time partnership between writers and programmers.
- Recognizing that technical writing is a teacher/student relationship.

As in any art form (and writing, be it writing novels or writing specs for a large software application, is certainly an art form), there is no "right" way to create.

More importantly, if you are writing technical pieces, give yourself time to really understand the issues and problem at hand. Define a voice and style of your own. The crucial thing is that you take time to make your writing better. After all, it is not enough for programmers to write code that works. Programmers must also write code that is easy to modify later; by the programmer himself/herself, or by the next programmer. To assist you here is an example of a technical memo dealing with debugging code.

Executive Summary for Technical Writing Memo for Debugging VB Code

TO: Code E. Joe
FROM: Dee B. Ugg
SUBJECT: Progress on Visual Basic (VB) Debugging Report
DATE: April 3, 2006

Introduction

This memo describes the progress I have made to date on my independent-study project of writing a report on debugging in VB. In this memo, I review the nature of the project and describe work I have completed, work I am currently engaged in, and work I plan to complete by the end of the project. As I described in my memo of June 21, 2005, this project will result in a technical report whose purpose is to provide readers with practical information on developing and debugging programs in VB, supplementary to the material in your textbook, *An Introduction to VB and its Implementation*.

Project Description

The report is aimed at students in computer science (undergraduate and graduate) who have previous programming experience, but are new to VB. The information in this report is needed because readers who have developed programs by using compilers for other languages may be unfamiliar with the approaches available with an interactive interpreter and debugger.

Project Scope

In my earlier memo dated December 16, 2005, I proposed to cover the following high-level topics:

1. Loading the debugging module into the interpreter
2. Applying backtrace
3. Saving and loading a customized heap image of the VB system
4. Debugging native code procedure-calls
5. Program design/implementation strategies
6. Differences between RVB and other VB systems
7. Establishing break levels
8. Managing dependencies
9. Debugging local definitions
10. Debugging when using functional programming style
11. Using stubbed procedures

In my current outline (sent via email), these are divided into three major parts, with an addendum for topic 11. The three parts are: (A) basic debugging procedures—topics 1 to 3, (B) advanced debugging procedures—topics 4 to 7, and (C) general program development strategies—topics 8 to 10.

Work Completed

I have completed first drafts of the sections in part A on loading the debugging module, break levels, and apply-backtrace. I intend to make note of additional material for these sections while working on the later sections, if further background information is needed.

Present Work

I am currently working on the sections in part B. Since these sections are highly interrelated, I am working on them roughly in parallel. I am also currently researching information on other VB systems for section 11; I have located information on Gambit and Dr. VB programmers. I expect the current work to be completed by the end of this week, April 7.

Future Work and Conclusions

Next, I will draft the sections in part C and the addendum on other VB systems. Finally, I will fully revise the entire draft, integrating further material where deficiencies have become evident during work on other sections. The final report will be ready for your review on April 16. Thus far, the project is proceeding well. I have not run into any major problems, nor do I anticipate any in the remaining work.

Summary

If you perform a task repeatedly, you can automate the task with a macro.

If you perform a task repeatedly in Microsoft Excel, you can automate the task with a macro. As was defined in the chapter, a macro is a series of commands and functions that are stored in a Visual Basic module and can be run whenever you need to perform the task. When you record a macro, Excel stores information about each step you take as you perform a series of commands. The macro can then be run to repeat, or play back, the commands.

When you create macros, VB stores each macro in a new module attached to a workbook. You don't necessarily have to learn how to program or use the Visual Basic language to create or make simple changes to your macros. VB's macro recorder automates simple macro creation. The Macro Recorder acts like a tape recorder to assist in developing Excel macros. As you work, the VB macro recorder records your keystrokes and mouse button clicks and translates them into Microsoft Visual Basic for Applications (VBA) code. More advanced VB macros can be developed by using the Visual Basic editor.

Using the Visual Basic editor, we can create any macro. In fact, this is how most programmers create macros. The simple macro we created changes the background color of a Microsoft Excel spreadsheet according to the color values you specify. This chapter illustrated the creation of some simple VB macros and the use of a few basic VB commands and structures, including the following:

- How to record a VB macro, using the macro recorder in Excel.
- How to declare object variables by using a Dim statement. Dim is an abbreviation for dimension, a leftover from the old Basic language days.
- How to define variable types as integer values in a range by using the Integer command.
- How to use the **InputBox** command to create an **input box** to accept data from a user.
- How to use and create a message box by using the MsgBox command to display a message back to the user.
- How to change the color of an entire Excel spreadsheet according to a user's preferences—i.e., allowing a user to input values for red, green, and blue to physically change the worksheet's color, using the **RGB** command.

Optimal Information Area

Albright, S. C. VBA *for Modelers: Developing Decision Support Systems with Microsoft Excel*. Pacific Grove, CA: Duxbury, 2001.

CodeGuru Visual Basic Web site at URL **http://www.codeguru.com/vb/index.shtml**.

David K. Every Web site at URL **http://www.mackido.com/History/History_VB.html**.

History of Visual Basic Web site at **http://www.johnsmiley.com/visualbasic/vbhistory.htm**.

Jeff-Net Visual Basic Web site at URL **http://www.visual-basic.com/**.

Real-world VBA projects at URL **http://www.beyondtechnology.com**.

Walkenbach, J. *Microsoft Excel 2000 Power Programming with VBA*. Foster City, CA: IDG Books, 2000.

Problems

1. Revisit the section "How to Record a Macro for Formatting Cells" above. Follow the instructions and record the macro the exercise illustrates.

2. Record another macro using the macro recorder to perform a copy and paste of a cell in Excel.

3. Record another macro using the macro recorder to perform a copy and past of a cell in Excel but turn on the relative reference option.

4. Within the Visual Basic editor, compare the codes from Problems 2 and 3. Comment on similarities and differences.

5. Rewrite the code displayed in Figure 10.12 so the numbers are multiplied together instead of added together.

6. Open Excel and two new workbooks. These workbooks will most likely be called Book1 an Book2. Go to the Visual Basic editor and make the Project Explorer window visible. Insert a module into Book1 and click on the plus sign next to Modules to see the module you just inserted. Now type the following subroutine in the Code window and then run it.

```
Sub ShowName()
MsgBox "The name of the workbook is " & ThisWorkbook.Name
End Sub
```

Then, go to the Project Explorer window and drag the module you inserted down to Book2. This should create a copy of the module in Book2. Run the subroutine in the copied module. You should notice that the name of the second workbook is displayed. In turn, note that copying code is as easy as copying a module from the Project Explorer window.

7. Open Excel and go to the Visual Basic editor. Open the Immediate window. A shortcut for doing this is Ctrl-g. Erase any code that is in the Immediate box. Then type the following lines pressing Enter key after each line. Can you figure out why it is called the Immediate window?

```
?Application.Name
?Application.Version
?Application.UserName
?IsDate("May 10, 2006")
?ActiveWorkbook.Name
```

8. Open a new workbook and type some labels or numbers into various cells. Then turn the macro recorder on and format the cells in any ways you can think of (e.g., bold, italics, change the color, etc.). Stop recording and open the code for the macro you just created and examine it. You will find that there are many properties set that you never intended to set. Does any code appear to be unnecessary?

9. Changing font colors is a very nice feature in Excel. The ColorIndex property of the Font object does this. For text that is red, the index is set to 3. However, remembering all these index numbers becomes intractable. So try the following: open a new workbook and type a label in a cell. Highlight

this cell, turn on the macro recorder, and change the color of the font repeatedly to different colors. Keep track of the order of the colors you chose. Stop recording and take a look at the macro you just recorded. You should be able to match the colors you chose with the indices that appear in the code.

10. In many business spreadsheets, numbers are often in dollar format with no decimal points. Open a new workbook and type some numbers in the first row of cells. Highlight the cells, turn on the macro recorder, and format the cells to be in dollar format with no decimal places. Stop recording and take a look at the macro you just recorded. Although this formatting could be done using the Format menu, the macro can now complete the job in just a few key strokes.

Appendix A

Useful Information

STANDARD NORMAL DISTRIBUTION TABLE

NOTE: Entries in the following table give the area under the curve between the mean and z standard deviations above the mean. For example, for $z = 1.25$, the area under the curve between the mean and z is 0.3944.

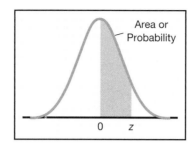

z	0.00	0.01	0.02	0.03	0.04	0.05	0.06	0.07	0.08	0.09
0.00	0.0000	0.0040	0.0080	0.0120	0.0160	0.0199	0.0239	0.0279	0.0319	0.0359
0.10	0.0398	0.0438	0.0478	0.0517	0.0557	0.0596	0.0636	0.0675	0.0714	0.0753
0.20	0.0793	0.0832	0.0871	0.0910	0.0948	0.0987	0.1026	0.1064	0.1103	0.1141
0.30	0.1179	0.1217	0.1255	0.1293	0.1331	0.1368	0.1406	0.1443	0.1480	0.1517
0.40	0.1554	0.1591	0.1628	0.1664	0.1700	0.1736	0.1772	0.1808	0.1844	0.1879
0.50	0.1915	0.1950	0.1985	0.2019	0.2054	0.2088	0.2123	0.2157	0.2190	0.2224
0.60	0.2257	0.2291	0.2324	0.2357	0.2389	0.2422	0.2454	0.2486	0.2518	0.2549
0.70	0.2580	0.2612	0.2642	0.2673	0.2704	0.2734	0.2764	0.2794	0.2823	0.2852
0.80	0.2881	0.2910	0.2939	0.2967	0.2995	0.3023	0.3051	0.3078	0.3106	0.3133
0.90	0.3159	0.3186	0.3212	0.3238	0.3264	0.3289	0.3315	0.3340	0.3365	0.3389
1.00	0.3413	0.3438	0.3461	0.3485	0.3508	0.3531	0.3554	0.3577	0.3599	0.3621
1.10	0.3643	0.3665	0.3686	0.3708	0.3729	0.3749	0.3770	0.3790	0.3810	0.3830
1.20	0.3849	0.3869	0.3888	0.3907	0.3925	0.3944	0.3962	0.3980	0.3997	0.4015
1.30	0.4032	0.4049	0.4066	0.4082	0.4099	0.4115	0.4131	0.4147	0.4162	0.4177
1.40	0.4192	0.4207	0.4222	0.4236	0.4251	0.4265	0.4279	0.4292	0.4306	0.4319
1.50	0.4332	0.4345	0.4357	0.4370	0.4382	0.4394	0.4406	0.4418	0.4429	0.4441
1.60	0.4452	0.4463	0.4474	0.4484	0.4495	0.4505	0.4515	0.4525	0.4535	0.4545
1.70	0.4554	0.4564	0.4573	0.4582	0.4591	0.4599	0.4608	0.4616	0.4625	0.4633
1.80	0.4641	0.4649	4,656	0.4664	0.4671	0.4678	0.4686	0.4693	0.4699	0.4706
1.90	0.4713	0.4719	0.4726	0.4732	0.4738	0.4744	0.4750	0.4756	0.4761	0.4767
2.00	0.4772	0.4778	0.4783	0.4788	0.4793	0.4798	0.4803	0.4808	0.4812	0.4817
2.10	0.4821	0.4826	0.4830	0.4834	0.4838	0.4842	0.4846	0.4850	0.4854	0.4857
2.20	0.4861	0.4864	0.4868	0.4871	0.4875	0.4878	0.4881	0.4884	0.4887	0.4890
2.30	0.4893	0.4896	0.4898	0.4901	0.4904	0.4906	0.4909	0.4911	0.4913	0.4916
2.40	0.4918	0.4920	0.4922	0.4925	0.4927	0.4929	0.4931	0.4932	0.4934	0.4936
2.50	0.4938	0.4940	0.4941	0.4943	0.4945	0.4946	0.4948	0.4949	0.4951	0.4952
2.60	0.4953	0.4955	0.4956	0.4957	0.4959	0.4960	0.4961	0.4962	0.4963	0.4964
2.70	0.4965	0.4966	0.4967	0.4968	0.4969	0.4970	0.4971	0.4972	0.4973	0.4974
2.80	0.4974	0.4975	0.4976	0.4977	0.4977	0.4978	0.4979	0.4979	0.4980	0.4981
2.90	0.4981	0.4982	0.4982	0.4983	0.4984	0.4984	0.4985	0.4985	0.4986	0.4986
3.00	0.4986	0.4987	0.4987	0.4988	0.4988	0.4989	0.4989	0.4989	0.4990	0.4990

STUDENT'S *t* TABLE

Degrees of freedom	Confidence level			
	80%	90%	95%	99%
1	3.078	6.134	12.706	63.657
2	1.886	2.920	4.303	9.925
3	1.638	2.353	3.182	5.841
4	1.533	2.132	2.776	4.604
5	1.476	2.015	2.571	4.032
6	1.440	1.943	2.447	3.707
7	1.415	1.895	2.365	3.500
8	1.397	1.860	2.306	3.355
9	1.383	1.833	2.262	3.250
10	1.372	1.812	2.228	3.169
11	1.363	1.796	2.201	3.106
12	1.356	1.782	2.179	3.055
13	1.350	1.771	2.160	3.012
14	1.345	1.761	2.145	2.977
15	1.341	1.753	2.131	2.947
16	1.337	1.746	2.120	2.921
17	1.333	1.740	2.110	2.898
18	1.330	1.734	2.101	2.878
19	1.328	1.729	2.093	2.861
20	1.325	1.725	2.086	2.845
21	1.323	1.721	2.080	2.831
22	1.321	1.717	2.074	2.819
23	1.319	1.714	2.069	2.807
24	1.318	1.711	2.064	2.797
25	1.316	1.708	2.060	2.787
26	1.315	1.706	2.056	2.779
27	1.314	1.703	2.052	2.771
28	1.313	1.701	2.048	2.763
29	1.311	1.699	2.045	2.756
30	1.310	1.697	2.042	2.750
Infinity	1.282	1.645	1.96	2.576

THE *F* DISTRIBUTION (UPPER 5 PERCENT POINTS)

The numbers in the table give the critical values cutting off 5 percent in the upper tail of the *F* distribution. The first row gives the degrees of freedom in the numerator while the first column gives the degrees of freedom in the denominator.

	1	2	3	4	5	6	7	8	9	10	12	15	20	24	30	40	60	120	Infinity
1	161.45	199.5	215.71	224.58	230.16	233.99	236.77	238.88	240.54	241.88	243.9	245.95	248.02	249.05	250.1	251.14	252.2	253.25	254.31
2	18.51	19	19.16	19.25	19.3	19.33	19.35	19.37	19.38	19.4	19.41	19.43	19.45	19.45	19.46	19.47	19.48	19.49	19.5
3	10.13	9.55	9.28	9.12	9.01	8.94	8.89	8.85	8.81	8.79	8.74	8.7	8.66	8.64	8.62	8.59	8.57	8.55	8.53
4	7.71	6.94	6.59	6.39	6.26	6.16	6.09	6.04	6	5.96	5.91	5.86	5.8	5.77	5.75	5.72	5.69	5.66	5.63
5	6.61	5.79	5.41	5.19	5.05	4.95	4.88	4.82	4.77	4.74	4.68	4.62	4.56	4.53	4.5	4.46	4.43	4.4	4.37
6	5.99	5.14	4.76	4.53	4.39	4.28	4.21	4.15	4.1	4.06	4	3.94	3.87	3.84	3.81	3.77	3.74	3.7	3.67
7	5.59	4.74	4.35	4.12	3.97	3.87	3.79	3.73	3.68	3.64	3.57	3.51	3.44	3.41	3.38	3.34	3.3	3.27	3.23
8	5.32	4.46	4.07	3.84	3.69	3.58	3.5	3.44	3.39	3.35	3.28	3.22	3.15	3.12	3.08	3.04	3.01	2.97	2.93
9	5.12	4.26	3.86	3.63	3.48	3.37	3.29	3.23	3.18	3.14	3.07	3.01	2.94	2.9	2.86	2.83	2.79	2.75	2.71
10	4.96	4.1	3.71	3.48	3.33	3.22	3.14	3.07	3.02	2.98	2.91	2.85	2.77	2.74	2.7	2.66	2.62	2.58	2.54
11	4.84	3.98	3.59	3.36	3.2	3.09	3.01	2.95	2.9	2.85	2.79	2.72	2.65	2.61	2.57	2.53	2.49	2.45	2.4
12	4.75	3.89	3.49	3.26	3.11	3	2.91	2.85	2.8	2.75	2.69	2.62	2.54	2.51	2.47	2.43	2.38	2.34	2.3
13	4.67	3.81	3.41	3.18	3.03	2.92	2.83	2.77	2.71	2.67	2.6	2.53	2.46	2.42	2.38	2.34	2.3	2.25	2.21
14	4.6	3.74	3.34	3.11	2.96	2.85	2.76	2.7	2.65	2.6	2.53	2.46	2.39	2.35	2.31	2.27	2.22	2.18	2.13
15	4.54	3.68	3.29	3.06	2.9	2.79	2.71	2.64	2.59	2.54	2.48	2.4	2.33	2.29	2.25	2.2	2.16	2.11	2.07
16	4.49	3.63	3.24	3.01	2.85	2.74	2.66	2.59	2.54	2.49	2.42	2.35	2.28	2.24	2.19	2.15	2.11	2.06	2.01
17	4.45	3.59	3.2	2.96	2.81	2.7	2.61	2.55	2.49	2.45	2.38	2.31	2.23	2.19	2.15	2.1	2.06	2.01	1.96
18	4.41	3.55	3.16	2.93	2.77	2.66	2.58	2.51	2.46	2.41	2.34	2.27	2.19	2.15	2.11	2.06	2.02	1.97	1.92
19	4.38	3.52	3.13	2.9	2.74	2.63	2.54	2.48	2.42	2.38	2.31	2.23	2.16	2.11	2.07	2.03	1.98	1.93	1.88
20	4.35	3.49	3.1	2.87	2.71	2.6	2.51	2.45	2.39	2.35	2.28	2.2	2.12	2.08	2.04	1.99	1.95	1.9	1.84
21	4.32	3.47	3.07	2.84	2.68	2.57	2.49	2.42	2.37	2.32	2.25	2.18	2.1	2.05	2.01	1.96	1.92	1.87	1.81
22	4.3	3.44	3.05	2.82	2.66	2.55	2.46	2.4	2.34	2.3	2.23	2.15	2.07	2.03	1.98	1.94	1.89	1.84	1.78
23	4.28	3.42	3.03	2.8	2.64	2.53	2.44	2.37	2.32	2.27	2.2	2.13	2.05	2.01	1.96	1.91	1.86	1.81	1.76
24	4.26	3.4	3.01	2.78	2.62	2.51	2.42	2.36	2.3	2.25	2.18	2.11	2.03	1.98	1.94	1.89	1.84	1.79	1.73
25	4.24	3.39	2.99	2.76	2.6	2.49	2.4	2.34	2.28	2.24	2.16	2.09	2.01	1.96	1.92	1.87	1.82	1.77	1.71
26	4.23	3.37	2.98	2.74	2.59	2.47	2.39	2.32	2.27	2.22	2.15	2.07	1.99	1.95	1.9	1.85	1.8	1.75	1.69
27	4.21	3.35	2.96	2.73	2.57	2.46	2.37	2.31	2.25	2.2	2.13	2.06	1.97	1.93	1.88	1.84	1.79	1.73	1.67
28	4.2	3.34	2.95	2.71	2.56	2.45	2.36	2.29	2.24	2.19	2.12	2.04	1.96	1.91	1.87	1.82	1.77	1.71	1.65
29	4.18	3.33	2.93	2.7	2.55	2.43	2.35	2.28	2.22	2.18	2.1	2.03	1.94	1.9	1.85	1.81	1.75	1.7	1.64
30	4.17	3.32	2.92	2.69	2.53	2.42	2.33	2.27	2.21	2.16	2.09	2.01	1.93	1.89	1.84	1.79	1.74	1.68	1.62
40	4.08	3.23	2.84	2.61	2.45	2.34	2.25	2.18	2.12	2.08	2	1.92	1.84	1.79	1.74	1.69	1.64	1.58	1.51
60	4	3.15	2.76	2.53	2.37	2.25	2.17	2.1	2.04	1.99	1.92	1.84	1.75	1.7	1.65	1.59	1.53	1.47	1.39
120	3.92	3.07	2.68	2.45	2.29	2.18	2.09	2.02	1.96	1.91	1.83	1.75	1.66	1.61	1.55	1.5	1.43	1.35	1.25
infinity	3.84	3	2.6	2.37	2.21	2.1	2.01	1.94	1.88	1.83	1.75	1.67	1.57	1.52	1.46	1.39	1.32	1.22	1

THE DURBIN-WATSON STATISTIC

Entries in the table give the critical values for a one-tailed Durbin-Watson test for autocorrelation. For a two-tailed test, the level of significance is doubled.

Significance Points of D_L and D_U at $\alpha = 0.05$ and Number of Independent Variables

Source: Durbin, J., and Watson, G. S. "Testing for Serial Correlation in Least Squares Regression," *Biometrika, Vol 38* (1951), pp. 159–177.

$K =$	1		2		3		4		5	
$N =$	D_L	D_U	D_L	D_U	D_L	D_U	D_L	D_U	D_L	D_U
15	1.08	1.36	0.95	1.54	0.82	1.75	0.69	1.97	0.56	2.21
16	1.10	1.37	0.98	1.54	0.86	1.73	0.74	1.93	0.62	2.15
17	1.13	1.38	1.02	1.54	0.90	1.71	0.78	1.90	0.67	2.10
18	1.16	1.39	1.05	1.53	0.93	1.69	0.82	1.87	0.71	2.06
19	1.18	1.40	1.08	1.53	0.97	1.68	0.86	1.85	0.75	2.02
20	1.20	1.41	1.10	1.54	1.00	1.68	0.90	1.83	0.79	1.99
21	1.22	1.42	1.13	1.54	1.03	1.67	0.93	1.81	0.83	1.96
22	1.24	1.43	1.15	1.54	1.05	1.66	0.96	1.80	0.86	1.94
23	1.26	1.44	1.17	1.54	1.08	1.66	0.99	1.79	0.90	1.92
24	1.27	1.45	1.19	1.55	1.10	1.66	1.01	1.78	0.93	1.90
25	1.29	1.45	1.21	1.55	1.12	1.66	1.04	1.77	0.95	1.89
26	1.30	1.46	1.22	1.55	1.14	1.65	1.06	1.76	0.98	1.88
27	1.32	1.47	1.24	1.56	1.16	1.65	1.08	1.76	1.01	1.86
28	1.33	1.48	1.26	1.56	1.18	1.65	1.10	1.75	1.03	1.85
29	1.34	1.48	1.27	1.56	1.20	1.65	1.12	1.74	1.05	1.84
30	1.35	1.49	1.28	1.57	1.21	1.65	1.14	1.74	1.07	1.83
31	1.36	1.50	1.30	1.57	1.23	1.65	1.16	1.74	1.09	1.83
32	1.37	1.50	1.31	1.57	1.24	1.65	1.18	1.73	1.11	1.82
33	1.38	1.51	1.32	1.58	1.26	1.65	1.19	1.73	1.13	1.81
34	1.39	1.51	1.33	1.58	1.27	1.65	1.21	1.73	1.15	1.81
35	1.40	1.52	1.34	1.58	1.28	1.65	1.22	1.73	1.16	1.80
36	1.41	1.52	1.35	1.59	1.29	1.65	1.24	1.73	1.18	1.80
37	1.42	1.53	1.36	1.59	1.31	1.66	1.25	1.72	1.19	1.80
38	1.43	1.54	1.37	1.59	1.32	1.66	1.26	1.72	1.21	1.79
39	1.43	1.54	1.38	1.60	1.33	1.66	1.27	1.72	1.22	1.79
40	1.44	1.54	1.39	1.60	1.34	1.66	1.29	1.72	1.23	1.79
45	1.48	1.57	1.43	1.62	1.38	1.67	1.34	1.72	1.29	1.78
50	1.50	1.59	1.46	1.63	1.42	1.67	1.38	1.72	1.34	1.77
55	1.53	1.60	1.49	1.64	1.45	1.68	1.41	1.72	1.38	1.77
60	1.55	1.62	1.51	1.65	1.48	1.69	1.44	1.73	1.41	1.77
65	1.57	1.63	1.54	1.66	1.50	1.70	1.47	1.73	1.44	1.77
70	1.58	1.64	1.55	1.67	1.52	1.70	1.49	1.74	1.46	1.77
75	1.60	1.65	1.57	1.68	1.54	1.71	1.51	1.74	1.49	1.77
80	1.61	1.66	1.59	1.69	1.56	1.72	1.53	1.74	1.51	1.77
85	1.62	1.67	1.60	1.70	1.57	1.72	1.55	1.75	1.52	1.77
90	1.63	1.68	1.61	1.70	1.59	1.73	1.57	1.75	1.54	1.78
95	1.64	1.69	1.62	1.71	1.60	1.73	1.58	1.75	1.56	1.78
100	1.65	1.69	1.63	1.72	1.61	1.74	1.59	1.76	1.57	1.78

For purposes of using the table, N is defined as number of observations and K is defined as explanatory variables.

WRITING GUIDE FOR BUSINESS DECISION MODELING

Business Decision Modeling Written Analysis Guidelines

- The executive summary is the single most important part of your analysis.
- Written analysis should be concise yet informative.
- Consider the information/space tradeoff.
- View yourselves as consultants presenting to prospective clients with the end goal of obtaining a consulting contract and getting PAID!!
- View the written analysis as a sales tool that is
  - a. Readable at many levels, e.g., executives, staff members, and managers.
  - b. Applicable to varying degrees of technical expertise, interests, and agendas.
- Ask yourself the following questions:
  - a. "What would I want to know from this Executive Summary?"
  - b. "What would grab my attention and keep me reading?"
  - c. "What information needs to be included for me or my group to make a decision?"
- Remember your are telling a story,
  - a. Think real life.
  - b. Brief the decision makers on the problem.
  - c. Provide them with a quantitative analysis.
  - d. State your results and sell your recommendations.

Business Decision Modeling Basic Presentation Guidelines

- Make use of the technology provided (i.e., data projector, computer, etc.) but always be prepared in case the technology doesn't work.
  - a. Concentrate on giving a concise yet informative overview.
  - b. Think of your group as consultants bidding for a contract.
  - c. Time is limited and you may be under pressure to get your ideas across.
  - d. Too much info and you risk boring the client to death, too little info and you risk being inadequate.
  - e. Strive to become more effective and efficient business writers and presenters.
- Items to remember:
  - a. Keep your slides simple.
  - b. Label all graphs, axis, and spreadsheets.
  - c. State your assumptions and stick by them.
  - d. Do not overcrowd slides (e.g., complicated spreadsheets usually confuse instead of enlightening the audience).
  - e. Use your time wisely, cover background material, but make sure you get to the results and recommendations with sufficient time left to discuss and make your sale.
  - f. Practice your presentation before you give it!

Executive Summary Tutorial

The business world uses what is called an executive summary. The following are a set of guidelines for writing executive summaries.

1. The executive summary must be short (i.e., one page).
   - An executive summary that is too long defeats its purpose.
   - An executive summary that is too short omits essential content
2. The executive summary must be a self-contained unit.
   - The executive summary must stand independently.
   - Most likely the executive summary will be separated from the report and be published or circulated independently.

3. The executive summary must satisfy your clients' needs.
   - The executive summary must contain a statement of the problem, the limitations placed on it, results, conclusions, and recommendations.
4. The executive summary must be objective, precise, and easy to read.
   - State the purpose or objective (sometimes called the thesis) of the problem clearly and early in the executive summary.
   - Clearly define assumptions and terms throughout the executive summary.
   - Reference visual aids included in the executive summary.
   - Display visual aids if they are referenced in the executive summary.
5. Rewriting is far more important than writing. Points to remember:
   - Spell-check your document.
   - Define all terms, do not assume your client "knows."
   - Have a third party read your work as a reality check.
   - Tell your story, sell and educate your client about your analysis.
   - Walk your client through the executive summary.
   - Link sections and ideas together.
   - Restate conclusions/recommendations—in words and in numbers.
   - Concise and effective executive summaries are never written; they are rewritten.
6. The executive summary should contain:
   - Headings.
   - Well-developed transitions between sections.
   - Comparison and/or summary sections.
   - Visual aids if applicable.

Visual aids such as graphs, charts, decision trees, and/or spreadsheets are highly recommended and should be used to help describe and define technical sections, comparisons, results, and/or recommendations.

Executive Summary Definitions

The following is a sample of what leading business writing scholars and practitioners have stated about executive summaries. Please read the quotes and use the references to improve your executive summaries and overall writing tasks.

An Executive Summary is a fully developed "mini" version of the report itself, intended for readers who lack time or motivation to study the complete text.

- Writing Long Reports, John Thill and Courtland Bovee

The Executive Summary, also called the synopsis, epitome, and précis, is the report in miniature. It concisely summarizes all of the report's essential ingredient . . . . It is designed chiefly for the busy executive who may not have time to read the whole report.

- Report Writing for Business, Raymond Lesikar and John Pettit

The Executive Summary is your most effective and important selling piece and deserves all the effort and attention you can give it. Remember, the client may receive dozens of proposals and may use the Executive Summary as an initial screening process,

- Handbook for Writing Proposals, Robert Hamper and Sue Baugh

The Executive Summary . . . should state the report in a nutshell—generally, it could include the purpose or objectives of the report, background, procedures or approach to the report, findings, and summary, recommendations, and conclusions (if any).

- How to Create High Impact Business Reports, Joyce Kupsh

Always include this [executive summary], whether you are asked for it or not . . . . Some readers will go no further, so it is important that you get the message across to them clearly. They are likely to include the more senior people who may have to take decisions based upon you report. It is vitally important to get it right.

- How to Communicate in Business: A Handbook for Engineers, David Silk

References

Hamper, Robert J., and L. Sue Baugh. *Handbook for Writing Proposals.* Lincolnwood, IL: NTC Publishers Group, 1995.

Holtz, Herman. *The Consultant's Guide to Proposal Writing: How to Satisfy Your Clients and Double Your Income.* New York: John Wiley & Sons, 1998.

Kupsh, Joyce. *How to Create High Impact Business Reports.* Lincolnwood, IL: NTC Publishers Group, 1996.

Lesikar, Raymond V., and John D. Pettit, Jr. *Report Writing for Business.* New York: Irwin, 1997.

Sant, Tom. *Persuasive Business Proposals: Writing to Win Customers, Clients, and Contracts,* New York: American Management Association, 1992.

Silk, David. *How to Communicate in Business: A Handbook for Engineers.* IEE Management of Technology Series 17, 1995.

Smith, Charles B. *A Guide to Business Research: Developing, Conducting, and Writing Research Projects.* Chicago: Nelson-Hall Publishers, 1991.

Tebeaux, Elizabeth. *Design of Business Communications: The Process and the Product.* New York: Macmillan, 1990.

Thill, John V., and Courtland L. Bovee. *Excellence in Business Communication.* New York: Prentice-Hall, 1998.

Index